KU-330-878

George Thomason was born and brought up in the English Lake District. He read degrees in economics and management in Sheffield and Toronto, before joining the staff of the Industrial Relations Department of University College Cardiff in 1953, where he obtained his doctorate in 1963. He held various research and teaching posts, before becoming Montague Burton Professor of Industrial Relations and head of the department of industrial relations and management studies in 1969. From 1960 to 1962, he was seconded from the College with a Leverhulme Trust Fellowship to work as Assistant to the Managing Director of Flex Fasteners Ltd and Porth Textiles Ltd. He was Dean of the Faculty of Economic and Social Studies from 1971 to 1973, and Deputy Principal for the Humanities from 1974 to 1977. He has been an external examiner in a number of British and Nigerian Universities and has served on a number of research and educational bodies in both England and Wales. He was elected a Fellow of University College Cardiff in 1980.

Since 1966, he has been an industrial relations arbitrator, first with the Ministry of Labour and later with ACAS and has been a member of the wages councils for boot and shoe repairing, pressed and stamped metalwares, retail food and road haulage, between 1967 and 1975. He is also a member of the pay review bodies for doctors and dentists and for nurses, midwives, health visitors and professions allied to medicine and was a member of the pharmacists' review panel between 1981 and 1984. He has also acted as consultant to a number of industrial and community organizations in Britain, Ireland and New Zealand. In 1983 he was appointed a CBE for his services in the field of employment and industrial relations.

He has been actively associated with the Cardiff branches of the Institute of Personnel Management and the British Institute of Management for many years, and has served on the IPM's Education Committee since the early 1970s. He was made a Companion of the Institute of Personnel Management in 1974. Professor Thomason is the author of a number of books on personnel management and community development, some published by the IPM, including *A Textbook of Personnel Management*, now in its fourth edition; *Job Evaluation: Objectives and Methods; The Management of Research and Development; Experiments in Participation* and *The Professional Approach to Community Work*.

He is married to a Cardiff solicitor and has two children.

R. Blackwell
Coventry Jan. 1985.

A Textbook of
Industrial Relations
Management

George Thomason

Institute of Personnel Management

For my wife, Jean

© Institute of Personnel Management 1984
First published 1984

All rights reserved. No part of this publication may be reproduced, stored in a retrieval system, or transmitted in any form or by any means, electronic, mechanical or photcopying, recording or otherwise without written permission of the Institute of Personnel Management, IPM House, Camp Road, Wimbledon, London, SWl9 4UW.

Note: The convention has been followed whereby *he* and *him* are used to cover *she* and *her* wherever appropriate.

Printed and bound in Great Britain by
Biddles Ltd, Guildford and King's Lynn

British Library Cataloguing in Publication Data
Thomason, George F
A textbook of industrial relations management.
1. Industrial relations
I. Title
658.3'15   HD6971

ISBN 0-85292-302-3

CONTENTS

v

Conclusions

List of tables and figures

List of tables

List of figures

Abbreviations

C	Appeal Court (Reports)
AS	Advisory, Conciliation and Arbitration Service
ER	All England Law Reports
A	American Management Association
EX	Association of Professional, Executive, Clerical and Computer Staffs
TMS	Association of Scientific, Technological and Managerial Staffs.
EW	Amalgamated Union of Engineering Workers
T	Association of University Teachers
M	British Institute of Management
C	Central Arbitration Committee
I	Confederation of British Industry
	Chancery (Court) Reports
R	Commission on Industrial Relations
C	European Economic Community
F	Engineering Employers' Federation
p Act	Employment Act
PTU	Electrical, Electronic and Plumbing Trades Union.
Act	Employment Protection Act
C) Act	Employment Protection (Consolidation) Act
P Act	Equal Pay Act
BATU	General, Municipal, Boilermakers and Allied Trades Union
	House of Lords
AW	Act Health and Safety etc at Work Act
	Incomes Data Service
R	Industrial Court (Cases) Reports
M	Institute of Personnel Management
R	Industrial Relations Law Reports
C	Iron and Steel Trades Confederation
	Industry Training Board
PI	National Board for Prices and Incomes
RC	National Industrial Relations Court
J	National Union of Journalists
AAW	National Union of Agricultural and Allied Workers
BE	National Union of Bank Employees
M	National Union of Mineworkers
R	National Union of Railwaymen

ix

NUT	National Union of Teachers
NUTGW	National Union of Tailors' and Garment Workers
NUVB	National Union of Vehicle Builders
QB	Queens' Bench (Reports)
TASS/AUEW	Technical and Supervisory Staffs / AUEW
TGWU	Transport and General Workers' Union
TLR	Times Law Reports
TULR	Act Trade Unions and Labour Relations Acts
UCW	Union of Communications Workers
UPW	Union of Post Office Workers
WLR	Weekly Law Reports

Preface

A book on the subject of industrial relations management must take a view of both industrial relations and management, both of which are regarded as important institutions in a modern society.

Industrial relations in the most general meaning of the term comprises all those human relationships which people develop within the work context. Some of these are rather informal, based on friendships and acquaintanceships which develop out of the sheer proximity of people at work. Others are much more formal, based on explicit status relationships and associated with significant titles like 'manager' or 'worker'. Industrial relations, both as a subject of study and as a practice engaging the attentions of people like managers and shop stewards, is usually focused on these more formal aspects.

The subject of industrial relations usually singles out for study the relations which are inherent in, or stem directly from, the organization of employment work around the concept of a contract of employment, and which are both intended to, and do in fact, influence both status and the way in which people (employers and employees) conduct themselves in the work situation.

The notion of a contract as a set of undertakings entered into by two persons or parties, establishes their basic relationships and, since those relationships are based on exchange of labour for remuneration, they are founded upon different, even antithetical interests. The idea of contract as an agreement is therefore one which looks towards securing co-operation in a situation in which difference, even conflict, is inherent. When this idea is then extended to embrace the notion of a collective agreement, the same kinds of notions carry forward: this too involves agreement to co-operation in a situation in which interests are different and may even be conflicting. Consequently, industrial relations is about both agreement and co-operation on the one hand, and disagreement and conflict on the other.

Those who 'practice' industrial relations are, in turn, usually concerned with establishing the 'status' on acceptable terms and with exerting influence in ways which will support improvements in it. Managers find themselves in the thick of industrial relations of one sort or another. At very least, they work with or through people and must necessarily develop some kind of working relations with them. But managers usually have a purposive and dominant role, not only in production, but in industrial relations processes as well. It is this which makes them such an important institution in modern societies. The manager's primary task may be to secure the production of goods and services, but he usually cannot perform that task without securing a measure of co-operation from other people. From this develops his or her concerns with industrial relations structures, procedures and processes, and with the containment of difference and conflict within the work situation.

Managers are expected, and are given power, to play some part in actually shaping industrial relations. Just what part that may be depends a good deal upon whether those with whom they work accord them legitimate authority to take decisions for them, or whether they demand to share of the decision making role. Over the past two centuries workers have tended to move from the one camp to the other, and in consequence managers have found themselves moving from the position where they took unilateral decisions in the confident expectation that they would be followed, to that in which they must share authority to decide with representatives of the workforce.

What the manager needs to achieve is an understanding of the people caught up in these relationships, a knowledge of the historical structures of industrial relations, a vision of what structures and procedures might generate a better future, and a skill in influencing people to accept changes which might be calculated to be for the better. What is attempted in this book is a presentation of our knowledge of industrial relations constraints, structures, processes and skills, on which the manager must base his decisions and actions. It deals with some of the main structurees and practices to be found in industrial relations, which are regarded as the patterned ways in which people try both to cope with what is and to change it for something better.

The book is in three main parts, following a brief introduction which sets the scene. The first deals with the main features of the constraints which are imposed upon action by the wider society: the values and norms which are built into our culture and institutions in order to guide and direct human activity into the preferred channels. The second concentrates on the main features of the devolved arrangements for taking the necessary decisions about industrial relations questions, particularly those concerned with respective statuses and roles of those who work in industry: this focuses mainly on the parties to, and the structures and processes of, collective bargaining through which status (including pay-status) issues are resolved. The third part examines the tasks which are mainly involved in the bargaining processes, and concludes with some indication of the kinds of pressures which are placed upon those who negotiate.

At the end of the excursion through the book, the student should have a deeper understanding of the values, institutions, norms, and practices of industrial relations. He or she should, as a consequence, be better equipped to embark upon the tasks of managing within such a context, although he or she will still need to 'practice' in order to develop the constitution and skills required of those who would shape our industrial relations of the future.

Skill must remain outside the remit of a book on management, because management is (in the ancient Greek philosophical sense) an art where books have to be writtten as if there were some underlying theory or 'science' of management decision and action. Management seeks to achieve concrete ends by deciding and acting on the basis, as Barnard lucidly indicated, of a welter of detailed and ephemoral facts within a situation. Textbooks, in contrast, are put together on the basis of systematic knowledge and aim to offer explanations of things or 'theories of causality'. The argument here runs that if there are (scientific) theories which explain the cause of things, then those who would, like managers, seek to cause things to happen, will benefit (become more effective) if they have some understanding of the theories.

Industrial relations is, in its nature, however, concerned with values and, indeed, with different values which people seek to have others adopt in their dealings within the work context. Workers have their values linked with notions of human dignity; managers have their values associated with efficiency and order. Each may be said to use what we identify as the industrial relations system for purposes of securing acceptance of their values by other party in order to improve the quality of working life or the efficiency of British industry, or something of that kind. For this reason, industrial relations, whether as a subject or as a practice, is not merely about creative arts and theoretical science; it is also concerned with ethics and morals. There can be no relegation of the subject or the practice to a concern simply with the theories of how control might be achieved, leaving out of account the ends to be served by doing so. I trust that the student will find in this book consideration all of these aspects of industrial relations in their turn.

Acknowledgements

I owe a considerable debt to the authors of the books I have read on the subject, the practitioners with whom I have worked and discussed industrial relations ideas and issues, and to my colleagues in the Department of Industrial Relations in University College Cardiff. Some of my friends have helped by reading drafts of the whole or parts of this book. I owe a particular debt to Peter Anthony for allowing me to bounce ideas off him from time to time during our long association. I have taken note of all comments but I fully accept that what now appears is entirely my responsibility.

The book has been produced by relatively novel method and I must also express my gratitude to Barbara Clargo for coping with the new word processor technology, as well as the usual eccentricities of an author.

Professor George F Thomason CBE
University College,
Cardiff
July 1984

1

Industrial relations in Britain

The industrial relations problem

The industrial revolution presented British society with a new
problem of work and work relations. The bonds of the preceding
feudal and mercantilist systems were swept away and workers
(as well as businessmen and employers) acquired the status of
'free men'; workers were now free to choose their kinds and
places of employment and free to contract with employers of
their choosing the terms under which they would supply their
labour. Even if the freedom was not as full as this statement might
imply, they were certainly emancipated in comparison with their
condition under preceding regimes (see Ashton, 1948).

The problem was now one of finding the methods appropriate
to securing the free workers' commitment to, and co-operation
in, work. The onus of resolving it fell largely upon the
businessman and employer who needed the workers' services.
He could no longer count on the legal enforcement of permanent
attachments of workers to their masters. He could no longer use
methods of coercion previously accepted but had to control by
means of incentives and/or persuasion. His problem and task was
to find a new moral order (or a new set of rules of work) to which
relatively-independent workers would subscribe, so that co-
operation in work could develop. By about World War I, it was
widely considered that the solutions had been found in 'the
British system of industrial relations' based on independent
worker associations (particularly trade unions) and free collective bargaining.

The story of British industrial relations is the story of how
voluntary commitment to work has been developed and how the
institutions which support it have been established within a
framework of values usually subsumed in the terms, 'individualism' and 'laissez-faire'. The scope of the 'subject' of industrial

1

relations has been defined by reference to this same problem of commitment and its institutional supports in trade unionism and collective bargaining.

The main features of the British 'system' had developed by about 1918, and it came to be seen (partly because Britain was the first nation state to industrialize) as an exemplary model which other countries would probably emulate. However, by about 1960, it was widely recognized that the system was not dealing adequately with the basic problem and was no longer producing the expected results. Industrial relations had itself become very much 'a problem'. The Donovan Commission Report (1968) provided a major diagnosis of and a number of recommendations as to what ought to be done to alleviate it. Not all of the advice was taken up, or taken up in the form in which it was given. Some changes *were* made, both in law and in managerial and trade union structure and practice, either on the basis of the Commission's recommendations or in response to situational pressures. In spite of these, there are many who would still regard the problem as unresolved.

THE TRADITIONAL MODEL

There was a time when the British approach to industrial relations appeared to be the model which other countries would naturally follow as they industrialized. It was not so much that it was necessarily 'good' or 'the best that man could devise', but rather that it represented the most fully worked out example of what naturally occurred as industrialization proceeded, and as the employers and workers established the conditions under which commitment to work would be forthcoming.

The arrangements developed seemed to deal with the fundamental problem created by the emancipation of both workers and businessmen. These entailed the decentralization of decision-taking about the issues of relative status and distribution of income which had to be resolved as a basis for co-operation, to the employers and workers themselves, and its eventual institutionalization into a structure (which we now refer to as that of 'collective bargaining'). They focused on decisions about:

(a) The quantities to be established within the contract of employment (the amounts of work and wages, on day-work or incentive rates, the hours of work and the holiday

2

entitlements, and the respective statuses of the employer and the employee which establish their respective rights and powers)

(b) The rules of conduct which would be accepted as governing the way in which employer and employee approached and addressed each other through representatives for the purposes of deciding these questions, and thereby established the rules which prescribed the roles of the parties in effecting any change in the *status quo*.

Managers and workers, initially as individuals but progressively as collectivities, were given some say in the determination of the necessary rules of work or of the terms and conditions of co-operation between them. The element of sharing (inherent in any concept of 'bargaining') was intended to secure the workers' commitment to work with the discipline which modern industry demanded of them.

The institutionalization centred on structures of unitary work organization which contained the employers and workers in an authority relationship, and on processes of 'collective bargaining' in which relatively autonomous associations of employees and employers (the independent trade unions and employers' associations) met and decided the issues which might be in dispute between them within a framework of guiding rules which was largely of their own devising. Importantly, the State held aloof from the processes of decision-making, although it established a basic structure of rights and obligations through the operation of the law. This apart, the agreements reached by the parties themselves were to be the major sources of regulating conduct in the processes of deciding.

Admittedly, this conception of a decentralized system developed in the days when industrial relations tended to be seen as a function of trade unionism, and when trade unionism in turn was seen to be an issue of industrializing out of capitalism (see S and B Webb, 1920; Cole, 1923; Phelps-Brown, 1959; Pelling, 1963). It was the apparent inevitability of this institutionalization of the labour protest which captured the imagination, and enabled England (it was usually 'England', rather than 'Britain') to be acknowledged as 'the classic land of trade unionism and her labor movement the model wherever workers began to organize' (Galenson, 1952a, p x).

The development in Germany (Veblen, 1909) was then seen

to have 'mirrored faithfully the industrial development of that nation' (Galenson, 1952a, p x) whereas 'Russian economic backwardness in the first two decades of this century frustrated unmistakable tendencies towards a 'normal' course of trade union development' (*op cit.* p xi). Later, and for a time, an American model involving an even greater degree of decentralization (to company and plant level bargaining) (see Slichter, 1955; Myers, 1962) seemed to offer a challenge to this. This substitute model did not endure long, because it came to be recognized that there was a *variety* of routes which societies might follow in industrializing and in structuring the consequential decision-making about terms and conditions of employment of new industrial workers. Nevertheless there remained a vague feeling that there was an underlying *basic* theme or pattern, if only we could discern it.

The system model

The 'British model' of industrial relations seemed to possess in its day general applicability to industrialized countries. A succession of descriptions of the arrangements in various countries to determine the status of workers and managers impressed many students with their similarities (for example, Richardson, 1933 and 1954; Marquand, 1934 and 1939; Jones, 1939; Norgren, 1941; Galenson, 1952a and 1952b; Flanders and Clegg, 1954; Slichter, 1955; Raza, 1963). Many of these writers perceived such regularities in these arrangements that they were led to adopt the term 'system' in their titles (see Boulding, 1956; Hanika, 1965; Buckley, 1967; and Kast and Rosenzweig, 1972). The idea therefore spread that industrial relations were not only handled in comparable ways in many different countries, but were capable of being appreciated in terms of system concepts; that, as Dunlop put it in 1958, industrial relations constituted systems of a more or less sophisticated kind wherever they were to be found.

This meant that there was now a theory which could help us to appreciate the essential nature of industrial relations. It reduced the complexities of the real world to a set of categories and categorial concepts which could enable us to discuss industrial relations in theoretical terms, rather than in the purely descriptive ones of the earlier accounts.

1   We could now identify three 'actors' within the industrial relations system:

   (a) the hierarchies of managers
   (b) the hierarchies of non-managerial workers
   (c) the specialized agencies of government or of the parties concerned with workers, enterprises and the relationships between them.

Some manifestation of each would always be present, argued Dunlop, although they would not necessarily appear in a highly organized form, nor all play equally important roles in the operation of the system (Dunlop, 1958, pp viii and 7). Where they *were* organized they were to be identified as trade unions, employers' associations and the State. This view emphasized the unitary or homogeneous nature (or the solidarity) of the three 3parties involved, Each was supposed to operate on the basis of a kind of internal consensus which allowed each to be seen as 'an actor' in its own right.

2   We could categorize the pressures in the environment in which they acted and which would constrain their opportunities for decision and action. The three environmental categories comprise:

   (a) the technology
   (b) the market or budgetary constraints
   (c) the statuses and power relations associated with them.

These were regarded as variable in time and space and for this reason they helped to account for the differences in the patterns of industrial relations which appeared between countries, or industries or enterprises (Dunlop, 1958, p 8).

3   The whole is cemented into a stable entity or system by the existence of a 'binding ideology', shared by the actors. This had the effect of ensuring that the actors held views as to the legitimacy and value of the arrangements themselves (and of the place of the others in them) and that they acted or behaved within them in accordance with the rules of the game which develop from these beliefs. Flanders was later to identify this ideology, in the British context, with a belief in the legitimacy and value of free or voluntary collective bargaining behaviour' (Flanders, 1965). It is this element in the theory which gives the notion of 'a system' its inherent stability (and

which has consequently attracted a considerable amount of criticism for assuming away the problem of conflict in relations; see Hyman and Fryer, 1975, and see p 46).

4   The system was then thought to exist and operate to produce the substantive and procedural rules by which the quantities to be determined within the employment relationship and the norms of conduct governing the interaction of the parties would be determined. This was the *output* of a system which took in the differences, disputes and disagreements which might arise within the contractual relationship between employer and employees and processed them through the machinery for discussion and agreement-making. They would usually take the form of:

'the regulations and policies of the management hierarchy; the laws of any worker hierarchy; the regulations, decrees, decisions, awards or orders of govenmental agencies; the rules and decisions of specialized agencies created by the management and worker hierarchies; collective bargaining arrangements and the customs and traditions of the workplace and work community' (Dunlop, 1958, p 16).

This theoretical perspective was then thought to explain what industrial relations existed to achieve and how it achieved this end. It existed to make the rules and (because of the involvement of those affected by them) to secure commitment to them (see Goodman *et al*, 1975a and 1975b). It did this by providing a forum for the discussion or working through of differences and disagreements between those (workers and employers) who possessed different interests and objectives, and for the reaching of compromise solutions between them in order that the co-operation might continue (see Wood *et al*, 1975).

These new perspectives and understandings allowed the system to be evaluated in accordance with the dominant cultural values of the society. In liberal democracies, for example, (whence, of course, most of the evidence for the model is drawn) it was likely to be evaluated in terms of liberal democratic values. On the same bases, the output of the system in the form of competitiveness or profitability and standards of living could be assessed both over time and between different economies.

The form of the system

The system concept manifested itself in Britain mainly in connection with the 'national system of industrial relations'. In the form advanced by Dunlop, of course, it could be applied to more 'local systems' such as that predominating in the USA, but in Britain, particularly in the inter-war years, it applied to the arrangements made on an industry-wide basis for making the rules and deciding the amounts of effort and reward. But it has had other manifestations, even in Britain. In the middle of last century, most of the decisions were reached in local and domestic negotiations (where they were not unilaterally imposed by the employer), but by the end of World War I, they were more often reached in national, or industry-wide, negotiations which set the conditions for the whole industry as defined by the employers (see Cole, 1923, pp 57-65).

The main actors in the national system were, therefore, the *representatives* of the national trade unions and the employers' associations, who met together as necessary to make, receive and resolve wage and other claims in a process of discussion and argument. Sometimes, the employers' associations and the trade unions might federate for this purpose, and sometimes individual employers and local trade union representatives might meet together domestically to decide these issues. But almost without exception, it was the meeting of the representatives of the employers' association or federation and the trade union or trade union federation, which produced the decisions.

The main onus of creating the necessary conditions for co-operation fell upon these actors. The third actor, the State acting through its agents of the dominant culture, was recognized as relevant but seen to play a relatively minor and peripheral role. It laid down a certain structure of rights and obligations for both individuals and collectivities which could be enforced in the courts (see below, chs 4-6); it occasionally stepped in to create machinery (as in the wages council trades, discussed below, pp 180-86) where voluntary association had produced none of its own; and it provided a service of advice, conciliation and arbitration to assist the parties to reach agreements when they had, by their own efforts, failed to do so (see pp 165-75 below). The State did little else directly, but constantly emphasized its policy of encouraging voluntary bargaining either by individuals or collectivities. Nevertheless, the concept of a voluntary system remained crucially dependent upon:

(a) the State maintaining a support in law for the voluntary processes
(b) the values and requirements of the law being accepted and upheld by the various actors in their industrial relations activities.

The State, by not becoming involved in the day-to-day decision-taking, was protected from direct challenge to these underlying rules which upheld status, except through the mechanisms of politics.

Within this framework of law, the relationships were largely subject to rule established in the agreements which the parties' representatives arrived at on their behalf. The individual rules were of two kinds, responding to the two major questions of industrial relations, given on pp 2-3 and usually referred to as the substantive and procedural rules, respectively (see Flanders, 1965, pp 27-28). Some of the particular rules are concerned directly with (and take the form of decisions about) amounts of effort (or contribution) and remuneration (or consideration) which shall apply. Some are concerned to set standards and procedures to guide conduct within the relationship.

These, as Dunlop's model allows, might be supplemented by other forms of rule, not necessarily established in the agreements of the parties, but by other councils or tribunals, created by legislation. But even these tended to fall within the parameters which the voluntary system established (see Flanders, 1968, p 112, on the comparison of arbitration awards with voluntary settlements) or formed supplements in aid of the voluntary system. There were few occasions when third party intervention occurred, simply because the decentralized arrangements worked reasonably well. This suggests that the rules agreed by the representatives found general acceptance amongst the constituents, who were willing (for whatever reason) to accept them as constituting an order which they had a duty to obey (see Charles, 1973).

This was the broad form of the much-vaunted system of voluntary collective bargaining which was thought to be so functional in creating the right conditions for co-operation. It came to be assumed that this degree of centralization-and-decentralization was about right for the times and the circumstances, and would generally ensure compliance with the rules made, and commitment to their application, if only because the people affected had had a say (through their own representatives) in making them. It was also assumed that this would avoid the necessity for much involvement by the third actor identified.

The achievements of the system

What the system achieved was something which reflected the values of society, or at least of those parts of it which had some opportunity and power to change it, if it was found wanting. These values had in their turn been changing over the last century. By about the turn of the nineteenth century, the value of 'pure individualism' had been so far replaced in practical terms, as to permit the subsequent half-century to embrace a collectivized approach to fixing the terms and conditions of employment, just as it allowed the growth of monopolies within commercial relationships. Nevertheless, the 'then-new' system was justified in terms of some of the same moral and material values as before, particularly those supporting devolved decision-taking, even if they now had a different form:

1 Decisions were to be left to the collective parties themselves (as in the institution of collective bargaining) and the State was able to remain aloof. Trade unions and employers' associations grew in numbers, membership and stature over the eight decades from 1870, (as shown in table 1 on p 10). Although not all members were represented for bargaining purposes, the trade union density amongst manual worker occupations indicated something of the extent to which collective representation had developed (see Clegg, 1972, p 59-60; Millward, 1983, p 281).

Consequently, by the 1970s, the position had been reached where at least half of the workers' terms and conditions of employment were settled in collective negotiation, and many others adopted settlements made elsewhere. Some of these decisions were still taken on an individual basis particularly in the managerial and other white collar and service worker areas. But only a minority (about 3.5 millions) had their wages and conditions fixed by the wages councils. The value of devolved or autonomous decision-taking (as this was defined) was largely satisfied.

9

Table 1
Trade union growth, UK, selected years, 1892-1979

Year	No of trade unions	No.of TU members. (000s)
1892	1233	1576
1894	1314	1530
1899	1325	1911
1904	1256	1967
1909	1260	2477
1914	1260	4154
1919	1360	7926
1924	1194	5544
1929	1133	4858
1934	1063	4590
1939	1019	6298
1944	963	8087
1949	742	9318
1954	711	9566
1959	668	9623
1964	598	10079
1969	563	10472
1974	507	11764
1979	456	13447

Source: Year Books of British Labour Statistics (DE, 1971 onwards); see also Bain, 1983, p 8)

2   Those in whose name the decisions were taken, the employers and the employees, had the opportunity to appoint and dismiss those who acted on their behalf in negotiations. The principle of democratic control was therefore apparently upheld by this devolved decision-making arrangement. People brought within it seemed content to follow the leads given and to honour the agreements thus reached. Whilst they could not then blame anyone but their own agents and representatives for the outcomes, the State was not pressurized to intervene to change them. Inequality of bargaining power was no longer a problem for a third party to deal with, as it was assumed that

Table 2

Indices of net national income of the UK* at factor cost and of the wages share, 1870-1950. Indices based on 1900 prices

Year	Price index (a)	Net national Income	Income per head (b)	Wages as % of national income
1870	120.9	43.8	57.72	38.6
1875	122.0	50.6	63.63	42.4
1880	115.4	52.9	63.21	39.8
1885	100.0	63.7	72.77	39.8
1890	87.8	81.5	89.43	41.5
1895	91.2	90.0	94.73	40.6
1900	100.0	100.0	100.00	40.7
1905	101.1	102.4	98.05	38.3
1910	105.5	111.4	102.04	37.8
1915(c)	135.2	109.1	97.63	–
1920	272.5	118.4	111.46	–
1925	192.3	117.9	107.55	41.8
1930	172.5	130.6	117.13	41.0
1935	157.1	148.9	130.70	40.3
1938	171.4	155.2	134.45	39.2
1940	–	–	–	38.2
1945	–	–	–	39.3
1950	–	–	–	41.9

* United Kingdom includes Southern Ireland between 1870 and 1919

it the organizations concerned did not effect changes in the distribution of structural power, then they did not wish to do so.

3   The provision of employment and of income were both controlled and accepted. The trade cycle affected both, but the causes of the boom and slump conditions were not attributed to the performance of the industrial relations system. The industrial relations arrangements effected order within that framework, and in spite of criticisms of the inequality of power and rewards which the system yielded, it could be assumed for practical purposes that order was

Table 3
Stoppages from industrial disputes, 1889-1981

Annual averages of years	No of strikes (a)	No of strikers (000s) (b)	Total striker days (Mn)	Days struck per striker	Strikers per strike
1889-91a	1050	340	7.1	21	250
1892-96	760	360	13.3	38	270
1897-1901	720	210	7.1	34	210
1902-06	410	160	2.6	17	240
1907-11	570	440	7.2	16	600
1912-16	890	660	13.2	20	600
1917-21	1120	1660	31.8	19	1330
1922-26	570	950	41.8	44	1600
1927-31	380	310	4.4	14	730
1932-36	520	250	2.5	10	400
1937-41	1020	370	1.6	4	270
1942-46	1960	580	2.4	4	240
1947-51	1590	430	1.9	4	220
1952-56	2100	680	2.5	4	290
1957-61	2630	830	4.6	6	320
1962-66	2260	1460	2.5	2	650
1967-71	2750	1520	7.8	5	553
1972-76	2514	1266	11.0	9	504
1977-81	1973	1815	13.0	7	919

Notes: a Three years only (reports probably less complete than in later years).
b Strikes, strikers, etc, refer also to lockouts, etc. The figures include workers 'indirectly involved' at the establishments where stoppages occurred
Sources: To 1966: HA Turner, *Is Britain Really Strikeprone?* (Cambridge UP, 1969), p 19; thereafter: *Employment Gazette*, annually.

preferred to greater equality. In good times, the employers were able to resist excessive trade union claims on behalf of the workers, whilst in bad times, the trade unions were able to act as a brake on wage cutting. In effect, the general pattern was less widely or wildly disturbed by the economic fluctuations, as the data on factor shares in the national income indicated (see Kerr, 1957; Phelps-Brown and Browne, 1968; and table 2, p 11).

4   This result was brought about by the containment of conflict, within bounds which, with the possible exception of the general strike of 1926, were considered acceptable. The values of individualism still influenced this evaluation at least

to the extent that such costs as were incurred in conflicts were largely borne by those in whose name they were conducted, not by society at large (see Durcan and McCarthy, 1974; Gennard, 1977). Provided that the strike did not threaten the State as an institution, the levels of conflict deemed necessary to achieve the objectives by the parties, were regarded as no more than a reasonable price to pay. Furthermore, the data available seemed to suggest that as the system settled down, the number of days' work lost in the conflict necessary for the purpose seemed to be declining (see Turner, 1969, p 19 and table 3 on p 12).

5   The industrial relations arrangements and activities yielded sufficient commitment to co-operation to produce an acceptable level of performance in the commercial system. Certainly, over this period, the dominance of Britain in world trade declined, as did the rate of growth of the national income. In real terms, the national income continued to increase as did the national income per head, and the wage-earner share of it held fairly constant (see table 2 on p 11). This was probably sufficient to prevent anyone from concluding that the arrangements for determining the shares of income to the factors of production were failing or that these decisions were detrimental to the economy. The opportunity which all appeared to have to exert their influence on pay and conditions, seemed to guarantee that the distribution which was effected would prove acceptable.

This national system of industrial relations was applauded by the Whitley Committee, 1917-18, and was developed and consolidated in the inter-war period. It was seen as an arrangement which allowed the commerce of the nation to continue in a stable social environment, and the problem of distribution to be resolved democratically, with a minimum of upheaval and without excessive State intervention The outcomes of the co-operation by the parties concerned fell within the socially-established limits of tolerance for the economy's performance, and it was regarded as successful. It seemed to demand little more than occasional lubrication and fine-tuning to ensure that it went on for ever. It seemed an effective system, given the values which society sought to preserve, and therefore one which ought to be preserved.

THE EMERGENCE OF THE PROBLEM

The system was regarded as successful only for so long as the decentralized arrangement performed in the traditional manner. In the period following World War II, the realization grew, gradually during the 1950s and explosively in the early 1960s, that the system was no longer working efficiently (in terms of its yield) or smoothly (in effecting decisions in an ordered fashion).

Efficiency in this context focuses mainly upon the benefits which the system distributed and the costs which it incurred in the process. Essentially, it was to be regarded as efficient if it continued to allow profits, wages and other incomes to be attained which satisfied the aspirations of the people concerned, and saddled them with costs which could be accepted as reasonable. On all these counts, the system seemed to be less than satisfactory during the post-war years (see Balfour, 1953).

These issues arise from a consideration of the size of the Gross Domestic Product (GDP) and of the manner in which it is distributed through the various factors of production. Between 1950 and 1980, the GDP almost doubled in real terms, and a simple division of this product amongst those employed in 1950, would have secured each an almost-doubled standard of living. The size of the labour force increased only marginally over this same period, but taking the increase into account, the GDP per person employed rose by about three-quarters (see table 4 on p 15).

This overall growth rate was relatively low compared with performance in competitor nations. By 1983, Britain's position in the European league table of per capita GDP (see table 5 on p 15) was close to the bottom. This supported the view that the British economy was failing to grow at a rate which would satisfy the material aspirations of the population. The explanation of the decline usually centred on the idea that there was an 'English disease' whose symptom was a reluctance to work with the intensity required to meet those aspirations in a competitive world without generating inflation. Its effect was, however, to produce a scramble for an increase in the standard of living and reduce the international competitiveness of the economy, which in itself exacerbated the problem.

During this same period, therefore, the shares of the GDP accruing to the various factors of production varied in a way which, for some, increased dissatisfaction from general sources.

14

Table 4

Indices of output per head, whole economy, 1950-80

Year	GDP at constant prices	Employed labour force	GDP per person employed
1950	100	100	100
1955	114	105	109
1960	128	107	121
1965	149	110	135
1970	167	108	154
1975	180	109	165
1980	192	108	179

Note: Gross Domestic Product (GDP) is calculated at constant prices before providing for stock appreciation
Source: Employment Gazette, September, 1968, and monthly thereafter

Table 5

Population, GDP and per capita GDP in EEC countries, 1983

	Population (1982) (million)	GDP (1982) (US$million)	Per Capita GDP(1982) (US$)
Total EEC	271.0	2,347	8,660
of which			
Belgium	9.9	83	8,380
Denmark	5.1	56	10,960
France	54.2	539	9,940
Germany	61.6	657	10,570
Greece	9.8	38	3,840
Ircland	3.4	18	5,180
Italy	56.3	348	6,180
Luxembourg	0.4	3	8,500
Netherlands	14.3	138	9,660
United Kingdom	56.0	469	8,370

Source: Abecor Country Report, June, 1983

Profits

A number of detailed analyses of profits as a proportion of the national income or of value added tend to confirm the earlier trend towards lower relative profits and show it to accelerate sharply in the 1970s (Glyn and Sutcliffe, 1972, pp 58-69; Bacon and Eltis, 1978 edn. pp 21-2).

Glyn and Sutcliffe showed that the share of profits in company net output, between 1950-54 and 1970, was almost halved, and that most of this process occurred between 1964 and 1970 (Glyn and Sutcliffe, 1972, p 58). They concluded from their analysis that the faster fall in the share of profits between 1964 and 1970 could 'be almost entirely explained by the combination of changes in wages and world export prices and the continuation of the tendency for the wages increase to have a greater and greater effect as international competition intensified' and that 'the basic reason for the decline in the profit share was the squeezing of profit margins between money wage increases on the one hand and progressively more severe international competition on the other' (Glyn and Sutcliffe, 1972, p 65).

Using a different method, and relating it to a later period, Bacon and Eltis showed that 'for companies as a whole profits were 17 per cent of value-added in 1964, 13 per cent or less from 1969 onwards, and only about 3 per cent in 1974 and 1975...' (Bacon and Eltis, 1978, pp 21-2). This trend was even more marked in manufacturing industry: the comparable figures given are about one per cent higher in 1964, and two per cent lower than the all companies' figures in 1970-72, four per cent lower in 1973, and nine per cent lower in 1974 (*ibid*). This was the basis for the 'profits squeeze' and for the 'export of capital' which occurred during this period as more profitable investments were discovered abroad.

Income from employment

The share of the GDP accruing to labour fluctuated on a year by

16

Table 6

Wage and salary bills, 1938-80

Year	Gross Domestic Income (GDI)	Index of GDI	Shares of Gross Domestic Income from		
			Employment	Self-Employment	Other sources
1938	4903	100	61.6	13.2	25.2
1946	8895	181.4	64.7	12.7	22.6
1950	12016	248.0	63.5	11.5	25.0
1955	17009	346.9	66.1	9.8	24.1
1960	22886	466.8	66.3	8.8	24.9
1965	31564	643.7	67.5	8.0	24.5
1970	44066	898.8	68.7	8.3	23.0
1975	97940	1997.6	70.1	9.1	20.0
1980	196848	4014.9			

Notes: Indices are calculated on the basis that 1938 = 100, but the accuracy of the resultant index diminishes with length of time.
GDP is calculated the this purpose in current prices before providing for stock appreciation
Source: Year Books of British Labour Statistics (DE, 1971 onwards)

year basis over this period, but the general effect for the period as a whole was to increase the labour share of the Gross Domestic Income (see table 6 above) at the expense of income from self-employment, rent and profits. Compared with the pre-war proportion of 61.6 per cent of Gross Domestic Income arising from employment (the equivalent Phelps-Brown figure is 64.4: see table 2 on p 11), the figure for 1975 was 70.1 per cent. Thus labour might be said to have achieved a slightly higher share of the increased GDP by this latter date.

The increasing share of wages and salaries in the GDP was thought to reflect the growing aspirations of workers for a higher standard of living and their increased power to secure increases in pay from employers in a period of full employment.

Over the period as a whole, however, this effect was not so sustained as to give a significant increase in living standards; workers had to run fast in securing money wage increases in order to stand still in real terms. By the end of the period,

17

Table 7

Survey of labour costs in manufacturing industry, 1981

Country	Index	(%)	Country	Index	(%)
Sweden	109.7	(40)	Denmark	86.0	(18)
Belgium	105.0	(43)	France	79.5	(45)
Norway	101.4	(32)	Italy	77.2	(52)
W Germany	100.0	(44)	Austria	71.1	(47)
USA	99.8	(28)	Japan	65.2	(21)
Switzerland	99.7	(32)	U.K	63.9	(24)
Netherlands	94.1	(44)	Spain	53.5	(37)
Canada	91.4	(26)	Ireland	53.0	(24)
			Greece	31.6	(36)

Notes: Costs for the various countries are expressed as percentages of the total labour cost per hour for West Germany, measured in Deutschmarks: the West German figure for 1981 was DM25.03, equivalent to approx. £6.00 and $10.90.
The figures in brackets indicate the percentage of labour costs accounted for by items other than the average hourly earnings (for example, social security contributions and holiday pay).
Source: Incomes Data Services (IDS): International Report No. 170, p 10; based on Institut der Deutschen Wirtschaft (IW): Annual Survey of Labour Costs in Manufacturing Industry, (IW, 1981)

therefore (as is shown by the international comparisons of labour costs and hours of work in tables 7 and 8 on pp 18 and 19) Britain had become the low wage country which many had been anticipating during the 1950s and 1960s. When coupled with the greater amount of time which the worker had to spend at work to secure this income, the comparison became even more unfavourable (see Incomes Data Services (IDS), *International Report* No 185, January, 1983, p 7, and table 8 on p 19). This was a measure of the incapacity of the British economy to produce results.

Set against the rate of growth in GDP, the changes in factor costs and incomes resulted in comparatively low profits, and low real wages even though in an internationally-high labour cost per unit of output (see tables 4 and 6). This was likely to affect the level of worker satisfaction with the payoffs obtainable from the existing arrangements and to produce in this group appreciable dissatisfaction with them.

Table 8

Hours of work, 1978

Country	Hours actually worked per manual worker	Customary hours worked per non-manual worker
Germany	1716	1820
France	1785	1886
Italy	1643	1851
Belgium	1527	1820
United Kingdom	1969	1827
Denmark	1694	1853
Holland	–	1654*

* the figure is for manual and non-manual combined.
Source: Incomes Data Services (IDS): International Report No. 144, p 6, itself based on the Eurostat Annual Survey

Lack of competitiveness

The central problem (from which much of the general dissatisfaction with the system flowed) was the lack of competitiveness of the British economy. By the 1950s data was being collected systematically on unit labour costs and it became possible to establish the direction and dimensions of change in both output (GDP) and labour costs per unit of output. The resultant time series appear in the *Employment Gazettes* (monthly) covering the whole economy, the index of production industries and certain manufacturing industries.

The figures in table 4 (p 15) suggest that if the economy were to demonstrate any kind of equilibrium, incomes to factors of production and their costs would all move over this period at the rate indicated in the third column. In fact, what happened was a massive increase in all money incomes (see table 6 on p 17) both reflecting, and contributing to, a high rate of inflation for most of the period up to the 1980s. The indices of growth of money incomes show a much greater increase than those indicated by the third column figures. Since the indices would all remain constant if the various incomes varied only with changes in total output and the size of the labour force, any acceleration beyond this may provide a measure of inflation, but not of changes in real living standards.

The fact that the indices for the different factor incomes, profits, incomes from self-employment, rents and wages and

19

salaries vary to different extents, indicates something of the relative changes in shares of incomes (and costs) in the British economy over this period. The feature of particular significance in terms of international competitiveness is the growth of labour costs per unit of output in relation to the growth of output and particularly output per person employed, compared with those of competitor nations.

Both the competitiveness of British industry itself and its measurement are complicated by variations in the international exchange rates and in the rates of inflation. A comparison of labour costs and export prices of British manufacturing industry and its competitors, making allowances for both of these factors, is made in figure 1 (below) taken from the *Red Book*. The general indication of these data is that Britain's international competitiveness has been generally reduced during the past two decades, in spite of the fluctuations. The trend and fluctuations around it, during the past decade, suggest that although recently there may have been a swing to a more favourable position, British industry (in 1983) remains less competitive than in the base year, 1975.

The evidence, considered generally, suggests that Britain has over this post-war period become increasingly uncompetitive in world markets and has failed to generate incomes to a level which

Figure 1

Relative unit labour costs and relative export prices, 1970-83

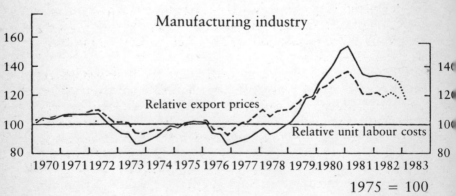

Source: HM Treasury: Financial Statement and Budget Report, 1983-4 (HMSO, March, 1983) p 13

20

either match those of foreign competitors or satisfy domestic aspirations. Such is a measure of the problem.

THE INDUSTRIAL RELATIONS CONTRIBUTION

If the economic situation was not particularly satisfactory, as these data indicate, the question which arises (and indeed arose during this period) is whether this was the result of failures within the industrial relations system (see EEF, 1972; Rhys, 1974). It certainly seemed that it was failing at this time to produce the commitment which the traditional arrangements had been thought to secure. At the time, there were many who were ready to find causes or scapegoats in the actions of the industrial relations parties (for example, Wigham, 1961, or Mant, 1977) or the operation of the system (see Flanders, 1965).

In the scramble to remedy the failures to meet aspirations, both management and workers could be expected to take any means which presented themselves. Investors took action to invest in domestic property or overseas enterprise. Workers took advantage of full employment to pressure employers for wage and salary increases of the kind that gave rise to wage drift. Both categories might be regarded as having done better in these ways than they might have done otherwise. In so far as they exacerbated the situation, however, they could be held blameworthy. In the process of 'scrambling' for advantage in a stagnating or declining economy, the underlying order of the industrial relations system was forfeited, and the 'scramblers' attracted the blame.

The two main scapegoats identified at the time were those which contributed to wage drift and unofficial industrial action, chiefly, it was seen, the workers and their shop-steward leaders. Management might have a responsibility, but it was often seen as a negative one: as the Donovan Commission Report suggested, the directors and managers had largely abdicated their responsibilities and thus 'allowed' the other problems to develop.

Wage drift

'Wage drift' was widely regarded as a major problem, but it was almost a non-fact and a non-event. It arose simply because it was rather naively assumed that national bargaining did and would

21

continue to fix the *rates* of pay for every job and worker within the respective national bargaining units. However, when bargaining took place increasingly within the company or the factory and produced a different rate which took the place of the national rate, the difference came to be treated as a measure of wage drift (see Landsorganisationen (LO), 1953, pp 55-56). However, the final rate fixed locally could have been regarded as the market rate for the job. The nationally-agreed rates could have been regarded as suffering from rate-lag, not that the local rates were suffering from wage drift.

Given workers' aspirations and what was happening to wage rates during the post-war period, it is not surprising to find them using any means to improve their position. The collective bargaining system did not, however, allow them much influence upon actual production performance, this being a matter reserved within the managerial prerogative, and the main impact that workers (through their unions) might have was through the wage rate. Wage drift, or something like it, meant for them the possibility of an increase in the share of the national income which accrued to labour, and more specifically to the wage earner, a possibility which became a reality, as figures which became available later demonstrate.

Wage drift symbolized not so much an economic problem as a political one. The gap (however it was labelled) indicated that the national collective bargaining institution was not producing the substantive results expected of it. Decisions about wages and other cost bearing conditions, once taken, were being retaken (and, as the Donovan Commission put it in 1968, thereby creating two parallel systems of decision-taking between which no rational relationship had been developed). Either might have produced its own unitary or equilibrium conception of order, but the two in parallel could and did not do so.

Whether or not one believes in the 'balance' theory with respect to shares of the national income, one has to acknowledge that during this period any earlier 'balances' were removed. The long-term stability of the share of the national income accruing to labour in the form of wages, which had been demonstrated by Phelps Brown and Hart (1952) and Phelps Brown and Browne (1964) appeared to have disappeared, and in doing so had rendered British industry non-competitive with the rest of the world in terms of both product price and yield on capital.

Unofficial action

Wage drift was accompanied by two other problems which suggested a similar conclusion, ie those of rejected leadership within the collectivity and of unofficial and unconstitutional actions initiated 'spontaneously' (as it was put) by workers and their local leaders (usually identified as shop stewards; see Eldridge, 1968).

The propensity of workers to ignore their official union leadership in the conditions of full employment in the 1950s was well aired in media reports. Wigham assembled some of the main reported events in which local groups appeared to be 'throwing off central authority' in their own unions (Wigham, 1961, p 105) and noted that the Trades Union Congress (TUC) had by 1960 come to 'advocate disciplinary action against members taking part in strikes contrary to the general policy and specific *advice* of their union' (*ibid*, p 112). The restoration of control and discipline by the national unions and their officers was seen at the time to be the most desirable and legitimate solution to what was widely acknowledged as a problem of the system.

The effect of this divorce of leadership and membership was manifest in the unofficial and unconstitutional strikes, called by the 'unofficial' leaders and carried through in defiance of the official union. 'The actions that are complained about,' Sir Thomas Williamson had said at the TUC's annual Congress in 1959, 'are unjustified breaches of agreement which under no circumstances can be condoned by the movement'. The actions were, nevertheless, unofficial and unconstitutional because no official body had made them otherwise; they were not any less real or consequential for that.

In the international league table, the level of strike activity in Britain was not particularly high (see *International Labour Review*, July, 1955, pp 78-91; Turner, 1969, p 7). The Ministry of Labour estimate that only about five per cent of the strikes were 'known to be official' (see table 9 on p 24) was taken as the indicator of the size of the main problem. But the fact that the *proportion of days lost* through stoppages 'known to be official' was much greater than the proportion of the number of strikes, served only to indicate that unofficial actions tended to be short, sharp and unpredictable. It was this unpredictability which became the basis of the 'disorder' central to the Donovan Commission's concern in its *Report* of 1968.

Table 9
Stoppages of work known to be official

Years	Average no of official strikes % of total	Average no of days lost % of total
1962-66	3.1	40
1967-71	4.6	38
1972-76	5.0	37
1976-80	3.1	56

Source: Employment Gazette, annually, 1961-81

At about the same time, the solidarity of the employers was also breaking down (although this tended not to attract disparaging epithets). Individual employers (usually the bigger or higher technology companies) increasingly took the step of severing or loosening their links with employers' associations, preferring not to be bound by the national, industry-wide negotiations with the unions but to make their own more localized deals. Such steps were not branded as unofficial or unconstitutional actions, but in effect they had a similar relationship to the existing bargaining relationships.

These 'spontaneous' developments in relationships stemmed, it was thought, from a change in the balance of power between management and workers. The workers, in a full employment situation, had the capacity to reduce uncertainty for undertakings and their managements by continuing to act within agreements and procedures, and to increase it by ignoring or breaking them. Many chose the latter course to press their demands, and in consequence, the situations became unmanageable and ultimately unmanaged as cost-push inflation began to run wild and profit margins to fall. Some, at least, of the decisions by companies to withdraw from employers' associations were a response to this (see pp 243-48).

Nevertheless, this process had gone neither as far nor as fast as the Donovan Commission would have preferred. Neither the local management nor the new joint institutions had taken over the control function from the employers' associations and the national collective bargaining institution, and for this reason domestic industrial relations remained disordered.

The Commission's analysis led them to define the main cause of the problem as the conflict between two parallel systems of industrial relations, the formal (or national) and the informal (or domestic) which had grown up in Britain in the post-war period. The 'formal' was that associated historically with the national, industry-wide bargaining system, and the 'informal' was that which had grown up around the local understandings and unwritten compromises negotiated by local management and union representatives mainly in response to local circumstances in the labour market and without reference to the formal national agreements and procedures. As they ran together, they produced the central problem as the Commission saw it:

> 'The central defect in British industrial relations is the disorder in factory and workshop relations and pay structures promoted by the conflict between the formal and the informal structures' (Donovan Commission Report, 1968, para 1019.)

The problem and its solution

The fundamental problem, as the Commission saw it, was that the behaviour of those who were most influentially involved in industrial relations, had ceased to be subject to any order. This was not confined to the behaviour of the shop stewards and their members, although there was clearly a problem here in the unofficial and unconstitutional actions. Workers, in the Donovan view, did and would continue to respond to the structures and rules which surrounded them at work. If those who were 'set in authority over them' did not provide the right structures and rules, workers could hardly be blamed for taking any kind of action which they considered might improve their lot, regardless of how disruptive that might prove to be. The problem was, in this sense, mainly one for the managers and the union leadership to tackle.

The Commission's main strictures were reserved for the directors of companies who were seen to have abdicated their responsibilities, preferring to shelter behind the 'facade' of industry-wide bargaining and agreements (Donovan Commission *Report*, 1968, para 169), behind which 'indecision and anarchy .... inefficiency .... and reluctance to change' were bred (*ibid.*, paras 1016 and 1018).

This view was not, however, one which emerged only with the Royal Commission. It was a view more widely held and applied to more general aspects of the managerial role. Mant, for example, castigated management for its generally poor performance and attributed this to an overconcern with status and the maintenance of a protective social distance between management and labour (Mant, 1977). Marsh had also foreshadowed the Commission's finding with respect to industrial relations particularly in his statement that:

1   'it has not been part of the traditional equipment of managers to understand industrial relations',
2   'managers do not find prestige in being skilled negotiators, handlers of grievance procedures, designers of systems of control and payments which minimize conflict between themselves and organized labour' and
3   'managers are rarely successful for their expertise in labour matters, and industrial relations is usually on the very edge of management education' (Marsh, 1965, p 144).

Such criticisms imply two things: first, that management is *expected* to perform adequately in respect of both wealth production and industrial relations; and, secondly, management was failing on both counts.

In the Commission's view, therefore, changes in perspectives (or theories) and in conduct were required if the national system was to be replaced by a local or domestic system to produce the desired order. This was possible they thought because at that level, *real* issues could be dealt with and the local parties could accept greater responsibility for the establishment and maintenance of *relevant* rules. Local management and shop stewards were the ones who would be required to assume control of industrial relations by incorporating the domestic system into new structures, via policies and procedures. To assist in this, some limited changes in central government policy, if not in law, would be needed.

However, the Donovan Commission's proposals amounted to a marginally reformist breaking up of the national arrangement into small change, not a radical proposal to change the currency used. It wanted to preserve many of the values (of stability and order) inherent in the national arrangements, by creating smaller-scale organization of an essentially similar kind (see Maitland, 1980; McCarthy *et al*, 1971).

Responses to the diagnosis

Following the Donovan Report's publication, some action was

taken by the main parties (as defined for example by Dunlop, see pp 13-15). Employers and trade unions took a good deal of notice both of the Royal Commission's conclusions and recommendations and of the changes in public policy which were subsequently made during the 1970s. But taking notice did not lead to a sweeping replacement of one (albeit bifurcated) system by another more consistent with the assumptions and beliefs of the Commissioners.

Throughout the 1970s, the economy was beset by many if not all of the same problems which had originally led to the setting up of the Royal Commission. At the time the industrial relations system was changing in a piecemeal fashion as the main actors responded to changes in law and in the market and social environments within which they had to operate. The long-term direction of any change was not, however, obvious.

State actions

In this interim phase, the State attempted to tackle some of the problems highlighted by the Royal Commission, but in doing so crossed and recrossed the 'meander plain' in order to find an acceptable course for the new river (see Pilkington, 1976). In their separate ways both parties in government have continued the process of increasing the individual worker's rights *vis à vis* his employer (and now *vis à vis* his trade union).

The Conservative goverments of the early 1970s and early 1980s tried by various means, and in quite different employment circumstances, to reduce the immunities of, and increase the legal curbs on, trade unions in order to redress the 'balance of power' in bargaining. Their first (and as it turned out, abortive) excursion into this field was with the Industrial Relations Act 1971; currently a succession of smaller Acts is re-establishing some of the principles which lay behind that Act.

The Labour administrations of the middle 1970s sought to give the trade unions the legal standing and status which they had had in the late 1960s by repealing the Heath Government's Industrial Relations Act 1971, and attempting marginally to extend their rights under the law (only to have most of them removed by the subsequent Conservative government). They also extended and consolidated the rights of individual employees, thus continuing the 'harmonization' with European practice begun in the 1960s.

27

In spite of recommendations from various bodies to governments to deal with the fundamental structure of enterprise in Britain in order to provide a more appropriate foundation for the development of co-operation in work (see, for example, Bullock, 1977) little has been done. The recommendation to develop 'enterprise law' on the continental European model, in place of separate company and labour laws (see Schmitthoff, 1975; Fogarty, 1965, p 187) little has been done (the main exceptions being ss 46 and 74 of the Companies Act 1980) to effect any significant alterations. If industrial relations is now quiescent, it is probably a reflection of the State's failure to mitigate the employment effects of world recession, rather than the result of more direct industrial relations policy measures.

Employer actions

Employers have, arguably, made more accommodations to the underlying problems and the Donovan recommendations than have the unions or the goverment, even if some of these have been wrung out of them by government policy and legislation. They have, perforce, had to orient their activities to the new laws, particularly those on health and safety at work and on employee rights, although that orientation may in some cases amount to little more than being willing to pay the price of transgression (see McCarthy, 1983). Their response to collective labour law has been largely to avoid it wherever possible.

Some managers (and managements) accepted the broad thrust of the Donovan criticism and sought to develop explicit policies of the kind recommended by the Commission in place of such espoused ones as they might previously have followed. In 1970, for example, Cowan advocated the acceptance by management of their responsibility of industrial relations policies, based on the principles of:

(a) management accountability, involving full acceptance by the management that they are responsible for the development of strategies and policies in industrial relations, as they are in other functional areas like marketing or production or development
(b) management initiative, implying that what is done is to be established on the initiative of management rather than in reaction to moves made by others, like the trade unions
(c) distinction of functions, as between the management and the

28

unions, allowing each to appreciate their rights and obligations in the area of industrial relations.

There were other examples of this kind of development during the ensuing years (see Cuthbert and Hawkins, 1973).

As management currently seek to cope with the (product) markets in which they have to operate, they may reveal either of two approaches to industrial relations. In the one, they confront the unions and their workers with 'the stark facts of economic life' and with demands for significant shifts in behaviours backed up by new agreements more supportive of managerial authority. In the other, the response may be more gradualist, aimed at ensuring that economic improvements are made in a more measured and agreed fashion, and developed on the basis of a more integrated local (enterprise-level) union organization. In both frames, significant improvements in the economic (productivity) situation in the undertaking have been effected and there is some evidence of both union de-recognition and local union incorporation at the enterprise level.

Trade union actions

Trade unions now operate within a different legal framework from that which applied to them at the time when the Donovan Commission examined the issues (see pp 140-54). They have also responded to some of the Donovan recommendations by, for example, giving greater formal recognition to workplace representatives in their constitutions and rule-books. They have also reduced their numbers by transfers of engagements and amalgamations, although the motivation for doing so has probably been to secure a stronger political or power base from which to develop pressures for change in employers' or government policies.

Trade unions are unlikely, however, to bring about major changes in either economic performance or the institutions of industrial relations. In both contexts, they are required to adopt essentially reactive, rather than proactive roles, largely because they do not possess a power base which rests upon anything other than the will of the members to act in a solidarist way in pursuit of objectives. This is notoriously difficult to mobilize and to maintain in a state of readiness for action, and can be destroyed by changes in economic circumstances. The unions are also, in their nature, likely to be slow to bring about changes in their own structures or in their objectives, because of the necessity for going through some democratic process in order to secure agreement.

Responding to the situation as they find it, therefore, the unions are probably more committed now to local or domestic bargaining than 20 years ago. There is strong evidence that in many industries 'national bargaining is still alive and well' (see Marsh, 1982, p 161) at least in certain industries other than engineering (see Daniel and Millward, 1983, pp 177-99). Workers' underlying attitudes and motivations may not have changed a great deal in the last few years, and they are still likely to want a more dignified status in work even if they now read the situation as unpropitious for realizing this aim. If worker/trade unionists are less aggressive and less active now than they were, this probably responds to the changes in the economic (labour market) climate within which they have now to operate, rather than to formal policy measures stemming from either government or employers.

Summary: the industrial relations problem

The two central problems of both the subject and the practice of industrial relations remain unresolved. They are the problems of securing sufficient worker commitment to work and co-operation in complex work organizations; and the problem of distributing the product of work activity amongst those who engage in it with all that this implies for status.

The particular forms which industrial relations took in Britain by World War I, came to be regarded as a manifestation of a universal model of 'industrial relations systems' through which the commitment and distribution problems could be resolved efficiently (and democratically). They were used as a basis for theorizing about the institutions of industrial relations, and the notion of a stable system was applied and developed.

By the 1960s, however, so many problems had appeared in Britain that doubts arose about whether there was a system (or even two systems) at all. But even if there was (or were) the main indices by which performance might be measured seemed to point to the fact that it (or they) were now performing most inefficiently in securing commitment or distribution in acceptable terms.

Developments since the Donovan Commission made its

report on the state of industrial relations and its recommendations for remedial action, suggest that at the level of national policy, different governments have chosen to wander widely over the meander plain. At the level of decision by the other two actors (whom Dunlop identifies), the suggestion is that pragmatism rules, while undertakings in diverse circumstances move in their different directions. All the main actors have taken some action, but it is difficult to see this adding up to a coherent pattern or system concept which has much similarity with the traditional model.

Perhaps the future lies with a resurrection of a national system, or perhaps it lies with a more highly decentralized arrangement of the American type. It is difficult to say with any confidence, because it is possible to detect countervailing forces in British society, some making for a more contingent approach to industrial relations structure to increase wealth, and some pressurizing for more solidarist organization to increase rights.

All of this may suggest that 'British industrial relations institutions are in a state of transition'. If this is the case, there is a very real need to analyse their nature and their underlying dynamics in order to make progress in what is clearly an area of importance to the well-being of the employed population.

Readings

On the general historical background to British industrial relations: Phelps-Brown, (1959); Flanders and Clegg (1954); Pelling, (1963).

On the background to the post-war period: Bacon and Eltis (1978); Elliott, (1978); Donovan Commission Report (1968); Cuthbert and Hawkins, (1973).

On the traditional conceptions of industrial relations: Dunlop, (1958); Flanders, (1965 and 1970).

On the current position: Daniel and Millward, (1983); Sisson and Brown, in Bain, (1983), pp 137-54.

2

Perspectives of industrial relations

The scope of industrial relations

Once something is seen to constitute a 'problem', money will be found so that somebody somewhere will be enabled to study it with a view to informing us about why it is a problem, what form it takes, and how it might be reduced (see Clay, 1929). Such has been the genesis of the subject of industrial relations.

As a subject for study, it* is relatively new, still without clear definitions of scope or content (see Barrett, Rhodes and Beishon, 1975, pp 6-39). It was obviously not possible to study industrial relations until modern industry itself acquired a distinct identity, and work relations became separated from those of the family or community (see Fox, 1974a, pp 175-81; Southgate, 1965, pp 344-66). It was also not feasible to do so on any scale, until someone perceived a problem and was persuaded that resources should be devoted to its study. A few people were able to give it attention before World War II, but only since then has it received much serious study.

The way the 'problem' is examined is likely to reflect the way it is perceived. The definition of the scope and purpose of the study is likely to vary with different perceptions (made by either the paymasters or the students themselves). At least two broad perspectives of the problem have been developed, one of which might be labelled the 'traditional' and the other the 'emergent' conception, and each steers study in a distinct direction.

These labels are adopted for convenience. By 'traditional' is meant only the way in which, *historically*, the industrial relations students have sought to define the problem as concerned with systems of rules (see Dunlop, 1958; Clegg, 1972). By 'emergent'

---

* The singular pronoun is used here to refer to industrial relations either as a 'subject' (studied by students) or as a 'practice' (carried on by managers and others).

is meant merely that the current emphasis on self-interested conceptions of man's approach to behaviours at work, whilst not new in itself, suggests a different (or non-traditional) definition and concern. This finds more room for the perspectives of social scientists other than those who have followed the traditional industrial relations path (see Deeks *et al.*, 1971, table 3). In this chapter, we will look at some of the ways in which the 'problem' of industrial relations has been examined by members of these different 'schools', the one traditional and institutional, and the other more widely based in the social sciences.

THE INFLUENCE OF WORK

Both schools are agreed, however, that work in its institutionalized form is influential upon both the human personality and human conduct. Work is seen to affect the *personality* of the worker *and* the way in which he or she acts or *behaves*. This is a common theme in the literature, where the influence of work is seen as a characteristic feature of the modern industrialized society.

For this purpose, work is regarded as an effort-requiring activity performed by people, in conditions of environmental uncertainty, usually in association with other people, in order that they may live, and, by extension, live well. It imposes a discipline on people by requiring them to behave, or to act, in some ways rather than others in order to realize their personal or the social objectives.

Those engaged in work are required to cope with three main aspects of the work environment, the physical, the economic and the social. The first demands a decision about the kind of work the individual is prepared to engage in. The second requires decisions about the amounts of effort or contribution he will make in response to the returns thought to be available. The third affects the terms under which the involvement will take place.

The physical aspects are usually considered under the heading of 'technology' but no matter how sophisticated this might be, it comprises essentially the materials and tools which have to be used and thus responded to by the individuals. Research has discovered links between the technology and behaviour (see Woodward, 1958; Sayles, 1958) and between it and the quantities of effort and reward realizable (see Doeringer and

Piore, 1971), thus suggesting that there is a patterned response to this feature.

The individual's work occurs within an economic environment but he or she may be protected by a mediating organization (whether company or trade union) from direct exposure to the market and its pressures. Nevertheless, the amount of remuneration he or she receives for his labours depends on the nature of both the product and labour markets within which the job is located. He or she is called upon to form some judgement of the market impact upon him or her, and (in the terms used in 'expectancy theory') this might affect his or her decision about how much effort to supply given the rewards likely to be available.

These demands are mediated through the social environment, that structure of norms and rules which determines the terms of the necessary co-operation. Thus technology and its demands on the person, is generally inseparable in its influence on people from that of the social relationships of work. Technology is both a cause and a consequence of the division of labour and both are the product of deliberate decisions by someone, who will also devise rules for co-operation to integrate what has thus been divided.

Comparably, the social structure cushions the individual from the direct effects of exigencies of the market, with the trade union providing a particularly good and generally-recognized example of this kind of process. But no matter how much representative arrangements for collective bargaining may shield individuals from market forces, some assessment of their own position in the market has still to be made. The social web around them does, however, help them to avoid some of the grosser uncertainties which might otherwise beset them as they seek to cope with the situation. But the social structure of norms and rules must then form the third element of the situation with which the individual must cope.

All of them therefore present 'problems' to the individual, and it is the process of coping or dealing with them that leads to the individual's personality and behaviour being regarded as shaped by work. The consequences may be discussed under these two headings.

Personality

The first idea is that work makes people what they are (see Miller, 1962). This might be simply because individuals spend a good deal of their waking hours engaged in it. Meakin summarizes one line of thought developed by many of the great thinkers of last century:

> 'Work ... and not least manual work ... is an integral part of our humanity and our intelligence. It dictates our relationship to nature, to our environment, but thereby also the working and scope of our consciousness itself, for consciousness is born out of that active confrontation with nature' (Meakin, 1976, pp 1-2).

But the idea is sometimes more focused than this emphasis on physical labour implies, upon the social control or the socially-imposed discipline to which working persons are subject.

Barnard has suggested, for example, that the unavoidable *relations* in work:

> operate on the individuals affected; and, in conjunction with other factors, become incorporated in their mental and emotional characters. This is an effect which makes them significant. Hence, co-operation compels changes in the motives of individuals which otherwise would not take place. So far as these changes are in a direction favourable to the co-operative system they are resources to it. So far as they are in a direction unfavourable to co-operation, they are detriments to it or limitations of it' (Barnard, 1938, p 40).

This links the control seen as inherent in the relations with the basic problem of commitment. The suggestion is that it is this feature of discipline or control which can (under appropriate circumstances) yield the personal commitment which organized activity demands of its members.

The same influences can also be regarded as resources or detriments to the individual as a human being, as well as to Barnard's 'co-operative system'. The Marxian thesis that the 'structure' of capitalism 'exploits' the worker in that it denies him the full development of his personality as well as the full product of his labour, whereas other structures which might be conjured up in the mind would provide more opportunities (and therefore 'emancipate' the worker), also illustrates this line of thought.

Behaviour

Burns suggests that modern industry deliberately *processes* people into resources of production and consumers of products (Burns, 1969, p 7) and thereby extends the idea to embrace the effect of involvement in work relations on the way people behave in or out of work. The way people behave at work is seen to be influenced by the nature and organization of that work.

Evidence exists at the small group level which suggests that the way people conduct themselves is influenced by the structures of relations in which they are caught up. The most famous such study (although not of an industrial setting) is that of the Norton Street Gang, studied by Whyte, in which the boys were seen to perform at bowls at a level which was consistent with their (informal) status in the group (Whyte, 1943; Homans, 1951, pp 156-71). The men in the Bank Wiring Observation Room at the Hawthorne plant were also found to conduct themselves differently but in ways which accorded with their group memberships (see Roethlisberger and Dickson, 1939). Sayles's discovery that patterns of grieving behaviour in groups tended to associate with their members' positions in structures of division of labour suggests a similar relationship (Sayles, 1958).

The explanation usually offered of these patterns is one which focuses upon the concepts of norm and expectation. A 'norm' is defined as a statement of how a person should, or is expected to, behave in a given setting, but it is always supported by some sanction which can be applied to punish or penalize the person who transgresses. People are *expected* to obey the norms of their group(s) and to do so, as it were 'voluntarily' or as a matter of course. If they do not, however, there is some means of expressing social disapproval, so that the abstract statement is backed up by something more compelling. Applied to the small group studies (p 56) the concept is used to suggest that there were in each case norms of conduct appropriate to each member, and they were expected to conform; but they knew that they would suffer some disapproval or penalty if they did not do so. Because group membership was somehow important to them and because they disliked the possible penalties, they tended to conform most of the time.

36

Human behaviour at work might be expected to respond to general norms or (more formally) to particular rules which apply to them in work. Formal works rules which carry appropriate penalties for breach, can in some circumstances, function in pretty much the same fashion as the norms of the informal group in compelling behaviour.

However, people's behaviours might also conform because of the pressures of the physical situation (whether it is rule-bound or not). There are, for example, a number of propositions about the association of technologies with behaviours, which imply that behaviour will conform to the 'law of the situation' rather than to any formal rules or informal norms (Woodward, 1958). The theories of strike-proneness in particular industries suggest that at the larger group level, something about the physical and or social structure creates a consistent pattern of strike behaviour (see Ross and Hartmann, 1960). The Marxian thesis that conflict is inevitable in a capitalist structure of industry also illustrates this same idea.

Thus, no matter which perspective is adopted, work and its concommitant relations and rules are seen to be significant because they are likely to have more influence upon both the well-being and the actual behaviour of people at work than other kinds of relations (such as the relations between family members or between persons who vote for the same party in an election). It is this which makes them worthy of study. As Fox has suggested, we can be as 'interested in the question of what work does *to* people' as producers of wealth, as in what work does *for* people in providing wealth and income (Fox, 1971, p 1). This provides one ethical orientation of the subject of industrial relations.

Roles and statuses

Explanations of how the work environment secures its effects make particular use of the concepts of role and status and motivation and incentive. These occur in the range of variables which are seen to influence behaviour (or, in the language more frequently used in the management context, performance).

The determinants of performance are usually considered under the three headings of role perceptions and prescriptions, abilities and traits of personality, and motivational level (see Thomason, 1981, pp 271-96; Steers and Porter, 1979, pp 210-46).

1   Role perception is partly a matter of how clearly the role is specified and its associated expectations communicated, and partly of the individual's capacity for perceiving and understanding the prescriptions.
2   Abilities or skills bring together conceptions of *knowledge about* and *know-how* related to the role in question, and personality traits to those displayed *behavioural predispositions* of the individual which may be relevant to performance in it.
3   Motivational level refers to the extent to which the individual *wants* to perform the role as specified or as he perceives it.

The first and third of these are considered further here, although this does not imply that abilities and skills are not relevant. However, these are usually acquired through a specific process of learning and are omitted from discussion here only because our concern will be more generally focused on 'socialization' (below, p 49).

The concepts of role and status are often used interchangeably to refer to the way in which the individual actor is normatively linked into complex organizations or structures of activity (see Argyle, 1972; Goffman, 1961, pp 85-95). The view is taken that man is caught up in many such structures, including those relating to work, and that these exert their influence upon man through his status (or the rights and obligations of his position) and his role (or the normative expectations as to what he will do in that status or position).

'Status' (or sometimes 'position') is defined as that set of rights and duties which are attached to the person in question and indicated (usually) by some title such as manager or worker (see Goffman, 1961, p 85). Barnard provides a longer definition which will be useful in later discussions of both individual and associational status. He suggests that status refers to:

> 'that condition of the individual that is defined by a statement of his rights, privileges, immunities, duties, and obligations ... and obversely, by a statement of the restrictions, limitations and prohibitions governing his behaviour' (Barnard, 1946, pp 207-43).

Status is what defines the individual's power (or authority) within a structure or organization of positions, such as that which surrounds work activity. A person's status establishes what he *can* do.

The concept of role is then defined as the dynamic aspect of a status or position. Role develops from utilizing the power which the rights and obligations donate in order to achieve some end, and constrains the individual incumbent to act in accordance with the norms of the group or organization within which the role exists. What ends are to be pursued, and what means will be adopted to do so, are subject to expectations formulated by others and transmitted to the individual to indicate what he or she ought to do or is expected to do whilst in that position (see Homans, 1951, p 11-12). Where the role is an important one (like manager or worker) it is likely to be defined by expectations which are given the form of specifications or *rules* which the individual is expected to obey on pain of being thought to be inefficient or lacking in capacity.

Role in the normative sense of what ought to be done is distinguished from role in the descriptive sense of role performance which establishes what the person actually does (see Goffman, 1961, p 85). Deficiencies under any of the three headings (above, p 38) might lead to a difference between the normative conception of the role and its actual performance. For example, the criticisms of management's performance in industrial relations (see pp 25-26) may exemplify an awareness of a deficiency in *role* performance, of a failure to come up to expectations. The manager might well respond, however, by suggesting that his authority ('rights and responsibilities') are now generally insufficient to enable him or her to conform to those expectations, especially where they are themselves the product of the classical definition of the management role.

Human motivation

Theories of motivation within both psychology and management seek an explanation of why man is willing to put an amount of energy into particular forms of behaviour within particular work situations. They tend to accept that, as Kelly has suggested, man acts (and is motivated to act) simply because he is alive (Kelly, 1963, p 37), that no other explanation of basic motivation is called for. He works because work is part of living. He may have to decide how much work or what kind in the anticipation of what returns, in the particular circumstances in which he finds

39

himself attempting to live, but in the general case, he does not have to decide whether to work.

Two broad approaches are to be detected in motivation theory. One places the emphasis on the individual organism, and seeks to explain human 'movement' or expenditure of energy in terms of some inner 'need' or 'drive', which is then seen to *push* the individual in some direction or another (for example, work). If the individual can be seen to have a set of 'needs' for material, social or mental satisfactions, then what he does may be explained in terms of his pursuing these as goals (see Maslow, 1943; Herzberg, 1967; Alderfer, 1972; Steers and Porter, 1979).

The other perspective of motivation stresses the importance of the external stimulus as the source of motivation, which then somehow pulls the individual along a certain path. In this case, something in the environment (which might be a coercive rule or the offer of a monetary reward) triggers off a response or reaction in the individual; he does what he thinks is appropriate to react to the stimulus, and what he does may reflect what he has through socialization *learned* to do in such circumstances (see Heneman and Schwab, 1972).

Kelly's approach attempts to bring these push and pull theories together, and to subsume them in a conception of the individual as a decision-maker. Man, he suggests, must take decisions after some fashion, in order to cope. He must use his innate and learned capacity which enables him or her to do so. Psychologists may subsume this notion of capacity under a label such as 'personality', but other concepts such as attitude, frame of reference, and ideology are often used to indicate the individual's holistic view of and approach to the environment.

The alternative views

A problem of perspective remains to be resolved: whether it can be assumed (or counted on) that these influences on man result from the operation of rules intended to bind human conduct in work, or from the way in which the individual forms his own views and takes his own decisions about how to conduct himself in the circumstances in which he finds himself (including, but not confined to, those indicated by rule). This is fundamental to the difference in approaches made to the study of industrial relations, and it focuses on the kinds of view taken of man and of the way in which he copes with or adjusts to the environment.

Another way of making the distinction is, therefore, to suggest that the traditional approach relies upon different assumptions from the emergent approach about what is important in the determination of behaviour at work. Both are ultimately concerned with the explanation, anticipation or prediction of human behaviour in the work context. But the question of just what it is that should be studied in order to do this can be answered in different ways which can be categorized to give the following two broad perspectives:

1   Everything which can be demonstrated to influence the behaviour of the person should be admitted directly to the study, which should itself focus on the behaviour of the individual as the final decider of action or the individual in an unavoidable socio-technical context.
2   Only those forces and factors which influence the nature of the values, beliefs, norms and rules by which people are assumed to live, need be included in the study, which should then focus on the rules, etc, and how they are established, maintained and implemented, on the assumption that the individual generally behaves in accordance with such rules.

These imply very different boundaries to the subject, and different assumptions about the nature of man and the way he interacts with the physical and social environment.

THE TRADITIONAL APPROACH

In the traditional approach (exemplified in the works of Dunlop and Flanders) the main focus is upon the 'rules' (or norms) which guide behaviour and the structures of relations which both express and enforce them. It is assumed that these are the important determinants of behaviour at work. If, therefore, we wish to study the influences upon human conduct or behaviour at work, we might, on these assumptions, go no further than to study the rules themselves. Writers in the traditional vein have tended to emphasize this as the scope and purpose of the subject.

Heneman has suggested that 'industrial relations is concerned with employment relations in an industrial economy' (1969, p 3). On the face of it, this suggests that every relationship in and around employment should be included, on the basis that all of them might have some influence. Allen attempts to define scope in much the same fashion, saying that it is:

> 'concerned with the individual at work, not in his home or during his leisure, unless it becomes clear that influences from these environments are determining his work-time behaviour' (Allen, 1971, p 12).

This too suggests that *all* the relationships in and around industry or employment are to be included in order to explain 'work-time behaviour' (see also Behrend, 1963).

Others take a more restricted view of scope, and change the focus in so doing. For example, Dunlop suggests that:

> 'the central task of a theory of industrial relations is to explain why particular rules are established in particular industrial relations systems and how and why they change in response to changes affecting the system' (Dunlop, 1958, pp viii-ix).

This introduces the concept of 'system' (see above, pp 4-5) but it also confines industrial relations to those processes which establish and maintain or change the rules which are thought to affect or *determine* some kinds of work-time behaviour. Flanders expresses a similar orientation more succinctly in his statement that 'the study of industrial relations may be described as the study of the institutions of job regulation' (1965, p 10), where 'institution' takes the place of Dunlop's 'system' concept, and implies a more restricted view of the field.

Flanders' conception leaves out, for example, the 'personal and unstructured' relations (such as those within workgroups mentioned on p 36) unless the condition identified by Allen (see above) applies (see Flanders, 1965, p 10). It also omits certain market or commercial relations, as for example those between firms or within cartels. It devotes almost exclusive attention to the formally-patterned (institutionalized) relations between categories (for example, workers and management) or organizations (for example, companies and trade unions) and to the rules which emerge from and are enforced through their interactions.

A systemic social relationship

This exclusivity follows from the perspective that industrial relations (and the human behaviour associated with it) can be regarded as operating in 'system' terms. It is postulated that industrial relations behaviours will be determined or structured in accordance with the rules made *to* determine that behaviour. Consequently, when the observation is made that large numbers of people behave in a patterned or uniform way, this, it is thought, can be explained in terms of the system 'working' in the manner intended: people behave consistently because they obey the rules which the industrial relations system creates.

This conformity is built into the system concept through the concept of 'binding ideology' (see pp 4-5). What, in effect, this means is that people necessarily accept that rules are to be obeyed and that they really have no discretion as to whether to obey or disobey. This basic assumption of the systems theory, thus removes any need to consider whether people will obey or not; it is taken as axiomatic that they will obey the rules. It is true that this assumption occurs in Dunlop's original exposition in association with a 'stable system' of industrial relations, and presumably the assumption is not meant to apply to 'unstable systems'. However, any industrial relations arrangement which reveals *any* pattern at all is regarded as a stable system, because it is the pattern of uniform behaviour that gives rise to it, and so this exclusion is not particularly helpful.

The operation of a stable system is therefore seen to depend upon the people involved accepting as a binding ideology that the rules created by the 'system' are to be obeyed. It may also be that these rules are only to be obeyed if they are made by the people themselves or their representatives; this would be consistent with that part of the perspective which these theorists take which posits that rules made by agreement are more likely to be regarded as morally (or ideologically) binding than those which are imposed (see Gouldner, 1955b, pp 19-20). However, where industrial relations is identified with systems of collective bargaining, this condition is assumed to be met, and the general theory can be applied to the operation of the system.

These theories of how the industrial relations system 'works' are dependent upon people learning their roles in interaction with others. This aspect is treated in theories of socialization which attempt to explain how it is that 'the individual earns the behaviour appropriate to his position in a group through interaction with others who hold normative beliefs about what his role should be and who reward or punish him for correct or incorrect actions' (Brim, 1966, p 9).

In broad outline, these theories of socialization or conditioning assert that, as the individuals mature, they learn what is expected of them in various positions within structures of roles and relations. This is done through the interaction with 'significant others' (people, like mothers, siblings, school-mates, work-mates, managers, who have a direct and influential relationship with the individual in some important context, like the family, school or work). From such sources, individuals learn what are the general and specific (role-linked) norms to which they are expected to conform.

This need not deny that individuals adjust to society in different ways, nor that in spite of the influence of society upon them, they may still manage to be creative or innovative and effect changes in the social order. But it does recognize that as these significant others 'do their best for' their children or their friends or colleagues, they consciously or unconsciously inculcate the values and behaviours favoured by the culture or society. By such interactions with others, people learn the behavioural expectations which these others hold. When, therefore, these individuals find themselves within some system of roles and relations which is governed by rules, they will tend both to know what the rules are and that they are expected to obey them on pain of some penalty or punishment for non-conformity (see Glazer, 1971).

A problematic social relationship

The main challenge to the view described above derives from Weber's social action theory, in which the questions of whether people obey rules and why are regarded as more of a problem to be examined. Weber regards a social relationship as consisting 'entirely and exclusively in the existence of a probability that there will be, in some meaningfully understandable sense, a course of social action' (Weber, 1947, p 118; 1968, pp 26-27). 'Social action' refers to action 'which takes into account the behaviour of others' in the *meaning* which individuals attach to their action (Weber, 1947, p 88). The individual's reasons or motives for attaching a particular meaning may vary considerably, just as workers may have different reasons or motives for attending work. But the observable fact of (pattern in) attend-

44

ance is what Weber seeks to explain in terms of meanings imputed to the behaviour.

We can, in other words, speak of a social relationship existing where the people concerned act or behave in roughly the same fashion because they have attached approximately the same kinds of social meaning to their actions. People may turn up to work on time because, for example, they see themselves as 'under a duty to do so' and regard doing one's duty as important. But they may do so out of habit, unthinkingly, and without any attribution of meaning which involves the concept of 'duty'. Pattern, says Weber, may develop for quite different reasons and be associated with quite different meanings, and, therefore, *why* people behave in a 'social' way is something to be explored, not (as with the systems theorists) to be assumed to stem from a perception of a moral duty. People may display common social behaviours because they orient their behaviours to the actions of others in one or other mode by which social meaning is assigned.

The traditional perspective only intermittently recognizes the problematic nature of social action. Rather it proceeds to examine the processes of rule formation on the assumption that the rules will constitute a a legitimate order to which people will (because of their conditioning) orient their work behaviours. This assumption is swept up in the concept of a 'binding ideology' whose intention and effect is to render it axiomatic that people will 'obey the rules', and will do so more especially if they have been produced democratically.

Weber would contend that this is one special case which occurs only where people accept that the rules constitute a legitimate order where, that is, rules are accepted as imposing a duty and where duty has a high moral value for the people concerned. The traditional approach to industrial relations and the recommendations put forward by the Donovan Commission are based on the assumption that the rules will serve as *law* in that they they will be accepted as binding upon the individuals and enforced by some functionally specialized agency. This directs attention to the rules, but, as Shimmin and Singh (1973, pp 37-42) have suggested, may then provide a very restricted focus for the study of work behaviour.

The underlying assumptions

This assumption that 'people automatically obey the rules' also directs attention and attracts recommendations for action which are comparably restricted. This effect can, for example, be seen in the analysis and recommendations made by the Donovan Commission where an edifice of assumption, drawn from this school, can be discerned in their analysis and, more particularly, in their recommendations:

1 that the primary end of working (for both individual and for society) is the production of wealth, and that what we refer to as industrial relations is therefore derivative from this and secondary and instrumental to this primary end

2 that the relationships of man at work constitute a constraining sheath or envelope, which both channels and restricts the individual's discretion to decide and act, and which, for this reason, may be evaluated as appropriate or inappropriate as an instrument

3 that the element of constraint or control is effected by establishing structures of norms (manifest specifically in individual roles) on the basis of applying some principles, norms or rules to the work process (and exemplified in the rights, obligations and restrictions associated with those roles)

4 that some men will have particular role responsibilities, backed by appropriate power or authority, for effecting the necessary arrangements, and that they, like everyone else, will discharge these role obligations in accordance with the built-in principles, norms and rules

5 that man will generally obey the rules, and particularly those which are applied to his or her role if only because the individual must make the best kind of coping decisions he can in order to live, or live well, and since the rules structure the environment within which he must perform the role, obedience to the rules may be seen as functional

6 that whilst generally men will obey the rules built into the structure of relationships, they are more likely to obey them if they are developed on their agreement or under their control, rather than autocratically by 'Masters' or impersonally (and therefore inhumanely) by the operation of the 'forces of the market'

7 that the best guarantee of willing co-operation in the processes of production is thus to be the continuation, even if in modified form, of the structure or system of industrial

relations which has been identified by the traditional label of voluntary collective bargaining.

It is not therefore surprising, given these basic assumptions, that the Commission should seek to exhort management (given their legitimate authority) to join with their worker representatives (because agreement is to be preferred over imposition) in developing policies and rules (to form a new legitimate order) which would bring behaviour in the 'informal system' (see p 25) into a new conformity (because people will automatically respond, because of their conditioning, to obey legitimate authority and to conform with legitimate rules).

This is the essence of the traditional, institutional perspective which necessarily leads to a reformist approach to the resolution of industrial relations problems. It is not unreasonable as an approach, if the assumption about general obedience to rules holds good. Clearly, if that is the case, and man does accept that work behaviour is instrumental in the way suggested, then the recommendations could well succeed.

THE EMERGING CONCEPTION

The emerging conception may be composited from some of the speculation about man's nature in the social sciences, some of the ideas which have been put forward in recent years about the maturation of worker attitudes and abilities, and some of the principles which underly some of the aspects of recent State policies.

Generally, this conception tends to elevate the significance of the individual as a decision-maker who is less bound by rules and more concerned with taking conscious decisions about the action which will fit the circumstances as they are perceived by him. This places the emphasis on the psychologist's concern to explain how it is that the individual in spite of the pressures of the society and culture, still manages to act individually and creatively rather than merely conformingly.

One view which emerges from a good deal of the kind of speculation about the nature of man (Maslow, 1943; Herzberg, 1967; Kelly, 1963) is depicted in table 10 on page 48. This treats man (which includes both managers and non-managers) as an organism which is required to cope as best it can with the

Table 10
A perspective of man

1   Man cannot avoid work (even if individual men can) since the word 'work' itself is used to indicate an activity which is inherent in living.

2   Man in his nature is motivated to work (even if some men are reluctant movers) since only by working will he acquire the necessities and the luxuries of life, although he is not necessarily motivated to work within any particular physical or social context which might structure the available work.

3   Man will generally seek to optimize his return (in material and non-material satisfactions) for any given expenditure of energy or effort, and will thus put out as much or as little effort as he considers is required to secure the returns as he perceives and defines them.

4   Man will develop perceptions and perspectives of the environment (his frame of reference) as a necessary foundation for making the decisions which must precede any coping activity on his part.

5   Because of the nature of the world in which he has his being, man's perceptions and perspectives will be influenced by the presence of other men as both competitors and co-operators as all try to cope with the environment in which they find themselves.

6   Man derives his knowledge partly as a consequence of coping with the world and partly as a result of socialization or indoctrination in the values and beliefs which his society adopts as appropriate to its circumstances, and builds into the institutions with which he must perforce interact.

7   Man's knowledge of the environment cannot be perfect or complete both because of its scale and because of its dynamic and changing character, which creates the fundamental conditions of uncertainty.

8   As a consequence of this, what man wants (from work or anything else) and how he sees himself as best able to secure what he wants from that environment, are both affected to an extent (unknown in each case) by his physical and psychological nature and his physical and social environment.

environment in which it finds itself, and endowed with a capacity to think, decide and act for itself even if in some contexts it may choose to act unthinkingly.

Something of this idea may also be found lurking in some aspects of social policy, although in that context it is not particularly new. Indeed, it could be argued that it is a perspective which applied more forcibly to the individual entrepreneur of the early stages of the industrial revolution. It is only new in our present context in that it has been revived in recent years both by academic thinkers (for example, Silverman, 1970) and by the State in the development of a more 'individualistic' policy-base for removing some of the constraints of rule from at least some of the actors in the industrial relations context, and exposing the individual more directly to the *pressures* of the market environment (see also below, pp 228-29).

The conception of man as a decision-maker implies that man acts according to the way he decides to act (see Simon, 1953, p 1), and decision-making is something which is personal to him. It also implies a particular conception of human motivation or will; it suggests that man will normally act as an individual, and will do so whenever the opportunity is presented. In doing so, he or she may orient his decisions and actions to others, thus accepting the rules, but the primacy of rule or rules in influencing behaviour is removed. This is to emphasize the types of social action linked with the habitual and self-interested orientations identified by Weber rather than those associated with external order (see pp 58-59).

Social organization and its associated rules, are but one element in the situation to which the individual is required to respond. There are other things external to man which provide him with a stimulus to which he both can (by virtue of his skills and abilities) and will (given his motivation) respond in some way. This stimulus has both physical and economic features, as well as social ones. It can be held that man is capable of responding directly to these without the mediating influence of organization or its rules. But it has also to be recognized that even the most competent decision-taker is likely to appreciate the role of the organization in reducing (by promulgation of norms and rules) the uncertainty within which decisions have to be taken. In this sense and to this extent, the emergent conception is not to be equated with a simple or primitive 'individualism' of the kind which animated policy in the first industrial revolution.

Man as decision-maker

The way in which the coping man approaches the handling of his environment is likely to be common for Kelly's scientist, the manager, and the worker on the shop floor. The individual manager or worker may not regard himself as 'a scientist' but the argument is that in seeking out the ways of coping with his work materials and his work relations, he does not differ too much from the scientist in the approach he adopts. He may not regard himself as particularly 'scientific' in trying to work out what decision is called for in given circumstances, but he may nevertheless use approaches which in the most generic sense are those of the scientist. In the present context, it might not be inappropriate to substitute the conception of a 'manager' rather than a scientist, given some similarity in the approaches made by the two to the problem of dealing with problems. Kelly suggests that the *social scientist* who seeks to understand this or any other kind of human behaviour might well start from this point.

How the means adopted are to be described has attracted a good deal of attention, particularly in the management literature devoted to this one special category of 'coping man' (Simon, 1957; Cyert and March, 1963; Braybrooke and Lindblom, 1963). There is also a growing body of literature on decision-taking in worker/trade union contexts (see, for example, Batstone *et al.* 1977 and 1978; Armstrong *et al.*, 1981). The theorizing about the process of decision-making has frequently focused on how managers do so (although there is also a whole psychological literature on decision-taking in other contexts, some of which is used in connection with studies of negotiation and bargaining: see pp 509-13).

The dominant view of decision-taking is one which, to whatever degree of sophistication, distinguishes a number of processes by which all kinds of information from all manner of sources are processed and turned into a predisposition to act. In Kelly's view, people, regardless of situation or role, all approach the task as what he calls, 'scientists' (Kelly, 1963, p 4), albeit with different degrees of methodological sophistication. They may not all reach the same conclusions, but they all seek to construe (or give meaning to) their situation in order to anticipate what might happen and forecast the most appropriate action. All of them must decide by some means to go for those outcomes which are considered necessary or desirable to them and to do so after

50

some kind of appraisal of the situation and its potential for yielding the desired outcomes.

Management decision-taking

The concern with management decision-taking arises because it is often regarded as problematic. It has usually responded to the recognition by economists that managerial capacity for decision is often an inhibiting factor in, for example, growth of enterprise scale (see Bridge and Dodds, 1975). Current thinking suggests that targets of not more than 500 people on any one site managed by a single management may be optimum. But the source of the problem may lie not simply in lack of capacity or skill, but in a failure to acknowledge how decisions (in management or anywhere else) are actually taken.

The traditional model is one which regards the process of managerial decision-taking as a 'rational' one which can be regarded as having objective characteristics. The 'rational model' of decision-taking postulates that there is a known objective, a number of alternative courses of action whose properties are known or knowable, and the task of the decision-maker is then to choose the optimal alternative from the range on criteria (for example profit) derived from the objective. This model may be articulated in a number of distinct ways (see Brown, 1971; Bakke, 1950: Falk and Clark, 1966) but it implies that the goal is one of finding optimizing solutions given a range of known alternatives, and that the approach of the decision-taker is one involving total rationality.

This model of decision-taking has three operational phases:

1 identification of a problem, or a departure of the actuality from the desired, which requires of the individual both recognition and definition
2 search for courses of action one of which might be adopted to resolve the problem (close the 'gap'). This requires not only their identification but their assessment in terms of their efficacy and the probability with which they will serve the purpose
3 choice of one such alternative from the range discovered and determination to act upon it in order to resolve the problem. For this the individual must possess a capacity for choosing in accordance with established criteria.

The *form* which this model will take in practice may well vary with the circumstances, the nature of the problem itself and the constraints upon the decision-taker in resolving it. But typically, it is depicted as a closed loop system, in which the feedback loop triggers the perception of a need to decide and a feed-out loop carries the resultant choice into action. The 'controller's' decision is reached by the systematic process outlined above, and in accordance with the criteria which derive from the objectives established for the system. By necessary implication, therefore, the manager as decision-maker is as much a cog in the decision process as is the worker in the production process (see figure 2 below).

Figure 2
A closed loop model of decision-making and action

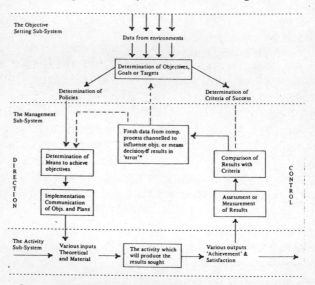

* In this model, any perceived departure of the achieved results from the intended ones, signals 'an error' and stimulates the controller to think or decide again. The error may indicate that the given ends are not attainable by the presently-used means or that they are not attainable at all and require change. In the one case, the 'loop' is closed without involving a consideration of the appropriatenesss of the objectives, and in the other through their reconsideration.

If the model is related to time, it might be better construed as a spiral through time, with each subsequent re-think occurring at a later point in time.

Alternative models

In recent years a number of alternative models of managerial decision-taking have been advanced. Allen (1977) has suggested

52

that because of this, the manager now has a choice of a number of normative and descriptive theories of decision-making, which purport either to describe what he does do or prescribe what he ought to do.

The three main alternative theories in this area are:

1   The 'bounded rationality' model (associated with Carnegie) which acknowledges that the manager (and by extension anyone) is usually not in the position of having such complete knowledge of either objectives or the means to their attainment. Instead he has imperfect knowledge and must seek to simplify his problem and the range of alternatives which he must consider. In this model (see Simon, 1957; 1959) dissatisfaction with what exists triggers the recognition of a problem (rather than an objective) and the goal of the manager's action is to reduce the dissatisfaction or to effect improvement. In order to do so he engages in a search for solutions but only to an extent defined by the probability that when he finds one which he thinks will be satisfactory he will adopt it without continuing the search for a better one. Instead of total rationality, Simon substitutes a 'bounded rationality', and instead of optimizing he substitutes 'satisficing' (choosing the 'good enough').

2   The 'social model' which extends some of these ideas, but acknowledges the social aspect of decision-taking, by recognizing that decisions are taken by 'coalitions' (Cyert and March, 1963) (of managers) rather than by individuals operating in isolation, and as a result of a negotiating (Abell, 1975) or a political (Pettigrew, 1973) process. In one extension of this idea, the garbage can model, (see Cohen, *et al.* 1972, pp 1-25) the problem itself emerges or is defined only as a consequence of the interaction within the social situation. This approach also implies that the members will consciously simplify the problems, the solutions and the processes by which they arrive at them, and that satisficing criteria will be employed to determine the solutions which will both help to reduce (but not eliminate: Cyert and March, 1963, p 117) the conflict in the coalition (as to what ought to be done) and move things forward only incrementally (allowing effects to be monitored closely).

3   The 'strategy of disjointed incrementalism' (Braybrooke and Lindblom, 1963) sometimes described more simply as 'muddling through' (Lindblom, 1959). In this conception, decision-takers are seen to stay close to where they are, to attempt only very marginal changes in the situation and to limit their search

to such alternatives as will be consistent with this. Objectives are not the determinants of methods, but the consequences of them, reflecting the attempt to reduce the unsatisfactory rather than to realize some previously-established abstract goal. Decision-making therefore proceeds on the basis of minimal or marginal change which can be agreed amongst the decison-makers themselves on the basis of their several perceptions of the problem and possible ways of handling it.

The differences between these are therefore mainly focused upon the extent to which the problem is defined scientifically and the extent to which the 'search process' is carried out systematically. The notion of man as decision-maker need not, therefore, imply that everyone behaves as rationally as the classical model implies (see Johnson, 1972, pp 344-45). The usefulness of that model and its alternatives lies in its capacity to focus our attention on those aspects of the person and situation most likely to be significant in shaping decisions and action.

Situational and personal correlates

These different conceptions of how decision-taking occurs, could conceivably apply to practices in different *kinds* of situation, for example public and private organizations (see Allen, 1977). In addition, as both Etzioni (1968) and Lindblom (1959) argue, the rational and the incremental models might be relevant to different *levels* of decision within the single hierarchical organization. Etzioni refers to this possibility as 'mixed scanning'. Such variations could arise simply because individuals in different contexts attach different social meanings to their actions, and in this they may be guided by the expectations or rules which apply to them in their different positions.

The source of the difference may not, however, lie in the roles (as these comments imply), but in personality variables; different models may be adopted by different types of decision-taker. Different people may well approach the taking of decisions in quite distinct ways, regardless of whether these ways are 'objectively consistent' with their roles or the environment in which they are taken (see Johnson, 1972, pp 378-80). Different individuals (whether they are managers or not) can be expected to reveal distinct approaches to the decision-making task, reflecting motivation and perspectives.

Motivation may be significant in that the individual's wants and desires may define problems for him and drive or impel him in some directions rather than others, according to how he sees his chances of success. These wants are not necessarily given by man's inherent nature and may well be shaped or moulded by the values and standards of the surrounding organization or society, but they are likely to attach uniquely to the individual (see Maslow, 1943; Herzberg, 1968; Steers and Porter, 1979, pp 31-89; Kelly, 1965; Brim 1966, p 11).

It may be important to the extent that the individual may construe external stimuli as constituting some kind of problem which he must resolve and as offering benefits of the kind he would like. This construction may be based on ideas which the individual has developed as a result of construing similar stimuli in past experience or as the result of intellectual learning in a more abstract fashion about the way the world 'works'. In either case, it could lead him to adopt a particular frame of reference for resolving the problem and to act in one particular way in dealing with it. Action would be associated with some variable of his 'personality' defined as a more or less stable condition of the individual (see Eysenck, 1960, p 2).

The individual's frame of reference

The focus on man as decision-maker demands some individually-holistic concept such as personality to provide the 'key' to the way in which individuals take their decisions about action. In the traditional approach to industrial relations, as we have already seen, the 'key' used is the web of rules which surround the individual at work and so provide a legitimate order which he regards as incumbent to obey. In this other conception, the key is likely to be provided by some holistic concept which indicates the individual's predisposition to act. Personality is one such construct and those of attitude or perspective could equally serve the purpose. Avoidance of a purely psychological approach might make it desirable to use that of the individual *frame of reference* (Fox, 1966; 1969).

A frame of reference has been defined as 'a conceptual structure of generalizations or contexts' which donate meaning to what is experienced and direction to individual action. In these terms, they have a clear affinity with Weber's concept of 'meaning' and with the manner in which this is related to 'social action' (see above, pp 44-45). Thelen and Withall expand their meaning of the construct by suggesting that the 'structure' embraces:

(a) 'postulates about what is essential,
(b) 'assumptions about what is valuable,
(c) 'attitudes about what is possible, and
(d) 'ideas about what will work effectively' (Thelen and Withall, 1949, p 159).

These elements are unique to the individual in the actual form they take, because they have been construed by him partly from 'direct social experiences' (Popitz *et al*, 1969, pp 317-18) and partly from more abstract learning as in socialization (see Brim, 1966, p 9; Slater, in Smelser, 1967, pp 548-600) which uniquely combine for any single person. As with the other main concepts which have been mentioned, it is activated by a combination of an inner drive (or motivation) and an external stimulus in the environment.

The individual frame of reference may therefore be regarded as either the consequence of interactions with the environment or the source of coherent and consistent decisions by which the person adjusts to it or alters it to accommodate himself, or both simultaneously. It equips the individual with a repertoire of ideas and values which he can use to guide his or her decisions about action. It thus mediates between perceptions of the world and choices or decisions which have to be made about coping with some apect of it. It enables the individual to make sense of his experience of the environment and to determine his mode of acting upon it.

This conception is consistent with the approach of 'expectancy theory' (see Steers and Porter, 1979) in which an attempt is made to explain how individuals come to reach their decisions about the amount of effort they will put into work (see also, Thomason, 1981, pp 271-92). This idea may however be generalized to include any decisions which individuals are called upon to make, since each such exercise involves some cost to the individual and looks for some future benefit or advantage. The perceptions which the individual makes of the availability of benefits, and of the relations which exist between any feasible course of action which he might take and the realization of any of them, are likely to be as important in the wider context as in the narrower one.

Adult socialization and frames of reference

There is an additional benefit in employing this concept within this approach. This is the possibility of finding a place as contributors of 'meaning' for the various work groups and associations of which the individual has membership. The individual's frame of reference is undoubtedly the product of his or her own experience and of his or her own 'meaningful construction' of the surrounding reality. But it is also something which is open (at least to some extent) to social influences from significant others; people, as adults, do 'change their minds' or 'their views' as a result of interaction with others (see Katz and Lazarsfeld, 1954). Any individual's frame of reference is in this sense likely to be subject to modification under the influence of both experience and interaction with significant others (see Paine *et al*, 1967).

The common nature of many experiences of workers and managers are shared. Many of the messages which reach them or are communicated to them (for example, through 'company policy' or 'union ideology') are common. For these reasons, the frames of reference of large numbers of individuals will be similar in significant respects. The frames of reference of large proportions of the workforce or of significant numbers of managers may for this reason exhibit common features. As they decide upon action in accordance with their frames of reference they are likely to come to similar conclusions about what to do. Pattern, as a probability of a course of social action, is likely to be established by this route as readily as by the systems route of the other school.

The existence of alternative sources of influence assumes relevance to this discussion. In the work situation, individuals belong to official and voluntary (or free) work groups, as well as to the undertaking or establishment and often to a trade union. He or she will probably belong to many other groups and organizations in and out of work, and in the context of all of them, interaction will occur with some potential for influence. It is highly improbable that all of these influences will be directed in the same way, and any individual becomes the centre of a web of competing and conflicting messages which only he can construe in a coherent and meaningful way. This establishes his uniqueness but uniqueness in construing does not necessarily mean that resultant frames of reference will be unique or idiosyncratic.

This approach readily finds a place for the differences discernible between people and the conflicting aspects of industrial relations. Differences in frames of reference held by individuals, and differences in ideologies coercively maintained through collectivities of which the individual is a member, reduce the emphasis of the systems theorists on persistence of pattern and on inherent stability and co-operation and allow more opportunity for exploring the processes by which change may occur.

The focus of study (or of practitioner concern) is now not upon assumedly-accepted rules, but upon decisions, the frames of reference which people rely on in making them, and the influences upon them to establish those frames of reference. It becomes unnecessary to assume that people in work accept a legitimate order as binding upon them in order to account for consistent behaviours, because individuals might well reach the same position, as indeed Weber's analysis provides for, by adopting other modes of orientation to the social situation.

Types of social action

The explanation of the emergent perspective is therefore attempted in the context of social action theory. This attempts to account for the same kinds of observable uniformity of behaviour but without *assuming* that human responses (by way of behaviour) are based on rules as manifestations of a legitimate order (see Weber, 1947; 1968; Silverman, 1970). Rather it is thought that social behaviour follows from the attribution of *some* social meaning to human action (which in turn implies the existence of an accepted social relationship) and that the meanings may vary across a range.

Weber argues that an observable uniformity of social action which Weber (1947, p 121; 1968, pp 29-30) identifies by the term 'usage' may appear for one or more of four main reasons. These are derived from the 'modes of orientation' (or the four main ways in which meaning may be attached to social action) and permit four *types* of social action to be identified. Two of these may be more directly associated with what we have referred to as the emergent conception of industrial relations, and two with the traditional model.

The first two types of social action allow for the individual actor to take his or her own decisions, either as a result of conscious thought or simply unthinkingly as a matter of habit:

(a) **Custom**; where the actual behaviour rests upon long familiarity with some set of rules which are 'devoid of any external sanction'. The individual conforms with them as a matter of his or her own free will, merely to avoid inconveniences and annoyances which might attend not doing so (Weber, 1947, p 121).

(b) **Self-interest**; where the individual decides his behaviour on the

58

basis of a rational consideration of the opportunities available to him and a careful calculation of the costs and benefits of acting in any given way. In this case, there is no conformity to a rule governing substantive behaviour, but there is a kind of conformity to the procedural rule which emphasizes the *rational* consideration of the options (Weber, 1947, pp 121-2; 1968, pp 29-30).

Both of these do, therefore, focus on 'rules' of a kind (either those inherent in customary ways of acting or those procedural rules which support rational decision-making; see pp 51-52). The important distinction between these rules and those in the other two categories is that they depend upon no external social agency for their enforcement.

The other two types of social action differ in that they depend on conformity to external rules which are seen to constitute the basis of a 'legitimate order' (that is one which is 'considered binding') to which the individual responds as being under an obligation or duty to obey:

(c) **Convention**; defined (in distinction from custom) by reference to the external guarantee of its validity 'by the probability that deviation from it within a given social group will result in a relatively general and practically-significant reaction of disapproval' (Weber, 1947, p 127).

(d) **Law**; distinguished from convention by the existence of a 'probability that deviant action will be met by physical or psychic sanctions aimed to compel conformity or punish disobedience, and applied by a group of men especially empowered to carry out this function' (that is, by a 'functionally specialized agency' of enforcement such as the 'bureaucracy') (Weber, 1947, p 127; 1968, p 34).

Thus, in these two cases, the rules are more explicit and characteristically they depend upon socially-administered sanctions for their maintenance.

The situation in which actors, particularly those within a social relationship, orient their behaviour to 'a belief in the existence of a legitimate order' (Weber, 1947, p 124) is thus to be distinguished from that in which they orient their behaviour on the basis of habit or self-interest. In the latter, individuals act without feeling that they have any binding obligation to others to act in a particular fashion, whereas in the former, they act because they regard the order as morally or legally binding upon them.

The individual may have a variety of personal motives for conforming to a set of rules or maxims, and he or she may indeed still orient his behaviour to such rules even though there is no conformity (a law-abiding citizen and a burglar both orient their behaviour to the validity of the criminal law). For a legitimate order to exist, the individuals must act in a way which suggests that they are aware of their subjection to it. They must see it as imposing obligations upon them *and* regard 'duty' as having an absolute value for them.

In this context of the emergent perspective, therefore, the individual may autonomously decide upon his or her action for a variety of reasons, and may adopt one of a range of different modes of orientation: to custom, to self-interest, to convention or to law. Any are possible, and only some of them direct attention to formal rules.

Summary: industrial relations

Two disinct perspectives of man at work or of industrial relations may be discerned in its literature and practice. These focus upon two distinct views which have been developed with the social sciences and in social policy. The one might be most directly associated with theories about human conditioning and social systems. The other is more aptly linked with theories of personal constructs and social action. Dependence on these focuses attention in different directions.

In the traditional approach based on the systems perspective attention is devoted to those relationships which establish, contain and apply the *rules* by which people (managers and workers alike) are expected to behave at the work context. This implies that man's behaviour at work is (generally) rule-oriented: that people will (generally) obey the rules. Because they do, it is most useful to consider how the rules are established, maintained and enforced. The rules in question are then identified as the ones which are inherent in, or stem directly from, the contract of employment, which is seen to operate as the most significant source of legitimate order, and as the foundation on which other conventional rules (as in collective bargaining) are based.

In the emergent approach, based on a wider range of social scientific theories, attention is devoted to the way in which individuals cope, both with work and with relationships, when work occurs within social structures (such as firms, plants, government departments, etc). Here the emphasis is upon the autonomous individual necessarily coping with the problems of relating effort and return and, incidentally to this, with the rules which may influence them. It is not assumed that the individual will generally obey the rules but that he will decide on his action as an autonomous (if constrained) decision-unit, taking the rules and many other factors into account. In the process of coping he comes up with his or her own particular actions or behaviours, which may or may not conform to the most salient rules and may depend upon a unique selection from a whole range of competitive rules.

Behind these approaches, there are clear differences of view as to the nature of man, the nature of the relationships (or organization) within which work is contained, and the relationship between the two, as these affect (or are expected to affect) behaviours. Which view is correct is not a question which can be answered except at the level of opinion. But some views may explain more or prove more useful in predicting and controlling industrial relations events. Both the student and pratitioner must make their own choice of perspective and approach, but may well do so selectively according to the purpose they wish to serve by the choice.

Thus, the two perspectives and approaches can be shown to influence the kinds of questions which students or practitioners think are pertinent to the subject. This focuses on what it is that the student of industrial relations is trying to explain by his theorising, and what constructs or theories the individual person (manager or worker) is applying to try to anticipate or predict what might happen in his industrial relations context. Clearly, different people (students or practitioners) may use different approaches and theorems and come up with different answers to the questions about status, conflict and control in the work situation.

Readings

Allen: (1977), pp 79-94. Jackson: (1977), pp 11-36.
Dunlop: (1958), pp 1-32. Hyman: (1975), pp 9-31.
Fox: (1971), pp 1-25. Thomason: (1981), pp 231-93.
Silverman: (1970), pp 126-74. Anthony: (1977a), pp 1-16.
Ackroyd: (1974), pp 236-48.
Flanders: (1965), pp 7-20; and (1970), pp 83-89.
Thelen and Withall: (1949), pp 159-76.
Shimmin and Singh: (1973), pp 37-43.

3

Society and industrial relations

Society, culture and the State

All societies, if they are to survive, must make some provision for both the production of the material necessities of life and the development of institutions which will order living in an acceptably civilized way. The one is focused on the way in which wealth is produced by, and distributed among, the members of the society. The other embraces a wide variety of structures of relationships through which a predictable order is achieved. They relate to what are usually regarded as *important* areas of social living (and of course there are other important areas with which here we are not directly concerned). Industrial organization and relations are concerned with the systems of production and distribution and the way in which the processes within them contribute to order.

Industrial relations is therefore concerned with the nature of the institutions through which both production and distribution are ordered (for example, those of the 'firm' and individual or collective bargaining) *and* with the nature of the underlying structure of value and norm through which the actual functioning or operation of these institutions is controlled in the manner in which society desires that they should be controlled (for example, the structures of law and convention as applied to these activities). The institutions are intended to ensure that the necessary decisions and actions are taken, and the underlying structures that they are taken in socially-approved ways and with socially-acceptable consequences or outcomes.

The manner in which different societies arrange their production and institutions varies, and leads to the identification of differences which may be important for both the (material) standard of living and the (cultural) quality of life. For a time, there were not only fears that industrialization would sweep over all the countries of the world and place its distinct stamp upon them but also hopes that the structure of industrial relations which had developed in Britain would become the universal model.

Neither of these is now seen as probable (see Marsh, Hackmann and Miller, 1981). In recent years the concept of culture has been resurrected as significant for explanations of differences in industrial relations practice (see, Maurice *et al.*, 1980; Sorge and Warner, 1980a; Mansfield and Poole, 1981). It is now thought probable that different societies and cultures will impose their own stamps on industrial organization (see Jenner, 1982). The British structure of industrial relations is already, and will continue to be, different (whether better or worse) from that of the Germans (see Saunders, 1979), the Swedes (Pratten, 1976b) or the Japanese (Abbeglen, 1958; Dore, 1973). This at least suggests that such separately identifiable societies as Britain, Germany, America or Japan deal with the question of securing commitment to action in the work context differently.

Society and culture

A number of different terms are employed to identify what is thought to be the 'cause' of these differences. Terms like, the people, the society, the culture, or the State are used to identify what is thought to account for the differences in the way the problems are tackled. These terms refer either to different aggregations of people or to different features of the way people are grouped together. In discussions of industrial relations theory, it is common to focus attention on the single concept of 'the State', which Dunlop (1958), for example, singles out as one of his three 'actors' in industrial relations (see above, pp 4-6) but references to society and culture are becoming increasingly common as more social scientific disciplines are brought to bear on the general area.

The relationships between these entities might be expressed in the following terms. 'Society' (or people) provides a convenient catch-all term which can be applied to those who somehow belong together, because of their geographical proximity, their use of a common language or their acceptance of common values, beliefs and norms. 'Culture' refers to the amalgam of their ways of doing things *and* the values and norms which help to hold these patterns of behaviour in place and to control the rate at which, and the procedures by which, they may be changed (see, Kluckhohn, 1962). Thus, culture may be said to refer to the preferred 'designs for living' which the people of the society prefer, in much the fashion that we can say that in Britain we accept or have a preference for collective bargaining over other ways of handling the issues of distribution in our society.

Societies establish values and norms to control conduct in the context of work, or wealth production, so that work is usually surrounded by a well-established set of norms by which behaviours relevant to these activities are to be perceived and judged (see, Newcomb, 1952, p 273). Values and norms of this kind have been long-established in British society.

At least since Tudor times, a major goal of British economic policy has been the enhancement of 'trade' (or increase of national wealth) and this has been upheld by the power of the State. This has been generally accepted as so desirable (valued) an end of human activity that steps have been taken to try to ensure that nothing will interfere with its realization. Like other societies, British society has also been concerned to maintain order in the way in which people work towards this goal. The authority of the society vested in the State has therefore been dedicated to the twin objects of increasing national wealth and maintaining order in the course of doing so.

The pursuit of these goals of public policy has been supported by norms which favour individualism or private enterprise as a means to this end. The individual pursuing his own ends and relying on his own means describes a valued personality type of western industrialized society. Private enterprise is widely regarded as a better method of realizing the general objective than any alternative system of organizing the means of production. The law, as the embodiment of the State's norms, is constructed in such a way that it gives support to these values, by stating what is acceptable conduct and by providing penalties and punishments for non-conformity.

Institutions, developed within public policy, law and convention, structure economic activity in ways which provide the opportunities which these heroic individuals require. With some major exceptions, industries are organized on the basis of *firms* (see below, pp 81-83) which have legally-established and enforceable autonomy to decide issues for themselves as if they were 'private persons'. Public ownership of the means of production has been advocated as an alternative but has

64

advanced only a short distance, and can be rolled back by appeal to higher values such as enhancement of trade or wealth.

For reasons of this kind, both workers and businessmen have found themselves restricted from time to time in their activities. Workers' trade unions operated for many years under the embargo of the Common Law which, by regarding them as 'combinations in restraint of trade', denied them legality (Wedderburn, 1971, pp 85-91). For similar reasons, combination amongst businessmen in cartels, trusts, or price rings was frowned upon as 'contrary to public policy' (see, Allen, 1968). Such actions by workers and businessmen were thought to go against the achievement of greater wealth or of an ordered and stable approach to its realization.

Comparably, it is believed that the methods which will be employed to increase wealth will most usefully be rational ones: individuals will decide on action by a rational consideration of the alternatives open to them in each case. This may be an open or a bounded rationality, (see, Johnson, 1972, pp 344-5) but it remains a rationality which supports and sustains the theories which are intended to guide economic action (see above, pp 50-55).

Those activities which form the subject-matter of industrial relations have, in their very nature and intent, frequently confronted and challenged this structure of legitimated objectives, norms and rules, which derive from the underlying culture (see England, 1971 and 1975; Hyman, 1953; Hyman and Brough, 1975). Over the past two centuries, for example, the values and norms of 'individualism' have been challenged and at least partially replaced by those of 'collectivism' or even, in some views, 'corporatism' (see, Pahl and Winkler, 1974; 1976). The process of making the challenge through unionization, joint negotiation and industrial action constitutes the basis of trade unions' activity during their 'struggle' to achieve a place in the body politic. Necessarily, much of that struggle has been to secure recognition for bargaining purposes and against the dominant values and norms of individualism which the State has attempted to uphold.

The State

If 'culture' refers to the values and norms of the society (and to their artefacts which embody these), the concept of 'the State' refers to that piece of formal organization which acts as the guardian of that culture on behalf of the society. The State concerns itself with maintaining the culture in being, both by providing for the reproduction of culture through successive generations and the mechanisms of enforcement of the formal rules (as in law) which uphold it.

It is commonly identified with the formal mechanisms through which a given society intends to assure order and governance. Within it are included the government as an active legislative and executive ingredient, and also the institutions of 'monarchy, the armed forces, the police, the law and the judiciary' (Crouch, 1979, p 125).

Each of these institutions has a characteristic function within civil society. The monarchy may serve as a symbol of unity, integrity and continuity, whilst the political element of government provides the mechanism for responding to differing and changing ideas amongst the population. The law serves as the embodiment of the moral values and norms of the society as interpreted by governments and the courts. The civil service forms the executive arm of government, technically 'under the Crown', and carries out the policies and programmes developed by governments. The judiciary adjudicates differences and disputes arising within the society largely in accordance with the norms expressed in law. The armed forces are intended to perform the function of protecting external interests, but may on occasion be called on to aid the civil power to uphold law and order within the society.

The State might exercise this function on behalf of the people as a whole (Jenks, 1919) or some class or category of them (Milliband, 1969). In a democratic society, elaborate arrangements may be made to ensure that those decisions respond in some way to the will of the members of the society. But whether democratic or not, the State machine or apparatus serves to ensure that, as far as individual socialization and social structure can achieve this, decisions are taken and acted upon in the preferred ways.

The view taken of the State's role and function, varies. There are three main perspectives.

1   The State is seen as the organized element of the unitary society and culture, the part which is equipped to ensure the

ordered survival and ordered change of valued ideas and behaviours.

2   The State is seen as the arena in which different factions compete and struggle with one another to secure acceptance of their ideas and values, and as an interested party in its own right in the development of an integrated culture.

3   The State is seen to be a creature of one such faction, notably in the Marxian view, of the exploiting or ruling class, and therefore representative and reflective of nothing more than the subcultural or ideological values and ideas of that one faction (see Hyman, 1975, pp 121-23).

Whichever perspective is adopted, however, the State remains a powerful instrument of decision and action, operating in the name of society. It must try to ensure that industrial relations activities, amongst others, are structured in accordance with those values and mores which are held to be good, either by the people or by the State (see, Anthony, 1977b, pp 105).

The culture, thus, provides a kind of envelope or framework for human action within a particular society, and the State machinery provides the organization whereby the cultural values are made known and upheld. For the manager or the shop steward, as for anyone else, this provides him with a structure of values and norms and customary ways of behaving which tend to operate as the taken-for-granted foundation on which he will operate. In taking industrial relations decisions, he is not free of constraint which develops from this societal or State interest.

THE ROLE OF THE STATE IN INDUSTRIAL RELATIONS

The State in Britain has used its power and authority to secure two broad ends (or values) in the area of industrial relations.

1   The end that those decisions which need to be taken on a day-to-day basis about the contribution of human effort to the production process and the remuneration which the individual will receive for it, are taken and implemented by someone other than functionaries acting on behalf of the State. Such decisions are necessary if wealth is to be created and distributed in some acceptable fashion but they do not have to be taken centrally by the State itself, although that is

one possibility. The State must however ensure that they *are* taken and 'our preference' has been to have them taken on a decentralized basis.

2   The end that whoever takes the decisions they will accord with the values and norms which the State is expected to uphold. This is partly a question of ensuring that the rules of the game are both known and complied with, and partly a matter of ensuring that the structure of social relations is such as to encourage some kinds of approaches and outcomes and discourage others. The main device which the State has available to it to effect these ends is, of course, the law: the law states what the rules are and provides the penalties and punishments for breaking them.

We, in Britain, are prone to talk of our 'system of industrial relations' as a 'voluntary' one, and to imply by this both that it rests directly upon the will of the parties, and that the State is 'abstentionist' in this area and has very little to do with it. In collective bargaining the decisions are taken by the representatives of the parties, not by the State or its representatives. But the very institution of voluntary collective bargaining itself is a creature of the State, and the options for decision by the parties are constrained by law as well as the conventions developed over the years by the parties themselves. There is delegation of decision-making authority, but retention of the power to structure the framework within which it is exercised.

Historical evolution of methods

Over the past three centuries, many different methods of resolving industrial relations questions have been adopted. They range from resolution within the executive arm of government, to that by affected individuals or their representatives. What we now see as the characteristic method, that of collective bargaining, is but one of many which are theoretically available, and this one does not necessarily apply to all circumstances even now.

In the later Middle Ages and early modern times, the magistrates were charged with the task of taking the legally-enforceable decisions about wages and hours on an annual basis as agents of the State. The decisions about how much work contribution should be made within the working hours for the remuneration laid down were left to the masters.

This centralized approach gave way to one which relied upon the forces of the market in which supply and demand were to fix the price of labour at a level which would 'clear the market' if every individual concerned took his own maximizing decisions. This seemed to allow the State to abstain as each individual took his own decisions according to his own preferences without any third party intervention.

The market mechanism probably worked only in special circumstances and for limited periods of time. The determination of the amounts of work and reward became the prerogative of the employer, supported by his legal property rights and his greater bargaining power. Devolution of these decisions to the arbitration of market forces thus probably meant devolution to the employer acting within *his* authority.

This prerogative power was challenged by the trade unions, and the market forces mechanism gradually gave way to the mechanism of collective bargaining. In this arrangement associations of workers demanded some influence upon the decisions and secured it by virtue of *their* enhanced bargaining power and the eventual grant of certain legal immunites which supported the joint determination of the issues. Although the unions have sought to influence both standards of reward and contribution, they have usually been more successful in influencing the former than they have the latter.

Collective bargaining has been supplemented, where trade unionism failed to develop adequately for this purpose, and where unacceptable quantities of effort and reward persisted in contracts, by tripartite arangements in which representatives of the employers, the workers and a third party meet together to come to joint decisions on questions of remuneration, again leaving the question of contribution to be determined largely by the employers (see below, pp 179-86).This should serve to warn us that there is nothing particularly sacrosanct about the currently prevalent method of collective bargaining. It happens that this is the preferred method over a sufficiently large tranche of the society to give the appearance of universality and permanence (see, Clegg, 1972, pp 59-60) and it may well persist (see, Blackaby, 1980). But it is only one of a number of methods which have been tried in the past and which persist in some circumstances to the present.

Flanders has offered a basis for classifying these different methods of taking industrial relations decisions, based on the three dimensions of who decides what, under what authority, derived from what source. This can be applied both to the historical and the current variations. He suggests that the various methods may be defined by reference to:

(a) 'the parties participating in the authorship of the substantive rules' (Flanders, 1965, p 21). Amongst these might be the workers, the employers (or managers), the agents of the State or the members of the society, acting unilaterally or in some combination, and with more or less formality.

(b) the structure of dependency or power which is relied upon in the decision-taking process itself. The parties taking the decision might meet in a context of equality or inequality, and they might have power to impose their decisions on others, or power merely to negotiate acceptance of their decisions.

(c) the relationships subjected to regulation in the process, and controlled by the rules once they are made. They may have responsibility for deciding only limited issues (for example, wages and hours) or for a wide range of issues (for example, the whole gamut of contribution and reward).

This taxonomy recognizes, in other words, that different agents may come together in different power relationships to decide some quantities and establish some rules intended to regulate some or all aspects of the relationships existing in work. It might also be extended to recognize that those who take the decisions might or might not be involved in their actual implementation and monitoring.

Societal and State regulation

The main aim of the society and the State in all this is to set the normative scene and to encourage the actors involved to comply with them. This is an indirect role in that it does not involve the State in what might be called the 'formal' arrangements for taking actual decisions. But it is no less significant for being indirect, and it can be argued that this influence is more powerful and pervasive than direct involvement would be (see, Bachrach and Barratz, 1962; Clegg, 1975; Lukes, 1975; Martin, 1971 and 1977).

Flanders makes a similar distinction to this between what he called State and societal regulation, which he saw as 'alternative methods to collective bargaining' (Flanders, 1965, p 22). He saw the one (State regulation) as relying on control through statute or common law and the other (societal regulation) on control through custom and convention (Flanders 1965, p 22). The one is relatively formal and open, whereas the other is more difficult to observe in operation because it depends upon less formal mechanisms.

State regulation

State regulation in its pure form would involve establishing all the rules and decisions at the centre (and probably also a complex inspectorate with powers of enforcement). At different times in our history, the State has been more or less involved in these activities, as we have seen, but the general role and function of the State in our voluntary system has been to set the scene for others to act out.

The State continues to be directly involved in the development and enforcement of those rules which we identify as 'law'. The rules in question provide the enforceable authority of those who are involved in the industrial relations decision processes. These may be made through legislation or court interpretation and are intended to be binding on all within the domain. People are involved in the process of rule-making only to the extent that any citizen is involved in this general process in a democratic society. They have more direct influence on legislation (through the democratic process) than they have on Common Law (which derives from judicial interpretations of law).

The traditional role of the Common Law has been to uphold individual *freedom* to contract in employment whilst ignoring any issue of inequality which might exist in relation to employment contracts (see Kahn Freund, 1977; and below, pp 92-96). In doing so, it has influenced both the forms of conduct in industrial relations (for example, trade union organization was necessary to redress the balance in the absence of judicial interest) and the substantive terms of the contract (by leaving the employer with greater power or opportunity to dictate terms), a not insignificant influence in spite of Kahn-Freund's conclusion that the Common Law in Britain has had little influence on industrial relations.

Legislation has usually tried to redress the imbalance of power by curbing the autonomy of the parties where necessary. It has

71

therefore chiefly influenced the shape of procedural rules. More recently, it has attempted to provide minimum substantive terms and by administrative action in the form of wages policies has increased this influence.

Societal regulation

Conversely, the State is not directly involved in devising or promulgating those rules which develop from the social norms within the society which are identified as conventions. These may be as important as or more important than the formal laws. These are enforceable through the exercise of social disapproval not the courts. This system is less formal, less codified, and less easy to discern, but may nevertheless control a good deal more of the day to day behaviour of people at work than law ever did or does (see, Anthony, 1977a, pp 136-64). It is frequently attested that formal laws and rules can treat only the extremities of the problem (see, Kahn-Freund, 1977, pp 18-24).

The questions of who is the author of the rules and what is the nature of the dependency established are questions not easily answered. Social regulation, operating through custom and convention, is as problematic as State regulation, in so far as the question of 'whose custom?' or 'whose convention?' can be answered differently over time and from place to place. Which customs and conventions have exerted influence on rules of procedure or substance, and with what force or strength, have varied over time, and a case might be argued for regarding this variation as a meandering search for solutions (see, Pilkington, 1976). But the strength of custom and convention in structuring relationships (and therefore the outcomes of interaction within those structures) cannot be ignored because the voluntary activities of the parties to industrial relations appear to be mainly regulated by them (see below, pp 327-337).

Both of these methods imply *imposition* of rules and norms upon the parties because 'in these methods industrial associations do not carry any direct responsibility for the rules' (see Flanders, 1965, p 22). They usually apply to the control of both competition (whether businessmen or workers *should* combine) and bargaining (whether the trade union *should* have a right to be recognized) and to substantive (what are *appropriate* subjects for bargaining) and procedural rules (how *should* the parties approach one another). In other words, they are seen to establish

72

broad norms or rules (of the kind which usually figure in the codes of practice produced by the Secretary of State or the Advisory Conciliation and Arbitration Service (ACAS)) which guide both the determination of the quantities of remuneration and reward and the conventions which influence the conduct of the parties in their relations with one another.

Delegated authority

Over the period reviewed above, the necessary decisions about industrial relations have been taken at different levels by different groups of people in various combinations. Where the State has not reserved the decisions to itself, it has, however, tried to ensure that ultimate control of the decisions is retained. It delegates authority to subsidiaries to decide, only on certain terms and conditions. These delimit their scope and serve as a reminder that the real power and authority still reside in the hands of the State.

The abstention by the State, therefore, relates only to the direct participation in decisions about standards of effort and reward, and does not occur in connection with the determination of the rules which are to be applied to the decision-taking process as these appear in collective labour legislation. As a consequence of this, those who 'volunteer' to determine their effort and returns in the prescribed way (or to have the determination made by representatives) do so only within the framework of norm and rule which is established by the State through the law.

The terms of the grant of authority to decide and act have varied on the issue of the matters to be determined. A major distinction made is that between authority to decide the broad quantities of contribution and remuneration and authority to decide the detailed relationship which will apply between them in the actual workplace. Within this framework, more detailed attention is usually given to the remuneration element than to the contribution element.

The decentralized arrangements have, however, given British industrial relations the cast of a democratic, 'voluntary' system in which those most directly affected by the decisions are involved (through their representatives) in the taking of them. What is delegated, however, is a limited power to decide within limits which are set, generally, by the operation of law. The role and function of the law in this area remains one of setting the limits to authority to decide on both the substantive and the procedural aspects of such decisions, by defining the status of the parties. Devolution is, in other words, always, 'on terms'.

DELEGATED DECISION-MAKING

These same values and norms which support this kind of societal and State regulation have also supported the delegation of decision-making to those who are more closely affected by the decisions. Thus, some of the day-to-day decisions of industrial relations are taken by the individual parties (employers and employees), some by the collective parties (employers' associations and trade unions) and in both cases, either separately or jointly. Historically, the collective has tended to take over from the individual, and the joint decision from the unilateral. The present pattern might, indeed, be regarded as a mixture of mechanisms which have either been left behind by the tides of history or have been constructed to meet some recognized exigency not fully met by generally-adopted arrangements.

Delegation of authority might be made either to natural persons, as is the case with workers and might be the case with employers, or to bodies (such as the company or the joint negotiating committee) which are given some legal or fictional personality in order that they might be regarded as homogeneous 'things' or 'persons' (when in reality they are made up of a large number of individual persons). Those involved in the industrial relations processes are:

1 individual employees who contribute services under the employment contract in expectation of remuneration
2 individual employers who contribute remuneration under that contract in return for services
3 the separate associations of individual employees (for example, the trade unions) which seek to influence the terms and conditions of employment under which their members will be employed
4 the separate associations of individual employers (eg trade or employers' associations) which seek to influence the terms and conditions of employment which members will be required to offer in the future
5 the central organizations of workers and employers which

generally seek to create the appropriate climate or ethos within which the other parties may effectively pursue their objectives.

Where individual bargaining takes place it involves workers as natural persons and employers as either natural persons or corporate bodies. Where collective bargaining occurs, however, these may become the 'principals' (or constituents) and the other three, in some sense, their agents or representatives acting on their instructions.

These may have a common interest in reaching an agreement as to terms which will apply within their respective domains, but they will also have different interests (as between workers and employers, for example) which they will seek to pursue in the bargaining process. Although both parties may want a decision about terms, what is an income or benefit to the one represents a cost to the other, so that the pursuit of distinct objectives by the parties to the contract must lead to some degree of conflict. The 'associations' to which these parties belong, are the means by which simple differences in interest and aim are turned into significant conflicts. These attempt, in various 'democratic' ways, to ensure that their objectives and approaches are in line with those of their principals or constituents. They may not always succeed in this, but at least there is some intention that what is done by associations reflects the wishes of constituents. To this extent, therefore, the differences of the individuals are carried forward as differences in formal objectives and are neither created not destroyed by the collectivizing processes involved.

Devolution to 'persons'

In the first flush of enthusiasm in the industrial revolution, devolution of decisions was made to individuals, as natural persons, and particularly to the entrepreneurs and inventors as well as to workmen. But it was later applied to companies and corporations who were given a fictional legal personality to allow them to be embraced within the philosophy of individualism, but not to trade unions. These individual persons were the ones given authority to decide issues for themselves in accordance with their own preferences and their view of the situation. They would, however, arrive at their economic (or exchange) decisions by way of bargaining with another, where 'bargaining' is defined to refer to the process whereby 'the antithetical interests of supply and demand, of buyer and seller, are finally adjusted' in an agreement as to the terms of the exchange (MacIver and Page, 1953, p 474).

Public policy and executive action, guided by classical economic theory, had to be directed towards the creation of a free market in both commodities and labour in which this individual bargaining could occur and in which market forces *would* control individual decisions within the supportive framework of rights and obligations established in law. No bureaucratic mechanism, other than that of the court system, was thought, however, to be needed to establish control because this would be achieved through the twin mechanisms of the impersonal forces of the market (which established the objective limits), and the law relating to enforceable status (which set the limits to personal authority to act).

This ideal was not realized in practice for a variety of reasons. A free market demands an infinite number of buyers and sellers to allow any individual a range of choice, such that if he cannot secure acceptable terms from one he can seek them from another. As the two parties to a potential exchange try to reach an agreement as to its terms and conditions, neither will have a whip hand over the other. Each party to a contract, whether in goods or labour, will have equal chances with the other. For as long as enterprise was small in scale and in the hands of the individual entrepreneur, this condition might nearly prevail, and a near-free market exist in labour. Labour price would be dictated by the interaction of supply and demand, not by any 'person', since none was in so dominant a position to dictate it. For this reason it was considered that the 'operation of market forces' yielded a superior morality as well as a price.

This could only be the case, however, if it could be assumed the individual would make his choices 'rationally' in the light of his own wants or preferences and his own reading of the market situation. The second of these requires, however, that individuals have a considerable knowledge of the market situation, and this is rarely the case. We also have it on the authority of Adam Smith (1776) that 'reading the market' would be difficult for the worker simply because the masters were always and everywhere in a 'tacit' (or hidden) combination to agree amongst themselves in advance of bargaining, what terms they would offer.

76

Nevertheless, for many years, it continued to be assumed that both of these conditions were met and would be translated through the medium of bargaining into decisions which would permit the development of co-operative activity. If in this process everybody acted rationally, the market would be cleared at the ruling market price, co-operation in wealth creation would be secured, and the greatest good of the greatest number would be the result. The conception of the market as perfect (completely comprehended by those who operated within it and free from any form of rigging in the interests of either buyer or seller) pervades the economic literature. It is made the assumption of much analysis and still serves to describe a former 'Golden Age' from which we have now passed, perhaps as a result of some sin (see Hutt, 1975, pp 3-33).

Where the two main conditions (of perfect knowledge and infinite choice) are not present, because one party either confronts a limited set of alternatives or is unaware of those which do exist, the assumption of equality of power to bargain (or 'higgle', as the Webbs put it) is unlikely to hold. In the extreme case, the single seller (monopoly) or the single buyer (monopsony) confronts the other party with a 'take it or leave it' type of choice. The monopolist or monopsonist can dictate his own terms for the exchange provided that he has a choice of buyers or sellers, respectively. This tendency was always present in the labour market, if only because, as Adam Smith pointed out (1776), the employer was able to 'wait' longer for the labourer to comply with his terms than the labourer could wait for the employer to alter them, so that he could always dictate the terms on which employment was available.

In these circumstances, wages and other terms necessarily become the subject of deliberate decisions taken by somebody or other. Usually in the labour market it was the employer as the dominant partner who took the decisions (see Pen, 1959, p 7) on the basis of what he thought he needed in terms of contribution and what he considered he could afford to pay. The liberal policies of the early part of last century supported this. As long as the employer faced little or no significant opposition to his decisions, he could dictate terms regardless of the effects of the operation of market forces. The individual worker was confronted with what was virtually a 'standard form contract' and with a take it or leave it attitude which he could do little to change.

Only when the trade union was grudgingly granted a freedom to reduce worker competition in the labour market through combination (1824) and a legally-supported authority to negotiate terms with the employer in collective bargaining were the decisions removed from the spheres of impersonal market determination or unilateral employer imposition. The trade union developed as the main challenger to these concepts and their underlying philosophies. It sought to replace the individual freedom with a collective organization in order to increase the worker's bargaining power in relation to the employer. Although the unions were not really given the same kind of 'fictional personality' as in law applied to the corporation, they were permitted some lawful authority to influence or decide some of the questions of industrial relations. Their power and authority had to rest upon a different base from that of the employers and businessmen, since, at least initially the law denied them lawful authority to act in this way. It depended therefore on a collective will amongst workers to be bound by their own majority decisions and the power of the collectivity itself to sustain them in the face of challenges by employers and others.

Unilateral imposition

Consequently, it is possible to recognize two approaches to the delegation of authority to decide and act, one to individuals and the other to organizations. The one focuses on the concept of contract and the assumption that its terms will be freely determined by any two individuals who will have equal power to coerce the other to agree (see below, pp 89-95). The other directs our attention to the negotiated agreement between organizations which will also be assumed to meet voluntarily to establish its terms.

But short of these positions, any party may be in a position to impose terms on the other party, a condition which Flanders identifies as 'unilateral imposition'. He identifies two such situations:

1   One in which rules are made by the employer or the employers' association and imposed not only on the members but on the other side as well. The historically more significant aspect of this is the situation in which the employer is able to dictate terms to potential and actual

employees. This effectively presents the employee with a 'standard form contract' about whose terms he can do very little. Flanders says that 'employers' associations may similarly impose regulation on the firms that belong to them' (*ibid*) and in doing so standardize the terms over a wider area. The effect of the combined unilateral imposition is to place restrictions on the demand for labour in the terms in which it might be on offer. This is an exactly similar process of developing solidarity to that recognized in connection with the trade unions. The employers' association then simply puts the strength of the association around the individual employer in the interests of standardization and solidarity.

2   Another is the situation in which rules are made by the trade union alone and imposed, not only on the members but upon employers and managements as well. 'Trade unions may ... unilaterally ... bind ... their members to observe working rules which the 'other side' has had no say in making' (Flanders, 1965, p 22) but which constrain the other side in what it can do.

Most of these rules relate to the trade union's need to secure itself in the workplace or to the worker's need to diminish the impact of competition. They replace the individual's vulnerability to immediate exigencies by a solidarist 'common front'. They commonly relate to apprentice ratios, recruitment to the occupation, association with non-members in the workshop, aspects of jurisdiction and demarcation. They have the effect of restricting the employer's power (see below, pp 473-76) to dictate terms by limiting the options open to him in recruiting labour and in the workplace.

Whether such rules can be imposed on the other party depends upon the distribution of power within and between the collectivities. The history of industrial relations, it might be said, is the history of the shifting frontier of control and power between the entities (see Goodrich, 1920). Although this has taken place under the control of law (for the most part), it has also involved the discovery of compromise solutions by the parties themselves.

Devolution to joint bodies

The resolution of this last question about capacity to impose usually lies in the development of collective bargaining. Historically, once trade unions (or other workers' associations) became powerful enough to challenge the unilateral decision-taking authority of the employer, a joint body composed of the employer and the workers' association(s) became a sensible mechanism for reaching compromise solutions. In time, this arrangement became institutionalized as a way of avoiding the head on collisions inherent in opposed attempts at unilateral imposition.

Collective bargaining

'Collective bargaining' may then be defined as a method of resolving conflicts which is characterized by its involvement of at least two opposed parties who have a different (even opposed) interest in the outcomes of decisions, but who come together voluntarily to decide matters of concern in the belief that by so doing they can achieve more than if they remained separate.

In more concrete terms, collective bargaining usually involves one or more trade unions on one side and one or more employers (often as members of employers' associations) on the other, coming together voluntarily to negotiate over some issue of distribution which divides them, and to reach a 'collective agreement', which establishes either the quantities or the rules for their determination.

In collective bargaining the parties whose activities are to be regulated by the decisions and rules thus participate in their production. Usually, two sets of decisions or rules are established. The substantive decisions or rules establish the terms on which the co-operative and distributive relationships between the buyer and the seller will be continued. The procedural rules establish how the 'bargaining' process will be conducted between them and how, therefore, the continual necessity to adjust the terms of the relationship will be handled. The parties approach one another on a more 'equal' basis than is implied in the arangements described as unilateral imposition. The dependency of one party on the other is at least reduced by the method, although possibly this reduction is to be correlated with the 'level' of the negotiations (see, Gottschalk, 1973, pp 37-38).

Tripartite regulation

Clearly, since the establishment of joint arrangements requires the assent of both parties, wide discrepancies in power between them may well prevent one or other from agreeing to join in such an exercise as collective bargaining. This possibility is a real one, and it has led to a number of different kinds of body being set up which associate these two (collective bargaining) parties with a third party (whose role is to encourage the development of collective bargaining). Identified as tripartite regulation, this was paired by Flanders with collective bargaining as one of two methods of delegated decision-taking or rule-making (see below, pp 377-82).

Tripartite regulation (see also below, pp 384-96) is to be found mainly in the trades where employer and worker organization and/or collective bargaining machinery has not developed spontaneously, and in those situations where one or both parties have an ideological reluctance to embrace such a system of deciding issues. The main examples are the wages council trades and certain professional occupations, mainly in the Health Service. A similar arrangement may also be embraced to bring normal collective bargaining back into existence after temporary breakdown by engaging the services of conciliators, mediators and arbitrators, as third parties.

Tripartite processes of this kind differ from collective bargaining in their consequences for autonomy-dependency and for the kinds of issues dealt with. In the wages council trades, for example, it is generally considered that there is high worker dependency because of the nature of the trades themselves. The 'third party' element is not independently powerful in this situation, but rather provides a power resource which the parties themselves can attempt to employ for their own advantage in their negotiations. The subject focus is usually restricted to a limited range of substantive issues as defined by the instruments of their establishment and the procedural rules are largely taken as given by the initiating legislation and the administrative procedures established under it (see below, pp 180-86).

The sites of industrial relations

The devolution of industrial relations decisions necessarily creates a number of subnational sites on which the activities take place. There are clearly many particular sites, but in the British context two main ones are to be found at the industrial and the undertaking/establishment levels of organization. These are neither homogeneous nor neutral in their consequences for decision and action since they are largely defined by the employer.

The industrial site, on which national or industry-wide bargaining occurs, can be associated with the conception of 'industry' as used for purposes of compiling national production statistics (see Florence, 1953, pp 15-22). This would allow us to distinguish service industries from manufacturing and extractive industries, for example, and the iron and steel industry from the coal mining industry and the education service. But such technical distinctions are not of great use or of great validity in the context of industrial relations.

This is because what passes for an industry in the context of industry-wide bargaining, tends to be that collection of plants, offices, etc, which the particular employers' association considers to form its actual or potential membership. Industry is *their* industry, defined by *their* criteria. Industries defined by objective criteria might well be either split or combined for collective bargaining purposes, largely on the insistence of the employers' associations. Trade unions may, in consequence, find themselves splitting or combining *their* memberships into national trade groups or into federations of unions in order to confront the employers directly.

The local or domestic site for industrial relations comprises not one but two levels of organization, one concerned with corporate government and the other forming a unit of account within some larger corporation. The one may be no more than an abstract conception which refers to the fact that a board governs a variety of activities, but the other is usually related directly to complex activities in production, marketing, etc which have to be accounted to some such unit of government.

In *private* manufacturing and service industry, these two levels may be identified by the terms enterprise and establishment (Bolton Committee Report, 1971, p 41f) or company and plant (Florence, 1953, p 22). In the public service sector, the distinction may be drawn between the Department of State and the local office, or between the unit of local government and, say, the education office. However, these terms are not universally employed and variations are permissible, although ultimately the two-level distinction is maintained in some terms or other. In order to identify this distinction for our purposes we will use the concepts 'undertaking' and 'establishment'. This will at least allow us to use common terms for the public and the private sectors of the economy.

These two sites are no more neutral with respect to the parties involved in industrial relations, because the domestic organization is also under the control of the employer. Management determines very largely not only the unit of government and the unit of account but also how the work shall be organized at this level (see Gospel and Littler, 1983, p 1). This helps to predispose workers to join one union organization or another, on the basis of status and role differences. Management also retains the power to define the bargaining unit in the light of employees' union affiliations, but without necessarily accepting these as the only basis for its delimitation (see CIR, Report No 85, 1973, pp 28-38).

Internal and external regulation

There are obvious implications for the autonomy of the principal parties, according to whether decisions are taken on one or other of these sites. Industry-wide and domestic bargaining imply different degrees of involvement for the local parties, and this kind of difference is also to be associated with bipartite and tripartite processes.

National or industry-wide bargaining, in which both the workers and the individual employers are represented, will yield an agreement which has, by definition, not been established within the domestic unit. Company- or plant-wide bargaining, on the other hand, enables both parties to be represented by known negotiators who might be expected to have a great deal more local knowledge: the resultant agreement might then appear to have been internally conceived. In tripartite regulation, by definition, some element of external intervention, however slight, must be involved.

Flanders has considered these differences in terms of the extent to which the regulation is perceived by the employer as internal or external.

External regulation refers to the process of reaching decisions within a bargaining unit which is more extensive than the particular establishment or undertaking and involves persons who are outside the assumedly-unitary undertaking. In industry-wide arangements, for example, the bargaining unit which contains the domestic undertaking will be defined as to its extent by the domain of the employers' association. It will embrace one or more unions representing the workers within that domain. The negotiations will be directed towards securing ageement as to standard terms and conditions of employment to apply to all the workers within that domain. In effect, therefore, such regulation will, by definition, have an 'external' origin from the viewpoint of the undertaking.

By internal regulation, obversely, Flanders refers to an arrangement in which the parties to the employment contracts in an undertaking attempt to resolve problems and issues without (much) recourse to such external bargaining agents. The single employer (at company, plant, or office level) will seek to settle relevant terms and conditions of employment by negotiating with representatives of his workers, with little or no reference to outside officials of the workers' association. What may be agreed is agreed within the domestic situation, even if, in some cases, it is then ratified by an external representative of the union or other association.

The extent to which the parties experience it as internal or external, will depend (mainly) on whether the employer is a member of an employers' association and chooses to allow the association negotiators to establish the terms and conditions of employment which will apply to his establishment or undertaking. Collective bargaining does not automatically involve external imposition or internal agreement. The union may be an 'external' agency but this does not wholly determine whether the decisions will be perceived as external ones.

Recent surveys (IFF, 1978; Brown, 1981; Marsh, 1982) suggest that many establishments are still in the position of experiencing external regulation, some of it from company or divisional level, but much of it still from national level. The prospects for the development of 'comprehensive and authoritative agreement' as recommeded by the Donovan Commission, would seem to be poor even in private manufacturing industry (to which these surveys relate).

The prospects for local negotiation in the public sector appear to be even more limited, as national bargaining continues to hold sway. The tendency for the national organization to be coincident with the organization of the employer in most cases outside the local authorities, offers some prospect that some kind of comprehensive plan might be evolved. Attempts to change are likely to be defeated by the sheer size and complexity of the undertakings to which such plans would relate. For most establishment level managers, therefore, regulation is likely to continue to be experienced as external, although without necessarily involving direct societal or State interference.

Summary: the State and industrial relations

The interest of society at large in industrial relations stems from the common human interest in both ordered and beneficent arrangements for dealing with industrial relations issues. The State may then be regarded (whatever interest group may acquire power to direct its activities) as the executive arm of the society which acts to uphold this interest. It may reflect the interests of 'people', as the conservative might argue, or the interest of a dominant group or class, as the radical might argue. It is expressed in terms of dominant values, norms and rules, enshrined in law, public codes of practice and government policies.

The problem for the liberal State is to maintain a relatively abstentionist posture whilst at the same time securing a foundation for co-operation. This may be expressed in three propositions (which underlie the discussion in the following chapters):

(a) there is a need to regulate the enforceable status of the potential co-operators in such a way that co-operation can occur on acceptable terms;

(b) there is a need to control the development of alternative mechanisms which are designed to change or increase that status and so interfere with the operation of the system; and

(c) there is a need to ensure that the co-operators themselves take all the decisions and action which are necessary to co-operation, thus obviating the necessity for the State to become involved.

The State has attempted to operate in accordance with these propositions, but (as we shall examine in the following chapters) the extent to which the State has been able to hold to them has diminished in the face of changes in social attitude over the industrial period.

Acting in the interests of society (in one or other of its conceptions) the State has sought to regulate matters in two main ways: indirectly (or normatively) through legislation designed to control the conduct of the parties to devolved decision-making; and directly (or coercively) through State-established machinery whose members take and enforce the necessary decisions following laid-down procedures (see Anthony, 1977a, p 136).

The State has the power and usually the authority to ensure that the issues are dealt with in accordance with the dominant values and beliefs. It can determine that a central State organization will take the decisions, or devolve decision-taking to 'persons' individually or to persons acting in some 'joint' capacity (as is the case with 'collective bargaining'). Its power to compel or encourage compliance is not dependent upon the State having to deal directly with the issues itself, although it retains a power to set the scene by postulating certain norms and rules, which constrain others' role performance.

Where authority to decide is delegated, however, those to whom it is given, are expected to perform certain functions (with the threat of direct State intervention if they do not do so). These functions are essentially those which different authors have attributed to collective bargaining:

(a) a function of determining the price (and more generally the relative status) of all involved in the production process
(b) a function of establishing the rules by which those intended to be subject to them are to be expected to conform
(c) a function of managing (deciding and enforcing) the decisions or the rules which are to be applied.

The State has been able to remain abstentionist because, generally speaking, the joint mechanisms have operated in the expected ways and because the parties themselves have developed conventions which extend the control which the law and other cultural norms initiates. For this reason, *convention* which forms the basis of Flanders' societal regulation, may be more significant than the *law* as the source of order or behavioural control. In workplace regulation both parties are comparatively freer to acknowledge the strength of such conventions in regulating their relations, usually under the heading of 'custom and practice' (see, Brown, 1973). In collective bargaining, the collectivities have been relatively free to order their relations on this basis, although the effect of the Donovan Commission's recommendations would have been to transpose much of this convention into formal collective agreements (see Marsh, 1982, p 151).

The power of the State is not, however, absolute, as the action of the management of the Grunwick Processing Laboratories in 1977 (see Scarman, 1977; Rogaly, 1977), or the members of the National Union of Mineworkers in 1974, in thwarting the State's intentions, must suggest. Where there is an unwillingness to be bound by law, conventions are at least as likely to be thwarted, and an unordered situation is the result. The manager, on the other hand, is more likely to find himself bound by expressions of company policy to obey the law, just as most trade union members are likely to respond to their association's policies with similar assenting behaviours.

Readings

Jackson: (1977), pp 218-40. Flanders: (1965), pp 7-20.
Milliband: (1969), pp 46-106. Crouch: (1979), pp 119-39.
Hyman: (1975), pp 121-49.
Anthony: (1977a), pp 136-64; 268-303.
Kahn-Freund: (1977), pp 1-47.
Thomason: (1981), pp 63-127 and 427-54.

4

Regulating individual status

The significance of the employment contract

The State may be said to attempt a fundamental control over industrial relationships by establishing the rights and obligations ('status') in law of those who are party to them. Although it elevates the principles of individualism, it sets legally-enforceable limits to the individuals' opportunities to act and to develop relationships. It does this through the law in two main ways:

first, by prescribing and proscribing in the criminal and civil law certain activities in which individuals might engage; and

secondly, by standing ready to regulate and enforce the important undertakings (or contracts) which people might establish between themselves:

The first establishes the rights and obligations of the citizen in general, and the second ensures that important private agreements about status are upheld.

The first set of prescriptions and proscriptions is, of course, extremely complex. It seeks to provide the individual with lawful opportunities to act and with limits to his authority to do so. It is established for the most part in Statute law, but it is usually expressed through the common law as the 'distillation of the customary rules of the people over the centuries' (see Padfield, 1972, ch 7). It establishes the individual's constitutional rights and obligations, that which he has lawful authority to do and every right to expect of others (see Dicey, 1939).

The second set is rather different and in many ways more relevant to our present concerns. It focuses upon the concept of *contract*, that 'characteristic legal institution of an exchange economy which is strongly market oriented and based on the use of money' (Fox, 1974a, p 153). This device permits individuals of their own volition to enter into agreements entailing mutual rights and obligations for a limited period of time. The function of the law in this context is to be prepared to uphold such agreements where they are sufficiently important to the parties and where they wish to have the terms enforced.

The parts of the law which most directly affect the roles of managements and workers are those which govern rights in or ownership of property and relationships or acts of economic 'exchange', particularly the ownership of the means of production and of 'labour' and the exchange of labour or effort for consideration (in the form of a wage or salary).

There are other kinds of economic exchange, for example of goods for money, all of which are covered by the law of contract, as if they were all alike. But there is a sense in which the peculiarities of the exchange of human labour for a wage or salary have been allowed to influence the basic principles applied, so that the law relating to employment contracts is somewhat different from that relating to commercial contracts.

Here, we will be primarily concerned with the law relating to employment contracts, in so far as this reflects the societal intention to set limits to the opportunities of the parties voluntarily to give up any rights of ownership in property or labour. The employment contract will be examined in two parts:

(a) the nature of the contract itself as this is established in law as an instrument for encouraging *and* controlling exchange relationships, and as a vehicle for upholding rights and obligations drawn from a diversity of sources
(b) the content of the contract in so far as this establishes the rights and obligations which people enjoy or suffer, and thus determines what they can count on in developing their work relationships (see also Armstrong *et al*, 1981, p 7).

These are examined in the present chapter and the limits placed on the manager's rights in the next one.

THE MEANING OF CONTRACT

At its simplest, the concept of contract refers to the voluntary establishment of mutual promises by two (or more) persons with

89

the intention that each will be bound by what is thus contracted for, and subject to penalty for breach. The factor which distinguishes contractual from other legal obligations (such as those imposed in the criminal law or the law of tort) is that contractual obligations are based on the *agreement* of the contracting parties themselves, not on the will of the society at large.

The agreement is usually based upon mutual promises by two persons. A promise, for example, to play a round of golf on Saturday morning may not be terribly consequential if it is broken, either for the parties or for society at large. One may be annoyed if the promise is not kept, but it is unlikely that life is much blighted as a result. A promise to deliver goods at a certain price might be much more important and consequential. The proposed recipient's business and economic well-being might be seriously put at risk if the promise were not kept. If people could renege on such promises without hindrance and with impunity, the whole commercial fabric of the society might be jeopardized.

This latter kind of promise is usually made within a 'business contract' which is distinguished in law from the 'social contract' illustrated above by the agreement to play golf. Business contracts may be recognized and enforced in law, where social contracts, or mere 'gentlemen's agreements', cannot be. The legal definition of a 'contract', therefore, makes it 'an agreement giving rise to obligations which are enforced or recognized by law (Treitel, 4th edn, 1975, p 1). It might equally apply to the exchange of goods for valuable consideration (money) or to the exchange of labour (or labour services) for comparable consideration (wages and salaries).

The concept of an 'employment contract' is, therefore, but a part of a much wider concept of 'contract' and is usually conceived as an essentially *voluntary* agreement to give up something in return for something else. Mansfield Cooper and Wood describe it as a:

> 'voluntary relationship into which the parties may enter on terms laid down by themselves within limitations imposed only by the general law of contract' (Mansfield Cooper and Wood, 1966, p 2),

thus establishing that employment contract law is subject to the same kind of legal principles and rules as that of the commercial contract.

The assumptions behind the contract

As a device facilitating exchange, contract rests upon the fundamental assumption that what each agrees to exchange is his or hers *to* exchange. This is easy to appreciate in connection with the exchange of goods for money: the one must 'own' the goods and the other must 'possess' the money and each must have come by them honestly. Where these conditions are met, and the parties intend that they should be held liable to meet the obligations they have agreed to assume, all that is required in the event of default or disagreement as to terms agreed, is some means of assessing and enforcing the claim of either party in the event of either dispute as to the terms agreed or default by the other party.

Contracts of this type have been distinguished as 'purposive contracts' and defined in a way which captures the idea that each involves a single, one-off transaction, in which what passes between the parties in either direction is of limited and tangible consequence, quickly and easily recognizable by either. Purposive contracts are:

> 'made to complete a specific transaction or to further a discrete objective. Only a tenuous and temporary association is created. The purposive contract is infused with the spirit of restraint and delimitation; open-ended obligations are alien to its nature; arms-length negotiation is a keynote' (Selznick, 1969, p 54).

In this form, it represented the device which freed men (entrepreneurs and workers) at the time of the industrial revolution from the more diffuse ties of obligation which had previously bound them to their lords and masters. Whenever this kind of contract is employed by free men it curbs their freedom in a limited number of respects and for a limited time. It does not bind the contractors to one another for anything more than its particular purpose.

As it applied to the exchange of goods, it was also relatively easy to make the assumption that the transaction would only take place if each of the two persons wanted what the other had to offer. They could then be assumed to meet one another as equals in setting up the contract. Ricardo, the high priest of individualism in economic affairs, declared, for example, that such contracts as were freely entered into would automatically be 'fair' as well. No interference by a third party, such as the State, was called for because there was no morality superior to that produced by the operation of unfettered market forces.

This presupposes, however, that the application of the law is as impersonal and as impartial as the operation of the forces of supply and demand and this may not always be so. But more fundamentally, it implies that the nature of the employment contract is the same as that of the commercial contract.

Employment contracts

The device of contract was initially regarded as adequate to contain the opportunities of contractors in employment. The existing civil law of contract was thought to be capable of enabling individuals to contract on their own agreed terms in employment, under the supervision of the courts in the usual (commercial) way. But this proved to be the case only if certain assumptions were made, both about what existed to be exchanged and about what obligations were necessarily incurred by the parties.

First, it was necessary to be able to recognize that each party to an employment contract owned something which could be exchanged. The worker clearly owned his labour, his labour power, or his contribution to work, and he could offer these to the employer as 'services' which the employer could make use of. The employer might well need such services and be willing to pay for them. But what did the employer own that he could exchange? In the simplest sense, he owned the cash which might form the 'valuable consideration' paid in the form of a wage or salary. But in a more real sense, he also had to be assumed to own the *employment* which the worker needed and wanted; without the employment there would be no transaction, just as without the worker's services there would be none.

Secondly, it was necessary to recognize that an employment contract was not, for reasons related to this, a simple purposive contract. Rather it involves obligations which are much more extensive in both content and time, than those usually found in the commercial contract. On the one hand, the ties (sought by both parties in different forms) are likely to be broader, and on the other, they are usually expected (again by both parties) to continue into an indefinite future.

The complexity and continuity of the mutual obligations are

indicated in Commons' suggestion that the employment contract is not so much a contract as:

> 'a continuing implied renewal of contracts at every minute and hour, based on the continuance of what is deemed on the employer's side to be satisfactory service, and on the labourer's side, what is deemed to be satisfactory conditions and compensation' (Commons, 1924, p 285).

This is a necessary view to take, because it is 'hardly practical to resolve what each employee was to do over the life of the agreement' at the point where the contract is first established (see, Young, 1963, p 246).

On this basis, therefore, an individual would find himself entering into quite distinct kinds of relationship with another, according to whether the contract related to the exchange of goods or of labour for consideration. Although the same device of contract is used, it becomes a device which establishes very different sets of mutual obligation. Consequently, the contract for the exchange of labour services may be regarded as more of a 'status' contract, although not completely so (see Leighton and Dumville, 1977). The status contract is much more general in the obligations which it establishes and continues much longer into the future, and has been defined by Selznick as:

> 'a voluntary agreement for the creation of a continuing relationship, especially one that affects the 'total legal situation' of the individual' (Selznick, 1969, p 54).

Agreements to become someone's kin, servant, follower, client or henchman, would provide more extreme examples than the ordinary employment contract. The statuses thus identified are much more general and longer-lasting than are those of buyer and seller of goods. What is agreed to, assumes that all the main elements of an individual's status are linked together as was the case in feudal structures, and the contract is not made to depend upon agreement to perform, or actual performance of, specific actions. Whatever 'freedom' is effected by the element of 'agreement', it is a very different one from that envisioned in the purposive contract.

Furthermore, it could not be assumed that this kind of contract would be established 'fairly', because it required the subordination of one party (the supplier of the services) to the other (the owner of the employment). As Adam Smith noted so long ago, the employer had a greater capacity to wait to secure the terms which he wanted in an employment contract, than had the labourer, and he was therefore much more likely to be able to impose his terms. Even if the free and fair epithet could be applied to the contract to exchange goods for consideration, it was much more difficult to see its relevance to the status, or employment, contract.

Strictly, a status contract may, in principle or in theory, involve an even-handed assumption of obligations by the parties. Those assumed by a master may be as extensive as those assumed by a servant, those by a leader as extensive as those by a follower, and so on. However, the emphasis put upon the need for freedom of the 'trader' (or businessman) in the industrial revolution led to his assuming much more limited obligations to his servants or employees whilst demanding that they assume more extensive obligations to him.

This lack of even-handedness was supported by the law, in both its legislative and common law manifestations. Under the old Master and Servant Acts, *criminal* penalties were imposed on 'workmen who failed to fulfil their duties' but failed to visit these penalities or punishments on the employer in breach (see S and B Webb, 1920a, p 249; Wedderburn, 1971, p 75). Vestiges of this distinction continue in law to this day. Although the last of the Master and Servant Acts (that of 1867) was repealed in 1875, the idea of a 'master' and 'servant' relationship involving differential rights and obligations, still persists (as do the terms themselves in the common law).

Although the position is now much less extreme, it was, in the early years of the modern period, difficult to perceive the operation of the fundamental principle of 'freedom of contract' in legislation or court decision applied to the contract of employment. This helps to explain some of the worker's reluctance to go to law for redress of any grievance he may have.

For these reasons, a number of eminent academic lawyers have cast doubt on the validity of the assumption that a contract involving limited obligations (as in commerce) provided an adequate instrument for a relationship which involved more complex reciprocities (see Kahn-Freund, 1977, pp 3-15; Rideout, 1966, p 112).

The rules of contracting

The influence of the law upon the definition of contract is already clear from what has been said. It arises because people accept (even automatically or without thinking) the legal requirements or rules applied to contracts. Where the parties find their *business* bargains important (as they undoubtedly do) they just accept that the rules designed to protect the institution of contract itself, will apply.

These basic rules are intended to establish who may contract, with what purposes and intentions, and how they shall do so, if they want the bargains to be recognized and enforced in a court of law.

1   The persons entering into the agreement must (in the eyes of the law) be competent to do so. There are limitations placed on competency in respect of age (minors cannot be bound by contract), mental health or dependency. But it was the admission of (specifically) adult males of sound mind to the ranks of the free contractors which ushered in the 'freedom' which is associated with the industrial revolution.

2   The objects of the contract must themselves be legal, as the courts will not enforce contracts which intend a breach of the law. Thus, an employment contract which contained a term which sought to evade responsibilities for income tax, would be unenforceable on this ground, and any other rights established in such a contract would be 'lost' because of the presence of an illegal object.

3   The parties must clearly intend that the agreement they are making will be legally-binding and give rise to obligations which they intend shall be enforceable through the courts. Generally, 'business' contracts are presumed to have this intent, but 'social' contracts (including collective agreements) are presumed not to.

4   There must be both 'offer' and 'acceptance' of terms. This means, in effect, that each party must offer something and the other accept it *in the same terms* before there is a basis for an enforceable contract. The offer by an employer of a job as, say, sweeper up for £50 a week, must be accepted in those same terms by the potential employee. 'I'll accept the job for £60' does not amount to acceptance for the purposes of contract law.

5   There must either be some consideration of an identifiable or

95

recognizable sort (such as money for labour services) or the agreement must be entered into according to certain prescribed forms (as in the case of promises by deed ... which are usually outside the scope of employment relations). Consideration is a relevant, but complex, requirement: it is defined as consisting:

> 'either in some right, interest, profit, or benefit accruing to one party, or some forbearance, detriment, loss or responsibility given, suffered or undertaken by the other'

or as requiring

> 'that something of material value shall be given or some other detriment sustained by the recipient of a promise, in order to make that promise enforceable' (Mansfield Cooper and Wood, 1966, p 37).

These amplify the legal definition of contract. They also impose a procedure to establish the individual's legally-enforceable status in the employment relationship.

STATUS: RIGHTS AND OBLIGATIONS

The *content* of an individual's status is established by the 'broad rule of the common law' that 'no one may interfere with or invade my person or property unless he has lawful power to do so'. Should he do so, he commits a wrong contrary to the common law and 'I may sue' (Padfield, 1972, p 17). This 'broad rule' covers the situation where an individual seeking to employ his capital or his labour in trade may not be interfered with by another unless he has lawful authority to do so. In such cases the courts will uphold the individual's right:

> 'to employ the capital he inherits or has acquired, according to his own discretion, without molestation or obstruction, so long as he does not infringe the rights or property of others' (Report of the Committee on the State of Woollen Manufacture in England; 4 July, 1806, p 12).

This statement may be applied equally to the owner of capital and the owner of labour. But to apply it to labour, it does require the acceptance of a fiction that the person 'owns' the labour service as an object which he may offer to an employer when contracting in employment, in much the same way that he might be regarded as owning exchangeable goods. Constitutional rights and obligations in employment are largely dependent upon this ownership of real (capital assets) or assumed (labour) property for the exchange of which the individual might lawfully contract.

The particular rights and obligations of the parties to the employment contract are derived from a number of distinct, but interdependent sources. These reflect the influence of different values and different agencies over a long period of time. The juxtaposition of the principle of freedom of contract and certain cultural values of the past two centuries has, in consequence, made the contract of employment an amalgam of different, sometimes contradictory, expectations. Over this same period, a number of different agencies have tried to change the balance of advantage and disadvantage, and have sedimented a number of other expectations and requirements into it.

The main sources may be listed as:

1   the express terms formally and explicitly agreed between the employer and the employee at the time of establishing the employment contract or subsequently
2   the express terms which may be agreed on behalf of the individual employer or employee by representatives negotiating (collectively) on his behalf and which may be imported into the individual contract under certain conditions
3   the terms implied on the basis of the well-established customs of the trade or industry concerned
4   the terms which will be implied by common law, if the question is tested before the courts, when the express terms do not indicate the full scope of the relationship
5   the terms which may be established by, or by reference to, legislation enacted (usually) to protect the worker in his employment relationship.

It has been argued that these, together, fill out the picture of the rights and obligations of employee and employer within the employment relationship. But none of these five categories of influence upon the terms of an individual contract of employment, alone or in combination, really establishes certainty as to the status of the parties, although some are more certain and predictable than others.

The express terms of the contract

The express terms of an individual contract of employment are those which stem from individual or collective bargaining over the terms of offer and acceptance at the time when the agreement was first reached or when amended. They may be established orally or in writing. Those normally entered into expressly are to serve the employer and to pay wages to the worker, and these will normally be sufficient to establish that a contract has been brought into existence.

Such a contract would, however, leave out more than it includes in defining the scope of the relationship or the mutual obligations actually assumed in 'the course of dealing' in reaching the agreement. A contract which might be deemed to have been established by conduct even if nothing was said about terms, would also have much in common with this. In both cases, the terms which would be read into the contract would normally be imported by reference to either custom or common law doctrines, and in these lies the greatest source of uncertainty for the individual contractors.

Individually agreed terms

With 'pure' individual bargaining (see above, p 74-78) the express terms are what the two parties agree to orally or in writing in establishing or modifying the contract, or those which they demonstrate by their conduct they have agreed to. With collective bargaining, the express terms are those which may be agreed orally or in writing between agents and representatives of the principals (provided that those parties have agreed in advance to their incorporation in the individual contract).

There remain many situations in which the initial terms of a contract are established between individuals (see Marsh, 1982, pp 153-54). This occurs in the so-called 'unorganized' trades and industries, (although in many of these the device of the wages council has been adopted to impose a statutory minimum in respect of wages, hours and holidays) (see below, pp 180-86). It occurs also in many managerial, professional and technical occupations, although these workers may be supported to some extent by membership of a 'professional association' (discussed below, pp 135-39) and there was some suggestion in the 1970s that some of these groups are becoming increasingly unionised (see, Hartmann, 1974; Shackleton and Davies, 1976; Bamber, 1976).

Individual contracting is subject to the 'rules of contracting' (above, pp 95-96). But in practice, the process of offering and accepting in agreed terms frequently does not have the clarity and precision about it which the law requires, and this may lead to both dispute and judicial 'interference'. The terms articulated may be off-hand in the extreme, and may not be accepted in the same terms as the offer. They may or may not exactly accord with the several intentions of the contractors, and they may intend to give rise to unenforceable rights and obligations. It is this which admits the implication of terms either from custom or from the common law doctrines themselves.

Collectively agreed terms

In the case of the collective agreement, the express terms are established indirectly by bargaining between representatives. A collective agreement is essentially a charter of rules governing the relationships between the employer (or the employers' association) and the employees' association (usually a trade union in the normal meaning of that term) and expressing the agreed substantive terms and conditions under which employee-members will work for the employer.

Over the years, the subjects dealt with in the substantive part of the collective agreement have increased in number. One or more documents may now cover many terms and conditions of employment which in an earlier period might well have been treated as customary. The subjects have generally expanded from wage rates and ratios of apprentices, to cover in addition hours, holidays, overtime and bonus payments, working arrangements, facilities (for example, for washing) and a range of fringe benefits, including pensions. These affect the substantive and express terms of the contract by substitution, so that regardless of what the individual parties may have agreed initially, they define their future status entitlements.

A trade unionist would tend to see these as most important in determining his rights and duties at work, rather than those associated with either the common law or legislation; but it is important to establish how they come to have any impact on the contract of employment terms and how they relate to the offer and acceptance situation.

Both the procedural and substantive agreements affect the relative status of the parties, but not all of what may thus be agreed (collectively) is necessarily enforceable in the individual contract. Most of the procedural terms would not be enforceable in law (except in so far as they establish, for example, terms of notice or conditions under which disciplinary action might or might not be taken). Most of the second set would in principle be enforceable, but only through express or implied importation into the terms of the individual contract.

There are two reasons for a distinction between the two kinds of collective agreement:

1 A collective agreement is not in itself a contract which the courts would enforce. This has been accepted since 1871, when the Trade Union Act ordered the courts not to entertain actions to enforce agreements between trade unions. Even where a single employer negotiated an agreement with one or more trade unions, it was assumed that it would still remain unenforceable. In 1969, however, the Ford Motor Company Limited sought to challenge this assumption in an action against the Amalgamated Union of Engineering and Foundry Workers (1 WLR 339; 2 All E R 481; 6 KIR 50) but the point was never determined for technical reasons, and the outcome was taken to confirm what had been the accepted view.

The position was changed, deliberately, by the Industrial Relations Act 1971, but has been re-established more explicitly in the Trade Union and Labour Relations Act 1974, s 18. This states that the whole or part of a collective agreement will be conclusively presumed not to have been intended to be a legally enforceable contract unless it is in writing and contains a provision which (however expressed) states that the parties intended that it (or some part(s)) shall be a legally enforceable contract. Any clause restricting a worker's right to take industrial action must meet additional conditions before it would be enforced, regardless of what may be said in such an agreement to the contrary. Lord Denning's recent judgement involving an interpretation of the meaning of this section, confirmed the general view that the agreement is still unenforceable (in Monterosso Shipping Co Ltd v International Transport Workers' Federation (1982) IRLR, 468).

2 The collective agreement and the individual contract must

both make explicit provision for incorporation. Even then enforcement of the substantive terms is not automatic; there are legal conventions governing express incorporation to be applied:

(a) the agreements reached between the employer and the trade union representatives cannot bind anyone but themselves. Therefore what is agreed can only bind others if the representatives are explicitly in an agency relationship to their principals. Thus, mere membership of a union does not place the worker in a position where the negotiators are his agents; individual members must provide an express authorization to the agents or there must be an explicit union rule to this effect which will have the same force. Thus, in the case of Rookes v Barnard the judge held that only because:

> 'the representatives were authorised by their executive to bind the union as a whole and the members individually, the terms of the agreement became part of the terms of each individual contract of employment between (BOAC) and the members of (the Union)' (1964) AC, 1129).

(b) there must also be either express or implied incorporation of the collective agreement terms in the contract of employment itself. A term in that contract may expressly state that the contract incorporates the terms of the relevant collective agreement (National Coal Board v Galley (1958) 1 All E R, 91). Such terms must also be capable of being translated into the individual's contract: procedural clauses obviously cannot be incorporated since they relate to the conduct of the bargaining parties, and others may apply only to union members or some other defined class or category of worker so that they could not influence the contracts of those not in the category.

(c) there must also be an absence of conflict as between different collective agreements which may conceivably be relevant. O'Higgins makes this point by saying: 'so far the (court) decisions suggest that the courts will only allow the worker to get the benefit of those terms in conflicting collective agreements which are least advantageous' (O'Higgins, 1976, p 35).

Implied incorporation may take one of two main forms.

1   The parties may be assumed to have intended that the terms of the collective agreement were so vital as to necessitate their incorporation into the employment contract.
2   Such incorporation may have been taking place in the trade or industry for so long that it could be regarded as established practice for this to happen, or the terms may have stood for so long that they have become part of the custom and practice of the trade or industry.

This tends to reinforce the first point made above that the collective agreement has some association with custom and practice (see Flanders, 1965, p 22).

Customary terms

Many individual contracts are established with very little being expressed on any of the terms and conditions. This is mainly because many terms and conditions are standard either for employment contracts in general or for those in the particular trade or industry. The universal standards are considered in the next section. Here attention is directed towards those which could be regarded as customary for the trade, industry or occupation, and which are often assumed by the contracting parties.

Both parties rely upon this notion of 'custom'. Employers frequently plead that certain practices are customary for their trade and seek to have the courts read them into the terms of the contract. Trade unions seek to preserve some customary way of proceeding or performing unless and until some new set of formal rules is agreed. In one sense, therefore, the collective agreement might be seen as either a 'successor' to unwritten custom or a 'codification' of it (see Brown, 1972, pp 42-61).

The common law has always been willing to take cognisance of custom and practice in imputing terms to an employment contract. But again the law imposes its own conditions: it requires that custom must be reasonable, certain, and notorious before it can be accepted as influencing the terms of the contract.

1   'Reasonable' customs must accord with the usual judicial views of what is reasonable: a custom of paying non-unionists less than unionists in a factory would probably be regarded as unreasonable and for this reason not provide an implied term in the contract.

2 To be 'certain' the custom must be precisely defined, so that none could interpret it in an alternative way to give a different conclusion. Since, almost by definition, customs are usually unwritten, there is an obvious pitfall here.

3 'Notorious' means that the custom must be well-known to people in the trade or industry or factory concerned, and certainly not something concocted or invented by either trade unions or employers on the spur of the moment to support their case.

But even customs which are reasonable, certain and notorious will be denied validity by the courts as sources of implied terms unless they are also reflective of an assumption of obligation on the part of the party. This is usually applied to the advantage of the employer; he may have followed certain policies for donkey's years because they are supportive of his business interests, but does not see himself as *obligated* to anyone to pursue them.

The *ex gratia* payment is an obvious attempt to permit money to be paid without creating any kind of customary precedent. But it can extend beyond this. The employer may pay gratuities or bonuses over many years, and do so from a sense of philanthropy not of obligation. It would be pointless trying to persuade a court that these should be regarded as customary terms and conditions of employment. However, in the process of collective bargaining such arguments may well be used and may succeed, and thus allow custom to be read into the contract by implication.

Other implied terms

The agreed and customary terms do not usually establish completely the range of rights and obligations entered into by the parties to a contract. Additional terms may be introduced by the courts in the event of dispute, or by legislation.

The courts will read into the contract terms which derive from the doctrines of the common law itself, where there is no other source of resolution of any dispute. These represent an important source of rights and obligations in themselves, and depend upon an accumulation of past legal interpretations of public policy as expressed in law. The doctrines of the common law as related to contract, and particularly contracts in employment, developed largely during the early part of the nineteenth century. In this process, the societal values of enhancing trade and of individualism were incorporated into the doctrines, with the result that they emphasize the rights of the individual in property and the obligations of the individual to serve the interests of 'trade'. Aspects of that public policy may be expressed in current legislation, but some of it is bound up in common law doctrines which derived from much earlier periods and situations, where public policy took very different forms.

This may be regarded as a source of irrelevance and uncertainty in spite of the contention by lawyers, that such terms 'may serve to indicate with greater certainty, the boundaries of (the) relationship' (Gayler and Purvis, 1972, p 57). Hepple has argued on this point that:

> 'Some of the employment cases in the law reports were decided in a pre-industrial society at a time when agricultural and domestic labour were the most common forms of gainful employment. Others were decided in the early stages of the industrial revolution at a time when the judiciary was anxious to allow entrepreneurs freedom to trade without interference from combinations of workmen and with little regard for the safety, health and welfare of children, let alone women and men. These decisions and the social philosophy which guided them have little relevance to a modern industrial society. Yet the orthodox legal view in England and Wales is that a proposition of law which forms the basis of the decision in a case cannot be held to have lost its force simply because it has become obsolete. ... It is misleading to rely on the older cases in which the judges were strongly influenced by the requirements of the criminal law (that is, before 1875)' (Hepple and O'Higgins, 1981, p 52).

As a consequence, the common law may be seen to impute terms which are derived from considerations of commercial convenience and reasonableness (as these concepts developed through the hey-days of mercantilism and individualism). However willing the lawyers may be to seek to capture the spirit of the present age in their inference of implicit terms of the employment contract, they are, unless excused by legislation or given opportunity by relevant collective agreements, bound by precedent.

Common law doctrines

Treitel suggests that there are three main doctrines which are to be found in the common law and which are applied where the express terms are absent or unclear:

1 In some circumstances the law will enforce what is *commercially* convenient (or 'reasonably necessary' to give efficacy to the contract from a business point of view) rather than what (one of) the parties might contend was the real intention of the contract. (Recently, Stephenson, LH, in an *obiter dictum* in the case of Mears and Safecar Security Ltd (1982), IRLR, 99; (1982) 2 All E R, 865) warned that this might change and that the 'convenience' of the employee might in some circumstances be given more prominence). The older doctrine has been justified on the grounds that 'great uncertainty might result if a person who appeared to have agreed to certain terms could escape liability merely by showing that he had no 'real intention' to agree to them' (Treitel, 1975 edn, p 1).

2 The courts will also act on the assumption that contractors will, unless they expressly agree otherwise, observe 'certain standards of behaviour' and will then read these standards into the agreement unless they are expressly excluded. These usually figure as *implied* terms of the contract (see Treitel, 1975 edn, pp 1-2).

3 The courts may also intervene to redress the balance of advantage between the parties, where, either it can be shown that there was misrepresentation, undue influence, or illegality, or there is a presumption of inherent inequality of bargaining power, such that in either case what may have been agreed acts unfairly to one party's detriment (Treitel, 1975, edn, pp 2-4). The doctrine of 'inequality of bargaining power' is a recent construction of Lord Denning, MR, in which he swept together a number of the hitherto distinct forms of inequality (such as duress of goods, unconscionable transactions, etc). It has not yet, however, been applied (or even thought about) in relation to the contract of employment, although critics of the judgements have recognized such a possibility arising in the future (see Seely, 1975; Carr, 1975).

Those who establish contracts are likely to order their behaviour (for example, when actually entering into a contract) in accordance with these doctrines simply because they can forecast that in the event of a dispute, the courts will apply them; they do not, in other words, have to be before a court for their influence to be felt.

It does not follow, however, that all of these doctrines will be applied to *employment* contracts although that is generally the case. Some of them are considered inapplicable (the doctrine of inequality of bargaining power, for example, has so far made no such inroads). Some are necessarily modified (for example to take account of the continuing relationship). But the possibility of the one influencing the other remains and the law of contract as it relates to employment contracting is made more uncertain than might be the case if the two were developed separately.

Common law duties

The employer's and employee's rights and duties *at common law* are derived from these sources. There is some evidence that the courts have shown some willingness to develop new rules to meet changed conditions (for example, Hill v C.A. Parsons and Co. Ltd. (1972) Ch, 305; Langston v AUEW (1974) ICR, 180, 190, 192). But there is probably much more change to be made before they meet the aspirations of many employees at the present time.

The statement of rights and duties under contract, may be presented in the form of the duties accepted by the two parties, with rights deriving from the reciprocals of these.

The employer is regarded as owing a duty to the employee:

1 to pay for work done or service rendered under the contract
2 to provide opportunity to earn remuneration and, in some circumstances, to provide work for example where 'practice' is important to maintain the value of the service
3 to take reasonable care for the safety and well-being of the employee whilst at work
4 to indemnify the employee for any loss sustained in the performance of his or her duties
5 to 'treat the employee with appropriate courtesy' (Rideout, 1979, p 35) in order to sustain mutual trust and confidence.

In so far as the courts will uphold these duties in the absence of a specific disclaimer, the individual employee may expect the reciprocals of these 'as of right'.

The employee, comparably, is regarded as being under a duty to the employer:

1   to be ready and willing to work
2   to provide personal service
3   to avoid wilful disruption of the employer's undertaking or, put more simply, to co-operate with the employer and facilitate the execution of the contract
4   to obey reasonable or lawful orders
5   to work only for the employer in the period during which he is being paid by him to work
6   to account for any profits received
7   to respect the employer's trade secrets
8   to take reasonable care of the employer's property when it is entrusted to him
9   to take reasonable care when engaged in the employer's service.

The employer can, comparably, expect the employee to behave in a manner consistent with these obligations, and, consequently, he can expect to receive loyal and faithful service from his employees, who, as a result, place themselves under the authority of the employer for the period of their employment.

There is a presumption that the judges will read these terms into employment contracts, unless the parties have expressly excluded them, or unless legislation has sought to deny their validity or to modify them. This provides the basis for expectations of the roles of managers and workers, given that they attach importance to them.

STATUTORY INTERVENTION

If some of the common law doctrines have avoided redressing advantage in employment contract terms, legislation (as well as collective bargaining) has deliberately sought to change it. The position early in the industrial revolution was one in which legislation tended to operate to the advantage of the master or employer, as the decks were cleared to allow the new individuals to make their contribution to the creation of trade and wealth. As Wedderburn records:

'From the Statute of Labourers 1351 onwards, various

enactments subjected workmen who failed to fulfil their duties to the master employing them to criminal penalties, including imprisonment. Similar penalties did not attach to employers who broke their contracts.... In 1867, the Master and Servant Act revised the law and made it somewhat less harsh but retained the sanction of imprisonment for 'aggravated misconduct" (Wedderburn, 1971, pp 75-6).

Some legislation has attempted to increase the status of the workman or employee. Kahn-Freund (1977, pp 32-35) has suggested three distinct stages in this development:

1   The first concern was to meet the needs of particular categories by imposing statutory duties upon the employer in respect of the morals, health and well-being of children, young persons and females. Only later and slowly, were these duties extended to other categories but they are now largely embodied in the Health and Safety at Work Act and the Truck Acts.

2   The later concern was to improve standards of treatment, including remuneration, by, for example, establishing minimum wages, hours and holidays of particularly disadvantaged workers by the Trade Boards (under the Trade Board Act 1909) which employers then had to meet. This legislative exercise was conceived as more deliberately experimental. Although it was applied to limited and defined areas or categories, it was conceived as capable of extension if extension appeared warranted.

3   More recently, legislation has tried to establish (almost) universal standards. This is exemplified in the Contracts of Employment Acts (1963 and 1972), the Redundancy Payments Act (1965), the Industrial Relations Act (1971) (ss 22 *et seq*), the Trade Union and Labour Relations Acts (1974-1976) and the Employment Protection Act (1975). The objective here is to make the statuory terms universal, whether in respect of periods of notice, reasons for dismissal or compensation terms to be expected in certain defined eventualities.

In effect, the terms agreed between the employer and employee are in appropriate ways modified by the legislation. Initially, the modification was seen to be made because the legislation imposed a 'statutory duty' upon the employer, with the one consequence that actions under it had to be commenced within a specified period of time. This still applies, for example, to the duties imposed under the Truck Acts, 1831-1940, and the Health and Safety at Work Act 1974.

More recent legislation in the 1960s and 1970s imposes duties upon the employer to observe certain specified minimum terms and conditions of employment, but imputes the terms as contractual:

> 'The parties to the contract of employment are, by a statutory fiction, deemed to make the contract on the basis of the statutory terms ... The terms of the statute can be contracted out only for the benefit of the worker and if the parties purport to agree on terms less favourable to him, they are nevertheless deemed to have contracted for the minimum, and the worker's claim for the difference is accordingly (by fiction) a contractual claim'.

The fiction is 'that the content of the statute was contractually intended by the employer' (Kahn-Freund, 1977, p 31).

Employee rights established by Statute

The general effect of this legislation has been to curb the rights of the employer to discipline and control the employee. In some cases, such as the Truck Acts, the Wages Councils Acts and the Health and Safety legislation, a duty is explicitly placed upon the employer to conduct himself in certain ways. In others, however, the duty is derived as the reciprocal of new, explicit rights which have been granted to the employee. The effect here is that the employee secures a closely defined 'right' without the employer losing his general right. For example, an employee's right to a specific period of notice does not take away the employer's right to dismiss his employee.

The main rights which qualified employees now possess as a consequence of statutory modification or extension of rights at common law are the rights:

1   not to be discriminated against on grounds of sex, marital status or race, whether in recruitment, or at engagement or termination, or during employment
2   to be paid for work done, (at a statutory minimum rate in some trades), and if a manual employee outside the public

sector, to be paid in full in coin of the realm unless he gives this up voluntarily and in accordance with the prescribed form
3   to join and belong to a trade union and to engage in its activities, (and by agreement with the employer to do so in the 'employer's time'); and to refuse to join a trade union under certain circumstances
4   to be given an opportunity to earn remuneration, and in some special cases, a right to compensation for lay off
5   to be provided with a healthy and safe working environment and with instruction in appropriate methods of safe working
6   to be given basic information about his contract and the manner in which remuneration is calculated, and about the reasons why he is being dismissed
7   to be given a minimum amount of notice commensurate with his period of employment with the employer
8   not to be dismissed 'unfairly' as this is defined in legislation and to be given reasons for dismissal on request
9   to have the industrial tribunal or the courts review the conduct of his employer in respect of any aspect of relationship which is governed by Statute.

The employee may need to have a certain minimum amount of service with the employer and to be within a certain age range in order to qualify for some (but not all) of these rights (see Thomason, 1981, pp 92-95). Some (particularly those which have been established in recent individual employment protection legislation) are deemed to be rights enforceable in contract, and are not to be compared in this respect with the rights under the Truck, Health and Safety and Wages Councils Acts. These are usually within the jurisdiction of the industrial tribunals (see, below, pp 206-18).

Thus, the general effect of this recent legislation has been to assure the employee of certain minimum rights in employment, and to modify certain of the implied terms derived from the common law. These constitute a floor of enforceable rights on which he or his trade union in negotiation may build.

Summary: the influence of contract

The contract of employment is an important element in structuring the behaviour and the relationships of those at work. It is intended to have a fundamental influence upon the kinds of relationship which those in employment (both employer and employee) can establish. Taken together the various sources of the parties' status in the employment relationship, contribute to the definition of what a worker, or an employer, *is* in the modern industrial society. Whilst it is not true that the whole of his status is determined by the contract of employment, this is clearly a powerful instrument for shaping both the nature of the work role and of the industrial relationship.

If either party is to have the protection of the law for the rights and obligations into which he is deemed to have entered voluntarily, he must both conform to the law's requirements as to form, and accept the validity of certain legal doctrines which have been applied by the courts. Their application, in the absence of explicit agreement to the contrary, establishes the influence of the common law upon the basic duties and obligations of the parties.

The common law, for the most part, establishes those rights and obligations which would accord with the old individualistic or liberal principles which were applied in the first part of the industrial revolution. It imposes duties upon both the employer and the employee, and it is largely with the discharge of the duty assumed under contract that the other party secures certain rights or benefits.

The terms which the competent parties may agree to may, however, obviate the necessity for implied terms to be read into the contract. Potential contractors tend, however, to use a kind of shorthand in establishing contracts, and *assume* that a good deal of what is customary or traditional will be read into the contract automatically without it being expressed. This, as well as simple forgetfulness, provides a role for the courts and tribunals whenever disagreement as to terms arises.

The effect of legislation on the other hand, has been generally to establish positive rights or benefits for one party or the other. Just which party was the recipient varied from time to time. In the early part of the period, both the Companies Acts and the employment laws (such as Master and Servant or Employers and Workmen) tended to establish positive rights for the employers and their agents, whereas in recent years it has tended to create more rights for workers or employees. The terms recently established by Statute and deemed to have been agreed to by the parties are sometimes more beneficial to the worker than those which they in fact agreed. These are more likely to establish employee rights than employee duties, although the rights of the worker impute a duty upon the employer.

In spite of the changes effected recently by legislation there is no very strong suggestion that the legally-defined status of the two main parties is now 'equal' in any meaningful sense. The disparities may be less great than they were, but the dependent position of the worker in the employment relationship remains. There may, indeed, be good reason for continuing this relationship of subordination, but it is generally regarded as providing one of the mainsprings of trade union challenge to the existing system, and might, arguably, be out of line with the kinds of norms which are being developed in a democratic society (see Goldthorpe, 1974).

Readings

Kahn-Freund: (1977), pp 1-47.
Rideout: (1979), pp 3-66.
Hepple and O'Higgins: (1979), pp 52-75.
Treitel: (1975), pp 1-7.
Fox: (1974a), pp 152-206.

5

Regulating the disciplinary function

Ownership and discipline

The purpose of contract is both to uphold individual freedom, and to facilitate the co-operation of free men in performing the tasks of economic enterprise. It does this by ensuring that the employer (and therefore the manager) has a lawful authority to discipline the worker. The rights and obligations embodied in the contract of employment include the right of the manager to manage *and* the necessary subordination of the worker to the requirements of the undertaking as these are defined by management. This is subsumed in the common expression 'the manager's right to manage' (see Daniel and McIntosh, 1972; Kipping, 1972; Wigham, 1973; Porter, 1954).

The right to manage (supported by the right to discipline) originates in the right of the owner to do what he will with his own and, as in that case, it is a derived right. The employer is primarily a businessman (or business corporation) and has a protected status in law and convention in order that he may effect the increase of the wealth of society (and incidentally of himself or itself). *In order to achieve these ends*, he needs to have the derived right to organize, direct and control (see Tannenbaum, 1949, pp 225-41) the resources of production, including that of labour. This right is then a necessary means to the realization of his main objective and task.

Express delegation of these rights to managers occurred under a number of early acts including those of Master and Servant and Truck. In the Truck Act 1831, and the Master and Servant Act 1867, the contracting powers of a wide variety of managers, supervisors and agents were expressly recognized as having authority to 'contract as employers' with workers, so that by extension, all managers acquired a comparably protected status in the area of employment and industrial relations. In spite of the

113

fact that some of these old acts have been repealed, this general managerial power to contract and to discipline remains with the management (see Redgrave's Factories Acts 1966).

In the early part of the industrial revolution, the right of 'ownership' was extended to cover labour as well as material goods, and was almost absolute. Over the past 200 years the right has been challenged (particularly by organized labour) and has been modified in consequence. The law has followed in the wake of the political challenge, and now upholds a much more truncated right than it did two centuries ago. The (almost) absolute right (see below, p 117-19) has been reduced to the present limited one in which the right to direct and control labour is hedged about with a number of restrictions (see below pp 120-31).

In spite of these changes, however, the fundamental right of the manager (as the owner's representative) to manage and to discipline is upheld. The principle that the employer determines and enforces the rules of work in response to the exigencies of his business is continued in all recent legislation, even though the limits of discretion are now fixed somewhat differently (see Collins, 1982). In this chapter we look at the legal basis for, and current form of, this fundamental right to discipline.

COMPANY ORGANIZATION

The particular philosophies which surrounded the formation of business organizations in the early days of the industrial revolution encouraged individual businessmen to satisfy the market demand by allowing them to retain whatever surpluses (of revenue over costs) their skill could secure. It was assumed that none of them would be powerful enough to rig or fix the market, and that market forces would therefore impose a discipline upon *them*. For this reason, it was thought that whatever surplus or profit they obtained would be a 'fair' return for skill and effort expended, and not the result of simple exploitation.

The entrepreneur was the archetypal hero of this age of individualism. He was the one who would bear the risks of any trading venture, and be liable to his last penny and his last acre for any debts which might be incurred in it. He was therefore supported by the grant of the status of sovereign in his own

114

domain, or of the head of the working family, endowed (as sovereigns and family-heads had always been) with a near absolute power to control what he owned.

As enterprise came to require larger aggregations of capital than the individual (or the partnership of a small number of such individuals) could lay their hands on, business promoters looked for other forms of organization which would allow aggregation of capital to occur. The device eventually adopted was the joint-stock company. Interestingly enough, this device was originally regarded with suspicion as providing a licence for reckless risk-taking with other people's money and for fraud. However, by 1844, this suspicion had been overcome to the extent that the formation of a company by mere registration and conformity to a set of broad requirements, was facilitated by the first Companies Act. Limited liability was added in 1855. By the time company law was consolidated in 1862, legal incorporation with limited liability for shareholders by mere registration had been established.

Coincidentally, the growth in scale and the tendency for the number of suppliers to reduce (see Allen, 1979) has given more market power to the firm and reduced the relevance of the 'perfect market' assumptions about what happens in practice. In effect, prices (whether of goods or of labour) became much more matters to be decided deliberately rather than 'givens' which were established by the interplay of market forces (supply and demand).

The company or corporate form of organization (now regulated under the Companies Acts, 1948-81) is, strictly, the direct successor of the businessman. In law, it is this corporation which possesses the legal, if also fictional, 'personality', and the rights associated with ownership. It is not the director or manager who is heir to the owner-manager of earlier years, but the company. In so far as this has any concrete form at all, it is as a 'constitution' comprised of the memorandum and articles of association, which set the objectives and regulate the relationship between the shareholders (as beneficial owners) and the board of directors (as the *de facto* and *de jure* agents of the corporation).

The powers of directors and managers

This origin has had a particular consequence for industrial

115

relations. Being designed for the aggregation of capital, the British legal conception of a company is an extremely limited one which defines it by reference to the shareholders whose interests are protected along with those of the creditors (see Hadden, 1977). The directors and managers who derive their authority from the corporate constitution created in conformity with this legislation, are therefore restricted in the interests they can lawfully serve. In effect, the board of directors are enjoined to give first consideration, in their decisions, to what is in the interest of the *company*, and of the shareholders as the beneficial owners of it.

The board of directors forms one of the two primary organs of the enterprise (see Gower, 1959, pp 139-60). The directors have virtually the final word on what should be done, a position which justified the Donovan Commission in criticising them for their omissions. Their decisions are subject only to the exercise by the shareholders in general meeting (the other primary organ) of such power as the articles of association reserve to them. This means, in effect, that the shareholders' interests remain paramount, but that the power of the directors is otherwise unrestricted.

In the normal situation, therefore, the directors must consider the interests of the property owners in preference to those of the contributors of labour or any other group. However, with the divorce of ownership from direct control and the entry of the manager who does not necessarily own any of the assets or the equity, the interests of the controlling group itself may also loom large in their decisions. There are various restrictions in law on the self-interested actions which the directors can take, but those apart, the interests of directors as a group may well obtrude. In fact, there are those who have argued that with the advent of the 'managed firm' (as distinct from the owner-managed business), managerial objectives have tended to replace shareholder objectives.

Consequently, the main objective of the firm (and therefore of the managers) is that of making money or making a profit as a means of protecting the assets. But this is only a part of what other interest groups might want the corporation to do. They might emphasize the production of commodities and services for the benefit of man, the creation of a symbiotic relationship with the physical and human environment, and so on. Thus, Brech (1975) argues, in line with this, that money-making is a derived

116

objective, one which stems from the more general purpose and objective of satisfying consumer demand. This broader conception and objective, it can be argued, holds true for the individual entrepreneur or businessman, as for the 'firm' or 'the corporate manager'.

It is not therefore surprising that business undertakings can be regarded as pursuing one or more of three distinct objectives in some combination (see pp 42-55):

1 profitability (as measured by return on invested capital)
2 growth (as measured by increased consumer-derived revenues)
3 stability (as measured by market position and any changes which occur in it) (see Bridge, 1981, ch. 5, and pp 223-24).

These place different degrees of emphasis on the interests of the owners and of the management as controllers. It thus becomes a more open question as to whether managers are expected to maximize profits, growth, service to the consumer, or something else as they carry out their roles. The variability makes it difficult to regard the firm's *behaviour* as dictated, either by 'the market' or by the objective of maximizing some single function, such as profit. But the directors' exercise of discretion which the present structure seems to allow still depends upon the legally-supported right of management to act, and particularly to contract, on behalf of the company.

Treatment of employees

In carrying out their basic tasks of organizing, directing and controlling the resources of production, including labour, managers thus have considerable delegated power to contract, and therefore to control. As the board of directors exercises its authority to contract on behalf of the corporation with the workers/employees, it *makes and enforces the rules* of employment which will apply in the undertaking, and thus assumes control of the human activities and relationships within it. If the worker fails to obey he may be disciplined by the management, and that disciplinary process, whilst subject to legal constraint, might well involve termination of employment.

In their treatment of employees, however, the directors have the power to act for good or ill, charitably or uncharitably, always provided it can be justified (in the minds of the directors

117

themselves) as being in the company's interest. The famous passage from the judgement of Bowen, LJ, in the case of Hutton v West Cork Railway Company (1893) (Ch D, 23, CA) illustrates this:

> 'A railway company, or the directors of the company, might send down all the porters at a railway station to have tea in the country at the expense of the company. Why should they not? It is for the directors to judge, provided it is a matter which is reasonably incidental to the carrying on of the business of the company ... the law does not say that there are to be no cakes and ale, but there are to be no cakes and ale except such as are required for the benefit of the company'.

The general meeting or the board of directors (dependent upon which is given authority to act by the memorandum and articles of association) *may* therefore take into account the interests of employees. But they may only do so when, in their opinion, it would be in the interests, and to the benefit of, the company. But 'charity has no business to sit at the board of directors *qua charity*' (*ibid*; see also Silberberg, 1968).

Changes made in company law in 1980 do now require that directors 'shall' take account of employees' interests in carrying out their (directorial) functions. But the amended s 46 of the Companies Act, 1980, still continues the directors' duty *to the company* rather than any interest group or section of the members. The problem about this change is that it is unlikely to be enforceable (since the initiation of the action would lie with either the directors, or the 'company' (shareholders in general meeting) or by means of a derivative action (which is generally regarded as difficult to mount in any circumstances) (see Prentice, 1981; Savage, 1980).

In this case, any test applied is likely to be whether the decision taken by the directors was in the best interests of the *company*. The other amendment introduced in the same Act (s 74) allows the company (regardless of its articles) to make provision for the benefit of employees or former employees in the event of cessation or transfer of the undertaking. But for this purpose, it is not necessary to justify the action on the basis that the action is in the best interests of the company.

The position of the worker/employee

This subordinates the interest of the worker/employee to other interests, and although recent labour legislation grants rights to workers and employees, this too maintains their subordinate or dependent position. This is inherent in the current legal definitions:

'Employee means any person who has entered into or works under ... a contract with an employer, whether the contract be by way of manual labour, clerical work or otherwise, be expressed or implied, oral or in writing, and whether it be a contract of service or of apprenticeship' (Redundancy Payments Act 1965, s 25, and continued in the EP(C) Act 1978 and the Employment Acts 1980 and 1982).

This is a narrower definition than that applied to 'worker', which includes employees, some self-employed persons and Crown servants:

'Worker' means an individual regarded in whichever (if any) of the following capacities is applicable to him, that is to say, as a person who works or normally works or seeks to work
(a) under a contract of employment, or
(b) under any other contract (whether express or implied and if express, whether oral or in writing) whereby he undertakes to do or to perform personally any work for another party to the contract who is not a professional client of his, or
(c) in employment under or for the purposes of a government department (otherwise than as a member of the naval, military or air forces of the Crown or of any women's service administered by the Defence Council) in so far as such employment does not fall within either of the two preceding paragraphs, and excepting those in the police service' (TULR Act 1974, s 30).

The special position of the public servant is reserved in this, as is that of the professional person (see below, p 135-37). Otherwise it is the nature of the contractual obligations assumed which is made to distinguish the category.

The language of 'service' is usually maintained, even though the associated concept of Master has been removed. In the

119

development of the legal test as to whether a person should be regarded as self-employed (and not, consequently in a dependency relationship) the concepts of service and control figures prominently. For a person to qualify as an employee (or a servant), he or she must:

(a) agree to provide his own work and skill in the performance of some service for his employer
(b) be subject to the other's control in a sufficient degree to make the other the master
(c) have a contract whose other provisions are consistent with its being treated as a contract of service.

This test is applied in three distinct stages, although they are not completely independent of one another. In spite of its inadequacies as a legal test (Hepple and O'Higgins, 1981, p 136) it does at least suggest that the elements of control and dependency are crucial to the definition of a worker's and, *a fortiori*, an employee's position *vis a vis* the employer. The basic distinction in status is perhaps summed up in Foulkes' comment that:

> 'An employee must obey those orders and rules which are within the scope of the work he agreed to do, and to find out what he agreed to do we look at the terms of his contract and the accepted practices of his trade and of the organization he works for' (Foulkes, 1971, p 103).

In effect, therefore, the businessman/employer has a privileged position *vis a vis* the suppliers of both capital and labour services to the undertaking. In relation to both categories, he has significant rights and a restricted range of obligations.

CURBS ON THE EMPLOYER'S RIGHT

A limited amount of legislation last century did attempt to protect workers from the harsher effects of the employer's exercise of this basic prerogative. This tried to deal with limited aspects of the problem in two distinct ways.

One set of Statutes was aimed at preventing the employer from contracting in certain defined terms, and thus from disciplining employees who did not comply with them. This was done in what came to be known as the Factories Acts. Originally, the aim here was to prevent the employer from requiring some categories of worker to work long hours or to work in unhealthy or unsafe conditions. Applied to children, young persons and females in turn, they were later extended in some respects to all employees. The original concern with 'health and morals' was also extended to cover many different elements of the physical working conditions. They gradually helped to reduce the harsher requirements and to prevent the imposition of employer sanctions for refusing to meet them.

Other legislation aimed to restrict the employer's power to use sanctions in disciplining his employees. The group of Acts which came to be referred to as the Truck Acts 1831-1940, were designed to ensure that workpeople were paid in coin of the realm. But they were extended to restrict the categories of penalty which the employer might visit upon manual workers (and in some cases upon shop assistants) for breaching rules devised by the employer.

The employer of these types of worker was barred from imposing fines, stopping wages or suspending without pay for breach of rule unless an express term permitting this was included in the contract of employment and certain other conditions, listed in the Truck Act 1896, were complied with. (However, in the case of suspension without pay, it was possible to rely upon the plea that it was customary in the trade or industry concerned, provided that it met the tests of certainty, notoriety and reasonableness discussed on p 102 above.) The employer of manual workers was similarly restricted in making deductions from pay for bad workmanship.

However, before 1965 the power of the employer to use the ultimate sanction of dismissal against an employee was not subject to much legislative restriction. Dismissal in breach of the terms of a contract might be held by the courts to be wrongful dismissal. For the most part, this simply meant that dismissal with notice was lawful, since it was for the employer to decide what was acceptable conduct, not the courts. In effect, dismissal *with notice* was something which the employer (or his agents) could determine upon unilaterally for a good or bad reason, safe in the knowledge that, without challenge from the trade union, no one could compel him even to state the reason for taking this step.

Partly because of trade union pressure to change, and partly because of changes in social values, disciplinary practices inside undertakings are now placed under closer supervision via the industrial tribunals and the courts. This process began with the Contracts of Employment Act 1964, which (in this area) did little more than fix the minimum amounts of notice which would be requisite for the termination of the employment contract. In the Redundancy Payments Act of 1965, the presumption that all dismissals would be deemed to be for reasons of redundancy in the absence of other stated reason, obliquely pushed employers into giving a reason for dismissal.

These acts merely initiated a movement, however, which was given considerable forward momentum in the Industrial Relations Act 1971, and continued and augmented in the TULR Act 1974, and the EP Act 1975, which are now consolidated in the EP(C) Act 1978 (see Bercusson, 1979).

The right of the employer to make rules governing the conduct of his business and the conduct of employees is upheld in recent legislation (EP(C) Act 1978; HASAW Act 1975) and is in fact extended by this last Act to establish a duty in relation to safety.

But by this legislation, and the interpretations of it by the courts and by codes of practice, the employer is constrained in his rule-making and -enforcing activities in a number of ways:

(a) the rules must be clear and unambiguous and related to the real requirements of the business and not so vague as to be meaningless
(b) the penalties for breach of rule must be indicated in unambiguous terms
(c) some procedure, however rudimentary, must be established to permit an individual to appeal against a decision of management or to process a grievance
(d) the rules and penalties must be applied in accordance with principles of natural justice and equity
(e) the rules, penalties and procedures must be effectively communicated to employees.

Taken together, therefore, these now amount to a 'code of conduct' which employers might be regarded as under a duty to observe in the exercise of their authority to enforce rules.

The rules of conduct

The legislative requirements were, and continue to be, supported by ACAS codes of practice. These do not have the force of law, but may nevertheless be introduced in proceedings commenced under one of these enactments. They may be regarded as an attempt to codify some of the *conventions* of industrial relations (cf Anthony, 1964; Mellish et al, 1976), rather than its law, even though they are supported by law.

The ACAS *Code of Practice on Disciplinary Practice and Procedures* (No.1 1977) identifies the object of establishing disciplinary rules and procedures as ensuring that standards of fairness can be set and applied, fully, speedily and effectively. The legislative provisions on discipline and unfair dismissal are considered to be met effectively by a systematic procedure for drawing up, publicising and applying the disciplinary rules. Management's responsibility for maintaining discipline is upheld in the Code, although it is suggested that the drawing up of rules and procedures might be done by involving employees.

However they are drawn up, they must be clear and unambiguous: they must indicate to the employee what it is that the employer considers to be necessary conduct and unacceptable conduct. This tends to oust the catch-all rule, in which 'behaviour contrary to good order' or 'conduct unbecoming' will be made offences. It requires a statement of *which* behaviour and *which* conduct. Although it is to be doubted whether rules can be drawn up to cover all circumstances and contingencies, it is recommended that rules should be specific enough to be clear to employees.

A first such restriction on the employer's right to make the rules is therefore that the rules decided by the employer must be both reasonable in themselves and justifiable in terms of the requirements of the business. Rules should, therefore, be particular, rather than universal: in food handling businesses, for example, rules which expressly forbid smoking, or the wearing of beards or of long hair, or finger bandages or plasters, may be justifiable even though they might not apply in all other working situations (see Singh v Lyons Maid Ltd (1975) IRLR, 328; Boychuk v H J Symons Holdings Ltd (1977) IRLR, 395). However, a general rule about length of hair or the wearing of ties might not prove enforceable (see Greenslade v Hoveringham Gravels Ltd (1975) IRLR, 114; Talbot v Hugh M Fulton Ltd (1975) IRLR, 52).

Problems of clarity and ambiguity usually arise less in connection with what the rule actually requires, and more in connection with the penalty which might be applied to a breach. This aspect has often been considered by the industrial tribunals in connection with, for example, clocking. It may be clear and unambiguous to state that it is an offence to clock another person's clock card at the beginning or end of a working period, but what happens if the offence is committed and apprehended? To say that this will 'render the individual liable to instant dismissal' might not be held to make 'instant dismissal' fair (Meridan v Gomersall (1977) IRLR, 425; (1977), ICR, 597).

This is, however, one of those areas in which it is difficult to forecast how the tribunals and courts will interpret conduct. Appeals in recent years have shown some tendency to take a more general view of what is 'fair' than occurred in these earlier cases but this tendency is not a very safe base on which to act (see Elliott Bros. (London) Ltd. v Colverd (1979) IRLR, 92; Taylor v Parsons Peebles NEI Bruce Peebles Ltd, (1981) IRLR, 119). To avoid problems it *may* be necessary to say that 'anyone found clocking another's card *will be* summarily dismissed' (Dalton v Burton's Gold Medal Biscuits Ltd (1974) IRLR, 45). Similar considerations arise in connection with rules about drunkenness or fighting.

Penalties

Once the rules have been established, the employer is advised to indicate what penalties will be regarded as appropriate to their breach. Some penalties involving fines or suspensions without pay may be unavailable to the employer under the Truck Acts, but there is a range of other penalties, from an oral warning or reprimand to summary or instant dismissal, which are. The Code of Practice recommends both that particular attention should be given to the determination of which offences might attract the latter, and that the others might be arranged in a sequence according to severity or frequency of the offence.

Instant (or summary) dismissal (that is, where no notice is given) is usually reserved for those offences which involve conduct antithetical to the basic terms of the contract. The position on this in law has changed over the years. Once it would be held that any refusal by an employee to obey a lawful order given by the employer was sufficient justification for it (Turner v Manson, (1845) 14 M and W, 112). Now it would be held that some acts of disobedience might be excusable, and instant dismissal in these circumstances might be 'wrongful' (Laws v London Chronicle (Indicator Newspapers) Ltd (1959) 2 All E R,

285; (1959) WLR, 698). Similarly, a single act of misconduct would probably not justify instant dismissal, unless it involved theft or some other dishonest act. Deliberate damage to or sabotage of company property, fighting, commission of a clocking offence, working for or assisting competitors, insubordination accompanied by offensive language, and gross incompetence, have also been held to justify summary dismissal although there is nothing automatic about this.

Giving notice, except in cases where it would not be conducive to good business or good order to continue the individual in employment, provides the employer with a defence in wrongful dismissal cases even where an offence is serious or where it occurs in a sequence to which lesser penalties have first been applied.

What is 'serious' in this context is, however, left to the employer to decide, provided always that he acts reasonably (and not idiosyncratically, arbitrarily or discriminatorily) in so deciding, and ensures that it is communicated effectively to employees (see Boychuk's case, above, and Meyer Dunmore International Ltd v Rogers (1978) IRLR, 167). The Code of Practice acknowledges that certain categories of offence may warrant summary dismissal, although it is counselled that this penalty should not be applied to trade union officials until further steps and discussions have been held (Code, p 4). For other offences it is recommended that the penalties should follow the broad principles listed below:

1   Where minor offences are established after the complaint has been investigated and the individual given a chance to explain his position, he should be given an oral warning and told that it constitutes the first formal stage in the procedure.
2   Where there is repetition of the same offence, and in more serious cases of misconduct, the individual may be issued with a formal written warning (again after investigation and hearing), setting out the nature of the offence, and the likely consequences of further misconduct.
3   Further misconduct might warrant a formal final written warning which would contain a statement that any recurrence will lead to suspension or dismissal or some other penalty, as the case might be.
4   Further or more serious offences might then result in disciplinary transfer, disciplinary suspension without pay, (where provided for in the employment contract as outlined

above, pp 119-20) or dismissal, dependent on their nature.

The intention is clearly that dismissal (the severest sanction available to the employer) should be applied as a penalty only as a last resort when all else has failed. It becomes necessary to contain enforcement within explicit procedures because it is now subject to closer judicial supervision. These generally accord with what the trade unions have sought as the means of both facilitating more just and equitable settlements of issues, and to ensuring that it is carried out in accordance with certain principles derived from, but not exactly similar to, those of the common law.

Procedures

At the same time, the legislation which has placed curbs on disciplinary processes, has also attempted to provide for the handling of employee complaints or grievances in very similar terms. The two processes might be thought of as reciprocals of one another. If the employer has a complaint about performance, there should be a clear procedure for handling it. If the employee has a complaint about employer performance, there should be a well-understood procedure for that too. The two procedures are considered below.

Disciplinary procedure

The legislators' intention that there should be a procedure for discipline was first expressed in the Contracts of Employment Act 1963 in connection with the requirement that a statement of contract particulars shall be given by employers to new employees within 13 weeks of engagement. This has to be accompanied by 'a note' which both specifies the rules applicable to the employment (or indicates where they might be found) and 'specifies by description or otherwise:

(a) a person to whom the employee can apply if he is dissatisfied with any disciplinary action relating to him; and
(b) a person to whom the employee can apply for the purpose of seeking redress of any grievance relating to his employment and the manner in which any such application should be made'

and if there are further steps the nature of them (EP(C) Acts 1(4)).

This requirement is amplified in the Code of Practice which lists the 'essential features' of any such procedure. It is recommended that the procedures should:

(a) be in writing
(b) specify the employees to whom they apply
(c) offer a speedy sequence of steps
(d) identify the disciplinary actions which may be taken
(e) specify which levels of management and supervision have what powers in relation to discipline
(f) provide for individuals to be informed of complaints against them and to have an opportunity to state their case before a decision is taken
(g) allow for the individual to be accompanied by a trade union representative or fellow worker as he might choose
(h) reserve dismissal as a penalty for gross misconduct and then only after the complaint has been referred to higher management
(i) provide for proper investigation of any complaint
(j) provide for explanation of the reasons for a penalty
(k) provide for an appeal and a procedure to be followed should the individual wish to avail himself of the right.

The authority of managers and supervisors to handle disciplinary matters must also be established and publicized. The immediate supervisor is usually able to handle the first stages, although he is now more likely to be required to record his action. Some indication must also be given of who is authorized to investigate and/or determine the penalty, and whom the individual can or should approach to obtain a written statement of the nature of the alleged offence. If the employee (provided he or she is qualified by having six months' service) asks for a reason for his dismissal, he is entitled by law to receive one from the employer (EP(C) Act, s 53) and care must therefore be taken to ensure that a factual and defensible reason is given.

Records of any established breaches of disciplinary rules and the action taken in respect of them are now more necessary than they were. Such records should be regarded as confidential, and provision might be made in agreements with the trade unions, or as an element of policy, that minor offences should be expunged from the record after a period of time.

This deals essentially with the mechanical aspects of the

127

problem. It sets up the rules and machinery of discipline. But clearly, there is no sense in having an elegant system if the employees themselves are not aware of it. The Code therefore recommends that the information on all of these be made available in the form of a written statement or handbook and that opportunity should be taken to explain the system to employees orally, probably in connection with induction. In all of this it is recommended that particular attention should be given to rules which, if broken, may lead to dismissal. It is possible for an employee to claim successfully before a tribunal that a disciplinary action was unfair because the employer had not made the information available to him.

Grievance procedure

A disciplinary code provides the employer with a basis for dealing with any complaints against the employees. But there remains a need for a code to govern the handling of any complaints that the employee may have against the employer. This may be referred to as a grievance procedure or a complaints procedure.

The *Code of Industrial Relations Practice*, issued under the Industrial Relations Act 1971, recommends a comparable procedure for handling grievances which are not necessarily disciplinary. This Code suggests that all employees 'have a right to seek redress for grievances relating to their employment' (para. 120) and that management 'should establish, with employee representatives or trade unions concerns, arrangements under which individual employees can raise grievances and have them settled fairly and promptly' (para. 121). This right is only obliquely established in legislation, since it may be upheld only in a supporting plea related to another substantive right, but in unionized plants it is upheld by the authority of the collective industrial action which the union may mobilize in its support.

The Code recommends that the grievance procedure should:

(a) state the level at which an issue should first be raised
(b) lay down the time limits for each stage of the procedure and make provision for their extension by agreement
(c) preclude any form of industrial action until all stages have been exhausted and a failure to agree recorded.

The number of stages which should be built into the procedure

128

will vary with the type of establishment and the type of bargaining arrangements applicable. The procedure may state:

(a) that the matter should first be raised by the employee representatives with the level of management directly responsible, or by the management with the level of employee representation most directly concerned according to union procedure
(b) the next stage of appeal in the procedure
(c) any further stages that may be gone through, even to the extent of appeal to an industry-wide arrangement
(d) whether the appeals machinery should terminate within the establishment, at industry level or with a reference to conciliation and arbitration, and whether the parties agree to be bound, in advance, by any award made there.

As in the disciplinary matters, however, the real test of a procedure is whether it allows the grievance to be dealt with speedily and equitably, so that whatever the final decision may be the individual concerned at least feels that he has had a fair hearing and a fair deal. In the longer term, it may well be that these ends will only be secured if the procedure is implemented and administered by the two parties jointly. For the moment, however, as with the disciplinary procedure, it is implemented and administered by the employer, but under the constraint of law and (usually) trade union surveillance.

Equity and natural justice

The changes which have been compelled by legislation and recommended through the codes of practice have also imported a greater concern with principles of equity and natural justice, into the employer's enforcement actions. It is not simply a matter of the employer stating the rules and the penalties he considers appropriate, nor of establishing a procedure through which the application of these principles might be facilitated and encouraged: he is also required to act reasonably in deciding to apply penalties, to take into account the facts of the case as he is able to ascertain them, and in so doing to adopt a commonsense approach to fairness or equity.

The supervision by industrial tribunals has thus imposed on the employer the onus of establishing that he has reasonable grounds for believing that the employee had committed misconduct, by carrying out an investigation of the fact (although not to anything like the extent which might be required in a court of law), and determining whether dismissal is a fair sanction to impose in the circumstances as revealed.

The main statement on the standards imposed by the tribunals was provided by the EAT in the case of British Home Stores Ltd v Burchell (1978) IRLR, 379; (1980) ICR, 303.

'What the tribunal has to decide every time is, broadly expressed, whether the employer who discharged the employee on the ground of the misconduct in question (usually, though not necessarily, dishonest conduct) entertained a reasonable suspicion amounting to a belief in the guilt of the employee of that misconduct at that time. That is really stating shortly and compendiously what is in fact more than one element. First of all, there must be established by the employer the fact of that belief; that the employer did believe it. Secondly, that the employer had in his mind reasonable grounds upon which to sustain that belief. And thirdly, we think, that the employer, at the stage at which he formed that belief on those grounds, at any rate at the final stage at which he formed that belief on those grounds, had carried out as much investigation into the matter as was reasonable in all the circumstances of the case. It is the employer who manages to discharge the onus of demonstrating those three matters, we think, who must not be examined further.

It is not relevant, as we think, that the tribunal would itself have shared that view in those circumstances. It is not relevant, as we think, for the tribunal to examine the quality of the material which the employer had before him, for instance to see whether it was the sort of material, objectively considered, which would lead to a certain conclusion on the balance of probabilities, or whether it was the sort of material which would lead to the same conclusion only upon the basis of being 'sure' as it is now said more normally in a criminal context, or, to use the more old-fashioned term, such as to put the matter 'beyond reasonable doubt'. The test, and the test all the way through, is reasonableness, and certainly, as it seems to us, a conclusion on the balance of probabilities will in any surmisable circumstances be a reasonable conclusion.'

This test was articulated at the time when the onus of proof was placed entirely on the employer (by s 57 (3) of the EP(C) Act). The amendment introduced by the Employment Act 1980, s 6, changed this and it is not now for the *employer* but the tribunal to establish the second and third elements in the test. Nevertheless, following the guidance laid down will make it easier for the employer to justify any dismissal whose merits and fairness are challenged before a tribunal, because the tribunal remains under a duty to judge on the basis of equity.

The recommendations of the Code of Practice with respect to procedures, designed as they are to give the employee the right to be told the nature of any charge against him, the right to speak in his own behalf, and the right to appeal to higher authority, also admit the possibility that an employer might lose a case before a tribunal on purely procedural grounds. Where he fails to acknowledge these recommendations, and to act upon that acknowledgement, he leaves himself open to an adverse finding on these grounds alone, even though he may have met all the other judicial requirements in respect of fair dismissal.

Summary: the nature of the curb

The managerial prerogative to manage is largely exercised in respect of the management of labour through the right or power to discipline (and ultimately dismiss) employeees for any breach of the rules which management is empowered, legally and conventionally, to make. This power is associated closely with the underlying principles of ownership as they are applied within the context of corporate organization as this has grown up in Britain under the supervision of company law.

This right stems from the more general right of an owner to do what he will with his own, subject only to a general supervision by the law. The idea of ownership in goods is readily comprehended. The idea of ownership in the labour of another is less so, partly because it is becoming anachronistic. It continues vestiges of ancient systems of slave ownership and feudal bondage, and of the conception of the workplace and its inhabitants as essentially an extension of the family.

The recent curbs upon the power to discipline workers has not taken away the right to make and enforce rules itself, and management is still left with considerable power over workers, who necessarily occupy a dependent and subordinate position in the structure of work relations (see Clayton, 1967). Recent legislation requires that management shall use its power reasonably, which tends to mean humanely and rationally as these are defined within our culture, or pay the price for breaking the law (see McCarthy, 1983, pp 97-98).

The changes respond to changes in social values, some of which have been brought about by the general propagandizing by the unions of their own case for a better deal in industry. They look towards more humane treatment of the worker to improve the quality of working life, itself a long-standing trade union objective and aspiration. The legislative prescriptions and proscriptions which develop from them are, however, based on the use of a third party (the industrial tribunals and the courts) to supervise the managerial exercise of its power and do not necessarily involve the unions themselves. But they also acknowledge (particularly in the codes of practice) the desirability of an extension of joint control (whether this is regarded as it is by Chamberlain and Kuhn (1967) as joint 'government' or 'management'; see below, pp 324-25) on the value-laden assumption that rules which are agreed are more likely to be accorded validity than any which are imposed.

The effect is to curb the employer's use of naked force or coercion in organizing, directing and controlling human resources. He is required to decide the rules and the penalties on a rational basis (that is, related to the requirements of the business, not to personal whim or foible). He is required to enforce them through machinery (procedures) which will themselves admit the application of the principles of equity and natural justice. He is not required, however, to establish criteria and procedures which replicate those applied in a court of law. Essentially, he is required to act openly, equitably and reasonably in his dealings with employees.

The exercise of the managerial prerogative is, in consequence, placed more directly under the supervision of the law. In one sense, the requirements as to conduct merely generalize 'best practice' from industry itself. But the generalizing process extends what some managements may have been prepared to give and unions eager to take in the past, to areas of employment not amenable to other forms of pressure to change. The withdrawal of some (shorter-service) employees in some employment undertakings (the smaller family businesses) from the

132

supervision of the law may however reduce the impact of this kind of legislation upon managerial morality and upon employee welfare.

These changes in law have not, however, been minimal, merely giving legal backing to what had been achieved in the larger employers' undertakings by virtue of trade union activity (see Clifton and Tatten-Brown, 1979; Daniel and Stilgoe, 1978). They do represent a major change of direction in State policy and a step on the road to a new mercantilism in which centralized control by the State is given high validity. In the development of our theme in this book, it does, therefore, represent a significant illustration of State interference with industrial relations.

Readings

Hepple and O'Higgins: (1979), pp 215-303.
Rideout: (1979), pp 84-156.
Thomason: (1983), pp 97-126; 239-61.
Hepple, in Bain: (1983), pp 393-418.
Anthony: (1977a), pp 105-36.

6

Control of
associational development

Associational freedoms

The device of contract was designed to secure co-operation in
work on the assumption that the co-operators would always be
identifiable persons. This obviously fitted the philosophy of
individualism and the circumstances of the early part of the
industrial revolution. The institutions of the State, including that
of law, were developed in support of this conception and
approach so that people were free to contract, but not to combine
into associations.

Not everyone accepted the values and principles of the new era
or the effects which it produced. Workers in the new factories
found themselves unacceptably subject to the vagaries of the
market as well as to the control of a 'master'. Now that no one
was any longer willing or able to accept diffuse obligations to
protect the welfare of the workers, attempts to secure these by
combination seemed a logical step. There were precedents for
association by workers, albeit in combination with 'masters'. As
the workers now attempted to reduce the exigencies by
combination against their masters, the State had to take a view
about the validity of this development.

In fact, workers collectivized in two distinct ways. Certain
groups (usually identified as 'professional' workers) did so
through the device of the 'professional association', itself a fairly
direct descendant of the former gild organization. This secured
protection in law and support in social institutions because it was
concerned with the control of *work activity* in the public interest,
much as the older gild and the more modern business corporation
did. Others (manual workers particularly), attempted to control
their *status* and *remuneration* through the device of the trade
union. This attempt initially fell foul of the law because such
associations were treated as unlawful combinations or conspir-

acies by virtue of their pursuit of an unlawful end (the regulation of *wages* 'in restraint of trade').

The industro-legal history of the nineteenth century is largely one of changing attitudes towards this new principle of collectivism. Change was not achieved without what the trade unionist refers to as a 'struggle' (see Williams, 1954; Birch, 1973) but it *was* achieved *and* in consequence, trade unions were subjected to some control by the law (see Fraser, 1974). Workers were accorded a bare right to organize in 1824 (Repeal of the Combination Acts, 1799-1800) and given a set of immunities in criminal and civil law in a number of acts passed between 1869 and 1876. These were consolidated and extended by the Trade Disputes Act of 1906 (which the Webbs described as 'the Charter of the Trade Unions'), after court interpretations had nullified some of the immunities thought to have been established in these earlier Statutes (see Griffith, 1981).

Some of these immunities remain today but some modifications have recently been made to these (Employment Acts 1980 and 1982). Trade unions are still protected in law, but are being subjected to a more detailed control of their internal affairs and external actions. In this chapter, we review (with a minimum of attention to the historical evolution) the manner in which the State, mainly through the operation of law, currently seeks to influence the status and actions of workers' associations in Britain.

THE PROFESSIONAL ASSOCIATION

The professional association is an association of workers which attempts to organize, qualify, and either maintain or improve the standards of performance of those workers, in order to maintain or improve their (relatively high) status (including pay-status) in society. The emphasis on performance tends to differentiate this type of association and its ideology from the trade union.

Traditionally, professional workers have performed service roles within society, usually (but not always) in relation to individual clients. Their performance has always been difficult to measure and therefore the possibility of exploiting their clients high. They are also difficult to control from an external source, whether that source be a corporate authority or the forces of the market (see Larson, 1977, p 40).

From the State's point of view it has always been undesirable that these workers should be left to exploit the market as best they might. But instead of placing them under the direction of a State agency, or a separate business organization, the State encouraged them (by the grant of high status to the individuals concerned) to form their *own* corporations to carry out this function of (autonomous) control.

By the end of the fifteenth century, such autonomous corporations had become universal outside agriculture (Unwin, 1908, p 172) and:

> 'professions were regulated much as other vocations; professional corporations were treated as other corporations ... at one and the same time, it was attempted to ensure that persons should be competent in their own line, should deal honestly with their clients, and fairly with those of inferior status, and should maintain discipline and exercise supervisory duties' (Carr-Saunders and Wilson, 1933, p 305).

At that time, there was not much organizational difference between these different non-agricultural occupations. The professional corporation regulated the conduct of the workers in scope and implanted the still-potent idea that a profession was to be *defined* as necessarily concerned with self-regulation 'in the public good' (Caplow, 1964, pp 113-23).

The workers were regarded as the corporators in a corporation essentially the same as any other. Their organization was conceived of as:

> 'an entity apart from its members, capable of rights and duties of its own, and endowed with the potential of perpetual succession' (Hahlo and Trebilcock, 1977, p 42).

As such, this body acquired 'powers, rights, capacities and incapacities' some of which remain incidental to every corporation:

1   'to have perpetual succession ... the very end of its incorporation...
2   'to sue or be sued, implead or be impleaded, grant or receive, by its corporate name, and do all other acts as natural persons may.
3   'to purchase lands and hold them...

4 'to have a common seal...
5 'to make bye-laws or private statutes for the better government of the corporation; which are binding upon themselves,
unless contrary to the laws of the land and then they are
void...' (Blackstone's Commentaries, 1813).

This amounts to a substantial grant of autonomy, but it also
provides the association and its members with a protection of
individuals who act in the name of, and with the authority of, the
association. The member, acting within his authority on behalf
of the association does not incur personal liability for his actions;
in effect he becomes an *agent* of the association. When the
business corporation was developed to fit what were seen as the
business needs of the nineteenth century, it also took this form,
but the corporators then were the contributors of finance, not of
service (or work).

In *both* of these cases the corporation acquired the same kind
of fictional legal personality and assumed the same kinds of
rights and obligations. The trade union, by contrast, never tried
to move down this road, and, for most of the past century, the
State has not tried to compel it to do so, in spite of pressure from
employers.

Society, through the operation of the law, has, in fact,
encouraged the maintenance of this distinction. During the early
years of the industrial revolution, the desirability of the
objectives of the professional corporation were never doubted
(Carr-Saunders and Wilson, 1933, p 327), and the law was
directed at their general protection, as long as they kept the
service ideal paramount. This occurred during a period where the
trade union was either outlawed in legislation (Combination
Acts 1799-1800, repealed in 1824) or was prosecuted under the
Common Law as a necessarily unlawful body by reason of its
objectives being treated as in restraint of trade and its method of
combination being indictable as conspiracy.

Before 1971 (when the Industrial Relations Act blurred the
long-standing distinction), cross-stipulations in the Trade Union
Act 1871, (now under s 2 (2) of TULR Act 1974) and the
Companies Acts (1948-82) prevented any association whose
objects would make it a trade union from registering under the
Companies Acts, and any registered company from securing the
kinds of immunities granted to trade unions as defined in the
Trade Union Acts 1871-76. Any association of workers therefore had to make a choice as to the kind of body it was going to be.

137

Types of professional association

Associations of professional people engaged in some service activity have developed from the original occupations of medicine, the ministry and the law. In the first half of last century, some of the new heroes (engineers, architects, builders) became incorporated, and in the second half, a large number of the new specialists (chemists, accountants, teachers, specialist engineers) organized in the same way. Initially, the mark of their legitimacy and dignity was the Royal Charter, but after 1862 many registered under the amended Companies legislation and obtained similar benefits without the cachet of being chartered (Millerson, 1964, p 88).

The professional association form lends itself to the organization of many quite distinct types of activity. Some concern themselves with little more than the study of some subject, others with study and qualification, others with control of professional (occupational) practice, and yet others (usually more recently) with the protection of relations between members and their employers. Millerson has distinguished four main types with a number of sub-types:

1   *The prestige association*
    (a) The exclusive prestige association
    (b) The non-exclusive prestige association. (Examples are the Royal Society, the Royal Academy and the British Academy)
2   *The Study Association.* (Examples are the Chemical Society, the Royal Statistical Society, the Royal Geographical Society)
3   *The Qualifying Association.* (Examples are the Chartered Institute of Transport, the various accountancy bodies and the Institute of Personnel Management)
4   *The Occupational Association.*
    (a) The co-ordinating association, which seeks to organize and co-ordinate professional activities in a limited field in order to assure improvements in practice. (Many local government officers whose negotiations are conducted by NALGO have developed such associations)
    (b) The protective association, which usually seeks to cover a wider field of practice and to maintain a more deliberate pressure on paymasters to improve working

conditions and remuneration of members. (The British Medical Association, which acquired trade union special register status in 1971 and many other bodies in engineering and health occupations are of this type).

Professional associations thus reveal a variety of objectives and forms of organization. As Carr-Saunders and Wilson comment:

> '...the variety of objects with which professional men associate together favours the multiplication of associations within each profession, so that the number of associations involved and the bewildering variety of types to which they conform have become a characteristic feature of the professional world' (Carr-Saunders and Wilson, 1933, p 320).

This is contrasted with the tendency to greater homogeneity of the trade union's purposes (*ibid*, p 319). Trade unions are regarded as single-mindedly concerned with *protection*, whilst this is seen as only one relatively insignificant purpose in a much wider range associated with professional associations.

Nevertheless, at the lower end of the above list, there are protective *professional* associations which might be said to be more concerned with the protection of remuneration status, and less concerned with public prestige or esteem as a main basis of position in society. But they tend also to avoid industrial action (see Jones, 1974-75) as is illustrated by the extract from the Rules of the United Kingdom Association of Professional Engineers.

Extract from the rules of the United Kingdom Association of Professional Engineers

Rule 2.1: The Objects of the Association shall be:

(a) to protect and promote the interests of members and improve the conditions of their employment, and to regulate the relations between them and their employers or between themselves and other employees.
(b) to provide benefits for members and employees and such other persons as the Association may from time to time determine.
(c) to provide for the promotion, teaching or extension of, or the interchange of views on, professional knowledge, science or practice within the engineering profession.
(d) to promote and maintain the unity, the public usefulness, honour and ethics of the engineering profession. (Rules, 1977, p 1).

139

THE TRADE UNION

The term 'trade union' is used to refer to a collectivity or association of workers formed around the objectives of improving the remuneration and conditions of work of members and their lot in society generally (see S and B Webb, 1920a, p 1). It is this concern with the protection and improvement of the worker's status which has both set them apart from other associations, and led to their being branded as unlawful by virtue of their purposes.

Trade unions may have a number of objectives, but it is this principal purpose of status protection (and improvement) which gives them their distinct identity and provides the focus of their distinctive ideology (see Blackburn, 1967, pp 9-48).

Classification of unions therefore tends to ignore purposes (because they are sufficiently alike to make this criterion unhelpful). Unions are usually classified by their 'organizing principles' and possibly the extent to which they see it as desirable to pursue their protective role into the political arena. Consequently, classifications of trade unions (see below, pp 270-74) reflect their openness or closedness to workers by grade/status, industry or labour market (see Flanders, 1968; Turner, 1962; Hughes, 1966; Armstrong, 1969). Only in the context of discussion of white collar unionism does the question of purposes assume relevance (Blackburn, 1967; Prandy, 1965), and even then they are usually found to overlap with those of the protective professional association (see Dickens, 1972; 1975; Gill *et al*, 1978).

Trade unions are also alike in their wish to remain 'voluntary unincorporated associations' rather than to become corporate bodies. Although trade unions may display themselves as craft or single occupational unions, industrial unions or general workers' unions, they have not sought to distinguish themselves by incorporation. This has remained a constant desire, in spite of attempts by employers to persuade both governments and the unions themselves to change their status and by legislators and judges to impose a change of status upon them. The desire to avoid the additional requirements of companies legislation (the main vehicle of incorporation in the world of business) or of any comparable, if *ad hoc*, legislation relating specifically to trade unions, has, however, held British trade unions to the course of avoiding even 'registration' unless it is 'voluntary' (see Weekes *et al*, 1975, pp 252-60). There are only a few professional associations which retain this form, so that this too tends to distinguish them from the unions.

Legal status

The attempt by the State to accommodate the desire to remain unincorporated whilst still keeping the trade union under some kind of supervision has produced the chequered history of the trade union's legal status in Britain.

The clear preference of trade unionists in the early years was for the union to be left as an unincorporated body. Such a body cannot have existence in law as an entity apart from the members. The members are held, in law, to be in the position where they have all contracted with one another as individuals to pursue certain objects, not with a separate entity called 'the trade union' (in our context). It can therefore neither sue nor be sued in its own name, nor be made the subject of proceedings in a court. It is possible to proceed only against the members, or against some of them as representative of the total. This form of organization exposes the individual member to personal liability for any actions which they may take on behalf of the association, and this can severely hamper the pursuit of associational objectives.

For this same reason, *it* cannot hold property because there is no *it* to hold it, (and property is therefore usually held through 'trustees'). Like any other association, it is bound (in the actions it can take) by its constitution and rules. But it could become difficult or impossible to change these (except on the unanimous agreement of all the members contracting amongst themselves), unless the rules make provision for some other way of dealing with the problem of changing rules.

The major advantage of remaining unincorporated is that the association thereby avoids the kind of supervision and control by the State, inherent in incorporation. This has not been, and is not now, complete avoidance, because there are common law rules 'governing the right of individuals to associate for the promotion of a common purpose' (Carr-Saunders and Wilson, 1933, p 327) which can be applied to them. Court interpretations of the intentions of the legislature (as in the Taff Vale case discussed on the following page) and the legislators' own attempts to impose incorporation (as in the Industrial Relations Act 1971 and the

141

Employment Acts 1980 and 1982) have all threatened the freedom from direct control.

The legislation of the 1870s effectively made a trade union a 'third thing' between the corporation and the unincorporated association. The trade union was not to have (as it did not want) the benefits of incorporation (above, p 136) but it did want, for example, to protect its funds from fraudulent officers. It did not want its internal relations to be subject to supervision by the courts, but it did want to hold property on behalf of the membership.

The trade union was allowed a kind of incorporation in relation to its property and those of its activities as were unconcerned with its main purpose of regulating relations between employers and workmen. Thus, common property was to be vested in trustees, and active and passive suability was made available in the names of the trustees (rather than of the union itself as an entity). Authority to act in relation to any member who decamped with the union's funds was also provided, from 1869 onwards, to protect them against a practice which had proved devastating for some of the early unions.

The unions were allowed (under the Trade Union Act 1871) to register with the Registrar of Friendly Societies (until 1971), if they wished. This secured them certain exemptions from taxation in connection with friendly society benefits, and certain benefits in connection with the protection and transference of property. Registration imported some obligations in respect of keeping the Registrar informed of the union's name, registered office and rules, and of providing some rules to cover aspects of the internal relationships (although the content of them was a matter for the union). The Donovan Commission regarded these as neither onerous nor vexatious, and as not going 'beyond what any well-run trade union would do in any event' (Donovan Report, 1968, pp 211-16). These are now administered by the Certification Officer.

The trade union was not incorporated in respect of its main purposes and activities in this early legislation, although the judges sought to effect this by interpretation (as in the Taff Vale Railway Company v Amalgamated Society of Railway Servants case in the 1901-2). The important issue in this case was whether *the trade union* as an entity could be sued in its own name for civil damages arising out of industrial action, and its funds made answerable for them. On appeal to the House of Lords, the majority view taken was that although the 1871 Act did not make a trade union a corporation or any other legal entity distinct from the generality of the members, *registration* under the Act imported a correlative liability to be sued in its own name for any tort committed in its name. Lord Brampton declared in his judgement that:

> 'I think a legal entity was created, under the Trade Union Act of 1871, by the registration of the Society in its present name in the manner prescribed, and that the legal entity so created though not perhaps in the strict sense a corporation, is nevertheless a newly-created corporate body created by Statute...'.

The Trade Disputes Act 1906, was enacted to overturn the effect of this decision, by immunizing the union from tort actions of this kind. The Act did not, however, change the standing of the trade union in law, and it remained the kind of 'third thing' which it had been previously.

In the Osborne judgement the question of whether a trade union as an entity could be said to have a contract with individual members was dealt with (Osborne v Amalgamated Society of Railway Servants, (1910) AC, 87, (HL)). It was held that such a contract did exist because the principal Act had stipulated what the lawful purposes of a trade union would be and any member was entitled to join with the expectation that these would form the purposes of the union he joined. Osborne therefore had the right to bring an action to prevent the union from applying funds for political purposes (which were *not* alluded to in the principal Act).

The Trade Union Act 1913, was passed to overturn this judgement. It provided that the trade union might have some 'principal objects' (essentially those related to regulating relations between employers and employees and providing benefits to members) which would be referred to as 'statutory objects', but also other objects of a subsidiary (and non-statutory) kind which would still be lawful. The trade union then became an association of either workmen or employers pursuing named objectives as statutory objects as well as a number of non-statutory ones. All of these had to be stated if the union applied to register or sought (under the 1913 Act) a certificate that it 'was a trade union' (even if not registered).

Both of these conceptions were aired in the Bonsor case

(1956), where Bonsor attempted to sue the union for damages for wrongful exclusion from employment. Lords Morton and Porter asserted that a union was capable of entering into contracts and of being sued as a legal entity, and that such a contract could be regarded as existing between Bonsor and the Musicians' union. Lords McDermott and Somervell took the view that the union was suable in its own name, not as a separate juridicial person, but simply because parliament (by the Trade Union Act of 1871) had in effect sanctioned such a course. In the event damages were awarded on the ground that the union had ratified the action of the Branch Secretary in expelling Bonsor for non-payment of subscriptions (Bonsor v Musicians Union (1956), AC, 104; (1955) 3 All E R, 518 (HL)).

By 1965, therefore, the standing of the union in law was subject to doubt. The Donovan Commission argued that the doubt ought to be removed by requiring all unions to register as a condition of being regarded as trade unions in law, and by giving them incorporation (with safeguards for temporary combinations). The Industrial Relations Act 1971, took up these recommendations but infuriated the trade union movement (see Weekes *et al*, 1975, pp 252-61) by requiring the unions to register *in order* to secure their traditional immunities. Registration brought incorporation, but whether organizations of workers registered or not they were to be treated as bodies corporate, with their funds at risk in civil actions for damages in connection with a larger range of specific torts ('unfair industrial practices') introduced by the Act. The repeal of the Act in 1974 returned the unions to their previous position with some small variations in respect of their property-owning status. But the removal of the blanket immunity from tort actions (given in 1906) by the Employment Act 1982, once again exposed the union's funds to liability of civil damages.

Current status

At the present time, trade unions are declared not to be, or to be treated as, bodies corporate (TULR Act, s 2(1)) although they are to be capable of making contracts, suing and being sued, and having proceedings brought against them in their own name, in respect of property and personal injury (which are long-established) and now under the Employment Act 1982, s 15(1) in respect of a new class of torts (unless the action complained of was unauthorized by a committee or person with authority to do so under the union's rules) (see below, pp 148-49).

The effect of the two Employment Acts has been to expose the unions to a wider range of possible actions for damages initiated by aggrieved parties because of the removal of the blanket immunity in tort and the redefinition of the limits of a trade dispute. The nature of the trade union in law is not particularly affected by this legislation, but actions for injunction or damages may be commenced both against the union in its own name and against officers and members in more circumstances than previously (see also, pp 196-201 below).

An employers' association, although defined as a trade union in 1871, may now be either incorporated or unincorporated. When it is incorporated it enjoys the advantages and suffers the obligations of any other corporation. When it is unincorporated it continues to enjoy the same status and the same immunities as the trade union (TULR Act, s 3). The new restrictions of the Employment Act 1982, upon trade unions' immunity in tort do not apply to the employers' association, since they are specifically aimed at the trade union.

ESTABLISHING LEGALITY

Professional associations and trade unions have had a very different legal history, largely because of the different views taken of their objects by society and the law.

The professional association seeking a charter or registration as a company had to establish that it was concerned in some way with the public good. There is usually no problem of principle to be overcome in this because the members tend to see themselves in this fashion, ie pursuing a service ideal. Professional associations have been granted corporate status and the privilege of monopoly control over their activities in the market, simply because their objectives accord with dominant social values. They faced no necessity for struggle because none cast doubt on their purposes.

However, the trade union did not have this advantage for a number of specific reasons, connected with the political and juridicial philosophies of the period.

Until the middle of the eighteenth century, the regulation of terms and conditions of employment of those outside the professions was in the hands of the magistrates (who in their Easter Vestry meetings fixed wages, hours, etc, for the next year, see Southgate, 1934, p 102).

During the period when this device was falling into disuse, but before the Statutes were repealed towards the end of the Napoleonic Wars, workers sought relief by petitioning Parliament to have the magistrates do their job properly (see S and B Webb, 1920a, pp 62-63). After the repeal the idea of worker organization for self-help was born. When the workers attempted to pressure employers for wage increases before the magistrates' role had been abolished, they placed themselves in the position of interfering with this lawful process. Later, such pressure was regarded as both undesirable and unlawful because it threatened to 'restrain trade' by pushing up prices.

Over this transitional period, trade unions (or any organized group of workers) were regarded as necessarily and inherently unlawful, therefore, either because they involved conspiracy to usurp the authority of the magistrates or to act in restraint of trade. The early members were prosecuted for both in their turn.

In time, attitudes to trade unions and to workers' right to influence on wage decisions, were to change, and changes in the legal position followed. But given their perceived nature in the conditions of those days, the changes were made chiefly by granting trade unions immunities from criminal prosecution and from civil actions for injunction or compensation which must otherwise apply to them under the doctrines of the common law.

These changes were made principally in the Repeal of the Combination Acts 1924 (and the Amending Act of the following year), the Trade Union Acts of 1871 and 1876, the Conspiracy and Protection of Property Act 1875, and the Trade Disputes Act 1906. These provided the basis for trade union immunities which, with only a few modifications, remained operative until 1971 (see Hanson, 1973). The Industrial Relations Act 1971, changed the position but was itself repealed in the Trade Union and Labour Relations Act 1974. This, together with the Act of the same name of 1976 and the Employment Protection Act 1975 (Consolidated, 1978), virtually restored what had been taken away in 1971 and added to the trade union's rights. Subsequently, the Employment Acts 1980 and 1982, have introduced further modifications mainly in the direction of reducing immunities.

The politics and drama involved in these changes need not

146

concern us here. What is relevant is the panoply of rights and obligations which currently apply. These are outlined in the following section, but a general indication of the origin is also appended in each case.

Present immunities

The general position at the present time is that the law:

(a) confers legality to the trade union in spite of its purposes (TULR Act, s 2 (5))
(b) gives immunities in criminal and civil law (TULR Act, s 13) to industrial actions in connection with
  (i) a trade dispute (as defined by s 29 of TULR Act, amended by s 15 of the Employment Act, 1982), and
  (ii) with picketing (TULR Act, s 15 as amended by s 16(10 of the Employment Act, 1980)), and also
(c) restricts the immunities in connection with secondary actions (EA 1980, s 17) and acts to compel trade union membership (EA 1980, s 18).

In addition to the limits now placed on the definition of a 'trade dispute', the Employment Act 1982, s 15(1), in repealing s 14 of the TULR Act, removes the broad immunity of the trade union from actions in tort, originally established in s 4 of the Trade Disputes Act 1906.

Legality of the objects

Chronologically, the first problem tackled was that of declaring a trade union lawful *in spite of* its purposes being regarded in law as in restraint of trade and combination to pursue those purposes being treated as unlawful conspiracy.

The immunities granted in 1871, are currently continued in s 2 (5) of TULR Act, which states that:

> 'The purposes of any trade union ... shall not by reason only that they are in restraint of trade, be unlawful so as ...
> (a) to make any member of the trade union liable to criminal proceedings for conspiracy or otherwise; or
> (b) to make any agreement or trust void or voidable; nor shall any rule of a trade union ... be unlawful or unforceable by reason only that it is in restraint of trade'.

Neither the trade union nor its members can now be prosecuted on these original grounds. But it (and they) can make lawful rules and agreements to bind members provided the processes of making them conform with the existing rules and these rules, in turn, comply with the requirements of legislation on ballotting and elections.

However, once the trade union had been made a lawful body, even though unincorporated, there was a distinct possibility that the Courts would seek to supervise its internal affairs. This was not originally intended and so it was declared in s 4 of the 1871 Act that 'nothing in this Act shall enable any court to *enforce directly*' the agreements which trade unionists might enter into amongst themselves or with employers. They were thus to remain enforceable only by 'voluntary means' and to be binding in honour not law.

This attempt to preserve the union's internal autonomy was generally effective, although the courts did find a way of *indirectly* enforcing some of them (see Donovan Commission Report, 1968, paras 809-15). But the effect of s 4 (until it was repealed in 1971) was to permit trade unions to operate effectively and without legal penalty in spite of their common law status (see Wedderburn, 1971, pp 314-5). Under the latest piece of legislation, however, the *content* of some of the union rules has to conform to a general requirement intended to facilitate 'democratic' control by the members.

Legality of the trade dispute

The trade union has traditionally relied upon the 'concerted withdrawal of labour' and the threat of it to secure its objectives in negotiations. Under earlier Master and Servant laws, such actions (for example, leaving work unfinished or without permission) by individuals were unlawful. If a trade union was to succeed in its objects, it needed protection not only from the criminal law but also from civil actions which might arise from members' attempts to induce other workers to act in this way. In 1875, immunity from criminal prosecution was provided by the repeal of the Master and Servant Acts themselves and the Conspiracy and Protection of Property Act, and in 1906, immunity from civil actions was conferred by the Trade Disputes Act (s 3).

This relates specifically to those circumstances where a 'trade dispute' is involved. Currently s 13 of TULR Act immunizes persons, and thereby their unincorporated trade unions, from actions in tort (that is, from actions leading to injunction or damages) which might arise from acts committed *in contemplation or furtherance of trade disputes*. Such actions are barred where the ground is:

> 'only that it induces another person to break a contract of employment or interferes or induces any other person to interfere with its performance, or that it consists in his threatening that a contract of employment (whether one to which he is a party or not) will be broken or that he will induce another person to break a contract of employment to which that other person is a party' (TULR Act, s 13).

Related subsections seek to ensure that the legislators' intentions override the older common law doctrines applied; but a third such subsection was removed by the Employment Act 1980:

(a) 'For the avoidance of doubt it is hereby declared that an act done by a person in contemplation or furtherance of a trade dispute is not actionable in tort on the ground only that it is an interference with the trade, business or employment of another person, or with the right of another person to dispose of his capital or his labour as he wills.

(b) An agreement or combination by two or more persons to do or procure the doing of any act in contemplation or furtherance of a trade dispute shall not be actionable in tort if the act is one which, if done without any such agreement or combination, would not be actionable in tort'.

In these ways the trade union member is immunized from civil actions provided that he is acting within the context of trade dispute.

From 1906 (s 4 of the Trade Disputes Act) until 1982, the trade union as a body, also enjoyed a curious blanket immunity from tort actions, even outside the context of a trade dispute (see Wedderburn, 1971, pp 320). In effect this meant that neither the union nor its members could be sued for damages for anything except actions to do with property or personal injury. The clause last appeared in TULR Act 1974, s 14. It denied any court the right to entertain any action in respect of any alleged tortious act committed 'by or on behalf of the trade union'.

This general immunity was removed by s 15(1) of the

Employment Act 1982. This Act also created two new torts by making the unions or their members liable if they engaged in actions to induce anyone to enter into or to break a commercial contract in order to discriminate between unionized and non-unionized labour or in order to compel recognition or non-recognition of a trade union (Employment Act, 1982, ss 12 and 13). In addition, other changes mean that the trade union's immunities in tort are now limited to actions undertaken in contemplation or furtherance of a trade dispute, itself now more narrowly defined. It therefore becomes important to recognize the limits set to 'a trade dispute'.

The limits to a trade dispute

The concept of a trade dispute (or 'industrial dispute' during the currency of the Industrial Relations Act (1972-24) was quite widely defined in the legislation of 1871 and 1906. The parameters were reduced by making certain kinds of industrial action (secondary actions and actions to compel union membership or recognition) unlawful (Employment Act, 1980). The removal of disputes between workers and workers (for example, jurisdictional and demarcation disputes) from the earlier list of protected actions, narrows them further (Employment Act, 1982, s 18). This same Act also excludes disputes relating to matters arising outside the UK unless those in the UK are likely to be affected by the outcome of the dispute. It still covers, however, a wide range of disputes, *and* a wide range of subjects.

As a result of these amendments, a trade dispute is now defined to mean a dispute between workers and *their* employer (amended by s 18 (2) of the Employment Act, 1982) which relates *wholly or mainly* to one or more of the following:

(a) terms and conditions of employment, or the physical conditions in which any workers are required to work
(b) engagement or non-engagement, or termination or suspension of employment or the duties of employment, of one or more workers
(c) allocation of work or the duties of employment as between workers or groups of workers
(d) matters of discipline
(e) the membership or non-membership of a trade union on the part of a worker

(f) facilities for officials of trade unions
(g) machinery for negotiation or consultation, and other procedures, relating to any of the foregoing matters, including the recognition by employers or employers' associations of the right of a trade union to represent workers in any such negotiation or consultation or in the carrying out of such procedures. (s 29, TULR Act, 1974, as amended).

The explicit stipulation in the TULR Act that a dispute between a trade union and an employers' association could involve *all* the members (workers or employers, respectively), in the dispute, was deleted by the Employment Acts 1982, s 18(5). Now, the question of who is lawfully involved in a dispute is for determination by reference to the other elements in the definition of the limits of a trade dispute.

However, the definition given to 'contemplate' allows that differences which may be settled without dispute are caught by the definition. Subsection 5 declares that:

> 'an act, threat or demand done or made by one person or organization against another which, if resisted, would have led to a trade dispute with that other, shall, notwithstanding that because that other submits to the act or threat or accedes to the demand no dispute arises, be treated for the purposes of this Act as being done or made in contemplation of a trade dispute with that other'.

Tort actions would therefore not arise in such circumstances.

Restrictions on secondary actions

The general intent and likely effect of recent changes in the legislation is to restrict lawful industrial action to the domestic situation. Lawful action is that which has some expected and direct consequence for the employer of those who take part in it. The trade union emphasis on solidarity of workers takes a knock as a result.

The changes respond to the examples of blacking, secondary action and picketing, of recent years (see Weekes *et al*, 1975; Elliott, 1978). In effect, they limit the immunities of trade unions and their members to those circumstances where employee-members have a trade dispute with *their own* employer (or employers' association) and the dispute is concerned essentially

151

with *their* terms and conditions of employment and industrial relations matters. In this event the dispute's boundaries are set with the employer's suppliers and customers. Outside these limits, trade unions (by virtue of s 12 of the Employment Act 1982) and their officers and members (as persons) are now exposed to the risk of actions in tort, and therefore to injunction and liability for damages (see below, pp 200-02).

For purposes of establishing immunity under s 13 of the TULR Act, therefore, the trade union and its officers must avoid inducing or threatening to induce a breach of an employment contract (or in the first case below a contract other than an employment contract):

(a) either, by means of a secondary industrial action unless under s 17 of the Employment Act 1980:

1   its purpose or principal purpose is to prevent or disrupt the supply, during a trade dispute, of goods or services between the employer who is a party to the dispute, and the employer whose employees are involved in the secondary action, *and* the secondary action is likely to achieve that purpose; and

2   its purpose or principal purpose is to prevent or disrupt the supply, during a trade dispute, of goods and services between the employer who is a party to the dispute and either associated employers, or customers or suppliers, *and* the secondary action is likely to achieve the purpose.

(This section is not intended to create a class of criminal offence, and any civil proceedings must be initiated by an aggrieved party. This is also the case with the restrictions imposed by ss 16 and 18.)

(b) or in order to compel the workers of another employer to become members of a particular trade union, *unless* the other employees involved are working at the same place as those threatening or inducing. This does not, however, remove the immunity from those workers who seek to induce breaches of contract by employees of an employer in order to compel other workers of the same employer to join a particular union (Employment Act, 1980, s 18).

(c) or in order to pressure an employer to act contrary to the intention of s 10, (by which any term in a commercial contract which requires that the contractor shall use only union labour (or non-union labour) in fulfilling the contract, is made unlawful). (The same section also makes it unlawful to terminate a contract, to exclude from a tender list, or to refuse to invite tenders or to make a contract with, any person on the grounds that those employed or likely to be employed shall or shall not be union members). Section 11 also withdraws the immunities from any who organize any action to interfere with the supply of goods or services on the ground that they had been produced or supplied with union or with non-union labour (Employment Act 1982, s 15).

This blow is softened by the imposition of limits to the amount of damages (see below, p 202) but it could prove serious to unions facing determined managements:

> 'If there is to be litigation on any scale as a result of both (1980 and 1982) Acts, I do not see how trade unions can be expected to avoid 'breaking the law' from time to time. Unless there are enough leading cases, unions will be quite unable to determine the consequences of acting in any other way (McCarthy, 1983, p 97).

Most employers (as the most likely aggrieved party) will probably avoid invoking the new laws, as they did between 1971 and 1974 and as they have done since the 1980 Act was passed, on the ground that taking their workers (or their unions) to court 'will not improve their industrial relations' (ibid) which, after all, remains one of the declared aims of government policy.

The legality of picketing

Picketing is a necessary adjunct to the union's attempt to use its concerted power against the employer. It too has had a chequered legal history. At present, in the context of a trade dispute, it is lawful if it confines itself to attendance by an individual (in contemplation or furtherance of a trade dispute):

(a) at or near his own place of work, or
(b) if he is an official of a trade union, at or near the place of work of a member of that union whom he is accompanying and whom he represents

for the purpose only of peacefully obtaining or communicating information, or peacefully persuading any person to work or abstain from working' (TULR Act 1964, s 15, as substituted by Emp Act 1980, s 16(1)).

This immunity is extended in the same section to allow for attendance of those who do not work at one place or who work at a place which it would be impracticable to picket, and to admit workers to the immunity who lost their employment in connection with a trade dispute. However, a restriction is placed on the union official elected or appointed to represent only some of the members, in that he can only attend the 'place' appropriate to those members.

In connection with the new restrictions placed on secondary actions, the same section provides that the prevention or disruption of supplies referred to is to be attempted or achieved only by picketing which is declared to be lawful by TULR Act, s 15, and carried out by employees of a party to the dispute or a union official accompanying and representing such employees (see also SI, 1980/1957). This reduction in scope is, again, consistent with a State policy of domesticating the industrial relations process.

It is thus possible that those who engage in picketing activity may (perhaps in an excess of zeal) commit criminal offences (for example, damage to property) and that they may go beyond *peaceful* persuasion or action specifically rendered lawful by this legislation. When they do so, they may render themselves liable to criminal prosecution or to civil actions for damages, under non-industrial relations legislation (see below, pp 196-201).

POSITIVE RIGHTS

For over a century, therefore, trade unions have enjoyed various immunities, but until recently have not been the recipients of 'positive rights', in the sense of rights which are reciprocated in another's duties. Such rights as 'workers' have possessed have had effect as legal or conventional norms which (for one reason or another) have not been challenged rather than as rights which could be legally-enforced against another. The trade unions have had few of either kind, but have depended largely upon the freedoms and immunities granted to workers.

The early unions were without a fairly clear legal status comparable to that of the corporation, and were in any event not encouraged to challenge the functions delegated to the business

154

corporation. It was difficult to accord 'rights' to or to impose legally-enforceable 'obligations' upon them, until in 1971, *legislation* for the first time gave the union corporate status. Once that happened, such explicit rights and obligations (as distinct from freedoms and immunities) could be established. Recent legislation has attempted to restore some of the position created in 1971 and closer control therefore remains feasible through the manipulation of rights and obligations.

We have already noted that its quasi-corporate personality has been reaffirmed in recent legislation. This incidentally gives some protection to the agents and representatives. But the law has not gone far in providing the union, as such, with that kind of security which is usually spoken of as 'the closed shop' (see McCarthy, 1964; Szakats, 1972; Hanson *et al* 1973; Gennard *et al*, 1980) which is now hedged around with requirements in respect of ballots (see, EP(C) Act, s 58A as amended and SI, 1758/1980).

Collective rights

Some positive rights are given to those unions which 'qualify' by establishing their independence of the employer (by obtaining a certificate of independence from the Certification Officer if they are not affiliated to the TUC which automatically qualifies them). Such unions which secure recognition from the employer then become entitled to a number of positive benefits and the employer is under a duty to provide them.

Recognition is something which the union can only achieve by using its own power to coerce or persuade the employer. In accordance with one of the reccommendations of the Donovan Commission, the EP Act (ss 11-16) gave the independent trade union the right to refer a 'recognition issue' (refusal by an employer or associated employers to grant recognition or an extension of recognition) to ACAS for conciliation, investigation, recommendation and report, and to seek an eventual award of terms and conditions of employment by the CAC in the event of the employers' continued refusal to recognize after the recommendation and report had been made. This provision had a chequered history during the 1970s (see the Grunwick case, p 171, below; and Rogaly, 1977) and was withdrawn in 1980.

The law gives positive support to the *recognized* independent union in securing *information* from the employer for purposes of improving industrial relations or collective bargaining, and information and *consultation* on redundancy, transfer of undertakings, and health and safety matters.

1 *The right to have information disclosed*

A recognized independent trade union has the right to:

(a) request (in writing if the employer so determines) information for purposes of collective bargaining where such information would contribute to improvement of industrial relations or its lack would impede the union to a material extent in carrying out collective bargaining, and

(b) the right to have such information disclosed (in writing if the union wishes) provided that

  (i) the information is in the employer's (or associated employer's) possession and its assembly or compilation would not involve the employer in a disproportionate expenditure of time or effort;

  (ii) its disclosure would *not* be against the interests of national security, involve the contravention of a prohibition imposed by or under an enactment, involve a breach of confidence, relate to an individual who has not given his consent to disclosure, involve a substantial injury to the undertaking for reasons other than those associated with the collective bargaining itself, include any information obtained in connection with legal proceedings (EP Act, 1975, ss 17-18).

Collective bargaining in this context has the same meaning as given in connection with a trade dispute (see TUC, 1970; CIR Report No 31, 1972, and above, p 150).

Enforcement is *via* complaint to the CAC which on further complaint may penalize the employer by imposing such terms and conditions of employment upon him as it considers appropriate (see pp 203-06). However, the qualifications which are built into the legislation to protect national and commercial interests are such that the employer has many grounds on which he can refuse and secure approval for so doing.

2 *The right to consultation about proposed redundancy*

A recognized independent trade union has the right to be

informed and consulted about a proposal to dismiss employees as redundant.

The employer's duty in respect of redundancy is to inform and consult 'at the earliest opportunity' and in any event at least 30 days in advance of the proposed redundancy where it involves the dismissal of 10 or more employees and at least 90 days where it involves 100 or more to be discharged within a period of 90 days (EP Act, 1975, s 99; and SI, 1979/958). The duty is in two parts:

(a) the employer shall disclose in writing to trade union representatives, by hand or by post:

    (i) the reasons for his proposals;
    (ii) the number and descriptions of employees whom it is proposed to dismiss as redundant;
    (iii) the total number of employees of the same description employed in the undertaking in question;
    (iv) the proposed method of selecting the employees who might be dismissed; and
    (v) the proposed method of carrying out the dismissals, with due regard to any agreed procedure, including the period over which the dismissals are proposed to take effect (EP Act, 1975, s 99 (5) and (6)).

(b) the employer shall, in the process of 'consulting':

    (i) consider any representations made by the trade union representatives; and
    (ii) reply to these, giving reasons for rejecting any of them (EP Act, 1975, s 99 (7)).

An appropriate trade union may present a complaint to the effect that one or both parts of this duty have not been discharged, to an industrial tribunal. The onus is then on the employer to show that he took all such steps to discharge the duty as were reasonably practicable in the circumstances or that there were special mitigating circumstances which prevented his doing so or both. If the tribunal finds the complaint well-founded, the remedy is a protective award to all such employees as had been dismissed or proposed to be dismissed (EP Act 1975, ss 101-3). This is limited to a week's pay (with a maximum amount provided for in regulations) for each employee affected for the part of the 'protected period' (that is, of the 30 or 90 days) during which the employer was found to be at fault.

3 The right to consultation about transfer of undertakings

A recognized independent trade union also has a right to be given information (and consulted) about any proposed transfer of an undertaking (in the UK) in which that union has members (under the Transfer of Undertakings (Protection of Employment) Regulations, SI, 1981/1794). The main purpose of these regulations is to ensure the continuity of individual contracts of employment and any collective agreements in force in the undertaking which it is proposed shall be transferred by one means or another.

The employer's duty is to inform the appropriate union(s) of the fact of the transfer and its proposed or likely date, indicating the legal, economic and social implications for employees and whether the transferor or the transferee proposes to take any measures in respect of the affected employees, and if so what they are to be. The information is to be given 'long enough' before the proposed transfer to enable consultation to take place with representatives of the union(s).

If measures of any sort are to be taken the employer is under a duty to consult with representatives, and the requirements in this respect are as in 2 (b) above, p 157). The remedies for failure which is not found to be excusable because of the circumstances, are also similar to those in the preceding section. The tribunal on complaint by the union(s) which is found to be substantiated, may award such compensation to affected employees as it finds due. The award under this and the preceding heading are not to be added where both compensation and a protective award may be appropriate, and neither is to be added to any other award of damages, as, for example, in the case of a successful breach of contract claim.

4 The right to consultation about health and safety

A recognized independent trade union has the right to appoint or elect safety representatives from amongst the employees, to consult with the employer and carry out such other functions as may from time to time be prescribed by regulation (HASAW Act, 1974, s 2 (4); SI, 500/1977, Reg. 3). Provided that the selected employees have been employed by the employer, or had similar experience elsewhere, for two years, they commence their duties as soon as the employer has been notified in writing of their appointment. No stipulation as to numbers is made in the Act or Regulations, but the Code of Practice indicates the factors which might be taken into account (see H&S Commssion, 1978b; Abell, 1979).

The trade union's right in this case derives directly from the stipulations as to the employer's duty, which is in two parts:

(a) to consult any such representatives 'with a view to the making and maintenance of arrangements which will enable him and his employees to co-operate effectively in promoting and developing measures to ensure the health and safety at work of the employees, and in checking the effectivness of such measures' (HASAW Act, 1974, s 2 (6)).

Regulation 4 of SI. 500/1977 reiterates the function indicated in the HASAW Act s 2 (6) and adds a number of other more specific ones:

(i) to investigate potential hazards and to examine causes of accidents;
(ii) to investigate complaints relating to the health safety or welfare of the employees he represents;
(iii) to make representations to the employer on these and general health and safety matters;
(iv) to carry out inspections after notice to the employer and with facilitation and assistance from the employer,
... of the workplace or part of it, not more often than three-monthly;
... of the workplace or part of it where there has been a change affecting it or new information published by the Health and Safety Commission or Executive relevant to it;
... where there has been a notifiable accident or disease or a dangerous occurrence has occurred (provided it is safe to do so and the interests of constituents might be involved (Detailed in Regulations 5, 6 and 7).
(v) to represent employees in discussions with inspectors or other enforcing authority;
(vi) to receive information from inspectors;
(vii) to attend meetings of safety committees.

The Regulations specifically provide that no function given by them to safety representatives imposes any duty upon them, and that where they act in this representative capacity, or undergo training for it, they shall be entitled to time off with pay, under conditions comparable to those relating to industrial relations duties. (Schedule to Reg. 4(2)).

Regulation 7 provides that on giving reasonable notice to the employer, safety representatives shall be entitled to inspect and take copies of relevant documents, and that the employer shall be under a duty to make available to them information within the employer's knowledge and necessary to enable them to fulfil their functions. There are, however, restrictions on this comparable to those relating to disclosure of information for purposes of collective bargaining (see, pp 156, above).

(b) to establish, in prescribed cases, and on written request by two safety representatives, a safety committee having the functions of keeping under review the measures taken to ensure the health and safety at work of his employees and such others as may be prescribed from time to time (HASAW Act, 1974, s 2 (7)).

Regulation 9 prescribes that the employer shall be under a duty to establish a safety committee whenever and wherever two safety representatives make such a request in writing. On receipt of the written request, the employer shall consult safety and trade union representatives in the appropriate areas, post a notice stating the composition of the committee and its coverage by areas of the workplace, and do so within three months of the request being made.

Individual rights of trade unionists

These are the main examples of statutory protection of the rights which trade unions have 'won' through negotiation with the employers. They are supported by rights given to individual officers and members of trade unions on account of their being trade union members (and not merely that they are employed persons).

Any employee who is an *official* of a recognized, independent trade union has a right to *reasonable* (see ACAS Code No 3) time off work with pay at his or her usual ordinary rate (day work) or average earnings (incentive working) in order:

(a) to carry out such duties as his official status ascribes to him in connection with the relations between his employer (and any associated employer) and his/their employees; or

(b) to undergo training in aspects of industrial relations which is both relevant to carrying out those duties and is approved by his union or the TUC (TUC, 1977).

Any employee who is a *member* of such a union has a similar right to reasonable time off (but without any right to payment) in order

(a) to take part in any activities of his trade union; and
(b) to take part in any activities in which the employee is acting as a respresentative of such a trade union,

provided always that neither of these involve taking industrial action. (Both of these rights are enforceable through the industrial tribunals, see below, p 207-11). Health and safety representatives also have rights to time off for training (H&S Commission, 1978a; see also TUC, 1978).

Powers to exercise options

There are two other examples of the way in which legislation has recently sought to uphold the value of voluntary negotiation of procedures and terms. The independent trade union is given two other rights which it shares with the respective employer: the right to apply (jointly with an employer and any other parties) to the Secretary of State for Employment to have a dismissal or redundancy procedure agreement substituted for the procedures required under the EP (C) Act, s 54 (see above, pp 126-27) given by s 65; and the right to conclude with the employer an agreement which abrogates the worker's right to strike (TULR Act, s 18 (4)).

1 The first of these requires that the Secretary of State shall be satisfied, before making an order which will put the substitution into effect, that:

(a) all trade unions party to the agreement are independent;
(b) the agreement provides procedures to be followed where unfair dismissal is alleged;
(c) the procedures are available to all within the class of employees to which the agreement relates;
(d) the remedies provided are at least as beneficial as those provided in the Act, without necessarily being identical with them;
(e) the procedure provides for independent arbitration or

161

adjudication in cases where, domestically, a decision cannot be reached for any reason; and

(f) the provisions of the agreement make it clear 'with reasonable certainty' whether a particular employee is covered by it or not.

Once an order is made, the terms of the substituted agreement will apply in all appropriate cases, excepting only that the dismissal provisions will not apply to any dismissal in connection with maternity.

2   The second right is intended to control the abrogation of the workers' right to strike through the terms of a negotiated agreement. Such a clause is made a void term of the individual contract, *unless* each union party to the agreement is independent, and the agreement is in writing, contains an express provision that the terms shall or may be incorporated in an individual contract, and is kept in a place reasonably accessible to the worker to consult during working hours, *and* the worker's contract expressly or impliedly incorporates the relevant terms of the agreement (see, also above, pp 99-102).

Summary: protection of associations

Thus, taking all together, some workers (professionals) are encouraged and protected in their attempts to control their own jobs and remuneration for themselves by incorporation which might support monopoly (and thus affect returns). Non-professionals do not enjoy this status, and what they have been able to secure has usually been achieved only after conflict or 'struggle'. The one group have usually been at some time 'independent practitioners' and their corporation has therefore been based on their own association. The other group have usually confronted a corporate organization whose members do not include the workers, and *their* association has therefore developed in opposition to the business corporation and as a challenge to its authority.

The protection of the worker's trade union as it made its challenge to the employer (as business corporation) has been more hesitant and precarious and based on a grant of immunities from the disabling consequences of the Common Law. The protection of the professional association has been based on the donation of positive rights, of the kind which the trade union has only relatively recently acquired.

The trade union's immunities (apart from the now-withdrawn general immunity in tort) are derived from the freedoms donated to 'workers' to withdraw their labour in concert and to persuade or induce others to do so in the circumstances of a trade dispute with the employer. These strengthen the power (and authority) of the trade union to impose sanctions on the employer in order to bring him to change his policies or practices in a number of areas defined as proper ones for collective bargaining.

The positive rights donated in more recent times to trade unions had to await the donation and acceptance of a quasi-corporate status to trade unions (one which is in some respects comparable to that of the business company and the professional association). These rights (mainly to information and consultation on certain defined matters) are intended to support voluntary negotiations, but not to coerce the employer to negotiate. This is left in the realm of 'voluntary' decision and action.

Public policy has never compelled the employer to recognize the trade union (or, indeed, to deal with a professional association). But there has, over the years been a growing moral pressure to do so. More and more workers have joined trade unions, and more and more of these have been recognized by the employer for purposes of engaging in joint determination of relative status and the quantities which enter into the contract of employment. The function of the State, operating through the law, has been to supervise this activity in a broad way, without seeking to compel such accommodation. The principles of a *voluntary* approach to the determination of status are thereby upheld.

Readings

On the nature of professional associations and trade unions:
Carr-Saunders and Wilson: (1964), pp 319-65.
Millerson: (1964), pp 26-46.
Blackburn: (1967), pp 9-43. Prandy: (1965), pp 30-47.
Turner: (1962), pp 233-51; and in McCarthy: (1972), pp 89-108.
On the legal aspects:
Hepple: (1979), pp 3-51.

Lewis, in Bain: (1983), pp 361-92.
Wedderburn: (1971), pp 160-221 and 304-409.
Howells and Barrett: (1982), pp 102-16.
Weekes *et al*.: (1975), pp 193-97.

7

Direct intervention by the State

Forms of State involvement

The major role of the State in industrial relations is that of establishing the limits to the lawful authority of the parties to make decisions. It is often asserted that, thereafter, the State abstains from involving itself directly in the decision-taking processes. There are some important exceptions to this abstentionist generalization. One early intervention which is not discussed here, occurred in the development of the Factories Acts. Apart from this, State intervention has otherwise occurred to support and facilitate the parties in reaching their own decisions, and to supplement and complement the activities of the unilateral or joint bodies to whom authority to decide is devolved. This 'other' category of intervention may be considered under four distinct headings:

1   the encouragement and facilitation of peaceful resolution of differences and disputes, by a public conciliation and arbitration provision
2   the facilitation of the extension of voluntarily agreed minimum terms and conditions, without the necessity for negotiation in each and every case
3   the determination (through some specially-appointed agency) of the minimum or actual amount of remuneration to be paid
4   the determination of changes in the quantity of remuneration to be paid, through a 'wages policy' or 'incomes policy'.

These, although not in chronological order, represent increasingly direct intervention. The first was originally intended to help the parties reach their own decisions; the second to extend these without State intervention to determine amounts; the third established a complementary means of setting minimum standards; and the last usually limited the amount of *increase* in remuneration to be paid in any given datum period (usually a year). They may be regarded as a set of experiments, acknowledged to be outside the mainstream of voluntarism, and therefore always at some risk of being abandoned.

CONCILIATION AND ARBITRATION

The least directly interventionist of the measures adopted by the State have been those which simply provide machinery through which issues and problems faced by the parties can be resolved without recourse to industrial action. The original legislation expressed as a principle that voluntary settlement of issues was to be preferred to any kind of State intervention, and this continues to the present time (for example, in the Employment Protection Act, 1975). The machinery it established for conciliation, mediation and arbitration is intended to facilitate the parties in reaching voluntary settlements of any differences. It is available for use at *their* discretion.

Initially, it simply copied existing voluntary practices. From the middle of last century there had been a spontaneous development of boards of conciliation and arbitration usually composed of equal numbers of representatives of employers and workers. The oldest of them is thought to be the Board of Conciliation and Arbitration for the Manufactured Iron and Steel Trades of the North of England (established 1869). Set up at either local or national level, such bodies functioned to hold stoppages at bay whilst the issues were considered (see Amulree, 1929). There was said to have been:

> 'an almost unbroken record of acceptance and loyal observance by both sides of the industries concerned, of the decisions of the umpires or arbitrators to whom their disputes were referred' (Ministry of Labour, 1944, p 26).

Their rapid growth in this period suggested that there was a need to be met. After the Royal Commission of 1891 had commented favourably on them as devices for avoiding open conflict, the Conciliation Act 1896 established a public provision of a similar facility. (Amulree, 1929; Turner-Samuels, 1951)

This Act did not make the voluntary councils redundant, and in fact there are still a number in active existence. The first

166

reaction of industry to public intervention was, however, not particularly favourable, although it was extremely well hedged about with restrictions to preserve the essentially voluntary character of the existing system:

> 'In the first instance, both sides of industry showed reluctance to accept Government interference, even to this limited extent, and the officers who were concerned with carrying out the purposes of the Act had to use the powers sparingly' (Ministry of Labour, 1944, p 19).

This was not surprising, since it remained entirely up to the parties to use the facility or not, as they wished.

The Conciliation Act

The Conciliation Act 1896, gave the Labour Department of the Board of Trade power to engage in a number of peace-keeping activities in industrial relations. With one major modification, it provided the foundation for the work of the Ministry of Labour conciliation and arbitration service from its inception to the 1970s (see Turner-Samuels, 1951). It provided for:

1 the encouragement of the parties to set up conciliation agreements voluntarily for themselves
2 the establishment of a means of inquiry into the causes and circumstances of a dispute where it seemed useful or expedient to do so
3 bringing together the parties to any dispute, either under a chairman of their own choosing or one drawn from the Department, in order to get negotiations under way
4 the appointment of a conciliator or a board of conciliation if *one* of the parties to a difference requested such
5 the appointment of an arbitrator if *both* parties requested this.

The first of these provisions emphasized the concern to foster voluntarism, and the second enabled the nebulous force of public exposure or opinion to be brought to bear on the parties and issues in dispute. The third retains the principle of voluntarism but recognizes that the parties might on occasion need, and even welcome, a push from an outside source, and the fourth makes a more formal provision for such help.

The fifth provision was potentially the most useful (in

avoiding open stoppages) but also the most potentially threatening to a voluntary system. But the built-in requirement that the parties must both want arbitration was a safeguard against undue interference from the government or any other third party. It also made it more likely that, where it was requested, any award made would prove acceptable, even though it had no legal force.

The Industrial Courts Act

The main modification was the establishment of a 'standing industrial court' under the Industrial Courts Act 1919. This created a permanent court in addition to the *ad hoc* arbitration bodies of the earlier Act, but did not otherwise change the principles on which it rested. The consent of *both* parties was still required for a reference to the industrial court, to boards of arbitration or to single arbitrators and the award was usually not legally binding upon the parties, even though it might be made by a 'court'.

The court was composed of equal numbers from the employers' and workers' panels maintained by the Minister of Labour, sitting under the chairmanship of an independent President of the Court or another independent member, appointed by the Minister. The intention was that the Chairman would have the powers of an umpire, but could seek an agreed award, and would have the benefit of the side members' industrial experience in reaching any decision.

During the 1920s and 1930s publicly-serviced voluntary and *ad hoc* arbitration was little used, possibly because of the economic situation but possibly also because of a lack of trust. Between 1920 and 1939, 315 cases are recorded, amounting to less than 17 per annum. The Industrial Court carried out 1,669 arbitrations (or 88 per annum), although these figures are inflated by unilateral arbitrations in the Civil Service between 1925 and 1936) (Flanders, 1952, pp 96-7). During this period, 1,199 settlements (63 per annum) were reached as a consequence of conciliation by the officers of the Ministry of Labour, and there were 20 Courts of Inquiry (16 of them appointed before 1926). The number of settlements reached by one of these means within the private or voluntary system is not known.

During World War II and the 15 years following, the usage made of this machinery is affected by the existence of alternative machinery established under Emergency Orders (see below, pp 175-77). In the 1960s, however, the level of usage of the Industrial Court was appreciably down but conciliations and *ad hoc* arbitrations up by comparison with the inter-War period.

With the exceptions mentioned, this constituted the public provision until 1971. In that year, the Industrial Relations Act changed the name of the Industrial Court to that of Industrial Arbitration Board (to avoid confusion with the new National Industrial Relations Court (NIRC)) but left both its powers and those of the conciliation and arbitration service of the Department of Employment largely unchanged.

By this time, however, some suspicion of the independence of the service had developed in the face of the administration of governmental incomes policies by that same Department. Because of this and the generally unhappy experiences of the Industrial Relations Act, a major reorganization of the machinery was undertaken in 1974.

The Advisory Conciliation and Arbitration Service

The Employment Protection Act 1975 repealed the whole of the Conciliation Act of 1896 but re-established most of its machinery under new auspices, and extended its role. It gave a statutory base to that which had been established quickly in 1974 by administrative means, namely the Advisory Conciliation and Arbitration Service (ACAS). The provision is much the same as before, but is extended slightly and run by a body independent of the Government.

Its independence is achieved by making ACAS a body corporate 'of which the corporators are the members of' the governing Council (a Chairman, up to three deputy chairmen, and six other members), which directs its affairs. The Council is appointed by the Secretary of State, who under some circumstances, (indicated in para 3(7) of Sch 1 of the Act) may terminate the appointment of a member. The six other members are appointed by the Secretary of State only after consultation with such employers and workers organizations 'as he considers appropriate', and the additional deputy chairmen may be appointed after consultation with these bodies. The Council is authorized to determine its own procedure, may elect its own Chairman in the absence of the appointed Chairman if the

Table 11

Usage of public Conciliation and Arbitration, 1963-82

Year:	Concil– iation	IC/CAC	Arbitration Board	Single	Total
1963	–	36	1	32	69
1964	408	35	0	24	59
1965	406	19	9	39	67
1966	447	22	2	43	67
1967	413	7	0	27	34
1968	412	12	2	42	56
1969	516	14	4	41	59
1970	647	9	4	48	61
1971	650	7	8	48	63
1972	716	15	17	48	80
1973	886	5	4	50	59
1974	1235	8	17	127	152
Sep-Dec					
1974	578	–	7	62	69
1975	2017	–	32	260	292
1976	2851	5	31	265	301
1977	2891	7	40	247	294
1978	2706	5	39	346	390
1979	2284	11	44	304	359
1980	1910	10	34	237	281
1981	1716	5	27	212	244
1982	1634	10	26	194	230
Av					
1963-73	500	17	5	40	61
1975-82	2340	7	34	258	299

Sources: 1963-74: DE: Industrial Relations Procedures (Manpower Paper No. 14, HMSO, 1975), pp 61-2. 1974-82: ACAS: Annual Reports.Figures on mediations, Courts and Committees of Inquiry and other forms of arbitration (Fair Wages Resolution, and under various Acts of Parliament not included). The figures for the earlier group of years are not strictly comparable with those for the later group. (see also, Table 17, p 359).

Secretary of State has not appointed deputy chairmen, and may determine its own rules as to quorum.

By s 1(2) ACAS is charged with the general duty of promoting the improvement of industrial relations, and in particular of encouraging the extension of collective bargaining and the development (and where necessary the reform) of collective bargaining machinery. The existence of two objectives, whilst clear enough for laymen, led to difficulties when the actions of ACAS were successfully challenged in the Courts (UKAPE v ACAS (1979) ICR, 337; (1979) ICR, 303; (1979) IRLR, 68, CA; (1980) 1 All ER, 612; (1980) ICR, 201; (1980) IRLR, 124, HL; and Grunwick Processing Laboratories Ltd and others v ACAS and another: *The Times*, July 30, 1977; CA: (1978) IRLR 38; (1978) 2 WLR, 277; (1978) ICR, 231; *The Times* 15 December, 1977, HL). The intention was to require ACAS to give priority to the first objective over the second, and the consequence to reveal how limited were its powers to act in a disputed recognition situation (see Mortimer, 1975).

Specifically, ACAS takes over from the Department of Employment functions which it previously carried out. These comprise the advisory function (compounded of the personnel management advisory service of the Department of Employment and certain functions of the Commission on Industrial Relations, abolished by the same Act); conciliation (previously Department of Employment conciliation service made up chiefly of full-time officers in the Department); arbitration (formerly provided partly by the Industrial Court/Industrial Arbitration Board and partly by a panel of arbitrators maintained by the Department) and inquiry (originally given to the Secretary of State by the Conciliation Act). In addition, ACAS was empowered to issue guiding codes of practice (see below, pp 173-74).

The EP(C) Act (ss 2-6) gave ACAS the authority:

1   To provide a conciliation service. Where a trade dispute is apprehended or in existence, the Service may either offer its assistance as a conciliator or provide such assistance at the request of one or more parties. The conciliators may be officers of the Service or independent persons: their role is to encourage the parties to reach a settlement by using any agreed procedures, and, whether such procedures exist or not, to help them to come to a resolution of their differences 'by conciliation or by any other means'.

This *collective* conciliation role is extended to embrace *individual* conciliation in respect of matters which are or could be the subject of proceedings before an industrial tribunal (s 2)(see also below, p 206-09).

2 To provide a service of arbitration. Where a trade dispute is apprehended or in existence, the Service may provide arbitration 'at the request of one or more parties to the dispute and with the consent of all the parties' to it. It may do this either by reference to a single arbitrator or a board of arbitration (made up of persons who are not officers or servants of the Service) or by reference to the Central Arbitration Committee (see pp 203-06, below). This power is restricted to those circumstances in which procedures are ascertained to have been exhausted and in which conciliation is judged not to be capable of resulting in a settlement, provided only that there are no 'special reasons' which justify arbitration even though the procedures have not been exhausted.

This section continues provisions of the earlier legislation, but by s 3(4) provision is made for publication of awards of arbitrators or boards of arbitration 'if the Service so decides and all the parties consent', and a more explicit basis for establishing precedent in arbitration awards is thus established (s 3).

3 'To inquire into any question relating to industrial relations generally or to industrial relations in any particular industry or in any particular undertaking or part of an undertaking', if it thinks fit. The Service is given powers to publish the findings of any such inquiry, together with its advice based on these findings, if the Service thinks that publication would help improve industrial relations, generally or specifically, and after submitting a draft to, and taking note of the views of, the parties concerned with the inquiry. This section of the Act continues the powers previously exercised by the Commission on Industrial Relations (CIR) (s 5).

A number of inquiries of this kind have been conducted by the Service. Reports have been issued on, for example, disputes at BL Cowley (Report No 1), difficulties in London Docks (No 2), industrial relations in the London Fire Service (No 7) and industrial relations at the St Stephens Parliamentary Press (No 14) amongst others.

4   To offer advice on industrial relations or employment policies, whether this is requested or not, to employers, employers' associations, workers and trade unions. It may also publish general advice on these same matters. The Act offers a list of matters which are considered to be within the scope of this provision:

(a) the organization of workers or employers for the purpose of collective bargaining;
(b) the recognition of trade unions by employers;
(c) machinery for the negotiation of terms and conditions of employment, and for joint consultation;
(d) procedures for avoiding and settling disputes and workers' grievances;
(e) questions relating to communications between employers and workers;
(f) facilities for officials of trade unions;
(g) procedures relating to the termination of employment;
(h) disciplinary matters;
(i) manpower planning, labour turnover and absenteeism;
(j) recruitment, retention, promotion and vocational training of workers; and
(k) payment systems, including job evaluation and equal pay (s 14).

These provisions continue the functions previously performed by the Advisory Service of the Department of Employment and the CIR. These advisory activities constitute a very substantial part of the total carried out by ACAS.

5   To issue, at its discretion, codes of practice aimed at improving industrial relations. When it does draft a code of practice, it is required to publish the draft and consider any representations made about it and may modify it in the light of them. The final draft must then be submitted to the Secretary of State who is required to lay it before both Houses of Parliament if he approves of it, or to publish details of his reasons for withholding approval if he does not. If, after the draft has been before both Houses for 40 days, no resolution to stay proceedings on the code is forthcoming, it may be issued by the Service, and will come into effect on such day as the Secretary of State may by order appoint. Revision of codes is also permitted and this must take broadly the same

course as in the original. Code No 1 on *Disciplinary Practice and Procedures* has been issued under this provision. The Act *mandated* the Service to issue two codes on:

(a) disclosure of information by employers to trade unions for purposes of collective bargaining (ss 17 and 18) and
(b) time off to be permitted by the employer to union officials or members (ss 57 and 58).

In these two cases, the procedure to be followed, whilst generally the same as that above, is different in that express approval by each House òf Parliament is required before the Code may be issued and come into effect on a date to be specified by the Secretary of State, by order (ss 6(2) and 6(5)). Both of these Codes have been issued (Code No 2 on *Disclosure of Information* and Code No 3 on *Time Off for Trade union Duties and Activities*).

(These Codes are separate and distinct from those, such as the *Code on Picketing*, which the Secretary of State himself is empowered to issue under the provisions of the Employment Act 1980).

6 To investigate the working of any wages council, at the request of the Secretary of State, with a view to determining whether it should be continued, modified or abolished. This power is transferred by the Act, to enable ACAS to perform this role in place of the *ad hoc* committees which the Secretary of State could appoint under earlier legislation. In the event, ACAS has investigated the operation of a number of such councils and issued reports on its findings and recommendations: for example, Road Haulage (Report No 6), Retail (10), Button (11), Toy (13), Fur (17), Licensed Residential Establishments and Licensed Restaurants (18), Laundry (19) etc. It has also examined the possible need for a new council in Contract Cleaning (20).

In effect, therefore, the various public provisions, previously administered in different ways by different bodies have now been placed under the control of one independent organization. It functions to investigate, advise, and facilitate, and it remains largely under the control of the joint parties to industrial relations. As the figures in Table 11 (on p 170 above) show, it has been significantly more used than the service which preceded it,

174

although the return to free bargaining since 1979 appears to have reduced this.

EXTENDING VOLUNTARILY AGREED TERMS

The role and function of the ACAS is to be distinguished from those of the Industrial Court and its successor, the Central Arbitration Committee (CAC) (see below, pp 203-06). These bodies have been more directly but not exclusively, involved in unilateral (or compulsory) arbitration, and their awards have had a purpose and scope not applicable in the ACAS context.

Compulsory arbitration has been adopted in conditions of emergency (during and after the two World Wars). Parliament's intention in both cases was to extend general or negotiated terms and conditions of employment to other workers and employers in the public interest, but *without their express consent*. The policy was later extended by legislation as a normal (non-emergency) means of ensuring that terms and conditions of employment in unorganized workplaces could be raised above levels considered to be too low by comparison with the rest of their industry. Both the original concept and the later extension stop short of direct State intervention to fix the terms of employment, although it does introduce under State supervision an element of compulsion into an otherwise voluntary system.

Unilateral arbitration

The form taken by compulsory arbitration in Britain has been that which allows one party to refer a difference or dispute to an independent body which then has the power to issue an award which will be binding on all parties. This modification of the normal practice (see above, p 168) has usually been made in two kinds of emergency situation:

1   Within an industry conditions might be so bad that something more drastic than pure 'voluntarism' was thought to be needed to save the situation. This is exemplified in giving statutory force to collective agreements in the cotton industry (in the Cotton Industry (Temporary Provisions) Act 1934) because of the 'possible collapse of the whole principle of collective bargaining' there.
2   More generally, wars and related emergencies have spawned

departures from the voluntary principle. Under the Conditions of Employment and National Arbitration Order (1305 of 1940), every employer was obliged to observe terms and conditions of employment not less favourable than those which had been settled *either* by agreements made 'between organizations of employers and workers in the trade in the district in which the employer is engaged' *or* by the decision of Joint Industrial Councils or similar bodies, *or* by arbitration awards.

The purpose of the wartime Order was to minimize stoppages in wartime by reducing the occasions when industrial action provided the only way that terms and conditions could be improved. It offered another way by which a union could secure improved terms and conditions and striking was made a criminal offence unless certain procedures were first followed (see, Turner, undated). It was intended that compulsory arbitration would ensure that questions relating to the terms and conditions which should be observed to meet the requirements of the Order would be referred to the National Arbitration Tribunal in the same manner as any other dispute. Providing that the party reporting any question was one which habitually engaged in determining wages and conditions for that trade or industry, it could secure an award which would be legally binding on both parties.

This wartime Order was replaced by another emergency Order 1376 in 1951. This was introduced mainly to remove the provision that it was a criminal offence to take part in strike action but also to limit the powers of unofficial or unrecognized groups of workers to report a dispute to the Minister. This new Order sought to secure the ends both of strengthening the voluntary system and of giving some real power to the third party machinery.

It discontinued the relatively simple requirement of the earlier Order that employers observe the recognized terms and conditions of employment (or terms and conditions not less favourable than these). Instead it was made possible for either party which habitually engaged in the settlement of such terms and conditions to report to the Minister, what the Order called, an 'issue', about whether a particular employer should observe them or not.

The Industrial Disputes Tribunal (which replaced the National Arbitration Tribunal of the earlier Order) was given a power which was later to be granted to the CAC in a similar connection

176

(see below, pp 203-06). It was empowered to award that an employer should observe either the recognized terms or such other terms and conditions as it determined to be not less favourable to the workers in question. The award was then to become an implied term of the affected employment contracts and could therefore be enforced by civil action in the courts in the same way as under the preceding Order.

Both of these Orders, therefore, made it possible, in a limited way, for workers to secure an improvement in their (or their fellow workers') terms and conditions of employment, without the necessity for either negotiation or strike action, provided that the foundation for these had been laid by voluntary negotiation (or by voluntary arbitration). Not surprisingly, the arrangement was not viewed very favourably by those employers who preferred not to recognize and negotiate with unions. Nevertheless, it was to be developed in later legislation in 1971 and 1975 before being abandonned, in response to employer criticism, in 1980.

Extension of terms and conditions

These emergency arrangements were abandonned in 1958, largely on the insistence of the employers who saw its application as biased against them. In the following year, however, the Terms and Conditions of Employment Act reintroduced the mechanism which permitted recognized terms and conditions to be imposed on the reluctant employer. The Act was mainly concerned with wages councils and their functioning, but in section 8 the 'issues' provision of the Order 1376/1951 reappeared, but without any provision for compulsory arbitration.

In effect, the new Act extended the principle and sentiment of the Fair Wages Resolution of the House of Commons (first moved in 1891, amended in 1909 and 1964 but now abandonned). The Resolution required employers *in receipt of government contracts or subsidies* to observe terms and conditions of employment not less favourable than those established by negotiation, or arbitration award, or those which were general to the trade or industry concerned. The new Act extended this principle to the general field of employment, regardless of whether government contracting was involved or not.

The parties habitually engaging in collective bargaining for a class of workers in a trade, industry or district (other than those in the wages council trades), were given the opportunity to request the Minister of Labour to extend recognized terms and conditions, to workers (and employers) in the trade etc, who were not party to the negotiations. They were empowered to do this either through voluntary machinery if this was possible or by reference to the Industrial Court if it was not.

Workers whose remuneration or minimum remuneration was fixed by enactment (other than section 8 of this Act) were, however, excluded, This made it impossible to use the provisions of this section to enhance the wages of workers in the wages council trades and industries. With this important exception, the new Act did make it possible for the parties to have recognized terms and conditions made a term of the contract of employment under an Industrial Court award.

The specific exclusion of the wages council trades from these provisions caused increasing concern to the trade unions during the 1960s. The Donovan Commission recommended that section 8 be removed in order to make it possible for voluntarily negotiated terms and conditions to be extended from the large scale employers in some of the wages council trades to the smaller (and usually unorganized) ones.

The change was made in the Industrial Relations Act 1971, so that the extension provision could now apply to these trades. An award of the Industrial Arbitration Board (as the Industrial Court was now renamed) might be secured. But this Act also introduced one other amendment to the 1959 Act (see Sch 7, IR Act, 1971, which replaced Section 8 of the 1959 Act). This made it possible for trade unions and employers' asociations to use this general provision, only if they were registered under the Act (and, of course, most of the TUC-affiliated unions did not register).

The Employment Protection Act 1975, codified the provisions for such extension of terms (in s 98 and Sch. 11). Where an *independent* trade union normally negotiated for workers of a like description, it might now pursue a claim through ACAS to the CAC for the extension of negotiated terms to an undertaking which did not follow them. Also a union could seek an award of terms which were general for the trade or industry or district concerned.

The CAC was given the power to award the 'recognized' (that is negotiated) terms or such terms as were established as 'general', and these would take effect as part of the contracts of the workers concerned in substitution for whatever might have been agreed between them and their employer. Claims under this provision and under the Fair Wages Resolution provided the major part of the work of the CAC during its first five years of life (see, p 203, below). This provision was, however, removed by the Employment Act 1980, s 19, simultaneously with the removal of the recognition provisions (by s 19), and with the abandonment of the Fair Wages Resolution. These matters were now to be dealt with in virtually unassisted free bargaining.

MINIMUM REMUNERATION

Britain still does not have a minimum wage law or policy (except in the sense that the TUC has a target of this kind). The State has tried to avoid involvement in this area and has succeeded in leaving *amounts* to be paid in wages to voluntary or tripartite bargaining.

Early in the industrial period, Parliament was impelled to legislate on the manner of computing and paying wages. The Truck Acts, 1831-1940, required the employer to remunerate manual workers outside the public service wholly in legal tender, and to make deductions (particularly fines) only under rather rigorously defined conditions (see above, pp 120-21). The Payment of Wages Act 1960, now permits payments to be made by cheque or money order, rather than in actual notes or coin, but the basic intention of avoiding remuneration in a form with lesser value remains (see, Thomason, 1981, pp 78-80). Currently, the view that such alternative forms of payment should be further encouraged is being widely canvassed in discussions between the Government, the employer organizations and the TUC.

A universal minimum

The *amount* of wages to be paid, has, however, been left to be determined either by market forces or voluntary negotiation by the parties themselves. Britain does not have a universal national minimum wage established by legislation, as do many other countries, but it does have statutory minima applicable to particular trades.

The question of a national minimum wage was last seriously examined in 1967, when an Inter-Departmental Working Party was set up to:

179

'examine and report on the social, industrial and economic consequences of introducing a national minimum wage, with particular regard to its effects on industrial costs, wages and pay differentials, its relationship to the Government's productivity, prices and incomes policies, and its relevance to the problem of families with low income' (Ministry of Labour, 1967).

The Working Party's Report suggested that there were three main arguments in favour of a national minimum wage:

1 it would be a useful means of achieving social justice, provided that its introduction was not immediately followed by a general upward movement in wages;
2 it would contribute to the relief of poverty amongst those in low paid employment, thus helping to alleviate the problem of the wage stop, although it would not and could not take family circumstances into account; and
3 it would tend to increase efficiency in the use of manpower, although this would have to be set against the cost of induced unemployment and labour turnover.

It also advanced two main arguments against the idea:

1 it would be inflationary, because the resultant upward adjustments in other rates (whose size would depend upon the level chosen for the minimum) would only improbably be met by increases in productivity
2 it would require comprehensive administrative arrangements to enforce the national minimum wage, and this would in itself be costly.

The Report effectively dampened any enthusiasm for the national minimum wage concept. Only the Family Income Supplement (FIS) paid under the Family Income Supplements Act 1970, to supplement particularly low wages by transfer payments related to family circumstances, can be regarded as a positive response on the part of the Government to the problems which the Report listed.

Statutory minimum wages

The nearest Britain comes to such a conception is in the form of the statutory minima established by tripartite wages councils for specific trades. These were established as trade boards under the Trade Boards Act 1909, and were gradually extended in both scope and coverage over the intervening years, becoming known as wages councils under legislation in 1945. They are now being considered for abolition on the ground that they maintain artificially high levels of wages in these trades (see Bayliss, 1962).

In setting up these bodies Parliament continued to apply the principle that the Government should not interfere directly in the determination of wage rates for any individual or class of individual. 'It has never been possible', Kahn-Freund states:

> 'for a government department to fix minimum wages without a proposal from an independent council or board ... Outside agriculture, the ultimate decision whether or not wages should be fixed rests with the Minister (of Labour), but he cannot determine the substance of his decision. It is not he who settles remuneration and holidays. This is done by the wages council ... concerned, and although he does not have to act on proposals made by the council ... (and may, if he disagrees, refer the matter back to them), he cannot in substance amend them' (Kahn-Freund, in Flanders and Clegg, 1954, p 71).

This he considers a distinctive feature of British labour law.

The trade boards

The trade boards were set up initially in a limited number of 'sweated' trades (originally ready-made tailoring, paper box making, chain making and machine-made lace and net finishing) to recommend improvements in rates of pay, which could then be enforced by the Wages Inspectorate as statutory minima. It was thought that they might also encourage by their example or practice, voluntary organization and collective bargaining. The rationale was that:

(a) certain trades revealed themselves as incapable of fixing adequate levels of remuneration, and for this reason some external intervention was necessary; but

(b) such intervention ought to allow as much opportunity for the development of local autonomy as possible, and for this reason the boards brought together equal numbers of representatives of employers and workers in the trade, with a third party providing continuity and a degree of expertise.

The first Act set down the main lines on which the councils have continued ever since.

1   The types of trades or industries which might attract this kind of interference. In all four of the original trades, the units of production involved tended to be small and scattered and there was a great deal of out-work and subcontracting, and neither employers nor workers were organized in unions or employers' associations or capable of developing voluntary machinery.

2   The form of the tripartite machinery, comprising two representative sides plus an independent side of three members (five in the case of the Agricultural Wages Board), and the practice of voting by sides in taking decisions.

3   The use of an inspectorate (originally under the Board of Trade, but after 1916 under the Ministry of Labour (now DE)) to enforce the minimum time rates of wages established by the Boards, by prosecution where the circumstances warranted it.

In 1917, the Whitley Committee recommended an extension of the trade boards to a wider range of trades which suffered from poor organization. This was incorporated in the Trade Boards Act of 1918, which empowered the Minister to set up a trade board if he was:

> 'of the opinion that no adequate machinery exists for the regulation of wages throughout the trade, and that accordingly, having regard to the rates of wages prevailing in the trade, or any part of the trade, it is expedient that the principal Act (of 1909) should apply to that trade'.

This gave the whole experiment a considerable fillip. Thirty seven trade boards were set up between 1919 and 1921 in poorly organized trades and industries and in 1924, agricultural workers in England and Wales were brought into the scheme. Thereafter, trade boards held their own but were little extended or developed, until just before World War II. Agricultural wages in Scotland were brought within their scope in 1937, and road haulage wages were made the subject of a special wages board in 1938, and a few other new boards were set up between 1938 and 1939, in, for example, baking, furniture manufacture and rubber manufacture.

182

The wages councils

The next major extension came during World War II, when their scope and powers were increased, by the Catering Wages Act 1943, (which created four new boards) and the Wages Councils Act 1945 (which created nine new boards in retailing).

The 1945 Act also changed the name of the old trade boards to wages councils, to remove any lingering stigma of being associated with the sweated trades. It also increased their scope to include the fixing of minimum remuneration rather than merely minimum rates. Their other new functions included advising the Minister on training, recruitment and working conditions. This meant, amongst other things, that wages councils were now able to tackle the problem of short-time employment in their trades, where employers engaged workers at the statutory rates but for limited periods of time.

Consolidation

Between 1945 and 1970, however, very little change occurred in the nature or coverage of the wages councils. Legislation served largely to change names of existing bodies and to make minor modifications and variations. Some new boards were set up (for example, retail bread and rubber proofed garments) and some of the former special boards were converted to wages councils. The procedures for abolishing boards or changing their field of operations were also changed. The councils became largely routine exercises of fixing statutory minimum remuneration, hours, and holidays which in reality affected a declining proportion of workers as voluntary agreements made greater impact.

The number of councils peaked in 1947, when 69 councils or boards determined the minimum terms for over four million workers. By the early 1960s, the figures were down. About 3.5 million workers were covered by 53 councils, in addition to the 400,000 covered by the two agricultural wages councils. If at this date the statutory minimum still remained a significant influence on the wages of workers in scope, it could have been said that the wages of one in every six of the employed population in Britain were fixed in this way.

However, it was generally known that the wages of many workers nominally covered by the wages councils had by this time become responsive either to voluntary agreements within the industry itself or to voluntary agreements in some closely associated industry which were, by agreement, followed in the trade concerned. Just how far this process had gone, and therefore just how relevant the fixing of statutory minima really remained, was something which could only be guessed at.

It was on the basis of such inspired guesses that the Donovan Commission questionned whether there was really any point, in the second half of the twentieth century, in continuing machinery which had been set up to deal with a beginning of the century problem. The Commission found little evidence that the wages councils generally exerted much impact on a worker's actual pay in the trades covered, and that market forces in the post-war period had probably done much more than the wages councils to improve wages.

The Commission did note that there were specific exceptions, and pointed to the position of agriculture as an example. They were, however, much more censorious of the role of the wages councils in encouraging or facilitating 'organization' in their industries, and declared that 'today, many wages councils are doing little to fulfil the aim of extending voluntary collective bargaining.' (Donovan Report, 1968, p 59). The thrust of the Commission's argument was that some examination should be made of the place of wages councils in the scheme of things (1968, pp 57-60).

This was carried out by the CIR and subsequently by ACAS (see p 174, above). Both bodies recommended a number of abolitions (on grounds of their being no longer necessary) and a number of variations in scope (usually to remove the better organized end of the industry). This led to a higher rate of abolition in subsequent years. Between 1953 and 1963 nine Councils were abolished (in chain-making, drift-net mending, fustian, rubber, rubber reclamation, sugar confectionery, tin box, tobacco and unlicensed residential establishments) and two separate country councils were amalgamated (in hat and cap making). Between then and 1973, only four were abolished (in baking (Sc.), baking (England and Wales), cutlery and paper bag).

Between 1973 and 1983, another 11 councils were disbanded, the two country-based councils in milk distribution, and the councils in hair, bass and fibre; brush and broom; boot and floor polish; paper box; holloware; keg and drum; stamped and pressed metal wares; road haulage; and industrial staff canteens all disappeared. In addition, the seven councils in retailing were replaced by two councils for food and retail (non-food). By the end of the period, only about 2.75 million workers were left in scope of the remaining 34 councils.

There was, however, during the 1960s and 1970s a strong feeling that since wages councils had not succeeded in taking the traditionally low paid workers out of that category (see NBPI, 1971) they ought to be abolished as having failed in their primary purpose. This failure was variously attributed to lack of boldness on the part of the independent members, of vigour on the part of the workers' representatives, or of diligence on the part of the inspectorate. Free collective bargaining, encouraged and assisted by the grant of rights to recognition and unilateral extension of negotiated terms and conditions of employment, would, it was confidently expected, prove more effective in this respect. When, however, Craig *et al* surveyed a number of trades whose Wages Councils had been abolished, they concluded that low pay persisted in them, and for some categories of worker might even have got lower (Craig *et al*, 1982, p 63).

Certain other problems remain. The variation in coverage which took the larger employers in the trade out of scope, raised questions about whether it would deny the 'rump' the opportunity to develop its own bargaining arrangement. It is generally considered that the small end of a trade has lowest potential for effective organization on either side (for example in retailing) and that the large end ought perhaps to be retained in the hope that it would spearhead industry-wide agreements of a voluntary nature which could then supersede the wages council minima. Abolition might only prove beneficial if some device like that provided by the EP Act, s 98, were to be retained or reintroduced (see above, pp 177-78).

Where the industry makes use of outworkers, the problem of minimum standards is ever more difficult to resolve. These are so dispersed that the problems usually advanced as salient in trades like retailing, are exacerbated. A number of the CIR's reports made reference to this problem, and in some cases, the wages council's continuance was recommended on the grounds that there would be no other way (short of minimum wage legislation *per se*) by which a control could be maintained over remuneration of such persons. In 1983, however, the Government was inclined to see wages councils as institutions for maintaining wages and other conditions in these industries at levels higher than market forces would produce and canvassed views on their possible abolition.

INCOMES POLICIES

An 'incomes policy' (sometimes referred to as a 'pay policy' or a 'prices and incomes policy') represents another mode of intervention by government in the processes of economic decision-taking. In essence, it attempts to secure a limit to pay increases for any (usually annual) round of negotiations. It may apply to everyone or to certain categories. It says, effectively, 'this year, pay increases will be limited to this amount or to this percentage addition'.

Incomes policies are usually adopted to control inflation in the economy. It is one of the options available from several: for example, fiscal policies (relying on variation in the rates of taxation), monetary policies (focused upon changing interest rates or the terms of hire purchase agreements) or exchange rate policies (effecting changes in the rate of exchange of the home currency for foreign currencies) are alternative means which, according to circumstances, might be used to tackle this problem. These are not necessarily discrete options, and may be melded together, as when in 1976 the Chancellor tried to secure restraint in demands for pay increases by varying the level of income tax established in the Finance Act.

Policies aimed at restraining increases in income in order to hold down money wage costs and thereby curb inflation, take one of four forms, distinguished according to the mode of orientation relied upon: the exhortative; the informative; the centrally-imposed; and the self-regulative (or negotiated) policies. Britain has experienced all four types over the post-war years (see Gennard and Wright, in Torrington, 1978, pp 157-93; Metcalf, 1977).

1 The exhortative policy

The exhortative policy is worked out centrally by the government, but issued as a set of recommendations (exhortations) to the pay negotiators to confine demands and offers to a range of pay increases, and particularly within an upper limit. The first of the pay policies in post-war Britain, that of 1948-50 relied upon such exhortation: the Government's *Statement on Personal Incomes, Costs and Prices*, 1948, argued that given the country's economic position, there were no grounds for general increases in pay. Negotiators were 'expected' to take this into account. In effect, this produced a period of voluntary wage restraint, which persisted until 1950, with TUC support for part of the period. During the next decade, exhortation was used in preference to any formal declaration of a policy.

Such exhortation is likely to be a constant feature of any incomes policy, even when stronger methods of persuasion or compulsion are introduced. Attempts at persuasion are thought likely to make the stronger medicine more acceptable; regulations require acceptance in a democratic or devolved decision-taking situation. But experience of incomes policies over the years gradually suggested exhortation by itself was insufficient, and other forms were adopted later.

2 The informative policy

The informative type of policy relies upon making *expert* information on the likely consequences of the actions or proposed actions available to the negotiators. The government will have a view as to the level(s) of settlement appropriate to the circumstances, but instead of relying on political persuasion, it appoints experts to monitor and comment on the likely effects of settlements. An attempt is then made to persuade the parties by increasing the amount of information available to them from a source other than the government *per se*.

This type of policy usually entails setting up some committee which will generate and disseminate the information. In 1957, the Government established the Council on Prices, Productivity and Incomes which became known as 'the Three Wise Men'. It was charged with keeping changes in productivity, prices and incomes under constant review and with issuing reports on these from time to time. The Committee had no power to interfere in actual negotiations or settlements. But it was thought that its activities would result in a fuller appreciation of the 'facts' of the economic situation, by both the public and the negotiators and, as a consequence, influence conduct in respect of incomes and costs. The underlying assumption was clearly that a better informed public would become a more responsible public, where 'responsibility' is to be understood as conforming with the Government's reading of the economic situation.

3 The centrally-regulative (imposed) policy

The next step is obviously one which entails the introduction of some kind of sanction to compel compliance with the Government's conceptions of what is appropriate. There are many particular variants of this approach ranging from that in which the Government secures power to refer specific claims or settlements to a 'neutral' body (as in the case of the National Incomes Commission, set up in 1962, when a 'guiding light' of 2 to 2.5 per cent increase was in operation), to that in which Government establishes limits and sanctions to back them by legislation (as in the case of the Counter-Inflation Act of 1973).

The Labour Government's incomes policy of 1964, entailed setting up the National Board for Prices and Incomes (NBPI) in 1965, with power to monitor changes in pay against criteria establised in tripartite discussion between Government and the two central organizations of employers and trade unions (see below, pp 250-52; and 278-81). However, after the first year, these bodies could not agree and criteria were established by government and given effect through legislation in the shape of the Prices and Incomes Acts.

In 1965, the Government threatened to compel notification of pay and price increases, but delayed for a year to give the TUC's own early warning system a chance to show whether it would work. But in 1966, the Government imposed a statutory control on incomes under the Prices and Incomes Act, 1966. Two more annual statutory phases followed, but then were abandoned in favour of exhortation once again. What began as a 'voluntary' form of policy became an 'imposed' one, and then reverted back again, continuing in this fashion until the Government changed and the NBPI was abolished in 1971 (see Clegg, 1971).

The Conservative Government (1971-74) began with the intention of having no formal incomes policy, and for two years attempted to use an informal exhortatory form. In 1972, however, the Government introduced a statutory policy under the Counter-Inflation Acts, 1972 and 1973, to back up a pay freeze. In 1973, it set up the Pay Board and established a Pay Code. All of this was dismantled with a further change of Government in 1974 (see Daniel and McIntosh, 1973).

The later Conservative Government (of 1979) also claimed to be avoiding any notion of a pay policy. Given its belief in monetarism and the efficacy of market forces, it relied on the operation of market forces in a recession to dampen wage demands in the private sector and a policy of cash limits to effect the same consequence in the public sector. Since the reliance on market forces is not to be equated with the establishment of a perfect market (in the economist's sense) both policies represent Government *decisions* to interfere with the manner in which the system was found to be operating. Furthermore, they are policies which are essentially imposed by Government, albeit on the basis of a claimed mandate from the electorate but without too much pretence at securing consensus.

4 The self-regulatory (negotiated) policy

The self-regulatory policy has been an aspiration of a number of governments, but has had only limited success. It stemmed from the belief that control of bargaining behaviours on the basis of agreement would be more likely to succeed than control attempted by imposition. The approaches made in this context have involved negotiation or tripartite bargaining between Government and one or more of the labour market partners in order to secure such agreement. Whenever this idea has been tried, however, it seems to work for a limited period, but (not unnaturally) to collapse when the changes in the cost of living continue seriously out of line with the norm for pay increases.

In 1974, the Labour Government sought to secure agreement to a pay policy from the trade unions and the employers. This attempt at a kind of consensus and a kind of self-control, came to be known as the Social Contract. This 'contract' promised that the Government would pursue certain fiscal, monetary, economic and social policies, in return for restrictions upon pay claims by the trade unions in accordance with guidelines developed by the TUC as its part of the bargain (see Elliott, 1978, pp 25-61; TUC, 1974)).

In the face of mounting inflation in the middle of 1975, the TUC suggested a limit of £6.00 per week increase for all but the higher paid, which was accepted by the Government in a White Paper, *The Attack on Inflation* (July, 1975). The TUC undertook to resist all claims outside this limit. The Government tried to make the policy stick in the public sector and encourage its adoption in the private sector by refusing price increases and contracts or subsidies to any company which breached its terms. This was thought to be a sufficient incentive to the employers to co-operate, even though they had been less involved in the Social Contract negotiations than had the TUC.

The exercise was repeated in the following year. The TUC's proposal of a general increase of five per cent subject to a maximum of £4 and a minimum of £2.50, was accepted by Government. This held, but the Annual Congress in that year called for a return to 'free collective bargaining' in 1977. The Government's White Paper of the following year indicated a limit of 10 per cent, with more for self-financing productivity deals, but this was set up without TUC support and in the face of continuing opposition to restraint. The 1978 White Paper was similarly devised by Government, and indicated a limit of five per cent, variable in respect of the low paid, 'severe anomalies' and self-financing productivity schemes.

The trade union opposition now reflected itself in many settlements outside the limits and in major disputes in the public and private sectors. In an attempt to resolve those in the local authority and health service sectors, the Government set up the Standing Commission on Pay Comparability, with the task of finding a way of relating pay in the public sector to that in the private sector. This issued a total of 15 reports and awards on pay in various parts of the public sector between 1979 and 1981 when it was abolished (see also below, p 414).

The idea of a Social Contract was not completely dead, and the Government continued to seek an agreement with the TUC (in particular). As late as February, 1979, these two parties issued a Joint Statement on *The Economy, the Government and Trade Union Responsibilities* which expressed a willingness of the signatories to try to reduce inflation to the lower level enjoyed in major competitor countries, but without suggesting any limit to pay increases. Nevertheless, taking the period as a whole, the Government found again that it had to become more insistent that the actual norms be adopted, so that the idea of an enforceable 'contract' effectively evaporated before the end of the Labour Government's term.

Mixed and partial policies

From what has been said, pay policies (whether coupled with

controls on prices and other factor incomes or not) frequently rely upon some element of each of these four types of approach. Even the most mandatory policy makes use of exhortation and information, if only to try to make the direction more palatable; all governments try to convince the various sectors that their actions are in their best (usually long-run) interests and seek (with whatever hope) to secure compliance. Every pay policy so far has spawned a mass of information which was generally disseminated. Succeeding policies then show a clear trend towards more centralized control. The debate has then focused on the advantages and disadvantages of securing control by imposition or agreement. The experiments with each have demonstrated a conclusive advantage with neither.

Some of the policies have also been directed at particular sections of the economy or the workforce. The Pay Pause, introduced in 1961, was intended to apply to the public sector and the wages council trades only. The 1979-83 Conservative Government also aimed its most direct controls in these same directions on the grounds that this was where the greatest sources of inflation and lack of competitiveness were to be found. In the Social Contract period, the policy was intended to be applied generally, but it bore differently upon the two sectors if only because of the position of the Government in relation to the public sector employees. In that sector, it could use instruction or direction, whereas in the private sector it was limited to the manipulation of various incentives.

In other cases, notions of fairness and welfare have affected the shape of the policies; in the Social Contract era, for example, the lower paid were allowed to make significant advances in their relative pay, whilst those in higher pay brackets were restricted more firmly. Some redistribution of income between the two categories was therefore effected, without producing any permanent change in the differential pattern, as the powerful battalions were able to restore their relative positions in subsequent negotiations.

Summary: the suspension of an experiment

During the past century, the State was persuaded to intervene in a number of largely 'experimental' ways to bolster the voluntary system of collective bargaining. Against the background of judicial supervision of the activities of the parties in determining how wealth is to be produced and distributed as income, the State has from time to time provided additional machinery to facilitate or complement the decision-making and to control or underpin the decisions made.

The most facilitating and least directing of these interventions has been that focused on the provision of a public service of advice, conciliation and voluntary arbitration, now since 1974 through the Advisory, Conciliation and Arbitration Service. This is an independent body which is designed to assist the parties to achieve their own ends without imposing its own, or those of government.

The intermittent ventures in compulsory or unilateral arbitration, and the carry-over exercise of extending recognized or general terms and conditions of employment to employers' undertakings without the employers' direct consent, is a much more interventionist exercise which certainly gave assistance to workers seeking but not securing recognition for their associations, but one which has now been abandonned along with the Fair Wages Resolution of the House of Commons.

The device of the trade board/wages council was always intended as a supplement to the ordinary processes of collective bargaining, and applied mainly to those trades where organization was difficult and recognition relatively meaningless. These bodies, established by a Minister where wages were low or organization poor, were designed to encourage the development of voluntary bargaining but to take the necessary decisions in the meantime. Generally, they have been thought to have failed to raise the low wages and to encourage organization; but this may reflect the nature of the trades rather than the will or the practice of the Councils themselves. These too are under consideration for abandonment.

Incomes policies are in a rather different category from these, since they are designed more deliberately as a control over the outcomes of the parties' interactions in bargaining. In this sense, they are perhaps more to be compared with the legislative restrictions placed on bargaining and strike behaviour. They do, however, bear upon the same kinds of activities which figure in the other cases, and illustrate some of the difficulties of securing support for general norms related to pay and conditions. In their 'pure' form these may too have disappeared, although the general economic climate may offer a substitute in the private sector just as cash limits provide a restriction in the public one.

At the present time, therefore, the State might be said not to give much assistance to workers or trade unions in any of these areas of unilateral imposition of their will or wish upon the employer who refuses to accept certain current conventions. The main rationale for the Government's present approach is that wages, as a price of labour, should, like all other prices, be directly subjected to market forces. In the belief that labour is overpriced in Britain, the Government attempts to expose wage fixing to these pressures, in the belief that they will thereby find their 'true' level in the competitive conditions. The level of employment is seen by Government as both a consequence of over-pricing and a factor likely to assist in reducing it. In the light of this, therefore, the Government's role must be abstentionist to an extent greater than we have become accustomed to in the post-war period.

Thus, the experiment of assisting the parties to industrial relations decisions to arrive at socially-acceptable standards, and of establishing a degree of societal or State control of their performance in the process, may be at an end, at least for the time being. Of the mechanisms of intervention which have been reviewed in this chapter, only that of ACAS remains virtually intact. Some reductions have been made in its work both by legislation and by the exigencies of the economic climate resulting from world recession and the Government's economic policies. However, removal of centrally-validated standards does not always assist the manager in his task. Without them, some managements found it difficult to work out the pay 'norms' which should apply in their situations. It may not prove easy to identify the new ethical standards which should apply in other areas than pay.

Readings

ACAS: (1980), pp 25-38. Lockyer: (1979).
Craig *et al.*: (1982), pp 1-64. Smith: (1962).
Gennard and Wright, in Torrington: (1978), pp 157-93.
ACAS: Annual Reports. CAC: Annual Reports.
Elliott: (1978), pp 25-61.
Bain: (1983), pp 179-208 (Pond); and pp 419-455 (Davies).

8

Enforcement: the judicial system

The need for enforcement

If everyone accepted that laws and rules were morally binding upon them, there would be no need for a separate mechanism for their enforcement. But rules are not always regarded in this way by those to whom they are intended to apply (see Anthony, 1977, p 136). They therefore have to be supported by penalties and punishments, administered through specialized judicial machinery, to increase the incidence of compliance.

Enforcement of any formal rules is attempted through what may be referred to generically as judicial machinery and judicial processes. Such machinery is likely to be established in connection with each distinct set of formal rules, whether within an organization or within a society. Where, as with the regulation of work behaviour, rules themselves have numerous origins, the number of distinct judicial mechanisms established will be correspondingly large.

Accordingly, the rules which exist in statute and common law are enforceable through the tribunal and court machinery, where the latter is a long established machine and the former a relatively recent innovation set up to handle enforcement of the rules governing individual status resulting from legislation since 1963.

The rules established and enforced by the authority vested in the corporation and its managers, are enforceable within the domestic unit (see above pp 113-33), although under the supervision of the industrial tribunals and courts. The rules established through voluntary collective bargaining are not normally treated in this fashion (and the means of enforcing these are looked at below, pp 372-85).

In this chapter, we shall be concerned with the machinery of the law as the means of enforcement of society's rules, as they apply to conduct in the work situation, and as they are handled in domestic tribunals. There are two relevant parts to this:

1   The county courts and High Court (together with the criminal courts, which have less direct relevance), with appeal to the Court of Appeal and ultimately the House of Lords.
2   The industrial tribunals from which appeal lies to the Employment Appeal Tribunal, with further appeal to the Court of Appeal and thence, to the House of Lords.

THE COURTS OF LAW

The courts of law administer both the criminal and the civil law and, in the particular context of contract, arbitrate disputes about conduct within private relationships. The court system comprises two parts which handle the first two types of case. Criminal cases are handled by a hierarchy of criminal courts and civil cases by a hierarchy of civil courts. Both may be relevant to contract cases, although contract is mostly a civil matter (see Walker, 1970).

The courts at the lower end of the hierarchy examine issues presented and may dispose of the smaller and less heinous or complex cases. The higher courts may take over the more complex ones from the lower courts and will deal with appeals from the lower courts.

Thus in the criminal hierarchy, the magistrates' courts deal with the more minor crimes and the Crown Courts with major or indictable ones, and appeal is possible to the Court of Appeal (Criminal Division) and thence to the House of Lords. Magistrates have the power to commit persons for trial in the Crown Court which may also hear appeals from the lower court (see, Howells and Barrett, 1975, pp 90-96).

In the civil hierarchy a similar sequence is involved although there are specialist divisions of some of the courts which complicate the picture. Actions founded in contract or tort involving claims of up to £5,000 (the current limit) would begin in the county court but claims for higher sums would begin in the High Court. Claims concerned with contractual rights and rights in partnerships and corporations would be dealt with similarly, although possibly in a different division. Appeal in the civil law area is to the Court of Appeal (Civil Division) and thence to the House of Lords (see, Padfield, 1972, pp 188 *et seq.*).

Both criminal and civil courts are relevant to industrial relations, although to quite different extents.

The criminal law applies to persons in their industrial roles as in any others, but it is now of less specific relevance than the civil law. Criminal offences were more common under the legislation applied to work relationships last century and although many of these were removed in 1875, some employer and worker offences still remain, so that the application of the criminal law cannot be ignored completely.

Civil law, particularly that concerned with torts and contract, is much more directly and frequently involved. This is where the law supervises the important bargains and relationships which people enter into (contract) voluntarily and provides remedies to private citizens who have been disadvantaged (or damaged) by another's conduct. In addition, the civil courts are involved in supervising the discharge of those statutorily imposed duties under which citizens are placed in their employment roles.

Criminal offences

There were many criminal offences which workmen might commit during the last century, which would now be regarded as anything but crimes (see, Wedderburn, 1971). From the 1870s, most of these have been removed. But employers and workers may still be charged with criminal offences which might be committed in the course of business or work activities. Personal conduct which occurs in connection with actions which are themselves labelled industrial relations actions, may give rise to offences (for example in connection with strikes and lockouts). But there are also some *business* crimes as well.

General offences

Once companies and trade unions became recognized in law as legal *persons* they could conceivably commit offences. These might be offences against the generality of criminal law or specific crimes or misdemeanours arising out of the conduct of business or trade union affairs. The crimes of fraud, theft or misrepresentation committed within the framework of normal business dealing are particularly relevant in this context.

Companies might, for example, be criminally liable in respect of actions undertaken in the normal course of their activities when, for example, the actions can be attributed to persons who have been made (by the Articles or constitution) responsible officers (cf Gower, 1977, p 147).

The officers themselves as *natural* persons may also be criminally liable for these and other actions. Thus, theft, misrepresentation and fraud are categories of offence which may arise in the course of discharging their duties. Directors knowingly misrepresenting something to be true (as for example in a prospectus) may be criminally liable under the Companies Act 1948 (ss 44 and 438), the Theft Act 1968, (s 19), and the Prevention of Fraud Act 1958, (s 13). If convicted, the persons concerned may be fined or imprisoned, and the courts may deny such persons, as well as undischarged bankrupts, the opportunity to serve as directors.

Labour legislation also admits certain offences in addition to these which arise in connection with corporations. The Employment Protection Act, 1975 (s 117) provides that directors and other named officers of companies may be guilty of an offence when it is proved that a corporate body has failed to notify the Secretary of State in advance of certain redundancies (s 100) or has failed to provide required information in connection with occupational pension schemes (now s 126 of the EP (C) Act, 1978). Trade unions and employers' associations, and their authorized officers, may be liable for offences in connection with keeping accounting records (s 10, TULR Act 1974) and rendering annual returns and audited accounts to the Certification Officer (s 11).

Specific offences

The Health and Safety at Work Act 1975 creates a second set of criminal offences. The provisions of the Act are mainly enforceable by the specialist inspectors, to whom the right to initiate proceedings under any of the Act's provisions is largely restricted. An inspector who finds something unsatisfactory within an undertaking may either serve a notice requiring that the position be remedied, or institute a prosecution alleging breach of a statutory duty, or both.

Offences may be committed by employers, owners, occupiers and others, either by contravening the provisions of the Act itself or by hindering the inspectors in the discharge of their duties. They are in two categories: summary offences (of a less serious and more routine type which do not involve endangering persons at work) and offences which may be tried summarily by the magistrates' courts or on indictment (that is, in a Crown Court before a jury).

Summary jurisdiction is applied, *inter alia*, to attempts to prevent an inspector from carrying out any investigation, or to obstruct him in carrying out his duties, or to prevent anyone from appearing before an inspector or answering questions put by him. Summary conviction carries a maximum fine of £400 (HSAW Act, s 33 (1) and (2).

Offences which may be tried summarily or on indictment include failure to obey an inspector's notice, contravention of general duties under the Act, of regulations designed to avoid endangering people at work, and of the requirements of earlier legislation still current. In these cases, the penalties on summary conviction are as in the preceding category, but those on indictment may in some cases involve imprisonment for a term not exceeding two years or a fine or both (HSAW Act, s 33 (3)(5).

Offences associated with industrial action

A third set of offences are associated with industrial action, where strikers or pickets may commit offences under legislation other than that which is strictly industrial relations legislation. Pickets have lawful authority to attend at or near *their* place of work to engage in 'peaceful persuasion', but in the course of this, they might well fall foul of other legislation and commit offences which are not, strictly, offences under industrial relations legislation.

The authority to picket is confined to a place 'at or near', but not 'on or in' a place of work. If pickets attend on or in the workplace without specific authorization, they may be liable for the *tort* of trespass (Larkin v Belfast Harbour Commissioners (1908) 2 IR, 214; Thompson and others v Eaton Ltd (1976) TLR, 18 May, 1976). The pickets may also lay themselves open to *criminal* charges even if they confine their picketing to attendance at or near their place of work.

'At or near' usually means 'on the public highway' (including its footpaths or pavements) and such attendance might interfere with the rights of the citizen (including the drivers of vehicles) to have access to these. A charge of 'obstructing the highway' (under the Highways Act 1959) might be brought against pickets, as it was in the case of Hunt v Broome (1974) 2 WLR, 58; 1 All E R, 314, HL).

The authority to picket is also subject to supervision by the police in their discharge of their general duties, which includes that of taking reasonable steps to prevent a breach of the peace. Failure to comply with a policeman's instruction to desist from an action which he has reasonable grounds for supposing might lead to a breach of the peace (Piddington v Bates (1960) 3 All E R, 660) might therefore lead to a charge of obstructing a police officer in the execution of his duty (Tynan v Bulmer (1965) 3 All ER, 99; (1966) 2 All ER, 133).

In addition, pickets may in an excess of zeal for their cause or for other reasons, commit other offences such as damage to property or injury to persons, intimidation or affray, and attract the appropriate charges for so doing. In all of these cases, the individual picket might risk a fine or imprisonment upon conviction (see, R v Jones (John) (1974), ICR, 310).

Civil actions

Civil actions may arise when one person behaves in a way in which he has no lawful authority to behave and, as a consequence, causes loss or damage to another. The 'lawful authority' may be created (and denied) in the voluntary formation of a business contract or by Statute (as in the above example of picketing).

Actions founded on contract

A common example in the first category concerns 'breach of contract'. Persons who consider that they have been dismissed from employment in breach of their employment contract terms, may, for example, take an action to the civil courts, for *wrongful* dismissal. The basis for the action is that the employer, in dismissing the individual, acted in a way in which he had no warrant to act, because the contract terms prescribed a different course of action. A court which found the complaint well founded would have three remedies which it could apply. The first two look towards the performance of the contract terms and the third towards establishing the amount of compensation for their non-performance.

1   The injunction (or order of the court) to restrain the employer from acting in the manner proposed, where the action has not already been commenced.
2   The order of specific performance by which a court might require the employer to restore the contract in its terms and thus continue the employment.

The courts are reluctant to make either of these kinds of order in *employment* contract cases, for two reasons:

(a) it would be difficult to supervise their enforcement (even if, as in the first case, there were time in which to make it)
(b) that it would mean ordering that two persons should continue in a personal relationship which might not be congenial to one of them (in the words of Fry, LJ, in De Francesco v Barnum: 'I think the Courts are bound to be jealous, lest they turn contracts of service into contracts of slavery' (1889) 43, Ch D, 165: 59, L J Ch, 151; 6 TLR, 59)

3   The payment of compensation for loss or damage, occasioned by the breach. In most breach of employment contract cases, this is limited to the amount given by multiplying the relevant notice period by the appropriate wage or salary; set against the likely costs of an action this provides little incentive to the individual to proceed.

This type of case has not been common in the past, for reasons which are obvious from the above discussion. Much more prevalent currently is the action for unfair dismissal, itself a concept created by Statute (originally in the Industrial Relations Act, 1971) but this is processed through the industrial tribunal and is discussed in that context below (pp 206-10).

Actions in tort

Actions in tort may brought by anyone who considers he has been threatened with damage or actually damaged by the unlawful actions of another. The onus is on the complainant to show that he will suffer damage, is doing so, or has suffered damage as a result of the actions complained of, and that the other had or has no lawful authority to act in this way. The court action is begun by the complainant supplying the court with the particulars of the claim (a brief resumé of the facts of the case) and an indication of the remedy sought (for example, injunction and/or damages and costs).

The law has established a wide variety of causes of action which may be started where someone acts to another's disadvantage when the person has no lawful authority to act. For example, many employers have, in the past, brought actions of this kind against trade unionists (usually the officers or strike leaders) or occasionally, as in the Taff Vale case, against the trade union. The employer has often faced the difficulty of naming individuals as defendants and this has often detered him from taking this kind of action. The individual worker is unlikely to take this kind of action because of the expense and time involved, although his union may assist in this (often in connection with claims for industrial injuries).

Recently, the removal of the trade union's *general* immunity in tort (by s 15 of the Employment Act 1982) has exposed the trade union to a range of actions not possible since 1906. The employer, as the most likely aggrieved party, now has opportunity to seek such civil remedies against the unions in the courts. The employer might, however, feel that in most circumstances, the initiation of such action is unlikely to prove helpful in the long run. He has usually to continue to live with the representatives of the union against whom he might proceed, and the limits imposed upon the liability for damages might in other cases make the effort not worthwhile. The upper limits are fixed in relation to the size of the union's membership:

> Up to 5,000 members: £ 10,000
> 5,000 – 24,999 members: £ 50,000
> 25,000 – 100,000 members: £125,000
> more than 100,000 members: £250,000.

These amounts could be devastating for any union which found itself involved in three or four such court cases, particularly when the damages and costs are added together. However, time must pass before a judgement can be made as to whether employers will see it as desirable to take advantage of the new opportunities, and a number of cases will need to be tried before an assessment can be made of the likely effect of awards upon the financial viability of the unions (see McCarthy, 1983).

THE NEW ARRANGEMENTS

Court procedures and rituals are complex and closely regulated by court rules and conventions, and the services of a solicitor are usually necessary to enable an individual to progress his action in conformity to them. All of this adds to the complexity and cost of the process and often acts as a deterrent to individuals with small claims (which are common in this area). In addition, the very formality of the court proceedings are often a deterrent to individuals seeking redress. The cost and formality of court proceedings were the main reasons for developing a tribunal system distinct from the courts, and for making provision to transfer to their jurisdiction all claims arising out of (or deemed to arise out of) the employment contract.

In the period since the Donovan Commission's *Report* was published, there has been a move to make it easier for workers (and their trade unions) to enforce the collective and individual rights which have been provided for in legislation. Both developments have their antecedents but most of the changes have occurred in this more recent period. The intention has clearly been to develop a Labour Code and Labour Court system, outside the traditional court system and less subject to protocol.

The enforcement of collective rights has been facilitated by the extension of the role and function accorded originally (by the Industrial Courts Act 1919) to the Industrial Court. The jurisdictions have been extended and the function has now passed (under the Employment Protection Act 1975) to the Central Arbitration Committee (CAC). Although this is not strictly a part of the court system, it has, by virtue of its discretionary power to award binding terms and conditions of employment, an enforcement role comparable to that of the courts themselves.

The enforcement of individual employment rights is largely in the hands of the industrial tribunals (from whose judgements there is appeal on points of law to the Employment Appeal Tribunal). These tribunals were originally established, with a more limited administrative-appeal role, in 1963, but their jurisdiction has been greatly extended since that time under a variety of Acts. The tribunals are more firmly a part of the judicial system, but in some respects their jurisdictions overlap with both the civil courts and the CAC.

The Central Arbitration Committee

The Employment Protection Act 1975, provided (s 10) for a continuation of the function previously carried out by the Industrial Court (and the Industrial Arbitration Board as it was renamed by the Industrial Relations Act 1971). Under the new title the Central Arbitration Committee (CAC) was set up in 1976 with comparable functions to its predecessors, and with some new ones introduced by the Act.

The CAC is made independent of government, and is not subject to its directions.

> 'The functions of the Committee shall be performed on behalf of the Crown, but the Committee shall not be subject to directions of any kind from any Ministers of the Crown as to the manner in which it is to exercise any of its functions under any enactment' (para 27, Sch 1 of the EP Act, 1975).

It may, however, be subject to judicial review where it exceeds its statutory powers or otherwise abuses its own procedures, but the courts must leave judgements of fact to the special expertise of the CAC.

This expertise is built into the composition of the Committee itself. It consists of a Chairman, a number of deputy chairmen, and a larger number of members selected for their experience as representatives of either the workers or the employers in negotiations. The Chairman and deputies are usually persons independent of the immediate concerns of the parties to industrial relations, but with some professional knowledge of industrial relations affairs (such as academics).

Any particular hearing of the CAC brings together a Chairman (or deputy) and one member from each of the two representative categories (although there could be more, just as there might also be 'assessors'). The chairman and members seek to reach a unanimous decision, but where this is not possible, the Chairman has powers of umpire. The decisions are published, where they are made under the Committee's statutory powers, in addition to being notified to the parties themselves.

Jurisdictions

The CAC's jurisdictions are now fewer in number than they were originally. Some of them (particularly those relating to trade

Table 12

Awards of the Central Arbitration Committee

Year	Vol arbit- ration	FWR	1959 Act & Sch 11	EP Act	Recog- nition	Discl- osure	Other Acts
1976	5	13	30	20	–	–	2
1977	8	115	167	16	2	0	0
1978	3	271	521	9	7	10	15
1979	9	243	307	5	5	14	11
1980	10	25	139	1	10	15	9
1981	8	16	9	0	–	2	0
1982	10	12	–	0	–	6	2
Average 1976-82	8	99	168	7	3	7	6

Notes:
1. FWR = Fair Wages Resolution;
2. 1959 Act and Sch 11 = claims for the extension of recognized or general terms and conditions of employment;
3. EP Act = references under the Equal Pay Act;
4. the 'other Acts' are those which require conformity of wages and conditions within a specific industry to those which are negotiated for or general in the industry concerned.

union recognition, and extension of general or recognized terms and conditions of employment), were removed by the Employment Act 1980. The jurisdiction in cases referred to the Secretary of State in respect of the Fair Wages Resolution of the House of Commons was also removed in December, 1982. Amongst these, those relating to the extension of recognized or general terms and conditions of employment and the application of the Fair Wages Resolution of the House of Commons, produced by far the largest number of applications (see table 12 above).

Its jurisdiction in respect of voluntary arbitration, is shared with ACAS. Parties to a dispute may seek arbitration by the CAC instead of by a single arbitrator or board of arbitration appointed by ACAS. ACAS also has an investigatory and conciliation role in respect of some matters which are to be referred to the CAC under Statute, and the two bodies might in this sense be said to complement one another. In these ways their jurisdictions overlap, but they remain *completely independent* of one another, neither being subordinate to the other.

The jurisdictions which remain exclusive to the CAC are:

1   Claims to the effect that an employer does not provide terms as required under various Statutes (such as the Films Act 1960, or the Independent Broadcasting Authority Act 1973).
2   Claims to have clauses in collective agreements or awards which relate to one sex only, amended, under the Equal Pay Act 1970, as amended by the Sex Discrimination Act 1975.
3   Complaints (and further complaints) about the failure of an employer to disclose information for purposes of collective bargaining, in accordance with the EP Act 1975, ss 19-20.
4   Resolution of disputes between employees' and employers' representatives on statutory joint industrial councils, under Employment Protection Act 1975, s 92(2). (See Hepple and O'Higgins, 1981, pp 170-72; EP(C) Act, ss 17-18).

The discretion and remedies available to the CAC vary through these different jurisdictions. In jurisdictions under 2 above, the remedy is the award of one or more specific terms and conditions of employment (which then become part of the individual contract of employment). With references under the Equal Pay Act, the CAC has the power to declare what amendments need to be made in the agreement or award to comply with Statute and to offer advice to the parties.

Information disclosure had greatest novelty about it during the 1970s, and the remedy for non-disclosure is the award of appropriate terms and conditions of employment to the employees concerned. Under this provision of the Act, an independent trade union may present a complaint that an employer has failed to disclose to representatives of the trade union such information as the employer is required by s 17 to disclose. If the Committee consider that this complaint might be settled by reference to conciliation, it is empowered to refer it to ACAS for this to be attempted. If this fails, or is not so referred, the Committee is empowered to hear the complaint and if it finds it well-founded to declare by what date the employer 'ought' to disclose the information specified.

If this does not produce the intended result, the trade union may present a further complaint to the Committee. If this is found to be substantiated, the Committee may award, after hearing the parties, *either* such terms and conditions as the trade union has sought at the time of or after its second complaint, *or* such other terms and conditions as the Committee considers appropriate. These will then, as was also the case in respect of well-founded recognition claims before 1980, have effect as part of the contract of employment of the employees specified in the complaint and the award (EP Act 1975, ss 19 – 21).

This aspect of the CAC's powers makes the CAC itself a body which sits astride the voluntary-compulsory divide in industrial relations, even though it is not, strictly, a part of the court system and is more usually construed as an extension of the role and function of ACAS. By virtue of the powers of enforcement given to it, however, it does, in these jurisdictions, serve as a specialized agency of enforcement in a way which ACAS does not.

Industrial tribunals

Since 1963, industrial tribunals have performed the function of *administrative* tribunals. This means that they have provided a mechanism for appealing against decisions taken within the framework of government administration. Their first role in this respect was in relation to levies imposed under the Industrial Training Act 1964, (s 12). Their jurisdiction in this regard has been extended, and they may now hear appeals or consider references regarding:

1 industrial training levies (Industrial Training Act 1964, s 12)
2 redundancy payments rebates (EP(C) A s 108) and equivalent rebates in respect of public servants (EP(C) Act, s 112)
3 improvement and prohibition notices served by the Health and Safety Inspectorate (HSAW A, s 2 (as amended))
4 whether any given work is to be regarded as dock work (DH Act, s 51).

The Contracts of Employment Act 1964, gave them the additional role of adjudicating on issues of individual rights established therein. This role has subsequently burgeoned under different pieces of individual rights (in work) legislation, the earlier pieces of which have now been consolidated in the Employment Protection (Consolidation) Act 1978. The jurisdictions and powers of the industrial tribunals are now established very largely (although not exclusively) by this one statute.

The intention and effect of this group of Acts is that in order to deal with individual rights arising out of the employment relationship, a separate, distinct, and relatively informal court is required. First, it should deal with all such disputes of individual right as might arise, including those connected with breach of contract (EP(C) Act, s 131) although this jurisdiction has not yet been transferred (see below, p 209). Secondly, it should develop its own body of relevant law and precedent, subject only to appeal to higher courts on points of law. Thirdly, it should deliberately try to avoid overawing individuals with the formality and ritual of law in order to facilitate the individual litigant to bring his own case (see, Donovan Commission Report, 1968, para 577).

These tribunals do not quite amount to a Labour Court system on the continental European model, but they are moving in that direction as Britain attempts to harmonize its systems with those of the European Economic Community. The recent legislation on individual employment rights (and status) has tended to usher in this new conception with its relatively informal tribunal and tribunal appeal system. In this respect it has something in common with the informality and expedition of the CAC. But the public machinery of conciliation, mediation and arbitration (as provided by ACAS) remains outside this machinery of enforcement, although at some points (such as the handling of equal pay claims) their involvements may be coming closer together (see above, p 171).

Tribunal jurisdictions

In addition to their original function of hearing appeals against decisions by executive bodies, industrial tribunals now mainly hear complaints or references initiated by individuals (and in some cases, trade unions) in respect of individual rights which have been established in subsequent legislation. These embrace complaints relating to:

1   the adequacy or the accuracy of the information an employer is required to give to an employee on his contract terms (EP(C) Act, s 11; on the make-up of his pay (EP(C) Act, s 11), and on the reasons for dismissal (EP(C) Act, s 53(4)
2   rights to compensation and the amount of that compensation in the event of redundancy (EP(C) Act, s 91(1)) and over similar rights granted to employees in the public sector

(EP(C) Act, ss 130 and Sch 10; Local Government (Compensation) Regulations 1974 (SI 1974/463)

3 unfair dismissal (EP(C) Act, s 67) or failure to give adequate or accurate information on reasons for dismissal (EP(C) Act, s 63(4))

4 any of the payments employees are entitled to claim under the EP(C) Act (guarantee payments, (s 17), entitlement under a protective award, (s 103), remuneration on suspension from work on medical grounds s 22), maternity pay s 36(1)), debts on insolvency of employer, (s 124)

5 whether an employer has given an employee time off with pay for ante-natal care (Emp. Act, s 13(6), to perform public duties (EP(C) Act, s 29(6)), or to look for work, (EP(C) Act, s 31(6)), to carry out trade union duties, (EP(C) Act, s 27,(7)), or engage in trade union activities (EP(C) Act, s 28(4)) and whether he has given safety representatives time off with pay to perform statutory functions. (Safety Representatives and Safety Committee Regulations 1977 (SI 1977/500), Regs 11 (1) and 11(5)

6 an employer's failure to follow the statutorily-established redundancy procedure (EP Act, s 101 (1)

7 alleged unlawful discrimination on racial grounds (RR Act, s 54)

8 alleged unlawful discrimination on grounds of sex or marital status (SD Act, s 63)

9 the effects of an equality clause in the contracts of men and women (Equal Pay Act 1970, s 2 as amended)

10 the question of whether there is equal access for men and women to occupational pension schemes (Occupational Pension Schemes (Equal Access to Membership) Regulation, 1976)

11 whether an organization is an independent trade union recognized to any extent for the purpose of collective bargaining, and whether the employer has complied with the requirements as to consultation on the question of contracting out of occupational pension schemes (Occupational Pensions Schemes (Certification of Employments) Regulations 1975, SI 1975/1927, Reg 4 (2) and (3)

12 an employer's action short of dismissal to restrict an employee's rights to belong to a trade union and take part in its activities (EP(C) Act 1978, s 23)

208

13 alleged unreasonable exclusion or expulsion from a trade union (Emp Act 1980, s 4 (4))

14 the employer's failure to accede to a request for a secret ballot in circumstances where it was reasonably practicable for him to do so (Emp Act 1980, s 1).

However, we might note that the common law courts and the industrial tribunals share jurisdiction with respect to dismissal claims. The courts have a jurisdiction in respect of 'wrongful dismissal' and the industrial tribunals with 'unfair dismissal'. Different claims might therefore arise from the same set of circumstances and turn upon the same set of facts, and might have to be resolved in two distinct 'courts'. In practice, proceedings in the tribunal would probably be stayed pending conclusion of the court hearing. Although the Lord Chancellor (and the Secretary of State for Scotland) has ben assigned the power (under EP(C) Act, s 131) to assign wrongful dismissal claims to the tribunals, this has not yet been done and 'breach' cases remain within the jurisdiction of the ordinary civil courts. It may not be done because, as Hepple indicates, there are a number of supposed benefits in keeping the two distinct (Hepple & O'Higgins, 1981, p 386).

The Employment Appeal Tribunal

Appeal on questions of law lies to the Employment Appeal Tribunal in respect of decisions by the tribunals under the Equal Pay, Sex Discrimination and Race Relations Acts and the Employment Protection and Employment Acts. Application is required within 42 days of despatch of the tribunal's written decision or order. (Appeal on decisions under the Docks and Harbours Act, the Industrial Training Act, and the Health and Safety at Work Act, conversely, lead to the Queen's Bench Division of the High Court, where the appeal is heard by a single judge.)

Appeal is important in connection with prediction of the likely decisions of the tribunals (as indeed is the case also in the courts). Since a higher court's decisions bind all lower courts, the decisions of the Employment Appeal Tribunal (EAT), on matters of law decided on appeal, are therefore binding on the tribunals (see Hepple, 1981, p 385), in their interpretation of the law (the facts could, however, lead to different judgements). The EAT would in turn be bound by the decisions of the Court of Appeal (Court of Session Inner House in Scotland) and the House of Lords, but not by the High Court (or its Scottish equivalent). As the number of appeals heard and decided increases, the interpretations of law by individual tribunals (the cause of very real difficulties experienced in their early years) are becoming more standardized and predictable.

The EAT is, like the tribunals, made up of three elements. Judges of the High Court or the Court of Session (in Scotland), one of whom is President, and any one of whom will hear a particular appeal in the company of two or four other persons. These other persons are drawn from two panels representative of the employer and the worker interest and usually experienced in actually representing these interests; one or two from each panel will sit with the judge to hear the appeal, although the judge with one appointed member may, with the consent of the parties, hear the appeal. The EAT has a central office in London, but may sit at any other place in Great Britain, as it has done occasionally. Its decisions may in turn be appealed to the Court of Appeal, and ultimately to the House of Lords, on points of law, and in this way, it is integrated into the general court system.

Procedures

The rules of procedure applied in these cases are those contained in the Industrial Tribunals (Rules of Procedure) Regulations, (SI No. 884, 1980), but separate regulations govern appeals both under the Industrial Training Act, the Health and Safety at Work Act, and against non-discrimination notices under the Sex Discrimination and Race Relations Acts. As Hepple summarizes this aspect:

'The method of getting a case before a tribunal is far simpler than the corresponding procedure for getting a case (even a small claim in the county court) before the ordinary courts; the average time it takes for a claim to come to hearing is about 9 or 10 weeks, compared with many months or even years in the ordinary courts; tribunals are relatively informal, not being bound by the rules of evidence which apply in the ordinary courts, interpreting procedural rules flexibly, and being designed to put the parties, particularly the unrepresented applicant or respondent at ease; and they are inexpensive ... because legal representation is the exception rather than the rule, with costs generally being awarded against a party only for frivolous or vexatious conduct' (Hepple, 1981, pp 361-2).

In order to commence proceedings the individual needs only to send an originating application to the appropriate Central Office of Industrial Tribunals (COIT) in London, Glasgow or Belfast. This will contain names and addresses of the applicant and persons against whom relief is sought, together with the grounds (and the particulars of them) on which relief is sought. Although a form exists for this purpose, it is not absolutely necessary to employ it.

The COIT will register the application and will serve a copy of it by post on the respondent informing him of the means of and time limits for entering an appearance, the consequences of failure to do so and his right to receive a copy of the decision. The respondent may enter an appearance within 14 days of receiving the copy, but the Chairman of the tribunals has the power to grant extensions of time, provided that he considers the respondent has reasonable grounds for seeking this. The entry of appearance must be in writing and give the respondent's full name and address, and it must state whether he intends to resist the application, and if he does, it must give sufficient particulars to indicate the grounds on which he will do so. On receipt of this, the COIT will send a copy to any other party to the case.

Before the hearing, conciliation officers designated by ACAS, will attempt to promote a settlement of disputed matters placed before the tribunal, particularly those of unfair dismissal, discrimination, and a number of statutory claims under the employment protection legislation. In unfair dismissal cases the officers are placed under a duty to attempt to secure reinstatement or re-engagement. Only if that is not possible do they try to secure agreement to compensation on terms appearing to them to be equitable.

Under the 1980 Regulations, the Chairman of the tribunals may decide upon or agree to a pre-hearing assessment (PHA) in which consideration is given to prospects of success of the application and an opinion expressed on this. The object is to weed out the hopeless cases, and save everyone time and cost; when the opinion is that an application should be withdrawn, the applicant may be warned that he risks having an order for costs

211

being made against him if he persists in his application.

The parties to a case are given at least 14 days notice of the hearing, but may agree to a shorter notice. Applications are heard by a tribunal comprising a barrister or solicitor chairman (appointed by the Lord Chancellor) and two lay members, drawn from two panels constituted after consultation with employers' and employees' organizations respectively appointed by the Secretary of State for Employment. In the absence of one lay member the tribunal may proceed to the hearing with the agreement of the parties.

All three members are equal participants in the decision-making process, although the decision itself is drafted by the Chairman and signed only by him. Usually the decision and the reasons for it are given orally at the end of the hearing and the written statement is transmitted to the parties later. The tribunal's decision need not be unanimous. Only when the decision is entered on the register does it become binding.

The remedies

Where the individual is accorded rights under the legislation, he has the opportunity to refer his complaint or claim for relief to the industrial tribunal. In some cases, the employer may also refer a disputed matter to the tribunal. Where the industrial tribunal finds that the claim presented by the individual is well-founded, it has authority to award a variety of remedies, appropriate to the right in question. However, their main sanction is an award of a sum of money, either 'as due' or as compensation for infringement of a right or for loss.

In some cases the tribunal may issue a statement which establishes what rights the parties have in some area. Where there has been a failure to act in accordance with those rights and obligations which the legislation requires to be stated, the tribunal may also order a payment to be made, as being the sum due:

1 A finding that the statement of particulars of the employment contract or that the statement of changes in these has not been issued or is incomplete, may be remedied by a statement of what ought to have been included and it will then be deemed that the employer had issued the statemnt in this form. (EP(C) Act, s 11).

212

2 A finding that the pay statement or statement of deductions from pay is incomplete or inaccurate in some regard, may be remedied by making a declaration to that effect, and where unnotified deductions are found to have been made, the tribunal may award that the employer pay to the employee as a maximum a sum equal to the total of the unnotified deductions over the 13 weeks preceding the date of the application. (EP (C) Act, s 11).

3 A finding that an employer either refused unreasonably to give a written statement of reasons for dismissal or that what he did give was either inadequate or untrue, may be remedied by a declaration of what it finds the employer's reasons to have been, and an award that the employer pay to the employee a sum equal to the amount of two weeks' pay (EP (C) Act, s 53).

In other cases, enforcement may be by way of ordering a payment which is due under contract terms required by Statute.

4 A finding that the employer has not paid the whole or part of a guarantee payment (EP(C) Act, ss 34-6) or of a protective award (EP Act, s 102), or the remuneration due under a suspension on medical grounds (EP(C) Act, s 22), or for time off with pay for trade union duties (EP(C) Act, s 30 (3), is to be remedied by ordering the payment of the amount found to be due. The amount due will vary, according to the entitlement stipulated in the statute. A guarantee payment, for example, is the normal or average day's pay (EP(C) Act, s 14), but with a maximum (curently £10) which is reviewed annually. Maternity pay is fixed at six weeks pay at the rate of nine-tenths of a week's pay reduced by the amount of maternity allowance payable (whether the individual is entitled to it or not) (EP(C) Act, ss 34-6), and a protective award of a week's pay for each week of the protected period.

Treatment of redundancy, and of lay-off and short-time working of sufficient duration to qualify is based on the principle of a fixed compensation for a loss of opportunity to earn remuneration for a reason which is not the employee's fault.

5 A finding that an employee was dismissed by reason of redundancy (including lay-off and short-time working under certain specified conditions in ss 87-89 of EP(C) Act)

213

determines in effect whether the employer must pay compensation and whether the Department of Employment must pay a rebate to the employer in respect of his redundancy payment. The redundant employee is entitled to receive compensation at the rate of his week's pay (up to the current limit of £145 per week) multiplied by the years of service and age formula (which also applies in the case of the basic award in unfair dismissal). This formula allows up to 20 years to be counted calculated backwards from the 'weightiest' ones:

(a) 1-1/2 week's pay for each full year of employment between the ages of 41 and 65 years (60 in the case of women);
(b) 1 week's pay for each year between ages 22 and 41, years; and
(c) 1/2 week's pay for each year between 18 and 22 years (EP(C) Act, s 72).

There are two sources of complaint in connection with rights to 'time off', one that time was (unreasonably) refused and the other that (in relevant cases) payment due was not made. Enforcement then involves 'just and equitable' compensation in the one and an order to pay the amount due in the other.

6 A complaint that the employer has not allowed the employee time off without pay for any purpose specified in the EP(C) Act, ss 27, 28 and 29, is remedied by an award of compensation in an amount considered to be just and equitable in all the circumstances having regard to the employer's default and to any provable loss arising from this (EP(C) Act, s 30). Such compensation is additional to any remuneration which may be due to a trade union official for time off.

7 This is similar to the remedies available for refusing time off and failing to pay for time off as required under the Safety Representatives and Safety Committee Regulations (SI 1977/500, Regs 11(1) and 11(5)). In the first case, the award is that compensation considered just and equitable, and in the second, the amount due (either normal pay or average earnings for the period (Reg 4 (c)).

8 In the case of time off to look for work or make arrangements for training in the event of redundancy, the tribunal may

declare the complaint well founded, and order the employer to pay the amount which it finds due to the complainant, that is the remuneration at his appropriate hourly rate for the period of time off or for the period when he or she was refused time off, or both, subject to the limit of two-fifths of a week's pay for the notice period applicable to the individual (EP(C) Act, s 31).

9 In the case of time off for ante-natal care, the remedy available is payment equivalent to the hourly rate for the period of time off where the employer unreasonably refused it, or the amount found by the tribunal to be due to her (the whole or part of the amount of the appropriate hourly rate for the period of time off) where the complaint was that the employer had not paid the whole or part of the amount to which she was entitled where time off was granted (EP(C) Act, s 31A).

The other major category of jurisdiction is that concerning unlawful discrimination. This is in two parts. The first concerns decisions to dismiss which are taken on the basis of considerations other than those derived from the requirements of the job, and the other discrimination on grounds of race, sex or trade union activity, membership or non-membership.

10 The preferred remedy where a tribunal finds a complaint of unfair dismissal to be well founded is an order for reinstatement or re-engagement at the discretion of the Tribunal and if the employee wishes (EP(C) Act, s 69). The employer has a counter argument that it is not reasonably practicable to comply but if he does not convince the tribunal, there is provision for the alternative remedy of compensation, and compensation is also to be awarded where no order is made.

Where reinstatement or re-engagement occurs (and therefore where the employee does not remain dismissed) but the employer does not comply fully with the terms of the order, the tribunal must award compensation up to a limit of £7,500.

Where no order is made for reinstatement or re-engagement, and where an order is made and not complied with, the tribunal is to award compensation in three distinct parts.

(A) A basic award calculated on the basis of age and length of service, (as outlined on p 214 above) but subject to a maximum of 20 years multiplied by 1-½ weeks' service pay at the going rate (currently £145) and subject to reduction for contributory fault (EP(C) Act, ss 72 and 73).

In cases where the principal reason was to do with union membership or activity, or non-membership, the basic award is subject to a minimum of £2,000 (currently, although variable by order), and is fixed at a minimum of 2 weeks' pay in certain redundancy cases.

(B) A compensatory award in such amount as the tribunal finds just and equitable up to a maximum of £7,500 (EP(C) Act, s 74). This is additional to the basic award but will be reduced by the amount of redundancy payment above the basic award in cases where both apply. The amount is also subject to deduction for contributory fault on the part of the dismissed individual. It is to be determined on the basis of estimated loss, (not by formula related to pay rate, age or length of service as in the case of the basic award) and can, therefore, vary from a zero award to the maximum figure according to circumstances.

(C) The third element in the award comprises either an additional award or a special award:

(a) in any case where the employer cannot satisfy the tribunal that it was not practicable to comply with a re-instatement or re-engagement order, an award will be made in one of the following forms:

(i) an additional award in an amount judged just and equitable within the range of 13 to 26 weeks' pay, to apply in any such case

(ii) an additional award in those cases where the reason for dismissal is connected with race or sex within the range 26 to 52 weeks' pay.

(b) in any case of unfair dismissal where the principal reason for dismissal is connected with trade union activities or membership or non-membership, and where the employee seeks reinstatement or re-engagement, a special award of one week's pay multiplied by 104, or £10,000, whichever is the greater, and subject to a maximum of £20,000 shall be made. This may, however, be reduced for the reasons listed above and must be reduced by at least the same fraction as the basic award where contributory fault is established.

If the circumstances specified in (a) and the conditions listed in (b) are met, the limits of the special award are increased to one week's pay multiplied by 156, or £15,000, whichever is the greater. The same reductions as above apply here.

The jurisdictions concerned with unlawful discrimination on grounds of race or sex, attracts a rather different range of sanctions. These are treated similarly and in both cases, the civil courts have a comparable jurisdiction in cases not concerned with employment.

11 In the areas of race and sex discrimination, where the tribunal finds that an act complained of is unlawful by virtue of Part II of the Race Relations Act or of Part II of the Sex Discrimination Act it has authority to award such remedies as it considers just and equitable from the range of:

(a) an order declaring the rights of the parties in relation to the act complained of

(b) an order that the respondent pay to the complainant compensation of an amount corresponding to any damages he could have been ordered by a county court or a sheriff court to pay, had the matter not been an employment case but subject to the limit imposed on the compensation element for unfair dismissal

(c) a recommendation that within a specified period, the respondent take such action as the tribunal considers practicable to reduce or remove the adverse effects upon the complainant of the act complained of.

In both cases there is a provision for individual conciliation at the request of both parties or where the conciliation officer thinks he can help achieve a settlement, before the matter progresses to the industrial tribunal.

12 Where the tribunal finds that a claim in respect of an equality clause and of arrears of remuneration or damages in respect of its contravention, is well-founded it may remedy the situation by awarding the arrears of remuneration or damages (up to two years' prior to the claim) (Equal Pay Act 1970, s 2).

Discrimination in respect of trade union membership is the third area, and this may conveniently be linked with the new sanctions for excluding or expelling a person unreasonably from a trade union.

13 In the area of discrimination against trade unionists, a finding that an employer took action short of dismissal against an individual for belonging to or taking part in trade union activities, empowers the tribunal to make such award of compensation to the employee as it considers to be just and equitable in all the circumstances having regard to the infringement of the right and any consequential loss, but taking into account any contributory fault on the part of the claimant and any expenses incurred or benefit foregone (EP(C) Act, ss 24 and 26).

An individual who is dismissed for non-membership of a trade union may secure remedies as listed in paragraph 10 above. He may 'join' the union in any such action for compensation for unfair dismissal, and the tribunal may award the whole or part of the compensation against the union joined. This is subject to a minimum of £10,000 (and will be added to the basic and compensatory awards). Equitable compensation for the employer's failure to hold a ballot is to be paid to the trade union.

14 A complaint to the tribunal that an individual was unreasonably denied membership of a union or unreasonably expelled from membership requires the tribunal to determine whether the union acted reasonably or unreasonably in accordance with equity and on the substantial merits of the case (and not merely whether it acted in accordance with its rules or not). If the tribunal finds the exclusion or expulsion unreasonable, it must make a declaration to this effect.

The individual may then make an application to an industrial tribunal for compensation, if he has been admitted or readmitted, or to the Employment Appeal Tribunal in other circumstances. In the first case, the tribunal may award such compensation as it considers appropriate in relation to the loss sustained by him. In the second, the Employment Appeal Tribunal is required to award compensation which it considers just and equitable in the circumstances, and in both cases subject to the rules of duty to mitigate any contributory fault.

Assessment of penalties

The processes and penalties for upholding the values which are embodied in law, are designed to focus the minds of those to whom they are intended to apply. Where individuals are not *persuaded* as to the validity of the legal and associated moral prescriptions, the penalties are intended to *compel* compliance. Of course, people do generally obey the law for a variety of reasons and the penalties for not doing so are for them mere academic matters. Where they do not do so, it is difficult to say whether the penalties are significant or not. They may compel compliance, but there is also a view that they have often become mere payments for the privilege of breaking the law (see McCarthy, 1983).

A consideration of the remedies which are actually awarded (as distinct from the maxima which are in principle available) suggests that they may have little power to compel employer compliance with the underlying philosophies of recent legislation. Although the amounts involved may be significant for the complainant, the average amounts indicated in table 13 (on p 220) may be a relatively small price to pay for breaking the law, in letter or in spirit. The median payment of compensation by the tribunals in 1982 was a mere £1,201, and in less than 2 per cent of the cases upheld was the maximum amount awarded. The preferred remedy of re-instatement or re-engagement was applied in only 2 per cent of the conciliated settlements and in only 1.1 per cent of the cases upheld before the Tribunals.

The costs in time and trouble in appearing before one of these bodies may be more onerous on the employer, particularly where he is small in scale or where he considers that it is 'important' that he should not risk losing the case. Many small employers have now been taken out from this system of regulation, and it is left to develop a standard for the larger ones. But, one is left with the possibility that employers may assent to these legally-expressed values largely for reasons to do with esteem, not cost; to be thought a 'bad employer' might be a more serious outcome of a complaint than to be 'fined' the relatively small sums which figure in compensation awards. To the extent that public esteem is important, the law may succeed in its primary purpose of regulating behaviour without having to rely directly upon penalties and punishments.

Table 13

Unfair Dismissal Cases, 1982

Category and amount awarded	Conciliation cases no	per cent	Tribunal cases no	per cent
All cases	21,600	100	11,509	100
Cases withdrawn dismissed	11,053	51.2	7,974	69.3
Cases settled upheld	10,547	48.8	3,535	30.7
Reemployment	425	2.0	136	1.1
Compensation	9,879	45.7	2,045	17.8
Other remedy	243	1.1	1,354	10.2
Compensation amounts				
Not known	–	0.0	36	1.8
< £50	149	1.5	9	0.4
£50-£99	638	6.4	35	1.7
£100-£199	1,860	18.8	108	5.2
£200-£299	1,739	17.6	110	5.8
£300-£399	1.118	11.3	117	5.7
£400-£499	698	7.1	99	4.9
£500-£999	1,950	19.7	404	19.8
£1000-£1999	944	9.6	525	25.7
£2000-£3000	472	4.8	434	21.2
£4000-£4999	99	1.0	51	2.5
£5000-£8999	147	1.5	111	5.4
£9000 and over	65	0.7	6	0.3
Median Award	£1,201			
Cases where basic award only	–	–	145	7.1
maximum award made	–	–	38	1.9

Source: Department of Employment Gazette, October, 1983, p 449

In spite of this, both those who obey and those who break the law may still be regarded as orienting their behaviour to the values which are embodied in it. He who breaks the law with the intention of paying the price for so doing, is at least as aware of the law as he who obeys its prescriptions and proscriptions. The values which it expresses are still, to some extent, influential upon his conduct.

Summary: enforcement

The mechanisms and remedies supporting enforcement which have been reviewed in this chapter represent two quite distinct approaches. In the one, the underlying thought is that industrial relations matters should be kept under some central (State) control, which would normally imply that control should be through the formal court system. This system continues to be relevant to both criminal and civil actions which are not especially concerned with employment matters, even if the criminal act or the civil wrong involved may happen to arise in that context.

The alternative view is that the court system should not provide the 'court of first instance' for specifically employment claims and disputes but that there should be some more informal means of securing resolution of differences with the higher courts taking over only if this fails in some respects. This still allows the hierarchy of the civil courts to be retained as relevant to appeals, but provides a different (and potentially less formal) starting point.

Some attempt has been made to develop this second alternative in recent years. A broad-brush distinction might however be made between the individual employee rights which fall within the jurisdiction of the tribunals, and the rights of workers and collective rights which may fall there but may also fall within the arbitration system.

Individual employee rights are dealt with for the most part through the tribunals as specially designed informal courts. These keep the enforcement process within the judicial system but aspire (albeit not always successfully) to administer justice on a more informal and less off-putting basis. There is a growing concern that this is not really being achieved as legal representation increasingly imbues the tribunal's proceedings with greater formality. There is also some concern that the remedies which are

221

available to the tribunal are not sufficiently significant to act as a deterrent to proscribed action, and the force of the law remains essentially moral.

On both grounds, therefore, ie the lack of bite in the remedies available to the disadvantaged employee and the tendency to greater formalization of the tribunal system, there are doubts being expresssed as to whether the much-vaunted revolution in employment law and employment rights has really materialized. For the employer, the system of enforcement does uphold certain principles of which he cannot remain unaware and may well accept as morally binding, but the degree of compulsion which the remedies effect may be small.

Collective rights or the rights which accrue to 'workers' in their collective orientations, are usually dealt with through the conciliation and arbitration process which involves machinery not, strictly, within the court system. This is, however, only a partial system and overlapping jurisdictions are to be found, with both the CAC and the tribunals enforcing collective rights or rights which are attached in some way to the trade union presence in different ways and by recourse to quite different remedies (for example, compensation in the one case and imposition of terms and conditions of employment in the other).

Readings

Hepple and O'Higgins: (1979), pp 361-87.
Rideout: (1980), pp 108-26. CAC: Annual Reports.
Howells and Barrett: (1982), pp 61-76.
Angel: (1984).

9

Employers' objectives and organization

The decentralization of decisions

In the British approach to industrial relations, decisons are taken by the employers and employees who are involved in them, (whatever the extent to which they are organized (see above, p 74)). The State's role is to establish their general status and the broad limits to their lawful authority to decide and act, and thereafter to leave the actual decisions to be taken by them, severally or jointly. The underlying principle that decisions ought to be taken at a level as close to the affected persons as possible, is strongly entrenched in British culture.

Delegation results in two main processes. This might be either individual bargaining between employer and employee such as in the establishment of the contract of employment. The main alternative is collective bargaining such as when the employer (or his association's representatives) seeks to reach agreement on terms with representatives of his (and possibly other employers') workers. Over the past two centuries both forms of bargaining have been emphasized at different times and for different categories of worker. Individual bargaining during the early phase of the industrial period was, however, virtually synonymous with what Flanders refers to as unilateral imposition' of decisions and rules acknowledging the situationally-induced inequality of bargaining power of the two parties which was not reduced by the operation of law.

As this gave way, progressively, to collective bargaining and to the introduction of an 'external' influence on the domestic decisions within the undertaking, the possibility of these decisions being taken at two distinct levels emerged.

Two broad-brush analyses have been made of this phenomenon in the literature on industrial relations.

223

1   The first reflects upon the traditional two-tier arrangement, in which a national bargaining structure existed alongside a domestic bargaining system of some kind. The one attempted to provide some standards which helped reduce some of the wage-benefit and labour-cost uncertainties for the individual employer. The other tried to retain local discretion to deal with the operational uncertainties *within* that national framework of rules and guidance usually on the assumption that at the sub-national level there was a homogeneous structure of single establishment undertakings (see: Clegg, 1979, pp 62-123; Marsh, 1965, pp 142-78; Flanders, 1970; Goodman *et al*, 1977).

2   The other concentrates attention on the position in multi-plant (and multi-national) undertakings (see Thomson and Hunter, 1975, pp 23-40; Gill, 1974, pp 22-35; Ramsey, 1971, pp 42-48; C I R 1974, (Report No 85); Department of Employment, 1971; Roberts and Gennard, 1970, pp 147-66; McCarthy, in Kessler and Weekes, 1971, pp 83-89; Hawkins, 1971, pp 198-213). Although these tend to identify a similar two-tier arrangement (now seen to be between oompany and plant levels) they also present a picture of greater complexity than a simple either-or characterization allows for (see Thomson and Hunter, 1975, pp 25-26).

It is, however, possible that actual practice emphasizes a mixture of these two, in that the type of two-tier organization adopted varies with the purposes of the parties and the subject matter of the negotiation. At the present time, both industry-wide and domestic 'two-tier' arrangements are to be found side by side, distinguished mainly by subject and purpose. Organization might, in other words, be regarded as a function of the 'project' which the employer wished to develop with the workers' representatives.

In both of these analyses, however, the individual unit of government (or undertaking) has been somewhat neglected, by the assumption in each case that undertakings and establishments need to be separately distinguished. In the one case, the national structures were seen as the prime agency, and the domestic unit as a residual; in the other, the domestic was equated with the plant or establishment almost to the complete exclusion of the company or undertaking in the multi-plant situation. The company may, however, represent the domestic in

224

the national context and the centre in the domestic context, and for these reasons should be considered in its own right.

In this chapter, we examine the objectives and organization of the employer at these different levels, looking first at those of the individual employer and then at those of the employers' association. A similar examination of the trade union's objectives and organization follows in chapter 10. These objectives and organization are then related to each other in chapter 11, to the functions of collective bargaining in chapter 12, and its outcomes in chapter 13.

THE INDIVIDUAL EMPLOYER

The 'employer' in the private sector is a 'businessman' first and an employer second. The primary task of the business is to generate wealth in some form, and it is the primary task of management to realize this objective by combining the various factors of production. In a market economy, the generation of wealth must necessarily occur within a market framework, and the nature of that market (in terms of its size and trends) is likely to constrain both business and industrial relations decisions. Because the business requires the services of labour (as one of the factors of production) the 'employer' concept becomes applicable and the size and composition of the workforce required can also be expected to influence decisions about policies and strategies. To speak of 'the employer' unduly personalizes the concept, because at the present time the employer may be a corporation or a company rather than a natural person. There are still many small companies and owner-managed businesses in existence run by individual businessmen. Where the business is a large-scale enterprise the only natural persons in evidence are the directors and managers who run it. They take the place of the businessman.

Employers' objectives

The employer's objectives in industrial relations are derived from his primary business function. A list of long-term industrial relations objectives (see Harbison and Coleman, 1951, p 7) is likely to be consistent with a description of the normal management objectives in enterprise. As a whole, however, these

225

objectives have to be seen as developed from a base of legalized and legitimated rights which have to be preserved in order to continue the business and management roles which have been assigned. For this reason the first objective is likely to be that of preserving the system on which the pursuit and realization of the objectives depend.

1   The preservation of the system of free enterprise as the main source of business and managerial prerogatives and freedoms. This is a far-reaching objective and one which has broader political connotations than the others, which are nevertheless likely to support it. This objective might also lead him to accept membership of an employers' association which acts as a political pressure group in order to preserve the general ethos in which he operates (see below, pp 248-53).

2   The preservation and strengthening of the business enterprise itself. This emphasizes the maintenance of the 'instrument' through which customer needs might be served, growth fostered and profits made. Whatever orientations might exist amongst the labour force and whatever the degree of unionization, the businessman/manager is likely to pursue such long-term objectives, either by avoiding involvement with 'dual' organizations such as the unions or in any dealings he may have with them (see Cyert and March, 1963: Drucker, 1961).

3   The retention of effective control over the enterprise, an objective which is likely to place the emphasis on the local situation and upon local initiatives by management to secure it. The manager might regard himself as being delegated the task (and duty) of efficiently allocating the productive resources of enterprise. In the light of this, he would seek to preserve his power and authority to control, if only to permit him to continue to discharge the duty. He might also, of course, wish to continue to enjoy the rights which go along with the obligations; but giving up control to any other, even joint, body could be expected to rouse resistance.

Thus, in dealing with trade unions representing his employees, the employer is likely to be mindful of this range of essentially business objectives, however they may be modified in the immediate situation and in response to short-term needs and problems. But once organized opposition is established, for example through the organization of trade unions which the employer then recognizes, he is also likely to develop objectives in relation to them. These in the long term are likely to tie in with the first and fourth objectives.

4   The establishment of 'stable and businesslike' relationships with the workers and any bargaining agents. In effect, these goals are likely to manifest themselves in attempts to secure union acceptance of, and support for, the above objectives (or at least the first three of them). Securing such ends, or preventing alternative goals from being pursued at the negotiating table, might help to achieve a stable and businesslike relationship with the union(s).

5   The realization of personal ambitions and goals which the businessman/manager might like to sustain and serve in any such interactions. Although these might accept the perspective of 'free enterprise' and recognize that progress depends upon meeting system targets within his own command, these are essentially his own goals, intended to improve his own well-being and to advance his own career.

The employer can be expected to pursue such objectives in industrial relations, regardless of the size and nature of his undertaking and of whether his employees are unionized. But how he organizes to pursue them is likely to vary according to the kind of situation (measured on market and organizational dimensions) in which he finds himself. It does not follow, for example, that the employer must always seek to realize industrial relations objectives through collective bargaining in the institutional sense. The fourth objective may depend upon some kind of organized opposition being present, but the others might apply to the employer in any situation. The first and fourth might lead the individual employer to consider joining with fellow employers in an association as a means of realizing them.

There is some evidence to suggest, for example, that some employers are developing a multiplicity of channels for the development of commitment by way of communication, particularly in the larger undertakings and establishments (see Daniel and Millward, 1983, pp 130-2). These involve distinct consultative, participative, or bargaining channels, and involve different combinations of management and worker representatives, each pursuing a distinct project. Discussion within them may focus on changes in product mix, division of labour, use of new technology, working practices, and similar issues.

The idea that industrial relations policies and practices are to be discussed in monolithic terms is to be pursued with caution, therefore, because different situations may so constrain decisions as to allow a number of different but parallel outputs to be generated, all comparably valid.

The influence of the organizational pattern

The employer can be expected to pursue the broadly-conceived objectives through a variety of strategies, which are likely to be influenced by the underlying pattern of the relationship to the undertaking to the market, that is, by business considerations (see Ansoff, 1975). Using either product-life or life-system models (see Lippitt, 1969) undertakings might be categorized into juvenile, economically- and organizationally-dynamic firms (often small or smallish), youthful and thrusting undertakings (large as the market defines large), mature and stably profitable corporations (usually large and well-established) and aged and stagnant or declining industries (usually fighting, however successfully or unsuccessfully, a rearguard action). Whilst these situational characteristics do not determine the organization and practice of industrial relations, they do constrain the decision-makers in such a way that some patterns are more likely outcomes than others.

The effect of these variations upon industrial relations organization and practice is usually considered in terms of the tendencies towards centralization and decentralization in the structure of decision-taking and bargaining and in terms of constitutionalism and 'ad hockery' in the way industrial relations affairs are handled. Accommodation of these counter-vailing pressures is usually seen to produce a two-tier arrangement and either an informal or a formalized system of activity.

The employer may have a choice between a highly centralized arrangement (in which all decisions are taken at the centre and serve as binding rules upon all subordinate units) and a highly decentralized arrangement (in which near-complete autonomy to decide is given to units with little or no control imposed from the centre). Some employers may see this choice as one between joining an employers' association and handling industrial relations themselves. These options may, however, be constrained by the nature of the business enterprise and therefore any description of the employer must be cast in terms of differences on these dimensions.

Size of undertakings

Businesses vary in size or scale as measured by their assets, their turnover, or their profits and this variation is in the broadest sense linked with the form of their business organization. Some are organized as individual traders, some as partnerships; the majority are, however, organized as registered companies, whether private or public. Under the new definitions introduced by the Companies Act 1980, the public company tends to be larger than the private, and both are probably larger than the partnership and the individual trader.

Impact on industrial relations features is more likely to be associated, however, with size measured in terms of the number of people employed. Whole industries may be characterized as large scale (like iron and steel) or small scale (like baking) in respect of the size of establishment (or plant). Large undertakings (or units of government) and small undertakings do not so readily characterize industries, because of the possibilities for both horizontal and vertical integration of plants. Large undertakings do, however, tend to be associated with large establishments and with multi-plant composition (see Bolton Committee *Report*, 1971, p 41 f).

Payroll size has been demonstrated to link, albeit tenuously, with morale and orientation to work (see Acton Society Trust, 1953/1957; Revans, 1960; Ingham, 1969). It is associated with a propensity to join trade unions and therefore with 'union density' (with larger establishments having a higher proportion of their employees in union membership) as well as industrial action (see Shorey, 1975). It is frequently held that 'small-scale' undertakings (as in retailing or many of the other trades embraced by Wages Councils) are notoriously difficult for the trade unions to organize. Conversely, the large-scale undertaking or establishment is frequently considered to be more likely to have trade unions and industrial relations problems.

Larger undertakings and establishments are also more likely to have both more specialist personnel staffs and increasingly elaborate machinery for handling industrial relations issues and problems (see Daniel and Millward, 1983, pp 130-2). They are also considered to be suitable cases for treatment by the introduction of formal structures of worker participation in strategic decision-making (Bullock Committee *Report*, 1977; EEC Fifth Directive). Size may also have some bearing on decisions to join or stay in membership of an employers' association (see below, pp 241-44).

Size may, however, be an accidental (if also partial) correlate. It may be because juvenile and declining undertakings are more likely to be associated with one range of sizes and youthful and mature firms with another, that size may produce the correlations it does. It may however mask the nature of the constraints which are imposed upon decisions about organization and practice.

Composition of undertakings

This possibility is more readily acknowledged in the discussions of the effects of the composition of undertakings upon industrial relations organization and practice (see Knight, 1969). This term 'composition' is used to refer to the extent to which and the manner in which processes within single establishments and between establishments within multi-establishment undertakings are alike or unalike, and complement or replicate one another. This factor might mitigate the simple effect of size if only because it might admit major differences in the pattern or mix of market relationships. Also, in both large private and the public sector undertakings (see also below, p 264 *et seq*), a multiplicity of establishments might reduce the consequences of sheer size for both structure and behaviour.

In the private sector, some units of government coincide with the units of account, as in the case of the single plant company. Such coincidence of the two units may produce large or small scale, but generally it would be expected that they would be subject to a unitary control, or control from the centre. But such single plant undertakings may contain a variety of products or services, although their integrated nature is usually acknowledged as contrasting with the multi-establishment undertaking.

The multi-establishment undertaking occurs frequently in both private *and* public sectors, and is generally regarded as producing a variety of forms with implications for the way the employer is organized to deal with industrial relations. (Multi-national undertakings may be distinguished separately, but the subdivisions relevant to industrial relations organization may be regarded as comparable).

Doyle, for example, identifies three distinct compositions for the multi-plant company: the conglomerate, the process-integrated, and the single-system enterprise. In the conglomerate, a number of separate establishments produce distinct products not in any significant way related to one another. The process integrated undertaking possesses a number of separate plants which are integrated into a single process which yields a variety of products. In the single system category, the plants tend to be replicas of one another differentiated only or mainly by size and location (Doyle, in Marceau, 1969, pp 24-31).

Domestic organization of industrial relations

The seminal work on centralization and decentralization *within* the undertaking is the American study made by Baker and France (1954). This examines the 'common problem' in human organizations of handling:

> 'the dichotomy between the pressure for centralization of authority to assure corporate integrity, and the countering pressure for decentralization in administration to secure efficiency through ready response to diverse conditions and human motivations' (Baker and France, 1954, p 5).

Essentially, the view is taken that, on the one hand, there is pressure to secure uniformity and standardization in practice and, on the other, a pressure to provide flexibility (see also, Thomson and Hunter, 1975, pp 26 and 35-36). Their terminology has continued to be employed, (for example by the CIR in its study of multi-plant industrial relations (CIR Report No 85, 1974) and by the Department of Employment (in Manpower Paper No 5, 1971)).

Baker and France examined 46 multi-plant companies, for example, and found that only 41 per cent (19 companies) operated with an exclusively single plant bargaining unit and the remainder bargained on both plant and company bases (see Baker and France, 1954, p 150). Thomson and Hunter estimated that in Britain in 1974-5, probably about one million workers could have been covered primarily by Company level agreements (as distinct from agreements with a wider or a narrower coverage) (see Thomson and Hunter, 1975, p 23 footnote). Daniel and Millward's more recent survey reveals that company bargaining was regarded as the 'most important' influence (by level) on both manual and white collar worker pay settlements, in between a fifth and a quarter of their cases and plant/establishment bargaining as the most important influence in slightly more cases in respect of manual workers and slightly fewer cases in respect of white collar workers (see Daniel and Millward, 1983, pp 181-3). They also point out, (p 189) that the pattern varies from sector to sector, and that the position in manufacturing industry in both their and the Warwick survey, is broadly that about 40 percent regarded multi-employer agreee-ments as most important and about 40 per cent plant agreements (see also: Brown, 1981).

These analyses establish the presumption that the arrange-ments for negotiation may incline towards one or other end of a spectrum, and any particular manifestation will represent a reconciliation of the countervailing pressures in the two direc-tions. Although the Baker and France study, being concerned with American practice, expressed the centralization and decentralization largely in company versus plant terms in multi-plant situations, the same concepts can be and have been applied in the British context in recent years.

The main options

Empirical investigation of the patterns of organization suggest that about four options are open to the employer in the organization of bargaining arrangements. These are usually distinguished by reference to the locus of power or discretion to decide or accept the terms and conditions which emerge in negotiations. The most convenient manner in which to locate this authority is that which pins it upon the *level* of management within the corporate organization, regardless of whether it is single- or multi-establishment. In order to relate these options to national or domestic situations, these levels are associated with the company, the plant, the division or department. This convention is, for example, adopted by both Baker and France (1954, pp 150-62), and Thomson and Hunter (1975, pp 25-6).

The main options in descending order of centralization of decision, are as follows:

1 The dominantly central structure

This is represented by the structural arrangement under which all issues which are considered to be important in principle are settled at the centre of the company, either by the main board or by a staff which acts with that board's authority. Issues which do not raise matters of principle, and the implementation and monitoring of the decisions (settlements) reached (including the processing of grievances which do not raise questions of principle) are then allocated for resolution in the individual plant of the multi-plant company or within the individual division or department of the single-plant company. It follows that what are defined by the company management or by them and the unions jointly, as the important or major questions are negotiated by teams representing the whole company or workforce (or complete categories of labour within it where negotiations are conducted on (usually) a separate skill or occupation basis). Characteristically, it is the control of settlements which is retained at the centre, even though some resolution of questions is permitted at subordinate management levels.

2 The co-ordinated decentralized structure

This structure is to be distinguished by the fact that negotiations are conducted by separate and distinct negotiating teams, at departmental level in single plant undertakings and at plant level in multi-plant companies. Any one such team may conduct separate negotiations on behalf of distinct occupational groups, but it is characteristic of this option that the terms of all such groups are not negotiated by the same team. This implies a relatively high degree of autonomy to decide and settle issues. But the distinguishing element in this category is the existence of a tight brief prepared for all the negotiators by the central authority. This brief is intended to function as a statement of where the limits of local discretion lie, and as an indication of the circumstances under which the negotiators must refer back to the centre. The co-ordination of the actions of the local negotiating teams is intended to be preserved by this device, even though some discretion is allowed (usually to settle within the stated limits).

3 The constrained decentralized structure

This arrangement is similar to that identified in the preceding paragraph, but a much greater discretion is allowed to the local or subordinate unit teams to make their own settlements. They may reach their own decisions and settlements on issues which arise with a degree of speed which would not be consistent or possible with reference to the centre. However, the element of central control is retained to the extent that the centre prepares (either unilaterally or in consultation with the local management) a general budget which sets the monetary parameters for the settlement without influencing the form of the settlement in any more detailed terms. Containment of any settlement within the budget becomes the criterion of success in negotiations, and no more particular justification of the composition of that settlement is usually required. Thus, the local negotiators have a considerable autonomy to decide and act, but this is constrained by the centrally-sanctioned budget.

4 The autonomous unit structure

The 'packaging' of the constraints upon the local management in the shape of a budget, as in category 3, represents a kind of central service as well as a central control. The situation in which no such service is rendered may also be recognized. In this case, the local management is left to work out for itself the constraints upon their decisions and actions which arise from market forces in both the product and the labour markets; it must render this service to itself and formulate its decisions accordingly. This represents, therefore, the least controlled bargaining arrangement which is consistent with a collective determination of outcomes in this field. A similar freedom may be taken by or allowed to the worker/trade union group, who must then work out its own market intelligence and determine its own objectives and strategies.

Although these broad distinctions have been worked out in terms of negotiations with representatives of the unions, there is nothing in this which suggests that any one undertaking must have only one such structure. Where the 'project' approach (see above, pp 228) is adopted, one such project might be decentralized where another is centralized. The nature of the *task* (or objective) set for the project might be expected to exert some influence upon the form of organization adopted to deal with it (see Brown, 1960, p 18).

Discretion to decide on arrangement

Research studies may identify such variations on the general theme, and suggest that management, or unions, or both together, have discretion to determine such arangements to suit themselves. The literature on the subject provides three distinct answers to this question:

1 open choice
2 constrained choice
3 determination by the nature of the situation.

The grounds for these assertions are broadly as follows.

1 Open choice

The conclusion of the Commission on Industrial Relations (CIR) from an analysis of its many separately-referenced cases, was that the arrangement adopted appeared to be largely a matter of choice, particularly for the employer or management:

> 'Management in a company with a number of plants can, for industrial relations purposes, elect either to develop policies and negotiate agreements which cover the whole company or treat each plant separately, and a group controlling a number of companies or divisions can do likewise' (CIR Report, No 85, p 28).

Trade unions appeared to have much less discretion because of their dependent position. They 'have to take management authority structures and negotiating policies very much as they find them although the influence unions can exert may induce changes over a period of time or assist or hinder changes initiated by management' (CIR Report No 85, p 29). For the trade union to exert an influence, it is necessary for it to develop a pre-condition of solidarity and to mobilize power openly and explicitly behind the chosen objective. These may prove difficult to achieve in the particular case both in an absolute sense and relatively to the opportunity which presents itself to management.

Thomson and Hunter have argued, however, that:

> 'the locus of collective bargaining is not properly a 'choice' either for management or union. The outcome will depend on the mutual reconciliation of their preferences, basically through bargaining, or at least by the gradual adaptation and adjustment of attitudes and machinery' (Thomson and Hunter, 1975, p 25).

Nevertheless, with that caveat, we may recognize that in the CIR report it is implied that management can select either a centralizing or a decentralizing objective, regardless of the amount of bargaining or adjustment required to realize it.

> 'The aim can be to produce industrial relations ... arrangements which .... are either mainly or wholly controlled from group level or mainly or wholly decentralized to plant (or divisional) level. Some companies have adopted a mixture of both kinds of industrial relations policy and negotiating arrangements with the industrial relations needs of some produce divisions or plants being dealt with by a different negotiating structure from those of the rest of the group' (CIR Report No 85, p 28).

Furthermore, companies were seen in the case studies by the CIR both to have opportunity to change their patterns of emphasis and to have availed themselves of it. This might effect a change to new circumstances, or it might imply the use of a proposal to change the bargaining structure as a ploy in negotiation itself.

> 'Over a period of time (a company) may move in one direction to achieve one purpose and move back again to achieve another. Group controls may, for example, be relaxed to achieve gains through local productivity bargaining .... A period of tighter group control may then follow if there are net gains to be had from greater uniformity and from eliminating discrepancies which may have arisen in the previous period' (*ibid*, p 29).

Thus, by inference, the management may be regarded as having a relatively unfettered choice in this respect, at least initially.

2 Constrained choice

Clegg's view that employers' past recognition practices have contributed to the present multi-union structure of in-company industrial relations, also implies that, in principle, the employer has a choice in the matter of structuring bargaining units (see Clegg, 1972, pp 65-66). However, it also implies that once the choice has been made and recognition given on the basis of the trade union's existing membership, the structure of bargaining units will tend to remain a barrier to change. Although the choice exists, it is, by implication, easier to exercise at the point of first recognition, and more difficult to re-exercise once a structure has been established.

This idea also appears in the CIR Report, where management's freedom to create an arrangement is recognized to be constrained by what already exists:

> 'The main restriction (on management's achieving a mainly centralized or mainly decentralized policy) is likely to be the company's existing negotiating and other industrial relations arrangements' (CIR Report No 85, p 29).

Amongst the 'other' arrangements might be included the organizational structure of the management's own personnel (or industrial relations) function, as well as the trade union composition and structure within the undertaking or establishment. The development of a variety of project organizations within the domestic situation could provide some stimulus to change in the main negotiating arrangements, but this might also demand some change in the staffing and organization of the specialist functions within the management structure itself. The historical constraint might also be supplemented by the constraint of the circumstances in which the undertaking or establishment (or both) is operating. In the present changed climate, there is evidence of some change on these various dimensions as undertakings seek ways of improving their productivity and profitability through increased employee commitment.

The probability of constraint is also indicated by the findings of the Baker and France study and the analysis which Doyle makes of the size and composition of undertakings. Whether these are seen as constraints or as determining factors depends upon how one reads them and what weight one wants to attach to the possibility that differences are the result of 'mistake'. Regarding them as constraints suggests that:

(a) An integrated or continuous production process yielding a single final product is likely to lend itself to greater centralization than is variety and/or batch production under one roof. The correlation here is probably closest between degree of decentalization and variety of products or processes, although there may be other reasons for devolving accountability.
(b) Where the single-plant under the control of a company is in reality a single location on which a number of different plants are located, the likelihood of decentralization is greater than where all such production operations are all 'under one roof'.
(c) In the conglomerate enterprise, in the multi-product single plant undertaking and in the unit and small batch producing plant, the organization of industrial relations is likely to emphasize devolved decision-making. The local manager and/or supervisor needs to be in the position to determine (albeit in negotiation with the unions) both the general agreement terms and the disposal of both disciplinary and grievance issues.
(d) In the integrated and single system companies and plants, and in the mass and process production plants, the industrial relations organization is more likely to emphasize the requirement of centralization, both of agreements and authority to decide and act. Within this category, however, there is likely to be a variation according to the extent of difference between production activities, effecting opportunity for the development of supplementary local agreements and for the devolution of decisional authority for them.

All of these factors are thus seen to constrain the discretion of the parties.

3 Determination by the situation

If, however, these variables of size and composition were to be regarded as determinants, there would be no grounds for supposing that management or anyone else had any discretion in the matter. If the nature of the product or the division of labour admits of no discretion to the management or the trade unions in the way they organize and act, then once the nature of the independent variable (for example, the market situation) is known, so is the appropriate approach to and arrangement of industrial relations activities.

The nature and size of units within an industry might also influence the organization and membership of employers' associations (to which we now turn), although the dearth of empirical data on these limits the opportunity to test hypotheses of this kind.

EMPLOYERS' ASSOCIATIONS

The employers' association may be regarded as the formalization of the tacit combinations of employers which Adam Smith noted. It is more often seen as the functional equivalent of the 'trade union' on the other side of the employment contract. Where the trade union is regarded as an association of 'employees' or 'workmen', the employers' association may be regarded as an association of the individual employers treated as 'persons' regardless of their size and composition. Indeed, between 1871 and 1971, employers' associations had a similar legal status to the trade unions. Not until the Donovan Commission reported on the situation and the Industrial Relations Act 1971 made some changes, was a significant legal distinction made between them.

The comparison can be taken further by recognizing that just as the trade union is concerned with questions of both distribution and authority or power, so too is the employer's association. Employers cannot escape a concern with distribution because they too are subject to the contractual rules about consideration, but neither can they escape the necessity to defend the claimed prerogative power to run the business in the way they see best. Such concerns are independent of, or prior to, the existence of a trade union as such. This is obliquely recognized, for example, in Adam Smith's comment that employers must always be in a tacit agreement to keep wages as low as possible, a comment made before trade unions appeared.

For this reason, the 'composition' of the employers in an industry might be expected to exert an influence on the kind of function which is assigned to an association, and, therefore, on its ideology. Different industrial structures (see Florence, 1953; Bolton Committee *Report*, 1971) might be expected to influence the dominant frames of reference of those who occupy the status and role of employer in these industries.

A distinction might be made between the entrepreneurs (those who are essentially 'masters' in the original common law conception of natural persons who have committed their capital to a venture and have entered into contracts of service with some workers) and the 'employers' who are the managements of the corporations themselves, merely abstract corporate constitutions, not persons as such. This touches upon at least one aspect of the market influence upon the way units are run.

Historically, the master was a more prevalent type of employer than he is now. In those circumstances, the common notion that the employers' association was or is the equivalent of the workers' trade union, was a sensible one to adopt (as indeed it was adopted by the legislators in 1871). In that context, the individual masters could and did join employers' associations as individuals and the association bore a strong resemblance to the trade union.

Currently, the corporate form of business organization tends to dominate most trades and industries. The decision to join an employers' association is a decision of the Board of Directors (or its equivalent in those public sector bodies which are not required to register under the Companies Acts). This may commit the corporation as an abstract entity (and do so in respect of a large number of employees) but membership will occur through the persons of the directors (or their nominees) who attend the meetings and take part in the activities. They are in a different position from the 'masters', and it is doubtful whether the perspective which sees them as joining the equivalent of a worker's trade union remains a sensible one (as the change introduced by recent legislation implies).

This distinction seems to be a useful one to draw, both in respect of their historical evolution and in respect of what Munns (1967, pp 26-30)) refers to as 'the mood' of the current ones. Thus, until the fourth quarter of last century the employers' associations were mainly masters' associations, and whilst some of these continue in some trades to the present time (see Goodman *et al*, 1977), those which have succeeded them since that date have increasingly become associations of corporate employers (see Gill, *et al*, 1978). The mix within associations might, however, account for some part at least of the differences in philosophy and approach discernible.

Distribution of membership

It is difficult to test the above hypothesis, however, given the paucity of empirical data on employers' associations. We know something about their incidence and size, but the surveys of distribution by industry tend to produce inconclusive results. The general distribution of membership within such organizations is often quoted as a disadvantage, as for example by Grant and Marsh (1977, p. 212) in their evaluation of the Confederation of British Industry (CBI) as a pressure group (see, below, pp 250-52). They regard the tensions arising from the different ideological positions of the different categories of members as detracting from its ability to speak with a single voice to Government.

At the time when the Donovan Commission made its asessment (1966) there were in existence in Britain about 1,350 employers' bodies, usually defined by 'industry', and some as 'federations' of local associations, and some simply as associations, whether local or national in scope. These bodies ranged tremendously in size. At one end of the scale was the Engineering Employers' Federation, which embraced about 4,600 separate establishments which between them employed about two million employees (See also Wigham, 1973, p 1). At the other end of the scale were the local associations, some independent (where the degree of industrial localization was high) and some members of larger federations (the National Federation of Building Trade Employers was made up of about 250 such local associations).

The Government Social Survey of Workplace Industrial Relations (1968) found that four out of five plants in its sample (258 plants or 81 per cent) were members of one or more associations. It found no significant difference between industries or between plants of different sizes, in spite of the assumption often made that large companies might find fewer advantages in belonging.

The Social Survey Division of the OPCS's Survey of 1972, asked senior managers whether their establishments were in membership of an association. Of the 85 per cent who gave an answer, two-thirds said yes (57 per cent of the 307 senior managers). In this survey, however, some variation across industries was noted: distribution showing membership in only 19 per cent of the cases, and the public sector in only 33·5 per cent, compared with percentages in the seventh decile in the

241

metal manufacturing, engineering and food drink and tobacco categories. In the office situations which were separately distinguished, only 47 per cent of the 49 senior managers declared their establishents to be in membership (Social Survey Division OPCS, 1972, p 17).

Separating the answers of the masters from those of the managers is not possible on the basis of these surveys. But they do indicate something of the attitude adopted by managers in the larger organizations which are more likely to be in one or other of the last three categories identified on p 228 above. The responses were obtained from works managers and personnel officers, in 1966, and from senior managers (some of whom might well have been owner-managers) in 1972, and are likely to show a 'managerial' attitude rather than an entrepreneurial one. In the 1966 survey, 82 per cent of the works managers and 92 per cent of the personnel officers, in establishments in membership of one or more employers' association, claimed to derive practical benefits from membership.

The advantages perceived were (for the 111 works managers) those of collective action and uniform decisions (28 per cent), technical information (28 per cent), advice on trade union matters (25 per cent) and representation/liaison with government and trade unions (24 per cent). For the 82 personnel officers, the order was somewhat different, with advice and information on Government or Local Authority regulations/ prices policy (27 per cent) coming third after representation/ liaison with government and trade unions (35 per cent) and advice on union matters (28 per cent) and all other items except collective action (24 per cent) being mentioned by less than a fifth of them.

Disadvantages were perceived by 20 per cent of the works managers and 35 per cent of the personnel officers. The main disadvantage was the limitation of freedom of action and the need to conform to the majority decision and practice (64 per cent). Eleven per cent of the works managers and 25 per cent of the personnel officers admitted that they had wanted to make concessions which were not approved of by the association. A number reported that they had, nevertheless, made them, and that in most cases nothing was done about this, although personnel officers reported that three firms had either left or been thrown out as a consequence of doing so. A small number saw some disadvantage *vis a vis* the non-member (14 per cent) and seven per cent identified the cost and four per cent the delays involved as other disadvantages.

The personnel managers were, however, rather more likely to criticize the employers' association when asked if they had any specific criticisms: 34 (or 34 per cent) of the personnel people and 69 (or 26 per cent) of the works managers admitted criticisms. Both categories made similar criticisms, although the emphasis varied, but the categorization of the personnel officers' answers makes direct comparisons difficult.

The other untestable hypothesis is whether these criticisms reflect managerial perceptions of a market-derived 'need' to move to a different structure which would facilitate the pursuit of different (and as perceived situationally more appropriate) policies. Nevertheless, it ought perhaps to be borne in mind that the sources or motives of the criticisms might indicate a genuine concern that the industrial relations handling processes of the undertaking are inappropriate to the circumstances.

Objectives of employers' association

The employer's decision to join an association may depend a great deal on the power which he can muster *vis a vis* his employees or their unions within the undertaking. The small employer may feel that the costs of resisting unions on his own are too high and that membership of an association to which the task of dealing with the unions can be delegated, is preferable. The larger undertaking with more control over the local labour market, and *a fortiori* the monopolistic or oligopolistic undertaking may feel this kind of pressure less strongly. For the rest, the employer's appreciation of the objectives of the association and of its power to secure them, is likely to bear upon the decision made.

Resistance to trade union demands might be expected to loom large in the range of objectives of the employers' association. This body is frequently viewed as a defensive organization of employers established in response to the development of opposing trade unions. It may, however, be more 'proactive' than this implies and there is some evidence that some such bodies preceded the establishment of trade unions (see Clegg, 1972, pp 120-23).

Adam Smith's long-standing (1776) testimony to the effect that employers, no less than workers, were prone to meet to discuss common problems suggests that they perceived a position which required protection and defence. Amongst these, doubtless, would be the problems of maintaining or improving the system under which they operated. Such defence of the system would not be a surprising function for a body of employers to engage in. Faced with what could only be regarded as a threat from organized labour, they could only increase their concern to pursue this objective more vigorously.

Munns suggested in his study for the Donovan Commission, however, that not all employers' associations are alike in the mix of objectives and functions which they pursue (1967, p 26). One obvious difference is to be found in the distinction between *trade associations* dealing with wider commercial matters (see Millerson, 1964, p 41) and associations devoted exclusively to industrial relations ends. The one must pursue a much wider range of functions than the other by its very nature. It is, for example, concerned with the development of standard forms of trading contract, the standardization of products in the trade or industry, and the financing of research into products and processes.

There are those who have seen the trade association form as a means of accumulating power which could then be deployed in dealing with the trade unions. But Wigham, in his study of the Engineering Employers' Federation (EEF), argues that a single-minded pursuit of industrial relations objectives is likely to be much more productive. Such single-mindedness he sees as contributory to the EEF's reputation for 'being the toughest employers' organization' (Wigham, 1973, p 1).

Munns draws another distinction between the association which sees its role as that of providing a common forum for swapping experiences for mutual benefit, and that which seeks to develop a more active programme for dealing with the trade unions and their demands. He cites the Multiple Shops Federation as being heavily oriented towards the first of these, and the Federation of Civil Engineering Contractors as more representative of the latter type of association. These distinctions are, however, marginal and scarcely amount to distinct ideologies. Like trade unions, employers' associations tend to be single purpose bodies in the sense of pursuing a single broad ideology.

Dominant orientations of employers' associations

Nevertheless, differences can be discerned, both in history and in contemporary practice, in the relative weight which these associations place upon defensive and offensive objectives. The implication here is that some associations deliberately orient themselves to one kind of approach, whilst others align themselves with a different one.

Defensive aims

Employers' associations are seen as predominantly defensive and responsive to the (prior) trade union organization. Which came first is probably unanswerable, particularly since trade unions are often said to have come into existence to defend workers against their employers: a whole edifice of Chinese boxes might be the likely product of this kind of search for origins.

In so far as they were established as defensive organizations, what they were defending was probably their competitive position. Although individual employers might well wish to avoid the attentions of the trade unions altogether, if they were subjected to a union demand which they could not resist effectively, they might well find themselves placed at a competitive disadvantage in respect of labour costs.

In addition, however, they were probably defending their authority to control labour in the workplace in the interests of efficiency and profit. Attempts at 'unilateral imposition' of certain union rules, (for example, with respect to apprentice ratios) not only had possible cost consequences, but took the deployment of labour out of the hands of the employer and manager.

Wigham sees these two concerns as the major imperatives of employers' association action:

> Employers' associations must seek to keep labour costs within reasonable bounds (even though they incur losses through stoppages in the process), and to maintain the controls they regard as essential for efficient management' (Wigham, 1973, p 1).

It is because these are of paramount importance that he subscribes to the view that such associations should pursue these objectives without deflection or diversion.

The pursuit of this kind of objective leads the association into the labyrinths of developing agreements and procedures as devices for 'containing conflict'. This is not to be seen as merely a matter of avoiding stoppages because they are costly, but rather as a means of securing acceptance of certain principles (the union accepts that managment has the right to manage its undertaking) and certain constraints upon the method of raising issues for negotiation as well as upon the content of those issues (the management accept that the union may raise questions of the following type by the following method).

Defence also calls for a political presence, particularly through pressure group activities. This may be related to the broad objective of preserving the system (for example, through the avoidance of detracting legislation) or to the narrower objective of securing closer restrictions on claims (for example, in the setting of incomes policy limits). Organization to ensure that this kind of pressure may be placed on central authorities is, consequently, one of the major roles possessed by employers' associations.

Offensive aims

Neither in their history, nor in their current approach to their task, have employers' associations been simply defensive and reactive to the trade unions and their demands. Offensive or proactive behaviour has tended to take two distinct forms: either the offensive has been mounted to crush or coerce the unions; or its purpose has been their more constructive containment through the development of procedures.

The 'document' (or the 'yellow-dog contract' in the more picturesque American terminology) was used in the past to secure the new employee's contractual promise not to join a trade union. Its use in the 1830s and 1850s in an attempt to destroy the early unions (albeit with little success) provides one example of the employers' attacking approach (see Clegg, 1972, pp 121-22; Wigham, 1973, p 279). Although the document has been little used in the present century, the device of the staff mutual benefit society (largely supported by employers' contributions) which offered high benefits to those who agreed to resign from unions, has been used with similar objectives (Donovan Commission *Report*, 1968, pp 62-63)

There are also numerous examples of straightforward battles between the employers' associations and the unions, in which the objectives of the former were to smash the latter or remove (what was seen as) a significant threat to managerial prerogatives. For example, the Shipping Federation was formed in 1890 in direct response to the Sailors' and Firemen's Union demand for a closed shop. In three years it reduced the union organization to a shambles in a series of actions which involved the use of strike-breakers on 'an unparallelled scale' (Clegg, 1972, p 125). Such battles over principles (as distinct from battles over wage claims) have also been less frequent in recent years.

Employers' associations have also shown themselves willing to take the lead in developing machinery and procedures for the joint resolution of issues and the ordering of common interests. Clegg suggests that some employers' associations did show some willingness to hold 'free and friendly communication with the representatives of (workers) with a view to the avoidance of strikes' (Clegg, 1972, pp 123-24). Much of this tended to occur in the period prior to World War I, when both Clegg and the Donovan Commission considered that employers' associations had shown themselves to be much more innovative than they have been since that time.

Such initiatives are in evidence in the establishment, following strikes, of neutral Conciliation Boards in hosiery and ironmaking. These pre-dated the development of a public conciliation service (see above, p 166). Some employers' associations in the 'new unionism' period began with a determination to destroy the unions, but ended up signing comprehensive agreements with them to regulate relations, as in the boot and shoe industry in the 1890s. The EEF developed in a similar way at this time, and from its activities the national procedure agreement evolved which persisted in modified form until 1970 (see Wigham, 1973, pp 285-89).

During this period around the turn of the century, the employers' associations were largely responsible for:

1   developing the shape and coverage of the national bargaining units, as they made the domain of jointly negotiated rules coterminous with their own organizational boundaries
2   developing agreements, particularly procedural agreements, designed to reduce the likelihood of industrial stoppages during the lifetime of the agreement
3   helping to make it at least unlikely that government would feel constrained to step in to determine the quantities and the rules of industrial relations.

In the period after this, however, the employers' associations went on the defensive, by seeking to preserve the national bargaining structure as the *status quo* of industrial relations (see Donovan Commission *Report*, 1968, paras. 75-82; Marsh, 1982, p 151).

> 'Any change, they had come to believe might be exploited by the unions, and their overriding concern was to resist further union encroachment, even after the defeats which the unions had sustained in 1926' (Clegg, 1972, p 133).

So they rested until the challenge from below, in the form of pressure for the post-war shop steward organizations, placed the whole conception of an employers' association in jeopardy, at least where large employers were concerned.

POLITICAL INVOLVEMENT

In addition to their bargaining role, however, employers' associations, like practically all other status-oriented associations, find themselves involved in propaganda and negotiations designed to preserve the position or status of the members, individually and collectively within the wider social or political context. This is the role which is normally identified as representing the employers' interest to other bodies and to the State, and which is usually regarded as important in preserving the prerogative base and social power of the members.

> 'All of the national organizations regard the representation of members' views to government as an important and growing part of the function. The general importance arises from the fact that much legislation has a direct bearing on industrial affairs and associations take very seriously their responsibility to seek amendments to existing or proposed legislation which would have a harmful effect on their members, or to improve the practical execution of the Government's intentions' (Munns, 1967, p 53).

The increase in this activity arises not merely because more legislation and more directly interventionist policies have been put out by governments, but also because many new bodies have been established on which provision is made for employer representation (for example, Economic Development Commit-

248

tees, and Departmental Committees). By this kind of contact, associations may not only influence policy but also secure information about intentions and meanings which can be used effectively by their officers in advising members.

All employers' associations, reflecting both their size and their 'mood' (in the term employed by Munns), play some part in this process of influencing others in the employer interest. Some of them are extremely powerful and influential, in this respect, but not all are particularly involved in this kind of activity nor particularly good at it when they are. The EEF tends to stand out as a body which takes every opportunity to express a viewpoint on behalf of what it sees as the major manufacturing sector of British industry and its management; it takes such opportunities as are offered to present evidence to government departments and royal commissions whenever the occasion seems to warrant doing so. Others, however, take the view that there are other associations, including trade associations, through which such views might be collated and expressed, and the employers' association as such is not the forum which should be used for this purpose.

A central employer body

A number of different bodies seek to represent the industrial and managerial interest to the State and the public at large. Some of these are the employers' associations at which we have just looked. But there are others. Some are similar in their representation of a defined industrial or service interest, as in the case of the Chambers of Commerce. Others are different in that they are professional managerial bodies as much as they are anything else; the main examples here are the Institute of Directors, the British Institute of Management and the many specialist managerial associations (such as the Institute of Personnel Management). These tend to represent more of an individual (manager) interest than do the industry-based associations. Yet others are designed to represent a much wider interest, such as that of 'industry as a whole' or 'commerce as a whole'.

The Government itself has played some part in trying to establish the later kind of representational body. For some purposes at least, government prefers to discuss general issues with representatives of the totality, and at different times has sought to encourage such bodies to develop. The success of a body in influencing governmental policy depends to some extent therefore upon a recognition on the part of government that a particular body is representative of some interest or other, and effective in expressing it, and is not merely a part of the Tower of Babel.

The Confederation of British Industry

The Confederation of British Industry (CBI) is a case in point. It has been described as 'one of Britain's most prominent interest groups' (Grant and Marsh, 1977, p 1), ranking alongside the TUC. It is, however, a recent creation dating only from 1965 when it brought together the Confederation of British Industries, the National Union of Manufacturers and the British Employers Confederation. Its formation at that time was strongly influenced by government attitudes, the Labour Government of the day making it clear that it preferred to deal with one association of business men and employers rather than three. That Government was at the time looking for tripartite discussions about the management of the economy, involving the TUC as a third party, but requiring an equivalent body on the employer side. It might therefore be said that the CBI was born with a dominant role of representing the industrialist's interest to government.

In origin, it was a pluralist body, representing the *commercial* interests of large and small firms as well as the interest of the employer *per se*. The pluralism was held later (by Grant and Marsh, 1977) to foster tensions within the Confederation, as the different types of businessmen and employers sought to persuade the CBI to adopt policies consistent with their distinct ideologies. The new body did not, however, represent the whole of the industrial and commercial sector of the economy. The Association of British Chambers of Commerce had been established in 1860 largely to develop the interests of the trader and it continues to represent this group to the present time. The financial sector was also largely outside the influence of the CBI and in spite of attempts to broaden coverage the CBI therefore remains largely restricted to the industrial interest. Even then small manufacturing businesses, represented through the Small Businesses Association (formed at the same time as the CBI) sought to avoid becoming associated with a body which they thought would become largely a tool of government in the development of economic policy.

250

The current membership of the CBI tends, therefore, to reflect the plural origin. The vast majority of members are industrial companies and a majority of those are small companies with less than 200 employees. Commercial companies form the next largest category, followed by employers and trade associations. There are also a small number of commercial associations and public sector members. The main contributions to revenue are made by the industrial bodies and more than 50 per cent is provided by large organizations in the industrial sector. The influence of the large industrial company predominates within the CBI in spite of various attempts to develop a more homogeneous membership and structure of representation.

The CBI still aspires to function as the government intended, providing the overall employer representation in tripartite discussions. During the period of tripartite management of the economy under successive governments in the 1960s and 1970s, the CBI represented the industrialist and employer interest on a number of tripartite bodies such as the National Economic Development Council.

Grant and Marsh (1977, pp 187-207) consider the extent and limitations of the CBI's influence on various issues which developed within the economy during its lifetime, and conclude that it had 'relatively limited impact on the major issues which have dominated British politics' since 1965. The main reason they give for this limitation is that the political environment was becoming increasingly unsympathetic to its aims and aspirations. The successes therefore were mainly confined to detailed concessions and did not extend to major changes in the directions of government policy. Since they carried out their study, however, a change of government in 1979 ended the tripartitism and may well have created a more favourable climate for the CBI to influence general policy. Whether it has succeeded in achieving its objectives must, however, await further study.

These same authors point to other reasons for such successes and failures as there have been. The size of the membership, they saw as an advantage, but the mixture of orientations as a disadvantaging factor. The attitude which the government adopted to it as the most representative body in manufacturing industry, they saw as facilitating its success but its failure to expand beyond this sector as a limitation. Inadequacy of resources to provide services, and lack of internal sanctions to compel compliance of members with central policies, were also seen to detract from the CBI's past and future success in its role.

The success which it did have might justify the treatment of the CBI as a pressure group within the political arena (the role which Grant and Marsh are particularly interested in). This does not deny the role of the CBI in providing legal and advisory services to members but many of these are available from the individual employers' associations and from government departments. But it does suggest that the involvement of the CBI in anything which might be identified as 'negotiation' is largely confined to relations with government on matters of policy and practice; it does not have any direct role, just as the TUC does not have any major role, in bipartite negotiations.

In spite of all, the CBI remains a relatively strong and well-established pressure group within British society and not alone because it is the only body which attempts to represent the interests of the industrial sector. It supplements the political roles of the individual employers' associations without supplanting them. It does not, however, engage directly in negotiations with the trade unions over terms and conditions of employment (which is left to the individual employers' associations) but it does help to set the scene for these negotiations whenever the political climate is sympathetic to this kind of tripartite bargaining.

Summary: employers

Employers may be regarded as having a hierarchy of objectives, ranging from the defence of the private enterprise system to the development of their own business undertakings.

They are also to be found in a variety of market and technological situations which will affect the ease or difficulty with which they may pursue these objectives.

Although the law and social conventions provide them with a protected and enforceable status, their power in the particular situation will be circumscribed by their market and political positions.

Their organization will tend to reflect the influence of these different variables, and although some generalizations can be made about the tendencies to centralize and decentralize to cope with industrial relations issues, the evidence seems to suggest a variety of organizational strategies which may be chosen carefully but with consequences which appear to be random in their incidence.

Nevertheless, the homogeneous undertaking and industry might be expected to adopt more centralized approaches to industrial relations than the heterogeneous ones. The small scale employer might be more likely to seek the strength of the association as an insurance or protection, if only because the large ones are more able to afford to buy their own expertise to deal with the problems.

Employers' associations serve a number of distinct functions, and for this reason may attract members from different contexts for quite distinct reasons, of which representation in bargaining or protection from union challenge may be but two attractions for the small businessman. Informational and political representational functions may attract quite disparate members.

However, the composition of the employers' associations might be expected to be reflected in the kinds of objectives and policies (or the 'moods') which they adopt and pursue. Like the trade unions, they may, as a category, reveal offensive and defensive, as well as more pragmatic aims and strategies, but individually place more weight on one rather than another.

Each such association may be regarded as playing some political role, in defence of the system or the industry's perceived interests. At the centre, the Confederation of British Industry represents the latest attempt to secure a single voice for the employer in discussions with government and with the TUC. Recent surveys show that it has had some successes and failures, and that it continues to have problems of an organizational and representational nature.

Readings

Anthony: (1977), pp 17-63. CIR Study No 1 (1973).
Clegg: (1979), pp 62-123. Munns: (1967).
Marsh: (1982), pp 150-82. Grant and Marsh: (1977).
Sisson, in Bain: (1983), pp 121-34.
Farnham and Pimlott: (1983), pp 135-82.
Beaumont and Gregory: (1980), pp 46-52.
Marchington: (1982), pp 35-51.

10

Workers' objectives and organization

The workers' goals

Workers, in common with the rest of humanity, have varying goals, hold varying views of the character of the environment and adopt distinct theories about the way in which, in that environment, their goals might be achieved. The fact of such individual differences not only confronts the employer who might wish to achieve standardization of worker behaviour in the interests of securing his objectives, but also the trade union (or any other worker association) which seeks to develop a standardized (solidarist) worker response to the employer or to other pressures from the environment.

Human goals

There are a variety of models of human motivation which purport to explain individual differences in relation to behavioural goals. They may be explained by theories of the general 'push' variety. In this view, the worker may want various outcomes from his action, in some fixed order of priority (Maslow, 1943) or as the occasion provides (Alderfer, 1972). These drives do not stem necessarily from the physiological and psychological constitutions of the person, but may be more dependently the products of learning during socialization. What is thus implanted may derive from the culture in some general sense, but it may also be taken from some more immediate group, such as the class or the trade union organization.

From any such group, the individual develops both a set of wants or goals and a view of how they might be pursued and achieved in his environment. That environment may be considered to have 'objective' character, but the individual will be called upon to develop his or her own perspective of it as a basis for organizing his action upon it.

Workers in Britain will usually realize their material goals through the operation of the *wage* system, a term used to identify the 'objective' characteristics of the mechanism through which most income is distributed. The term 'wage' may need extension to include salaries, and the whole concept may need to be considered as a mechanism for distributing *status* in a wider sense, which includes non-material elements. It is inherent in the system that, for example, the worker's obligation to serve in a dependent relationship to the employer, and his right to expect the employer to protect his health and well-being at work, are established by the same mechanisms as yield his wage. In this sense, therefore, 'the wage system' distributes not only income (which establishes the individual's *pay* status) but a complex set of rights and obligations (which establish his broader politico-social status: see above pp 38-39).

Over the last two centuries, the worker has been free to enter into such contractual arrangements which establish his status as the law permitted and as he could secure in the circumstances given the power and ability he possessed. In the early period, he was expected to establish his contracts and accept such terms as he could secure *as an individual*. In order to remove some of the disadvantages inherent in individual bargaining, he attempted to develop associations which would act on his behalf and *collective* bargaining came to replace the earlier process for many workers. This change did not, however, replace the 'wage system' as the device for distributing economic status; it merely attempted to alter the balance of power between the contractors. This required that workers should give up some of their 'freedom to contract' as individuals and to accept the discipline of 'solidarity' with their fellows as a means of increasing their 'power to contract' as a collectivity. The history of the later period of industrial relations is therefore one of developing such solidarist foundations for the process of bargaining over worker status.

The worker will therefore develop a view about the capacity of this system, and its various elements, to satisfy his wants or goals, and his behaviour will tend to reflect the view which he takes of it and the orientation (or 'mental set') which he then adopts in relation to it. Individual differences in this goal-seeking behaviour may be masked by socialization and, as a result, large groups of persons may display common orientations to action and common behaviours (see Steers and Porter, 1977; Thomason, 1981, pp. 262-93).

Goldthorpe *et al*, in their Luton study, for example, suggested that it was not possible to understand workers' comments about job satisfaction, without establishing what 'meaning' the workers gave to their work. This meaning is classified into three overlapping 'orientations to work', which they call instrumental, solidaristic and bureaucratic (Goldthorpe *et al*, 1968, 37-42; Daniel, 1969; 1971). Different *groups* of workers, they found, displayed different orientations which reduced the significance of individual differences within those groups.

An instrumental orientation is displayed where the workers see the job as a means to some other end, such as 'living', and work does not attract deep personal commitment. A solidaristic orientation is displayed where people experience work as a group activity, and derive a good deal of emotional reward from involvement in its relationships. This group could be the enterprise or the class or trade union or simply the working group. A bureaucratic orientation is revealed where the individual sees work as a career based on service to an enterprise which will steadily increase his rewards for the service rendered (see also Beynon and Blackburn, 1972).

The point of this type of categorization is to suggest that the way people will be predisposed to act will reflect this kind of ordering of priorities in relation to work. The instrumentalist will *calculate* whether a given action is economically worthwhile, whilst the solidarist will *assess* the effects of an action upon the continuity of emotional gains, and the bureaucrat *evaluate* an action in terms of its implications for service and reward (see Goldthorpe, *et al* 1968, pp 36-42). The implication is that within any group such differences are likely to be found and there is a presumption that those with similar goals will exhibit some propensity to associate, thus providing some foundation for concerted opposition.

Frames of reference

Workers might also be expected to develop distinct frames of reference through which they represent their view of the way the world is and their appreciation of what actions might be expected to yield what consequences within it. Popitz *et al* have, for example, indicated something of the variety of view amongst workers about the nature of their work reality, and their predispositions to act within it (Popitz *et al*, 1969, pp 281-324; Bulmer, 1977, pp 6-7). They attempt to identify the distribution of class images held by a group of German workers. Their classification is based on the ways in which respondents saw the social structure within which they lived and the view that they took of the way in which it might be coped with.

The two largest groups (who gave positive responses, see table 14 on p 258) saw the social world as either a 'progressive order' (ordered and generally improving) or a division into classes which sank or swam together, somewhat fatalistically). The other main views emphasized the unchanging and impervious nature of the order or the order as one which might be challenged by individual action. Those revealing views of the world which suggested that class divisions needed to be changed by collective action were few in numbers – but it has to be remembered that a large proportion gave no views which could be categorized in any of these ways.

They conclude, therefore, that people are different in the images of society which they hold and the priorities for action which they see as consistent with these views. The differences are, however, not idiosyncratic because they derive from at least partially-shared experience of the same reality, and because the socialization processes tend to emphasize the same sets of values and norms. Consequently, coherent patterns of response to stimuli can be expected to flow from these frames of reference, and because those with like views will tend to come together, they are likely to coalesce into associations which will *coercively maintain* the view of the world and the priorities for action which brought them together in the first place.

The differences in individual frames of reference may therefore become associated with ideological differences at the associational level. Associations tend to adopt focal goal orientations and action-theoretical positions (see Gamson, 1968, pp 1-19; Sayles, 1958) which provide a kind of rallying point not only for existing members but also for those who might, if the ideologies are congenial to them, become members. In the world of work, associations of employers and workers provide the main examples of formal organization which adopts this role of providing rallying points for those with similar orientations and frames of reference. The members are then likely to have different priorities as to the ends to be pursued and attained (see

Table 14

Workers' images of society

Type	Total no of respon- dents	%	% of types 1-6 only
1 Type one (static order)	60	10	14
2 Type two (progressive order)	150	25	34
3 Type three (dichotomy as collective fate)	150	25	34
4 Type four (dichotomy as individual con- flict)	60	10	14
5 Type five (reform of the social order)	12	2	3
6 Type six (class warfare)	6	1	1
7 No image of society	120	20	–
8 Records of insufficient quality	12	2	–
9 Intermediate cases, excluded	30	5	–
	100	100	100

Source: Bulmer: (1975), p 10

Crouch, 1982; Munns, 1966), and about the means to be employed in pursuing them (see Stinchcombe, in Smelser, 1967, pp 157-60). Given the distribution of differences, it is therefore not surprising that such organizations reveal a variety of objectives and ideologies.

THE TRADE UNION AND ITS PURPOSES

Both professional associations and trade unions provide examples of associations formed around some perceived common orientation and frame of reference. Because these bodies recruit members whose experience of status and roles tends to be different, they might be expected to develop distinct objectives and ideologies (as we noted above, pp 135-39). Each might be said to pursue ends which are different from, and possibly in opposition to, those of the employer and his association whose given status and whose experiences are likely to be different.

The trade union is generally regarded as spontaneous in origin, a creation of workpeople to alleviate their lot in the early factories, maintained now as an insurance against the vicissitudes of working life. From early origins, the trade union movement has now grown in scale, and although its roots may lie in common worker perceptions of the world and its ways, we might (on the basis of the preceding discussion) expect these organizations to contain within them a variety of orientations and objectives because of their sheer scale (see table 15 on p 260) even though they may be capable of identification with common objectives and orientations.

The nature of the trade union

The trade union inherently is an association developed for the purposes of maintaining that which the worker considered valuable and effecting improvement in worker status. The Webbs supplied the trade union with its well-known definition, and in the process indicated its broad purpose:

> 'a continuous association of wage earners for the purposes of maintaining or improving the conditions of their working lives' (S and B Webb, 1920a, p 1).

It identifies a category of citizen (wage-earners) (which may now need extension to accommodate the growth of white collar worker unions), indicates its form of organization (continuous association) and spells out its purposes.

Much has been written about the 'nature' of the trade union, and particularly about whether, in its nature, it is an association concerned with, or even dedicated to, collective bargaining. In the Marxian view, it is necessarily a creature of capitalism, bound

259

Table 15

Numbers and Membership of Trade Unions by Size, end 1981

No of members	No of unions (000s)	All percentage of		No of
		Members unions	No of members	
Under 100	69	4	16.4	0.0
100- 499	113	28	26.8	0.2
500- 999	45	32	10.7	0.3
1,000- 2,499	54	86	12.8	0.7
2,500- 4,999	37	132	8.8	1.1
5,000- 9,999	25	167	5.9	1.4
10,000- 14,999	4	54	1.0	0.4
15,000- 24,999	18	354	4.3	2.9
25,000- 49,000	17	617	4.1	5.1
50,000- 99,999	14	978	3.3	8.0
100,000-249,999	14	2,175	3.3	17.9
250,000 and more	11	7,555	2.6	62.0
All members	421	12,182	100.0	100.0

Source: Department of Employment Gazette, 91 (1), January, 1983, p 26.

by the constraints imposed on it by the system which gave rise to it, and therefore of limited use in effecting revolutionary change. In the more conservative view, it is usually regarded as concerned essentially with bargaining as the currently most effective method of realizing the kinds of purposes which the Webbs set for it.

The contrast with the professional association

It may be contrasted on important dimensions with the professional association which also embraces 'workers'. The trade union, conceived for the protection of members, necessarily operates as a pressure group (in relation to management or government) and cannot escape the ideological consequences of so doing. The professional association, having originated in high status occupations, remains supported in its more élitist position and approach, has some chance of acting more as an interest group, and may seek to distance itself in terms of objectives and methods from the trade union. The distinction is often found to have the practical consequence of leading representatives of different worker groups to refuse to meet together in bargaining with the employer.

The fundamental distinction carrying over from their origins is fostered by other distinctions which arise in the course of operation. Millerson, for example, has suggested that they are also different in that:

(a) professional associations are usually incorporated under the Companies Acts or by Royal Charter where trade unions are unincorporated

(b) professional associations tend to be multi-functional and concerned with both social and economic status, in distinction from the more singular function of trade unions

(c) professional associations may contain employees, self-employed persons, and employers within the one body where trade unions usually contain only employees

(d) some professional associations, particularly the qualifying association, tend to contain a number of different grades of membership reflecting differences in competence (as indeed do some unions although most do not)

(e) most professional associations do not attempt direct negotiation of remuneration or working conditions, and usually eschew direct industrial action in furtherance of their claims, even in those cases where (as in the protective association) some attempt is made to influence remuneration directly. Most unions do aim to negotiate and to back this with industrial action.

Given the existence of such differences, it is not surprising that at the present time, professional bodies and trade unions frequently find themselves at loggerheads. The associations at the beginning of the professional association list (above, pp 138-9) are unlikely to display any features in common with trade unions, but those at the end may begin to look much more like them in the kinds of objectives they adopt and the functions they perform. Such bodies may be prevented from acting like trade unions by their Articles and Bye-Laws and may in any case not want to resemble the trade unions, or to act as pressure groups.

'Accordingly, associations principally devised to qualify, or to study, usually act as interest groups, not pressure groups. Associations aimed to protect remuneration and working conditions ... are normally pressure groups' (Millerson, 1964, p 32).

Any aspiration to maintain member status on the assumption that society will somehow 'automatically' recognize good works is likely to keep the association distinct from the trade union (see Roberts *et al*, 1972).

'Unionateness'

Worker groups with different statuses and experiences may well have different ideas about how they might secure their general, and possibly shared, ends (see Kleingartner, 1968; Lansbury, 1974). This is clear in Blackburn's attempt (1967) to produce a criterion measure of what *real* trade unionism amounted to. In his study of bank staffs, he tried to set up a measure of the extent to which white collar unions had developed a trade union ideology, that is whether they could be regarded as equivalent to manual workers' unions. He attempted this in two parts.

The first part involved a measure of 'completeness' of unionization. This depended on the extent of membership recruitment within the particular population, and yielded a measure of union density. The second part entailed description of the 'character' of unionization. This attempted to compare the similarities and differences between unions supported by these two categories of workers (Blackburn, 1967, pp 16-20), in much the fashion considered above (see pp 261-62).

Blackburn developed, in this second part, what he referred to as a measure of 'unionateness' or 'the commitment of an organization to the general principles and ideology of trade unionism' derived from a consideration of manual worker unionism (Blackburn, 1967, p 18). His measure was derived from the extent to which the following seven characteristics might be ascribed to the organization:

1 'it regards collective bargaining and the protection of the interests of members as employees as its main function, rather than, say, professional activities or welfare schemes
2 'it is independent of employers for purposes of negotiation
3 'it is prepared to be militant, using all forms of industrial action which may be effective
4 'it declares itself to be a trade union

262

5 'it is registered as a trade union (rather than as a corporation under the Companies Acts)
6 'it is affiliated to the Trades Union Congress
7 'it is affiliated to the Labour Party'. (Blackburn, 1967, pp 18-19).

Blackburn acknowledges that the first three of these items are different from the others in that they can be scaled, and that there are difficulties in the way of using any or all of them to produce a 'measure'. They capture, however, something of the historical difference between workers' organizations, even if currently these historical distinctions may be becoming more indistinct. They are clearly derived from historical perspectives, but they do nevertheless make it possible to highlight the nature of the difference, if not between different unions, at least between unions and professional associations (where, however, as Blackburn himself says, the difference 'is by no means clear') (*ibid*, p 26).

This then indicates something of the orientation and frame of reference (or the ideology) of the trade union in Britain. By implication, it is a relatively homogeneous category of association, singlemindedly pursuing a set of distinct objectives by means (including collective bargaining and industrial action) which are themselves characteristic. But unions come in a variety of shapes and sizes, often reflecting their origins, and pursue a variety of specific objectives (as distinct from their general purposes) by means which have been variously described as defensive or offensive, reformist or revolutionary. Containment of individual differences is a difficult process.

Trade union objectives

Useful as the Webbs definition of the nature of the trade union is, it does little to indicate what particular objectives the trade union can be expected to pursue. The TUC, in its evidence to the Donovan Commission has amplified the Webbs' definition, by indicating the unions' most likely objectives:

1 improved terms of employment
2 improved physical environment at work
3 full employment and national prosperity
4 security of employment and income
5 improved social security

263

6 fair shares of national income and wealth
7 industrial democracy
8 a voice in government
9 improved public and social services
10 public control and planning of industry.

Some of these are related to material standards of living (1-6), some to the dignity and power of labour (7-8), and some to the form and purpose of the economic and social system within which they live and work (9-10). The list may be broadly indicative rather than exhaustive, and it could be expected to change with change of circumstances. Hughes and Pollins, for example, suggest that the list might unjustifiably underplay the goal of the unions in providing workers with opportunities for becoming involved in governmental processes within the unions themselves (Hughes and Pollins, 1973, pp 35-6).

The union's general purpose, therefore, might be interpreted as the mobilization of the strength of the collectivity around the worker against the power of the employer, in order that his lot might be improved (see above, pp 119-20). Within such a general characterization of purpose, however, a number of distinct objectives can be identified. These reflect the varieties of objectives and orientations which a cross-section of workers might reveal if asked. Whether this is so because the workers have arrived at these spontaneously as a consequence of experience or because they have 'learned' them from the trade unions is not a question which can ever be answered. All that can probably be said is that workers who join are likely to be in broad agreement with the ideology, but that the union, like any other associational entity, must have some interest in continually mobilizing and maintaining members' support for that ideology (see Batstone, *et al*, 1978).

Short and long-term goals

Unionism does, as Blackburn's measures indicate, depend upon the recognition of a fundamental difference between the interest of the employer and the interest of the worker. This is usually associated with, and explained by, the act of exchange, in which one party is a buyer and the other a seller. It can be extended, *via* 'exchange theory' (see, Adams, 1963; 1965) to embrace the giving and taking of 'status' in its wider meaning. In either context, the interest of the worker is not coincidental with that of the employer, even if their interests are neither completely opposed.

Some interests necessarily coincide, whilst others remain antithetical, and because of this a foundation exists for *both* co-operation and conflict, as well as for the containment of such conflict as is unavoidable within a general framework of co-operation. This perspective might be said, for example, to lie at the root of the collective bargaining relationship itself: this is essentially conflictual, but the conflicting parties generally accept that there are limits (which are spelled out in commonly accepted conventions: see pp 327-36, below) beyond which the conflict does not extend.

Dependent upon which aspect of the relationship one wants to highlight, it is therefore possible to perceive unionism as not only oppositional but also revolutionary, or to see it as essentially co-operative, even as a 'creature of capitalism'. Because each of these perspectives rests upon one aspect of the relationship, there can be little agreement on just how significant the more revolutionary goals are in comparison with the unions' practical or pragmatic objectives (as listed above, pp 263-64).

The recognition that any particular union might pursue either at different times may be explained by reference to the existence of long and short term goals. Indeed, the objectives of either party in industrial relations may be divided into general or long term and immediate or short term. The long term goals may be linked to a need to maintain or improve, through the vicissitudes of many negotiating episodes, the general position of the workers in membership. The short term goals may be related to solving some immediate problem or resolving some immediate issue which develops between them.

In the short term, the union is generally regarded as having a limited range of immediate aims which focus mainly on the *protection* of living standards or jobs but with a margin left for their improvement. In the long term, the union may have more radical and revolutionary goals, focused on the overthrow of the system of control and subordination. The possibility that the pursuit of the short-term goals may detract from the achievement of long-term objectives is frequently noted, and forms the basis for the radical's distinction between class consciousness and trade union consciousness.

Crouch argues that a choice of trade union strategy is not just a choice between goals, but one between goals 'set in the context of the means needed to secure them' (Crouch, 1982, p 139). In this sense, therefore, goals would not usually be set in advance of the circumstances becoming known. Consequently, the purpose may be to protect members against exploitation, improve the general conditions of life of the members, or replace the capitalist system in the long term by a socialist (or some other) one. What any union may aim to achieve at any one time, say in any one year, may well be determined by the current circumstances of that time, and have only the most tenuous relationship to the general purpose. In fact, many (including Blackburn) see unions 'in their nature' as having much less 'ambitious' goals than this listing suggests.

Defensive goals

The defensive goals of the union are those which seek to preserve what the union has already secured for its members – whether in the form of relative share of the national income, relative level of wages in comparison with comparator workers and jobs, degree of employment security, level of contribution required in return for remuneration, extent of fringe benefits, or whatever. Crouch argues that 'it means accepting the conditions found on entering employment, but preventing any worsening of them' (Crouch, 1982, p 120).

This type of goal is associated with a perception of relative weakness in the union's position *vis a vis* the employer. It implies that the costs to the union of seeking to secure significant improvement are likely to outweigh the gains which might be secured by taking more offensive action. This is not, however, the same as saying that workers will not use their collective strength to resist strongly any attempt to cut down on the conditions which are available (see Crouch, 1982, p 121). This, as Crouch argues, has been a significant goal of trade union activity, particularly among the semi- and un-skilled workers, through-out union history (*ibid*). Even radical leaders, like those of the Clyde Workers' Committee, found themselves restrained by this perspective on the part of the members (see Hinton, 1973, p 161).

This defensive, conservative approach has also been discerned in worker behaviours directed towards the State. Runciman has developed the argument that it is not absolute levels of hardship which provoke militant action, but attempts by the authorities to reduce the existing standards. He cites the example of the Unemployment Act of 1934, which cut unemployment benefits as an example (Runciman, 1966, p 65). He also comments later that:

> 'Manual workers certainly felt that they had a claim on the State. But their demand was not 'soak the rich' so much as 'work or maintenance'. It was in terms of working class comparisons that their deprivations were felt' (Runciman, 1966, p 69).

There is a case, therefore, for recognizing the validity of the first part of the Webbs' definition of trade union purposes (the *maintenance* of living standards).

The revolutionary goals

However, 'defence of existing positions does not exhaust the catalogue of union goals' (Crouch, 1982, p 127). At the other extreme, as at least trade union rhetoric rather than actual day-to-day behaviour suggests, are the more revolutionary objectives. Despite their rhetorical associations these have real significance and influence. The radical literature on trade unions is replete with examples of possibilities of revolution which never quite materialized (Thompson, 1965, pp 320-21) although some attempt was made. It also contains many assertions of the un-revolutionary nature of British trade unions, with the blame for this being laid at the door of the artisans, the workers in general, or the trade union leaders. It may however do no more than confirm that trade unions usually adopt the *maximin* approach to goal setting (see Bridge, 1981, p 98).

Nevertheless, examples can be found of *expressions* of revolutionary objectives, in the statements of the union rule books and the pronouncement of union leaders. What is usually meant by the use of this adjective are those aims which would overthrow or otherwise replace or transcend the existing capitalistic system or structure of production, distribution and exchange. Where the system is seen to deny the benefits which the workers seek from their labour, it ought to be overthrown or replaced by one more in keeping with the workers' real interests and aspirations. The solidarist organization of workers in trade unions or political parties, then, offers some scope for the pursuit of this type of 'revolutionary' end, as well as, or instead of, the end of reforming or improving terms and conditions of employment within the system.

Hyman and Fryer point to a number of examples in support of their contention that the objectives of the trade unions are not confined to those of negotiating with employers over terms and conditions of employment (Hyman and Fryer, 1975, pp 172-80).

> 'There is no necessary reason ... why trade unions should pursue their members' interests solely through the channels of collective bargaining. Trade union action might properly be oriented towards the establishment of rules with the greatest possible independence and freedom from constraint: unilateral control rather than joint regulation. 'Invasion, not admission, should be the trade unionist's watchword' is a sentiment with deep roots in the British labour movement (Goodrich, 1920, p 253). It may involve two distinct assumptions: that indpendent action is the most acceptable means by which workers collectively can defend and improve their conditions *within* capitalism; and that trade union action should aim ultimately at *transcending* capitalism altogether' (Hyman and Fryer, 1975, pp 180-81).

Hyman and Fryer quote a number of statements which serve to indicate that some trade unionists, usually in leadership positions, have expressed this kind of sentiment on occasion in the past, but acknowledge that, as Crouch also argues, 'such ambitious objectives have often been eroded in the actual practice of trade unionism' (*ibid*, p 181) largely because the negotiators have become committed to the maintenance of the system of collective bargaining for its own sake.

The strategic or 'intermediate' goals

Crouch suggests that between the defensive and the revolutionary goals of the trade unions fall those which he describes as 'intermediate'. 'These', he says, 'can be seen as advances out of defensiveness' and involve 'taking an aggressive plunge forward where it seems that something can be safely achieved' (Crouch, 1982, p 138). These may be described as 'strategic' goals in the sense that they are the ones pursued when the opportunity presents itself and the approach to decision-taking is another

268

example of the use of the *maximin* method.

Crouch suggests that this kind of goal seeking strategy is consistent with the worker's position and perceptions. It implies a bounded rather than a complete rationality (see above, pp 51-52).

> 'many of the factors determining their environment are unknown to them; much has to be taken on trust; their position is, always, one of subordination to capital and fear of bumping against a rigorous demand curve for labour' (Crouch, 1982, p 138).

It may also be regarded as fitting the 'logic of his situation' (*ibid*).

The goals which fall within this category still constitute a 'bewildering variety: higher wages, reduced working hours, improvements in many different aspects of working conditions, reductions in the degree of supervision, a share in managerial control, increases in manning levels, improvements in work rules' (Crouch, 1982, pp 138-39). This characterization by Crouch comes close to outlining the main features of the typical collective agreement (as outlined, for example, by Muir (1981) or Davey (1951)). By implication, it is these lurches forward which determine the 'shape' and content of collective bargaining (see Phelps-Brown, 1959, pp 344-67).

Crouch also identifies a category of procedural goals, not merely in the sense of establishing a procedure to be followed, but rather in the sense of trading off a substantive achievement against the right to control its provenance. His illustration is the situation in which a possible rise in a pay rate may be traded for an acceptance by management that the shop stewards shall have control of the allocation of overtime (Crouch, 1982, p 149).

This identification of procedural outcomes as a source of 'rights' (in this case, the right to control overtime) is then represented as an outcome which is concerned with control, particularly with control over work and its rewards: 'to demand a right rather than a particular gain is to demand predictability, assurance, something on which one can insist, and thereby, impart control' (Crouch, 1982, p 150).

The personal goals of leaders

Much has also been made of the actual or potential difference between the goals of the union and the goals of the leaders. They are seen to have personal goals, involving either advancement of their own status or their own careers, or protection from the consequences of member disapproval. They have also been regarded as too slavishly supportive of the institution of collective bargaining because of their greater and more direct involvement in it (see, Hyman and Fryer, 1974). This may, however, do no more than recognize that union leaders by virtue of their differentiated roles are subjected to a number of role-constraints which do not impinge upon the membership.

To the extent that union leaders (or negotiators) regard themselves as bound by the expectations of the members or of the union (as an abstract entity), they might pursue as goals those listed by Harbison and Coleman (1951, p. 7). In this they are expressed in a way which finds a place for both the institutional and the personal goals (and incidentally corresponds with the goals given by them for management, above, pp 217-20):

1   the preservation and strengthening of the union as an institution
2   the realization of the objective of getting more for the membership
3   the acquisition of a greater measure of control over jobs to help realize 1 and 2
4   the pursuit of certain broad economic goals (for example, that of human welfare before profits, or greater equality in distribution).

Union leaders may well 'internalize' these goals, making the goals of the union their own, or, in ordinary language, they may 'live, eat and sleep the union'. It is possible that in doing so, the leader is able to achieve goals which are much more personal to him or her, at least to the extent that achieving the union's goals is necessary to his or her own self-fulfilment.

WORKER ORGANIZATION

The generally subordinate position of the worker in modern enterprise, limits his autonomy to organize to meet the employer in bargaining. Workers and their associations must respond to management's decisions about how work will be organized and undertakings and establishments run. Although they may also

270

respond to other features of their situation, such as the nature of the labour market as they perceive it, it remains difficult to escape the view that a good deal of the historical organization of trade unions has responded primarily to the way in which work has been divided by the employer at the particular stage in the development of industry. Once established their organizations have not been willing to modify their shape and form simply to suit the changing circumstances of business or employer organization. The perception by managements of a problem of multi-unionism is partly a carry over from this historical evolution.

There is considerable evidence that workers usually organize themselves into associations of a more or less informal and a more or less oppositional kind within their workplaces. Such organization will usually develop around the formal division of labour within a workplace, but without following this slavishly (see, Roethlisberger and Dickson, 1939; Homans, 1951; Lupton, 1963). Their distinctiveness usually does not ignore the official organization; most frequently, the unofficial organization builds onto, or extends from the official organization, in much the fashion that the unofficial organization of the men in the bank-wiring observation room in the Hawthorne plant of the Western Electric Company did (Roethlisberger and Dickson, 1939).

Some of this unofficial organization may be 'personal and unstructured' in the sense in which Flanders uses these terms (Flanders, 1965, p 11); it merely makes life more tolerable for the members. It may or may not oppose the official structure of the undertaking or establishment (see Lupton, 1963); it may function as the basis for oppositional association or form a part of the organization of the trade union (see Sayles, 1958; Dalton, 1959). There is, thus, a strong suggestion in these many 'small group' studies that there is an informal organizational base for opposition even in those circumstances where no trade union has established itself.

Trade union organization

The more formal and permanent associations which we know as trade unions may also be seen to respond to the official organizational pattern in the sense that they were and are often based on occupational and role differences. Thus, historically,

271

the craft unions organized around the principle of admitting time-served men, and the general labour unions around the principle of embracing all semi- and un-skilled workers in a labour market who were not already organized by the existing (usually craft) unions.

Today, these same organizing principles remain pertinent although time and technological change have tended to blur the original distinctions. What was inherent in the original approach has, however, continued into the new conditions; unions still seek to organize into one association those who either might otherwise be regarded as competitors in the relevant labour markets, or might be useful sources of strength in any conflict with the employer. Thus, both craft and general labour unions have extended themselves into something closer to industrial unions (without ever having succeeded completely in this). The grade and single occupational associations are less frequently found amongst the manual workers, although equivalents are still found amongst white collar workers.

A general classification

The development of white collar workers' unions (see Bowen and Shaw, 1972) makes it more desirable than before to produce a classification which embraces *all* unions (and even the 'protective' professional associations) according to their organizing principles. The different concepts adopted by Flanders (1952), Turner (1962), and Jackson (1982) might be merged to give four types of union.

1 The single-occupational union. This represents the first stable form to appear, often on a highly localized basis. Their pattern of growth was usually from the trade club into district and then national forms, but subsequently they often merged with other unions of a like type. They include some of the older craft (Flanders) and closed (Turner) unions. The Bradford and District Power Loom Overlookers' Society and the Grimsby Trawler Officers' Association are examples of the first form. The Association of Patternmakers and Allied Craftsmen, and the National Union of Scalemakers are examples of the national form. Amongst white collar workers, the AUT and the NUT provide similar examples.
2 The single-status/multi-occupational union. This represents

272

the outcome of merger. One strong motivation for merger was to present a united front of, for example, craftsmen, against the threats posed by the unskilled and semi-skilled workers introduced by the employer to increase substitutability. Such mergers also helped accumulate membership and income, a factor of some importance since viability requires a minimum of both. The Union of Construction and Allied Technicians is an example of merger of originally-distinct single-occupational unions (England, 1979, pp 1-18) faced with declining influence in both their industry and the TUC.

3   The vertically-integrated union. This is made up of two types of union, distinguished according to the manner in which they reached their position. Some unions (the single industry unions as Jackson calls them, (1977, p 48) set out with the intention of recruiting everyone in a particular industry, with the NUM, the NUR, and the UCW providing examples. Others arrived at a similar position by process of merger or extension of membership eligibility. Some of the original craft unions have extended downwards through the skill hierarchy in this fashion (for example, the AUEW) whilst other unions have extended upwards in the skill hierarchy (the TGWU for example amalgamated with the National Union of Vehicle Builders). More recently, a number of the manual worker unions have extended upwards into the white collar sector, often developing distinct white collar sections for the purpose. None actually amount to 'industrial unions' (see Bell, 1949) and are more in the category of 'single industry unions' (Jackson, 1977, p 48) because they share the industry's employees with other unions.

4   The conglomerate unions. This is the product of merger, amalgamation and transfer of obligations. It is represented by those unions, general in their membership potential, which tend to cover many occupations and industries. The more obvious examples are the general worker unions (TGWU and GMWU) but examples are to be found amongst white collar unions (ASTMS and APEX) which may seek to retain a white collar orientation but otherwise embrace appropriate workers at appropriate grades in many different industries. Two organizing principles are involved, one emphasizing the single grade coverage and the other stressing the desirability of 'one big union' regardless of grade as well as industry.

Through this range the unions are increasingly 'open' (in Turner's sense), but they are also decreasingly concerned with control of particular labour markets. They are likely to be more concerned at the conglomerate end of the range with the accumulation, not only of 'industrial' power (power to influence employers in negotiations) but also with 'political' power (power to influence public opinion and the State) by developing a considerable membership 'constituency'.

Multi-unionism

Nevertheless, there is little in the development which will remove what the employer sees as a problem of multiple unionism (see Armstrong, 1972, pp 31-52; Daniel and Millward, 1983, pp 46-51). In national, industry-wide negotiations, the general effects of merger and transfer of engagement may be to reduce the number of separate unions involved. Similarly, the growth of very large unions may give them predominance in local or national negotiations. As they seek to dominate, they are likely to fight out their power battles in the negotiating arena itself, to complicate if not prevent effective negotiation (see Aldridge, 1976).

However, the separate unions are frequently federated (or confederated) for purposes of national negotiations and the employer is presented with some semblance of unity on the worker side. Unity will not always hold, as different individual union policies may lead to different approaches to action under different circumstances but for much of the time and purpose, one or other of the 40-50 union federations will confront the employer's side as a single body, with the larger unions probably taking it in turns to present and argue claims.

This same national federal structure may carry through to the domestic situation. Even where it does not, it is now less uncommon than in the past to find the unions being willing to group into joint shop stewards' committees to face the employer with local claims and even grievances. Some of these develop from the stewards' perception of the source of their advantage in bargaining, and some of them from pressures by management (see Gregson and Ruffle, 1981). At the corporate level, the 'combine committee' has effected a similar organizational effect, although most often it is not recognized by the management, or in many cases, by the union.

However, the appearance of multi-unionism which is given from the figures on number and size (see table 15 on p 260 above) belies what exists in the practice of negotiation. If the individual trade unions have not responded by amalgamation to the changes of recent years in the occupational structure and the skill mix they have often done so on a less formal basis, so that the realities of trade union structure are closer to what the employer's pattern of organization might suggest as appropriate.

Domestic organization

Some mitigation of the employer's problem of multiple unionism is, therefore, found at the domestic level of negotiation. This results less from mergers and take-overs than from the development of 'domestic organization' by the several unions which may be recognized by the employer. Sometimes the employer may deliberately create or foster this, but in any event, some predisposition on the part of the workers' local representatives to combine amongst themselves in order to increase their bargaining power seems now to exist.

This has led to the development of the 'joint shop stewards' committee' which may serve to bring together the elected or appointed representatives of the workers in the particular undertaking or establishment for purposes of negotiating more effectively with management. The 'natural' extension of this grouping is the combine committee, which, in spite of any particular political connotations it may have acquired, seeks and serves to bring together such diverse union representatives in a multi-plant company.

The management which seeks to develop a single bargaining unit, or a structure of units which bears more resemblance to the structure of the undertaking or establishment, is likely to find itself facilitating these kinds of 'spontaneous' developments in worker organization. But this is not easy to achieve, either for the unions themselves or for managements.

Securing *joint* negotiations immerses management in a number of problems. The first concerns which employee associations can be expected or persuaded to sit together. The traditional form of this difficulty has centred on the production versus service worker distinction which often had a craft versus general union connotation as well. Each group often prefers to negotiate on its own, regardless of how many different unions might be involved. Management has usually connived at this for reasons of its own.

As a result of inter-associational tensions brought into the open, after 1971, by the Industrial Relations Act, separatism has focused upon the distinction between the TUC-affiliated union and the non-affiliated association, and between some affiliates which registered under that Act and those which did not. The effect of later legislation on trade union certification, independence and recognition may support continuing this kind of distinction, but could force the non-affiliated employee association out of the arena in due course.

This affects the white collar and public sectors most particularly. Some professional and managerial associations prefer procedures which do not depend upon strike activity in defiance of professional norms of conduct. This increases both the desire for separate negotiating status and separate agreements, and the difficulties faced by management in securing a generally applicable constitution.

The extent of external control

Achieving unity may depend upon separating the local representatives from the union's full-time officers. Boraston, Clegg and Rimmer, in their study of the relationship between workplace representative and union full-time officers, throw some light on this issue. They started out with the hypothesis that this relationship would be affected by the 'scope available for autonomous workplace bargaining' (something largely within management's discretion to modify). They found this to be a significant factor in developing independence in workplace organization and bargaining. The scope itself, they found to depend upon the extent to which centralized administrative arrangements had reflected themselves in 'tight' (restricting) agreements negotiated outside the workplace (for example, at company or national level).

They defined a tight agreement as one covering 'a wide range of issues' specifying 'in some detail what is to be done', entered into 'with the intention that its provisions are standards to be observed rather than minimum requirements which may be exceeded, and ... supported by arrangements to make sure that the intention is realized' (Boraston, Clegg and Rimmer, 1975, p 6).

Conversely, a loose agreement 'covers few issues, is phrased in general terms, and, whether explicitly or implicitly, prescribes minimum requirements only' thus leaving the door open for 'domestic bargaining to fill in the gaps or to go beyond the minimum requirements' (*ibid*).

Other things being equal, therefore, a tight agreement would limit scope and in so doing limit workplace independence of the full-time union official and of the wider union organization. But other things are not always equal, and in some cases even a tight agreement was found to increase independence, by allowing a small, and perhaps inexperienced local group to exercise greater independent control within the limited area of negotiation allowed to it, than it could possibly cope with under other circumstances (Boraston, Clegg and Rimmer, 1975, p 188).

They also found that the size of the workplace organization plays the largest part in determining the degree of dependence. This had an important effect on the resources at the union domestic organization's disposal, but they found independence also requires support in a consciousness of solidarity, in relatively high member status as employees, and in a history of autonomous bargaining experience. Nevertheless, the small domestic union organization might achieve similar ends by attaching itself, almost parasitically, to a larger and more powerful domestic group (see Boraston, Clegg and Rimmer, 1975, p 187).

However, dependence could also be modified by deliberate decision by the wider organizations involved, particularly where these affected the control of the resources available to the domestic group:

1 the trade union could vary the amount of the full-time officer's time and services made available to the domestic organization, so that if these were restricted the local group had to sink or swim on its own
2 the management could vary the amount of office space, meeting space, communications, facilities, and time-off, as well as the status accorded to the representatives, so that it could vary the ease or difficulty of the group's attempting to do its own thing.

But they suggest that whether an agreement is tight or loose (and therefore whether scope for local bargaining exists) is a matter largely determined by management: 'tight agreements are found where management is centralized' (Boraston, Clegg and Rimmer, 1975, p 8). This suggests that however much graduation there is to be found between tightness and looseness, it is management structure and policy which largely affects the issue of what kind of domestic organization exists on the union side.

The political role of the trades union congress

Trade unions, no less than employers' associations have an interest in developing an ethos which is supportive of their activities. Individual trade unions are involved in propaganda and in discussions with governments to preserve the position or status of the members, individually and collectively, just as the employers' associations are. But as with the employers, so with the unions, a central organization co-ordinates this function and engages in political activity on behalf of the movement as a whole.

On the worker side, and corresponding to the CBI on the employers' side (see above pp 250-51), stands the Trades Union Congress (TUC). This body was not in any sense a creature of government, and was not developed for any reason other than a wish on the part of trade unions to have a voice which could speak up on their behalf in respect of needed political action and changes in government policy. It was given political recognition and a national role by becoming involved in planning during World War I, much as were the predecessors of the CBI (see Richter, 1973).

Such involvement has since been subject to some vicissitudes, but the broad trend has been in the direction of more, rather than less, involvement with government (see Chandler, 1983). Although it has a role in relation to the internal regulation of the trade union movement, it does have a political representational role as a pressure group, focused on attempts to persuade governments to act in a way consistent with the trade union or worker interest. As the TUC's treatment by the Conservative Government of 1979-83 indicated, however, its success is dependent upon the willingness of governments to accept it in a pressure group role.

The first Trades Union Congress, held in 1868, was conceived differently from what the TUC eventually became. Originally, it was aligned with the trades councils and intended as a rather genteel (almost academic) debating chamber. It quickly moved into a position where it concerned itself with practical, day-to-day issues and with Parliamentary action on behalf of the unions, and eventually (1895) it was to exclude the trades councils as being vehicles of dual representation now that the national unions formed the affiliated members. As Roberts said of it in 1956: 'The functions of the TUC today are extremely diverse .... They embrace almost the whole gamut of industrial and political activities in which trade unions take part' (Roberts, 1956, p 426).

Structure

The TUC is now composed of affiliated national unions and draws its funds from the affiliation fees paid on a per capita basis by them. The affiliated membership is lower than the numbers of unionists given in table 15 (on p 260, above) but the larger unions are usually members whilst the smaller ones are less likely to be. The affiliation fee gives the unions a right to send delegates to the annual congress in proportion to their affiliated membership (although not all members are included in the affiliation and not all entitlements to delegates are necessarily taken up).

The supreme policy-making body is the Annual Congress which is made up of delegates. It usually conducts its business by debate on reports and motions put forward by the General Council or by affiliated unions. Decisions are usually taken by a show of hands, but a card vote may be called for on important issues. Delegates are accorded one vote for every 1,000 members and this results in the mammoth voting figures which are frequently quoted.

The main task of the Annual Congress is to approve the report of the General Council which provides a report of stewardship and indicates any special problems or surveys which may have been done during the previous year. Congress also decides on the main lines of policy which the General Council will be expected to follow and in recent years this policy has most frequently involved guidelines on the relations between the TUC and the Government or government policies. When incomes policies existed, the TUC's reaction to them was an obvious matter for discussion at least annually. Similarly, in the face of proposals for new legislation and its annual enactment, guidance on the TUC's approach and reaction have proved obvious subjects for consideration in the past 20 years. In addition, Congress elects the new General Council, a General Purposes Committee, and the fraternal delegates to other organizations.

The General Council is the body which runs the TUC's affairs between annual congresses. It operates through a number of sub committees, some of which are required to be established by rule and others are established as occasion demands. Members are elected by vote of the entire Congress, but the membership of the affiliated unions is divided into 19 groups and the elections are for representatives of each group. This is designed to ensure that the General Council is made up of representatives from a wide range of the affiliated unions and to prevent the very large unions from securing election of their nominees to the exclusion of others. The groups are however defined largely by reference to industry (with groups for non-manual workers, general workers, and women workers) and there is currently concern about the adequacy of representation of white-collar workers given the upsurge in membership of this category in recent years. Proposals for change in this respect are currently under debate.

The specific duties which are imposed on the General Council by rule include the review of all legislation affecting labour, adjustment and adjudication of disputes between affiliated unions, the formation of a general policy on such industrial matters as wages and hours of labour, the development and propaganda on behalf of the labour movement, and the maintenance of relationships with trade union movements in other countries.

Authority

To carry out these functions the General Council is given authority to invest and administer funds. It also has authority to levy affiliated unions on a pro rata basis to defray any legal costs which may be incurred in cases of vital concern to the trade union movement as a whole. It may also sanction affiliated unions in the event that they are in breach of TUC policy, but this is used sparingly (see Lerner, 1961). It was used in the period of the Industrial Relations Act to bring unions into line with TUC policy with respect to registration under the Act (see Weekes *et al*, 1975).

The internal organization of the TUC is under the control of the General Secretary who operates through assistant general secretaries and assistant secretaries. The General Secretary is usually the spokesman for the TUC on matters of general and public interest and he usually represents the TUC on international organizations of trade unions. The position is a potentially powerful one although he must operate within the framework of policy laid down by the General Council. The assistant general secretary usually carries a major responsibility for economic issues and the assistant secretary for organizational questions.

The work of the TUC is divided amongst a number of departments, chief of which are the production, research, economic, social insurance, industrial welfare, international, education, organization, and finance departments. Some of these, particularly the economic committee, are much more influential than others in relation to the development of national governmental policies. In addition, the TUC has a press and publicity department which has an important role in maintaining the public relations of the trade union movement with the media.

The TUC is able to provide the representation of the trade union movement on national committees whether governmental or otherwise. A number of such joint committees exist also at a regional level within the UK and, to organize the nomination of trade union representatives on these bodies, Wales and Scotland have their own TUCs and the regions of England have regional advisory councils whose members are elected at an annual meeting of affiliated union officers. The trades councils which exist in many towns have a much looser relationshp to the TUC than either the regional advisory councils or the trades councils themselves had in the early days of the TUC. This relationship has not been an easy one over the life of the TUC but a degree of co-operation, particularly in the development of local policy and in education, is now generally attained.

Summary: worker organizations

Workers have a variety of objectives and strategies for achieving them (which reflect their reading of the nature of the world in which they operate). They also 'possess' different statuses within work organizations and outside it. Because of this variety it is not surprising that they seek to associate in different ways in different kinds of organizations.

A broad distinction may be drawn between professional associations and trade unions, even if in the intermediate area

281

there may be some overlap. This is partly because within either group there is some variation in preferred objectives and strategies; although trade unions may be regarded as more homogeneous than the professional associations in this respect, there are still variations, particularly in the area of white collar employment which help account for similarities.

Trade unions, like the employers' associations examined in the preceding chapter, may be regarded as having some goals which are both offensive (revolutionary) and defensive, and perhaps more which are pragmatic. This does not diminish the significance of the first group, but it does perhaps suggest something about the views taken of the reality and the kinds of decision models and approaches used.

The way in which they are organized also demonstrates a wide variety of forms, many of which hark back to the conditions in which some of them were established. This might help to account for the fragmentation and multiplicity of unions within single establishments. Changes in circumstances, particularly those of post-World War II origin, seem, however, to have brought about adjustments of a less formalized kind which nevertheless reduce the problems of multi-unionism in the actual operating situation. The professional association versus trade union relationship may, however, replace this definition of the 'problem' in some and particularly the public sector work situations.

Trade unions, also like employers' associations, are necessarily involved in wider 'political' activity, as they seek to establish conditions in which they can, independently, pursue their intra-industrial goals. For this purpose (and others), the movement is equipped with a central organization, the TUC, which, again like the employers' central organization has a limited power *over* its members, but potentially considerable influence with government in so far as it can appear to speak for 'labour' as a whole.

Readings

Popitz et al: (1969), pp 281-324.
Goldthorpe: (1968), pp 36-42.
Crouch: (1979), pp 168-76; (1982), pp 120-89.
Hyman and Fryer: (1975), pp 150-213.
Roberts: (1956), pp 57-22; 395-458.
Blackburn: (1967), pp 9-66.

Clegg: (1972), pp 41-76; (1979), pp 165-227.
Bain and Price, in Bain: (1983), pp 3-34.
Armstrong, in Kessler and Weekes: (1971), pp 32-52
and 121-26.
Allen: (1958).

11

The bargaining relationship

Bargaining for objectives

The objectives of the several parties to industrial relations are only to be achieved through interaction between them. For example, what the employer may wish to attain is realizable only with the consent of the employees, individually or collectively. A similar statement might be made about what the workers and their associations seek. This is so because those caught up in the employment relationship have both complementary and antithetical interests. They must co-operate with one another because each needs (or wants) what the other has to offer, but they are opposed to one another because their interests in relation to the respective offers are different and divergent. These requirements both hold them together and (simultaneously) generate opposition and conflict between them.

This places them in the position where they must attempt to achieve their objectives by interaction in which each seeks to persuade, cajole, pressurize, coerce or compel the other to adopt or accept a particular course of action which accords with his objectives. This can be identified as dialogue, discussion, debate, or argument, but is more usually referred to in this context as 'bargaining'. Bargaining is fundamentally a process whereby the 'antithetical interests of supply and demand, of buyer and seller, are finally adjusted' in an act of exchange (MacIver and Page, 1953, p 474). It involves the bargainers in a:

> 'process of argument, persuasion, threat, proposal and counter-proposal by which the potential parties to a transaction discuss its terms and possibly reach agreement on them' (Brown, 1972, p 50).

The bargainers may be individual persons acting in their own interests or representatives of some association, and this distinction is usually indicated by the two adjectives, 'individual' and 'collective' applied to 'bargaining'.

In this view of bargaining, the process is regarded as serving a purely economic or material purpose, namely, the fixing of the two quantities which make up the 'consideration' necessary to the existence of a contract (see above, p 96). Bargaining is seen to occur only where it concerns itself in whole or in part upon these quantities. These constitute a fixed sum, so that whatever one secures, the other must lose.

In an alternative view, the process is regarded as one of *negotiating* the terms of both their mutual co-operation and the handling of their inevitable differences. This is much wider in its meaning than 'pure' bargaining, and can be defined to include all the other processes listed above, thus providing a much wider conception of the process. It might be used to apply to all types and forms of interaction within the context of the employment relationship, and it is in this sense that the term is used in this present chapter. It may focus on the purely economic aspects of the relationship, simply because the fundamental feature of that relationship is one of exchange. But the wider conception at least allows the possibility that the focus could be upon non-economic aspects of co-operation and containment. It might be thought of as a process of producing a constitution or a set of conventions (a kind of 'private' law) to govern the relationships within which decisions about the purely economic aspects can be taken (see chapter 12).

A PATTERNED RELATIONSHIP

The consequence of this is that the parties are unlikely to escape the necessity for developing an institutionalized relationship of a reasonably permanent kind within which they may interact to attempt to secure their aims. Over the industrial period, the pattern developed in Britain has changed from a highly decentralized to a highly centralized (but still voluntary) one, and then back to a more decentralized one.

Once collectivization occurred on the worker side and controlled the workings of competition between workers, it was probably inevitable that the employers would also collectivize, substituting formal association for the informal and (as Adam Smith (1776) expressed it) 'tacit' agreement of employers to hold down wage rates. The possibility of two collectivities confronting one another in a bargaining relationship was thus created, if only as a means of allowing each collective party to share in the process of controlling decisions about the labour price, through collective bargaining (in the term applied to it by Beatrice Webb (1890)).

However, at different times, this bargaining between collectivities has taken very different forms, starting with domestic and district arrangements, moving through a phase of national (industry-wide) bargaining, and most recently reverting to arrangements which placed greater emphasis on bargaining within the workplace. In domestic the representatives who meet to bargain are drawn predominantly from the undertaking or the establishment itself, and outsiders are drawn in little or not at all. In national or industry-wide bargaining, in contrast, the representatives are essentially external to particular undertakings and establishments, and the agreements that they might reach are generally regulatory of a much wider domain.

District and industry-wide bargaining

Between 1850 and 1950, it might be said that collective bargaining in Britain moved from one end-state to another. Initially, the parties attempted to secure district rates of pay and hours of work (together with certain manning ratios, as in the case of apprentices). The Webbs suggest, for example, that during the period up to World War II, the unions in particular attempted to 'secure recognition of certain broad principles', of which one was to the effect that:

> 'over a whole area, certain standard rates of wages should be paid, and certain recognised terms and conditions of labour respected, and that these wages, hours, and conditions should be determined by negotiation between the trade unions and the employers concerned' (Cole, 1923, p 7).

Establishing these standard or minimum rates to give uniformity in the labour market relevant to the trade was, in their view, the main problem faced at this time by the unions. The employers were themselves not averse to this outcome, because if they had to deal with the unions at all, they preferred to ensure that the consequential costs would be standardized to prevent 'unfair' competition between them as businessmen.

From World War I more emphasis was placed by both parties on securing national rates and conditions through a more highly centralized, industry-wide, bargaining machinery and process. The change was thought to have come about because of the increased governmental intervention in industrial affairs during the War. For example, Flanders talks of the:

> 'displacement of district by national or industry-wide negotiations, a trend already existing but greatly accelerated by the First World War and taken further by the Second' (Flanders, 1965, p 29; see also Goodman and Whittingham, 1969, pp 142-44; and Flanders in Flanders and Clegg, 1954, pp 272-87).

This may form a simple logical extension of the attempt to secure a district rate. Alternatively, it might represent a sensible accommodation of the problems posed for workers in a period of depression (as occurred during a good part of the inter-war period). It also aggregated the bargaining power of the workers (see below, pp 377-85) to an extent apparently sufficient to strike a balance, and at the same time provided a voluntarist bulwark against direct intervention by the State in industrial relations affairs (see Flanders, 1965, p 30). It came to be interpreted as a movement towards the establishment of a 'national system' of industrial relations which retained the decisions in the hands of the representatives of the affected parties but served to produce a system of regulation on an industry-wide basis.

It is well-recognized that the collective determination of *pay* and *hours of work* on a district or national basis is much easier than the determination of other quantities and particularly those relating to effort and contribution (other than such as might correlate with hours of work). Boraston, Clegg and Rimmer, for example, comment that it is:

> 'easier to determine rates of pay in an ... industry agreement than to regulate jobs. (It) can specify the rate for the job and the rate of overtime pay, but it cannot easily determine the amount of overtime working required to do the job' (Boraston *et al*, 1975, p 173).

This emphasis on pay rates helped to create and sustain the view that collective bargaining at these levels was essentially individual bargaining writ large. But no matter what the level of negotiation, there was a strong tendency, reflective of the practical difficulties, as well as the managerial ideology, to leave the job to be done for the manager to determine, the matter being dealt with 'by custom and practice arrangements at the plant' (*ibid*).

Although individual workers and employers still *established* their own contracts of employment, their representatives could be regarded as establishing the rules and the limits which they should observe as they did so. The national negotiators also established their own rules and procedures to govern *their* relationships as well as those of their constituents:

> 'Almost every industry with voluntary arrangements for collective bargaining has some kind of agreed procedure for dealing with local disputes ... An agreed procedure for collective bargaining is adopted in order to avoid industrial conflict' (Flanders, in Flanders and Clegg, 1954, pp 293-5).

National bargaining arrangements thus came to look like a kind of private law-making process as well as a bargaining arrangement.

Domestic bargaining

In the changed market situation after World War II, the tendency to develop domestic (undertaking or establishment) bargaining re-emerged, so that by the 1970s it was considered (probably erroneously) that this was completely replacing the national system (cf Elliot, 1980) whilst still incorporating many of its conventions and rules.

There has probably never been a time during the period since the industrial revolution, when no collective bargaining took place at the factory or company level. Over the period, there have been great changes in the subjects dealt with and there may have been a general trend (at least up to about 1950) towards greater centralization but there is an argument that suggests that both employer and trade union power 'has remained where it began in the eighteenth century, on the shop floor' (Cuthbert, in Cuthbert and Hawkins, 1974, p 3). As their power was affected by economic and technological changes, they might divest themselves of authority to negotiate to higher officials or they might retrieve it (as in the post-World War II situation).

In the face of full employment in the post-World War II situation, managements were often persuaded to engage in supplementary if not outright substitutional bargaining with local union representatives in the company or plant itself. In spite of the push in this direction given by the Donovan Commission, there seems to be relatively little domestic bargaining which is 'complete' in itself, either at company or plant level. Marsh, for example, concludes from his survey that:

> 'company-wide bargaining, strictly defined, is practised by only about one-in-ten of multi-establishment companies. In some cases, divisional level bargaining exists in addition, or as an alternative. It seems likely that there has been no significant move towards company-wide bargaining in British manufacturing as described and defined in the survey, although there has undoubtedly been a development of *partial* bargaining and even more head office involvement in settlements at lower levels... Some evidence in the survey suggests that companies have been actively decentralizing their bargaining to establishment level, reserving for themselves at head office a role as co-ordinator rather than direct bargainer' (Marsh, 1982, p 162).

This tends to indicate that some bargaining goes on at a number of discrete levels, from national to establishment, but that at no level is there is a complete absence of some, partial bargaining. There may still be enough such bargaining taking place at the local level to justify its examination as a significant element in the British pattern.

The more attention is focused on the domestication of collective bargaining, (whether in the form dominant in America, or in the partial form here), the more likely it is that an inference can be drawn that collective bargaining is a process of 'management'. At this level of negotiation, not only are the parties involved in the policing (in Britain) of the application of national agreements, but they are also dealing with real, day-to-day issues which call for decision and action. This involvement locks the union representatives into a *management* process.

The various contexts of bargaining thus involve the parties in different functions and different structures, ranging from legislating (laying down the rules) to managing (taking day-to-day decisions and implementing them). These contexts then

289

demonstrate what Walton and McKersie refer to as 'relationship patterns'. Those which they identify they regard, following Selekman, Selekman and Fuller (1958, pp 4-8), as reflecting different attitudes and ideologies related to the basic question of how the approach is to be made to the necessary interaction between them. The several parties are treated as adopting distinct attitudes towards the bargaining partner and the bargaining relationship itself which help either to sustain or to modify them.

Walton and McKersie suggest that a broad indication of the character of each 'pattern' is provided by the labels which they give to the five they isolate: 'conflict, containment-aggression, accommodation, co-operation, and collusion' (Walton and McKersie, 1965, p 185). We are concerned here with the nature of this relationship and with the foundations on which it is based although slightly different terminology is used to identify the different positions taken up in the British context.

Attitudes, orientations and ideologies

How the parties approach this relationship may, however, vary. Not only do they seek to achieve different objectives, but they may also display very different attitudes towards the relationship within which they, perforce, find themselves in seeking to achieve them. How they behave within the relationship can be expected to vary not only in response to the objectives which they have severally set for themselves, but also in accordance with the attitude which they hold to the relationship.

Walton and McKersie see the relationship as based on 'the modal attitudes' (*ibid*, p 185) of the parties. The concept of 'attitude' (see Allport, 1935) is probably better reserved for association with the principals (the individual employers and employees) as persons. They may be expected to reveal an array of attitudes towards both the opponent and the relationship. The survey evidence that we have (see Popitz *et al* 1968) suggests that this is likely to be distributed normally such that one broad central set of attitudes or predispositions will be more frequent, and therefore dominant, than others.

The concept of 'ideology' (what Walton and McKersie refer to as 'social beliefs') seems more pertinent and more comparable at the organizational level to the concept of 'orientation' or mental set applied at the individual level. The attitudes or perspectives which collectivities are usually seen to maintain coercively

290

amongst their members amount to an ideology which that organization expresses. Giner describes an ideology as 'a conception of the social world, explicitly and coercively maintained by a collectivity' (Giner, 1972, p 218). Corbett describes it in a way which links it more closely with 'attitude'. It is, he says:

'any intellectual structure consisting of:
– a set of beliefs about the conduct of life and the organization of society;
– a set of beliefs about man's nature and the world in which he lives;
– a claim that the two sets are interdependent; and
– a demand that these beliefs should be professed; and that claim conceded by anyone who is to be considered a full member of a certain social group' (Corbett, 1965, p 12).

Such 'a pattern of beliefs and concepts (both factual and normative) which purports to explain complex socio-political choices facing individuals and groups' (Gould and Kolb, 1964), predisposes the holder to think, feel and act in particular ways, as does the individual's attitude; it provides the base for their cognitive, affective and behavioural predispositions (see Lemon, 1968, pp 16-18), and justifies our association of the two concepts in the present context.

Walton and McKersie single out one salient and a number of subsidiary features of the parties' modal attitudes or ideologies as being particularly relevant to the kind of relationship pattern which develops between them. They regard the 'motivational orientation and action tendencies toward each other (competitive-individualistic-co-operative)' as the most general and complex (Walton and McKersie, 1965, p 185).

It covers what each party wants *from* the other and from engagement *with* that other in the relationship and what each party regards as the preferred behaviour (strategic and tactical) to adopt within that relationship. It must therefore encompass those perceptions and perspectives which are developed as a result of considering the capacity of the other in the relationship to yield, or facilitate the securing of, that which the party seeks. It implies a view of that part of the 'world' which is enshrined in the relationship. The other elements, 'beliefs about the other's legitimacy, feelings of trust toward each other, and feelings of friendliness-hostility toward each other' (*ibid*) are then seen as supplementary to this.

A description of the main ideological positions and of the relationship patterns may be identified in the industrial relations context on this basis. All of these may occur at some time and place, but some with greater frequency than others.

THE UNIONS' POSITIONS

Much material on which such a classification of trade unions according to their modal attitude can be based, has been assembled in many studies over the years (see S and B Webb, 1920; Dunlop, 1944; Crouch, 1982). Unions have been characterized on this basis as essentially oppositional to (see Clegg, 1951; Hyman and Fryer, 1975, pp. 170-82) or as essentially accommodative of (Batstone, Boraston and Frenkel, 1977; Beynon, 1973; Goodrich, 1975) management in particular or capitalism in general. Their orientation has also been variously labelled as indicative of revolutionary, overthrow, oppositional, business and racketeering unionism. Some of these labels may be more appropriate to some national cultures than to others, but the terms have been developed to highlight modal attitude or orientation as employed by Walton and McKersie (see table 16 on p 293).

Broad generalizations about workers' associations being necessarily opposed to the employer, and the equally broad generalizations about their being hooked on collective bargaining as the only possible relationship with the employer may be recognized as part of the rhetoric of industrial relations, and as only partially true. Any attempt to depict and describe the relationship patterns to be found in practice, would, consequently, have to provide space for a number of different orientations. Trade unions, no less than the workers whom they recruit and mobilize, are likely to display a number of different ideologies and attitudes along with congruent strategies for securing their members' positions in interaction with the opponent. Many different 'ideological' positions might be taken up.

It is possible to find examples of attitudes on the worker side which might fit the categories of revolution, rebellion, competitive association, and co-operation, as well as specific examples of associations which seek to engage in illegitimate collusion with the employers against the interests of some third party.

292

Table 16

Salient values and management and trade union ideologies

Corporate (employer) philosophy	!	Salient values of parties congruent relation	!	Trade union (worker) philosophy
Individualism paternalism	F R E E	REJECTION CONFRONTATION	F A I R	Revolutionary overthrow unionism
Boulwarism & similar abrasive ideologies		OPPOSITION		Permanently oppositional unionism
Demotivated abdication		a)PASSIVE ACCEPTANCE		Apathetic unionism
Status quo maintenance		b)ACCOMMODATION		Status quo maintenance
Constitutional-ism; plural-ism		CO-ORDINATION		Business unionism
Corporatism	F A I R	RE-INTEGRATION	F R E E	Non-political unionism

Based on Walton and McKersie, 1965, p 189

1 Revolution

An orientation towards revolution characterizes those associations which have been described as oriented towards the overthrow of the existing system of production and relations. The workers or their association or both deny 'the legitimacy of the other party's ends and means' (Walton and McKersie, 1965, p 186). Consistently with this, the association is likely to develop a predisposition towards confrontation and industrial action as a way of coercing the employer by unconventional means which are usually regarded as illegitimate if not unlawful.

Surveys of worker orientations have suggested that some, usually relatively small, proportion of a worker population reveals one of this type (see Popitz, 1969; Goldthorpe, 1968). Usually, the orientation is expressed in terms of a class-conscious dichotomous view of the world which calls for remedy by revolutionary means. Given the existence of such orientations amongst the workforce, it is not surprising that they carry over, in some cases at least, to the collective organizations of which they are members.

A number of episodes in the history of British radicalism provide examples of such value orientations amongst worker representatives and organizations (for example, the shop stewards' movement of the Clyde in World War I (Pribicevik, 1959, ch 6), aspects of the 1926 General Strike (Page Arnot, 1949) and some more locally-bounded developments in the motor car industry after World War II (Marsh and Coker, in Marsh, 1963; Friedman and Meredeen, 1980; Cliff, 1970).

2 Rebellion

An orientation to rebellion may be distinguished from that to revolution (as it is by Albert Camus and Jean-Paul Sartre respectively). It appears more readily to characterize British manual worker trade unions which have been described as a permanent opposition in industrial government (Clegg, 1951, p 24). In this view, the union may see itself and be seen by others, to demand the right to challenge the decisions of management, whilst still accepting management's right to take them. This implies that the workers' association accord a grudging legitimacy to the ends and means of the employer, but demand the right to oppose, that is to restrict the employer's freedom of action. In effect this means that in negotiations, the agenda is sometimes accepted and sometimes challenged by the unions. Agreements which emerge from them represent a succession of truces which never turn into peace treaties.

In both of these orientations, the conception of the relationship with the employer will be one predominantly based on *conflict* as the normal mode. What distinguishes them are the ultimate objectives sought and the 'degree' of conflict regarded as desirable or legitimate. However, cases also exist amongst workers' associations (and particularly amongst those which may not regard themselves as trade unions in the usual ideological conception) which suggest an orientation to *co-operation* with the employer, although again, the 'degree' of co-operation and the ultimate objectives may differentiate them.

3 Competitive association

We can distinguish an orientation to competitive association which reduces the salience of this type of conflict (as in the case of what has been described as 'business unionism'). Here the union accepts some of the aims of the employer as legitimate both for him and for the union itself, but reserves the right to challenge him on the means and particularly on the distribution of the benefit secured through the relationship.

The 'pure' form of unionism advocated by Gompers and the American Federation of Labour (AFL) and the frequently quoted actions of the International Ladies Garment Workers' Union (ILGWU) in the New York fashion trade, provide examples of this co-operation. The actions did involve co-operation on some matters, but the relationship thus initiated, did not deny their separate interests nor eliminate the possibility of conflict between the parties over the distribution of benefits. The unions did not offer such help in all circumstances nor were all of them accepted by the employers (suggesting that some of them had quite incongruent motivational orientations).

4 Co-operation

Trade unions and other associations may well display an orientation which is essentially co-operative. It is based upon a more complete acceptance of the values of the employer and of the means which he might use to secure his ends as equally valid for the union (association) and its members. It does not question the ends of the work undertaking, and does not expect there to be much dispute even about distribution. However, the orientation implies that the 'price of democracy is eternal vigilance' and that for this reason a 'democratic' means of curbing possible (even if unexpected) excesses on the part of the employer should be developed and maintained. For the radical, at least, this might be branded as an example of 'false class consciousness' suggesting that in relation to these values, the orientation involved is somehow illegitimate, even though in terms of others' values it could be accorded complete legitimacy.

The underlying value orientations of some of the white collar and managerial/supervisory associations provide examples. Some unreservedly accept the ends of management as their own, and seek only to develop a constitutional constraint upon the employer's exercise of his discretion. A main aim is to establish and preserve the quasi-independent status of the employee group concerned, and to provide a mechanism for the handling of grievances, either against the management or other organized groups of workers (see Thomason, Doughty and Spear, 1977).

These four positions are not necessarily completely distinct from one another. In practice, they may shade into one another and also provide justifications for different positions taken up by the same associations at different times. The same association or group might equally adopt quite different positions for different purposes or in relation to different problems or issues; it might, for example, adopt a rebellious position on discipline and a co-operative one on safety (see, for example, Gouldner, 1955b).

The bigger gap occurs between the first two and the last two. The first two are broadly oriented towards collective (even class) conflict, where the other two have a much more individualistic connotation. In between them may lie an orientation which is much more passively directed towards acceptance of the status quo, and which may be less fervent in the advocacy which it evokes and in its consequences for the relationship. The differences within each pair are then much more a matter of degree. But they do enable some systematic treatment of the workers' associations' orientations and attitudes to the bargaining relationship, which may then be set alongside the orientations of the employer.

EMPLOYERS' POSITIONS

Fewer studies have been made of the employers' positions in industrial relations. Some generalizations about the attitudes which employers bring to industrial relations are possible on the basis of general theories and of the material we do have available. Some use can be made of the two basic theories which underlie the legitimation of managerial authority, the *residual* theory and the *trusteeship* theory.

The *residual theory* sees the employer or manager as endowed

296

with all the power and authority which originally accrued to the sovereign head, except for that which he may have given up voluntarily. It forms the basis of the claim frequently written into collective agreements to the effect that the managemnt remains possessed of all such powers and rights as are not expressly given up or assigned to others (unions or joint bodies) within the agreement (see Hill and Hook, 1945). It emphasizes the power of the directorate or management over and above all others associated with the undertaking (see Friedman, 1963; 1977).

Application of this concept gives the directorate a powerful position, which has to be defended against any attempts (by law or the trade unions) to curb it. It tends to commit the management to a defensive posture in relation to other interest groups, whether shareholders or workers, and thus to the maintenance of a conflictual relationship with any group which challenges their authority. This theory supplies the foundation for the unitarist conception, in which the role of management is seen to be essentially autocratic and authoritarian (see Fox, 1966).

The trusteeship theory regards the manager as the trustee of the manifold interests associated with the undertaking. It emphasizes more the idea of a partnership or of a democratic structure of authority at least to the extent that it allows autonomy to the other interest groups. Such powers and rights as the manager may posess are, therefore, seen as held *on trust* for the various interest groups: shareholders, employees, the community, etc. Nevertheless, it is not usual to regard management as merely another interest group (which in some senses they are), but rather as an interest group which, by virtue of its co-ordinating and controlling role, must be superior to the others. This theory then forms the basis for the 'pluralist ideology' (see Fox, 1966; 1973; 1979; Nichols, 1974; Clegg, 1975; Hyman, 1978) and the conception of the 'statesman' role of central managers (see Walton, 1967; Beesley and Hughes, 1978).

Neither of these conceptions denies managers their dominant position in modern society (Drucker, 1955, p 1), nor their role as a 'rule-making and rule-enforcing body' (Harbison & Myers, 1959, p 19), on behalf of the undertaking as the superior entity. Both theories regard the undertaking as essentially co-operative, even if it is also recognized that from time to time, differences will arise between the co-operators. But they do allow for two very different attitudinal or ideological positions to be taken up with respect to the place to be accorded to trade unions in the processes

297

of handling industrial relations issues, and these could respond to perceptions of need in the situation.

It follows that, according to perspective, the machinery considered by management as appropriate to the fostering of co-operation and the handling of differences will vary. In the one case the expectation will be that problems will be solved by management acting in everyone's interest. In the other they will be dealt with by management applying the jointly established rules for their solution worked out in discussion with representatives of the trade unions and perhaps other worker associations. They therefore contrast with the radical theory which denies management legitimacy as a 'superior' authority in the employment context (see Hyman, 1978; Nichols, 1974).

The major positions which can be derived by this method extend along the individualistic/paternalistic – collectivist /corporatist axis, much as in the case of the trade unions. But they do not extend over the whole spectrum to embrace the radical ideology. Consequently, the positions taken up by management do not exactly match the spectrum of positions taken up by the workers. The two ranges reveal themselves, therefore, as skewed in relation to each other.

1 Individualism/paternalism

One end of the spectrum is defined in terms of unitarist models of organization and leadership. This is historically derived, drawing upon the values of individualism and the principles of sovereign authority in structures of familial organization. It is most often identified with a unitarist frame of reference, or ideology. This emphasizes the relevance of family-type models of enterprise, and leads managers to *assume* that all members of the undertaking will be motivated to deal co-operatively with any differences on a problem-solving basis and within a framework of interpersonal co-operation and consensus. This then provides the foundation for the managerial prerogative.

Concretely, the unitarist denies the need for any alternative or external organization within the one happy family. This is manifest in the attitudes adopted towards trade unions or any other alternative organization seeking to develop a bargaining relationship with the employer. Thus, Walton and McKersie's illustration of their 'conflict' relationship pattern identifies the company which:

'is determined to refuse to deal with unions if at all possible... and ... recognises the union only to the extent imposed by law and union power. In the company's pursuit of this policy it is constrained only by the letter of the law; ... it is certainly not constrained by the spirit of the law. Co-existence is not a policy but a temporary state of affairs.' (Walton and McKersie, 1965, p 186).

Such companies are also to be found in Britain. For example, the Scarman Report (1977) on the Grunwick Film Processing Company's dispute in 1976-77 describes the attitudes and values of the Company in terms almost exactly the same as those employed by Walton and McKersie. It refers to the attitudes of unconcern for the other's internal affairs, distrust of the other's motives and action, and disrespect for the 'spirit' of the law. Another example, with some parallels, is to be found in the Roberts-Arundel dispute of the late 1960s (Arnison, 1970) and some of the more graphic disputes of 1983 carry similar connotations.

2. Combatative competition

Another and less extreme orientation is that which manifests itself as a combatative competition with any alternative organization. The view is taken that such association may be a fact, but that it is nevertheless both misguided and a hindrance to the realization of the associators' best interests. These are served by maintaining loyalty to the single (employer's) organization of the firm. It is then seen as a duty upon the employer to do all that is lawful and within his power to woo the backsliders back to the ways of righteousness.

In the USA, the approach to unions referred to as Boulwarism illustrates this attitude (see Northrup, 1964; Walton and McKersie, 1965, p 187; Anthony and Crichton, 1969, pp 108-9). Boulwarism involves recognition of unions (as may be required by law) but a continuing intransigence towards them. The objective is to destroy the union in the interests of restoring individual bargaining; it is mitigated only by the legislative requirement of recognition and good faith bargaining (in the USA).

Intransigence is usually manifest in the maintenance of open communication lines to the employees in competition with the unions, and by communicating management's last (and only) offer in any negotiation to the workers directly rather than *via* the trade union officers. It is not unknown for other employers to use a comparable strategy from time to time, seeking to break a union's hold by a direct, competitive appeal to the workforce, as in the strategy adopted by Sir Michael Edwardes in British Leyland during the early 1980s and by a number of other employers subsequently.

3 Pluralism

Employers, and perhaps more particularly managers, do not necessarily adopt a frame of reference which is as individualistically-oriented as these first two examples suggest. Where they represent the large corporation, they are as likely to adopt 'bureaucratic' orientations (see Goldthorpe *et al*, 1968, pp 39-40) or attitudes which give salience to the objectives of achieving ordered performance by whatever means may be necessary or expedient. Within such orientations, recognizing and dealing with the workers' associations may represent an acceptance of what are seen as the realities of the situation which they are called upon to manage.

This is frequently identified as a pluralist frame of reference. This entails recognizing the existence of a number of different interests and viewpoints. It is likely to lead managers to accept that these will need to be reflected and represented in separate independent bodies (such as the trade unions or professional associations) and that differences will need to be resolved through a bargaining process, between, if not 'equals', at least independents each deriving their power from separate sources.

This kind of orientation, regardless of how particularly it may be labelled, gives much more emphasis to the collectivity or the organization than the unitarist. The aim becomes not the denial of the alternative organization its place in the sun but the development of some constitutional or procedural arrangement by which its status is protected. This is the essence of the original pluralistic perspective (Fox, 1966). It places the manager in the 'statesman' role (see Walton, 1967; and above, pp 115-18 and 298), that of reconciling the varied interests pursued through distinct organizations.

An outstanding British example of this approach is to be found in the Glacier Metal Company experiment of the immediate post-World War II period (Jaques, 1951). Without changing the status of the company as a free enterprise corporation, Wilfred Brown as managing director sought quite deliberately and relatively successfully to provide an elaborate constitution to codify and contain the relationships between management and the workforce. Part of this constitution reserved certain roles and functions to the Board of Directors (as required by Companies Acts) but the other part, on the making of conditional policy (as distinct from the reserved 'definitive policy') and supporting machinery, sought to co-ordinate the interests of the company and the unions. (The theory supporting this venture is expounded in Brown, 1951.)

The initiative in the above case was taken by the Company. The union(s) and the workforce as a whole accepted the proposals after widespread discussion, but never gave up their right to strike (see Kelly, 1968). Many other managements have, over the years, sought to develop similar but less thorough-going constitutions in the form of elaborate procedural agreements (see for example, GKN-Shotton, 1973: and below, pp 451-52) with varying success in terms of the response of the trade unions involved.

4 Corporatism

Such an approach by management may easily extend to embrace objectives and strategies which could be regarded as illegitimate (not sanctioned by social norms) or illegal (contrary to the law). This represents a degree of collusion (the term used by Walton and McKersie) to reintegrate the workers into the system, but now under the control and discipline of the corporation *and* the union. It is the element of double-headed coercion which distinguishes this orientation, and depends upon the managerial acceptance that the union can be legitimately recruited to serve ends which are properly those of the management or the employer.

In recent years, that extension of constitutionalization and acceptance of the aims and means of the opponent which focuses on the closed shop or union membership agreement, illustrates both of these. Many managers have shown themselves in favour of signing such agreements with the unions, often on the grounds that it 'makes control much easier'. However, the objectives of the management and the unions in this matter have not gone

301

unchecked; sanctions of disapproval were often applied (see McCarthy, 1964; Department of Employment, 1983). Initially, there developed a highly critical public concern about the practice as offensive to broad societal norms. Later attempts were made in various pieces of legislation (in 1971 and 1980-2)to outlaw it by one means or another.

Thus at this pluralist end of the spectrum of orientation and attitude, two discrete positions are recognizable, where there is a discernible orientation towards the social or collective rather than the individual. On this 'side' therefore, one can recognize a number of distinct employers' positions which are equivalent to, but do not necessarily match or reciprocate those adopted by workers' associations.

THE CONGRUENT RELATIONSHIPS

Any combination of these employers' and employees' positions is theoretically possible. Some of them in juxtaposition, can be expected to prove more congruent with one another than other combinations. There seems to be no a *priori* ground on which it might be asserted that any one orientation of one party will necessarily be associated with any one of the other party. In practice, one such orientation in the relationship may prove to be dominant, in the sense that it renders the orientation of the other inoperable. But which proves dominant may also depend on how the procedural (as distinct from substantive) conflict between incongruent orientations is handled in the particular situation.

Walton and McKersie, however, imply that as a result of some natural selection or shake-out process, congruent relationship patterns will develop. They state that 'the parties *share* a relationship pattern, by which we mean a set of reciprocal attitudes salient to the parties in their interaction' and that the particular attitudinal components identifiable 'are assumed to be crucial to the parties' joint dealings, to be interrelated, and generally to *vary together* in the labour management context' (Walton and McKersie, 1965, p.185; *italics added*).

These statements are generally unexceptional in so far as they indicate merely that the parties, whatever their attitudes and orientations, must be involved in a relationship or a relationship pattern, whether one of individual or collective bargaining or some other. However, in so far as they depend upon the attitudes

302

being 'shared' or 'reciprocal', and the components of these attitudes 'varying together', they are less so. It must be the case that sometimes attitudes are not shared or reciprocated, even when a relationship pattern of some kind exists (as Fox's discussion of the patterns resulting from the conjunction of various ideologies indicates (Fox, 1974a, pp 297-313).

This does not preclude the possibility of recognizing certain congruent or consonant patterns of relationship, in the sense that certain conjunctions might be more likely to occur or to be viable. Based on Walton and McKersie's scheme, five such congruent patterns can be identified in association with the positions adopted by the parties (although the opportunity for 'mixed relationship patterns' rather than congruent ones to develop is not thereby denied). The five can be identified and described, in terms more relevant to the British situation, as: confrontation; opposition; accommodation; co-ordination and co-operation.

1 Confrontation

The first congruent pattern is identifable as confrontation (rather than as conflict which is the concept used by Walton and McKersie) where the term is chosen to highlight a likely consequence of the juxtaposition of individualistic orientations shown by the employer and revolutionary ones by the workers' association.

Given the current conventions surrounding labour relations, both parties may orient their behaviour to a revolutionary value, which not only involves 'a denial of the legitimacy of the other party's ends and means' but a dominant belief that he must be obliterated. But the direction of the revolutionary movement sought by the two parties will be opposite: the employer may seek to return to a condition of unfettered individualism amongst workers, in the interests of 'freedom'; the union may try to advance to a condition of workers' control (in which the employer concept is eliminated), in the interests of 'fairness'.

The consequences for the relationship pattern can best be described as creating a situation of confrontation. Regardless of the attitudes adopted by the other party, the adoption of attitudes of this kind by one party, can be expected to lead it into a situation of confrontation (in which there is a denial of legitimacy, as suggested above, pp 292-93 and 298-99). This extreme attitudinal position may for this reason, beget matching strategies on

303

the other side and where this occurs a congruent relationship could develop.

2 Opposition

A second congruent pattern might be described by the term opposition, recognizing the usual characterization of the relationship of manual worker unions and employers in Britain over a good part of their history. Walton and McKersie refer to this as a 'containment-aggression' relationship, in which the parties are seen as competitive in their relationship, grudgingly accepting the other's legitimacy, and as oriented in their action to restricting the other's scope of action (which then tends to limit the 'subjects' considered jointly). Each party is seen as predisposed to do the other party down in circumstances where this would not result in high costs to itself. Generally they are thought to regard one another with suspicion which leads to scrutiny of all acts of the other with a view to challenging them, often in a competitive struggle for the allegiance of the workers themselves.

In the British context, each party tends to reveal a basic and continuing acceptance of the probability that the opponent will pursue divergent ends and adopt a vaguely non-coperative posture within the relationship. For this reason, the parties may 'in their choice of means...., accept any limits of the law, including minimum definition of the spirit of the law as they understand it' (Walton and McKersie, 1965, p 186) and normally the limits set by convention (although this is less invariate). The limits of convention are frequently written into agreements and understandings in the form of acceptances of management's right to manage and the trade union's right to represent the interests of its members (and in the now defunct national agreement in the engineering industry: see Marsh, 1965, p 72-111 and 250-318).

This arises because the regulation of collective bargaining in Britain is less the consequence of legislation and more usually the conventions developed by the parties in the industrial relations situation itself. It is the 'spirit' of *this* law which is accepted as a minimum. This law is interpreted in accordance with the values of rebellion and may from time to time produce what others might consider its breach. But the rebel in this characterization requires two things: an institutional framework which will

304

(whilst, as it were, he is not rebelling) carry the action forward (this is the element of acceptance); and the opportunity, legitimately within that institutional framework, to challenge both that action and if need be the institution itself from time to time, in order to satisfy some end of 'adjustment' or of 'reform'.

3 Accommodation

The third relationship pattern identified by Walton and McKersie is described by the title of 'accommodation'. They see it characterized by 'individualistic orientation', 'recognition of the legitimacy of the other's ends and means' (amounting to an acceptance of the status quo), 'reasonable amounts of respect for the other's representatives', 'limited trust' and 'neutral affect' (that is a kind of 'calculative involvement' in Etzioni's (1975) phrase).

This provides a reasonable description of a middle position in the continuum of bargaining relationship patterns, but there could be a case for recognizing middle positions with either high or low affect. The reason for this is that it is possible to conceive of a relationship in which the *status quo* is maintained, as it were, by default, simply because no one has any motivation to make any kind of change. But it is also possible to effect this result by deliberate and positive action designed to achieve just that end. Generally apathetic (or low affect) orientations on the part of the parties might be associated with the development of this relationship pattern , but a deliberate commitment to a middle road could do so too.

The example of positive orientations used by Walton and McKersie (1965, p 188) of the mutual accommodation of the US Steel Company and the United Steelworkers of America in the early 1950s, showed, as they put it, 'some overtones of co-operation'. Other examples of desultory relationships between managements and workers are to be found in the period of apathy in the 1950s which defended a status quo which the Donovan Commission were to castigate in the 1960s. On the management's side, the 'demotivated manager' syndrome of the middle 1970s may prove to have contributed more to the absence of change in industrial relations than any other single factor.

4 Co-ordination

Walton and McKersie say little about their fourth category, 'co-operation', and their fifth, 'collusion'. This could reflect their association with assumedly non-modal orientations on the part of the two parties, the consequent dearth of examples in reality if the assumption is correct, or an inadequate terminology and characterization.

Over the range of workers' associations and corporate organizations, neither the assumption nor the lack of evidence seem to hold good. There are examples of both kinds of relationship pattern. But on the third score, these two points on the scale might be thought of as 'co-ordination' and 'reintegration' in that order.

The term 'co-ordination' is used here to mean roughly what is indicated by the use of the term in Kahn-Freund's discussion of the legal structuring of the relationship between employer and employee.

> 'The characteristic feature of the employment relation is that the individual worker is subordinated to the power of management but that the power of management is co-ordinated with that of organized labour. The regulation of labour results from the combination of these processes of subordination and co-ordination, of the rules made unilaterally by the employer in conjunction with those agreed between him or his association and the union through collective bargaining' (Kahn Freund, 1972, p 13).

However much conflict may exist, there is in the circumstances of industrial relations a need for a minimal degree of co-operation. Whatever the orientations of the parties, their interests will not and cannot be exactly similar but in any orientation which accepts these as problems to be solved, a degree of co-operation will be requisite for solving them. Some differences will exist to be dealt with even in the best regulated situations. There can be an acceptance, not merely of the legitimate expectations and interests of the other, but of the need to co-operate in the interests of solving these problems.

A relatively high degree of trust is both necessary and given in these circumstances, but it is not a trust relationship deriving from dependency unilaterally-defined. There is also a respect for both the law and the relevant conventions which regulate such relationships. They will however tend to be seen as instruments which may be used to protect such mutuality as is desired from an arbitrary use of structural power.

But most importantly, the parties will be strongly motivated to accept one constellation of objectives as being common to both parties even if there are then others which divide them. There will, in other words, be a predilection to co-operate up to a point and this might be better identified as a relationship characterized by the 'co-ordination' of the partly common and partly diverse ends of the parties.

There are cases on record of companies which seek to develop their relationships with the workers and their trade unions in a highly constitutional way. This is intended to permit the legitmate aspirations of both parties to be served, protected and even fostered by the same 'constitution'.

5 Co-operation

The relationship pattern which I have chosen to refer to as 'co-operation' differs fundamentally from Walton and McKersie's 'collusion'. In their view, collusion refers to the formation of a coalition of the two parties to pursue objectives which extend beyond their legitimate interests, to embrace exploitation of both principals and third parties by means outside the law and the usual conventions applied.

Consequently, in their conception, concern with the internal affairs of the other party, trust for the other, and friendship with him (in the sense of the phrase 'sweetheart relationship') are all high. They may be so mainly to preserve the cohesion of the coalition in the face of actual or potential threats from those parts of the environment which would not accord it legitimacy (Walton and McKersie, 1965, p 188). This relationship pattern does not, therefore, attract much support or legitimacy from those who orient their thinking towards the dominant conventions and laws which surround this institution.

There does, however, seem to be a relationship pattern based possibly on a congruence of orientations and values which on the employers' side involve a conception of social responsibility which is at least beyond the spirit of the Companies Act (although legitimate) and on the worker side a conception of a separate but co-operative relationship with the employer which is beyond the spirit of recent labour legislation in Britain (although legitimate).

This notion of 'extension beyond', should not, however, lead us to suppose that it is any more to be deplored than the attitudes and values discernible at the other end of this spectrum. Our predilection for voluntary collective bargaining may reflect a dominant social value, but at least as yet, we have not yielded to the temptation of demanding a completely conformist pattern of social action.

What can be recognized here as distinguishing the category, therefore, is a predisposition to co-operate, to trust the other because of a perceived accord of interests (rather than because of created accord) and a regard for the other as pursuing legitimate but distinct ends by legitimate but different means.

The motivation of the party to pursue these as objectives may be high, and not merely the result of an unthinking acceptance of the status quo of organizational life. Those who organize and maintain trade unions not affiliated to the TUC may be as keenly dedicated to the values which such organizations uphold as the TUC-affiliated unions may be to their values; those companies which seek to develop 'commonwealths' and comparable structures of authority in work regulation may equally have a strong dedication to these as alternative forms to the registered company (see Blum, 1968).

INCONGRUENT ORIENTATIONS AND PATTERNS

Congruent relationship patterns may be more likely because the attitudes, ideologies and orientations of the two parties are more consistent with one another, and therefore viable. Some orientations may, in turn, be more likely because they are perceived to be more relevant to the underlying market situation. However, this perspective implies a structure which is too rational and too tidy; in reality, the parties are unlikely to reach the same conclusions from their reading of the situation, and relationships are unlikely to fall together as readily as Walton and McKersie's analysis suggests. There are clearly other juxtapositions possible, and the theoretical possibilities of relationship patterns are exhausted only in a totally interconnected network of the different positions.

The question then arises as to whether such other combinations are any less likely to occur than those which have been identified in the preceding section.

The first ground for thinking this is that which accepts that the orientations at each end of the continua are likely to be more intensely held than those in the middle. The actors involved are more likely to hold strong convictions about the rightness or legitimacy of their positions. Walton and McKersie rely upon the adage that people will tend to 'fight fire with fire' to support their suggestion that the personality structure of the negotiators will influence the relationship pattern. They see the individual's predispositions and his perceptions of what the other intends as important determinants of the kind of relationship which emerges. Accepting that this is so, it also follows that the extreme positions are likely to be the most difficult to shift and the juxtaposition of an extreme position with a non-extreme one might not lead to any compromise but to confrontation.

One consequence of this could be that where one party adopts an extreme position, the other will (as a result of frustration, for example) be drawn into a more congruent (because more extreme) relationship pattern. High commitment to an extreme position might be expected to beget a corresponding response from the opponent. This might result in responses at the technical or strategic level rather than in fundamental changes of ideology or attitude. As the Scarman Report (1977) on the Grunwick dispute shows, the orientations of two parties at the outset of an interaction may not correspond, but the less entrenched party may be forced in the course of interaction to develop strategies and tactics which are more apposite to those of the opponent. In the Grunwick dispute, the APEX union found itself in a situation in which more militant strategies and tactics (not particularly characteristic of that union, nor, seemingly, intended by them at the outset) were 'developed' in the face of the Company's attitude.

Similarly, it could be argued that the underlying orientations of the Ford Motor Company to a constitutional approach changed scarcely at all at the time when it took steps to eliminate from its payroll certain shop stewards whom it adjudged to be oriented in a way not supported by its workforce in general and whose continued presence it considered inimical to its purposes (see Friedman and Meredeen, 1980; Beynon, 1973). This same episode could, however, be interpreted to suggest that the power of management to dismiss can be used as a counter to an extreme position taken up by a union, equivalent to the use by the workers either of a strike weapon or of a voluntary severance, to effect a change of strategy if not orientation on the part of the management.

Thus the effect of such juxtapositions as these could be to force the other party to adopt a congruent orientation. This might not carry the other party all the way across the spectrum. For example, the response of the undertaking to a behavioural pattern oriented towards revolutionary values could be better described as rebellious than as revolutionary. In these circumstances, however, the rebellious orientation could, as in the Ford case mentioned, prove temporary, and be detectable in strategic rather than fundamental terms.

In such circumstances too, the response could be interpreted as 'irrational and extreme behaviour' stemming from the 'considerable anxiety' that a mismatching produces. This may reflect incongruence and dissonance, not a coercion towards mutuality in value orientations.

Management may be able to tolerate many more positions that might be taken up by the workers' association, than the union can. It might be on general grounds, that management tends to be ideologically deficient but possessed of power to effect compliance with its will. There is evidence to suggest, for example, that management may take up a different position according to what it faces. Many adopt conventional positions and pursue conventional objectives in interaction with blue collar unions, but adopt and pursue different ones with reluctantly militant white collar staffs (Roberts *et al*, 1972), without finding this inconsistent.

The possibility that management in the larger undertaking will adopt an extreme position at the corporatist end of the range, seems for this kind of reason to be relatively small. To do so would have the effect of challenging the basis of the relationship between the workers and their trade union leaders, since it would involve the latter in a process of control which might not be supported by their ideology. The likely consequences of this might be either the kind of illegitimate collusion (which Walton and McKersie identify) or the replacement of the union leadership in the wake of membership resistance. In other words, unless reciprocation occurred, the union might be expected to move into a more conflictual orientation, which would be more detrimental to the realization of the management's objectives than would be the adoption of a much lower profile.

It should also be recognized that in very many cases, management is in the position where it has the power to compel the unions to leave their more extreme ideological baggage at the door of the bargaining chamber. In this it may be aided by appeal to a different part of the spectrum of worker orientations and the effect this might be to deny support for union representatives in the negotiating situation.

All of which suggests that the juxtaposition of the value orientations of the parties does not produce an even pattern of relationships. The unions' positions are generally more oriented to opposition, conflict and competition than are those of the management, a conclusion which simply reflects the different role constraints involved. Partly as a consequence of this, the factor of 'struggle' for an independent voice on the part of the workers, is likely to ensure that emotional commitment on their part is likely to be higher than that of management.

Summary: relationships

Against the background of a developed (institutionalized) pattern of interaction between the parties to the employment relationship, it is possible to identify a number of *positions* which any and either party to the relationship may take up. These are likely to be based on the party's reading of the world and how it works, particularly that world which encompasses the necessary interaction which occurs within the employment situation.

A basic matrix of about five positions which can be recognized as applicable to the two parties can be drawn up and both congruent and incongruent relationships between the different positions identified. This implies that, dependent on the under-lying attitudes and ideologies of the parties *as these are applied to the subject of the interaction at the time*, some relationship patterns will prove more viable or persistent (even productive in terms of the goals of the separate parties), and some will prove destructive and unstable (as well as unfruitful) in terms of the parties' objectives.

The possibility that the same parties might adopt different ideological stances in relation to different aspects of the relationship means, however, that it might be unrealistic to give the dog a particular name (good *or* bad) and assume that the name must apply to every facet of the relationship. The matrix used here is useful as a tool of analysis, but it has to be applied to each subject and facet to determine what strategies for changing underlying attitudes and predispositions might be required or useful.

Readings

Walton and McKersie: (1965), pp 184-209.
Popitz et al: (1969), pp 281-324.
Goldthorpe et al: (1968), pp 144-73.
Newby and Bell: (1977), pp 83-97. Munns: (1967).

12

The functions and conventions of bargaining

The context of bargaining

The fact that what each party seeks can only be realized by interaction or bargaining, possibly against the wishes of the other, need not imply that what is being played is a zero-sum game, in which one can only win what the other loses. But this does, at least, imply that one cannot achieve his ends without some concession or compensation to the other(s) (see below, pp 506-07).

This process of interaction takes place within a context which can be construed in a number of ways. First, the interaction may be seen as taking place within a situation whose 'objective' qualities limit the possible achievements: it occurs within a market and political situation which has a limited capacity for meeting the objectives of the parties whether these are regarded jointly or severally. These 'objective' factors may, however, only make their impact through the perceptions of the parties engaged in interaction, and thus do not have a direct and untrammelled influence upon either the interaction or its outcomes. But they are nevertheless separately distinguishable.

Secondly, the capacity of the parties to interact in a useful way may be construed as limited by their enforceable rights and obligations. We have already seen how the limits to this authority are set by law and the conventions and rules which have been developed within the relationship, and the internal and external mechanisms through which each of these is upheld. This structure of rights and obligations provides another part of the context of the bargaining or negotiating process through which the parties are obliged, because they are free agents, to try to secure their diverse or even conflicting interests and objectives.

Thirdly, the form of the interaction will tend to reflect the attitudes of the individuals and the positions taken up by the

313

parties as collectivities. These may encompass orientations to very different ideologies, and may result in very different approaches being made to the interaction with the other party. They are not unlikely to be influenced by their reading of the situation in which each party finds itself, but there is never a suggestion that different parties must necessarily come to similar conclusions from reading any given situation. The opportunity for diversity of orientation is always present.

Definition of bargaining

Bargaining tends to take widely-recognized individual and collective forms. These two methods, of individual and collective bargaining have been the ones which, at different times, and in different combinations at any one point in time, have been relied upon to mitigate the exigencies of the forces of the market as they impinge upon any specific labour market. They ensure that the necessary decisions are taken and that business proceeds even when the conditions for the free and perfect market do not obtain. In the analyses of these processes, the forces of the market can be treated as pressures or constraints upon either individual or collective decisions and bargaining as a process of evaluation and persuasion backed by differential authority and power.

The development of collective bargaining led, because of the nature of what is involved in it, to the development of complex structures of conventions and rules which the parties accepted voluntarily as governing their relationships. The first set of rules were necessary to order the collective relationships between those who actually met to engage in the bargaining process. These established who recognized whose authority to do what and what form the discussions between them would be expected to take. The second set of rules were required to govern the relationships between the principals or constituents on whose behalf the negotiators were acting. These took the form of procedures which these principals would be expected to follow.

The fact that the approach to and content of bargaining has changed over the industrial period, provides understandable reasons for taking divergent views of its functions and purposes. In the literature, three distinct views emerge which allow collective bargaining to be seen as:

1   a *collective* substitute for individual bargaining (a means of arriving at the terms of the contract in bulk)
2   a system of industrial government with the emphasis on producing the domestic equivalent of legislation
3   a method of management with the emphasis on both policy-making and implementation in the interests of control.

Each has different implications for the way in which the process is to be modelled, although the last two might for most purposes be taken together as being essentially similar to one another.

COLLECTIVE BARGAINING AS A MARKET MECHANISM

The function and purpose of collective bargaining may be interpreted as a simple substitution of collective for individual bargaining. The term itself was first coined by Beatrice Webb, but she did not define it. The Webbs later provided examples of what the term meant (S and B Webb, 1920). They showed that an individual worker, attempting to fix the terms and conditions of his employment in bargaining with the individual employer, found that the kind of bargain he could secure was subject to 'the exigencies of his own position' in the labour market (S and B Webb, 1920, p 178) and those of the employer.

However, by combination with fellows to negotiate with the employer, he could use the shop club and the trade union (in turn) to iron out some of these exigencies. Thus, the advantage of the individual could be enhanced by combining on a scale greater than that of the individual factory or workshop, thereby 'excluding from influence on the bargain the exigencies of particular firms or particular districts, and not merely those of particular workmen in a single establishment' (*ibid*, p 179), providing always that the association could secure recognition from the employer and engage in representative bargaining.

Although the Webbs *gave* no definition, Flanders infers that:

'For the Webbs, collective bargaining was exactly what the words imply: a collective equivalent and alternative to individual bargaining. Where workmen were willing and able to combine, they preferred it to bargaining as individuals with their employer because it enabled them to secure better terms of employment by controlling competition among themselves' (Flanders, 1969, p 13).

This conception implies that a trade union is essentially a *labour cartel* (see, Milne-Bailey, 1929, p 4) which sells labour and attempts to fix both the supply and the price of the labour under its control (see also Keenoy, 1981). The early unions attempted to do this through the two broad categories of rule which the Webbs saw as embracing all the particular devices which they adopted – the 'restriction of numbers and the common rule' (S and B Webb, 1920, p 704).

Their examples of 'restriction of numbers' were the apprenticeship quotas and the restrictions on the employment of women and 'illegal men' (those not fully trained for the work) (see, Jefferys, 1946). Those of 'the common rule' were those rules which fixed 'a standard rate, a normal day and definite conditions of sanitation and safety' (S and B Webb, 1920, p 704). Together these regulated competition between the workers themselves and helped to raise the price at which labour would be offered to the employer.

The effect of such regulation was to take the determination of the price of labour out of the assumedly perfect market, in which decisions were taken only by individuals. The trade union as a collective body then sought to participate with the employer in taking these decisions. This participation results in an agreement and this, in turn, focuses on the basic contractual quantities.

> 'Broadly considered, collective bargaining deals with remuneration and jobs. Remuneration includes everything that goes into the pay packet or the monthly salary cheque, and also holiday pay, pensions, sick pay, redundancy pay and so on. Jobs include the grading of posts and the qualifications for the job; recruitment, training, promotion and redundancy; the speed of work and the quality of work. Even discipline is mainly concerned with permitted behaviour on the job and penalties for falling short of the required standards' (Boraston *et al* 1975, p 172).

Flanders suggests that this is an inadequate conception and definition, however, because the trade union does not intend or function to sell labour. This is still reserved to the individual (albeit within the framework of pricing rules established by the

316

unions in discussion with the employer). The terms of the act of exchange remain embodied in the individual contract, as indeed is envisaged and enjoined by law. What the trade union does do, he suggests, is, first, regulate the competition between workers and, secondly, regulate the terms on which the employers' offers will be made. Nevertheless, the view that collective bargaining is simply individual bargaining in bulk remains pervasive.

Economic models of bargaining

Economists have attempted to model the process in both product and labour markets in individualistic and market terms (see Fisher, 1971). They have tried to predict the price which might obtain under conditions of both perfect and imperfect competition and to demonstrate the effects of different market structures on the commodity price and wage level (see Dunlop, 1944, pp 72-94; Hicks, 1932).

Individual bargaining in a condition of perfect competition presents no great problem in logic: provided the assumptions hold in reality, the theories can and do predict price level in the different supply and demand conditions. It is not the logic of the model which is a problem, but the relevance of the assumptions to actual markets.

Recognizing that they do not hold, economists have tried to model negotiations between employers and trade unions as if they presented a manifestation of bilateral monopoly, ie in which the firm is treated as a single buyer and the union as a single seller of labour, in what is otherwise a competitive market. Each has to accommodate costs (wages in the case of the employer and unemployment levels in the case of the union) and benefits (value of production in the case of the employer and wages in the case of the trade union) in a way which optimizes the overall advantage for the party in question. This model is not however, able to predict the actual wage rate which has to remain indeterminate: it will lie between the two parties' *preferred* positions, but just where between them it will not be possible to predict.

To try to predict this with greater precision, a *collective bargaining* (as distinct from the free market) model is developed, in which a place is found for 'bargaining power'. In this model, the actual wage rate which will be fixed by negotiation will be that which is 'dictated' by the relative bargaining power of the parties. It is recognized in this model that there are costs to both

Figure 3

A Model of Bargaining

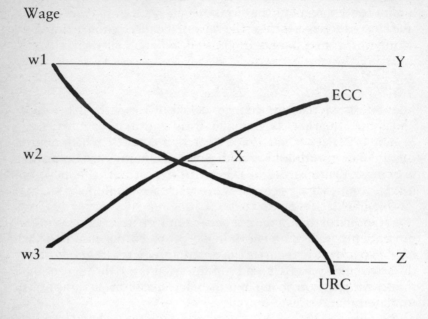

Wage

Expected length of Strike

parties of *both* agreeing and disagreeing with the opponent, and it is postulated that bargaining power can therefore be assessed in terms of the ratio of these two costs. The costs of agreeing are the wage levels not attained in each case, and the costs of disagreeing are the respective costs of industrial action.

Hicks has developed a model which relies upon the subjective perceptions of the parties as to the costs and benefits which might be associated with any particular wage claim (see figure 3 above). In his view, the trade union will claim a wage rate (Wl) higher than the one the employer is willing to concede (W3). The employer faces the options of either paying the demanded rate or of refusing to do so and risking the costs of strike; both of these will be more costly than the acceptance of his offer (W3) would have been. Any settlement above (W3) will involve a cost of

318

agreement (the higher wage rate conceded) but no *settlement* will involve costs of disagreement.

Hicks then relates these to the expected length of a strike, suggesting that the extent to which the employer will be willing to make concessions to the union will vary with the length of time the employer expects the strike to last. This permits the drawing in of the employers' concession curve (ECC); for any given length of strike, the employer will be willing to concede a rate of wages higher than his initial offer. It is implied that if there were to be no real threat of a strike, the employer would pay the rate (W3), but that if there were a real threat of a strike with different possible durations, then the ECC will slope upwards to the right.

The other curve, the union's resistance curve (URC), represents the wage rates which the union would be prepared to accept when faced with a strike of different possible lengths. If the union could obtain a wage rate without a strike, it would stand out for (Wl), but will be prepared to settle for lower amounts according to the length of strike which the union thinks the employer will be prepared to tolerate without concession. Hicks shows this to slope downwards to the right, reflecting the increasing costliness of a strike to members.

It is the bargaining power of the two parties which is then seen to determine the positions and slopes of these two curves. The thesis here is that the higher the costs of disagreement relative to the costs of agreement, the steeper will be the curve. Where, for example, the firm is carrying high stocks of finished goods the cost of disagreeing with the union's claim will tend to be lower (relative to the cost of agreeing) and the ECC will tend to be less steep (with smaller concessions being forthcoming for any given increase in the likely length of the strike). In comparable fashion, anything which might decrease the costs of a strike to the union (such as the retrieval of tax already paid or an increase in social security payments to the strikers' families) the shallower the URC might be expected to be.

Given this analysis, the problem of determining or predicting the wage rate which will be fixed by negotiation, is resolved by regarding the point of intersection of these two curves as that which, in the absence of error and mistake, will constitute the settlement rate (W2).

The dilemma in the model

The above analysis, however, produces a dilemma. On the one hand, if the final settlement rate can be predicted in this fashion, why do the parties not settle at this rate without striking and even without negotiating? If, on the other hand, the model does not suggest a final settlement rate, then it does not enable us to predict the outcome any more closely than before.

This is usually explained by saying that strikers do not necessarily relate bargaining and striking activity in an obviously rational fashion and that as a result of incomplete or imperfect knowledge of the preferences and intentions of the other party each makes miscalculations about the shape of the other's curve. These are the usual answers which are given when any positivist analysis fails to predict the outcomes of human behaviour. In essence, the suggestion is that irrational conduct cannot be explained by rational means (see Bartos, 1967).

Nevertheless, attempts continue to be made to identify and map the external factors thought most likely to have a bearing on the outcomes of negotiation. There is a presumption that such 'objective' factors must influence the outcome, and they are, in any event, easier to measure than the negotiators' subjective perceptions (see Gerhart, 1976).

Those who adopt the systems approach usually identify a number of relevant contextual variables. Dunlop, for example, sees the system as comprising three actors (government, employers and their associations, and employees and their associations) who are bound together by an ideology which supports an approach to resolution of differences, and whose interaction yields the 'web of rules' governing the workplace and work community. But these interactions are seen to be litle more than processes of mediating the effects of certain defined contextual variables, those associated with the market, status and physical (technological) environments, which in the last analysis are what determine the web of regulation (Dunlop, 1958).

A number of writers have pointed out that these may or may not subsume all the variables which ought to be identified. Anderson, for example, acknowledges the influence of the wider economic, political, legal and social systems which are not necessarily subsumed in these. He suggested that 'the objective conditions of the environment have a substantial impact on the costs of agreement and disagreement both for the union and management' (Anderson, 1979, p 131). But in his attempt to measure the influences on outcomes in local government negotiations, he found it necessary to see these as having influence through the mediating variable of perceived bargaining power.

He found, for example, that his results generally support the relationships between, on the one hand, the demand for city services, the demand for labour, the level of comparator private sector wages, the higher the erosion caused by inflation, and the level of unemployment, and on the other, the ratio of the cost of disagreement to the cost of agreement, and, 'thus, the bargaining power of the union' (Anderson, 1979, p 131). However, the hypothesis that the employer's ability to pay for wage and benefit increases would have similar consequences is not borne out. Thus, at this level of analysis too, the possibility of predicting outcomes from a knowledge of the strength of objective variables, seems small.

Objective and subjective factors in outcomes

An alternative view, however, stresses that conduct is more directly and consciously influenced by the conventions and rules which have been developed as a result of past experiences of voluntary negotiation. These at least supplement, and may supplant, the rules which are contained in law or other forms of external regulation. They influence the 'tastes' and the 'pure bargaining power' of the parties (see Dunlop, 1944) and thereby structure the conduct of the parties independently of the influence of the objective variables, which in turn will be perceived in the light of the conventions themselves.

There may not be a single, homogeneous set of game rules which apply to all these distinct forms of action. The rules accepted as governing strike action may be different from those which govern going-slow or banning overtime, and the rules of the negotiation may be different again from all of these. The denial of managerial authority in the context of the work-in, etc, implies yet another set of rules, which are obviously different from those applicable in negotiations where some legitimacy is accorded to management's role. The rules are not necessarily accepted in the same terms by both parties, although they are likely to be seen as relevant even when not acted upon (see Friedman and Meredeen, 1980).

Non-economists amongst the social scientists have tried to develop alternative models of the bargaining process which *do* find a place for such subjective perceptions. Indeed, it might be said that these models are based on the idea that bargaining is no more than an interaction around subjective perceptions, and that outcomes, whether wage rates or anything else, are no more than results of seeking to persuade the other as to the rightness of one's own perceptions and the wrongness of the opponent's, *within the context of understood and accepted conventions.*

These models tend to take discussion away from any simple notion that 'external forces' of the market or anything else determine the outcomes of negotiations. These are treated as constraints which may be more or less well perceived by the interacting parties, dependent upon how much 'distortion' is introduced by adherence to conventional behaviour. They also suggest that bargaining is a game (in game-theory terms) which is played according to (conventional) rules, which may themselves be more of less well perceived by those interacting. Outcomes, thus, come to depend upon the perceptions of both situational factors and the values and norms which limit the bargainer's opportunity to make use of his situational power.

This conception of 'bargaining' is, however, distinctly different from that adopted by either the Webbs or those economists who have attempted to model individual or collective bargaining in terms of market processes. It is *wider* in so far as it can be described as 'a continuous, dynamic process for *solving problems* arising directly out of the employer-employee relationship' and as 'an institutional process the principal object of which is negotiation between company and union representatives in an attempt to reach agreement on the terms and conditions of employment, ie wages, hours and working conditions' (Davey, 1951, p 6). But in addition, such extensions of meaning imply a quite distinct perception of what 'collective bargaining' is. They imply that it is, in the words of Dunlop and Flanders, a continuous rule-making (or 'governmental') process which is regulated not merely by procedures but also by conventions of the parties' own making.

A MECHANISM OF GOVERNMENT

Flanders' view of collective bargaining is that it is concerned with

322

job regulation, or a process of making the rules which will be accepted as controlling the job and the behaviour of the worker engaged on it. He rejects the Webbs' perspective and suggests that collective bargaining would be better named 'joint regulation' *because* it is essentially 'a rule-making process', with 'no proper counterpart in individual bargaining' (Flanders, 1969, p 14). In this conception, therefore, collective bargaining (or joint regulation) serves the purpose of making in advance the rules which will govern both status and the amounts of contribution and remuneration demanded and offered in the individual contract along with any other conditions which shall apply.

It is easy to find examples of such rules which guide the decisions about amounts themselves. A rule which requires overtime or shift premia to be calculated as a ratio of whatever the basic rate may be, is one such example. One which seeks to establish differentials according to fixed ratios is another. Where, particularly in the context of industry-wide bargaining, there are many exigencies to be dealt with, there is no doubt a good case for fixing such guidelines without seeking to interfere too directly with the actual quantities themselves (see below, pp 355-60).

However, the procedural agreements, often more complex than the substantive agreements reached, are more consistent with the idea that collective bargaining is a process of legislating. These agreements are designed to regulate the conduct of the parties to negotiations, but not exclusively those who are in the position of representatives. Some procedures are directed towards control of conduct in presenting and dealing with annual wage claims, but others are directed towards controlling, for example, the way in which either management or workers generally will proceed in disciplinary or grievance cases. In the latter case, therefore, it is not merely the representatives whose conduct is being restrained by procedure. Procedural agreements are, therefore, better conceived as rules which govern the way in which the principals *and* their representatives will approach one another in those areas which have been identified as properly controlled by negotiation.

These considerations lead Flanders to see collective bargaining (and again particularly where it seeks to deal with an underlying variety of circumstances, whether in industry-wide or multi-plant company-wide arrangements) as a private governmental or law-making process, comparable to the processes

323

which occur at the level of the nation-State. Because collective bargaining developed partly as a replacement of State control, this metaphor of a decentralized governmental process appeared apposite.

This is the source of the view of collective bargaining as a process of devising rules or promulgating regulations, rather than as a simple substitute for individual bargaining. But it is possibly more than mere legislating and an alternative conception allows that it is equivalent to the *whole* function of industrial government, such as is described, for example, by Brown (1951) to include legislature, judiciary and executive arms.

A method of management

Chamberlain and Kuhn (1965, pp 108-40) accept these two conceptions of collective bargaining as possible perspectives to adopt, but add a third. This was originally (lst edn. 1951, p 121) referred to as 'a method of management'. In their later edition, however, it was described as a method of conducting industrial relations, a procedure for jointly making decisions on matters affecting labor' (Chamberlain and Kuhn, 1965, p 130). This may not be too distinctly different from the 'job regulation' perspective. This governmental conception may be linked closely to Flanders' conception of it as a kind of private law-making process, by giving salience to the analogy of law-making and administration in the State.

In this third view, however, collective bargaining is seen to involve 'union representatives in decision-making roles' (Chamberlain and Kuhn, 1965, p 130) not as an act of volition on their part but by virtue of what is inherently involved in it.

> 'The bargaining conference that negotiates the agreement exercises final and binding authority in those areas with which it concerns itself. Union representatives meet with owner representatives to reach joint decisions which are incorporated in a written agreement and which cannot be overruled or rescinded for the period of the agreement, except by another joint conference possessing similar authority. Union representatives alone are powerless to modify its terms; owner representatives (those whom we describe as management) are equally without authority to alter the joint agreement. It is subject to change only by

mutual agreement of these two groups of representatives' (Chamberlain and Kuhn, 1965, pp 130-1).

This 'mutuality' is then complemented by joint involvement in the policing of the terms agreed, through the 'procedures' which are usually established in it or under it, and which allow representatives or constituents to test the validity or legitimacy of the actions taken by either party.

Bargaining and negotiation

This moves the concept of collective bargaining well away from the perspective which sees it simply as a collective alternative to individual bargaining and at least complements the view that it is analogous to legal regulation. But it also emphasizes the view that collective bargaining results in the sharing of such managerial power and authority as is accorded by companies and labour law, albeit on a foundation which is itself not juridicial in origin. It may be contended that what happens in this process is something which is upheld by social conventions subscribed to by the parties, with some disregard of the formal legal position.

As a private rule-making process, however, collective bargaining might be better thought of as collective *negotiation*. As in the quotation from Davey (above, p 323) the term 'negotiation' is often used as a substitute for the term 'bargaining'. The differences in meaning are not always consistent, and it is desirable to establish whether there is any difference between them which needs to be acknowledged.

The dictionary offers one distinction followed in broad outline by many students of the subject:

(a) negotiation is used to indicate a process of conferring with another or others with the aim of establishing, in the form of some kind of treaty, the rules which will be accepted as guiding the conduct of the parties in the future (see Pedler, 1977, p 19)

(b) bargaining is used to indicate a process of higgling or of establishing the terms of give and take in a zero-sum game, in which one gains what the other loses, and which may be undertaken in order to reach a decision or an agreement between the parties as to the terms of some transaction or exchange.

Negotiation may occur where neither transaction nor exchange is contemplated. The negotiation might do little more than provide an arena in which each party may engage in propaganda, aimed at the other party or at a wider audience. Negotiations may then be modelled in terms of purely verbal interaction, in which differences are present but not necessarily in conflict or opposition.

Bargaining may then occur within this context. Morley and Stephenson suggest, for example, that negotiation may be reserved for the process of 'verbal communication between two or more parties which is at least ostensibly aimed at reaching joint agreement on some course of action or verbal formulation' (Pruitt, 1969, p 2), and bargaining for the give and take process involved in the actual achievement of agreement (see Morley and Stephenson, 1977, p 26). Gottschalk also reserves 'bargaining' for the 'process of demand formation and revision' occurring on the route to reaching an agreement, and 'negotiation' for the 'situation within which bargaining occurs' (Gottschalk, 1973, p 38). 'Situation' then refers to the context of the relationship within which bargaining (the reaching of agreement) occurs.

Industrial relations negotiation involves more than mere discussion. The discussion must concern outcomes (whether treaties or contracts) which have different values for the people concerned. It relates to a discussion where some contemplated courses of action 'are better for one party than for the other' (Nicholson, 1970, p 67). Consequently, negotiation comes to include 'all forms of discussion in which parties to a conflict exchange information relevant to the issues which divide them' (Morley and Stephenson, 1977, p 20), and bargaining refers to the more bounded process of give and take. The distinction leads Jensen to argue that there may be a number of models of negotiation, one of which might be a bargaining model. For bargaining to exist, therefore, the process must involve give and take, involving a 'willingness to make concessions in order to enhance agreement' (Jensen, 1963, p 522). For other kinds of negotiation, this may not be necessary.

In the real world of collective bargaining, this 'serious' (bargaining) element within negotiations is underpinned by industrial action. This may be commenced by either party, employer or workers, and may take any one of a number of forms. All of them are, however, undertaken in order to coerce the other party in some way to engage in the process of 'give and take' in the interests of securing agreement as to terms. The conception of industrial relations negotiation must therefore include not only the bargaining element as a necessary part of the whole, but coercive industrial action as well. The latter may, in addition, be seen to be more closely and directly related to the bargaining aspect of the negotiation.

Industrial action as an inherent part of the process of negotiation is as much 'a form of human behaviour' (Karsh, 1958, p. 2) as any other part. By and large, people are willing to strike or lock-out in support of matters which, up to that point in time, they were willing to negotiate about. Industrial action may therefore be influenced by the same kinds of social pressures and it may be constrained by a set of rules. These, in turn, may so constrain the actions of the negotiators as to prevent the 'objective facts' of the situation, including those of the relative power of the parties, from determining or dictating an outcome.

This seems to be the main distinction inherent in the two concepts of bargaining and negotiation. It is often maintained in the attempts to model the two processes. These models focus on the central process of bargaining or give and take, but accept that processes of verbal discussion surround it which are themselves constrained by customary and conventional ways of proceeding. This extension makes it a negotiation model which incorporates bargaining as a subprocess. When, for example, Pedler presents his 'negotiation map' we find the bargaining tasks tucked into the middle of a sequence of other activities (see Pedler, 1977, p 20). Kennedy also associates bargaining with one phase of the wider negotiation process (Kennedy, 1978, p 190).

CONVENTIONS

The discussion of 'rules' within the context of industrial relations tends to regard them in two distinct ways. They may be seen as the rules which guide decisions (as for example about wage rates to be applied), or they may be seen as guides to the conduct of any and all parties to the co-operative relationship which is based on the contract of employment.

All of the actions which are subsumed under the headings of 'bargaining' or 'negotiating', or which we identify as industrial action including strikes and lock-outs, may be said to constitute 'forms of human behaviour' (Karsh, 1958, p 2). We can therefore expect it to be guided (where it is not merely a spontaneous response to perception of self-interest) either by tradition, custom or habit, *or* by a set or sets of norms and rules which, in so far as they are coherent for a particular kind of action, may be regarded as the rules of a (distinct) game. In fact, negotiation, bargaining and industrial action may all be treated as one or more games played according to conventions (or rules of the game). The processes of threat and response-to-threat and of preparing or mobilizing for industrial action constitute areas of overlap between these.

A negotiation (in this wider sense) may be conceived as an episode in a set of continuing relationships, so that the episode will reflect a history and will look forward to some future (which may involve using sanctions to compel agreement). The length of time that the parties have recognized one another as legitimate opponents, the number of occasions that they have indulged in such negotiating episodes before, and their experience of the input-output relationships involved in them, are likely to have some bearing on what happens. But these are likely to make their influence felt through the perceptions which the parties have developed of one another and of the process in which they engage.

The conventions (or accepted rules) of negotiation built up during past episodes are likely to be particularly important in this regard. Previous negotiating outcomes, good or bad, are likely to exert some carry-over effect on subsequent episodes. In fact, with the long development of the collective bargaining relationship, it is possible to induce conventions which have broad general validity through a wide range of bargaining situations. These serve, in the voluntary area, as general guides to conduct, much as law might in the official area, although it is not to be inferred that these constitute absolutely binding orders in the Weberian sense in either context.

The conventions of negotiation

The parties' prior experience with one another and with the negotiating process is likely to deposit in the minds of the negotiators, certain conventions intended to guide the actions of negotiators. Thus, any attempt to outline a process of negotiation must not only entail the description of procedures, but also take into account the general and the particular (or local) conventions, which apply to it.

These conventions represent a set of norms which indicate what would be regarded as normal and acceptable conduct by those engaged, and for this reason they do provide the negotiators with guidance as to their own conduct and a basis for making judgements about the other party and his position. They also carry the 'sanctions of disapproval' of which Weber speaks in connection with his definition of convention (see Weber, 1947, p 127-8). These may range over a wide spectrum from verbal disapproval (anger or derision) to industrial action (temporary withdrawal from the game).

The major conventions of this kind to be found in association with collective negotiations serve either to protect the continuous relationship (nos 1-3 below) or to render the actual processes of bargaining reasonably predictable (nos 4-9 below):

1   The negotiation relationship will be governed by the understandings and agreements which have been reached by the parties prior to the commencement of any particular episode of bargaining. This is usually manifest in an understanding or agreement about mutual recognition and about mutual respect for the status of the other party. But it continues beyond these, and establishes that what has previously been admitted as a matter which can be negotiated shall continue to fall into that category. It then becomes possible, for example, for the parties to predict (judge) the likely reactions of the other party to raising an issue; either it can be assumed to be negotiable or it will have to made negotiable by negotiation.

2   What has been agreed in the past shall be accepted as binding on both parties until such time as a new agreement supercedes it or notice of intention to rescind it expires. This is designed to prevent either party from taking steps to introduce change *unilaterally*, and thus to reduce 'uncertainty' for the other in the relationship. It may, and often does, happen that one party will break an agreement in order to take advantage of bargaining strength; when it does so, it increases the uncertainty for the other party and ultimately for itself. Prediction becomes much more difficult.

3   The processes of negotiating for a new agreement or for the change of an old one are prescribed and (by this token) made

329

predictable. This is usually manifest in a procedural agreement which lays down the period of notice of intention to claim or to change something, and the period of time over which the resultant negotiation should stretch as a maximum. This is usually fixed at a length which is not so long as to cause an issue to become stone cold before it is dealt with, nor so short that the opposing party has insufficient time in which to manoeuvre to make a response. Issues vary in their 'shelf-life', however, and the more perishable ones will often lead to breach of this convention.

4   A first statement of claim or offer should normally indicate a position which the party making it is prepared to move from during the course of the bargaining (which will occur on the way to reaching an agreement). The alternative to this, known as Boulwarism, is the convention of making the first offer the final offer, so that negotiation and bargaining are concerned only with 'take it or leave it' rather than 'give and take'. This convention of subsequent movement is an extremely important one in negotiations; without it, strategical interaction of the common type would be impossible. From this convention the concepts of ideal settlement (IS), realistic settlement (RS) and fall-back position (FBP) are derived, to indicate the stages in strategic development.

5   Closely associated with this is the convention that the movements made subsequently to the opening moves in order to facilitate agreement will involve approximately equal amounts of concession (or 'give'). This is related to a notion of *fairness* in negotiation (for example, that it is only fair that each side should make approximately equal sacrifices in order to obtain agreement). This then works back on the decisions about the opening position to adopt; this must allow, if possible, roughly equal amounts of movement to reach the 'most realistic settlement point' in the range (Bartos, 1977, p 573).

6   The methods of influence which may be used in negotiation cover a very wide range of legitimate activities, not all of which would necessarily secure approval outside the negotiation process. The use of deception and bluff is sanctioned, along with the use of adjournments for strategic and tactical purposes, but these have to be contained within the

conventions of bargaining and should not descend to outright lying and cheating.

7   Only some sanctions and some approaches to settlement are permissible within an exercise of bargaining. Thus, certain bans (as for example on overtime) may be tolerated as means of pressuring the other party, but calling a strike in the middle of negotiations would probably be taken as a decision by the union to play a different game from that implied in negotiation. Similarly, during the course of negotiation, an employer's attempt to secure a settlement by a direct approach to the union members, would probably be taken as an act of 'breaking off negotiations' and entering upon a different 'game'.

8   Bargaining should be undertaken in a manner which protects the integrity of the bargainers themselves. This takes a number of forms. Information which is exchanged informally or under a cover of conventionality should be treated as being intended to facilitate the bargaining, but not to be used in a settlement or bandied about outside. Agreements reached after long negotiations should generally allow each party to claim some degree of victory, however slight that may be in fact.

9   Actions within the negotiation should follow the procedural conventions, particularly those which govern 'bargaining in good faith' (displaying a willingness to bargain on an issue no matter how restricted the concessions made may be), and acceptance of the idea that when unconditional offers and acceptances are made in the course of bargaining, they will not subsequently be withdrawn (Bartos, 1977, p 575). This does allow the counter-ploy that all offers and aceptances are made conditionally until the final settlement point is reached.

These may be embodied in the form of agreements already reached by the parties in previous negotiations, or they may derive from 'general' understandings about negotiations. Taken together they establish something of the ritual of negotiations, on which so many writers have commented. They may or may not be functional from the standpoint of one party or the other, when the opponent wishes to achieve some end which is not served by following this ritual. They neverthless serve to make the process predictable for both parties when there is no need or desire to escape their confines for strategic or tactical reasons.

These conventions can be regarded as ones specific to collective bargaining. They supplement a number of purely behavioural conventions which may be taken as applying generally and therefore to behaviour within a bargaining framework particularly. Thus, conventions which require that debates and arguments should be conducted without 'personalizing' them are applicable here as elsewhere, as are conventions which attach respect to judgements which are made on the basis of superior or expert knowledge and information. These may nevertheless be subjected to particular constraints in the negotiating context (expert knowledge and information may have to be proved, for example, and cannot be assumed present by virtue of title or position: see below, pp 470-73).

Conventions of industrial action

A number of conventions which govern industrial action (and which are usually based on industry-wide bargaining processes) can also be recognized. These are usually accepted by at least one party and frequently by both, although there is usually no universal agreement on, or acceptance of, them.

1   Industrial action is not commenced by either party without some prior attempt to discuss and negotiate the issues involved. This is almost an article of faith on the part of management (see Friedman and Meredeen, 1980, p 343) but it is generally followed by convenors and stewards (*ibid*, p 315) when the issue is not seen as perishable (incapable of resolution unless done immediately) (see Batstone, Boraston and Frenkel, 1977 & 1978).

2   Industrial action which involves the suspension or breach of a legal duty (as distinct from a voluntarily assumed obligation) is not commenced without notice being given by the party of his intention to do so. The greater ease with which the single employer can be sued by the union or the workers leads management to accept this convention more often than the union leaders who recognize that the employer has considerable difficulty in using the courts to uphold his legal rights where large numbers of employees are involved. For this reason, unions may dispense with the formality of

notice, and may, even when in communication with management, remain vague about their intentions at the commencement of an action, not only in cases where the issue is perishable.

3   While industrial action is in progress, negotiations will not take place, since to do so would qualify as negotiation 'under duress'. This too is more an article of managerial faith than of the union, but its relevance is recognized by both sides when they adopt the practice of 'having talks about talks' during a strike or lock-out. But from the union's standpoint, getting management to agree to talk about the issue may be one of the main objectives of striking, whereas management is more likely to institute a lock-out to secure acceptance of its terms and conditions of employment, than merely talks about them.

4   Industrial action will embrace those forms of conduct which are sanctioned in law, and eschew those which are proscribed. This, in effect, means that trespass and criminal damage will be avoided, and that action to prevent the other party doing what he wishes to do will be confined to persuasion. Obviously, these limits are not always observed, but it rarely happens that the unions will sanction such conduct, just as the provocative use of blacklegs by management is now an infrequent occurrence.

5   Industrial action will be conducted (as an extension of the previous convention) in such a way that the resumption of normal working relationships will be facilitated (or at least, not prevented). This convention is best illustrated by the provision of 'safety or emergency cover' in industrial action so that a resumption of work is more easily effected when the dispute is settled. This again does not always happen, and breach of this convention, either by threat or actual implementation, may be used as a game-ploy in industrial action itself.

These conventions (or ones very similar to them) can be seen in many industrial actions, but their strength (and the extent to which people see themselves as bound by them) varies considerably (see Arnison, 1970; Lane and Roberts, 1971; Friedman and Meredeen, 1980; Batstone, Boraston and Frenkel, 1978). It is clearly no more possible to predict particular outcomes here than in connection with the wage rate.

Conventions and the control of negotiating behaviour

The conventions discussed above (nos 1-5) (or something like them) serve to constrain the conduct of those who engage in collective bargaining and negotiations. They do this by operating as an accepted set of norms or rules with which the negotiators abide, either because they see themselves as bound in duty to do so or because they accept them as defining customary ways of proceeding. To the extent that they do so, they predispose the bargainers to act in some ways rather than others, so that the outcomes of their actions are constrained by these as well as by any 'objective' considerations.

The first likely consequence of their existence is that the day-to-day conduct of the negotiators will be structured broadly in accordance with them (see, below, ch. 17). But a close second is that the matters which are settled by these processes are likely to be confined to those which can be handled in these ways. Flanders has, for example, argued that:

> 'Terms of employment have had the greatest interest for trade unionists, as they determine their share of income and of leisure. Consequently, they have always been in the foreground of collective bargaining' (Flanders, in Flanders and Clegg, 1954, pp 306-7).

Similarly, Boraston, Clegg and Rimmer hint at a similar acceptance of convention in their suggestion that:

> 'Historically, employers have been more willing to negotiate with unions about remuneration than about jobs. They have taken the view that once the rate of pay was settled, the job to be done was for the manager to determine' (Boraston, Clegg and Rimmer, 1975, p 173).

This is the same process as that referred to as 'guessing' the acceptable levels by Baldamus (1961). With a different set of conventions both the issues and the manner of dealing with them could well be different.

In time, such conventions tend to become part of the fabric of the industrial relations scene, and function to structure custom. People become habituated to seeing or doing things in ways which are structured by these conventions and supported by those organizational arrangements which have developed from them. This conclusion is supported and illustrated by Batstone,

Boraston and Frenkel's description of the normal manner of handling grievances in situations in which the domestic organization of the union is strong and well-accepted by management:

> 'if a member has a grievance, the normal 'way of doing things' will be to go through the steward. Typically, therefore, if a member is primarily concerned with resolving his grievance, it will be sensible for him to adopt this method, whether he believes in the union or not. If he attempts to pursue his grievance by himself, he is likely to face opposition both from management (if only because they fear the reaction of the stewards) and from the stewards. In other words, the easiest way to resolve problems is through the domestic organization' (Batstone, Boraston and Frenkel, 1977, p 10).

In the contrasting situation where the union domestic organization is weak and unsupported:

> 'the chances of a worker resolving a grievance may be greater if he ignores the steward and approaches the relevant manager himself' (*ibid*, p 10-11).

Although the manager and the steward are important actors in the two situations, it is not their *personal* predispositions and predilections which are highlighted, but the system or the 'way things are', itself made up of a set of conventions and customary way of acting.. Making the best of the way things are leads to two quite distinct patterns of conduct.

Such conventions are, however, not merely to be regarded as rules of personal conduct. They also serve to structure the organized behaviours of people and the institutions which grow up to contain them. Turner *et al* (1967) carry this thesis forward to account for the strike levels of the car industry in terms of the weakness of the trade unions and the inadequacies of the procedures available for dispute settlement. The undoubted tendency for the vast majority of workers and managers to negotiate rather than engage in industrial action might reflect a similar internalization of conventions such as these and the generation of a 'customary' way of proceeding which turns the notion of strike-proneness on its head (see Ross and Hartman, 1960; Kerr and Siegel, 1954; Knowles, 1952; Kuhn, 1967; Turner, 1968).

It is this which provides the major control for collective bargaining. Collective bargaining is, without much doubt, the main (and the preferred) method used in Britain to determine the quantities involved in the contract, the rules by which the contractors will abide, and the allocation of mutually-accorded statuses in the actual situation of industrial relations. It is regarded as a voluntary process whether it is also perceived as a mechanism for bargaining 'in bulk', a kind of private law-making to lay down the rules for decision, or a process of joint-decision-making about rights and obligations and the manner in which these will be taken up in the workplace.

It is, however, controlled not so much by law as the expression of some kind of general societal norm, as by conventions which have been developed by the parties themselves. These conventions have served to develop a conventional or customary way of proceeding, serve to protect the system as it has evolved and to prevent wilder excesses of conduct in the employment of power which might bring that system into disrepute. Over time, the widespread acceptance of these conventions has given them customary force. Not everyone accepts them, and not everyone therefore orients their industrial relations behaviour to them. However enough do, to give British industrial relations its stability and pattern.

Such conventions can also serve to prevent changes which are seen as desirable from taking place. The Donovan Commission implied that so many people followed these conventions and customs that they had become barriers to change. Both the Commission and the governments which responded to their recommendations, had to try to nudge the system out of its customary mould by various means, not always successfully.

Undertakings face similar problems. Some have attempted to break the mould by drastic actions, such as shaking up the management structure or dismissing the union leaders (see Friedman and Meredeen, 1980, pp 27-37). But as Gouldner's study of an American 'wildcat strike' (1955) illustrates a change of the rules through a change of managers and technology might so alter the customary way of conducting affairs that the workers might feel impelled to strike as the only way of securing a redress of their grievances (Gouldner, 1955a). Such is the strength of custom.

Summary: the limits of bargaining

Two types of factors might be expected to influence events in and outcomes of negotiations: what constitutes the underlying structure (as deposited by history) and what is happening contemporaneously within other parts of the system. (The system in this context may be conceived hierarchically, to include the immediate work station, the department, the factory, the corporate organization, and the local or national labour markets. At any of these levels of organization, events could be taking place currently which might shape both the formulation of the difference and the approach adopted to its resolution.)

The parties to industrial relations have lawful and legitimated authority both to make policies and to take the decisions which are defined as falling within industrial relations. In the nature of that authority, they have only a restricted opportunity to impose their own objectives, policies and decisions upon the situation or upon the other. The limits are fixed both by law, custom and convention, and by the degree of acceptance of one party's authority by the opponent.

The interaction also occurs within a framework of a kind of objective reality which may be perceived to have different capacities to deliver outcomes to either or both parties. This also provides limits to what each may achieve together or separately.

The ends which the parties seek are likely to reflect their reading of the capacity of the situation to deliver what they might wish to achieve. In this way, their orientations to the other(s) and to the processes of interaction are likely to be coloured.

The processes of interaction which have generally developed within this context are those of individual and collective bargaining (or negotiation) each applicable to different sets of circumstances. Either of these can be seen as a process which is narrowly focused upon the 'pay and effort' status of the parties to the relationship: put simply, they involve determination of how much contribution will be required or given for how much remuneration.

Each can be seen also as a process which is much more widely aimed at establishing the generalized status of the individuals who are party to the fundamental contractual relationship, and of the collectivized parties to the collective bargaining relationship. Thus the first focuses upon decision-taking about the main quantities which have to be exchanged in the co-operative relationship, and the second much more upon some notion of 'rules' which will guide the conduct of the parties to the employment relationship.

In order to structure the relationship and the interaction in a way which allows predictions to be made about future events and possible outcomes, the several parties have developed and secured agreement to a number of 'conventions' which are widely (but probably not universally) accepted as guiding the behaviours of participants. These can be expressed in game theory terms for each of the main elements in the collective bargaining process.

These, in turn, acknowledge that within the relevant framework of cultural value, some processes of securing compliance and consent are preferred over others, and society will stand ready to enforce the limits. But much of what society might thus establish as limits is concerned with the nature and extent of the power which the parties might legitimately use in the process of bargaining.

The method of securing control or compliance which is least acceptable is that which is based on what Simmel refers to as 'naked force' (with not even a pretence at persuasion) (see Etzioni, 1975, p 5). In this case, one party relies on the use of power to compel another to a course of action. This might manifest itself in a number of different ways, from coercion of the individual to industrial action against the collectivity or its agents. It is this use of such power to *compel* or *coerce* which generally finds disfavour in our society, although vestiges of it support the manipulation of utilities and the processes of 'persuasion' involved in negotiations.

The manipulation of utilities is a more common and more acceptable alternative method. It relies upon the use of power to change the availability of benefits and penalties within the individual's environment, whilst leaving it to the party to reach his own decisions about how to act in the light of what is available. This is more consistent with the view that the individual should be left free to reach his own decisions about action, where the freedom is nevertheless constrained by the structuring of the environment.

The preferred alternative is that which focuses upon some process of persuasion, but persuasion set within a structure of variable power which can be used strategically or tactically to 'compel' agreement. This moves the process on from a mere individual response to the environment, and emphasizes the necessity for a special kind of (persuasive or bargaining) interaction, in which the relative power of the parties is crucial to the final stage of reaching agreement.

In this case, issues are resolved by direct negotiation or higgling between the two parties concerned. This may occur in two distinct modes. The one involves inter-personal negotiations, as might apply, for example, in the establishment of managerial or professional contracts or in securing compliance to an instruction. The other entails interaction of representatives of the parties with an institutionalized structure (as in collective bargaining). The identification of the 'preference' implies that, generally, we expect this method, governed by these conventions, to be used instead of any other.

Readings

Levinson: (1966), pp 1-18. Pen: (1959), pp 91-112.
Dunlop: (1944), pp 1-32. Ross: (1944).
Kochan and Wheeler: (1975). Anderson: (1979).
Walton and McKersie: (1965), pp 2-10.
Marchington: (1982), pp 94-108. Poole: (1980).

13

The content of voluntary rules

The rules of work

The mechanisms of control reviewed in the preceding chapter find their expression in various kinds of rules upon which they rely for their effect. Those which govern the relationships between the organizations as such, find their expression in procedural rules embodied in the collective agreement. Those which govern the relationships of individuals in work, whilst they may be determined by individual or collective bargaining, are ultimately embodied in the individual contract of employment although they may find first expression in the substantive rules of the collective agreement. Both the collective agreement and the individual contract will, in consequence, contain decisions (and rules governing decisions) about wages and work contribution.

The rules which are produced by this devolved decision-making process are necessarily more diverse in their form than those which are enshrined in law which is intended to have a universal application. They represent the compromises between the aims of the different parties and between them and the capacity of the situation to provide what each and any may seek from it. As compromises which respond to the immediate situation, they are likely to reveal considerable variety.

Nevertheless, the rules produced in this way do reveal some consistency (although not as much as the legal ones) as legal regulation, custom and fashion influence the negotiating activities of the parties. The negotiators of agreements do not start with a clean slate and unbridled opportunity to decide their own rules. There are, as we have already seen, some norms and rules which are laid down in law to sustain the broad cultural values; there are also many conventions which govern the way in which the negotiators deal with one another. The first of these is intended to be general in its coverage, but the second is more fully developed within the context of industry-wide bargaining and reveals greater variety between one industry and another. Both set a limit to what is legitimate behaviour and therefore to the opportunity for establishing new rules.

In this chapter, we look at the kinds of rules which are made through voluntary collective bargaining, but commence with some consideration of the relationship between the collective agreement and custom and practice. In some views of the subject the latter provides the 'source' of a good deal of what passes into the realms of formal rule.

The collective agreement

A collective agreement embodies such parts of the objectives of the parties to it as they have been able to realize through negotiation with the other(s). It represents the compromise that they have come to after setting the power of the employee against the power of the employer or that which provides by a process of joint determination a mutually-sought basis of co-operation. It will usually establish four things:

(a) the status that each party is prepared to accord to the other(s) within the limits set by law in respect of the employment relationship
(b) the substantive terms and conditions of employment which will be applied through the individual contracts of employment
(c) the negotiating procedures which the collective parties will follow in their dealings with each other
(d) the managerial or monitoring procedures which will be followed in maintaining or changing the employer-employee relationships themselves.

The actual content of any of these will vary from situation to situation, reflecting the history of negotiation and the circumstances in which the agreements are reached.

When collective bargaining is seen as a collective alternative to individual bargaining, the emphasis is placed on the first two of the above functions. The question of pay status is then but one aspect, however important, of the more general concern with rights and obligations which go to make up status. Nevertheless, as Flanders has indicated, it is common for these two elements to

341

be considered as if they were one *and* subsumed in considerations of the wage-effort bargain:

'... Today the vast majority of agreements -- apart from those dealing with bargaining procedure -- are mainly concerned in one way or another with wages and hours of work. They do not, of course, relate only to minimum or standard rates of wages and length of the normal working week, but also to piecework arrangements and other systems of payment by results, to overtime and payment for holidays, and sometimes include provisions for a guaranteed week. Other matters ... dealt with ... include the employment of apprentices or juvenile labour, training schemes, job demarcation and the distribution of work, discipline and promotion' (Flanders, 1952, pp 79-80; see also, Flanders in Flanders and Clegg, 1954, pp 298-307; Boraston, Clegg and Rimmer, 1975, p 173).

But since (in the absence of statutory rules governing it) this agreement-making process has to be supported by voluntarily agreed procedures the third function has also to be covered. For this reason, the collective agreement must concern itself with voluntary donation of status to the two parties *to* negotiate, and with the procedures which will govern the making of claims by one party upon the other, and the handling of any disagreements about the manner in which the agreement terms and conditions have been applied. The fourth may be said to represent the logical extension of this general process in a situation in which management has to be achieved by consent. The function can also be covered more easily where the collective bargaining process is domesticated, and the parties to the agreement making process are those who represent immediate interests.

The agreement may be considered by the parties to be the foundation for a permanent and stable relationship or as no more than a 'temporary truce' (Allen, 1971) in an on-going process of securing improvements judged from the one interest or the other.

The agreement on 'substantive terms' (working conditions and wages) is more readily seen as a temporary truce than are the agreements on 'status' and 'procedures'. The status agreement has usually stood for a long time and shows little sign of variation. The procedural agreement has developed by gradual modification and accretion. It may be brought to an end, in the typical case, by either party after notice, but this occurs relatively infrequently, and when it does happen, it is usually replaced by a similar but better one. The agreement on substantive terms is, however, more often intended to be a temporary agreement; with high and varying rates of inflation in the post-war period, it has been common to set up the agreement for a year although at other times the period has been different.

Such agreements are reached by a variety of joint bodies and consequently reveal a wide variety of forms from industry to industry or from undertaking to undertaking. They are necessarily less standardized than are the legal rules. Nevertheless, the contents of different collective agreements show some similarity because they do develop in unison. New subjects for negotiation tend to appear like fashions, leaving behind new customs and conventions about what are negotiable subjects. In Goodrich's phrase 'the frontier of control' (1920) moves forward, leaving behind a residue of negotiable issues and acceptable ways of resolving them. Nevertheless fashion is not always taken up by everyone, and what is acceptable in one context may be so in another, so that variety remains.

Custom and practice

The rules of the formal agreement are not, however, the only norms which may govern work relations. Accepted customs which are not expressed in any form except in the conduct of the people who orient their behaviour to them, lie at the base of the informal system of industrial relations which the Donovan Commission distinguished from the formal system based on the express articulation of new rules of conduct in formal agreements. The informal system is seen to be based upon unwritten customs and understandings which support the continuation of a co-operative work relationship.

In one view of the provenance of formal agreements, these customary rules are seen to provide a reservoir from which specific rules, in either original or modified form, are drawn. Formal agreements thus represent a way of either formalizing existing custom or deliberately breaking with it. Some of these new rules may, for example, merely codify in more formal terms what already exists in the informal system in unwritten custom and convention. Others may be intended to break with traditions and to bring in some completely new rules to guide behaviour in the new circumstances of the future.

343

Few attempts have been made, as Brown acknowledges, to define custom or 'custom and practice' (C&P) (Brown, 1972) partly because, being unarticulated, it is difficult to get at and partly because there is apparently so much of it (see, Flanders, 1967, pp 69-70). It is, however, widely acknowledged to be a potent and conservative factor in the structuring of work behaviour. It can be argued that what has been the custom should continue simply because it has served its turn previously. Wootton, for example, suggests that 'the strength of conservatism is that it is held to justify itself' (Wootton, 1962, p 162), and the same might be said of custom.

Custom tends to be 'owned' by somebody, usually by the worker group who protect and defend it whenever the perceive it to be under attack from the employer who is seeking to introduce new ways of working and new rules to govern them. One good example of this is the differential rate between unskilled and skilled or manual and white collar workers. Brown implies that C&P (whatever its origins) may be captured by the workers or their trade unions, who then assume a proprietary right in it, and use it to trade with the management for improved practices in other areas.

Flanders, who regards C&P as a set of rules, considers that management has no say in making them but must tacitly accept them, presumably because the workers will demand such a course of action (Flanders, 1967, pp 69-70). Fox takes this further in suggesting that where the power situation is appropriate, the 'collectivity may be able unilaterally to establish norms of its own ... in the form of C&P' (Fox, 1971, p 136) and that 'acquiescance and tacit acceptance of the work group C&P (may become) the normal management stance' (*ibid*, p 171; see also above, p 310).

The kinds of rules which are to be found in collective agreements are of a different order entirely from those associated with C&P. The distinction between them is essentially that which Blackstone drew between written and unwritten law in his *Commentaries on the Laws of England*:

'For since the written law binds us for not other reason but because it is approved by the judgement of the people, therefore those laws which the people have approved without writing ought also to bind everybody. For where is the difference whether the people declare their assent to the law by suffrage, or by a uniform course of acting accordingly?'

Where a formal (written) rule is adopted to supersede a custom (unwritten) it requires a more *conscious* decision from those within its domain to accept or to reject it as a source of duty binding upon the individual. It cannot be followed without thought simply because it has been followed as a matter of tradition (see Weber, 1947, p 121). Where the rule is entirely novel and the result of deliberate and creative decision, it establishes a new fashion, to which a new and deliberate orientation of this same kind is invited. It may be that if the rule is agreed rather than imposed, it may be expected to command more immediate and loyal acceptance. Nevertheless it has the quality of a new fashion to which individuals will be called upon to make a decision about whether to accept it or not.

National and domestic agreements

The Donovan Commission's recommendation that the informal should be formalized was intended to ensure that the domestic situation should be brought more firmly under explicit control of this type. People at work should be offered the opportunity both to participate in the making of new rules and to commit themselves to them. In the Commission's view, the informal and customary was a constant source of misundertstanding and friction, because of the different interpretations possible and the inadequate knowledge of its implications. They thought it ought to be codified more explicitly so that the new rules would serve as an order to which those within the domain of the agreement could owe a duty. If the rules were worked out jointly, there would be a greater chance of their being accepted than if they were to be imposed. It followed that they might be expected to command greater acceptance if they were developed locally rather than nationally.

In spite of the pressure for the development of more domestic agreements of a more comprehensive kind, in the post-Donovan era, the latest evidence suggests that even this is not happening with any great frequency (Brown, 1981; Marsh, 1982; Daniel and Milward, 1983). The amount of fragmentation in bargaining may be less than had previously been thought (Moulding and Moynagh, 1982, pp 38-41) and there may be examples of comprehensive agreements being put together (Gregson and Ruffle, 1980, pp 62-64) but the overall picture remains one of considerable variation of practice.

These agreements seek to regulate certain basic relationships over the whole of their domain, which in turn is usually defined by the employers' definition of it. Traditionally, the national agreement(s) has/have sought to provide a standardized procedure for the 'industry' and a set of standards to apply to the quantities of effort and reward to be read into the industry's individual employment contracts. In the nature of this kind of joint decision-taking, however, the amount of detail which can be regulated by the resultant agreement must be limited. This, indeed, was one of the main reasons why the Donovan Commission considered that they ought to be, if not replaced, at least supplemented, by comprehensive domestic agreements (which would be able to deal with more detail on the basis of local knowledge). As Marsh recently commented, national bargaining and national agreements remain very much alive (Marsh, 1982, p 161).

Formal domestic agreements have nevertheless appeared more frequently in recent years (see Armstrong *et al*, 1981). These may either replace or simply supplement national agreements. Domestic bargaining offers the opportunity to make these agreements much more comprehensive than is possible at the industry level. Even if the domestic agreement does not form a single comprehensive document or constitution, it may in time add up to this if all the distinct local agreements are considered together. They may then determine the rights, procedures, conditions and quantities of remuneration for themselves, quite independently of any other agreement in the industry.

In the 1960s, there was a strong tendency for the larger employers in an industry to engage in substitution but the smaller employers generally were less well placed to do this and tended to go in for supplementation. Foreign capital has often been associated with attempts to establish domestic agreements in complete separation from national negotiations. In some of these undertakings, particularly in some of those which are American-owned, there has also been some attempt to establish 'collective contracts' on a more comprehensive basis, in the American mode (thus severing themselves from the underlying legal and social conventions which normally apply in Britain).

The alternative to this is that the domestic agreement might amplify and apply those rules and rights which are established in the national agreements. It was this feature which, in the late 1950s and 1960s, was seen to account for wage drift (see above, pp 21-22). This building-on was also practised in respect of other elements in the relationship, so that the locally-established rights and obligations were more precisely defined than they were in the more general national agreements.

Boraston, Clegg and Rimmer (1975) have attempted to determine just how much scope there might be in various industries for domestic negotiations to take place. Given their definitions of tight and loose agreements negotiated externally to the domestic unit (see above, pp 276-77),they found a 'gradation from the extremely tight provision in the civil service through various stages of loosening' in the rest of the public sector, although 'all of them must be classified as at least moderately tight' (Boraston, Clegg and Rimmer, 1975, p 174). They also found that the agreements in the steel, building and printing industries could be classified as moderately loose, whilst in chemicals, clothing, engineering, hosiery and rubber, they were generally loose 'without qualification'.

At the company level, the small number of agreements were found to vary over the range, as they impinged upon the separate plants of the multi-plant undertakings (*ibid*, p 175).

> 'Most of the multiplant companies in the case studies left collective bargaining to the plants, but a minority had negotiated company agreements ... there was a link between management collective bargaining and managerial organization, for the companies with relatively tight agreements stood out as having more centralized managerial methods' (*ibid*, p 177).

In the public versus the private sector analysis, they offer an explanation of the differences in terms of public visibility and accountability. Within the private sector itself, the explanation of the difference probably lies in the different degree of homogeneity of product or process within the unit. But whatever the explanation, the scope for domestic bargaining within multi-establishment undertakings, whether in the public or the private sector is likely to vary according to the tightness of the 'external' agreement. This implies that the adherence to different conventions in different industries has resulted in distinct approaches to the questions of what rights and obligations should be established and how they are to be determined.

AGREEMENTS ON MUTUALLY-ACCORDED STATUS

The fundamental requirement of any agreement, national or domestic, is that the parties shall recognize one another for purposes of negotiating to reach agreement (see CIR Studies Nos 3 and 5, 1973 and 1974). This is, indeed, the essence of the so-called *voluntary* agreement; the parties enter into the agreement-making process freely and of their own volition. This must therefore be referred to in the agreement itself, and the preamble to most agreements will therefore state that the parties recognize one another and accord each other certain rights and obligations within the relationship. It will identify the status of the parties who are willing to enter into a relationship with each other, and indicate what steps each will take to facilitate the other.

The preamble may do little more than identify the parties and delimit their respective domains in relation to it (see *Code of Industrial Relations Practice* (1972)). It may, however, give a more detailed description of the parties and how they will constitute themselves in approaching and dealing with one another. Where this is stimulated or dictated by legislative enactment (as, for example, in connection with redundancy or health and safety procedures), certain conditions may have to be met by the parties (for example, the union may have to be 'independent') in order to comply with legal or policy requirements.

National agreements

In the national agreement there is usually an acknowledgement of mutually-accepted rights and obligations which forms the preamble to the procedural rules themselves (see Flanders, 1965, p 11). For example, in the Manual Workers' Procedure Agreement in the Engineering Industry (1922) negotiated between the Engineering Employers' Federation and various trade unions, the first two clauses deal with this aspect under the heading of 'General Principles':

348

(a) 'The Employers have the right to manage their establishments and the Trade Unions have the right to exercise their functions.
(b) 'In the process of evolution, provision for changes in shop conditions is necessary, but it is not the intention to create any specially favoured class of workpeople.'

The first of these statements may not, in itself, offer much practical guidance to conduct, but in the course of the agreement itself, more specific statements of 'right' are to be found. For example, at various dates between 1932 and 1944, the Federation accorded the *right* of trade unions to negotiate on behalf of certain workpeople employed on staff conditions, and the nature of the right is spelled out in each case. The more specific content of these rights is usually given in the body of the procedural agreement.

Procedural agreements may also provide rights to the two parties incidental to the provision of a procedure. Recently, the parties have responded to the legislative requirements concerning information disclosure for purposes of collective bargaining or to those concerned with consultation about redundancy or health and safety, by developing procedures to handle these issues. In the course of this provision, the agreement will also explicitly or tacitly acknowledge the rights of the parties. The employer may recognize the unions' right to information, and the unions the employers' rights to preserve confidentially of certain kinds of information. With the future implementation of proposals of the kind found in the EEC Fifth Directive and the Vredeling memorandum (see below, pp 582-83), rights of this kind might become even more prominent in procedures and other arrangements for participation. However, given the general thrust of these, they are better considered in the context of domestic agreements.

Domestic agreements and negotiating status

In the domestic agreement, more scope exists to deal with bargaining status and the facilitation which flows from it. The agreement may do no more than identify the parties, in the sense of recording who is covered by it, but it may also indicate who is competent to agree on behalf of whom. It might state, for example, that:

'The Company recognizes the Union as being the sole Union to represent those members of the staff who are members or wish to become members of a union, given that they are directly engaged in the establishment on operations (as detailed) and it also recognizes the Union's right to raise any matters on behalf of employees so engaged who are members of the Union'.

'Apart from the personnel employed in the (Company's) Depot nothing in this Agreement shall alter the existing Agreement (dated) between the Company and (another named) Union, which, in accordance with its terms, gave that Union sole recognition throughout the Company. It follows that all other personnel, engaged other than in the (named location) are unaffected by this Agreement'.

It frequently happens (as in this example) that the management will recognize one trade union for a particular grade or category of staff and enter into an agreement with it through the respective agents or representatives. The possible consequence that where a number of different unions are recognized for different grades and categories, a number of quite separate and distinct agreements exist. The management may then endeavour to have each agreement conform to a 'standard form' in respect of its main terms. It may also attempt to secure joint trade union acceptance of a single procedure agreement, even if separate negotiations are retained in respect of substantive claims. Once procedures provide for 'joint' representation, however, the question of who is competent to agree on behalf of whom takes on a new dimension.

The mutually accorded status in the domestic agreement is usually a straightforward, if more detailed, copy of that in national agreements. It usually expresses a right to manage in some form: the trade union(s) recognizes the right of management to manage the undertaking, including the right to maintain or improve efficiency and to maintain discipline within the undertaking. In the period around 1970, the unions frequently sought to have a *status quo* clause inserted into such agreements, in order to restrict management's right to introduce changes without prior discussion with the unions. It sought to maintain the *status quo* on both sides until such time as the discussions had occurred (see IDS, *Status Quo*, April, 1971).

The agreement will acknowledge the rights of the union to

serve members' interests. Minimally, this involves recognizing the named unions to represent their members in claims or other disputes with management. It is now likely to deal with the question of facilitation, ie the provision of office facilities and time-off for shop stewards or other local (for example, health and safety) representatives, and the provision of a check-off arrangement for the collection of union dues under prescribed conditions (see CIR Report No 17, 1972; ACAS Code of Practice No 3; Ramsay and Hill, 1974, pp 9-13).

Provision is now usually made for a defined number of shop or office representatives (who are usually required to have a service qualification) related to constituencies within the undertaking, to be recognized by management. The agreement is also likely to stipulate what duties such representatives will undertake during working periods. These are composited usually from what is contained in the union rule book and the expectations that management holds of their activities as a *quid pro quo* of recognition. This part of the agreement is likely to deal with the question of what will be considered reasonable time off, and increasingly often, it will also deal with the question of how ballots will be arranged (for example, in connection with shop steward election or on issues such as the closed shop).

Domestic agreements and consultation status

The domain and range of domestic agreements makes them more appropriate for the development of procedures relating to consultation. Consultation is a process more relevant to the undertaking or the establishment than to the industry as a whole. With the growth of domestic negotiations in the post-war period, the distinctions between consultation as traditionally-conceived and negotiation have tended to become blurred. This is partly the result of greater acceptance by the employer of union organization as a mechanism for communicating with large groups of workers and recognition that tensions are likely to develop where two distinct representational systems are run side by side.

Recent legislation (see above, pp 155-56), and likely future developments arising out of EEC proposals on participation (see p 353 below), have had their influence on employers' willingness to consider the formal incorporation of consultative procedures into their general structures of communication. In the unionized establishments, this has necessarily required them to consider the relationship between union representatives and the consultative process, and, therefore, the status of the different kinds of employee representative in relation to it.

The *Code of Industrial Relations Practice* (1972) made a hesitant attempt to revive a flagging interest in joint consultative committees and councils. It exhorted management to initiate them in all establishments and certainly in those with more than 250 employees, and to seek joint agreement with employees on composition, structure and function of the committees and on 'the range of subjects to be discussed' (Code, 1972, p 17). However, on the subject of the relationship between joint consultation and negotiation it has little to say beyond noting that the two are closely related 'but distinct processes', and suggesting that:

> 'Management and employee representatives should consider carefully how to link the two. It may often be advantageous for the same committee to cover both. Where there are separate bodies, systematic communication betrween those involved in the two processes is essential' (*ibid*).

A reluctance to tackle the problems of who should represent whom and what the committee should be encouraged to discuss, reduced the impact of the Code's reommendations.

The Consultative Document on the proposed Code, issued in the preceding June (1971), was much more explicit on the subject, setting out three distinct alternatives:

(i)   a unified system combining both functions (of consultation and negotiation)
(ii) separate processes for the two functions with the same representatives on both
(iii) separate processes with totally or partially different representatives.

The document did refer to the need to establish machinery appropriate to the local circumstances, such that for example, where 'there is a substantial union membership the first or second of the above procedures is likely to give better results'. Representations to the Department of Employment on this subject were sufficiently numerous and sufficiently unidirectional in their suggestions to lead to a reduction in emphasis on separateness in the final version published.

352

The revival of interest in the 1970s awaited the EEC suggestion that participation be increased by setting up works councils and supervisory boards on the German or Dutch basis. The TUC has repeatedly denied the relevance of works councils on the German model, preferring instead to develop participation through trade union and collective bargaining organization. More recent amendments to the EEC's Fifth Directive on participation, opens the way to advancing on the basis of the British preference for developing voluntarily from a collective bargaining base. Although employer organizations have expressed themselves more in favour of works councils, it would not be too much of an exaggeration to say that their support has been lukewarm and qualified. The survey of practice by Daniel and Millward (1983), however, suggests that there is currently a considerable amount of development occuring on this front in industry.

Much of the experience to date suggests, however, that the maintenance of a distinction between negotiations (with the unions) and joint consultation, has limited validity. Its main value to management may lie in the opportunity which it provides to disseminate information amongst the union representatives and the workers generally. There is evidence that the trade unions may view joint consultation as a useful means of communication (see Anthony, in Balfour, 1973a). In this vein, joint consultation may be seen as contributory to the development of both congruent attitudes and mutual trust, but not as any very effective substitute for negotiation.

This does not mean, however, that there is no room for consultation which is conceived separately and distinctly from negotiation. On the one hand, consultation provides a supplementary (if not an alternative) channel of communication. On the other, it admits the possibility, even when the same personnel are involved, of segregating common interest problems from divergent interest issues, and of discussing some of these latter issues in a framework other than that of distributive bargaining (as, for example, in *preparation* for an annual negotiation).

Successful ventures involve two features which may be important to the success of any excursions into joint consultation in modern industrial organizations:

1   they acknowledge the fact of trade union existence and trade union attitudes, and seek deliberately to resolve the non-

unionist issue (either, as in the Glacier Metal Co experiment with consultation, by restricting representatives to trade union members or, as in the GKN-Shotton experiment, by founding the whole exercise on the trade union representational and negotiating machinery). Both give a consultative status to the existing unions and their representatives

2   they define the subjects with some precision and make them matters for decision by the consultative bodies rather than simply for discussion, by codifying the definitive policy and the conditional policy decisions required with the latter allocated to the consultative machinery for decision (albeit with a proviso that decisions must be unanimous in order to prevent inconsistency in the two sets of decisions), or by defining in advance certain areas of bilateral interest which may range all the way from trade union bargaining subjects of a traditional sort through safety, welfare and discipline to forward manpower planning (see also below, pp 491-99).

It is now more common for agreements to include lists of topics for regular discussion (albeit outside the framework of negotiation *per se*) between named representatives of the management and trade unions. These give a constitutional basis for this type of activity and may be coupled with the procedures for disclosing information as required by legislation and detailed in the ACAS *Code on Information Disclosure* (see above p 174). Disclosure and consultation can in this way become integrated with overall strategies and policies. In effect agreement is reached on which matters shall be discussed inside and outside the negotiating machinery and on what shall constitute the agenda of the consultative committee.

The mutual recognition and facilitation thus built into the domestic agreement establishes the negotiating and consultative status of the parties, providing them with a basis for developing a relationship. It is intended to provide a foundation for co-operation and/or the containment of conflict within the undertaking. In larger establishments, the recognition and facilitation of senior stewards or convenors effectively places these personnel in roles which are essentially managerial, making them lubricants rather than irritants. The preambles to many agreements openly acknowledge this, in their reference to the desirability of containing conflict and to the probability that such appointments are likely to facilitate this end.

354

AGREEMENTS ON SUBSTANTIVE TERMS

The substantive terms of an agreement are, in essence, those terms which could substitute for the existing terms of a contract of employment. They cover the two quantities of effort or contribution and reward or remuneration. In the more common language of agreements themselves, these two quantities are often referred to as 'working conditions' and remuneration or pay. Together they indicate something of the status of the individuals who are 'covered' by the terms of the agreement, as for example in the sense of 'pay-status' and 'job-status'.

National agreements

At the national level not all issues which might arise in industrial relations are necessarily negotiable. What is, is usually confined to what is readily quantifiable and controllable. This tends to focus on certain basic amounts of working conditions and wages (see Flanders, 1954, pp 306-7; Boraston, Clegg and Rimmer, 1975; p 173; and above, p 316).

A typical national agreement will contain clauses (or separate and distinct agreements) which establish certain 'working conditions' which will apply for the time being. These normally focus upon hours of work in general and specific patterns of hours (such as shift-hours or overtime hours) and usually make provision for meal times and the manner in which they are related to basic hours. Working conditions are also affected by whether pay is based on hours or on some method payment by results, and the requirements of work from PBR workers are often specified. Some reference is also likely to be made to part time working where it is a feature of the industry.

It is also usual for these to be prefaced by some statement which indicates the jointly-accepted objectives which underly such clauses (or agreements). For example, in the Engineering industry agreement on the working week (1947) the 'preamble' reads:

> 'The following Agreement is to be read and construed in relation to certain general principles which the parties accept as fundamental:
> (a) the need to maintain and develop maximum produc-

tion in the interests of the domestic consumer and the export market;

(b) the necessity of keeping prices at such a level that purchasing power will be maintained or improved. This consideration involves consumer goods at home, export trade and the buying power of the pound sterling;

(c) the inter-relation of industries in some of which there is an inherent inability to speed up by mechanical production, involving the consideration that a loss of hours means a loss of output'.

These are then to be taken into account in interpreting the ensuing clauses or agreements on the length of the working week, shift-working, holidays, payment by results, part-time workers, joint production committees and various miscellaneous conditions.

Another part of the national agreement will deal with the remuneration of those within its scope. Some attempt is usually made to ensure that rates are standardized for categories of worker (for example, craftsmen and labourers, in the engineering agreement) and either for the industry labour market as a whole or for areas of divisions within it. Both the employer and the trade union has some interest in rate standardization where the work done is itself sufficiently standardized. In recent years, the tendency for individual establishments to pay 'over the rates' in order to attract scarce labour in different localities (or in response to powerful local bargaining by the shop stewards) has complicated the provision of standard rates and has often resulted in national agreements stipulating the amount of increase rather than the final wage rate itself.

This part of the agreement may well be extremely detailed. It arises because the agreements about rates may have to provide for different categories throughout an industry: persons by age or seniority, persons according to employee status (for example trainees and apprentices versus fully-trained adult workers), and persons according to the nature of the contract terms (for example, whether engaged on some payment by results scheme or straight hourly rates). The agreement will also make some reference to rates applicable for overtime and part-time working. Separate provision will also usually be made for remuneration in connection with shift-working and short-time working and for guarantee payments in the latter event. The intention is to ensure that as many of the contingencies will be covered as possible by a formula or a rule in the national agreement which can be applied in the local circumstances.

The national agreement has been subjected to two countervailing pressures over recent years. From one direction, there has been pressure to make the agreements more comprehensive, so that they do amount to a complete code governing these kinds of relationship. From another, there has been pressure to reduce the regulatory function of these agreements in the interests of transferring control back to the domestic level where decisions can the more readily be taken in the light of local circumstances. As a result, the number of subjects alluded to in the national agreement has tended to increase over the years, but their detailed content has tended to decrease.

Domestic agreements

In the transition to a system of collective bargaining based on the domestic unit, the substantive terms of the individual contract of employment may continue to be negotiated nationally, and merely implemented locally. Dependent upon the strength of the local union organization, however, these nationally agreed terms may become 'the floor' on which the local negotiators will then build the particular (and usually higher) rates which are to apply in the particular undertaking or establishment. Where the domestic unit is not part of a wider bargaining unit, the complete set of substantive terms will fall to be determined locally, but in this case there may be some tendency to 'follow' the pattern established externally.

In either eventuality, the local agreement will tend to specify for the undertaking or establishment, what terms will apply there for either 'the foreseeable future' or the next negotiating period, (which has usually been one year for some time). The quantities which are dealt with will therefore be intended to have a minimum fixed life. This will be true of the hours of work and periods of holiday fixed, and of the rates of payment to apply to various jobs or categories of them under the different circumstances (for example normal hours, overtime hours, shift-hours, stand-by hours and call-in periods, as well as those of incentive and non-incentive working).

In the context of domestic bargaining, however, these

quantities may be fixed in much greater detail than would be possible in national agreements. Only administrative convenience is likely to prevent the quantities for each individual job being specified, but nothing in principle would prevent this, since the individual jobs concerned are 'known'. It is more probable that the quantities will be fixed for the various job grades or classes, *and* that the development of such classes will become an issue which will itself be brought into the negotiating process. For example, in the post-war period, there has been an increase in the use of formal job evaluation plans (see Thomason, 1980a, pp 118-24) and within that general increase an increase in the extent to which such plans are developed and maintained on some joint basis (see Edwards and Paul, 1977).

With agreement about the grades and classes, the negotiation of distinct rates for each becomes more feasible, and domestic negotiations more detailed as a consequence. In these circumstances, the variations in other terms and conditions of employment (for example, starting and finishing times, hours of work, eligibility for overtime working and overtime payment, etc) which often distinguish blue and white collar bargaining units, become difficult to accommodate in negotiations, and pressures arise from the employer side, if from no other, to harmonize them, so that pay differentials come to reflect differences in the job content (see Thomason, 1980, p 3) where all other conditions of job demand and job reward are rendered constant (see Gregson and Ruffle, 1980, pp 62-64).

The development of domestic bargaining has, for this reason, tended to bring many more such substantive issues within the purview of the negotiations. In a situation in which sick pay and pension schemes, holiday entitlements, medical insurance plans, overtime and shift obligations and entitlements to premia, and clocking requirements vary for different classes and groups of workers, any intention by management to standardize this (by 'harmonization') is likely to bring them into negotiations with one bargaining agent or another. Once incorporated in order to secure consent to harmonize, they are likely to remain so, and for all groups (and not just the ones which had to be persuaded to change).

Flanders' conclusion that the national bargaining had some responsibility for 'the poverty of subject matter' (Flanders, 1967, p 13) and left 'considerable scope for further growth' was prophetic (Flanders, 1967, p 15). A good deal of what he saw as custom and practice, and as 'fringe benefits', then still outside formal bargaining, has now been brought within the range of subjects bargained over locally. This often happened because attempts were made to find ways of reducing incomes policy constraints on the movement of wages.

Productivity agreements

The development of productivity bargaining in the 1960s and early 1970s altered a number of features of industrial relations activity. In particular, it brought into domestic agreements a number of clauses on employee contribution which served as a kind of *quid pro quo* relationship with the clauses on remuneration and reward. It also had the effect of both changing custom and practice in the domestic organization, and of taking certain conditions out of that category and depositing it in the formal agreement.

The NBPI examined seven major agreements of 1966-67 and concluded that they were concerned with:

> 'a reduction in overtime, freer interchange of tasks between different groups of workers, the removal of restrictions on output, manpower reductions and changes in patterns of work' and 'as a counterpart to these changes in working practices, changes have been made in levels and structures of pay' (NBPI, Report No. 36, p 3).

In their early study, using data from the Engineering Employers Federation and Incomes Data Service covering the period 1967-69, Roberts and Gennard concluded that the main subjects covered in productivity agreements were:

> 'reform of wages structures and incentive schemes, changes in working practices and more flexibile use of labour. Coming next in importance seem to be the development of fixed term agreements, then overtime...' (Roberts and Gennard, 1970, pp 1578).

A later more comprehensive study by McKersie and Hunter (1973) used a modified form of the Department of Employment's six categories of reward changes and seven categories of changes in working conditions (grouping them respectively into three and four broader categories) to develop their analysis.

They suggested that productivity bargaining was mainly about the issues listed below:

1   *Reward elements:*
    (a) wages or increased earnings
    (b) leisure resulting from overtime reduction
    (c) job guarantees and status.

2   *Achievement elements:*
    (a) nature of the work, emphasizing skill utilization and worker flexibility as between specialisms and between labour grades (as well as the DEP categories of organization and responsibility)
    (b) hours of work, including shift patterns and overtime reduction
    (c) effort utilization or manning, including questions on quantity of work in respect of both intensity and duration
    (d) methods, including work measurement and control, wage payment systems, and wage structure revision, all conceived within the framework of methods, by which the efficiency of the work system is kept under review on a continuing basis (McKersie and Hunter, 1973, p 117).

They divided their agreements by period, one running from 1960 to 1966 and the other from 1967 to 1970. They show that in the first period management usually took the initiative in proposing changes and these were accepted largely because the associated rewards were relatively high. In the second period, however, the unions usually demanded maintenance or improvement of their reward status, and management found productivity improvements to justify these (McKersie and Hunter, 1973, pp 158).

The effect of these developments has been to establish all of these items mentioned above as negotiable issues in many bargaining units. It does not follow that the original productivity improvements will always flow, but once introduced, the subjects tend to remain negotiable (in accordance with the usual conventions). This has proved one way in which the rights and obligations of the principals on whose behalf the negotiations are conducted, have been extended by negotiation.

AGREEMENTS ON PROCEDURES

Agreements on procedures are those which specify in more detail how the representative and principal parties to the agreements will approach and deal with one another. Even if they do not articulate the conventions of the previous chapter in so many words, they usually do give a more concrete expression to them by spelling out what rights and obligations each side assumes in the actual processes of joint rule-making and control. Such procedures are of three main types:

1   Procedures relating to claims in respect of matters of interest, indicating what matters may be negotiated on a joint basis and how that process will be gone through, and thus establishing how negotiations shall be conducted.
2   Procedures relating to matters of right, indicating how the parties will deal wih problems of interpreting and applying what is intended in the original agreements, and thus establishing how complaints and grievances shall be handled.
3   Procedures relating to the managerial process in respect of those contexts which the parties have agreed shall be subject to some kind of joint supervision or control.

Many of these have 'just grown' out of the negotiating experience of the parties and many have simply been copied from other situations. Changes in law and public policy have stimulated some of the developments, and the only coherent statement on practice in this area is that found in the *Code of Industrial Relations Practice* (1972). This is now somewhat dated, but is gradually being overtaken by the new codes of practice which have been developed by ACAS. Nevertheless, it remains the most focused *general* statement of 'best practice'.

1 Procedures relating to claims

Once the preliminary clauses regarding status have been inserted, the procedural agreement will usually make provision for dealing with interest claims by either party. These usually look towards some change in that status or the status which is accorded by the substantive agreements. This procedure normally covers such questions as what may be negotiable between the parties (at any or every level) and how they will be dealt with in negotiation.

The first of these requires two distinct kinds of decision. First, what matters are to be subject to negotiation in any event and circumstance. Secondly, how are these to be allocated for joint determination to the various levels of bargaining which will apply.

The first of these touches on management's general desire to preserve its right to decide certain questions and the union's general interest in bringing more of these questions into a joint decision framework. It also stands astride what may be discerned as the general process of expanding the number of subjects which fall within collective bargaining as domestic bargaining takes over the central role formerly assigned to industry-wide bargaining. The general trend is touched on above (see pp 14-30) but as it relates to procedures, it might be seen to involve a progressive transfer of subject matter from consultation to negotiation (see also below, pp 499-510). There is nothing automatic about this; transfer takes place only because the union seeks it and the management agrees to it for whatever reasons. Deliberate decisions are involved at both stages.

The second must necessarily accommodate the circumstances in which the undertaking finds itself. From one direction, the undertaking may be in membership of an employers' association and the parties accept that the agreements reached by that association in negotiations with the trade unions shall apply; consequently, certain subjects will be dealt with at that level and 'applied' within the undertaking, simply because of the circumstance of membership. From another direction, the undertaking may be single- or multi-establishment in form, and in the latter case may be conglomerate, single-system or unitary in composition, and these factors will tend to influence the extent to which domestic bargaining will be centralized or decentralized (see above, pp 226-39).

The problem of allocation of subject matter will thus be characterized differently in each circumstance (reflecting the kinds of consideration which are identified on pp 285-90 above). Nevertheless, the procedure to be followed at each and every level, will necessarily deal with questions of:

(a) what (which terms and conditions of employment) is a proper subject for consideration at this level
(b) which representatives of the two sides will be involved in the discussion of such subjects; (this frequently indicates approximately how the management team will be composed and

comparably on the union side what role is to be allocated to the full-time officer(s) in the negotiating process)

(c) the timing of any claims which may be presented within this area, together with the form and notice requirements which will apply (it is, for example, usual to indicate the date on which annual negotiations will start in order to produce the annual agreement in time to apply the new terms on the anniversary date)

(d) the phasing of discussions which the parties will intend or aim to adhere to in the absence of difficulties and disagreements; (this usually takes the form of setting down the periods which will be 'allowed' to each side to consider the demand(s) and response(s) of the parties and the frequency with which necessary negotiating meetings will be called within the 'negotiating period' leading up to the annual settlement)

(e) the courses of action which will follow a failure to agree or breakdown of negotiations; (the object here is to provide for a phased process of appeal or further consideration, leading possibly outside the undertaking to district conferences and the like or to conciliation and arbitration, as a means of preventing industrial action by either party at least until all avenues have been explored).

Procedures such as these do little more than provide a constitution for the better ordering of relationships: whether they work or not must depend upon the willingness of both parties to abide by them. It can be, and often is, argued that trade unions will only do so when it suits them. But it should neither be assumed that management is always willing to follow procedure nor that what management sees as a conforming course of action on its part will necessarily be seen as such by a group of shop stewards (if, for example, they are faced with frequent adjournments of meetings held to discuss claims or grievances).

2 Disputes and disputes procedures

A dispute is essentially a difference between two parties which has been elevated to the level of institutionalized conflict by the parties themselves. This is sometimes referred to as a difference or a dispute over *rights* which the parties have under existing agreements or in association with custom and practice. A difference between a worker and his supervisor over the allocation of work might, for example, be taken up through the kind of individual rights (or grievance) procedure outlined on p 128 above. But it could also be taken up by the union (as an institution) and represented to management (as an institution) as a matter of principle or rule which needs to be resolved other than by purely inter-personal means. In these circumstances, the two parties may readily mobilize their 'power' to confront each other over what now becomes a (collective) issue.

In a dispute, therefore, two formally defined hierarchies (of the management and the union) are made to confront one another within an unashamed power framework (see Terry, 1977, pp 81-87). Both are concerned with control, albeit in reflection of different values, of the situation in which the difference first arises.

The management's representatives aim to maintain or re-establish their control over the processes and flows of finance, materials and manpower through which management's complex objectives may be achieved. They need not be particularly or directly concerned with the maintenance or establishment of control over the industrial relationss processes and flows themselves; these only move within the purview when they threaten to interfere in an unacceptable way with the manpower flows and processes which management would see as falling within their 'prerogative'. (It is generally accepted that in industry-wide bargaining control of the amounts of work or effort was left to the on-the-spot management to determine (see Donovan Report, 1968; and above, pp 341-42.)

The trade union's representatives have similar aims. They too seek to maintain or establish their control over the flows and processes of protest within the situation. Without this the unions could not mobilize power to perform their functions, and their officers could scarcely carry out their roles successfully. If on the management side, there is a recognizable prerogative which justifies their involvement, on the union official's side there is also a recognized right to 'carry out trade union functions'. These status-according clauses repetitively preface annual or main agreements because they are so important to the parties.

The widespread acceptance of the benefits of disputes procedures tends to suggest that they serve both negotiating parties interests. Hawkins, for example, suggests that:

'In essence, procedures impose restraints on the use of power .... Fundamentally they reflect an agreement by both sides to be bound by a code of 'Queensberry Rules' in their day-to-day relationships' (Hawkins, 1978, pp 199-200).

Power being something which exists only in the relationship itself, the constraint may be seen to operate in both directions. Marsh has amplified this in his suggestion that a disputes procedure performs three distinct functions:

(a) 'a 'safety valve' against the spread of disputes...;
(b) a means of recognizing the negotiating rights of trade unions in the workshop while at the same time bringing strong pressure to bear against their misuse...;
(c) a means by which, in the event of failures to settle issues at workshop level, conciliatory forces outside the factory can be brought to bear on the situation' (Marsh, 1965, p 112).

The second of these supports and controls the mutually-recognized prerogatives and rights and the other two provide for the containment of differences (see above, pp 348-55).

The disputes procedure established to contain these differences usually looks like a combination of a grievance and a claims procedure. Depending upon its importance, the matter in dispute will be 'put in procedure' at the appropriate (lowest) level and proceed from there upwards through whatever arrangements exist for resolving it. The formal dispute over a broad issue of principle at the establishment or undertaking level is likely to begin with the body which normally handles the main claims. It will proceed from there through the agreed stages for dealing with unresolved claims. Where the employer is a member of an association, the issue could well move through the stages provided for in a national procedural agreement (see Marsh 1965, pp 260-61).

The more bargaining becomes a domestic matter, the more likely it is that all these procedures will attempt to stipulate some of the basic rules which the parties will agree in advance to abide by in the event of breakdown in negotiations over matters of interest or of right. Changes in the law relating to striking and picketing, and the dubious legal status of the lock-out (see below, pp 385-88) together with changes in the nature of trade union demands (for example, for payment of workers who have been on strike on the grounds that the employer played some causal part in the strike) make it more likely that the breakdown itself could become a negotiatiable matter which could be constrained by rules agreed in advance.

In the National Engineering Industry Agreement (see Marsh, 1965, pp 250-317) the 'Procedure for dealing with questions arising' amounts to a lengthy statement on the extent to which (and the procedure by which) the employer is prepared to give up his 'right to manage' in the interests of securing agreement with the workforce representatives and the extent to which the union will be allowed to represent its membership to the employer in defined circumstances of disagreement or dispute.

For example, the employer's right is modified by the following clause in the procedure:

> 'Where any alteration in the recognized working conditions ... contemplated by the Management will result in a class of workpeople being replaced by another in the establishment, the Management shall, unless the circumstances arising are beyond their control, give the workpeople directly con-cerned or their representatives in the shop, not less than ten days' intimation of their intention and afford an opportun-ity for discussion, if discussion is desired, with a deputation of the workpeople concerned, and/or their representatives in the shop. Should a discussion not be desired, the instructions of the Management shall be observed and work shall proceed in accordance therewith. Should a discussion take place, and no settlement be reached at the various stages of procedure which are possible within the time available, the Management shall, on the date intimated, give a temporary decision upon which work shall proceed pending the recognized procedure being carried through. The decision shall not be prejudicial to either party in any subsequent discussion which may take place'.

Other parts of this same procedure set out the provisions for the organization and time of such discussions and for the appoint-ment and functions (that is, their rights and limitations) of shop stewards and works committees.

3 Agreed procedures on management methods

With the growth of domestic bargaining and agreements, it has become possible to develop joint agreements and procedures which relate to approaches and methods of managing. These methods would in former years have been adopted and applied within the management prerogative. If these are applied less now, it is probably because of the frequently recognized need to share control in order to increase it, given the changes in fundamental attitudes towards work and its control in recent years (see Elliott, 1977; George and Elliott, 1979).

The procedures which are most often developed in this fashion are ones which relate to methods of determination of remuneration or to proposals for change in the 'technology' of the undertaking which might direclty (and seriously) affect the kinds of contribution made by workers or even whether they would continue to be employed at all.

It has, for example, become increasingly common in the past two decades for job evaluation schemes to be decided, implemented and monitored jointly by the two parties. The development of procedures governing these processes becomes a necessary step towards ensuring that the approach is measured, consistent and controlled. The procedures therefore identify the roles of the several parties, the methods of selection of those who will exercise an executive role, the steps which these executives will take to carry out their assigned tasks, and the steps which others (managers or workers) will be expected to take in order to relate themselves to these joint managerial procedures (see Edwards and Paul, 1977; Thomason, 1980a).

Procedures relating to work measure and the application of methods of incentive payment have sometimes been treated in a similar fashion. Here the objective has usually been that of reducing the number of disputes which tend to occur in PBR and particular piecework shops. It is hoped that by setting up jointly agreed procedures, or even procedures which give both parties an executive role, some of this aggravation can be removed.

The other major example of the joint-managerial agreement is provided by the so-called 'new technology agreement'. New technologies in the shape of chip-based machines threaten two main consequences: that the nature of the work to be performed will be changed drastically; and jobs may be eliminated by their application in the absence of a rising market trend. The new technology agreement is therefore often based upon a no-redundancy or restricted redundancy pledge and provides for the development of necessary training programmes and the protection of earnings in a transition period. Its main purpose might be

367

said to ensure the smoothest possible switch-over to a new system of working with new technology. In that sense it is, like the other examples, a case of a procedure which is agreed to cover a process which has been traditionally regarded as a part of the managerial role and task.

The scope for the development of more agreements of this general type, in which management 'voluntarily' gives up its rights to impose such plans unilaterally upon the workers, is clearly wide. Any managerial method which impinges upon either effort or reward elements could conceivably be put under some kind of joint procedural control in this general fashion. If this trend continues, the contention of Chamberlain and Kuhn that collective bargaining or agreement-making is a 'method of management' might be made more demonstrably correct. However, there remains a good deal of reluctance on the part of the trade unionists to become directly involved in the monitoring process which forms an inherent feature of the managerial role. For that reason, joint management, as distinct from joint agreements as to procedures which will govern a managerial process, may remain somewhat distant.

Summary: management and change

Developments towards more comprehensive and more detailed agreements may be readily seen as attractive to the unions. They imply that the four categories of rules (distinguished on p 341 above) are now becoming more systematized as custom and practice is gradually, but probably inexorably, replaced by more formal rules. They also imply, given their origins in the application of the union's bargaining power, greater acceptability to them.

As Batstone, Boraston and Frenkel have suggested , however, agreements may be perceived to have variable legitimacy in the eyes of both parties to it, including the unions and their members. This legitimacy is associated with the nature of the agreement itself and the interpetations which are made of it as it is applied.

First, the agreement may be perceived as legitimate in itself if it is seen to deal honestly and fairly (within the existing power structure) with a real issue or problem. An annual pay agreement usually acquires the cast of legitimacy in this sense, even though the parties may consider that it might have paid more or less (according to the objectives of the side). Other agreements may command less respect. Agreements on lay-offs can as in the example quoted by these authors, acquire the brand of a 'blackmail charter' or a 'blackleg's charter' and tend to be denied general legitimacy. Similarly, Friedman and Meredeen refer to the branding of the 1969 Ford income security plan being perceived as a 'confidence trick' (Friedman and Meredeen, 1980, p 258).

Secondly, the terms of the agreement have to be interpreted in order to apply them. Agreements on pay increases may be interpreted fairly easily, as it is clear that this year's figures replace last year's. But given the plethora of formal and informal rules which surround the work process, other terms may have to be applied within a network of existing norms and rules which may or may not (be intended to) take precedence over them. In this process, charges by one party that the other is adopting a view contrary to the 'spirit and intention' of the agreement, are not uncommon. In those circumstances, it is not the legitimacy of the agreement as such, but that of its several interpretations which is in question.

In spite of this, the general development of the rules may still be regarded as owing more to worker and union pressure than to simple benevolence or situational accommodation by management. The changes did not, and do not, occur without the consent of management. The question is why management should assent to them when they deplete the managerial prerogative in so far as they bring more subjects within the purview of joint control.

One answer to this question might well be that management has agreed to the changes because it has had no real alternative in the face of workers' attitudes as aggregated into union power. The 'growing power' of the unions might be regarded as a sufficient explanation in spite of the fact that there are many who have argued that the unions either have little power or that it is a house of cards.

Another could be that managements see their best interests served by developing these more detailed and elaborate constitutions. They might bind managements in some respects but they also bind the trade union representatives and possibly also the trade union members. This answer rests on the supposition that management sees its own interest as served by securing the co-operation of the unions in controlling or disciplining the workforce.

The argument here is that closer control is seen to demand that management secures the co-operation, not of the full-time officers as in national bargaining, but of the local representatives in domestic bargaining. This having been secured (with the growth of domestic bargaining during the 1950s and 1960s) the next tranche of required co-operation calls for employer support of the unions as institutions through the grant of some degree of union security (for example, the closed shop and check-off facilities). This granted, the next step requires some greater degree of harmonization of both procedures and substantive terms, to reduce the conflict arising on this score for both unions and management.

In effect, therefore, the translation of union power into concessions might be effected because management sees a means of developing greater control by incorporating the unions into the management system, (along the lines implicit in the Chamberlain and Kuhn suggestion that collective bargaining is a process of management).

But whatever the cause, the consequence has been the elaboration of domestic agreements along the lines suggested, leaving the subject matter of bargaining a less poverty-stricken affair than it might have been at the time when Flanders expressed his view about national bargaining.

Once brought into national or domestic agreements, however, the subjects provide both parties with a set of conventionally upheld rights and obligations enforceable on the basis of the sanctions available to the collective parties. They also give legitimacy to grievances in the event of breach by the other. Where management is in breach of a procedure, or the union members in breach of conditions, the other party may seek to secure redress on the moral ground that the other has breached a promise made and may ultimately back this up with industrial action.

However, each party is likely to see itself as 'bound' by the rules mainly when it perceives it to be in its interest to do so. This frequently means that it will seek to have the rules treated as morally binding on the other when it is otherwise in a strong enough position to breach them with impunity. This has frequently occurred in the full-employment period when the unions ignored procedures and management tended to cry 'foul' and in the recession situation when management tore up procedural agreements and the unions cried 'foul'.

370

This suggests that rules are binding to the extent that people see themselves bound by them for some good reason. This in turn may have more to do either with morality than with the fact that they are enforceable in the 'arbitrament of private war'.

Readings

Muir: (1981), pp 1-42 (on recognition and procedural agreements); p 36 (on status agreements); pp 43-74 (on shop stewards' credentials) and pp 75-112 (on redundancy agreements).
Singleton: (1975). Sisson: (1977).
Marsh: (1965), pp 72-141 and 250-318.
Marsh, Evans and Garcia: (1971), pp 121-35.
Marchington: (1982), pp 109-24.
Jackson: (1977), pp 140-63. Anthony: (1977a), pp 183-218.
North and Buckingham: (1969), pp 1-69.
Daniel and Millward: (1983), pp 129-58.

14

Enforcement processes

Assessment and enforcement

The customs, conventions, rules and decisions which are created by the parties in the bargaining process have to be monitored and enforced by actions of their own. The judicial machinery of the State will not directly enforce the rules which are erected voluntarily on the legal foundation (see above, pp 99-101). The parties themselves must acquire and apply sanctions against anyone in breach of them. These are likely to be the same sanctions as are used in the establishment of the conventions and rules in the first place.

Even where the State has acted to make the actions of the parties subject to control by the operation of law and by the courts and tribunals, the need for voluntary enforcement has not been removed. Action to enforce agreed rules (whether that action is undertaken jointly or separately) requires:

1 The assessment of the conduct of the parties to determine whether it is in accord with the conventions and rules which are intended to apply to it, is likely to be carried out by the parties themselves. It is likely to result in the identification of a grievance about the other's conduct. Partridge has suggested a model of how a grievance is articulated in an uncertain group context by a shop-floor leader (a steward) and brought to a successful conclusion.

   (a) 'When an individual has a grievance, he wants a collectivity with power to support him and progress his grievance. Therefore, he makes use of a collective representative, such as the steward.

   (b) 'The steward then has to mobilize commitment to action, or least a potential commitment, from a collectivity that has some bargaining power.

(c) 'The steward has to legitimize the grievance amongst his members by accessing some system of values and beliefs. In this sense the grievance can be said to define the group. This process of defining/legitimizing the grievance is simplified if there is one dominant system of values and meanings amongst the workforce. Obviously, it is made more difficult when there is a variety of value and meaning systems within the workplace' (Partridge, 1978, p 189).

(This might also be applied, *mutatis mutandis*, to the development of a manager's grievance, for which he might have to secure the backing of other members of the management group.)

2 The communication of the conclusions of the evaluation to those whose conduct is in breach along with a request that it be brought into line. At a minimum, this requires that each party shall have access to a relevant channel of communication and capacity to make effective use of it. (This is considered within the general case of negotiation in chapter 19).

3 The pressuring, through the use of sanctions, of those in breach to coerce them to change their minds, attitudes or conduct to bring it into line. The main sanctions available to the two parties are:

(a) the employer's sanction of denying the worker(s) opportunity to continue in employment (and therefore to earn a wage or salary); this may take either of two forms: the dismissal of the individual or the group from employment, or the temporary suspension of the offer of employment, as in a lock-out

(b) the worker's sanction of denying the employer his services, either by quitting the employment (individual withdrawal) or by combining with fellows in a temporary suspension of the offer of services, as in a strike (a collective withdrawal).

The sanctions to coerce agreement or compliance are not, however, simple equals and opposites. The employer's *main* sanction is dismissal (seen as the ultimate sanction at the end of a disciplinary chain). This, as we have seen, continues to be upheld (if also curbed in its application) in law (see above, ch. 5). It may be used either as an individual or as a collective sanction. Its collective use occurs at least partly by extension of the right in the individual case and not merely as an extension of the legally-supported collective sanction of the union.

The sanctioning power and authority of the trade union, as the workers' agent in these matters, is also to an extent founded upon a legal base, even though it may not be wholly determined in this manner. The workers' main sanction is withdrawal of services, which he is free to do under the law of contract. But the making and enforcement of the rules of work which may be *jointly* agreed, is largely effected outside the formal systems of law, although enforcement through industrial actions of the parties are subject to judicial supervision.

Each of these is associated with different parts of a general rule enforcement process which takes many different forms in different industries and undertakings.

MONITORING

Both parties need a monitoring mechanism to determine how existing rules are being applied (as the parties have a right to expect) and whether new ones (more in the party's interest) are desirable. (The process of monitoring grievances preparatory to composing a claim by the trade union is discussed extensively by Batstone, Boraston and Frenkel (1978) who show how the one process feeds into the other.) Both parties need also to have access to an established procedure (for example, a grievance or claims procedure, of the kind discussed in the preceding chapter) through which views can be communicated to the other party. Both need to have sanctions available to apply, and sufficient power to do so, in order to compel the other to accept the grievance or complaint and make the necessary changes.

Internal roles and machinery

Internal machinery of this kind has always existed in some form. Originally it supported the exercise of unilateral managerial authority. Traditionally members of the management team made the rules for the workers to follow and they evaluated and adjudicated on their conduct. The machinery involved was inherent in the normal exercise of the manager's or supervisor's authority and the roles were non-specialized in the sense that any manager was expected to carry out these tasks as part of his normal job. Brown recognized this in his argument that all undertakings engaged in a kind of private 'judicial' process, even if they were unwilling to identify it in these constitutional terms (Brown, 1951).

The traditional role of the unions has been one of pressurizing management to change both the values which it applies in this process and the procedures which it adopts in relation to it. This too was recognized by Brown (1951) as a major factor in stimulating the need to develop more formal machinery and procedures to determine the fairness or otherwise of decisions taken or proposed by management. Much of the trade union's ideology in this respect has now been reflected in legislation (see ch. 5).

The effect of legislation where management still seeks to retain in its own hands as much of its disciplinary or prerogative power as possible, and allows as little 'joint' influence as it can get away with, has been to make the unilateral management decisions more equitable and more humane, at least where the management is willing to accept the values inherent in legislation (see above, pp 129-31). The main example is provided by disciplinary action (which forms the main sanction available to the employer) where the requirements of the law has led many undertakings to improve on their pre-existing arrangements (see above, pp 115-23). It has also tended to nudge more managements (who do accept its underlying values) into a more 'joint' approach to decision and evaluation.

Gradually, therefore, joint approaches under the control of agreements have tended to overtake unilateral ones. Brown's 'judicial' machinery is now more likely to reflect the success of legislation or the union in modifying the original approach. Two distinct patterns are now visible:

(a) that in which the judicial machinery continues to be established by the employer to enforce the domestic rules applied to the undertaking; this may be more or less formal, but by whatever means it usually serves to subject employee action and managerial decisions on it to scrutiny in the interests of good order, efficiency, fairness and/or natural justice

(b) that in which the judicial machinery established jointly by the employer and worker association(s) within either the industry or the undertaking, for the purposes of evaluating and ruling upon the actions of management or workers under the 'rules' of the collective agreement or the conventions of the workplace.

External roles and machinery

Where the new controls do emerge from joint negotiation, their inception and their internal supervision is usually effected through procedural agreements of the kind which have already been outlined. These allow for the shop stewards to engage in a monitoring and representational role. They provide for persons to hear complaints from either party and to take action on them. They seek to guarantee the rights of the injured party in so far as a procedure can ever provide for this. ACAS has issued a considerable amount of guidance on this aspect, through the formal codes of practice and its advisory service to industry. The effect is to produce a more measured approach to the whole question of grievance and discipline within undertakings.

In this context, each party must function as a monitor of the other: each will seek to evaluate the action of the other party to ensure that interests are not denied and that rights are not infringed. Members of management or the union officers come to serve the 'judicial' process associated with the voluntary system. They engage in evaluation (pure monitoring), communication (or negotiation) and the enforcement of remedies (essentially that of getting the offending party to change its mind, attitude or conduct). This machinery is usually maintained by the two parties separately, and only in the negotiation and subsequent stages does it require a joint approach and structure.

In effect, the employer's conduct is subject to a degree of *external* control by the union and by the joint conference much as the workers' conduct always has been by 'the management'. This observation relies upon treating the trade union as a body external the (unitary) undertaking, as does Flanders (1965, p 15). The legislative developments referred to above (pp 374-76) have had the incidental effect of either creating or developing the roles of (particularly) the shop steward and the personnel manager in relation to these judicial and enforcement processes. In a clear sense, both of these roles and functions are *external* to the traditional conception of the unitary organization.

Shop stewards and industrial relations managers

The shop steward began life as a recruiter of members and a collector of union dues, and as a liaison person between shop and branch. His tenuous position in relation to both local negotiations and his own union was noted by the Donovan Commmission, who made recommendations that he should be more clearly and firmly incorporated into both. Their survey of the role suggested that a majority were essentially 'shop floor bargainers, using all the opportunities presented to them to satisfy their members' grievances and claims' (McCarthy, 1966, p 30). The subjects bargained about varied, but generally included any one on which the management was prepared to bargain (see, Clegg, 1972, pp 1-40; Goodman, 1971).

Coincidentally with the growth of a role for shop stewards has gone the development of a role for a specialist personnel or industrial relations manager, at least part of whose job was to deal at some stage (indicated by the relevant procedures) with these same grievances and claims, and also with issues of discipline and dismissal. If the Donovan Commission could see the shop stewards more as lubricants than as irritants, these specialist managers might be seen in the same light. Very often they do not possess direct responsibility for the matters at issue, this being the concern of line management, but they do stand ready to advise on how the matters might be handled and to play some part in the course of any appeal. It is in this advisory role that the externality of the personnel specialist is established.

The machinery involved is, however, only external in so far as it involves the two parties in a joint negotiating conference. As such, it belongs to neither party exclusively, and brings an external consideration to bear on any issue raised. In addition, it cannot be seen as necessarily a new integral body in itself, because it depends essentially (as does all negotiating) upon opposition and necessary conflict. Although it may, in respect of other functions which the joint conference might perform, serve a co-operative purpose, it serves an oppositional and conflictual one in this context of adjudicating upon the conduct of the 'other' in respect of discipline and grievances.

Tripartite regulation

The establishment, by or under State auspices, of bodies which

377

engage in 'tripartite regulation', has introduced a new 'external' dimension to the voluntary system of collective bargaining. In many respects, this acknowledges the values which support that system, but more importantly introduces a *third party* into the processes of both securing agreement and commitment, and in some cases (the wages councils, particularly) into the process of enforcement. The main difference, however, is that the power of the first two parties to establish the rules through agreement is replaced by the power of the third party to influence them or (in the case of pay review bodies and arbitrators) to determine them.

Any external arrangement (such as that which involves reference to national bargaining committees) might be taken as a form of tripartite regulation, from the standpoint of the domestic organization. But the main manifestations of it in Britain are the pay review bodies, the wages councils, certain other former pay monitoring bodies, and the machinery of conciliation, mediation and arbitration.

These bodies tend to deal with a limited range of issues: wages, hours, holidays and certain other conditions reflecting either what the parties sought the tripartite body for, or what was considered to be the scope of bargaining at the time when the initiative was taken. The employer in these contexts, retains his sanction of individual and collective dismissal, but the workers in most of them either cannot or will not muster collective power to withdraw labour (and where, therefore, all threats uttered by them would be empty ones). In these circumstances, the third party has been introduced into the bargaining arrangement to effect some redress of power.

In all of this machinery, a third party is involved but the principle that the parties retain the power to decide whether they make use of the machinery or not is usually maintained, in order to retain the link with 'voluntarism'. The procedures adopted attempt to leave as much power to determine outcomes in the hands of the first two parties, not the third party, for the same reason. But in spite of these apparent similarities, there are differences, the main one being that outcomes are subject to some (admittedly variable) degree of third party influence. Its main effect is to alter the allocation to the parties of roles of legislating, executing and adjudicating.

Each party has to plead or bargain in the presence of a third person or side, and possibly with the opposing side present. Moreover, the third party usually has the ultimate power of decision. One side of the wages council, for example, cannot easily adopt the posture that it will first try to influence the opponent, and only when it has failed in that attempt, seek to convince or negotiate with, the third party. To do so would be to give up a position or an image (see Pruitt, 1969, p 11) too early in the proceedings. The two main parties in these tripartite negotiation must, therefore, attempt to handle two negotiations simultaneously.

This is less of a problem for the parties in either the pay review bodies or in conciliation, mediation and arbitration, since they are more directly concerned to influence the third party (almost regardless of the effect on the directly opposite party). In the case of conciliation, the parties are usually apart, at least initially, and thus speak 'privately' to the conciliator. This may happen in mediation too, but this increasingly popular device (see table 17 on p 380) tends to stand astride both conciliation and arbitration, embracing elements of both. In the case of arbitration, the parties usually appear before the arbitrator together, and thus hear all that the other party may have to say, but to the extent that an arbitrator has any kind of judicial function, the parties have to recognize that he (or she) is the one to be convinced, not the opposing party.

Tripartite arrangements also change the position with respect to sanctions which might be applied to secure an agreement or a settlement. In the context of collective bargaining, the parties can use industrial action to secure their ends. In tripartite bargaining, the parties either do not possess these options or have voluntarily given them up for the time being and in relation to the outstanding issues.

Consequently, power, including the power to sanction, resides largely with the third party. The other two parties would presumably not be there if they considered that they not only had the power to exact agreement from the other side but also the authority or right to use it in this way. But this does not mean that any of these 'third parties' has a power which can be used to ride roughshod over all the parties (together). They might side with one or the other, basking it might be said, in the sunshine of that side's power and protection, and in this way secure some legitimacy for a particular course of action. But they are unlikely to find themselves with any power if they seek to go against the wishes of the two other parties together. These kinds of tripartite bargaining entail the first two parties voluntarily giving up

Table 17

Usage of mediation

Year	Single mediation	Board	Court of Inquiry
Sep-Dec 1974	5	1	–
1975	8	3	3
1976	15	2	1
1977	27	4	–
1978	28	1	1
1979	31	1	1
1980	26	5	–
1981	12	–	–
1982	15	1	1
Average, 1975-82	20	2	1

Source: ACAS Annual Reports

power, but not the donation of absolute power to the third party involved.

Tripartite arrangements vary as to the relationship between the negotiating and policing agreements. In some cases, enforcement is internal (by the parties) and in others, external (by some specialized agency outside the ranks of the parties themselves). In the case of the wages councils, the policing is done officially by the Wages Inspectorate, and in some of the Incomes Policies adopted in the past-war period a separately-established monitoring body was set up to police it. In the case of the other tripartite arrangements, however, the policing is left to the parties themselves to carry out their normal role, based on the identification and processing of grievances, in this respect.

OBJECTIVES AND SANCTIONS

Grievances and objectives

The identification of management or worker grievances is usually regarded as a necessary trigger to any process of enforcement (as otherwise there would presumably be nothing to 'enforce'). This is the assumption behind the collection of official statistics on strikes, namely that a strike is caused by an identifiable grievance associated with one or more individuals. This provides the basis for action, even if it does not actually *cause* industrial action rather than some other (such as quitting the job or working without enthusiasm).

Grievances may be of two types, external and internal. By 'external' grievance, in this context, is meant the sense of grievance which can arise when, even though the individual is receiving every consideration to which he is entitled under existing contracts and agreements, he or she nevertheless considers that external events (cost of living, comparative earnings of others, etc) have placed him or her in a less than desirable position. This kind of grievance is likely to give rise to a claim for enhanced 'rights', and may be identified as concerned primarily with the individuals' interests.

By 'internal' grievance on the other hand, is indicated that grievance which can arise because an individual considers that he or she is not being accorded the rights which have already been agreed. This might apply to both management members and trade union members. This is the more usual meaning of the concept of grievance, one which focuses upon 'rights' issues (as distinct from the 'interests' of the previous case). These grievances may, of course, 'add up to' a claim in certain circumstances, and indeed may be made to do so by the union leaders. But whichever conception of grievance is considered, it may be asserted that grievances in one sense or the other will trigger a claim or a complaint to the other party.

The only category of *remedy* which is available to the parties is a change of thinking, feeling or conduct on the part of the other. This, generically, is the 'objective' of either party. It may, however, be supported by other more particular and immediate objectives.

Objectives are usually firmly embedded in the parties' structures of values and norms and industrial action may be undertaken to secure a number of distinct advantages which surround the immediate issue but do not depend upon it. Lane and Roberts, for example, point to a variety of non-specific and non-immediate objectives in the Pilkington's strike of 1970 (Lane and Roberts, 1971, pp 235-8). Many commentators on strikes attach importance to the need for often minor grievances to 'build-up' into a 'critical mass' which must then release itself in action (see, Batstone, Boraston and Frenkel, 1978).

A union may decide that a strike is called in order to teach management (and sometimes government) a lesson, to demonstrate the solidarity of the workforce behind the union's values, or, more pragmatically, to secure redress of one or more specific grievances. Part of the motivation might be to develop a greater trade union consciousness amongst the membership, where it is considered that this could be achieved without too great a disruption of the relationships with the management. Management may call a lock-out or engineer a strike in order to gain some respite in the face of a falling order book, or to stop a union in its tracks during a difficult negotiating period.

This must be taken to suggest that strikes neither have a single 'cause' even at their outset, and certainly they are very likely to develop new objectives as the breach of relationship continues and the parties make their separate and several pronouncements on the position and conduct of the other party. For this reason, statements made in the course of such disputes are likely to benefit from a careful prior consideration of what it is that the party wishes to achieve by making them and whether they are likely to assist in securing *that* objective.

The clear implication of this is that strikes are rarely as automatic or as spontaneous as might at first appear, nor are they likely to depend upon the simple, single issue which the statistics collectors might delight to secure. Strikes may be much more complex activities than this suggests, involving more complex aims and means, and therefore demanding of more careful orchestration than the simpler conceptions suggest.

Sanctions

The parties may severally monitor the other's performance and collate their findings. They may jointly communicate these to one another and by doing so jointly seek to persuade one another of a correct conclusion and remedy. But this latter process depends ultimately, not merely upon their abilities to persuade, but also upon the power which they can mobilize in the form of sanctions against the other. These sanctions, in turn, focus upon some form of disciplinary or industrial action, undertaken by the employer in the one case or by either party in the other. Sanctions entail the withdrawal of co-operation from the other party, and are used to bring about a change of mind, attitude or conduct on the part of that other (which, generically, is the only *remedy* which is available to them in this context. From the employer's side, the sanctions involve the withdrawal of employment or the opportunity to earn remuneration either from individuals (dismissal or suspension) or from the workforce as a whole (a lockout). From the worker's side, they involve either the individual withdrawal of services (voluntary termination or unmotivated performance) or the collective withdrawal of labour in total (as in a strike). Although the individual forms of these are important, they belong more with the traditional conceptions of enforcement than with those associated with collective bargaining, and here we concentrate on the latter.

These same means of coercion have to be relied upon to compel agreement to the conventions and rules in the first place and to ensure that they are followed once that agreement has been established. This creates some conceptual difficulty in comprehending the uses and functions of industrial action in enforcing agreement or enforcing compliance with its terms. The two are kept separate usually by distinguishing between action to pursue interests and that to enforce rights. In the one case, the sanction seeks the remedy of agreement by the opponent to a different approach to some problem, whereas in the other it looks for the remedy of the other acknowledging or granting the rights accorded to the other under a previous agreement.

Collective enforcement requires that some machinery (the collective bargaining machinery) shall exist to permit the two parties to attempt to persuade each other to a particular course of action, or to apply sanctions to the other to compel his agreement to a course of action. These take the ultimate form of a concerted withdrawal of labour (a strike) or a refusal by the employer to continue the employment of a group of workers (a lock-out).

A strike is defined in the EP(C) Act as:

> 'the cessation of work by a body of persons employed acting in combination, or a concerted refusal or a refusal under a common understanding of any number of persons employed to continue to work for an employer in consequence of a dispute, done as a means of compelling their employer or any person or body of persons employed, or to aid other emplyees in compelling their employer or any person or body of persons employed to accept or not to accept terms

or conditions of, or affecting, employment' (EP(C) Act, 1978, Sch 13 para 24).

In the same place, a lock-out is defined as:

> 'the closing of a place of employment, or the suspension of work, or the refusal by an employer to continue to employ any number of persons employed by him in consequence of a dispute, done with a view to compelling those persons, or to aid another employer in compelling persons employed by him, to accept terms or conditions of or affecting employment' (Sch 13, para 24).

In the past, industrial relations students have tended to regard strikes and lock-outs as equivalents in that they merely suspend contracts of employment for their duration. It is generally accepted that workers intend no more than this when they strike, although the employer is at liberty to treat it as repudiatory breach of contract and to refuse re-engagement. This would rely upon the employer's exercise of his normal right to dismiss, with or without notice according to circumstances.

This lumping together of the two types of action may be appropriate within the context of conventional control, but inappropriate and productive of unwanted legal consequences if this is carried over into a legal framework. The main question in this is 'what happens to the contract of employment in the event of a lock-out?' The answer depends upon the way in which the employer decides to implement it. He faces a choice in this respect.

1 The employer may be experiencing a concerted action by (some of) his employees which amounts to a repudiatory breach of the contract of employment on their part. In the normal situation, it is up to the employer to decide whether he will accept or reject this repudiation: if he decides to accept that there is a repudiatory breach and decide upon a lock-out as a means of responding to it, he may well be interpreted as having intended to determine the contract, the effective termination being coincident with the initiation of the lock-out.

2 In similar circumstances, the employer may inform the employees concerned that they are to be dismissed and that with the institution of the lock-out, the employees will be denied access to their workplaces and to their work. This may

384

be interpreted as a straight-forward determination of the contract, occasioned and justified by the repudiatory breach, to which the 'lock-out' as such is incidental.

3   In similar circumstances, the lock-out may be interpreted as an intended suspension of the worker without pay, rather than as dismissal or acceptance of a repudiatory breach of the contract of employment. This is only lawful where the employment contract itself provides for suspension without pay, and may amount to constructive dismissal where this is not the case.

The lock-out as a sanction is not, therefore, an exact equivalent to the strike in law, since the worker may be presumed to intend to suspend both work *and* pay, where the employer *may* in a lock-out intend to suspend only the pay.

Other forms of industrial action

The strike is but one form of sanction, even if an important one, which workers can apply to secure employer compliance with a demand. From the trade union's point of view it is not without its costs: an official strike may attract strike pay from the union's strike funds, but even without this some of the union's resources will be devoted to maintaining and to ending it and the workers will lose their earnings. It is also more efficacious in some situations than in others: it relies for its success upon a denial of labour to the employer causing him a relatively high loss (for example when the order book is full) in either the short or the long run.

It is not therefore to be undertaken lightly. There are, in any case, other sanctions which the trade union (or workers) can apply without going this far along the road (see Johnston, 1975). In fact, any co-operation which workers voluntarily offer to the employer in order to facilitate the performance of the work contracts may be withdrawn as a bargaining weapon. Voluntary overtime or bonus rate and incentive working fall in this category. Withdrawal of the offer to work overtime, and fall-back to non-incentive working on flat time rates, may be carried out with impunity. Withdrawal from joint consultation has also been used as a kind of sanction in some situations, particularly in nationalized industries.

Working without enthusiasm, working to rule, and going-slow are frequently used as weapons. In these cases, the workers

385

perform less work than is common, normal or customary, either by simply holding back or by paying meticulous attention to the detailed rules, but expect nevertheless to draw their normal rate of pay. These weapons are in a different category from those involving withdrawal of co-operation which has been offered voluntarily, and have been held to be of doubtful legality because they threaten (at least) to undermine the terms of the contract of employment. They may nevertheless be effective in so far as they are often difficult to detect in the individual case even though their overall effect on performance may be readily discernible.

Such 'cut-price' industrial actions on the part of the workers can be used where a strike is unlikely to be supported officially because only the workers immediately involved think it likely to persuade management to take a particular course of action.

A number of industrial actions, other than simple dismissal of the individual or group and the lock-out, are also available to management. The undertaking may, for example, impose lay-offs or short-time working under appropriate product market conditions as means of changing worker commitment. The opportunities which the undertaking has to transfer work to other establishments are equivalent to the workers' opportunities to limit their co-operation, and may be used as a counter-threat to pressure from the union side. The opportunity to close down the plant may not be a common one, but it can serve a similar purpose and it can prove a difficult ploy to counter with any collective action (see Fox, 1966a).

The form which the management sanction takes has variable implications for the trade union or the workers. Dismissal of some individuals is not always easy to assign to a category of provocative or reactive industrial action. It is easier to do so if, for example, the individuals dismissed are shop stewards or leaders of some kind. Similarly, transfer of work to other establishments may also prove difficult to place under this heading. Compared with a 'declared' lock-out, these make the decisions about appropriate responses more difficult to arrive at.

A strike may have limited utility in those situations where the employer proposes closure of a work situation and the workers seek to uphold their job property rights against these odds. Workers have on occasion sought to 'take-over' the employer's 'property' in such circumstances, by means of 'the sit-in'. This is used as a generic term to over three different types or forms of action which interfere with the employer's property rights, as distinct from his rights in contract.

1   The 'work-in', in which the workers occupy the premises and thus guarantee free entry and egress to their fellows, but in which also the workers attempt to continue the operation of the establishment, albeit under some form of exclusive or joint workers control. The main example of this was provided in the Upper Clyde Shipbuilders' work-in between July, 1971 and October, 1972, where with a kind of 'dual management' the workers sought to continue operations on the employer's orders; but there have been others which were less clear cut than this, such as the Briant Printing experience in 1972, which might fall into the third category.

2   The 'sit-in' proper in which the workers occupy the premises and cease working, thus removing themselves from the authority of management. Managers are nevertheless allowed to remain on the premises and carry on with their work in so far as they can in the circumstances. They may be prevented from removing plant, and sometimes products, from the establishment. The first example of this in time was the Allis-Chalmers Sit-in in January, 1972; but this was followed by a whole host of others including all the Manchester engineering sit-ins which sought to pressurize employers to sign a new agreement, and a number of others besides.

3   The 'worker occupation' of the plant in which the workers occupy the premises on a round-the-clock basis and expel the management and prevent them returning to the plant, The first example of this variant was the Fisher Bendix occupation in January, 1972, but others have since occurred; by virtue of the departure of the management in the Briant Printing situation because of bankruptcy, and the hostility shown to the liquidator, that might be considered to fall into this category.

Some of these forms of industrial action are lawful and some not, but they have all been used at one time or another for some purpose or other and with varying degrees of success in helping the party to achieve objectives. Because they are potentially available in any dispute situation, they can also be used, by way of a threat (see below, pp 529-31), in the course of negotiations.

Whether threat *or* bluff *or* industrial action itself is used will depend upon perceptions by the two parties of their relative power in relation to one another. It is not unusual to treat management as being synonymous with 'control' based on the legally and conventionally supported right to make and enforce rules of work, and to regard the very existence of the trade union as a mechanism for aggregating workers' power, by controlling competition in the external labour market or by replacing individual worker dispensibility by a collective indispensibility. But *in the dynamic situation*, the power available is likely to depend upon the factors which are listed below (pp 479-83) *and* upon the capacity of the workers or their leaders to mobilize it (since it cannot be assumed to exist 'automatically').

There is likely to be some reluctance or even opposition within each side to taking either disciplinary or industrial action, either because of the moral undertones or because of the costs involved. It is frequently regarded as lying outside the realms of acceptable strategic action. For these reasons, it is usually necessary for the management or the union leaders to engage in persuasion of their colleagues or members that such a course of action is necessary and desirable. There is also evidence to suggest that a similar process of persuasion may be called for to prevent individuals or groups processing grievances in this way outside procedure or to process them as part of a strategy. It is not uncommon, for example, for the union leadership and the management negotiators, in preparing for, say, the annual round of negotiations, to list and process a number of different 'grievances' which might then be used to support the main thrust of the negotiation. At such times, for example, the chief stewards may be most active in encouraging workers to present some grievances and to delay some others which do not fit the master plan (Batstone, Boraston and Frenkel, 1977).

It is in this context that the basic differences in the authority structure of management and the union are likely to show themselves most strongly. Management is usually organized on a hierarchical basis with the superordinate in a position where he can coerce, manipulate material and other rewards, and command the attention of subordinates (see below, pp 463-88). The shop steward, on the other hand, 'has few, if any, sanctions which he can use against his members or to reward them'

(Partridge, in King *et al*, 1978, pp 188 and 197) and he does not necessarily have ready access to them to allow him to persuade them. His authority is continually open to challenge from his constituents, so that ensuring solidarity or internal consensus is a differently-based activity for the two categories.

Mobilizing management action

Although management has the authority to do so, it does not proceed against individual workers or groups of them in every case where a disciplinary sanction might be appropriate because of some transgression of the rules. 'Action' of a formal kind frequently follows the *build-up* of frustrations over a period in which minor or isolated infringements have been allowed to go unchecked. In these circumstances, it becomes necessary to secure a *general* management commitment to taking action, not completely dissimilar from the commitment usually considered to be required of labour.

Such a process of build-up has been noted in connection with the development of custom and practice (see Brown, 1972, pp 42-61) and the operation of 'the indulgency pattern' (Gouldner, 1955b, pp 45-56). It happens that management (particularly junior management) will allow practices which are outside the formal rules to develop in order to maintain or increase co-operation. This may often involve an active collusion in rule-breaking or bending. Nevertheless over a period of time, management may come to the conclusion that the workers are taking advantage of the indulgences for *their* own ends, or that this has been going on for so long that it threatens some basic principle of organization or control, and may embark upon a process of reinterpretation, and convince itself that there is a cause for action.

It is not uncommon for management to discover occasions for a 'grievance' with the performance of the individual workers, which are not allowed immediately to result in action against either individual or group. The issues may be resolved informally, and in spite of enjoinders from codes of practice (see above, pp 126-31) may not even be noted in any formal way as an event of any consequence. Over a period of time, however, management may come to the conclusion that 'enough is enough' and that some formal action may be necessary to restore control by management. A process of 'reinterpretation' of previous events may then be set in train.

Friedman and Meredeen have suggested that such a build up may lead to the development of new objectives which may emerge from the developing situation (1980, p 345) and illustrate this by reference to the developments in Ford during the 1960s and 1970s.

> 'In the post-war period, Ford persistently failed to deal with its relatively poor performance in the management of a greatly expanded and widely dispersed labour force. It was only after the economic losses of a rising trend of internal disruption and the public humiliation of two official Courts of Inquiry in the space of six years that top management came to grips with its failures. It professionalized its industrial relations; appointed its first Industrial Relations Director; set up a Forward Planning Team to develop a new and more appropriate industrial relations strategy ... which ... contributed significantly to the development of more mature industrial relationships in the late seventies' (Friedman and Meredeen, 1980, p 345).

Both parties may derive immediate (or pragmatic) objectives from the accumulation of these individualized grievances. The action which follows is likely in the most general sense to be directed at redressing the wrong or putting right what has gone wrong. If the grievance is over the actions of management, the objective sought will be a change in management practice in the relevant area; if it is over some alleged 'fiddling' by the workers on piece-work, the objective may be to introduce a new piece-work arrangement.

Mobilizing worker solidarity

For similar reasons, the spontaneous or automatic strike in support of a grievance must be considered to be a rare bird, although some such may occur (see Lane and Roberts, 1971, pp 223-24). Not all so-called wild-cat strikes are likely to be quite as wild as the term might imply. Rather, strikes might have to be prepared for, mobilized or eased into existence if only because of the presence of an element of 'concert' in a strike. Unlike the management hierarchy, the trade union hierarchy is less well

390

endowed with material means of influence, and must rely more upon 'persuasion'.

Were that not to be the case, there would doubtless be many more of them, since every issue or grievance would result in either industrial or procedural action. On the evidence, this is patently not the case (see Lupton, 1963; Batstone, Boraston and Frenkel, 1977 and 1978; Sayles, 1958). On similar evidence, it is not even the case that every grievance is handled through the institutions and procedures which are designed to contain or curtail such open conflict; as Batstone et al (1978, pp 55-56) indicate convenors and stewards frequently deny members the opportunity to move in either direction (see Friedman and Meredeen, 1980, pp 315-16).

Another reason for doubting the frequency of the spontaneous strike is that, as has been noted often in studies of actual strikes (for example, by Lane and Roberts, 1971, p 16), people tend to hold inhibitions about going on strike, for moral as well as economic and political reasons.

All strikes involve short-run sacrifice undertaken in the hope of long-run net benefit, and there are clearly those whose calculation of economic self-interest would lead them to avoid strike action because of the value they attach to the potential sacrifice. Strikes also occur in a context, and there are circumstances in which it would be politically inexpedient to strike, and individuals might seek to avoid striking on this ground. It might be thought, however, that more people would have moral scruples about a strike, because of the damage it would do to someone, unless they could see that it had some altruistic purpose.

Batstone, Boraston and Frenkel argue on the basis of their evidence that the development of a will to strike does not take place necessarily in an accepting framework of attitude. Particularly amongst the union *leaders* in their study, there existed a good deal of doubt and ambivalence both about the general desirability of striking in order to win concessions and about the probability of the membership giving it the support which might prove necessary.

The development of the necessary attitude had therefore to be accomplished against opposition within the side. Because not everyone either saw the situation in terms of striking being morally correct or regarded strike action as desirable or sufficiently certain in its outcome, the mobilization process involved argument and debate. The network of relationships developed by the stewards over the years assisted them in this exercise; it was possible to leave much of the debating to those influentials within the sections and groups rather than necessary to undertake it all themselves.

Their evidence suggested that far from strike action being spontaneous, it had to be mobilized. Through the process of argument and debate, the 'explosions of consciousness' or 'emotion' so often noted (Batstone, Boraston and Frenkel, 1978, p 2; Friedman and Meredeen, 1980, p 13) have to be created. Such explosions might be expected to occur spontaneously only infrequently, and then only after a build up of grievance (Lane and Roberts, 1971). More probably, they are likely to develop under the influence of group norms and pressures which replace the inhibitions with a will to strike.

There is a thesis that strikes, and particularly wildcat strikes, are *caused* by hot-heads and militants. No doubt there are instances of this (see Baker, 1980), but the general run of the evidence suggests that the relationship between leadership and followership is both more positive and more complex than this thesis implies. Thus, in his study of leadership on the shop floor, Partridge is led to conclude that style of leadership or action demonstrates great variability':

> 'The steward's treatment of a member's grievance varies from one grievance to another. The steward's choice of definition depends, in part, on his ability, his constituents' values, attitudes and beliefs, and the previous experience of those constituents acting together as a collectivity. Other situational variables will include the power of the collectivity and past management reciprocity. Just because the steward is effective in legitimizing a particular grievance is no guarantee that he will be able to legitimize other grievances in the same way' (Partridge, 1978, p 199).

This does not deny that the leadership has a role in the mobilization of industrial action, but it does deny that leaders simply manipulate unthinking pawns. But as this same author suggests, the shop steward must rely upon his skills 'of communication and interaction' to secure whatever ends he seeks (Partridge, 1978, p 188). This role is likely to be one which is constrained by the widely reported group processes which occur within the workplace (Roethlisberger and Dickson, 1938; Katz and Lazarsfeld, 1953; Sayles, 1958; Lupton, 1963). It is because even informal groups are found to be equipped with a leadership structure, and it is this which leads us to expect a role for leaders amongst shop floor groups (see Cartwright and Zander, 1953; Maccoby, Newcomb and Hartley, 1958) but not necessarily one which allows them licence.

The mobilization process

The mobilization of commitment to industrial action is likely to require action to:

(a) remove inhibitions against striking
(b) provide a rationale for engaging in such action
(c) secure commitment to engage in the action.

These actions are consistent with the view which Lewin takes of the steps involved in bringing about attitude and behavioural changes, where he suggests that 'a successful change includes ... three aspects:

(a) unfreezing, if necessary, the present level
(b) moving to the new level
(c) freezing group life on this new level' (Lewin, 1953, p 299).

Removing inhibitions

It has often been remarked that people are reluctant to strike, even inhibited from striking, for reasons of morality. This is not widely different from the often-noticed reluctance of supervisors and managers to take action which might result in employees being dimissed. There are inhibitions on both sides, and in the event that such action is contemplated by somebody, it may be necessary to remove them. In line with Lewin's theory, there is a need for a reordering of preferences and priorities and a for a relaxation of the inhibitions, equivalent to the 'unfreezing' process which has been noted in connection with the learning of new behaviours (see Lewin, 1953, pp 287-301).

In the context of mobilizing support for a strike, inhibitions against striking might be reduced by one of two main methods. One method is to command support via solidarity, either by autocratic decision of the leadership or by majority vote of the membership. On the basis of Lewin's model, this would lead to an increase in tension as all (autocratic) or many (democratic) of the individuals might consider themselves to have been steamrollered into the action against their will (see Bavelas. 1953).

Another method might be to allow resistance to action to wither, as it were, spontaneously, in the face of events (including the 'events' of interpretation of the conduct of the management). In the one case, the actions of management might themselves 'put people's backs up' sufficiently for the resistance to crumble. In the other, (as in the original experiments on which Lewin relies), spontaneity of support might be engineered by the use of 'group discussion and decision' methods (where ordinary conversations within work groups come to assume a more serious and strategic purpose) (see Lewin, 1953). Reliance is placed more upon the informal discussions which might occur in the workplaces than upon either autocratic decisions or formal meetings.

Rationalizing the cause

To build up positive emotional support for a strike may, however, require more than the identification of a grievance and the removal of inhibitions against industrial action. It may also be necessary to develop, as Batstone et al (1978, p 3) suggest, a consciousness of a will to win by this particular means. What is clear from their narrative, is that the leadership recognize the need to mobilize the thinking and feeling of their members to support the action, to be achieved by a process of 'education', which in turn required a rationale and a vocabulary of communication (see Bean, 1975).

This rationale may be developed amongst the workers themselves, or it may be implanted and developed by the leadership; in order to facilitate this, the workers and the leaders need a vocabulary which will legitimize the inferences to be drawn about the situation and will convey the appropriate 'meanings' in support of action.

The blameworthiness of the management for the event or events which trigger the grievance assumes significance, providing the basis for the necessary catharsis. The prior actions and present position of management need to be presented and accepted as being blameworthy and against the interests of the workers. It is necessary to develop a strong perception of managerial blame for any and all the ills being suffered at the time. This involves a reinterpretation of past actions with the inferences drawn that they are not mere accidents but a part of management's new 'hard-line' or of management's unwilling-ness to honour existing agreements or accepted custom and practice. This makes it a prior condition of strike action that the immediate cause of the grievance shall be attributable to some management fault (in the case of worker grievances), and be capable of being expressed and accepted in these terms. Individuals might develop grievances at work as a result of actions by many 'others', but these are only likely to effect industrial action where they can be attributed as a fault to management, however indirectly.

Batstone, Boraston and Frenkel for example provide a second sub-set of reasons which are more abstract in principle and more directly associated with managerial fault, and thus expressed through a distinct vocabulary. Amongst these are illegitimacy of management actions, illegitimacy of management's responses to the actions of the workers, unfairness by comparison with someone else, and infringement by management of what are perceived as the workers' job property rights. These amount to two thirds of the reasons given, leaving only a third of the total to be spread through more immediate issues. They may be distinguished from the first sub-set in that they emphasise more some matter of principle as distinct from some immediate and probably individual issue or motivation.

> 'During the movement towards strike action, particularly if this occurs over a number of days, this process of interpreting past events is often clear. Things which at the time were considered merely coincidental now become defined as part of a larger strategy on the part of management. Such reinterpretations might include mobil-ity, apparently technical problems, and so on' (Batstone, Boraston and Frenkel, 1978, p 51).

In similar vein, Hiller has suggested that the mobilization process:

> is accomplished by accepting or creating interpretations of the situation which encourage action: supplying justifica-tions for striking and minimizing the hazards of the undertaking. Justifications are provided by rehearsing grievances and claiming merits' (Hiller, 1969, p 49).

Friedman and Meredeen couple this process with their discus-sion of obedience of rules and acceptance of procedures. Against the general background of a willingness to seek 'a solution via the established channels', they point out that:

> 'Notwithstanding that fact, specific occasions occur from time to time which offer the opportunity of extending the frontier of workers' control and encroaching on management prerogatives. Then you feel entitled to take a short cut, to disregard the rules in order to achieve a particular objective ... There's no question of pangs of conscience about it. If such an opporunity presents itself, the standard practice is to 'review the troops' and if they're ready and willing to take action to bring about certain changes from next Monday, so be it...' (Friedman and Meredeen, 1980, pp 315-16).

A similar condition may be seen as necessary to the taking of action by management, whether that action is against individual workers or against the collectivity.

Securing commitment to action

If this rationale shows a new path for the group to follow, there remains the necessity for securing commitment to the recommended action. This commitment is required not merely at the level of argument but also and more importantly at the level of conduct: once the decision to act in this way is taken, the workers need to come out on strike or to adopt an overtime ban, or whatever.

This commitment may be forthcoming where the workers are already 'conscious' of the need for opposition to the employer and for solidarity, but not all workers have this 'trade union consciousness' and it may have to be secured, if only on a temporary basis. This is usually done by using the group pressures (which exist within most if not all working groups) towards conformity of member behaviour. Once the group norm of 'striking' is adopted, then these pressures can be relied upon to secure conformity in the majority of cases, since few are willing to put themselves outside their workgroup. The problem in many cases is to ensure that the norm *is* adopted in the first place.

Summary: sanctions and bargaining power

The devolution of decision-taking to subordinate levels raises important questions about the basis on which that decision-taking will be effected. In particular, it raises questions about the capacity or the power of the parties to influence the decisions, whether these be about wages or other terms and conditions of employment. In this area of enforcement of voluntarily-established conventions and rules, it is, however, the same power base which is relied on to enforce the rules as that which compels their agreement in the first place.

It is generally accepted that workers are usually placed at a disadvantageous position in this respect, compared with the employer. This disadvantage can be reduced, for labour generally by conditions of full employment, and for members of associations by combination to control entry into the job category. It can be reduced for more particular groups by the accident of their location in an interdependent structure of roles. But these are likely to prove short term improvements, given the power of management to substitute capital for labour or one type of labour for another.

The main opportunity to effect changes (which workers have developed largely for themselves) is that offered by collective bargaining based on the collectivities' sanctions of strikes and other forms of industrial action. Collective bargaining is essentially an arrangement by which workers can (with the employer's agreement) substitute in the industry or workplace, rules and conventions, binding on both parties. These will increase their status and, therewith, their power to influence the conditions of their working lives and the relationships within which they experience them. This, as we have seen, can overturn and supplement the status which is otherwise available to them under the laws and conventions of the society, and within the institutions as they are structured.

Ostensibly, management confronts the union and the collective bargaining process with a similar set of sanctions: the lock-out appears to have the same value as the strike, and suspension may have some equivalence to some of the other forms of industrial action. However, this is more apparent than real, and the difference lies in the still-enforceable right of the employer, under the law, to dismiss employees either individually or *en masse*.

Neither the pressure from the trade unions nor recent legislation has taken away from the employer and managers the main sources of their power to run their undertakings in ways

397

which they consider appropriate. They merely add some further constraints to the decisions. Their bargaining power tends to remain at least equal to that of the workers, in spite of all these changes, and in the long run, it is likely to prove to be greater (see below, pp 479-82). In any one particular episode of negotiation with the workers or their unions, however, they may well find themselves with considerably more or considerably less, dependending on the circumstances. But in the light of the above discussion, it is difficult to sustain the argument that the workers or the trade unions, generally, have 'too much power'.

In some cases, as we saw, the power of the workers is so low, relative to that of the employer, that the State has found it politic to introduce tripartite arrangements under which, effectively, the third party's power to influence decisions or the nature of the rules established, takes the place of any collective sanction which the worker side would otherwise rely upon. The third party in these circumstances must remain subject to direct influence by the parties acting in their own interest, in order to ensure that either the decision or the vote (as the case may be) can serve as a power base for the parties themselves. Tripartite regulation at least attempts to ensure that this vote or decision, consistent with the underlying conventions of voluntarism, will be made on the basis of what the parties argue, rather than on any other basis, so that the bargaining here is essentially a process of influence, not coercion on the basis of sanctions of the conventional kind.

Readings

Hyman: (1972), pp 52-139. Eldridge: (1968).
Kelly and Nicholson: (1980), pp 20-31.
Anthony: (1977), pp 17-63. Partridge: (1978), pp 187-200.
Batstone, Boraston and Frenkel: (1977), pp 54-76; and (1978).
Goodman, in Kesler and Weekes: (1971).
Clegg: (1979), pp 251-17.

15

The public sector

The private and public sectors

Industrial relations in the public sector has a good deal in common with industrial relations in the private sector but there are some important differences which focus on the status and role of the State as employer. Private undertakings are subject to some degree of State regulation through legislation, but public sector undertakings owe their very origin and continuation to the State. The division is not absolute, because there are some hybrids (as in private companies in which the State holds some part of the equity, or the privatized parts of what was previously a public service) but the distinction is well understood.

The public sector comprises that area of government and economic activity whose controlling organs are creatures of government rather than of private persons and is usually thought of as made up of three main parts:

(a) the executive organization of the central government under the government's direct control through a Minister who is accountable directly to Parliament
(b) local authorities, in which the body concerned has a limited geographicaly-defined domain and range of activity, power to raise funds through local taxation (rates), and an obligation to make annual returns of income and expenditure under the Local Government Act
(c) public corporations, bodies corporate created (usually) by specific Act of Parliament, to engage in trading activities in defined areas (whether in the nationalized industries or in the provision of broadcasting services, etc) (see Thomson and Beaumont, 1978, pp 3-6).

Together these account for a large enough proportion of the total employees in the country to make them a significant influence upon patterns and trends in industrial relations. The number of employees in the public sector as a whole exceeds six millions (see table 18 below) but of these about a quarter are employed in the nationalized industries. About a tenth of them are civil servants who come directly under the central government, and almost a fifth are engaged in the health service; almost a half are engaged in education and local government. A high proportion of them are professional and white collar workers, which gives the sector a special significance.

Table 18
Employment and union membership in the public sector Great Britain, 1979

Employment	Union membership (000s)	Union Density (000s)	(%)
Public sector	6,297.2	5,189.9	82.4
National govt	639.5	583.8	91.3
Loc govt & edn	2,879.9	2,232.0	77.5
Health services	1,317.9	971.2	73.7
Posts & telecom	428.1	427.6	99.9
Railways	208.9	204.2	97.8
Air transport	92.5	78.5	84.0
Port & inland water transport	71.9	59.8	83.2
Gas	105.8	95.5	90.3
Electricity	179.9	178.3	99.1
Water	66.2	61.4	92.7
Coal mining	306.6	297.6	97.1
Manufacturing	7,385.8	5,157.4	69.8
Construction	1,415.2	519.7	36.7
Agriculture etc	378.3	85.8	22.7
Private services	7,283.6	1,214.5	16.7

Note: Road transport and sea transport are not included in this table. The nationalized steel industry is listed under the private manufacturing sector, which also includes other mining and quarrying. 'Private services' comprise insurance, banking and finance; entertainment; distribution; and miscellaneous services.
Source: Bain, (1983), pp 11, 14, and 15

The first two parts (identifiable as the public *service* sector) call for particular consideration (the third being for most practical purposes more directly comparable with the private sector) because:

(a) the size and composition, along with the non-trading nature of most of their activities, gives rise to special problems associated with taking decisions about pay and other aspects of status

(b) the current conception of the traditional authority of the sovereign affects the way in which relations within the services are organized

(c) the development of the State's policies, *as an employer* in relation to its employees, has exerted some influence upon the development of industrial relations in the private sector.

Although the State as employer has attempted to distance itself from private employers in industrial relations affairs, the sheer size of the public payroll now denies it its traditional marginal influence and threatens to upset the balance which has previously sustained the idea that the two sectors were separate *and* independent of one another.

THE CONGLOMERATE NATURE OF THE SECTOR

The public sector as a whole, and each of the three subsectors listed on page 399, reveals considerable diversity in the nature of the services offered and in the types of skill assembled to provide them. At both levels the public sector appears as a conglomerate organization, and it might be expected that it would behave like the conglomerate undertaking of the private sector.

This, however, presupposes that the public sector is subject to a single 'unit of government'. They may be regarded in this way in the sense that all parts of it are either answerable to Parliament through a Minister of the Crown (even in the case of local government authorities, although here the position is more complex by virtue of their elected nature). But the State (or more technically, 'the Crown') is the direct employer of only a part of the total, that being confined to the first of the three parts identified. In the other cases, some other body (either elected or appointed by the appropriate Minister) is the employer, even though these bodies may act with the authority of the State.

All that unites them is the fact that at some time it has been decided that they should be provided under the direct authority of the State, instead of being left to private enterprise to develop them. This creates the presumption that they will operate in a fashion distinct from organizations in the private sector. It faces the sector with the need to recruit loyalty to the service(s) and commitment to the tasks involved in terms which are somehow distinct from those applicable in the private sector. If this were to be achieved it might provide a foundation for the distinctiveness of 'the public sector'.

Diversity of service provision

Each of the three subsectors when viewed as a single entity exhibits diversity of service or activity and of the skills which it must bring together in order to engage in it. Viewed from the standpoint of single services which make it up, however, some greater homogeneity can be discerned.

The national civil service as a whole embraces a variety of functions and tasks even if it is also closest in conception to the traditional public sector. It includes all those departments whose expenditure is charged directly to the supply votes, plus a few others. The main Departments of State (for example, Home and Foreign Offices, Departments of Education and Employment), and smaller bodies like ACAS, the Registry of Friendly Societies or the Public Record Office (about two dozen in total) are included in the first category. Other bodies, ranging from the National Health Service and the Atomic Energy Commission to the Research Councils do not have their expenditure directly charged, but they are subject to audit by the Comptroller and Auditor General and to financial control through the Public Accounts Committee of the House of Commons. Particular departments and services may display more homogeneity than the generality, but what comes under the single 'unit of management' is varied.

The local government sector is similar. This includes authorities with general and specific administrative powers. The larger of the two categories, measured by expenditure or numbers employed, is the local government authority (including metropolitan area, county and district authorities elected by universal suffrage) with general administrative authority over a wide range of locally-provided services. They provide (chiefly) services of education, housing, refuse disposal and sanitation, protection (police and fire service), transport, and welfare, and may, under permissive powers, supply other services (see Jackson, 1976, pp 180-241). The smaller sub-set consisting of specialized boards which may be charged with local regulation of markets, oversight of licensed activities, or the provision of transport (on a scale larger than that offered by a single local government authority) along with the particular departments of local government, may be more homogeneous in their specialization, but again the general picture of wide variety is present (see Thomson and Beaumont, 1978, pp 3-6).

The nationalized industries also present a picture of conglomerate organization if taken as a whole. The nationalized industries may be considered homogeneous only or mainly to the extent that they can be regarded as concerned with the *basic* commodities (coal or electricity) or services (a national airline or a broadcasting) of an industrialized economy. Otherwise, there is no particular reason why they should be grouped together.

Their origins are themselves diverse. Some of them have been developed out of ones which were previously private (for example, coal, steel) and some out of municipal undertakings (for example, gas, water, electricity). Some were created *ad hoc* with the development of a new technology (for example, atomic energy). Some deal with 'tangible' products (such as coal or electricity or water) some with less tangible services (such as broadcasting and television) or finance (as in the case of the Bank of England).

Within any of these, there is an homogeneity comparable to that found in individual departments of State or in individual local goverment departments. In all three sectors therefore there may be pressure for local autonomy in the 'single-system' units of account, as consideration of the pressures in comprable private industry undertakings might lead us to expect. Since the nationalized industries are usually run by relatively autonomous boards (whose members are appointed by a Minister of the Crown) they are more likely to be able to assert their autonomy in this respect than are the comparably homogeneous departments of State.

Diverse objectives

The diversity of objectives and tasks in public service sector undertakings is well illustrated by a roll call of the titles of the departments and boards included. But the objectives of any one tend to be more focused and to provide a degree of integration which is not apparent at the aggregated level of analysis.

Traditionally, the State articulated public policy through the organ of government, and attempted to maintain order at home and abroad, employing the civil and military services for the purpose. The civil service element of this carried out all the tasks required for ordering the civil society, including those of collecting the revenues. The modern conception of this function is more complex, but the principle of Crown employment remains, as does the general principle that a civil servant is a civil servant and not a specialist in any one department or activity (see Fulton Committee Report, 1968). This principle of a universal role is one of the unifying factors in what is otherwise a diverse structure of activity.

With the growth of the so-called mixed economy, the State has made ever greater incursions into the business area than before. This has occurred in two ways: first, through the increase in amount of regulation of private business activities and organizations; and second through the development of public corporations which are expected to engage in some kind of trading activity which would otherwise fall to private organizations to provide. The traditional distinctions between business and government have become blurred as a result (see Galbraith, 1974). Local government has also ramified in similar directions, although the acts of nationalisation took away some of their former trading activities.

What each of the less traditional elements is established to do may be identified by some grandiose phrase, such as care and cure of the sick; education of the young; rescue of social casualties; maintenance of the environment. These may be no more than broad indications of purpose, necessary to the development of integrity of action, but they do indicate the broad scope of public activities at the present time. Pursuit of such objectives is, however, subjected to a different kind of constraint from that which one would find in private enterprise.

The nationalized industries partially excepted, the public sector is usually not subject to the disciplines of the market, and the market mechanism does not set limits to action by limiting budgets. This places these undertakings under a different kind of constraint. In this sector, money is voted, which means deliberately decided by some personalized authority. There is therefore always some possibility that more (or less) may be secured by negotiation or by fiat. The effect is that outcomes are even less predictable than in the case of market analysis.

The services which are associated with elected authorities, and to a different extent the public corporations, are subject to public scrutiny in a way in which private corporations usually are not. This introduces the policy 'objective' which staff are expected to follow: that of avoiding embarrassment to the elected representative or the executive head. In the Civil Service this is often referred to as 'protecting the Minister' from the embarrassment of the parliamentary question, but it has its equivalent in other services. This could be a hangover from the past, a device to protect the omniscient and omnipotent sovereign. But it is also highly functional in that, given the need to negotiate over resource allocations, such embarrassment could be calculated to decrease chances of success. Its major consequence is to introduce a degree of caution into the actions of public servants.

The sovereign employer

Amidst the diversity, however, the notion persists that there is a kind of unity in the public sector which is usually identified by the concept of the 'sovereign employer'. This principle provides the source of legitimacy of the State's authority as an employer. It carries implications for both individual and collective relations. This is most directly relevant to the civil or public service part of the sector, but it has some *relevance* to the other services, including those of health and local government. In recent years, the differences from the private sector have been reducing, but there remains enough of a gap to give the impression that this sector is still distinct.

The State as it is currently conceived is the successor to the much older conception of a unitary kingdom governed by a sovereign, and it still carries connotations of sovereign authority and power. Once, as Jenks has suggested, the sovereign's power was absolute:

'it was the unquestioned right of the King, as of every feudal

405

lord, to insist upon the personal attendance of each of his direct vassals: and any refusal to attend a personal summons was a deliberate defiance, or repudiation, of the feudal lord, which involved forfeiture of the benefice' (Jenks, 1919, p 161).

Much may have happened to the *monarch's* prerogative power since feudal times but the sovereign power is still associated with the State. The part of the public sector which is concerned with national government, retains vestiges of this traditional conception of sovereignty which has two main manifestations of relevance to industrial relations. The first is the position of the 'Crown employee' and the second the State's attitude to delegation of authority to decide matters hitherto within its 'prerogative power'. In other parts of the public service sector, similar (but less extreme) expressions are to be found, either by virtue of enactments which are stated not to apply to them or by virtue of the exclusion of some types of 'office' from general legislation.

The public servant

Those engaged in the public service tend to be regarded and to be treated somewhat differently from the generality of employees. Some are regarded as being 'in Crown employment', that is, 'in employment under or for the purposes of a government department'. This includes industrial and the non-industrial civil servants, the members of the armed forces and holders of judicial and political posts. Members of the armed and police forces are not employees at all and legislation which applies to 'employees' therefore does not apply to them (see Hepple, 1981, pp 72-73). Although the employees of the National Health Service, local authorities, and public corporations (nationalized industries and other commonweal services) are *not* in this category, those in the public service sector are frequently treated differently in individual labour legislation than employees in either the private or the public corporations (see Fowler, 1980, pp 218-44).

Traditionally, the employment relationship in this sector was based upon the protection of the prerogative power of the Crown. This was incorporated to some extent into the industrial relationship of Master and Servant in the early part of the industrial revolution, but its relevance in public employment remains direct. In the local government service, a similar protection of the prerogative power of a 'democratically-elected body' has been much in evidence in recent discussions of worker participation.

Consequently, the Crown employee was not emancipated in the same way and to the same extent as other workmen at the beginning of the industrial revolution. He was not made free to contract in employment. There remains some doubt (see EP(C) Act, 1978, s 138 (7) (b)) whether a person in Crown employment has a contract of employment, although 'the balance of legal authority' is now that there is one (Hepple, 1981, p 73; Rideout, 1979, p 17). The effect of this change may be that the individual employee now has a remedy in any claims or arrears of pay. But Crown employment may still be subject to an *implied* term, by which the individual is dismissable 'at the will of the Crown' with or without notice (Hepple, 1981, p 73) and is denied the right to bring an action for wrongful dismissal (Rideout, 1979, p 17).

It remains a basic principle that the Crown is not bound by legislation unless the Statute says so expressly. On this basis, Crown employees now have (under EP(C) Act, s 138) the right of appeal to an industrial tribunal against unfair dismissal, the right to maternity pay and rights arising in the course of their employment. They are not given rights in respect of statements of the particulars of contract, nor in respect of the notice provisions of the Act (s4). The question of whether the rights relate to a contract of employment is avoided by making all references to 'contracts of employment' in the Act as they relate to Crown servants refer simply to the 'terms of employment' of these persons (s 138 (7) (b)).

Health service employees are not Crown employees, but have in the past been excluded from some of these provisions. Local authority employees are usually covered but some of the legislation relevant to this service places the employee under certain duties and accords certain privileges which again 'distinguish' them from the private sector employee (see Fowler, 1980, pp 218-22).

Organization for negotiation

The State now follows a general policy of negotiating issues of pay and conditions with employees through the Whitley councils (see pp 411-13). This called for decisions about organization for

407

bargaining purposes. These have to acknowledge the special features of the sector (its special and distinct service nature, its overall size, its composition, and its public visibility, as well as its ostensible unitary nature in certain sub-sectors at least). Taken together these produce countervailing pressures, towards centralization and towards decentalization.

As we have already noted (see pp 232-34) only a limited number of options exist in structuring collective bargaining, if operating requirements are accepted as of major importance. The major influences upon the decisions about structure are the perceptions of the need to reconcile the requirement for consistency or standardization (as a means of reducing uncertainty) and that for autonomy or flexibility (as a means of increasing the opportunity to deal with contingencies as they arise). It is implicit in this that action or relations cannot exist in either condition (of complete rule-bound certainty, or of completely unguided discretion or autonomy to decide in the light of circumstances). In the central government element of the public sector, however, the existence of a notional single employer or paymaster (the government) must compete for influence upon this question with the demands for operating flexibility and autonomy. Size and composition might be expected to influence the way in which management seeks to establish control, both generally and in connection with industrial relations particularly.

The character of the conglomerate undertaking which is relevant to the organization of industrial relations, emphasizes the disparate nature of the products made or services provided in the various departments or other forms of unit of account. In the nature of conglomerate formation, it is likely that the different units will have different tasks, traditions and customs, and that the workers as well as the operating managers (perhaps in different ways) will be predisposed to work in with these.

The need for operational flexibility in the conglomerate appears to demand decentralization of decision-taking by management, and decentralized negotiations between management and the local union representatives. As Doyle says (using American industrial terminology):

'...the ideal contractual arrangement is a series of individual contracts that have separate expiration dates and are negotiated with different unions..... the bargining advantage is that, if there is a shutdown in one plant or industry, the remainder of the enterprise can still function normally. Loss of income is thus minimized and the amount of pressure the union is capable of bringing to bear is therefore limited. With separate expiration dates, a whipsaw situation is less likely to occur. With separate unions, negotiations are more likely to be with people sympathetic to the problems of the particular business' (Doyle, in Marceau, 1969, p 25).

But this also requires acknowledgement by the centre of the need for both flexibility and autonomy (Doyle, 1969, p 31-32). The tendency to emphasize the 'unity' of the State (or local government) service, leads to their rejection, and what we find is that most public services are subjected to a highly centralized decision-making process in the Whitley councils.

The nationalized industry or the single infinitely-replicated office of the central government department seems to contrast with this in the demands which it makes. The unitary or single-system service provides a different set of operating conditions from those found in the conglomerate. Now the emphasis is likely to be upon common policies and practices. The management decision-taking structure is likely to emphasize central co-ordination serving the end of securing relatively standardized conditions of employment. In industrial relations, the emphasis is likely to be upon the negotiation of a department or service-wide agreement, and preferably upon one which embraces all the unions involved.

In effect, the solutions adopted to the organizational problems provide the traditional sectors with service-wide organization and agreements and the newer sectors departmental organization and agreements. The sovereign employer concept is thus maintained in the traditional elements and modified in the non-traditional. In the face of the government's acceptance of the Whitley recommendations, the countervailing pressures have produced distinct effects according to the operational demands of the particular service provided.

The State's concern to maintain the authority of the 'sovereign employer' in the face of employees' demands to join trade unions and secure recognition for negotiating purposes produced problems which were only resolved by the State's acceptance of the principles advanced by the Whitley Committee.

The State initially found it difficult to accept the relevance of trade unionism or collective bargaining to its employees. As sovereign employer, it felt it could not relinquish its authority to decide any matter, including pay and conditions, to any external body. It was thought sufficient that civil servants should have the opportunity to complain to their superiors in the department or the Treasury to obtain redress of any wrong. The power of decision would have to remain with the management, not some negotiating or arbitral body.

This changed with World War I. First, a Civil Service Arbitration Board was set up in 1917 as a temporary wartime measure to deal with claims from *lower* paid civil servants. Secondly, the Whitley Committee's recommendations (to establish joint bodies at all levels), originally intended to be applied in private industry, were, after much hesitation and argument, accepted by government as applicable to government service and adopted in 1919. A Whitley Council for the Civil Service, composed of representatives of the two sides, was set up to deal with general issues, including pay, and this was augmented by Departmental Councils. Although the Whitley recommendations were also accepted in many private industries, 'Whitley machinery' is now (after the many extensions which have been made since 1919) more characteristic of the public service sector than of private industry.

The Whitley Committee's recommendations

The main recommendations of JH Whitley's Committee on Relations between Employers and Workmen, 1917-18, were that all industries (public and private) should develop sound, national-level bargaining and consultative machinery embracing their organized employers and workers, and that similar machinery should be set up at regional and local (domestic) levels. These were spelled out as a set of principles which all industries should follow:

1   The employers in an industry should combine into a strong association for purposes of negotiation and consultation with representatives of their workers.
2   The workers in an industry should combine into trade unions, in order to provide a representational base for discussions with the employers.
3   The unions in turn should form a coherent bloc or federation which could meet the employers' association representatives.
4   These bodies should establish national, regional and local (domestic) machinery through which both negotiation and consultation might take place on a regular and continuing basis.
5   Determination of terms and conditions of employment should be by negotiation and agreement between the representatives of the parties.
6   In the event of failure to agree the parties should hold themselves ready to resort to conciliation and arbitration rather than industrial action.

A good deal developed from these and the Committee's other recommendations: national joint industrial councils in many industries (although fewer regional and domestic ones); a growth in joint consultation within undertakings; an extension of the coverage of wages councils to facilitate 'organization' by both sides; an extension of the (then) Ministry of Labour's conciliation and enquiry service; and the creation of a standing Industrial Court (as an arbitral body). These probably did something to increase collective organization on both sides, to increase the amount and coverage of national bargaining, to resolve differences by peaceful means, and to encourage joint consultation. But their impact on the public sector was greater and more permanent than in the private sector, although that influence was by no means insignificant.

The Whitley councils

Practically all the public service sector has had some experience with national Whitley councils, and many of them continue to operate. The main exceptions are the industrial civil servants (whose machinery antedates the Whitley recommendations and continues in modified form) and the teachers (most of whose pay and conditions are determined through two Burnham Committees establishd by the Secretary of State for Education under the provisions of the Remuneration of Teachers Act, 1965). The police and the armed services have their own arrangements appropriate to their special position: police pay is determined by a main police negotiating board and five standing committees (covering the pay of the different ranks) established in 1979; the pay of the armed services is determined by the Armed Forces pay review body (which operates on roughly the same basis as the other three, see pp 414).

The pay and conditions of non-industrial civil servants (other than those at Under Secretary level and above) are determined under the aegis of the Civil Service National Whitley Council. This is composed of an official side made up of senior serving civil servants and 63 representatives of the nine civil service unions who come together in the Council of Civil Service Unions. The full Council meets rarely, as most of the negotiations take place formally or informally in a network of standing and *ad hoc* committees which bring together representatives of the official side and the separate unions covering different grades or categories of staff.

In the conglomerate local authority area, there are no less than 40 such councils and committees dealing with the pay and conditions of occupational or status groups within the various job families represented in local authorities (see Fowler, 1980, pp 78-104; Terry, 1982). There are 25 main councils and 15 others, but by far the largest (covering over a million workers) and occupationally the most heterogenous (cleaners, refuse collectors, drivers, school meals staff, roadworkers, gardeners, etc) is the National Joint Council for local authorities' services (Manual Workers) (*ibid*, pp 299-301; see also Levinson, 1971).

In the National Health Service, which is apparently a more focused set of activities repeated geographically through the country, there are eleven councils, one general (dealing with common conditions of employment such as travelling expenses, leave etc) and ten functional (dealing with pay and conditions for separate status groups (see McCarthy, 1977; ACAS, 1980, pp. 250-58).

1 Medical and (Hospital) Dental Council
2 Dental (Local Authorities) Council
3 Optical Council, with four Committees, A-D

412

4 Pharmaceutical Council, with three Committees, A-C
5 Nurses and Midwives Council
6 Professional and Technical Council, A
7 Professional and Technical Council, B
8 Administrative and Clerical Staffs Council
9 Ancillary Staffs Council
10 Ambulancemen's Council.

Not all of these are actually used for the prime purpose intended; the doctors and dentists, and the nurses, midwives and professions allied to medicine (Professional and Technical Council A) now have their separate pay review bodies which recommend levels of remuneration to the Prime Minister. Some groups, like the builders, operate largely outside the formal council structure preferring the kind of direct negotiations which they, like the industrial civil servants and the manual employees of the nationalized industries, had already established prior to the development of the Whitley machinery.

The pressure for alternative machinery

There is clearly a problem of securing acceptable machinery to resolve some of the issues which public employees consider to be important. The Whitley machinery has been generally accepted by most of the employees in the sector (apart from the employees of the nationalized industries who continued their old machinery into the nationalization period). But it has not always been seen to serve their interests. Some continue their old machinery outside the Whitley structure and some have pressed for new forms of machinery which they consider more in keeping with their (usually) professional position. In the 'winter of discontent' in 1977, the apparent subservience of the Whitley machinery to government pay policy produced more general criticism.

The perceived failures of the existing machinery to deliver has led public servants to engage in industrial action although there has been a general acceptance of the principle that they should not do so. Whatever the merits or otherwise of the Whitley machinery as a forum for discussion and determination of terms and conditions, therefore, the predominantly white-collar employees of the public sector are likely to attach some value to an alternative to industrial action as a way of resolving failures to agree.

Since World War II, a number of expedients have been adopted to try to overcome this necessity for backing negotiation with industrial sanctions. Many but not all of these have been related to professional and white collar groups. The variety suggests that there is no very obvious solution to this problem.

The main expedients adopted in this period have involved:

(a) reference to arbitration where this was not blocked by government or employer
(b) resort to direct negotiation with the responsible Minister or the Prime Minister, effectively employing him or her as an arbitrator
(c) use of some formula, such as change in cost of living or earnings level, as a means of securing determination without further recourse
(d) reference to *ad hoc* review bodies which provide a set of recommendations for a settlement in a particular case at a particular time (one example being the reference of the pay of nurses to the Halsbury Committee in 1973)
(e) reference to external *general* review bodies, like the National Board for Prices and Incomes, or the Clegg Comparability Commission, in order to secure a recommendation which it would be difficult for the employer or government to turn down
(f) reference to a *specific* standing review body specially created to resolve issues by an acceptable arbitral process after hearing argument and considering evidence presented by the parties.

The number and variety of expedients tried suggests that there is some need to consider establishing a trustworthy body as a means of resolving such issues in the face of government reluctance. This might, in the current climate, be offered as a *quid pro quo* for giving up the right or opportunity to strike (as has happened with the establishment of the Nurses and Midwives Pay Review Body). Alternatively, it could be provided without interfering with that right, relying on the attitudes of the people concerned to support it in preference to striking if it established that its decisions were fair and/or rational.

External review and recommendation

A number of pay issues to the Standing (Clegg) Commission on

Pay Comparability, set up in March, 1979, and disbanded in March, 1981, responded to this same issue. The Commission's main brief was to examine the terms and conditions of employment of various groups of workers, on reference by the government after securing agreement from the employers and unions concerned. It examined 14 references and issued reports on them, together with a general report. These included a number of manual worker references relating to the public service sector: local authority and university manual workers, NHS ancillary staffs and ambulancemen; university technicians; local authority building workers; municipal airport manual workers. They also included a number of references relating to white collar employees in the same sector: nurses and midwives; professions supplementary to medicine; teachers; justices' clerks' assistants; chief officials of local authorities in Scotland; university computer operating staff and university technicians.

The main intention in these references was to secure a sound basis for dealing with the private sector - public sector comparability question but Bain has commented that the Clegg Comparability Commission's long-term objective 'to report on the possibility of establishing acceptable bases of comparison' of public sector pay remains unattained (Bain, 1983, p 170) because it was abandonned by a Government which wanted to diminish the significance attached to comparability in the determination of public sector pay.

The same consideration lies behind the establishment of the pay review bodies which recommend pay levels for the Armed Forces, the doctors and dentists and the nurses and midwives, health visitors and professions allied to medicine, as well as the Top Salaries Review Body, which deals with senior levels of the judiciary, senior grades of the Higher Civil Service, and senior officers of the Armed Forces (and which may have referred to it the pay of other groups, such as MPs).

These groups (or some large parts of them) generally find it difficult to engage in negotiation over pay either for technical or ideological reasons and the independent review bodies provide a forum in which they can make their views on pay and conditions known without actually engaging in negotiation with anyone. The review bodies consider any evidence, written or oral, which is submitted to them, and make judgements on the levels of pay which appear to them to be appropriate. These are passed as recommendations to the Prime Minister who undertakes, on

415

behalf of the government, to accept the recommendations 'unless there are obviously compelling reasons' for not doing so. It should be said that the government has found such compelling reasons on a number of occasions, and recommendations have often not been accepted, or not accepted in full, in recent years.

These bodies can and do examine the relative position of the occupational groups in the league tables of remuneration, but they can only do so for the particular groups in scope and not generally, as was intended with the Clegg Commission. They can and do, also, look at other factors which affect pay, but they are in no position to make alterations to the conditions or the other terms of the contracts of these groups, which continue to be negotiated directly by the groups themselves, where appropriate (see ACAS, 1980). Some kind of compromise is thus effected between negotiation and non-negotiation for groups who find it difficult to engage in full-bloodied negotiation of pay and conditions on the basis of the usual sanctions.

The pattern of organization

The public sector as a whole reveals some diversity within a general framework which is intended to preserve a kind of integrity. The diversity may be explained as responding to differences in services provided and skills employed. The integrity responds to the perceived need to preserve the authority derived from the (sovereign) people who elect the governments at the two levels. These different objectives reveal two main consequences. In one, a common form of organization is adopted to resolve questions of pay and conditions. In the other, a variety of centralized and decentralized arrangements is permitted to allow some flexibility where this seems to be demanded by the operating system. This produces some standard features, both of service and conditions, but admits some carefully controlled variations which can be justified by the exigencies of particular services.

The councils and committees usually follow the same general pattern of organization. They bring together a variety of representatives from professional associations and trade unions to handle those issues which might be considered to be common to the group in scope. Each separate council tries to achieve a judicious grouping of workers for purposes of negotiation. The ten specialist Whitley councils in the National Health Service are set up to determine terms and conditions for the major occupational categories, on the assumption that these have common interests not necessarily shared by all the other groups. There are also a large number of negotiating bodies in local government which handle terms and conditions for separate occupations. In the national Civil Service, on the other hand, the single general council tends to serve as a legitimating organ for the separate formal and informal negotiations which take placed by the employer and the various interest groups under its aegis.

Representation on these bodies is controlled to allow a geographical spread (special provision is made for Welsh and Scottish representation, for example), and to give a voice to specialist groups, whether professional or trade union, central government or employing authority. Numbers on each side varies considerably from one council to another. This does not affect the 'voting' on issues, because voting is 'by sides' not by heads, but it does affect the voting within the side on 'the line to be taken' and for this reason is important (especially where, for example, professional and trade union bodies are represented in different proportions). Particular professional associations or trade unions may dominate on some councils, according to their density of organization, but it is generally thought that on the employer side, central government representatives and particularly the Treasury representatives, have ultimate power (see McCarthy, 1977; Loveridge, 1971).

In essentials, the structure is the same in each of the public service segments identified above. The general principle followed in the public sector is that standard terms and conditions will be determined centrally for both national and local government employees. To this end, the traditional civil service has its own Whitley council, and the local authorities have theirs. In the case of the independent local authorities, however, the establishment of *national* bargaining machinery is the result of a conscious decision by the authorities themselves, since they do not constitute a national organization, as does central government or, say, the Health Service. Nevertheless, the general principle is breached where there is a reasonable ground for supposing that the necessary standards should be maintained on a single service basis. Thus in the areas of education and health, and in the nationalized industries, autonomy is accepted as relevant at the industry or service level, but standardization is then demanded within the service (see Walsh, 1981).

417

In each case, the machinery is designed to ensure that there are recognizable standards which can and will be applied from Land's End to John o' Groats. This indeed is one of the 'problems' which is identified with collective bargaining in the public sector. This is most clearly illustrated by the mandatory nature of the decisions reached in negotiations within the various segments. When a settlement is reached by the parties, and (where required) accepted by government, it is normal practice for this to be implemented without variation. This is applied in the Civil Service, for example, where it might be considered justified in terms of the principle of unitary authority. It is also applied in services like health and education, where the justification is expressed in terms of the pragmatic need to develop or maintain standards of service. In the nationalized industries, the same kind of single system requirement might overturn the alternative considerations.

This attempt at securing standard conditions is often seen as a problem because it denies local management and union representatives the discretion to agree variations which might resolve local difficulties without recourse to any higher (joint) authority (such as the provincial councils in the local authority area). Such possibilities of variation as are written into Whitley Council agreements (discretion to appoint at levels within a grade, or to vary bonuses on the basis of work study) are unlikely to provide much leeway for disputes' settlement at local level.

The problem of securing some devolution of power from the central bodies, in the face of an overarching desire to maintain uniformity and standardization of terms and conditions, and of a significant divergence of interests between professional and trade union bodies is characteristic of the public sector. The development of joint union negotiating committees at the establishment level is usually fraught with tension as different employee associations find it difficult or impossible to sit at the same negotiating table with others. The possibility of developing the equivalent of private industry's joint shop stewards committees is reduced by the tendency to hold power at the centre. This is a particularly difficult problem to cope with, and as McCarthy's examination (1977) of the Health Service structure suggests, there are likely to be limited opportunities for change given the objectives sought by the parties.

A relationship between a central industrial relations function and the peripheral divisional or departmental managers and

418

supervisors appropriate for the operating conditions seems, therefore, to be remote in the face of the persistent emphasis on unity and standardization.

THE INTERACTION OF THE TWO SECTORS

The public sector is now so large that it can scarcely avoid influencing the private sector. This possibility has helped to ensure that the government has attempted consistently to adopt policies and practices which will have least damaging impact on the private sector. In spite of this, some influence must occur, if only because of the present size of the sector.

The industrial relations objectives and policies in the public sector assume significance because of their implications for industrial relations practices in general, a factor which was alluded to in the terms of reference of the (McGaw) Inquiry into Civil Service Pay (Report, Cmnd 8590, 1982). The State, in its concern to secure general compliance with its approach and policies as regulator of the economy, must constantly concern itself with the impact of its own approach as a significant employer. At very least this implies that the government as employer will obey its own edicts as regulator of the economy (see Jones, 1978). Workers and their unions within this sector have persistently objected to the government's use of it in this way in connection with pay and benefits, and in some cases have secured assurances that this will not be done (for example, in connection with 'cash limits' policies).

The effects of its regulator policies are likely to differ as between the three subsectors identified. General policies (as for example in the case of incomes policies: see Balfour, 1972a) are likely to bear most heavily upon the central government organizations, and less heavily and less directly upon the public corporations and the local authorities. Other policies may, however, be adopted by all three subsets: the Fair Wages Resolution of the House of Commons, during its currency between 1891 and 1982, was sometimes copied voluntarily and sometimes imposed by statute (see Clegg, 1972, pp 348-49).

The State has attempted, in addition, to achieve two conditions within its own undertakings, in an attempt to minimize the impact of public employer on the private sector employment relationship:

419

1 to maintain as a matter of public policy that State employees proper are still to be regarded as somewhat different from the run of employees in the private or public trading sectors and therefore capable of being treated differently in respect of pay and conditions

2 to develop policies which reconcile that difference with the need for the State to be perceived as a 'good employer' comparable to others (although neither lagging behind nor advancing beyond them) (see Beaumont, 1981).

The public sector has adopted a number of general industrial relations policies which serve both of these ends, whilst at the same time holding the State's approach relatively close to the broad streams of thinking about industrial relations matters in the society generally. The general policies adopted tend to reflect the general trend in the economy towards collectivization of decision-taking about terms and conditions of employment, although in their insistence on national bargaining they may be somewhat dated. They are expressed in a number of specific principles which are generally followed in public sector industrial relations practices.

The general policy of encouraging the organization of workers and of seeking to settle industrial relations issues by negotiation has existed in the public sector since the end of World War I. This policy tends to set the tone of industrial relations approaches for the country as a whole, and it has also had the effect of encouraging the growth of white collar unionism during a period in which it developed little in private industry (see Bain, 1970). Use of mediation and arbitration in the event of failure to agree has had a more chequered history, but generally speaking the public interest has been used at different times to justify special arbitration arrangements and to justify refusal to countenance it.

Similarly, the policy adopted with respect to public sector pay, that it should broadly match but not advance beyond comparable pay levels outside the public sector, has been pursued particularly in respect of government industrial workers, hospital ancillary workers, or local authority manual workers where comparable jobs exist outside but where pay is generally considered to be higher (see NBPI: Report No. 169, 1971). The McGaw Inquiry addressed itself to this question, but recommended that comparability, *per se*, should in future have less of a role in pay determination, and that the need to recruit, retain and motivate civil servants, and to maintain or improve their efficiency should be more strongly pushed by the government as employer in pay bargaining (McGaw, 1982).

The curb on free bargaining

The first condition (see p 420) is achieved very largely by maintaining the fiction in law that the civil servant is not employed under a contract of employment, and by restricting the freedom of the negotiators to act exactly like those engaged in the private sector. This is supported by an aspiration to secure in the various negotiating bodies, an acceptance of a trade-off between public sector security (including things like index-linked pensions) and private sector pay and benefits.

The sovereign employer concept has tended to get in the way of both developing effective negotiations and providing adequate machinery for resolution of differences. Its influence is still felt in the limits which are placed on the negotiating process. Although the councils bring together representatives of workers and employers within a particular area of service, to negotiate terms, this does not create a negotiating situation like any other in private industry. It is not a completely free and unconstrained negotiation of the kind found there.

In the early discussions of the possibility of setting up Whitley councils in the Civil Service, government sought to retain this sovereign employer principle, but eventually gave it up and allowed these bodies to 'determine' rather than merely 'discuss' the *principles* of pay. Even then, the overriding authority of Parliament and of government was retained. In the centrally-run services, therefore, the Whitley Council is asked to reach agreement on a recommendation to government, as to what the pay or other conditions should be.

This has been referred to as 'consensus' bargaining, to acknowledge the requirement that in some of these councils at least, the parties are expected to develop a consensus about the best settlement. In the local authority case, the position is different, but the negotiations between the Local Authorities' Conditions of Service Advisory Board (LACSAB) staff and the unions, effectively produce a recommendation which must secure acceptance of the elected members, as of the unions' members, before it is implemented.

Consensus is made the more difficult to achieve because of the presence, in some councils, of either a Treasury (in the case of civil service councils) or Departmental Minister (in other cases, such as Health), or both. This presence may be experienced somewhat less directly in the case of local authorities; pressure from the Department of Environment or the Treasury is likely to be applied by the Paymaster (given the proportion of local authority revenue which comes from central government sources). But whether the influence is direct or indirect, this presence brings a representative to the bargaining table who is possibly not an employer but a paymaster. There is a thought that this representative may neverthless have the ultimate authority to determine the outcome.

The problem arises in the event of a failure to agree or to reach a consensus on what ought to be recommended to the political masters. The presence of powerful paymasters may ensure that anything which is not acceptable to government does not secure agreement, and this may involve 'no movement' on the part of the employer. The staff side may then face the option of accepting an impossible situation (one of non-bargaining, it could be said) or of accepting an equally impossible settlement. It is this which makes the question of how arbitration is to be established in the public sector so important.

External arbitration

Any form of arbitration necessarily involves placing a decision with cost implications in the hands of an external third party. This is serious enough in private industry, where an arbitrator could interfere with budgets and cash flows. But in the context of the public service where there is the additional concern about sovereignty, a process of third party adjudication in the event of failure to agree (or to reach the required consensus) would provide a direct challenge to this.

From the beginning, however, there was a need to provide for the resolution of disputes on which the parties could not agree in the Whitley Council. The government's hesitance in dealing with this question also showed the difficulty of moving away from the sovereign employer position. But the decision to make this kind of provision was taken. The Arbitration Board of 1917 was continued until 1922. After an inter-regnum of three years, the Industrial Court was then given the task of resolving issues which the parties could not resolve for themselves. In 1936, a separate

Civil Service Arbitration Tribunal was set up to deal with this special category of employment.

At this later date, however, certain matters were excluded from the arbitration process to protect the State's position. Some subjects, such as salaries above a certain level, questions of granting established status, and superannuation, were to be excluded from any reference to arbitration. Additionally, awards were to be subject to the overriding authority of Parliament, and to what the government of the day determined was 'national policy', but would be implemented where neither of these was invoked (see Clegg, 1972, pp 376-79). These same issues still complicate the processes of reaching negotiated settlements of claims within this sector.

This question was most recently aired by the McGaw Inquiry Report (1982), which stressed the desirability of avoiding industrial conflict, and suggested that if disagreements could not be resolved in any other way, they should, wherever possible, be referred to voluntary mediation or arbitration. The qualification, 'wherever possible', does, however, highlight the hesitation always present in this sovereign employer context. The problem here is that the government should probably be made no more and no less liable to refer unresolved disputes to arbitration than any other employer; but the insistance on a basic difference tends to reinforce the feeling that automatic reference to arbitration is a necessary *quid pro quo*.

The exclusive employer

The realization of both this condition and the second is both facilitated and complicated by the fact that the public sector employs virtually all who belong to certain occupations. Many of these are also 'professional' occupations oriented towards a service ideal which marries with the orientation to public service in most public sector organizations. These are usually the occupations which are associated with the main product of the undertaking. Thus, civil servants are virtually confined to the public service, teachers to the public education service, coal miners to the nationalized mining industry, and doctors and nurses to the National Health Service. Not everyone employed in the public sector is similarly affected. In the case of pilots, for example, there are job opportunities outside the nationalized undertakings, as there are for maintenance fitters or clerical and

423

administrative workers. Clerical officers may be readily inter-changeable with the private sector, but the character of their jobs may still owe something to the fact that they are performed in the public sector. Public sector employers are often also monopsonistic (single buyer) employers (see NBPI, 1969: Hughes and Moore, 1972), because many of the public sector undertakings are effective monopolies, and many of the skills they utilize are industry-specific.

This might be expected to increase the workers' sense of solidarity: not only do they perform the same tasks, but they also do so under a single organization, whether that is a Board or Department of State or some central authority like the Whitley Councils for the various services. It also creates problems in connection with the determination of appropriate pay rates and other conditions for these workers. It is not necessarily a problem, since many undertakings must establish rates without having the benefit of comparability; but it becomes a problem in its association with the government's declared policy of seeking to provide terms and conditions of employment to its employees which *match* those of private industry without exceeding them. Where no private industry equivalent exists, how is the provision to be measured and adjusted? (see Beenstock and Immanuel, 1979)

The problem of comparisons

These parts of the public sector would share this with any employer who was in the single buyer position. The problem is how to establish pay comparability between employees in the public sector and workers in the private sector, given that there are no private industry comparators. This problem is often exacerbated by the absence of a market curb since the public sector organizations may not engage in trading. The State's declared policy of 'paying at the market rate' in order to be thought a good employer (see Report of the Royal Commission on the Civil Service, the Tomlin Commission, Cmnd 3909, HMSO, 1931, p 85) presents those who seek to determine pay with a seemingly impossible task in the circumstances.

The establishment in 1955 of a Civil Service Pay Research Unit (CSPRU) to gather the facts on the pay of outside staffs engaged on broadly comparable work, as recommended by the (Priestley) Royal Commission on the Civil Service (Cmnd 9631, HMSO,

1955) was one attempt to resolve the difficulty for one group of public sector workers. The evaluation of these discovered facts was to be left to the negotiators on the Whitley councils.

Where there were no comparators ('outside analogues') identifiable by their job titles, pay for the civil servants was to be fixed by reference to 'internal relativities', linking them internally with jobs for which there *were* analogues. The reluctance of governments to adopt any settlement which might seem to deny them the final say, has produced a slightly chequered history for this body, and in 1980 it was abandoned by a government which sought to get away from 'comparability' as a basis for pay settlement on the grounds that it was inflationary.

The McGaw Inquiry proposed the establishment of a wholly independent Pay Information Board to supervise the collection of data to be provided to the negotiating parties. Unlike its predecessor, this was not to include among its member any representatives of either government or the Civil Service unions. It was also to make use of independent consultants to gather, collate and summarize data (using job evaluation methods if considered necessary to determine the relative 'weight' of jobs). These data would then be made available to the negotiators to enable them to engage in what the Inquiry called 'informed collective bargaining'.

By this they meant that the parties would accept a degree of restriction on their freedom of manoeuvre in negotiation by accepting that certain kinds of information (on market position, on efficiency, on the requirements of the public interest, and on comparative benefits) should be taken into account in reaching a settlement of differences (McGaw, 1982). Much of the thrust of this seems to be directed at the senior civil servants who represent the employer interest: it seems to be for them to adopt more strictly business or managerial criteria and to urge them more strongly in the bargaining process.

In local authority services, where a similar problem exists, a comparable, but less detailed, role to that performed by the CSPRU is carried out by the Local Authorities' Conditions of Service Advisory Board (LACSAB). This also assembles the data on comparability on which the negotiations must work. But here, and in the National Health Service, there has been some tendency in recent years to make use of job evaluation to secure pay data for jobs which, whilst not comparable by title or even job family, have been assessed (usually by consultant organizations) as making the same levels of demand upon the incumbents (see Thomason, 1980, pp 97-124). This has usually occurred under the auspices of an external review or arbitration agency (such as the National Board for Prices and Incomes or the Standing Commission on Pay Comparability) to which the problems of public sector pay have been referred (see Clegg, 1982, pp 3-12). The central government's control of this bargaining process is, however, much less direct, and currently operates largely through the imposition of cash limits on funding and therefore on local authority budgets.

The problem remains unresolved in spite of the variety of expedients adopted. Bain has commented that a number of these (particularly the Clegg Commission) have been adopted only to be abandonned 'on the basis of successive governments' short-term political calculations' (Bain, 1983, p 170). Only the particular example of the pay review bodies remains to try to deal with this kind of problem in their spheres. Elsewhere, 'free' bargaining is constrained by 'cash limits' policies, which, like all budgetary controls, offers only a blunt instrument for dealing with specific problems.

Summary: reconciling tensions

The relationship between the public and private sectors is one fraught with tensions if only because of the scale of the former and the consequential carry over of practices from it to the other. The State sector is forced to consider its impact as employer on the private sector and to order its own internal employment and industrial relations affairs in a way which is consistent with its other more general roles.

The State's role as a regulator of the economy is not now unaffected by its role as a paymaster and as an employer of some scale. The exercise of the latter role both complicates and is complicated by its role as regulator of the economy and society. Either role might with advantage be pursued in isolation, but pursuit of the two together tends to generate conflict.

The government has sought to reconcile the conflict by continuing to treat the traditional public sector employees differently both individually and collectively. The policy of encouraging unionization and joint negotiation responds to what was the main strand of thinking in the period around World

War I, but its unmodified continuation may prove disadvantageous. The policy of matching the average private sector employer (however hypothetical that concept may be) as to terms and conditions of employment is intended to remove a source of tension which might affect both internal and external relations.

The only cogent argument which is now advanced in support of this separate treatment of those in Crown employment is that of 'public policy'. This, however, must be taken as a kind of euphemism for a desire to retain a prerogative power for the executive arm of government, perhaps in the national interest but perhaps for its own sake. Where the national interest involves national security, there is usually an express term in the employment terms which would allow the matter to be dealt with. Where there is not, however, the prerogative power is probably a useful antidote to the *de facto* if not *de jure* security of employment which Crown employees enjoy.

Although Crown employment and other employment are not yet treated exactly alike in terms of the rights which workers might enforce through the machinery of the law, the process of bringing the two into line is now well advanced. It is therefore possible, with few qualifications, to consider the status of workers and employees *vis a vis* their employer in both sectors in broadly similar terms.

Preserving the Whitley principles

The continued acceptance of the Whitley Committee's recommendations by the State has probably helped to preserve the principles which they articulated, but it may also have hindered the development of a more appropriate structure of bargaining and negotiation within the public sector. The continuation has helped to ensure that a structure of 'national' bargaining is preserved during the period in which considerable pressure was exerted by both private employers and the trade unions to establish domestic bargaining in private enterprise undertakings. Even if this has not resulted in the replacement of one by the other, it has gone some way toward allowing a more focused discussion of the contribution side of the bargain than national negotiations in any sector have ever permitted.

Originally, the recommendations led to a whole ramified edifice of national joint negotiating bodies, established in the years immediately after the World War I, and these have been added to over the years, particularly after World War II. The Ministry of Labour called together the two sides of most industries not nationally-organized, in 1918, and exhorted them to establish such machinery. Consequently, 73 councils were set up before 1921, although some of them disappeared soon afterwards. The problems of production in World War II gave them another fillip, and 56 were established on this formula between 1939 and 1945, so that by the latter date, there was, effectively, a *national* system of bargaining in Britain (see Clegg, 1972, pp 203-6).

They were not immediately accepted by government as relevant to their employer situation, but after strong representations from staff, they were adopted with some caveats. Consequently, negotiations in the various public services are now, still, largely conducted on a national basis, through the kind of Whitley Councils which were then advocated. Whatever pragmatic solutions might be indicated by the nature of the services involved, the national, standardizing approach is retained.

Resisting decentralization

Despite pressures to fragment bargaining in industry generally following World War II, the national system has persisted in the public sector, without being confined to it. Marsh has suggested, for example, that the Donovan Commission 'gravely distorted the role and status of industry-wide agreements' and, indeed, his own recent survey suggests that they:

'are alive and well ... in the sense that the improvements in pay and conditions provided in them continue to be widely applied ...especially at establishment level' (Marsh, 1982, pp 151-62).

Nevertheless, private industry developed domestic bargaining to supplement the national system and provided itself with a mechanism for considering the contribution side of the bargain. This was what failed to develop in the public sector to any appreciable extent. There has, nevertheless, been some pressure from the trade union interest, at least, to devolve some of this decision-making. This has been resisted, and the McGaw Inquiry tended to support this view, with its recommendation against both productivity bargaining and decentralization in any other respect than in connection with London Weighting (McGaw, 1982, chapter 13).

Over the post-war period, there have been changes in the subjects dealt with in bargaining in private industry but this development has tended to by-pass the public service sector. This might be explained by the probability that bargaining in that sector began as a centralized, national system, whereas in private industry it reached that stage only after passing through a domestic phase. It can be said of private industry that there has never been a time when no domestic bargaining took place, but this is probably not true of the public sector. Similarly, the power of the unions in the public sector may depend upon public authority recognition, at the centre, whereas in private industry both employer and trade union power 'has remained where it began in the eighteenth century, on the shop floor' (Cuthbert, in Cuthbert and Hawkins, 1974, p 3).

This assumes particular significance in connection with attempts to resolve differences over pay and conditions through the standard Whitley Council machinery. The incidence of industry-specific occupations within the public sector leads to difficulties in determining the appropriate comparators as a basis for negotiation in a situation in which market controls are not available. The negotiations permitted through these councils are of a different order from those associated with free bargaining in the private sector, as are the arrangements conventionally-sanctioned for resolution of failures to agree. The arrangements are clearly not adequate to deal with issues likely to be presented, except in so far as the staffs concerned are willing to accept flawed arrangements as preferable to engaging in industrial action.

The assumption that the arrangements will continue to be accepted as adequate cannot be made about public sector employees. The 'winter of discontent' dramatically shattered illusions of this type. There have been many other episodes on a smaller scale which have also called in question whether the machinery available in the public sector is adequate. A variety of alternative mechanisms for resolving basic questions of pay and conditions have appeared from time to time, but it is to be doubted whether these could be regarded as anything other than temporary and *ad hoc* expedients. The need for a more coherent strategy remains.

A number of problems arise in connection with Whitleyism as applied in the public sector. From time to time, these surface in connection with particular disputes, and in some cases they have led to the adoption of alternative methods of fixing pay, if not other conditions of employment (for example, in the case of the pay review bodies). Society has not yet resolved the direction in which the system should move in future to reduce some of these tensions between this sector and private industry and within the public sector itself. Serious doubts must, however, exist about the relevance and acceptability of the 'sovereign' concept in this sector, given the likelihood that public sector workers share with others a desire for greater autonomy and control over their working lives.

Readings

Clegg: (1972), pp 200-06; 376-395.
Fowler: (1980), pp 78-122.
Winchester, in Bain: (1983), pp 155-78.
McGaw: (1982).
McCarthy: (1977).
Carpenter, in Sethi and Dimmock: (1982), pp 139-67.

16

The context of local bargaining

Recent trends

It is widely believed that industrial relations has become increasingly domesticated during the post-war period, even if national or industry-wide bargaining has not been abandoned altogether (see Marsh, 1982, p 162). The process may have begun with 'informal' developments of the kind noted by the Donovan Royal Commission, but may have become more 'formal' with the passage of time if not with the acceptance of the recommendations of the Commission. The effect has been to deposit much more local (undertaking and establishment) joint negotiation into the system.

The trend towards more localized collective bargaining may be a product of Britain's changed economic position in the world, an attempt at accommodating the trends and pressures (noted in chapter 1). These phenomena may not have 'caused' the development. It is more likely that the action has been stimulated by the constructions which both workers and managements have placed on their experiences of the situation. This action may then be consistent with a move towards more local control of industrial relations activities and outcomes, intended to reduce the uncertainties and improve the outcomes.

A move towards the assumption of greater local control over industrial relations affairs in the private sector has manifested itself in two main developments which have attracted attention and comment. First the development of more explicit industrial relations policies managements unilaterally. Secondly, the extension of local negotiation over *both* elements in the work contract, contribution and rewards. There is evidence of both in the three recent surveys (Brown, 1981; Marsh, 1982; Daniel and Milward, 1983) but the extent of each development remains somewhat indistinct, probably because of the difficulty of accommodating the differences on these dimensions which every survey reveals.

The reality, it can be speculated, may be more complex than these broad generalizations imply. It is not unlikely that as both managements and workers try to cope with the situations they find themselves in, they develop frames of reference which stimulate changes in behaviour. As these 'catch on', they assume the form of a new pattern of relations, and where this new pattern is different from what has gone before, it seems to presage the emergence of a general trend to which all will be subjected. The variety of behaviours found in these surveys may nevertheless attract an explanation which emphasizes different constructions of reality and variable decisions as to action, each of which remains valid according to situation.

The influence of markets and technological change

Whatever may, in general, have been happening to British markets, and however broad the developments have been in technology in this post-War period, they have not affected all units in the same ways or to the same extents. It is this factor which admits the possibility that various 'solutions' to the productivity and industrial relations problems may be found, only to show up in the survey results.

Managers and workers in undertakings (or establishments) which are involved in developing relationships with growing markets and seeking to increase their relatively small market shares, may well consider it legitimate to deal with industrial relations questions, either informally (or even peremptorily) or externally (accepting nationally-negotiated terms etc). Managers may justify this in terms of a need to maintain flexibility in productive activity (along with a need to diminish the significance of wage competition in relations with other undertakings). Workers may accord this legitimacy for a variety of reasons of the kind that Fox adduces in his discussion of the 'Traditional Paternalistic' pattern of relationships (Fox, 1974a, p 297). Where this is associated with a worker ideology which seeks a place for the trade union, the conditions for the development of a 'Classical Conflict' pattern, could well exist (ibid, p298).

Those in undertakings (or establishments) which have got over this juvenile hurly-burly and secured prosperity by having increased their market share in a still-growing market may seek to formalize the arrangements for dealing with industrial relations questions and make more explicit and detailed the policies and strategies on which action will be based. This can be allied by management (or workers) with a unitarist or a pluralist philosophy, and the issue of whether the handling of industrial relations finds a place for the trade unions will depend upon which is adopted. It will be justified in terms of securing order within the undertaking (etc) as a basis for maintaining the high market share, and the prosperity on which all stakeholders depend. In Fox's categorization, this situation might emphasize the 'Sophisticated Paternalist' or the 'Standard Modern' (ibid, p 307) patterns, according to the juxtaposition of the legitimating ideologies adopted by the parties.

These features and factors are likely to be reinforced when the undertaking moves into the mature phase or situation. Each will be strengthened by the need to maintain the prosperity of the undertaking in conditions which might emphasize a stagnating market and the need for more sophisticated production technology to maintain the competitiveness and hence the market share. The need for sophisticated means of ordering industrial relations affairs and for securing commitment may then be perceived more strongly than before, and a more sophisticated modern pattern may result. However, whether this results in management according legitimacy to the union as a bargaining partner, could well reflect the 'culture' developed uring the earlier phase, as well as the personal predilections and predispositions of the key managers.

The undertaking which faces an ever-dwindling share of a declining market and which, as a consequence, faces the need to retrench, has been common in post-War Britain, and in the current recession, it has become even more prevalent. In this situation, the sophistication of the well-placed oligopoly undertaking becomes a possible hindrance to the securing of such prosperity as is possible; the need is for retrenchment and redundancy of labour, and for sufficient managerial freedom to effect this when occasion warrants it. Under the circumstances, the union which might previously have won many 'concessions' from management, giving it a high degree of job regulation, becomes a liability unless it is prepared to yield. A situation of 'Classical Conflict', in Fox's phrase, could well develop, as, in the common managerial phrase, the 'union is rolled back'.

It would be idle to pretend either that this is a proven

relationship, or that even if it were managements necessarily construe situations in these ways and act accordingly. What the discussion does do is offer one possible explanation for the variety of patterns and the possible trends which are found in surveys recently made in Britain and locates some of the prescriptions for change towards 'good' or 'improved' industrial relations (which usually depend upon some greater domestic constitutionalization) within a broader business framework.

THE PRINCIPALS' OBJECTIVES AND POLICIES

It is useful, in discussing the approaches made by the parties to industrial relations to treat the undertakings and unions as if they took decisions and acted. This reifies the abstract conceptions, but it is used here merely as a heuristic or as a convenience, without meaning to imply that decisions are taken and acted upon by anyone other than the managers and union officers involved.

However well or badly these managers or officials read their situations, and however appropriately or inappropriately they conceive of their plans of action, they do develop ideologies and theories in the process of coping with their problems, which they then express in the form of policies and strategies regarded as those of their respective organizations.

The principals can be said to have industrial relations objectives which they will expect their agents and representatives to pursue, usually within the framework of accepted law and convention. They will frequently have to pursue these against the competing or opposed objectives of the other interested parties. The likelihood that the members of either side will not share the same objectives and approaches provides the foundation for both the dissensus and the intra-organizational bargaining which Walton and McKersie (1965) recognize (see below, pp 445-48).

The objectives are likely to have both an economic and a political component. The employer's economic aims will be to keep the cost of any agreement or decision as low as possible consistent with policy. 'Policy' is relevant in that management faces a choice as to the kind of labour market in which it wishes to operate (affecting the level of wages it considers ought to be aimed at) and the kind of employment contract it wants to offer (affecting the reputation as an employer it seeks to acquire). The worker's economic aims will be to secure the highest possible return for the expenditure of effort which is consistent with continued employment. Workers and their organizations also face a choice as to the trade off between wages and employment they want to make and as to the kind of union image which they wish to generate.

On the political side, the aim of both parties is likely to emphasize the establishment of a sufficient degree of order to make the future operation of the system reasonably predictable. Each party will want to secure order on its own terms. Management again faces a choice between securing control on management's own terms (the authoritarian or unitarist principle) and securing control by sharing control with other interest groups like the unions (the pluralist principle). The workers' and the union's objective is usually to secure greater order and predictability in relations by securing management's agreement that its decisions (about remuneration and discipline, for example) will be subject to the kinds of rule which normally appear in collective agreements. What the union faces is not so much a choice in this matter as a decision as to how far to proceed along this road of joint regulation of what have traditionally been management's prerogative decisions.

The parties are also likely to have ideas both about what approaches might bring about what results, and about which approaches ought (in a more moral sense) to be developed in their name. These are usually formalized as strategies and policies which are considered consistent with the realization of the parties' goals.

A strategy is a statement, prepared in advance of action, which details the actions to be taken at some time in the future in order to move towards the stated objectives. It constitutes a plan of action. It is composed as a result of establishing which methods or means of action might best secure the ends (where the criteria of what constitutes best are derived from the objectives of the parties) and on the basis of some set of theories which link ends and means).

'Policy' is sometimes defined to include statements of objectives (see Hawkins, 1971, p. 205 and Cowan, in BMC, 1970, pp. 18-19), and thus to have a kind of affinity with strategy. Where it does not it provides a set of principles governing conduct by which those within its domain may answer the question of what

435

to do or how to behave in this or that set of circumstances (see Shackle, 1970). This is clearer in Brech's definition of policy as:

> 'the modes of thought and the body of principles laid down to underlie and to guide the activities of the firm (or other organization) towards declared or known objectives'. (Brech, 1975, p 37)

This draws a kind of distinction between all three concepts of objectives, strategies and policies, even though a relationship is clearly established between them.

The unitarist approach

In those circumstances where management correctly perceives a need to retain power to act quickly and flexibly to meet the demands of the market, it is likely to adopt a unitarist approach to the ordering of industrial relations. The unitarist approach is based on the view that the interests of management and workers are essentially, or sufficiently, the same. It implies that what workers want from their work is either high or 'fair' pay, dignified treatment and opportunity to express their views whether these are positive or founded in grievance, and either a job which is interesting in itself or which obviously contributes to an achievement which is prestigious, and that all of these can be secured through positive or pro-active management, if it is allowed to act with flexibility (which usually means unilaterally).

Management's intention in adopting this approach will usually be to establish or maintain the power balance within the negotiating relationship which is implied in individual bargaining. This has been referred to as 'managing without unions' or as an 'open shop policy', in both of which, the specific accretion of a bargaining power which is associated with worker combination into unions is denied to them (see Myers, 1976).

Management might then adopt a policy which encourages agents to act in such ways as will preserve the managers' authority in the face of all challenges (for example, from the trade unions: see Dean, 1954). Such an authoritarian policy would be consistent with a unitarist frame of reference and has much in common with the concept of 'sovereign employer' as used in the context of the public service (see above, pp 405-07). It would assert managerial rights and prerogatives, emphasis central (managerial) decision-taking and diminish the need for consulta-tion, and seek to achieve ends by essentially coercive or utilitarian means. Such a policy could exist both where the intention was to 'keep the unions out' and where the union was already recognized for purposes of collective bargaining. The effect of the strategy would be different, but conduct could be responsive to the same values and norms.

Where the policy is adopted to deny unions recognition or a power based within the undertaking, management will have to articulate its objectives, strategies and policies with greater precision and more deliberate reference to best practice than in the case where it conformed more closely with the collective bargaining norms. In order to recruit the commitment of the workforce the undertaking must state what its pay, profit and price targets are, the means by which it will seek to realize these and the principles which will be applied in their administration. Furthermore, procedures for consultation (including sugges-tion) and for grievance will also have to be developed and (under the guidance of policy) utilized in the manner intended for the purpose of drawing people fully into the process of running the undertaking.

The undertaking will probably be a relatively high payer, particularly where the proportion of final cost which is attributable to labour is low. The provision of jobs which are in themselves interesting might prove more difficult to achieve in practice, dependent on the nature of the industry and its technology. Where there are close limits to what might be achieved in this area, management may have to develop methods of recruitment, incentive and supervision which might be calculated to minimize their consequences. This might not prove adequate by itself and proactive policies designed to allow those performing uninteresting jobs to participate in more prestigious aspects of the undertaking's activities may then have to be developed as compensation.

Where a union is recognized, a policy designed to protect and preserve the managerial status and role can rest on similar unitarist foundations. In this event, the stress is upon the possible manipulation of the institutions of collective bargaining to achieve this end. Management's representatives would be encouraged by this policy to allow the mechanisms of collective bargaining to operate, but to deny the workers' representatives the opportunity to claim victories by giving increases in pay and benefit outside them. General management activity would be directed towards a diminution of any challenge to prerogatives and managerial decisions. The effect might therefore be similar in that pay and benefit levels might be relatively high and joint consultative machinery which is not based on union representation, might be developed strongly.

The paradox in all this is, therefore, that an undertaking which seeks to avoid unionization of its workforce may be forced to simulate or improve on the benefits and representative systems which the unions commonly urge upon employers. Such undertakings frequently develop joint consultative and disciplinary procedures and practices to ensure that employees are drawn into decision-taking. They may even go as far as encouraging employees to develop and take an active part in employee or staff associations (which do not have affiliations to the externally based trade unions) and encouraging the associations themselves to be aggressive in representing members' interests in discussion with management. These then afford management the opportunity to discuss and develop strategies and policies with representatives of the workforce rather than with 'employees' in some amorphous and general sense (see Hawkins, 1979, pp 37-50; Myers, 1976). Paradoxically, therefore, the worker's power to secure *some* improved terms is increased by avoiding combination where combination is the norm in other undertakings.

The pluralist approach

The major policy alternative to this is a pluralist one in which the union (or other worker association) is seen as a useful mechanism for ordering relations. The policy therefore emphasizes the desirability of bringing worker representatives into the decision and implementation processes across a wide range of subject-areas which might otherwise generate conflict and disorder. It also usually involves machinery for communication which can be used on the route to decision-taking, and for monitoring performance once the decisions had been implemented.

This is an alternative to pursuing simple individualism in domestic relations and is one which depends upon sharing decision-taking processes and authority with representatives of the non-managers. This goes beyond inviting representatives into consultation (which reduces managements discretion hard-

438

ly at all) and entails giving up authority and discretion in the interests of greater control of work behaviour or higher commitment to work tasks.

Fox has referred to this as the 'sophisticated modern pattern' of management. Within it,

> 'management legitimizes the union role in certain areas of joint decision-making because it sees this role as conducive to its own interests as measured by stability, promotion of consent, bureaucratic regulation, effective communication or the handling of change ... it recognizes that its discretion is being limited in certain areas of decision-making, but it legitimizes these limitations and therefore does not counter with low-trust behaviour and attitudes (Fox, 1974a, p 302).

This amplifies Flanders' earlier suggestion that 'management must share control to regain control' (Flanders, 1970, p 96).

Purcell also accepts that this 'sophisticated pattern' will, almost inevitably, be adopted by the managements of the modern corporation, because of its inherent benefits to managements. He then proposes a managerial strategy which, partly based on the values emerging from legislation and government policies in the 1970s, can be built up from a consideration of corporations' responses to those requirements.

His eight 'core elements' in the strategy are designed to offer a place in the corporate scheme of things to the workers' own associations, (elements 1-3), to develop policies and procedures for the containment of inherent conflict (elements 4-6), and to establish control over the operation of the collusive structure (elements 7-8).

The eight elements are:

1 'The encouragement of union membership and support for the closed shop where appropriate.
2 The encouragement of membership participation in trade unions.
3 The encouragement of inter-union cooperation and development of joint shop steward committees.
4 The minimization of areas of avoidable conflict.
5 The maximization of areas of common interest.
6 The institutionalization of irreducible conflict.
7 The reduction of the power of strategic groups.
8 The development of effective control systems' (Purcell, in Purcell and Smith, 1979, p 29).

This may still involve little more than heading off the Indians at the pass, even if it makes the attempt at a more sophisticated level than does managing without unions. Its sophistication lies in a more apposite construing of the realities of power in the modern corporation; if workers are predisposed to seek the strength of unions around them as an insurance, then give them the insurance (and assurance) so that the control may result, at least partly on the employer's terms. However, since this approach entails cost, the undertaking must be profitable enough to afford it, or some other strategy will be adopted.

This is also expressed by Fox, who sees the satisfaction of the workers' 'marginal aspirations' as a device to strengthen 'the legitimacy of the system in the eyes of those subordinated to it, thereby enhancing rather than weakening managerial effectiveness' (Fox, 1974a, p 302). A mechanism, jointly devised to deal with issues jointly, suggests that the employer stands ready to act in the worker interest when issues are brought to his attention. More fundamental conflicts do not have the same opportunity to develop on the backs of these grievances.

The whole is properly referred to as a strategy for industrial relations since it is designed to achieve tangible results (the control of work behaviour) rather than as a policy by which certain values are upheld. Nevertheless, the development of the strategy calls for the development of policies which support achievement of these ends without infringing certain ethics contained in the culture (or the law) or any relevant ideologies. In each case, there is a necessary objective which is acceptable to management, given its wider aims, and a set of means (expressed in policies and plans) by which it is expected that these can be attained.

Undertaking policies in industrial relations

There is probably no such thing as a typical undertaking or a typical undertaking's policy. A medium-to-large-scale undertaking might well pursue a policy which contained some or most of the following principles (which must be assumed to take into account its market, physical and power environments). These are now more likely to be explicit than in the middle 1960s, but some are still espoused rather than articulated (see Brewster *et al*, 1981, pp 3-4).

The hierarchy of aims

The first set of principles will link the industrial relations objectives and practices to those of the undertaking as a whole, that is, to business objectives in a private or to service objectives in a public sector undertaking. A hierarchy of aims might be developed in which:

1   Industrial relations policies and practices are consistent with personnel or employment policies in both the short and the long term.
2   Personnel and employment policies are consistent with the long-term objectives of the business or the service undertaking and if possible contribute to them in the short-run.
3   Business (etc) objectives and policies will be based on research and investigation and will seek to serve the short-term and long-term interests of all those who are associated with the undertaking (for example, shareholders or other beneficial owners, managers and other employees, suppliers and customers or clients, and the residents of the communities in which the undertaking is located).
4   It follows from these principles that industrial relations practices and activities will conform strictly with the requirements of the law and (central and local) government regulations as these relate to business, employment and industrial relations.

As these relate to one another, therefore, each preceding objective or principle is 'nested' in each succeeding one, thus ensuring that each is consistent with what is required at some higher or wider level.

Handling employee relations without unions

Since industrial relations is particularly concerned with employees, the undertaking's policy will spell out how, in principle, the employer or management proposes to structure and develop this relationship. Here, the management has to make a fundamental choice between dealing with employees on an individual basis and dealing with at least part of the relationship through union representatives.

'Managing without unions' (see Myers, 1976) is one approach which some managements prefer to adopt. It is one which is easier to adopt in the private than in the public sector and in private undertakings with low unit labour costs than in those with high unit labour costs (which, of course, also tends to discriminate between public and private). Its consequences are likely to be (in a situation in which union recognition is the norm) that the undertaking will be one which pays relatively high wages and provides better than average benefits, and which necessarily spends a relatively large amount of managerial time and energy on the maintenance of 'good (and direct) communications' with employees. An expression of appropriate policy guidlines in this context might be:

5a Management will take the initiative in structuring industrial relations within its undertakings, and will do so in the belief that the interests of employees are best served by direct negotiation of terms and conditions of employment and of individual grievances between the employee concerned and the appropriate manager.

6a Management will accept the freedom of employees to join trade unions or other associations of their choice, but will continue its policy of not recognizing unions for negotiation purposes until such time as a majority of employees in any area within which a community of interest in employment exists, demonstrates in a secret ballot, a wish to be represented by an appropriate trade union.

7a Management will take all necessary steps to ensure that direct communication between individual managers and employees is facilitated through all channels so that employees are fully acquainted with the undertaking's policies and requirements.

8a Management will establish additional channels of communication with interest groups within departments or sections and with representatives of employees through joint consultation, so that employees are able to make their maximum contribution to the development and well-being of the undertaking.

Such a policy is not generally supported by the operation or law or conventions for the vast majority of manual and routine white collar employees in undertakings other than the very small ones in Britain. For that reason, it tends to be exposed to risk, and requires extra and continuing effort on management's part to maintain it in viable form.

Handling employee relations with unions

Managing with unions is (for reasons of history if no others) the only feasible option open to many managements. In these circumstances, the undertaking has to establish the principles on which management will recognize and deal with union representatives. These will relate to both the industrial relations practices which will be accepted and the structures within which they will be carried on. They will, nevertheless, carry forward and continue the principles expressed in paragraphs 5a-8a, and those which accommodate the union's presence will therefore be additional to them. The conventions which have grown up around the collective bargaining relationship (see above, pp 327-37) will also be incorporated (even if in partial or modified form) into any statement of undertaking policy.

5b Management will seek to retain the intiative in structuring and directing industrial relations activities within its undertaking(s), but freely accepts that dealing with the representatives of trade unions and other employee associations which might develop spontaneously is likely to contribute to 'good industrial relations' within them.

6b Management recognizes employees' freedom to associate in trade unions or professional associations, and will in principle recognize an obligation to deal with such associations where to do so is consistent with 'good industrial relations' provided that employees and their representatives in their turn recognize management's freedom to communicate its views on industrial relations issues directly to its employees. (Management representatives and any other employees who have access to strategic information about industrial relations will be excluded from these arangements for representation and collective bargaining).

7b Management will endeavour to develop a collective bargaining structure which is based on the recognition of bargaining agents and representatives where employees have a community of interest in their relations with management, and which can be calculated to faciliate ordered industrial relations and to preserve the authority and bargaining power of the management of the undertaking.

8b Management will continue to be accountable for achieving business (service) results and will be expected by all employees to make the necessary operating decisions, but the

443

function of employees' representatives is recognized as being able to act in the interests of their constituents and to protect their constituents' rights under agreements and law.

This set of principles subsumes much which is conventional in the unionized sectors of the economy. The principles may be spelled out in greater detail in collective agreements (see above, ch. 13) but their broad purposes are indicated by these four statement.

Conduct of collective negotiations

A third set of principles relates to the manner in which management agents or representatives will conduct themselves in negotiations with representatives of the workers. Assuming a unionized undertaking, management will seek to establish principles on which it can proceed to defend its interests and secure its objectives where this has to be done with the (at least potential) opposition of the union representatives.

9   Management will make information on commercial and industrial relations developments within the undertaking available to employees individually and to negotiating representatives in order to facilitate discussion of these questions.
10 Management recognizes that differences and disputes are likely to arise with employees from time to time, but will work to ensure that these are kept to a minimum in so far as management action can accomplish this. Where disputes do occur, they will be dealt with using the procedures agreed with representatives.
11 Disputes of interest will be dealt with through negotiations, conciliation, mediation, or third-party fact-finding or in the event of failure by industrial action. Disputes of right will be resolved by management decision (where this is acceptable) or by arbitration or other external forms of adjudication.
12 Management will not negotiate in circumstances where industrial action is threatened or in progress. In the course of negotiations, any concessions which will be made by management will be offered in return for some advantage or concession advanced by the other party, not merely to ward off some threatened action.

These principles may be expanded considerably beyond this.

444

They reflect the norms inherent in both legislation and convention, and for that reason could well include many more details from either source (see above, pp 154-62).

The status and nature of agreements

To secure order through the operation of agreements freely arrived at by the parties in negotiation calls for a policy to be expressed on the way management proposes to arrive at such agreements and to regard them once they are established.

13 Management will avoid expedient settlements of disputes that can be calculated to prejudice the long term interests of the undertaking or its management. Management will also refuse to countenance or sign any agreement which if made known to employees, other employees' representatives, the public or government, would attract significant disapproval and render it nugatory.

14 Collective agreements will be established for fixed terms and will proscribe disputes of interest during their lifetimes. The obligations entered into by the signatories to these agreements are intended to be acted upon during the lifetime of any such agreement and breaches will be subject to sanctions.

These principles seek to preserve the sanctity of agreements, and particularly those procedural agreements on which management rely to secure order in an area of potential conflict, and the unions to secure control by rule in any area where otherwise decisions would be taken entirely on the basis of managerial values.

The whole policy is, however, designed to ensure that people (managers or workers) know where they stand in this area and can act in a coherent and consistent manner in the face of any resistance to their will. Consequently, the policy needs to be communicated in comprehensible terms and in a manner in which the intended meaning will be drawn from what is communicated. This is a major part of the task of the specialist personnel or industrial relations function, but is not necessarily confined to it.

The probability of dissensus

It is, however, extremely unlikely that consensus will exist or develop automatically on *either* side. Their compositions and

445

structures are usually so complex that a variety of objectives and approaches is likely to develop amongst the principals. It cannot, therefore, be assumed that each side is homogeneous in its objectives, orientations or attitudes, even though, for purposes of negotiation with an opponent, this impression may be given. Expressed policy is one method of establishing an appearance of unity and consensus, but it may mask a variety of attitudes and motivations relevant to the negotiating process.

Walton and McKersie see the dissensus and potential conflict existing within a side as taking one or both of two forms, according to the circumstances:

1   It may reveal itself simply as a difference of view between individual members of the side. They may have different views of what is desirable and what is feasible in the circumstances. They may seek to persuade others to adopt their views as to objectives and strategies. This implies simple inter-personal difference and conflict.

2   It may reveal itself in attempts by one category or group within the side (for example, a group of 'small employers' within an employers association, or a departmental interest within an undertaking (see Dalton, 1959; Sayles, 1964; Armstrong and Goodman, 1979) to secure interests against those of another category or group within the side, where the negotiation with the opponent appears to offer a strategic opportunity for this. This leads to inter-group conflict based on perceptions of a common interest.

The implications of these for the development of consensus within the side are clearly different: in the one, it is necessary to convince individuals, whereas in the other it is necessary to convince groups who may have a solid foundation for their frames of reference for their position within the structure (see Blake and Mouton, 1961; Frey and Adams, 1972).

Walton and McKersie suggest that these differences reflect differences in motivational forces, or of perceptual factors. The first of these suggests that different individuals or groups within the side will actively want different ends, and the other that they see the actual and potential situations in different ways.

Status differences within the constituency are likely to be reflected in different motivations and goals. These may reflect differences in hierarchical position (as between the Board and the executive management or between craftsmen and semi-skilled workers) or differences in work position (as between line and service managers or between day-shift and night-shift workers).

The quantity and type of information available to different individuals and groups within a side (together with the ease or difficulty of relating it to the situation) might also spawn differences of view. This might occur independently of any differences in goals or wants which might be discerned. Different groups inevitably receive different amounts of information about the situation or about proposed actions to be taken in it. This usually reflects their central position in the communications networks. Night-shift workers or out-station managers are frequently disadvantaged in this respect, as are those groups of union members which do not have ready access to shop-stewards. Those who receive less information might be expected to develop different perspectives of situations and proposed actions.

Some people are likely to be disadvantaged more by the nature of their situation than by the sheer amount of information available to them. The decisions which they have to take may emphasize novelty and lack of structure, with necessary consequences for perceptions (see Simon, 1965, pp 58-61). People in these inherently more complicated roles are likely to find information more difficult to relate to their positions, and they may need *more* complex information to enable them to relate it to their situation.

Walton and McKersie suggest that this kind of problem is more likely to occur within labour organizations because of the operation of the democratic process (Walton and Mckersie, 1965, p 281) than on the employer's side. But where an employers' association bargains with the union(s) (as happens more often in Britain than in the USA) such divergence is also likely to appear on that side too. It is in other words a phenomenon of association, whether that association is a trade union, an employers' association or even a corporation.

It is also to be expected (see above, pp 225-32) that these problems are more likely to appear in the conglomerate and diversified undertakings than in the integrated and single-product ones. The opportunities for disagreement and conflict are likely to occur more frequently in dispersed conglomerates than in undertakings on a single site. What initially causes the problem may also make it more difficult to resolve.

The conglomerate union (see above, pp 272-73) is likely to face similar difficulties in securing solidarity across the union, although there are probably few occasions when this is required for negotiation purposes. However, the diversity of the locations of a multi-plant undertaking is likely to present problems to the union as to the management. The development of combine committees in the 1950s and 1960s was partly an attempt to cope with such problems and to provide a better communication structure to foster solidarity at the undertaking level. In the establishment, on the other hand, the joint shop stewards' committee is an attempt to develop solidarity within a side composed (frequently) of many different unions (see above, pp 274-76).

THE NEGOTIATORS

In both management and union organizations, the opportunities for resolving these problems by purely organizational means are probably limited. Consequently, responsibility for doing so lies with the specialist functionaries whose roles have often developed because of the need to engage in local bargaining (see above, pp 260-61). In any event, resolution is usually focused in the specific roles of those who must deal with both their own principals and the opposing principal's representatives.

This is because the terms and conditions of employment of a majority of employees are established in a process of bargaining or negotiation between representatives (see, Clegg, 1972, pp 59-60; 1979, pp 177-82). Some of these represent the employer, and are usually identified as 'managers' although their relationship is strictly one of *agent* of the company or corporation. Some of them represent the workers in the whole or some segment of the undertaking and are usually identified as full-time officials of the union (or other association) or as shop stewards. In spite of attempts in recent legislation to change their status, these worker negotiators usually have a more limited agency relationship to their constituents (see above, pp 99-101).

Each party has an interest in establishing his negotiating team to suit his situation defined by reference to objectives and the need to 'cover' all interests which have to be accommodated. But he also has some interest in the composition and structure of the opposing team and in its relationship to its constituents, if only because knowledge of these factors might have a bearing on the approach he makes to the negotiation.

The need for an effective management team to meet the union representatives is probably obvious. They go in to protect the position of the total management cadre in the face of grievances or claims put forward in the name of the employees. Whether they succeed or not depends upon the opportunity which managers and supervisors will have in the future for continuing to deal with the workforce in the hitherto customary fashion.

The managerial interest in the organization of the opponent may be less obvious, although widely attested. Evans, for example, concludes his study of the engineering industry with the suggestion that 'many managements see advantages in having a well-organized and authoritative system of worker representation in their plants' (Evans, in Warner, 1973, pp 85-6) and goes on to suggest that for this reason management might be willing to concede more union security (as allowed at the time by the Industrial Relations Act) in order to foster this.

The negotiating teams

Negotiations, whether these occur at national level on behalf of workers in an industry or at local level in respect of those in an undertaking or establishment or part of one, are usually conducted by two relatively small teams of agents or representatives. There is no precise number which can be predicted or demonstrated to be more effective. In practice, a team may be larger or smaller dependent on circumstances, but still small in comparison with the number of constituents. It may have a hierarchical structure with some people having more active roles than others. A 'chief negotiator' is commonly designated as team leader who may carry the brunt of the argument and who has authority to involve or exclude other members.

Management teams tend to be smaller, even if supported by experts or specialist back-up. They are also hierarchically structured, although practice in this respect varies. Goodman, Armstrong, Davis and Wagner, in their study of the footwear industry, identify five 'leading spokesmen' for the employers in the national negotiations between the British Footwear Manufacturers' Federation and the Footwear Unions (Goodman, *et al.*, 1977, p 90). These five were: the chairman of the employment and social policy committee, the two chairmen of its two sub-committees on industrial relations and time study, the full-time director of employment and social policy, and the full-time director general of the BFMF. They occupied the pivotal roles in negotiations, although they were not the only members to sit in on them.

Domestic negotiations on interest claims are sometimes led by a senior line manager supported by personnel or industrial relations managers, but sometimes leadership is with the personnel manager (see Marsh, 1971; Eaton, 1977; Beaumont and Gregory, 1980). Handling grievances seems more often to involve the personnel or industrial relations managers in the middle stages, with line management being involved at the outset and at the final appeal stages.

The unions are frequently represented by a larger team if only to allow a watching brief to representatives from all of the unions where members are involved. Full-time officials (such as general secretaries) usually lead, but the team is likely to be composed of other full-time officials and lay representatives or delegates to national councils. One full-time officer of one union usually leads in any negotiation, and only a small number of the others present may take any active part in the process. However, it is not uncommon for the leadership to change, possibly on a rota basis, between one negotiation and the next, unless one union is clearly dominant numerically or politically within the industry.

In domestic negotiations, the unions' negotiating team is *either* made up of shop stewards, possibly led by the chief steward or convenor, with the full-time official in the area or district joining in for the final stages and the actual signing of the agreement; *or* led from the start by a full-time official accompanied by shop stewards (with the Branch Secretary sometimes substituting for the full-time official in each case) (see Boraston, Clegg and Rimmer, 1975, p 153 and p 157).

Size of team is likely to be a function of the size of the undertaking (and of the payroll) and the requirement of expertize in the team. Honzik has suggested that on the basis of American practice, and depending on the size of the undertaking's operation, one or two or ten or more negotiators might form the team on the management side. But it is not the number of representatives that counts, but the spectrum of knowledge and experience that they encompass (Hoznik, in Marceau, 1965, p 85).

This reflects the common desire to ensure that the team

contains those who have expertise over a spectrum of employee relations questions as well as over general policy. Hoznik says that in America management will tend to draw its team members from the areas of 'industrial relations/personnel, management/ operations, attorneys, and outside counsel/consultants' (Honzik, in Marceau, 1969, p 80), each of which might contribute relevant expertize. Although it is not a case of drawing one member from each area, the legally-binding nature of the American collective contract does import the lawyers into the negotiations with greater frequency than would be the case in Britain.

Trade union teams tend to be somewhat larger, therefore, not because the smaller number will not possess the necessary knowledge and skill, but because some representatives have an assured place on the team by virtue of the importance of their constituencies for the final acceptance or rejection of any decision reached. This principle of democratic representation could also apply to the employers' association, but is more strongly entrenched on the trade union side where it may serve to increase the size of the bargaining team.

Selecting the team

The manner in which the negotiators are selected for their roles varies according to the level of negotiations and the principal under consideration. Where negotiations are conducted between two associations the negotiators are likely to be chosen from a group which is either elected or appointed by the constituents. The members of either the employers' association or the trade union(s) will elect a number of people to positions from which the members of the bargaining team are chosen, although in either case, certain full-time officers may be appointed for their skills and experience to lead the negotiations.

This is generally the position on the union side also in domestic negotiations. The membership, organized into constituencies of some kind, will elect a number of shop or office representatives from whose number the actual negotiators will be selected, probably by the representatives themselves acting as a kind of electoral college. The likelihood that a full-time negotiator will be selected to lead is in this case smaller, unless either it is customary to bring in a full-time official or there is a full-time convenor of stewards who will assume this role.

451

On the management side in domestic negotiations, the manner of composing the team is likely to follow different principles. In this case, the team is likely to be composed on the say-so of the board of directors or the senior management acting within their given authority. They (or one of their number) will determine just how many managers shall be involved, and who they shall be. The decision about who shall lead is also likely to be taken in the same way. The broad options vary between using a personnel (or industrial relations) specialist to lead, or placing the lead in the hands of a senior line manager who will then be assisted by the functional specialist (see Marsh, 1971).

This difference is likely to carry some implications for the way in which the opponent party will view the resolution or firmness of the side. Where the fiat of the management is accepted as the base for appointment, the other party is likely to form one view of the solidarity of the management team; where a process of election has resulted in a small team being presented, there may be a suspicion about the solidarity of the side and doubts about the 'representativeness' of the negotiators. In both cases, however, the fact that the agents or representatives present themselves on someone else's behalf is generally thought both to increase their power to coerce, and to depersonalize any interchanges which may take place in the bargaining process. Their power base may, however, have to be 'mobilized' as it cannot necessarily be assumed to exist automatically.

Those who thus come to acquire specialist roles are more likely than their principals to treat their activities as ends in themselves and to evade or even reject the constraints imposed by their principals where these may interfere with the realization of their immediate industrial relations (or bargaining) goals in the negotiating context itself.

This potential for divergence of aims between principals and agents is a commonly recognized source of uncertainty and tension for those who engage in negotiation and bargaining. This makes it imperative that the principals and their agents and representatives should seek an understanding of one another's viewpoints by a process which Walton and McKersie have labelled 'intra-organizational bargaining'. It leads to the further observation that the actual negotiators may find collusion between them *against their respective principals* to be a necessary device to reduce or remove what might otherwise prove to be an intolerable and dysfunctional encumbrance in carrying out their roles.

Composition of the team

In a general sense, the negotiating team has to be composed in such a way that all the manifold tasks can and will be accomplished with a degree of competence and that the inherent stresses and strains of negotiating will be borne. Some of the required tasks are 'technical' in that they are instrumentally related to winning in argument, and the negotiators as a group, must therefore:

(a) command all the knowledge and know-how required to cope with all the aspects of the negotiating process
(b) carry out all the strategic tasks which are involved, including that of concluding an agreement on acceptable terms.

Composition may also reflect the need to deal with potential intra-organization conflicts, before, during and after the negotiation episodes. It may also reflect the desirability of reserving arbitral power located at some other point in the organization in order that impasses might be resolved later if necessary. The actual selection of the members is, however, likely to reflect not only these requirements, but also the principal's need to 'trust' his negotiators to act in his best interests in the process.

The criteria of selection will focus on the possession of a range of knowledge and skill, including communications and judgemental skills, which is required to conduct a negotiation. The numbers involved are equally likely to reflect the possibility of securing such skills required in the smallest team possible. In some circumstances, not exclusively on the union side, some members of the team may be selected not because of their skills or knowledge, but because of their representative position and the potential power which they possess by virtue of this position to influence parts of the constituency.

The possibility of finding all of the relevant knowledge, know-how and skills in a single individual is relatively small. Consequently, it is usual to put together a team which will contain people who between them have the range of skills needed. One member, perhaps one with acknowledged authority or with special skills in negotiation, will usually be designed chief negotiator or spokesman, and he or she will be expected to 'lead' the team through the various stages of the process.

The managerial team is likely to incorporate professional managers from a number of separate levels and areas of the organization, but within those parameters an attempt will be made to secure abilities for coping with both the tasks and the stresses involved. On the trade union side, although the vocabulary is different, there is also some tendency to draw in representatives of the major areas of interest to the team. Thus shop stewards in important or simply large constituencies are likely to be incorporated, regardless of their particular skills, and in national negotiations involving a number of unions, full-time officers (at least) from the different unions (areas of interest) are likely to be incorporated for the purpose.

It is likely that the chief negotiator will be selected as having the ability to 'interpret the effect of all bargaining decisions' upon the total business or union operation, an awareness of 'current trends and legal implications' and a capacity to take 'decisions within the framework of company (or trade union) policy' (Honzik, in Marceau, 1969, p 79) in order to establish a base of trust for the act of delegation.

The definition of the overall task of the team in a negotiating structure might simply refer to the necessity of 'winning' as many of the principal's objectives as possible. A more sophisticated definition might be expressed in terms of the organization's written statement of objectives and policies. It might even be possible to describe the job to be done by the chief negotiator and this might in itself be one method of attempting to reduce the possibility of the specialist negotiators adopting situationally-derived goals of their own making, rather than those of the principal.

A chief negotiator's role description

The chief negotiator's role is likely to form but a part of some managerial job or trade union office, and is unlikely to constitute a whole-time job in itself. Although, therefore, there is no sense in writing a job description for a chief negotiator, it is useful to write a *role description* for the management's chief negotiator to summarize the kinds of task which are most commonly found.

Post: General Manager / Personnel Manager
Role: Chief Negotiator

Principal Functions:

To advise senior management, on the basis of a knowledge of the situation gleaned in interaction with the representatives and from research, on the approach to be adopted in negotiations between the Company and the trade union representatives on any matter covered by existing procedural agreements and on the objectives to be pursued in each such negotiation; and within the limits agreed with senior management to seek through negotiation with the trade union representatives the optimum solution to any problems presented.

Principal activities

1 To take necessary steps to ensure that all parties to existing procedural agreements work within the procedure laid down for the resolution of differences over rights and interests.

2 To review the operation of existing agreements regularly in order to detect areas for improvement or modification in the light of experience.

3 To evaluate the respective positions of the undertaking and the unions at regular intervals with respect to bargaining advantage, to establish the optimum timing of negotiations with the unions.

4 To review the patterns of settlement and dispute within the relevant sectors of industry and commerce to establish the likely demands to be made upon the undertaking by the unions in annual bargaining rounds.

5 To advise the Board, through the Managing Director, on the likely demands and their timing, and the possible responses, including recommendations as to the objectives to be sought and the strategies to be adopted, which the undertaking might make to these.

6 After clearance with the Managing Director, to engage in negotiations with the union representatives, with the object of securing the optimum benefits to the undertaking from them; this will involve presenting the management's position and case, and controlling the development of the negotiations from this point.

7 To determine whether it is appropriate during the course of negotiations to proceed or break off discussions, and to invoke third party assistance or permit industrial action to occur.

455

8 To represent the undertaking in any representations to third parties who may become involved, and to seek optimum benefits from so doing.

9 To reach agreement with representatives and to advice all interested parties on the outcome and contents, and any requirements for action which may apply to them as a consequence.

10 To monitor the implementation and consequences of any new agreement.

It should, however, be stressed that this is designed as a rather idealized model, not intended to apply to a particular role within a particular situation. In actuality, the dimensions of the situation to which it was to apply would influence the form which such a description would take.

The team's authority

The authority of the bargaining team, is likely to prove important to the outcomes if only because the authority vested in the negotiators is likely to be perceived by the opponent as indicative of their power. Where, for example, a trade union is convinced that the management negotiators are merely front men or 'talking heads' without the authority to conclude agreements, they are likely to assume that the opposition's principals are staying in reserve until 'the real negotiating starts'; in the circumstances, the union negotiators are likely to expect *more* to be forthcoming at the point where the prinicipals are brought in, in spite of what the front men may seek to argue (see Winkler, 1974, pp 134-6).

Ideally, from this point of view, the team should be delegated the authority and the power to carry through all the tasks which are involved in a negotiation, including the actual conclusion of an agreement. Delegation in any context is usually difficult to effect. Delegation of authority is usually dependent upon the existence of trust in the ability of those to whom it is devolved. This does not always occur, and often for acceptable reasons. Reference back, either to the membership in the case of the trade union, or to higher authority in the case of the management negotiators, at once provides a safety net (in the event of things going wrong) and a means of varying the opponent's perceptions of the power of the party.

456

This raises questions about the team's authority which need attention even if the team does not have complete and absolute authority to settle. A fine balance may have to be struck here. On the one hand, 'the team members should know the extent and limits within which they can bargain, and should be permitted to use their judgement within these limits and not be mere puppets'. But on the other, there are occasions when reference upward for decisions to a higher authority may be desirable for the reasons stated above (Honzik, 1969, p 84).

The distribution of authority within the team itself is an additional question which has to be settled. Usually the role of chief spokesman or chief negotiator is well-defined. He or she normally has an absolute authority to bring in or leave out other members of the team in the actual progress of negotiations. In this way, he or she is better able to control the development of the strategy. To this end, individual members of the team have to be warned of the kinds of issues they will be expected to deal with (at the chairman's request) and the kinds of negotiating role (aggressor, informer, tension reducer, etc; see below, pp 510-13 and 537-41) which they may be expected to adopt.

The authority of the team and the chief negotiator is thus something which is likely to prove difficult to define in advance. It is likely to respond to the ways in which the principals or constituents read the situation confronting the side. The negotiators themselves are not without power to influence these decisions about their own authority, but they are essentially the recipients of power and will be expected to accept it in the terms in which it is given. The contrary pressures upon them may also lead them to use their power of position to manipulate the expectations of their principals or constituents.

Summary: the context

The context of negotiation is given partly by the environment within which it occurs, taking into account, for example, the variables identified by Dunlop (see above, pp 4-6) and partly by the frames of reference of the parties (these being defined in such a fashion as to include objectives, strategies and policies).

Just as the external environment presents a variety of constraints, so the parties themselves may adopt any one of a variety of positions. Those adopted by management are frequently considered under the two headings of unitary and pluralist approaches, although there are a number of variations possible on this general theme. The two main orientations do, however, lend themselves to rather different industrial relations policies (whether explicit or espoused), and may also be expressed in terms of the ways of dealing with a union or avoiding all such involvement.

There is some reason to suppose that, whilst policies may offer general guidance, they rarely secure complete acceptance, and some dissensus is likely to occur on each side. It is the task of the leadership in each case to try to remove the dissensus, or at least keep it so controlled as to prevent it from interfering with the negotiations with the 'other side'. Part, at least, of this task will fall to the negotiating team and particularly to the chief negotiator to carry out.

Negotiating teams do not have a predictable size, although union teams do tend to be larger because of the constraints imposed by the democratic nature of these associations. They tend in their composition to reflect the twin necessities of establishing an undivided authority and of providing a skill cover for all the tasks which the team can be expected to perform on the route to securing agreement. Something of the kinds of skill which will be required are considered in the following chapters.

Readings

Brech: (1975), pp 9-44. Hawkins: (1979), pp 37-50.
Thomason: (1981), pp 11-16. Fox: (1966b).
Atkinson: (1975), pp 6-58. Anthony: (1977), pp 17-63.
Rubin and Brown: (1975), pp 157-96.
Honzik: (1969), pp 78-85. Marsh: (1973), pp 135-54.

17

The processes of influence

Choice of strategy

Management's task in relation to labour is to secure either compliance with its instructions and rules or commitment to the ends and means proposed for the undertaking (or some combination of the two). The one will depend upon management's possession of sufficient power to compel compliance, against the wishes or the interests of those whom it is intended shall comply (see Lukes, 1974). The problem to be overcome is that of securing such compliance as will satisfy the ends sought, without the use of 'naked coercion'. The other will tend to demand persuasive dialogue and will tend to be a more favoured option where management must manage 'by consent', but cannot rely upon the existence of such supporting attitudes.

People as people may be as predisposed to co-operate with co-workers (whether managers or not), unless deterred by experience, as they are to challenge them (see McGregor, 1960, p 10). Either is possible, dependent upon circumstances. But which is probable is likely to reflect the way in which participants' experience has been structured. Long exposure to coercion by rule may predispose them to respond with challenge or opposition. Long experience of persuasion as the main mode may similarly predispose them to respond with demands to be convinced.

The need for co-operation within work undertakings in order to realize the purposes of organization, provides people with one foundation for motivation and attitude (see Dubin, 1956). Some people will see their work roles as ones which demand co-operation, either for self-interested or customary reasons, whilst others will adopt a comparable perspective because they perceive themselves as being under a duty or obligation to do so. Any of these provides a basis for co-operation, but to the extent that obligations are accepted simply because of the fear of consequences for non-compliance, the basis is likely to prove brittle and ephemeral.

The need for individuals and groups and classes of them to protect their positions and pursue their separate interests in the workplace provides people with another, distinct foundation for attitude and motivation. Some people, at least some of the time, will attach primacy to their positions as buyers or sellers or labour, and consequently see themselves as opposed to those in the alternative category. Herein lies a basis for opposition and conflict, and where the capacity of the work undertaking to buy off the opposition is low, the conflict is likely to acquire a degree of permanence.

Management may build on either type of foundation. Where its frame of reference permits (or demands) it, management may seek to develop a 'team' approach to the resolution of difficulties and differences which inevitably arise in large-scale organizations, or it may try to create a negotiated system of order where the negotiations occur between independent bodies any of which, it is assumed, may deliver commitment in response to the agreement of the rules. Dependent upon whether the undertaking is unionized or not, these two broad options may take distinct forms, as management searches for the necessary commitment of free men to the ends of the undertaking.

Supportive attitudes

Historically, management has sought to develop co-operation on unitarist principles. Originally, this relied upon communication within the usual chains of command in hierarchical organizations, and upon workers' acceptance of the legitimacy of management's authority to 'command' in this way. This was put into effect by managers and supervisors through the face-to-face communication processes of instruction, persuasion, and suggestion, backed up by an enforceable legal right. It gave rise to the idea that managers and supervisors performed a 'boundary role' between the organization and the employee.

The classical conception of organization (see Cartwright, 1965, pp 1-2) emphasizes the crucial importance of social influence emanating from 'the top' or from management to the individuals at the bottom. Only if this is efficient is the performance of the organization as a whole thought to be assured. The classical view of organizations (which we owe to Weber, 1947) has frequently been challenged in recent years, and it is now recognized that other social influences (for example, from trade unions) play a major part in influencing individual behaviour and organizational performance. But the significance of the role of the management in securing compliance with the operating rules is not thereby diminished, but merely placed in a more competitive setting.

In the classical approach, however, the managerial capacity to exert influence was seen to rest upon either the ownership or control by management of economic, political, social and personal resources which were valued by the subjects and potentially available for distribution to them by management, or the control of relevant information flows, or both. Taken together, these constitute the *power base* (see Dahl, 1957, p 203) of the would-be influencer, which has been widely recognized in the social scientific literature. But the efficiency of their operation is crucially dependent upon the existence of attitudes in those subjected to influence which are supportive to its exercise by management. It is this which makes underlying attitudes or 'frames of reference' of such importance to all processes of influence.

Supportive attitudes are always both necessary and present to some degree in organizations: without them in some measure 'organization' could not be said to exist. Any successful influence depends upon the initiator possessing the opportunity to utilize the recipient's attitudes towards, and expectations of, being influenced by him in the circumstances (see French and Raven, 1959, pp 150-67; Harsanyi, 1962, pp 67-80). It can be exemplified in the expressions that 'a manager's instructions are to be obeyed simply because he *is* a manager' or 'a worker expects to obey the instructions of his manager'. Where this condition exists, it is unnecessary for the initiator to use the other kinds of resources in order to secure compliance. The recipient is predisposed to accept the initiator's values and his instructions. Consequently, 'the superior frames and transmits decisions with the expectation that they will be accepted by the subordinate. The subordinate expects such decisions and his conduct is determined by them' (Simon, 1953, p 11; see also, Barnard, 1938, p. 163).

Because there is no open offer and acceptance of other visible resources, this power has been referred to as constituting part of

461

the 'deep structure' (see Clegg, 1975) of social organization. It is essentially a hidden resource which can be relied upon. It may still have to be created by socialization or by the constant manipulation of information, and reinforced by giving rewards for compliance, so that individual attitudes and predispositions become permanently structured in a supportive way. But it is one of the functions of law and convention, and one of the consequences of organizing relationships in accordance with these that congruent attitudes develop as people discover which approaches will 'work' for them and which will prove ineffectual.

With the growth of the scale of organizations, and the reduction in strength of the supporting attitudes, it proved desirable if not necessary, to supplement this with machinery which brought together *representatives* of the workforce and management to deal with the problems of relationships. This spawned the arrangements referred to as 'joint consultation' which allowed management to communicate with and through representatives of the labour force rather than with every individual. Its introduction was often associated with deliberately avoiding trade union involvement in managerial decision-taking. It gave, at its least, the opportunity for management to discuss problems with representatives of the workforce before reaching its own decisions about them, and at its best, involvement of the representatives in a problem-solving mode of decision-taking.

Progressively, however, with the growth of unions joint consultation has come to operate as a parallel, and often truncated, forum for discussing matters left over from bargaining with trade union representatives. Gradually, the process of consultation has been incorporated into collective bargaining at the domestic level, and the earlier distinction between the two processes has become at least blurred. When it is practised alongside negotiation in an unionized undertaking, it may also serve as a medium of communication and a facilitator of co-operation.

INFLUENCE IN ORGANIZATIONS

Passive attitudes provide the condition for the exercise of an absolute authority in which neither *exchange* nor *persuasion* is required in order to *bring about* the desired changes in thinking,
462

feeling or behaviour (although they may be important to their maintenance). It is one in which passivity and acquiescence are the dominant characteristics of the attitude of the recipient. It produces *obedience*, provided the communication of the instruction is clear.

The power base of the the initiator in this case is the control of, or the access to, the only or the main channel of communication (which, in classical organization theory, the manager is usually seen to possess). Provided that the initiator is organizationally-linked to the recipient and thus has access to the relevant channels of communication, his only 'problem' is the purely technical one of making sure that the message transmitted is clear in its meaning and capable of being interpreted correctly by the recipient. The recipient's supportive attitudes may then be relied on to produce the looked-for compliance.

The models of communication and influence are similar, however, in the central elements which are singled out as significant. The terms and forms used differ in the two models. The two are nevertheless related. There is a sense in which communication is instrumental to influence but not necessarily influencial in itself.

Communication

The model of communication (like that of influence) implies the existence of an independent communicator (or initiator) and a receiver (or recipient) which (or who) are linked together by a method or process of communication (or influence). Each of these three elements has both a technical and a human or social character which affect the outcomes in either communication or influence.

Communication can be thought about in terms of the physical aspects (the transmitter, the receiver and the channels linking them) and described in engineering, to emphasize that some part of the process is purely technical. Each of the three elements has a capacity, for transmitting, receiving or carrying messages. Successful communication requires that each has a capacity related to the requirement placed upon it. Clevenger and Mathews offer a transmission model which identifies other technical elements of information, codes and signals:

'Transmission passes a *Message* consisting of a sequence of

Symbols from source to destination in some *Code* which is appropriate to channel employed. The function of the transmitter is to *encode* the message (translate the symbols into code) and the function of the receiver is to *decode* the message (translate symbols out of code). Thus, it is the signal or the coded message which passes through the channel rather than the message itself' (Clevenger and Mathews, 1971, pp 176-77).

Although some of these terms scarcely seem relevant to communication between two human beings, there is a sense in which it is worthwhile to regard the initiator as a transmitter whose role it is to encode messages (in symbols which the recipient can understand), choose channels which are appropriate to the message and the recipient, and to monitor the decoding activities of the recipient. The human transmitter is usually trying to convey meaning through language (a kind of code) and the language is conveyed by oral expression (a channel or medium). The listener (receiver) is expected to draw meaning from the language (decode) and there are obviously occasions when he might not be able to do this (because he does not understand the symbols or language employed).

The engineer's concepts indicate something of the demand which communication makes upon the parties involved. Where the aim is no more than ensuring that communication is effective in the sense that the intended meaning is successfully transmitted to another, the initiator must ensure that the messages are appropriately constructed in the right language for the channel and the recipient and the right channels used. Both of these require attention to the recipient's capacity for receiving messages of this kind.

Technical demands of communication

The first requirement is to ensure that the intitiator is clear in his own mind about the meaning which he wishes to convey. The second is to examine the language (code) which might be used to convey it: the language which the initiator might use in one context might be too simple or too complex to convey the meaning in another. After examination, the initiator must, thirdly, choose a form of expression which will best convey the intended meaning.

Attention is then required regarding the medium or channel to be used. Some communications are better expressed in writing and some in speech: the initiator must choose that medium which he considers most appropriate to the objective. Some channels do not necessarily link to the intended recipients (a good example being the use of the shop stewards as a channel of communication to employees, which reaches only to union members) and it may on occasion be necessary to create channels to carry the messages which have to be got across. Part of the problem here is that of 'noise' in the channel, which means that the message may become distorted in some way as it passes through and different people play a part in filtering and amplifying the original message.

Whether this kind of distortion has occurred is something which can be detected by monitoring the extent to which the message as transmitted has been received at the other end. This is where face to face communication is most useful: it is comparatively easy to watch the facial expressions and listen to the comments of the recipient and draw inferences about how clearly the original message has been received. In other cases, monitoring is more likely to focus upon whether behaviour (of any kind) has been modified as intended by the message, and this is more difficult because of the variety of influences playing upon such behaviour. Nevertheless, some evaluation of the efficiency of the communication needs to be attempted in some terms.

Influence

Successful influence may occur as a result of efficient communication where it can be assumed that supportive attitudes do exist. Supportive attitudes of an absolute kind cannot always be relied upon in the normal work situation. *Some* clearly do exist for some purposes, but usually not for all. In the usual situation, existing attitudes are more likely to support the exercise of influence in either or both of two alternative modes, each of which allows more choice to the recipient than the above discussion implies.

1   Influence which involves a *manipulation of utilities* (whether material or social) in which something is offered by the intitiator and, after calculation of whether it is worth it, accepted by the recipient.
2   Influence which entails *convincing* the recipient that a

465

particular thought, emotion or behaviour is appropriate for him in the circumstances.

The first of these embraces the whole field of incentives and the second the whole subject of communications.

Influence via exchange

Manipulation of utilities, like supportive attitudes, relies upon conditions inherent in the recipient. In this case, it is his preferences or his wants which are important. The individual may want material wealth, political power, social prestige, friendship, opportunity to learn or simply to associate, and anyone else who can and will make any of these available to him could expect to have a base from which to influence him in his thinking, feeling or behaviour. Whether influence were to prove successful would, however, depend upon how strongly the individual felt the need and how relatively he valued what was potentially on offer. Putting these together, however, it is possible to derive the main bases of influence which would-be initiators can use.

The resources which have been identified as actually or potentially relevant include economic, political, social and personal resources. Their relevance will be enhanced where supportive predispositions do not already exist, but motivation to want the resources in question does. These resources are then linked to the main *methods* of influence which initiators might attempt. It is usual to identify four main methods. One of these involves the utilization of supportive attitudes, already mentioned on p 460 above. The other three, which are discussed in this section are coercion, manipulation of utilities, and persuasion.

Coercion

Coercion involves increasing or restricting the freedom or opportunity which the recipient has to think, feel and act. This is usually most graphically illustrated by reference to the imprisonment of the deviant or to the coercion of the person by a bully, but other shorter-term and less drastic restrictions such as suspension from work or reorganization of the work group may be found in ordinary work-life. In both of these cases, the intervention is made on the assumption that the intervenor has the power to overcome any resitance that the recipient might offer, and therefore that the initiator occupies (and therefore *owns*) a position within a structure of positions and roles, which in addition to giving access to means of influence, permits the promotion or the physical restriction of the recipient. This gives the occupant power to use what Simmel (1955) has called 'naked force' to bring about change, even if it is used in a hidden or a socially-sanctioned way.

This mechanism tends to be disapproved for all but the correction of severely deviant social behaviour. It is usually both protected and constrained by the operation of norms and rules. In its more obviously restrictive form it is seen to be close to a form of slavery. In its less obvious form of restricting people to work stations for long periods of time, it still occurs, but has certainly become less prevalent in the past half century as social conventions have changed.

Manipulation of utilities

This involves manipulation of the material and social rewards and penalties which are offered to the recipient of influence to reward conformity and compliance. This process is commonly illustrated by references to industrial incentive systems and the application of penalties which deny the worker the opportunity to secure benefits. However, there are many other benefits (and costs) than those which fall into the economic category. The offer or denial of esteem, prestige, recognition, and the like might equally fall into this area. This has often been described as a democratic method of intervention because it allows the recipient to make up his own mind as to whether 'it is worth it' to comply; he can exercise choice.

The initiator requires bases which are appropriate to this mechanism and to the form of exchange involved in it. It is usual to distinguish three which cover the main types of exchange transaction.

(a) Possession of wealth (material resources) as a power resource is necessary for the manipulation of material rewards. This aspect has been emphasised in many widely different treatments of the subject. It underlies the observation by Adam Smith that the employer can wait longer than the worker to establish an employment contract, simply because the former has more wealth on which he can live through the interval. It underlies the observations of Marx about the exploitative dependency relationship in which workers are forced to subsist in a capitalist system. It enables compliance, or conformity, to be bought where there is motivation in the recipient to acquire this resource. More recently writers have suggested the substitution of control of wealth as an equally valid resource (see Berle and Means, 1933; Berle, 1960; Russell, 1938).

(b) Possession of, or control over, networks of power or prestige relations, through which the initiator might (by a successful exercise of influence on his part) secure social acceptance, prestige, power, or something comparable for the recipient. This is very similar to the resource of supportive attitudes but it does depend upon successful manipulation of the network by the initiator and perception by the recipient of the probability that the initiator can mediate these kinds of rewards because of both his position and his skill in utilizing it.

(c) Possession of personal traits or attributes regardless of the role he occupies or the economic resources to which he has access, may also provide the initiator with a power base. As Cartwright points out, little systematic research has been carried out on this aspect, but he quotes some of the research carried out by Gold (1958) amongst schoolchildren to ascertain what personal attributes they found valuable in others to suggest that some such personal resources might be expected to prove useful in influence exercises where the recipient valued the opportunity to identify or associate with persons with these attributes (see, Cartwright, 1965, p 6).

These external or 'objective' factors can thus, in the possession or control of the initiator, serve to facilitate influence in so far as they are valued and desired by the recipients. It is important that something different is exchanged between the would-be influencer and the recipient in each case. In this sense the processes involved in the attempt to influence are more open and visible than in the case of reliance upon supportive attitudes. But they necessarily depend upon the would-be influencer being in possession or control of the kinds of resources which have been identified and the recipient being without either.

Where the recipient is a worker, however, this assumption cannot hold absolutely. The worker is possessed of his labour, or his labour power, and this being valuable to and valued by the potential employer, provides him with his 'material resource' which he can exchange. 'Bargaining' becomes possible over the terms of the exchange of the labour service for valuable consideration. The contribution of this material resource to the worker's power to influence the employer as to these terms is, however, vitally affected by the opportunity which the employer has to substitute an alternative labour service for it. Unless the employer wants that particular unit of labour (because of its particular skill or capacity or because there is no substitute for it available to the employer) its contribution of 'bargaining power' to the individual may be extremely limited. Because each has something which the other wants to offer in exchange, there is a basis for bargaining over terms. In this fashion, attempts to secure influence on the basis of exchange turns into a process of negotiation between persons. (We return to this question below in the context of negotiation.)

Persuasion

The third main category of influence mechanism is that which involves the management or manipulation of symbols which convey meaning to the recipient and which aim to secure the other's conviction of the rightness of what is being proposed. Its intended effect is to modify the knowledge and understanding, beliefs and feelings or accepted courses of action of the recipient by making information available only in certain ways and in certain amounts. Both the content of the message and the form of its presentation become important sources of influence in themselves.

The central element in this process is the management or manipulation of information to secure conviction by persuasion or suggestion (or something similar) rather than by reliance upon appropriate attitudes or the manipulation of utilities. As Simon has well argued many years ago, this produces a very different ethical approach to securing compliance within structures of authority.

'The verbs 'persuade', 'suggest', etc., describe several kinds of influence which do not necessarily involve any relationship of authority ... A person who receives a suggestion accepts it as only one of the evidential bases for making his choice -- but the choice he will make depends upon conviction. Persuasion too centres around the reasons for and against a course of action. Persuasion and suggestion result in a change in the evidential environment of choice, which may, but need not, lead to conviction. Obedience, on the other hand, is an abdication of choice' (Simon, 1953, pp 126-27).

Essentially, what is attempted here is the persuasion of the recipient that it is right, or in his own best interests, to accept what is being urged by the initiator. If the recipient accepts, he does so from conviction.

This need not, however, imply that the initator is now providing *all* information which might conceivably be relevant to the process of convincing the other. In fact, it is much more likely that conviction will be secured by disseminating *selected* information and withholding some of it. Nor it is unlikely that this process of convincing will remain unsupported by other devices will are adopted to convey meaning in a more manipulative (or less open) fashion. Etzioni, for example, has suggested that this method of influence is usually supported by:

(a) The management or manipulation of *symbols* which convey meanings in themselves. This can be done by placing influence attempts in the hands of those with titles like expert, manager or shop steward. The quality of being expert and the connotations of the titles enable them to exert influence more successfully than would be possible if these designations were not involved.

(b) The management or manipulation of *ritual*, where the arrangements themselves (as is the case with collective bargaining, for example) carry their own meanings and come to have their own influence on behaviours regardless of what the individual actors may transmit or receive within them.

Conviction is thus likely to be effected by what is made available and by the manner in which it is made available (see Etzioni, 1975, p 5).

This brings us back to a consideration of the role of communication in the influence process but with the emphasis now placed much more firmly on the social aspects rather than

470

the purely technical ones. Any potential initiator must either possess or have access to the information necessary and command access to the channels of communication which will allow that information (or the symbols) to be transmitted in appropriate form. But now a place has to be found in the model (of communication) for the factor of power in its social meaning. The usual phrase which illuminates this base is the one that 'information is power', but the hidden element in this is that it becomes a power base only or mainly where the possessor is able to control its transmission to suit the intention of any influence attempt.

Where the recipient possesses or has access to alternative sources of information, this means of influence must change into a process of negotiation. The initiator's informational power base is reduced by the existence of an alternative source available to the recipient. This situation obtains once workers have unionized and can use their union as an alternative source of information.

Constraints on the choice of means

These various means of influence are not, however, equally available and open to the employer or management to use within organizational settings. We have already noted that the use of 'naked force' is unapproved, as is the more clandestine (or 'manipulative') use of any of the other mechanisms. There are also some legal requirements in respect of disclosure of various kinds of information for various purposes. These are supplemented by social conventions which carry some degree of disapproval. Although, as Cartwright says, 'little research has been directed to ascertaining the nature of the determinants of choice of means' (Cartwright, 1965, p 21) a number of constraints can be identified.

The initiator is, typically, as subject to the same kinds of social and environmental pressures as anyone else. Consequently, he might be expected to be restricted to some extent and in some combination, by the pressures of tradition (or custom), and by the sanctions which uphold the conventions and the laws. In addition, he is likely to have his own way of reading the situation and of determining what a right-minded, or rationally-thinking, person might properly do in those circumstances.

Choice of means is therefore likely to be constrained by the general theory of human nature which he accepts, which may be varied by consideration of the positions which he and the recipient hold within the social structure. If he believes that workers are motivated only by money, for example, he might be predisposed to use a method which entails offering the kinds of material incentives which he considers the individual will respond to. He might, however, consider that this would prove less efficacious if it were to be used as a basis for influencing a manager or a professional person. His reading of the nature of the attitudes which the recipients hold in relation to forms of influence is also likely to influence the kind of apporach which he makes. Regardless of whether these views are in any sense 'right', they might be expected to influence the choices made.

Choice is also likely to be influenced by the intitiator's ethical evaluation of the means available and this might be augmented by an evaluation against the requirements of the law (see, Cartwright, 1965, p 21). There are codes of ethics which are enshrined in conventions and in law which the individual might well subscribe to as his own, and use in making a choice. The general convention which disapproves of the use of naked force or the restriction of the individual's personal freedom, leads many managers to look for more approved means of influence; the particular conventions that support 'collective bargaining' as a means of deciding on the distribution of the product of industry leads many managements to accept that their influence on these issues must be exercized in association with workers' representatives.

In addition, choice of the means of influence is likely to be constrained for more technical or pragmatic reasons. The means have different technical capacities and capabilities and may be selected or rejected on these grounds alone. The choice of means may respond to the theories which individuals hold about their sheer efficiency and about their short and long run costs. This focuses on the more technical aspects, such as the most effective means to use for different purposes, and the cost which it is considered worth incurring in order to effect influence. All individuals hold some theories which enable them to predict these, but such theories are often built into undertaking policies to guide subordinates in making their choices.

Choices are also affected by the environmental conditions in which they are to be exercised, and particularly so where these conditions affect the nature and strength of the objectives (or demands) of the persons or parties concerned and therefore their perceived capacity to offer or resist particular attempts at influence. The initiators' and recipients' relative indispensibility either within the *market* or within the *organization* will affect the cost-benefit ratio and thus limit the opportunities to choose different means. This alters the relative capacity of recipients to disagree or to resist and affects the potential efficacy of any particular means. For example, a shortage of employment will tend to lower the cost of securing compliance and a shortage of labour will tend to have the opposite effect. This may occur generally.

> 'Group bargaining strength is high in periods of full employment when almost all grades of labour are scarce, as is shown by the high level of work group activity in both world wars and in the years since the second world war' (Clegg, 1972, pp 30-1; see also, Cole, 1923; Donovan Commission Report, 1968; and Lupton, 1963).

It may also occur in more limited contexts, where, for example, particular skills are in short supply or the skills of the long service employee are difficult to substitute because of the length of time needed for familiarization.

The unionization of the employees may also increase the workers' capacity to resist influence of this kind. This may arise because the union places an embargo on certain means of influence (for example, the resistance to the management's direct communication with their employees on 'union matters'). It may also arise because the presence of the union as a bargaining agent may make it impolitic to operate in a way which might be considered desirable in its absence (for example, in respect of disclosure of information).

COMPETITIVE INFLUENCE

Since the choice of means and their efficiency appear so closely related to the capacity of the intended recipients to resist influence, the extent to which they can increase that capacity is clearly a relevant factor in any attempt at influence, even within the context of the assumedly-unitary organization. As we have already noted, this capacity to resist can be increased by workers when they unionize and effectively substitute the strength of the collectivity for the weakness of the competing individuals. *A fortiori*, the workers' capacity to influence the employer, through the mechanism of collective bargaining or negotiation, requires not only the solidarity of combination to change the market position, but solidarity of purpose to provide a power base in negotiation of treaties of co-operation with the employer.

A propensity to reduce competition amongst either buyers or sellers is to be found amongst both businessmen and workers. It is perhaps not to be regarded as unnatural, aberrational or surprising behaviour on the part of either category. Competition, except perhaps in the purest of pure forms, is likely to contribute to the uncertainty within which the individual has to take his decisions, and consequently denies him control of his activities. Restraint of competition and its effects is therefore likely to decrease it, and make the outcomes of decisions more predictable, although by no means certain. A propensity which businessmen and employers on the one hand, and employees on the other, display may be no more than a natural or human propensity to reduce uncertainty by aggregating power to cope with the antithetical interests ranged against them.

The major difference is, however, that the worker is usually seen as disadvantaged *without* association. The employer (if not always the businessman) is commonly seen as having a favourable balance of advantage in bargaining with labour even without further association beyond that which is implied in the concepts of partnership or company. The employer who progresses towards monopsony in the labour market, whether by simple business amalgamation or growth or by becoming a solidarist member of an employers' association, is then seen as either securing an additional advantage or as restoring an advantage which might have been reduced (by, for example, association of workers into a trade union). Association is a necessity for the workers, an advantage for the small employer, but of more marginal benefit to the large one.

There is, however, nothing automatic about the development of a propensity or a will to combine in this way. The growth of what the radical frequently refers to as 'consciousness' is a necessary preliminary, and is the equivalent in this context of the development of the attitudes supportive of unilateral influence within organizations (which we noted above, pp 78-79). Without such a development, there is no more likely to be a development of 'collective bargaining' than there is likely to be

474

support for managerial influence in the other case unless there are attitudes which support it.

Purposes of combination

For the worker, the act of combining has two main purposes. The first is to secure control of competition between workers in order to provide the collectivity with a power base. This rests on the possibility that the solidarist collectivity may represent itself as owning or controlling labour services 'in bulk' (even if the union is not to be regarded as a cartel which buys and sells labour) (see pp 315-22). This is brought about largely by securing control over entry into employment, and by establishing a union 'jurisdiction' over certain jobs. This expedient is intended to operate in one or both of two ways:

(a) Rules may be adopted within the association and pressed upon the employer with the intention of restricting the entry to the occupational group, as in the regulation of the ratio of apprentices to journeymen or the control of entry upon professional training. The aim here is to create for the group within the occupation, a degree of scarcity which would otherwise not obtain, in order to affect bargaining power.

(b) Rules may be adopted and pressed upon other workers' associations, with the intention of denying the employer the right to substitute (whether in the guise of 'imported blacklegs' or staff take-over of the work normally carried out by workers). This manifests itself in two ways. On the one hand, it may simply be against the work groups or the trade union's principles to accept such substitutes, so that where its writ runs, substitutability is decreased. On the other, any given work group or union may secure a much broader writ than its own organization could secure by making alliances (temporary or permanent) with other work groups or employee associations (see, Batstone, Boraston and Frenkel, 1978, pp 28-9; Boraston, Clegg and Rimmer, 1975, p 178-86).

Persuasion by representatives within the workplace and by pickets in a dispute situation can be employed to decrease the possibility of other labour being brought in in substitution for a particular work group or union membership. By persuading others to take or to support some form of industrial action in support of a grievance, a particular group may, temporarily at least, reduce its substitutability and increase its 'power' to disrupt the flow of production (see Batstone, Boraston and Frenkel, 1978, pp 29-30).

Collective bargaining or negotiation is a second aim which tends to follow on from the realization of the first one. As a means of influencing those decisions which are less susceptible to the control of market forces, this still depends on the same solidarity to provides the *power* base for influencing the employer in his labour policies and practices. Once the solidarist base is established, the union will pressure for, and (in the large-scale organization) usually secure, recognition for negotiation purposes. This provides the workers with access to a channel through which to exert influence on the operating decisions of the employer as these affect labour. Given the attempt to impose union rules upon the work situation, the employer may also be predisposed to enter into a bargaining relationship, in order to influence their application.

Influence based on exchange

Once the workers have secured organization and recognition, they have the power and the access to channels which allow them to attempt to influence the employer. Organized workers will generally seek to defend their different interests and objectives either by imposition of their rules or in 'negotiations' with the employer. To the extent that their power base (see above, p 315) is associated with exchangeable resources, these will properly be described as 'bargaining' activities; to the extent that they move beyond this and seek to bring about changes of thinking, feeling and conduct on the part of the employer, they might be more pertinently described as 'negotiations'.

The technical means by which 'workers' in general or trade unions in particular, may employ to do this may be the same as those open to management. They may not be able to count on congruent attitudes (except perhaps after a long period of joint negotiations) but they can use means based on *exchange* (withdrawal of labour to restrict the other, offer of continued co-operation in production to 'reward' the other) and they can seek to *persuade* the other in negotiations to adopt alternative policies and practices. The major difference is that both the

476

employer and the employee representatives must now attempt to influence the other (by whatever means) against his wishes; there is a necessary conflict of interest which expresses itself in bargaining or negotiation.

Bargaining may be described as the process through which differences between the parties are resolved and a basis for continuing co-operation between the parties found in discussion and argument which in turn rests upon the potential exchange of resources in the possession of each party (see Blau, 1964). It follows, therefore, that the parties must each possess some material or symbolic resources, (although not necessarily of the same kind) which they can exchange (see Morley and Stephenson, 1977, p. 259). Rubin and Brown outline the nature of this process in their seven requirements that:

(a) at least two parties (who may be defined as persons or as roles and in the singular or the plural) are involved (Rubin and Brown, 1975, p 6)

(b) the parties have a conflict of interest with respect to one or more different issues (*ibid*) although their attitudes towards each other must exhibit some convergence as well as divergence in order to sustain the interaction

(c) the parties come together voluntarily for the purpose of bargaining or an exchange of resources which they possess, regardless of how long they may have operated in a similar relationship in the past (*ibid*, p 7)

(d) the parties must receive some outcome from the exchange, and that outcome must be interdependent with other possible outcomes, particularly with those available to the other party

(e) the outcome might concern an exchange of something or a resolution of some issue with differential consequences for the parties. As Rubin and Brown put this: 'activity in the relationship concerns (a) the division or exchange of one or more specific resources, and/or (b) the resolution of one or more intangible issues among the parties or among those whom they represent' (*ibid* p 10)

(f) the process must typically involve the presentation of some demand or proposal by one party, the evaluation of that demand by the other(s), and the presentation by the other of some counter-claim or offer. In this sequential process, the response of the other is always partly determined on the basis of the first party's earlier behaviour in the sequence (*ibid*, p 14).

These amount to a description of a process which is based on potential exchange. What the parties have to offer each other, may in one sense remain the same as before, but what is emphasized in the context of collective bargaining is the development of control of the power base through which a kind of coercion can be used to bring the other to agreement. For this reason bargaining, and particularly collective bargaining, is primarily concerned with increasing control over such power bases as lie to hand, either by combination or by strategic utilization of position (or status) (see Bacharach and Lawler, 1981).

Increasing power

Power to exercise control is increased to the extent that individuals can reduce their substitutability or increase their indispensibility to the other party to any exchange or mutual influence activity. This end may be brought about fortuitously by the operation of 'factors outside the control of the individual' or by deliberate decision (as in the case of unionization).

The first set of causes are associated with the market condition in which the individual may find himself (and by extension, in which union negotiators may discover that their members find themselves). A shortage of a particular skill is likely to increase the value of the individual possessing it to any employer and thus increase his opportunity to resist. This may develop for the individual who has been employed in a particular establishment for so long that he has skills which are peculiar to that establishment but difficult to substitute from outside. This illustrates the hypothesis advanced by Mechanic, to the effect that 'other factors remaining constant, a person difficult to replace will have greater power than a person easily replaceable' (1962, p 352). This may be applied to substitutability as it applies within a labour market (see Hill, 1981).

The employer may adopt policies which will increase the substitutability of workers and so reduce their power. He can do this by, for example:

(a) substituting capital for labour where this is technically and economically possible, and where the consequences of so doing may be calculated to avoid delivering the employer into the hands of a non-substitutable group of workers

(b) deskilling the work which he requires to be performed, in an attempt to make the 'pool of labour' available to perform it larger than it would otherwise be, were he to continue to rely upon highly skilled groups (see Blackler and Brown, 1978).

Either might be calculated to increase potential substitutability of the employed labour force, and thus affect the relative bargaining power.

The union may reduce substitutability by the devices discussed on page 475 above although these do not amount to direct counter-strategies to those adopted by the employer.

Internal power sources

Substitutability also has an intra-organizational connotation. For example, Dubin has commented that 'for any given level of functional importance in an organization, the power residing in a functionary is inversely proportional to the number of other functionaries in the organization capable of performing the function' (1963, p 20). This is usually seen to explain and, possibly, justify the higher rewards accruing to those with longer investment in skill training. 'Generally speaking, the more skilled the worker, the greater difficulty in replacing him' (Clegg, 1972, p 31), becomes a generalization which indicates that other things being equal skill will be associated with greater difficulties of substitution and therefore with relatively higher rewards.

It also illustrates the importance of the location of the worker in a work flow sequence for assuming countervailing power. This may depend upon the ability of the individual or group to create or absorb uncertainty for others in the production process (Crozier 1964; pp 108-9 and 145-74). Whether the individual can assume this power depends in turn upon the division of labour in modern organizations (which is itself a decision taken by the employer at some stage in their development). The consequences of role performance are central to the issue (see Hickson et al., 1971).

This is because taking on *any* role in an interdependent set of roles, does not leave others unaffected, but the extent of the effect may be variable across a wide range. Maintenance workers

(Batstone, Boraston and Frankel, 1978, p 31; Dalton, 1959, pp 31-52) are frequently singled out to illustrate the manner in which one group of workers may have a particular influence upon the uncertainty experienced both by themselves and others by virtue of their concern to repair (make certain again) machines which have broken down (causing uncertainty) (see also Crozier, 1964, pp 145-74).

Individual differences might account for some of the variation. Workers adjacent to one another in a work sequence may, by working faster or slower, produce gluts and shortages which increase the uncertainties of the other group. Those falling early in a sequence may produce effects which ramify a long way through it. Dependent upon storage possibilities, those late in the sequence may produce effects which work backwards through the system. Sayles indicates the manner in which this operates.

> 'Therefore, when the group just ahead in the sequence lays down its tools, all the preceding operation must stop. There is no place for the completed work to go. There are similar production stages in the non-assembly-line manufacturing processes. Lacking any adequate bank of materials with which to work, other areas close down almost simultaneously with these bottle-neck operations' (Sayles, 1958, pp 61-62).

For similar reasons the perishability of the product may enhance bargaining power:

> 'If a colliery is stopped for a day or two the loss of output can probably be made good during the next few days. If an air-line is stopped for a day or so its passengers turn elsewhere. ... A stevedoring company in the docks may lose relatively little through a strike, for it saves the wages which are its major cost, but the shipper with a perishable cargo may bring pressure to bear for a quick settlement in a dock dispute and thus reinforce the bargaining strength of the dockers' (Clegg, 1972, p 32).

Even the relatively unskilled grades can exercise considerable bargaining strength when they occupy 'a strategic position in the production process from which they can quickly bring a whole department or a whole factory to a standstill' (Clegg, 1972, p 32).

480

Power and breach of rules

The most significant source of power is, however, the opportunity which the workers have to keep to, or to break, the rules which apply and to do so with relative impunity. What either of these imports for the others in the system then constitutes a resource which can be made available or withheld in order to support any attempt at influence (see Hill, 1974). Where the workers cannot avoid the penalty, however, the cost-benefit calculation would probably lead to abandonment of the attempt, so that the 'strength of the union' is a necessary means of avoiding such an impasse.

Breach of the employer's rules, or of the expectations which people more generally might have of the people in the role, has frequently been noted.

> By conforming to rules, any one group reduces the level of uncertainty for others, but if the rules are not conformed to, then the degree of uncertainty increases' Batstone, Boraston and Frenkel 1978, p 31.

Disconformity to rules may take many forms (for example, from colluding in applying the tricks of the trade in spite of the formal rules, to working to rule, going slow or going on strike in the other). It is not, however, necessary that workers should actually break the rules because it may be sufficient that the potential for disruption and increase in uncertainty is there and can be used as a threat. As Batsone, Boraston and Frenkel comment on the collusion to break formal rules in the interests of speedier work:

> 'Managers are often ready to pay extra allowances either in recognition of such co-operation or in order to ensure that its removal is not used as a sanction' (Batstone, Boraston and Frenkel, 1978, pp 31-32).

These authors also recognize, however, that the power of work groups deriving from this source may be reducd or overturned:

> 'because some groups are important in the production process, it is possible for management to stir them to strike action to avoid having to pay those laid off when breakdowns occur, markets slump, or supplies run short. Power deriving from an important position in the production process may be turned against the group itself' (Batstone, Boraston and Frenkel, 1978, p 31).

As a creation of management, group working can be destroyed by management. Management has the power to introduce new technology or new methods of working which might reduce the potential of the work group to disrupt. The same processes of substituting capital for labour (where the labour is expensive enough) and of deskilling work to increase the supply of capability, apply here as in the other case.

This is to use capacity for both co-operation and disruption as a power base in influence based upon exchange. Instead of resting the exchange upon the basis of labour for wage (or wage for work) it is made to turn upon offer and acceptance of co-operation (and the avoidance of disruption). In this manner, not only action, but threat of action, becomes a factor which can be used strategically to coerce the other into agreement with one's own terms.

Negotiation as mutual persuasion

Once the parties recognize one another for purposes of negotiation, however, they also place themselves in the position where they will seek to 'persuade' the other. This is directed, not merely to the terms of the agreement, but also to securing acceptance of definitions of the situation and the value and validity of different ways of dealing with that situation. In other words, the conflict between the parties is verbalized rather than expressed in conflictual actions, but this verbalization involves a conflictual aspect which is best exemplified in the concepts of bluff and threat, the one related to definitions of situation and the other to possible actions.

This verbalizing activity implies that issues between the parties are resolved by exchanging influential information and argument, rather than missiles of a more tangible type. The parties seek to present information in ways beneficial to their several causes, and to marshall persuasive arguments. Inevitably, they do this in a competitive situation. Even within structures of authority, it is difficult for an initiator to secure a monopoly of information and, more crucially, of meanings which can be associated with it. The development of the trade union, and of trade union consciousness amongst workers, vitally affects this process, partly for the reason that more information becomes available and partly because alternative power bases can be used by the workers' representatives in their attempts at persuading

482

the employer to a course of action (see also pp 473-77).

In individual negotiation, the interaction might be seen to be based upon attempts by two persons of roughly equal capacity and ability to *persuade* each other as to the rightness of a conclusion, an attitude or a course of action. Each would rely upon his 'persuasive powers' to bring about his preferred end against the wishes of the other. Although we might assume that each is equal to the other in his possession of these powers, it is most unlikely that they would be exactly so, if only because of the existence of 'individual differences' (see, Anastasi, 1965). The assumption of an exchange based upon equality could provide a useful starting point for analysis, but it is unlikely to prove very realistic in any social context and more certainly not in the context of bargaining over pay.

Collective bargaining (or negotiation) also involves attempts at 'persuasion' by the union representatives as well as by the employer's representatives, but they are now based on a different foundation of relative power. The requirement for *collective* bargaining is met where the workers in particular are represented by their association officers in the negotiation process. It may also be the case that the employer is also represented through his employers' association but this need not be so. But where the individual employer is a corporation, he (or it) will be represented through agents in the form of designated managers, in a way in which the individual worker could not be represented *unless* through his union (see above, pp 114-18). In both cases individuals with a representative and power base greater than their own confront one another in the negotiating arena.

Representation of an interest group changes the *power* base on which the negotiators rely to get their way. The individual acting for himself can command only his own skill and resources; the representative individual acting for an interest group can command the power resources of the group in addition to his own power and skills. It is this which adds the new dimension to collective bargaining over individual bargaining, even if they both remain essentially interactive processes, based on interpersonal communication undertaken with the object of influencing the other by persuasion.

Alternative strategies

The underlying attitudes of the parties can, however, be regarded as predisposing the parties to negotiation in one or other of two distinct modes. Where the attitudes are supportive of a co-operative approach to resolving differences, the basic strategy of negotiation might emphasize a joint approach to problem-solving, or what Walton and McKersie identify as 'integrative bargaining' (using the adjective first advanced by Mary Parker Follett (see Pruitt, 1981, p 137). Where they emphasize a conflictual approach, the mode of resolution adopted is more likely to be that of 'distributive bargaining' (Walton and McKersie, 1965) or 'conjunctive bargaining' (Chamberlain and Kuhn, 1967).

Walton and Mckersie define integrative bargaining as one form of joint decision-making concerned with problem solving, and in more detail, as:

> 'the system of activities which is instrumental to the attainment of objectives which are *not* in fundamental conflict with those of the other party and which therefore can be integrated to some degree' (Walton and McKersie, 1965, p 5)

In integrative bargaining, the purpose is likely to be the solution of some *problem* which will enhance the advantage of the two parties together, leaving some room for manoeuvre as to just how the advantage is to be distributed between them. Skills will be used to try to secure an advantage over the environment in association with the other rather than over the other party.

Distributive bargaining, on the other hand, is a distinct form of joint decision-making which is concerned with the resolution of issues of difference and disagreement between the parties, and as:

> 'the system of activities instrumental to the attainment of one party's goals when they are in basic conflict with those of the other party'. (Walton and McKersie, 1965, p 4)

Both of these are 'hypothetical constructs' and, as experience with productivity bargaining indicates, they may not be discreet forms, but approaches which succeed or interchange with one another during a sequence of negotiation.

The distinction between these two kinds of bargaining may also be made by recognizing that they simply refer to bargaining over the two sides of the wage-effort bargain. But even if this is accepted, it does little more than suggest that the employer's interest in securing increased contribution (or effort) in return for

484

the consideration is likely to lead him to seek to develop an integrative approach whilst the trade union usually has an interest in the alternative because of the significance of distribution amongst its purposes. However, given the conventions of bargaining as these have grown over the years of national bargaining, it is possible to argue that for management to move in this direction in local negotiations, it will find itself having to share power or control as a prerequisite.

Problems versus issues

Integrative bargaining is found in situations in which the parties are willing to regard a difference between them as a problem, and proceed to a possible agreement on the manner in which it might be solved. This relies upon a distinction between problems and problem-solving on the one hand and issues and issue-resolution on the other. The one is associated with integrative bargaining and the latter with distributive bargaining.

Walton and McKersie define 'issues' as those differences between the parties which focus upon a fixed total amount of value being available to them and which stimulate disagreements as to the manner in which the value is divided between them. Distributive bargaining is then defined as the process by which the parties seek to influence the amount of value which accrues to each (Walton and McKersie, 1965, p 13).

They define 'problems' as those matters on which there can be a difference of view as to what ought to be done, but which focus on the probability of an increase in the total amount of value which might become available to the two parties jointly, if they succeed in handling the matter effectively. Integrative bargaining is the process by which the attempt is made to maximize the value available, without prejudice to the manner in which subsequently, the parties might negotiate to distribute it.

The two processes, therefore, rest upon a difference between a zero-sum (where the gains of one cancel the losses of the other) or a fixed-sum (the two must share what exists) game and a variable-sum game (where the total sum may be varied in the negotiation to give both some possible gains). The variable sum game of integrative bargaining is regarded as requiring different strategic behaviours from the zero-sum game.

Summary: influence

Influence occurs all the time in organizations as people seek to cope with both the physical environment and with one another. Influence processes may take a number of very different forms, dependent upon the would-be influencer's power base and the frame of reference he adopts with respect to the process. Assumptions about the legitimacy of unilateral influence based on physical coercion, manipulation of utilities, or selective disclosure of information, could lead to a generally manipulative and one-sided approach to influence. Assumptions about the legitimacy of mutual influence based on more open exchanges of either symbolic or material resources, could lead to generally more 'rational' and open approaches.

Influence processes may be seen to depend upon a nested set of processes, beginning with those of communication, and moving through those of persuasion and terminating with those processes which depend upon a coercion of an informational, utilitarian, or physical kind. In the context of negotiation, where the principals and the negotiators have different positions and interests to defend and advance, all the elements of the processes are brought together.

The parties will be called upon to exercise social or interactional skills, but these will rest upon some underlying power base, from which compulsion of the other can be generated. They will exercise these skills, not in a casual way, as in ordinary chat, but in a way which can be described as 'strategic', that is done deliberately and with a purpose related to the wider enterprise.

This suggests that negotiation is defined by reference to the parties, the perspectives and objectives which they hold, and the manner of proceeding in the resolution of differences which they regard as legitimate in the context of all the social norms which impinge on this process. Whether the parties will be prepared to regard the inevitable differences between them as problems (to be solved) or as issues (to be diputed over and resolved by a coordination of relative power) then becomes a crucial question to be answered before consideration can be given to the issue of what strategic behaviours are appropriate. This implies that what is crucial to bargaining or negotiation is either the set of attitudes which the two parties hold or the capacity of each to secure power to give sufficient control over the options which the other party might consider he has in the mutual influence process.

Readings

Cartwright, in March: (1965), pp 1-47.
Walton and McKersie: (1965), pp 11-57; and pp 184-209.
Anthony: (1977), pp 53-63.
Clegg: (1979), pp 251-57.
Bacharach and Lawler: (1981).

18

Joint consultation and co-operative bargaining

Assumptions and strategies

The parties in negotiation face the choice of a number of strategies which they might adopt to guide their interaction. These, in their turn are likely to respond to the assumptions which they make about the capacity of the 'system', as they perceive it, to yield outcomes of the kind which they seek. These take into account both the physical and the social elements of that system, but they may be thought of as crystallized in attitudes, ideologies or frames of reference which are brought to bear in the strategic decision-making process.

The frames of reference which both management and workers bring to the situation thus mediate between the perceived environment and the mode of securing co-operation which will be adopted. The managerial ideologies are likely to influence which mode will be *attempted*, and the worker/trade union ones which will be *accepted*. In either case, the frame of reference adopted may be derived directly from an ideology or from a more empirical construction of the reality or 'reading of the situation'. Thus management might simply 'believe' that a unitarist approach is desirable in a moral sense, or it might 'construe' the situation to be such that workers possess attitudes and frames of reference which would uphold such an approach. Workers may believe in the inevitable opposition of the interests of workers and managers, or they might see reasons for co-operation in their immediate situation.

Thus, where workers either possess views of the world which fit one of the first three categories in table 14 (on p 258) or are thought by management to do so, the kind of strategy which might be adopted to secure co-operation is one which reflects a unitary frame of reference and emphasizes some kind of 'team' approach. Where the reality or the perspective taken of it fits more readily the more dichotomous and conflict-oriented images of that same table, the strategy is likely to reflect a pluralist approach.

As approaches and actions become institutionalized within organizations, it becomes feasible to suggest that the institutions and supporting norms will reflect such underlying predispositions as these. Action in accordance with a unitarist frame of reference has tended to spawn joint production or joint consultative structures through which management is enabled to deal with representatives of the workforce whilst retaining power to decide and workers give their consent and commitment after a more open communication of the 'facts' material to the decisions.

Action in accordance with a pluralist frame has been more conducive to the development of a relationship of negotiation with independently-established representatives of a unionized workforce. Where this is acceptable to workers or their trade unions (see pp 292-96) the power to decide, if not transferred to a joint (negotiating) body, is at least subject to challenge by the workers' representatives. Commitment then hinges upon the principle that decisions made by agreement are more likely to be accepted as morally-binding rules upon those who agree.

For the purposes of this discussion of the processes of negotiation, two distinct situations may be considered. In the one, the assumption can be made that the attitudes of the people involved are such as to sustain the exercise of the managerial prerogative to decide issues of status. In the other, the relevant assumption is that the people involved hold attitudes which predispose them to challenge that prerogative in order to secure joint participation in the decisions about relative status. The first may be considered under the heading of joint consultation. The second will be considered separately in the following chapter, but in the present one, we look further at the development of integrative bargaining as a kind of composite of the two.

Both approaches try to preserve or re-establish management's prerogative to manage. They seek either to prevent the development of an outright conflictual bargaining approach, or to return the parties to a co-operative bargaining relationship. They must necessarily involve the maintenance or development of attitudes and frames of reference which support the approach in which differences to be resolved are treated as 'problems' not as issues. The approach adopted is therefore essentially a 'problem-solving' one.

JOINT CONSULTATION

The first managerial strategy which management might adopt to improve commitment and compliance in complex organizations is that which entails supplementing the ordinary 'channels of command' by some joint consultative arrangement, which provides additional channels usually involving representatives (although some joint consultative arrangements do embrace *all* employees). This is to emphasize the need to secure additional 'channels of communication' but to assume that the existing power distribution is capable of sustaining any move to secure greater commitment (see Banks, 1963).

The extension of this concept into joint production and other 'joint' problem-solving arrangements goes beyond this mere duplication of channels. It changes the relative status of the parties, at least to the extent that it admits as relevant the views and theories which the non-managers may have about the courses of future action to adopt. In this context, the workers are accorded some 'right' to suggest, even if the right of ultimate decision remains with the management (see Hawes and Brookes, 1980, p 353). In principle, this extension allows the worker representatives, if not the workers themselves, to feel a greater sense of ownership in the ideas for action which are adopted. The theory behind this is that if work people are involved in problem-solving processes with the management, then what appeared as barriers to communications previously are reduced with consequential and predictable improvements in their contribution to the management objectives (for example, in productivity).

As the term, 'joint consultation' is used in Britain, it may be defined as a formal arrangement accepted by management and workers through whose medium the two parties identified can converse purposefully with one another about matters of common interest. In more simple terms, it can be said that joint consultation is a contrivance to enable management and workers in relatively large and depersonalized work situations to talk to one another about matters of common interest.

Joint consultation has usually taken one of two different styles. It has been used either as a supplementary mechanism for communicating information and managerial inferences from it to the workforce, in order that they might then become better 'informed' about the position and problems of the undertaking,

490

or as a mechanism for jointly solving problems of performance within the undertaking.

Joint consultation is founded on the assumption that effective communication by management of the facts known to them (by virtue of their position) will yield consent to management's policies and rules. The exercise becomes essentially one of communication, albeit through representatives, to the workforce as a whole. The message of the Harwood Corporation case study (see Coch and French, 1948), however, seems to be that involvement, to work effectively, must encompass all involved. The message most often received by management has usually been other than this. The constraints of time and money (presumably) in following this out has led management to try to solve the problems by involving workers on a representative basis rather than as a whole, and this may be one source of problems.

Joint consultation also follows the basic principles of the influence process (see pp 462-71) and attempts to apply them on a scale greater than that of direct face-to-face interaction, associated with the supervisory role. In fact, it establishes a separate channel of communication between agents and representatives (in supplementation of the usual channels) usually to deal with the communications problems of scale or social distance. But it usually confronts the problem of communication between representatives and their constituents. A good deal of effort is therefore devoted to attempt to ensure that the representatives can and do act as true representatives, communicating on appropriate matters to their constituents (see Jaques, 1951, pp 129-35). Where the workforce is organized into trade unions, the union's 'domestic organization' is concerned primarily with just this task, but without such organization, it is a problem for management to resolve.

In most applications of joint consultation, the attempt to resolve the communication and influence problem has to be made on the basis of using representatives as filters and amplifiers in the communication process, thus placing the onus of success upon a sheer process of communication. It is frequently set up on the assumption that the necessary conditions of mutual trust and shared motivation exist throughout the undertaking. It is mainly under pressure of the threat of supervisory boards that management, through the mouth of the CBI, has begun to acknowledge the value of participation in the day to day management processes of organization.

The causes of failure

Joint consultation has had a chequered history, and the general conclusion from experience with it is that sometimes it works effectively, but many times it does not. The variables which might conceivably contribute to this result are many. Because controlled experimentation has not been carried out, the attempts to explain the reasons for success or failure are also many and varied. Nevertheless, the main categories of reason given for failure are of a nature that they reinforce the message that the 'facilitating conditions' (and particularly that of mutual trust) are not present for some reason. The causes of failure may be summarized as:

1   Insufficient commitment on the part of the management to the idea suggesting a lack of trust and motivation.
2   Indifference on the part of the non-management to the idea for similar reasons.
3   A tendency for joint consultation to focus upon subjects which are:

    (i)   residual (after negotiations have claimed all the main subjects)
    (ii) 'non-controversial' (and therefore possibly less interesting) reflecting the unwarranted assumption that all are motivated to solve problems in this way.

4   A failure to come to grips with the real problems of representation, usually focussed on the problem of getting worker representatives to communicate with their constituents to the extent thought necessary, thus reducing the likelihood that the conditions of open and effective channels of communication will be met.
5   Deliberate sabotage, either by management (as with a change of top manager or a change of management style) or by trade union representatives (by withdrawing from consultation or refusing to sit with non-unionists, again reflecting on the motivational question, and possibly also that of trust).
6   An inherent tendency for joint consultative committees to regress from their original position (with respect to objectives or subjects) rather than grow or mature from it (the 'sinking to the level of canteen tea discussions' syndrome),

implying that even if the facilitating conditions were once met, they have since ceased to be so.

The high failure rate of joint consultation as a device for ensuring harmony by discussing non-controversial problems, focuses attention on the underlying trust and motivation. If there is insufficient motivation to make it succeed or insufficient mutual trust to allow it to do so, it may not be the substance that causes the failure.

If, therefore, this represents the best information we have on why joint consultation has not worked effectively in the past, it provides a number of questions for decision.

1   How much commitment (personal backing, time, money and other resources) is (a) the management; and (b) the non-management body (together with its separate associations) prepared to put into it?
2   What objectives will be formulated for joint consultation to be advanced to match the motivations of the parties involved?
3   What conditions will be provided to ensure that trust and necessary information is forthcoming?

Since most of the evidence and argument about joint consultation tends to be negative it may not provide the best basis on which to offer suggestions for change. The few positive examples of joint consultation then have to bear too heavy a burden of justification.

A number of reports on experiences do, however, offer more positive conclusions about, first, the structure of representational committees which might sustain it, and, secondly, the processes which are necessary to it successful conclusion. These are to be found in undertakings like the Glacier Metal Company (Jaques, 1951) and GKN-Shotton (GKN-Shotton, 1973).

The Glacier case

The Glacier experiment in joint consultation began as a conventional joint production committee during World War II. Originally, it involved the usual pattern of constituency representation and concerned itself with the usual subjects of joint consultative bodies.

As it was developed, it evolved a distinction between

493

'definitive policy' decisions which must, under Companies legislation, be reserved to the board of directors, and 'conditional policy' decisions which were available for allocation to the works council. These definitions and allocations were worked out by the works council itself (although it should be noted that a number of company directors did sit on this body at the material time). The fact that the distinction did evolve in this way may be of some significance in determining success, but here it is possible only to indicate the outcome.

The distinction was embodied in a Company policy document (given in full as an appendix to Jaques, 1951, pp 321-29). This makes a number of definitive points about policy and provides for the establishment and running of a variety of joint consultative bodies in the works, but specifically reserves certain decisions (for example those relating to finance and financial control, the appointment of directors and senior executives) to the board, whilst at the same time making other decisions (for example those about manning and terms and conditions of appointment of staff) open to discussion on the works council between the managing directors (as the representative of the board) and the workers' representatives before resolution.

The distinction drawn is the one known to pluralist confederations, although in this case the necessity for concurrence from the managing director in any conditional policy decision provides a safeguard against a total application of this confederal principle. It provides that matters which are not specificially reserved to the board by the Companies Acts and the Articles of Association, etc are made the concern of the works council and the workers' representatives (who were ultimately drawn from the ranks of the unions' domestic officials). Nevertheless, with the above proviso, the Company policy document does create certain rights in matters of decision (of the 'binding in honour' variety) which moves the frontier of control and responsibility forward from it usual position in work organizations.

The main works council is composed of seven union-member representatives of the hourly paid grades of staff, three representatives of the junior white collar staff, two representatives of the foremen and middle management, and one representative of the senior management, together with the managing director who holds his position *ex officio* because of his crucial liaison role in policy making.

In addition to this committee, however, there are other

494

representative committees similarly constituted on a departmental basis, in which more local policy and implementation issues can be discussed and from which suggestions for changes in conditional policy affecting all staff can be put forward; the shop stewards themselves also meet formally in a works committee which serves to co-ordinate approaches from the worker side.

The GKN Shotton case

The GKN-Shotton experiment was instituted following a period of unhappy industrial relations which culminated in a strike and a major lay off. It attempted to institutionalize the kind of approach associated with some forms of productivity bargaining. The *Charter for the Workpeople* identifies a number of distinct areas of decision which will be reserved for resolution within a structure of five permanent committees.

The main committee is charged with reviewing the operational performance of the Company and the future need for research and development (R&D), manpower, training, rehabilitation, and with promoting and monitoring productivity agreements, as well as co-ordinating the work of the four subcommittees. These have separate functions. The first and major one identified is to consider 'normal trade union bargaining matters' including all matters related to manpower planning and employee resoursing. The other three committees then deal with matters of safety, health and welfare; employee benefits, suggestions and leisure activities; and all aspects of discipline from the definition of works rules to the provision of an appeals channel for any employee who feels aggrieved at a disciplinary decision.

In the GKN-Shotton case, the structure consists of a main committee composed of eight management representatives and eight 'shop representatives' elected from amongst the paid-up trade union members willing to stand for election, together with four sub-committees whose composition is broadly reflective of the distribution of staff in the enterprise. The *Charter for the Workpeople* stops short, however, of giving these representatives a clear constitutional obligation to communicate with their constituents; rather they are treated as shop stewards and whilst they are assured of all facilities and protection of earnings whilst engaged on representative business, they are not specifically required to keep their constituents informed of matters discussed in the various committees.

495

Although, therefore, this codification extends the control frontier little beyond the traditional one in bargaining, it does attempt to join traditional joint consultation and conventional collective bargaining, based on trade union representation, and to codify the distribution of authority.

Successful structures

In each of these situations described the structure of joint consultation is essentially similar. In all cases, there is a main committee which is generally-representative and supported by other committees which may be specialized by function or by geographical area. There is also some attempt to designate authority for decisions and to legitimize the roles of the committees in decision-taking within the undertaking, incorporating union and other associational leaders in the process.

The two factors: incorporating union representatives and detailing the subject matter for decision (see p 349) help to avoid the introduction of resentments and rivalries which will increase the noise and the resistance in the communications process, and to make the subject matter of the discussions sufficiently real or vital to motivate people to discuss them and communicate conclusions to their constituents. There is the additional rationale for their introduction which asserts that it is desirable, even necessary, for management to 'give away' their traditional prerogative to control in these areas in order to assure greater order in the work situation.

In view of this, it may be desirable to treat the whole 'communication-involvement-commitment' process as a form or mode of bargaining, which involves the formal union leadership and accepts that there are ideological differences which have to be accommodated. This shows that the boundary between joint consultation and *integrative* bargaining (in Walton and McKersie's phrase) is a decaying one, at least in large-scale organizations, and that a more integrated managerial strategy (linking the two concepts, as was attempted in some of the experiments in productivity bargaining in the late 1960s) might be more desirable and more productive.

Reconstituting channels of communication

The experiments referred to above effect a reconstitution of the representative arrangements concerned with joint decision-taking (whether they were joint consultative or negotiative in form and nature). They depended on appropriate attitudes of trust and motivation being present to a sufficient extent. But they also sought to reinforce the message about the need for co operation between partners, as distinct from co-operation between bosses and subordinates. The new models were based on union representatives and allocated legitimate authority to take certain types of decision.

Consideration of the successful experiments allows the following general principles to be drawn:

1 An attempt is made to identify the subject areas for discussion in joint consultation, and these are then introduced as matters which the participants have a moral right to discuss.

2 An attempt is made to make these subjects issues on which the committee must decide, even if this has to be done within what is a normal pattern of constraint on any decision. In some cases there is an implicit or explicit *status quo* provision which applies when no decision is reached.

3 An attempt is made to ensure that decision-taking processes are 'informed' either by the presentation of information by management and (usually and perhaps more importantly) by the development of a working party structure by which matters for decision are worked through in more detail than a single committee meeting can normally aspire to.

4 Each situation acknowledges the actual distribution of loyalties amongst the people concerned, such that where the trade unions are well entrenched in the workplace, representatives are required to be trade unionists, thus avoiding the tensions of trade unionists being required to sit alongside non-unionists from the same occupational category; and that foremen and middle managers are not left out or ignored.

5 In each case, communications are seen to require a ramified structure of representation which is not satisfied by the creation of a single committee, and in the more extreme forms of communication structuring, a deliberate attempt may be made to establish communications with everyone in the organization.

6 In all cases, therefore, representatives are given some form of executive role (that is, they have something to do which is

over and above merely sitting and listening and talking) and the danger of producing a talking shop in the joint consultative committee is at least recognized.

7   Finally, the attitude of individual managers towards joint consultative arrangements is allowed less influence than normal because in these examples the creation of rights and the redistribution of authority places the manager in the position where he must participate in order to carry out his role successfully.

Most of the points which can be made in a list of this kind tend to support the generalization that a good deal of the success or failure of these kinds of communications and problem-solving experiments depends on the attitudes, motivations and predispositions of the parties involved in them. Such conclusions as these, together with the fact that experimentation in this area has tended to move the frontier forward in recent years, help to explain why the matter is now more often considered as a form of bargaining.

CO-OPERATIVE (OR INTEGRATIVE) BARGAINING

This new approach has usually emphasized the desirability of putting the communications/consultative arrangements together (in one 'constitution' but not necessarily within the same 'organizational arrangement') in order to allow matters of both common interest and diverse interest to be dealt with within a single structure of enforceable mutal influence.

Such development acknowledges that management and workers have some divergent interests, particularly those which focus on the distribution of the product of enterprise. It therefore also acknowledges that the assumptions which can be relied upon in any attempts by management to secure commitment by influencing the hearts and minds of workers, are not necessarily those which recognize and accept a common order, but rather those which recognize dichotomous fates in one mode or another (see table 10 on p 48). For this reason, the development is not concerned simply with the provision of supplementary channels of communication, but with the production of a different structure of mutually-accorded status (see pp 349-54). This raises the question of the need to recognize the representatives of the 'independent' organizations of workers as speaking for the (unionized) employees, but underlying this is the recognition that workers and their representatives share with management the status of influencers of outcomes of the decision processes.

The variable which is crucially involved in this change of perspective is that of *power*. This is one of those terms which always has a disputed meaning, but broadly, it refers to the capacity of one person to effect a change in the thinking, feeling or conduct of another in circumstances in which the other would not (for whichever of a variety of possible reasons) make the change without that intervention.

It is frequently asserted that the trade unions developed spontaneously as a mechanism for redressing the balance of power between the employer and the worker, into a situation in which the authority of the employer was absolute (or nearly so) because the countervailing power of the worker was zero (or nearly so) (see, for example, Shafto, 1971, p 213; Harvey, 1971, p 293; Burkitt and Bowers, 1979, pp 2-3; and Hutt, 1975, pp 3-33). They first controlled the competition between workers as a means of increasing worker power, but eventually secured recognition as participants in the decision-taking process. This produced, 'voluntarily' as the phrase has it, a structure of divided or shared authority to determine status, although it is not the only one which can be identified. Where circumstances give some power to workers in their dealings with the employer, a division of authority to decide exists.

Negotiation does not, however, *require* that the people concerned shall be organized in trade unions or any other kind of association. Nor does it not follow that every employer must recognize trade unions to become involved in negotiations. He must, in any situation short of one in which he has absolute power, 'manage by consent' and this means that he must engage in negotiation with employees in one form or another. What *form* the negotiation takes will, however, depend upon the power dispositions of the persons or parties involved and it is in this context that the desirability of recognizing an *independent* association in order to assure the *power* of the representatives becomes significant.

Productivity bargaining

One form of negotiation (or bargaining) which has developed in recent years is that which, following Walton and McKersie, is now referred to as integrative bargaining, or following Chamberlain and Kuhn, as co-operative bargaining (see also, Ulman, 1974). These refer to essentially the same kind of institutionalized process, but may be considered in two distinct contexts. On the one hand, the process may involve a distinct approach to the resolution of differences between parties. On the other, it may form a broad part of the process of distributive bargaining, that part which is concerned with a movement towards agreement in a conflict situation.

In the first context (which is the one usually considered under the heading of integrative bargaining), it implies a *total* approach to both problem-solving and issue-resolution (not the replacement of the second by the first). It aims to deal 'constructively' (see Deutsch, 1973, p 17) with both the wage and the effort sides of the contractual relationship (or more generally with the status of both of the two parties), and with both the creation and the distribution of product within the organization. It is therefore oriented towards securing a higher 'social' pay-off (that is, a higher return to both parties together) in order to foster the kind of integration of which Follett speaks (see Metcalf and Urwick, 1941, pp 71-94).

The experiments which, following the Fawley productivity agreements (Flanders, 1965) came to be referred to as 'productivity bargaining', developed under the influence of the National Board for Prices and Incomes in the late 1960s carried these developments forward to embrace considerations of what formed appropriate agendas. It started from different assumptions from joint consultation, but some of the lessons which emerged from it were consistent with those learned from it. It attempted to deal with the problems of excessive overtime working, trade union restrictive practices, and demarcation, and often offered harmonization of manual and white collar conditions as a benefit. In the process, it highlighted the questions of trust and motivation, and in a rather more developed way indicated the role and function of communications and channels of communications.

In these experiments, less attention was given in advance to drawing up a detailed constitutional arrangement, because it proceeded on the basis that collective bargaining arrangements usually existed and were to be used for the purpose. These arrangements were therefore accepted as the starting point, even if they were often supplemented with other channels of communication through which mutual influence could occur.

The prime focus of the exercise was almost exclusively upon the question of how the management and workers' representatives could together work out methods of increasing productivity treated as a 'problem' rather than an issue. The undertakings which engaged in the exercise usually initiated discussions with the union representatives on ways in which productivity might be increased in order to meet growing international competition, to the mutual benefit of the parties. This approach had the intended effect of making the environment of the undertaking the source of any problems, and the reason why changes had to be sought in productivity.

However, many undertakings found that they were quite unable to embark upon this kind of deal. The attempt was made in more circumstances than those which succeeded in producing worthwhile new apporaches (see National Board for Prices and Incomes, 1977, Reports Nos 36, 83 and 83 Supplement). One reason for this could be that the underlying conditions of trust and motivation were not present on either side, or on the side of the trade unions particularly who preferred to engage in distributive bargaining in a conflictual or collusive way even if the result was a 'spurious' productivity bargain.

Progress towards participation

In 1977 it was possible to recognize a number of stages in the development of what might be termed 'full integrative bargaining' within the context of productivity bargaining. These represented distinct modes of recognizing the representatives' status as intervenors in the productivity problem-solving process in addition to their (already-established) status as bargainers over the distribution of the product. Mr J Fleming (the Personnel Manager) mapped the points along this route, with the final point representing the stage reached in his own undertaking, BP Plastics at Barry (see Thomason, 1971).

His model, in fact, contains three main variations, with the third subdivided into three more variants on the broad participation theme.

1 Employee participation only at the final negotiating stage on a package of productivity improvements and remuneration benefits already established in broad outline: the company meets trade unions at national level to design an agreement which is then sold to local officers, shop stewards and employees, in exchange for a predetermined patterns of manpower utilization.

2 Participation at various levels in the development of an agreement on the contents of a predetermined package of productivity improvements and remuneration benefits: the undertaking design the detailed framework covering salaries and wages payable, together with improved fringe benefits (for example staff status, and then invite personnel in individual establishments to work out the optimum way of applying it to that establishment).

3 Participation at various levels in the process of working out the features of the agreement, that is, without prior determination of the contents: the undertaking can lay down broad policy and then leave it to the individual establishment negotiating committees to work out their own agreements in compliance with this broad policy.

In following out this process, however, a number of variations are possible:

(a) participation only at the final stages: local management design a package with senior union officials which is then 'sold' to employees

(b) participation only by local representatives: the undertaking's management representatives work out agreements with the union's representatives, and the information on the agreements is communicated to employees through ordinary union channels (for example branch meetings)

(c) participation by all employes in developing the content and form of the agreement: the usual negotiators agree in advance to involve all constituents as well as the domestic leadership in the process of developing ideas for consideration by specially established working parties and monitoring groups, on the method of distilling a final agreement, which might then have to be sold to full-time officials of union or employers' association, but not to the employees themselves (see Thomason, 1971, pp 32-33).

A productivity agreement arising out of this kind of discussion usually moved the frontiers of control and responsibility forward, and brought in new 'subjects' for bargaining. 'Productivity' in this context was often defined in terms of 'job enlargement', 'management by objectives', the 'harmonization of employee status', the introduction of 'flexi-time', and changes in the methods and amounts of payment (annual wages for example). The concept of a 'blank sheet of paper' at the beginning of the discussions thus tended to yield a Glacier-type re-allocation of authority to decide.

In the typical productivity bargaining situation, there was usually some overall committee which co-ordinated activities. Sometimes this was the main negotiating committee, but where bargaining was fractionalized the joint consultative committee was often used to co-ordinate discussions where it was composed of trade union representatives. In other cases, this particular exercise of productivity bargaining was co-ordinated by a special sub committee of the main committee. This recognizes the potentially specialized nature of productivity bargaining and the likelihood that productivity bargaining is not the total area of concern of either a negotiating committee or a joint consultative committee.

However, the main co-ordinating committee was usually supplemented by a large number of other committees (the productivity working parties or teams) whose existence was necessary to ensure that communication and mutual influence was widespread and effective and that capable of being monitored effectively by all parties. In this framework, therefore, the requirements of integrative or co-operative bargaining are tackled in the context of new conceptions of status, new levels of mutual trust and motivation, and new organizational arrangements through which the power and authority of the several parties could be allowed to influence outcomes in a mutually-beneficial way.

Preparatory tasks

From such experiences as these, it can be asserted that integrative bargaining requires both a set of predisposing conditions with respect of mutual trust, a development of appropriate motivation in the parties, and a new approach to the structuring and utilization of the channnels of communication between management and workers. If these do not 'exist' they have to be created, but the question of whether they exist may first have to be ascertained.

Any attempt to initiate integrative bargaining will therefore require as a first step, that management (and the union representatives) should make some assessment of whether the predisposing conditions exist, and determine whether they can be introduced if they do not. Walton and McKersie define the main facilitating condition or pre-condition as a sufficiently high level of mutual trust and support between the parties to enable problems to be resolved rationally.

The requirement of an appropriate level of mutual trust is something which could be argued in connection with any mode of bargaining. Each is likely to make its own particular level of demand on this score. The emphasis in integrative bargaining is, however, upon a relatively high level of such trust, sufficient to prevent the parties moving to a distributive (and less trustful) mode. It is this relatively high level which is the *sine qua non* of integrative bargaining, and which has been demonstrated to be crucial in the success of both joint consultation and productivity bargaining.

If these mutually-supportive attitudes of trust exist, then the parties may proceed to co-operative bargaining; where they do not, a considerable amount of preparation (possibly extending over a number of consultative sessions or episodes of distributive bargaining) may need to be carried out, in order to develop greater mutual trust and motivation to operate in this way.

In an undertaking where practice and organization emphasize control, rather than commitment, and distributive bargaining has been the accepted mode of resolving issues, the option of integrative or co-operative bargaining may not be readily available. This is because the different strategies require distinct facilitating conditions, and particularly those which directly influence the degree of trust which exists between the parties. Integrative bargaining is seen to require the existence of an 'open' management approach to the workforce and the union representatives, whilst distributive

504

bargaining depends upon a harder management style which will facilitate the development of worker solidarity.

Furthermore, in the immediate context of the episode of negotiation, the power of either party to establish the mode of bargaining will depend a good deal upon whether he is in a position to make the opening move. The party which makes the first move has the opportunity to establish this, whilst the other can only respond to the move. Thus, management may (as was the case in the productivity bargaining era of the 1960s) open with a move in integrative bargaining, whilst the trade union(s) most frequently open with a demand for distributive bargaining, although this is variable. But the opening move does place the onus on the other party either to accept or to argue for a different game.

Motivation

The need for an appropriate motivation, or a motivation to solve *problems* in a co-operative or integrative way is also almost part of the defining characteristic of the mode of integrative or co-operative bargaining. If both parties are not prepared to tackle the matter 'as a problem' which could be solved by joint (and co-operative) effort, then integrative bargaining is unlikely to prove feasible. Again, the evidence from both joint consultation and productivity bargaining seems to support this view.

The development of motivation to engage in this form of bargaining is likely to be as significant as it was found to be in connection with successful joint consultation. It will call for a careful working out of the benefits to both parties. It is part of the definition of this form of bargaining that the *total* pay-off to the two parties together will be greater than with distributive bargaining. This is referred to by Pruitt as 'higher joint benefit' which he sees as possibly occurring in one or other of four different ways: by cutting one party's costs of agreement; by compensation by the other for costs incurred; by packaging the outcomes in a way which allows a mutually-beneficial trade-off; and by finding solutions not otherwise in contemplation which allow both to gain or to avoid loss. Both parties remain interested in the distribution of any benefit which accrues, even if they find an interest in jointly securing a higher social benefit.

It is not necessary to assume that the two parties will secure equal benefit as a result of the process, nor even that both will acquire some benefit in order, either to identify integrative bargaining in the abstract, or to secure its acceptance by opponent in the reality. However, there must be some net gain to the parties together, however it might be distributed. Walton and McKersie idenfity three categories of situation differentiated by the kind of pay-off involved.

1 The position of absolute and equal gains by the two parties, which implies that the two parties order their preferences (or utilities) in identical fashion.
2 The position in which both parties make gains, but the gains to the one are different in amount from those of the other, implying no such identity in the manner of ordering preferences.
3 The position in which one party makes a sacrifice of a marginal kind, but the other makes a gain sufficient to allow him to compensate the other for the loss and still retain a net gain overall.

These are subsumed in two kinds of pay-off (the cost-cutting and compensatory) which Pruitt (1981, p 141) identifies. He suggests, however, that there are two other forms of pay-off which can occur. Where, as commonly happens, the parties have a number of different objectives which they seek to secure in some order of priority in any episode of bargaining, the possibility of trading off the lower priority objectives of the two parties may exist in a way which leaves each with their higher priority objectives intact. This is referred to as 'logrolling', and necessarily involves the parties in moving somewhat from their original positions with respect to their goals.

Where the parties can change the nature, or the level of abstraction, of their objectives without at the same time sacrificing them, some possibility of securing a pay-off in these other terms or at this higher level of abstraction, may exist. For example, an impasse in a conventional claim/counterclaim situation might be avoided if the parties could agree to raise the level of abstraction by engaging in 'productivity bargaining' to redefine the parameters of the economic exchange problem within which any increase in wages had to be found. Alternatively, the packages of demands or offers might be given a different priority order to bring about the same result.

506

A number of distinct forms of pay-off can, therefore, be expected to fall within integrative bargaining. Nevertheless, these pay-offs are thought to be least likely to arise in negotiations over money value, and more likely to be associated with negotiations over rights and obligations (status). Walton and McKersie illustrate the latter concern by reference to negotiations over 'job security' (Walton and McKersie, 1965, p 129), but this might have to be interpreted more widely than this. It is the underlying structure of status and control which is most likely to lend itself to this kind of integrative bargaining, rather than the delegated activities of determining shares accruing to factors.

We should therefore expect to find a number of forms of joint-decision-making in work undertakings which can be included within the process of integrative bargaining. In particular, many (but not by any means all) of the exercises of joint consultation which have been carried out in British undertakings, and (more obviously) many of the exercises of productivity bargaining perpetrated in the 1960s and 1970s might be regarded as qualifying by virtue of their assumptions of consensual decision-taking between representatives.

Open communication

More important from a practical point of view, is the need to establish both open channels of communication and unrestricted availability of relevant information for purposes of this kind of bargaining. As Walton and McKersie recognize,

(a) free channels of communication between the parties, unencumbered by status differences and considerations of social distance; and
(b) free availability of information pertinent to the problem and the manner of its solution (Walton and McKersie, 1965, pp 139-43)

are essential prerequisites of this approach (and contrast with the requirements for successful distributive bargaining). Where the first two mentioned above (p 503-04) are oriented to values, these two are more technical and strategic and generally supportive of the required processes.

The necessity for open and unencumbered channels of communication and for the free flow of information through them,

507

is a consequence of the approach adopted. Where the parties want to solve the problem co-operatively, they will find it in their interest to meet these related requirements. Without a means of communication and without the relevant information, the problem is not likely to be solved in the most effective and expeditious fashion. Because integrative bargaining relies upon a degree of rationality in problem-solving or decision-making, it must perforce ensure that the informational life-blood of such decision-taking is made available to the joint parties. This too may be inferred from experience with both of the processes which have been mentioned above.

The Barry plant of the BP Company adopted new channels of communication for purposes of its bargaining exercise. It set up a number of special joint committees, as well as a structure of meetings between managers and subordinates which allowed 'cascading discussions' to take place within the normal chains of command to departments and sections, but involving the union representatives at all levels and stages.

This led to the development of unusually 'open' discussions. Management did not seek to impose their views on how or where productivity could be improved, but left it to the committees and working groups to find their own answers. Some structuring of the discussions was, however, attempted in other undertakings (NBPI, Report No 36). In some cases (although not by any means all) the 'blank sheet of paper approach' was used with management declaring themselves willing to accept *any* suggestions even if they might involve capital investment. In other cases, a limit was imposed on the amount of capital investment used as a basis for a suggestion (see Oldfield, 1966; Thomason, 1971). Unlike the Glacier Company case, these made no attempt to spell out in principle or in advance the limits of participation in decision taking. In practice, such limits operated, however, and took roughly the same form as in the Glacier Company.

This does not by itself place management and workforce representatives in the position where a co-operative approach is necessarily adopted to resolving their problems. For this to happen, it is necessary for the underlying attitudes of trust and motivation to exist or to develop, and these (particularly, the first of them) may be extremely difficult to achieve. It is much more likely that the parties to these kinds of relationship may be more amenable to changes in actual behaviours than to

508

changes in objectives and predispositions, and the behaviours involved may be capable of development, at least *'pro tem.,'* and prior to more fundamental changes occuring in attitudes and predispositions.

Associated behaviours

The various approaches to integrative bargaining rely on an acceptance that there are problems which can be solved co-operatively, and the existence of some agreement or understanding as to what (at least some of) the problems are. They proceed on the basis there are methods by which groups of people, with different frames of reference or even ideological positions, can handle problems of this kind.

The processes of problem-solving in small groups of individuals have been examined closely by Bales (1951) and by other resources who have used his, or a slightly vaired, method. The findings of this work provide information on the kinds of activities which are involved for the participants, as well as the kinds of sequence through which they will move in reaching their goals.

Processes

Bales' (1951) main conclusion from the application of his methods of 'interaction process analysis' is that:

> 'under ... specified conditions, the process of problem-solving tends to move through time from a relative emphasis upon problems of orientation, to problems of evaluation and subsequently to problems of control; and that concurrent with these transitions, the relative frequencies of both negative and positive reactions tend to increase' (Bales and Strodtbeck, 1951, in Cartwright and Zander, 1953, p 399).

The concepts used in this are used in the interaction process chart which Bales used to record behavioural events in groups. This instrument first divides activity into instrumental and affective classes, and then into a further six subcategories: communication, evaluation, control, decision, tension-variation, and integration. Each of these has a positive and a negative or an asking and a giving aspect (see table 19 on p 511).

The most rational way of conceiving the sequence of such behaviours is that which follows the table of activities, that is, from top to bottom. But research using the method has indicated that human behaviour in problem-solving groups does not always follow this simple sequence, but continually move up and down in often abortive and tension producing attempts to handle the technical problems.

Groups do not move directly through such a sequence and do generate emotional reactions as they cope with the instrumental tasks. They do not move from the top of the chart to the bottom in a simply ordered sequence, although there is behavioural movement from the top half to the bottom half as tensions are created by handling the orientation, evaluation and control tasks, and reduced. The emotions, in fact, serve as an indicator of the strength of (divergent) feelings which are aroused at any technical stage in the decision-taking process.

Groups have also been found to differ from one another on practically every dimension. Some moved faster through the sequences to the decision stage, some generated much more emotion on the route to the decision, some involved many and some few individual participants in the total process. Although the broad development tends to be constant, considerable variety of form exists within this.

When this approach was applied to a simulated negotiation (as distinct from a simpler problem-solving group assembled in the laboratory) by McGrath (1966), he was able to demonstrate that successful negotiating groups revealed certain characteristic forms of proceeding. The successful negotiators were distinguished from the less successful on two main counts: the display of positive or negative affect; and the display of structuring and controlling behaviours.

Successful groups showed more frequent and shorter interactions, less negative affect, more affectively neutral types of communication, and (in the final stages) even more positive and neutral affect and even less negative affect. The unsuccessful groups showed less frequent and lengthier communications, more negative affect, more emotionally-charged communications, and (in the final stages) a tendency to replace positive and neutral affect with negative affect.

The most direct implication of these findings concerns the

Table 19
Types of interaction and role in problem-solving groups

1 Asks for orientation Initiator Recorder Commentator Questioner	7 Gives orientation Co-ordinator Orientor Commentator Summarizer
2 Asks for opinions Opinion seeker Questioner Prober	8 Gives opinion Opinion giver Assessor Standard setter
3 Asks for suggestions Answer seeker Catalyst Enabler Expert	9 Gives suggestions Contributor Elaborator Gate-keeper Procedural expert
4 Disagrees Rejector Blocker	10 Agrees. Follower Compromiser
5 Expresses tension Aggressor Help seeker Self-confessor	11 Attempts tension release Appeaser Articulator of emotions Joker
6 Expresses antagonism Recognition seeker Playboy Bully Pleader of sectional case	12 Expresses solidarity Energiser Encourager Articulator of group feeling Sage

Key:
Interaction categories: 1-7 Problems of communication
2-8 Problems of evaluation
3-9 Problems of control
4-10 Problems of decision
5-11 Problems of tension
6-12 Problems of integration

Types of reaction: 10-12 Positive reactions
7-9 Attempts at answers
1-3 Questions
4-6 Negative reactions

Adapted from Bales, RF: Interaction Process Analysis
(Addison-Wesley Press, 1950) p 9

511

appropriate behaviours of negotiators in any context (which we return to below, ch. 20). For the present, however, we use this approach largely to illustrate the main accepted beliefs about the way in which problem solving groups proceed. From the classical decision-making model, and the group processes involved in decision-taking, we can infer that there are likely to be characteristic processes involved, which we might expect to find in problem-solving consultation or in integrative bargaining.

Summary: communication, consultation and participation

The managerial strategy which best fits the unitarist frame of reference of the employer is one which produces a sequence of approaches, beginning with communication, moving through involvement (or consultation) and concluding in participation.

These differ in the extent to which they both depend upon and reflect the attitudes of the employees involved. Where it can be realistically assumed that workers will accept management's right to manage without challenge, management will secure returns of approval if they carry out a role which communicates the necessary information which contributes to decisions. Acceptance of this same right, when coupled with a view that management is not necessarily omniscient, might then support a more involving, problem-solving approach in which management not only communicates but seriously consults workers for their views and ideas.

Where, however, the assumptions about the workers' assent to managerial prerogatives no longer holds good, the workers themselves are likely to demand consultation, but to do so *via* demands for recognition and negotiation. As collective bargaining has developed, management's decisions about *some* facets of industrial relations have been replaced by joint decisions. When *in those circumstances* management seeks to develop a strategy for commitment, it is likely that it will have to focus upon participation of the workers, probably through representatives, on the basis that they have a 'right' to participate in decisions as 'co-equals'. If *this* is to be achieved by way of a managerial strategy, it will probably require productivity or integrative bargaining methods to be developed on the basis of *mutual* influence.

The actions which are then required of the parties are likely to contrast at many points with those associated with distributive bargaining (see below, pp 538-42), but in essence they demand a more open approach to a party which is accorded both high trust and high status in the mutual influence process.

Readings

Guest and Fatchett: (1974), pp 7-46.
Brannen: (1983), pp 33-65.
Hawes and Brookes: (1980), pp 353-61.
Walton and McKersie: (1965), pp 144-83.
North and Buckingham; (1969), pp 1-69; 131-71.
Thomason: (1971). Cliff: (1970), pp 9-38.
Pruitt: (1981), pp 137-200. Pedler: (1977/1978).
Marchington: (1982), pp 150-161.

19

Distributive bargaining

The prevalence of distributive bargaining

When the term collective bargaining is used, it is usually distributive bargaining which is intended. This term 'distributive bargaining' is used by Walton and McKersie to identify that bargaining process which occurs when two antithetical interests are pursued in a voluntary exercise of mutual influence, which, in the end, culminates in an agreement regarding the terms of an exchange or in an exchange itself. It is, in fact, this process which is most frequently discussed in the industrial relations literature whenever 'processes' are under consideration (see, for example, Atkinson, 1973; Kennedy, 1978 and 1980; Pruitt, 1981; Morley and Stephenson, 1977).

This is not surprising for two main reasons. First, much of the actual practice of collective bargaining is concerned with wages and hours of work and related subjects, in which the whole object is to reach an agreement on terms of exchange. Second, even when the practice of other forms of bargaining (such as productivity bargaining or integrative bargaining) are under consideration, it is necessary to recognize that these must culminate in some agreement about *division* or *exchange* of any enlarged product. It is difficult (in the context of industrial relations) to get away from this kind of bargaining for long (see Armstrong *et al*, 1981, p 17).

For this reason, many models have been developed to describe the manner of its operation, and the way in which differences are resolved in this process of mutual influence. Not all of these models are in agreement with one another. It would indeed be surprising if models of such widespread and complex practices all focused on the same limited range of possibility. Nevertheless, it is possible to produce a general guide to the processes which are involved, even if it is also admitted that there are many variations on the general theme.

The outline of such a model is given by Pedler (1977). His negotiation map depicts the broad sequence from preparatory phases through Walton and McKersie's four modes of bargaining to implementation. This is modified here (see below) to substitute the stages occurring in the distributive 'bargaining' process for the four modes. It presents a map of a single bargaining episode, in which the objectives are related to outcomes through a series of interconnected steps, each of which has its own inputs and anticipated outputs (as influences upon the final outcome). It thus represents a particular concept of causality and is put forward as a guide to negotiating processes and conduct.

This map is based on a concept of rational planning (see pp 51-53). It begins the sequence with a definition of objectives derived from a perception of need. It proceeds with the identification of a strategy which depends not only on the nature of the objectives but also of the situation in which they are to be realized. This, along with the tactics, is presented in a written case

Figure 4

A negotiation map

The stages, processes, and activities in distributive bargaining

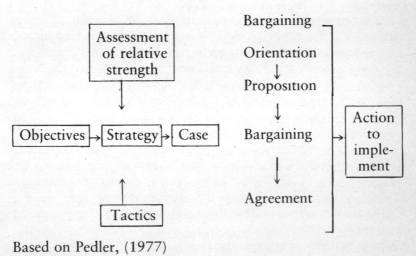

Based on Pedler, (1977)

515

intended to guide the negotiators in the various types and forms of bargaining in which they will engage in order to achieve their goals.

The original map shows that the bargaining process itself may take many forms: accommodative, collaborative, distributive, competitive, etc. In this form, it finds a place for the processes of orientation, proposition, bargaining (proper) and agreement, which are derived from various approaches which different authors have made to resolving this problem of how to depict the 'bargaining' process. What the map does not do is indicate where the sanction of industrial action fits into the whole, as a basis of the parties' power in securing the agreement of the other.

The occasions for negotiation

The issue in any particular case may be one (or group of them) from a wide range. The officially-identified causes of industrial disputes (as published, for example, in the *Employment Gazette*) may provide some rough indication of the matters over which the parties might be expected to conflict (see table 20, p 517) but this is unlikely to provide an exhaustive list. What people may be prepared to strike over is likely to constitute a more limited range of subjects than they want to negotiate about. But even this list offers *some* suggestion as to the likely issues.

These are likely to reach the bargaining table in the form of a claim for an increase in wages, a reduction in hours, an end to short-time working, or something similar. Presented as a demand on the other party, the claim will set the mode of bargaining. It will be an exercise in *distributive* bargaining, unless the employer can sustain a counter-demand that the issue is not negotiable. If it is accepted as negotiable, however, the mode is determined, and the behaviours called for will be significantly different from those associated with integrative bargaining.

Once the decision is taken and the mode accepted, the exercise has to be conducted within a framework of maintaining or securing control of the issue or the problem. Distributive bargaining is about competition for control, if only of the decisions on wages and other conditions of employment. Integrative bargaining is about co-operation to bring the problem under the joint control of the parties. The employer is usually perceived to be in control (that is, possessed of the

516

Table 20

Causes of industrial stoppages

Cause	No stoppages	No workers directly in— volved
Pay – wage rates and earnings levels	580	1,952,000
Pay – extra wage and fringe benefits	34	9,800
Duration and pattern of hours worked	88	40,600
Redundancy questions	111	286,200
Trade union matters	86	24,700
Working conditions and supervision	160	31,300
Manning and work allocation	256	74,800
Dismissal and other disciplinary measures	139	40,300
All causes	1,454	2,259,700

Source: Department of Employment Gazette, 1983

necessary power to get his way) and the union is seen to be in the position of challenging that control (mobilizing such power as it can on the way). The main aim will be to secure advantage over the opponent so that the outcome will be favourable to the party and less favourable to the opponent.

It is possible to develop an ideal-typical model of distributive bargaining because, in the absence of mistake or misinterpretation, the behaviours involved are 'strategic'. For this same reason, it becomes possible to present a view of the behavioural steps or stages of distributive bargaining negotiation which are most likely to occur. This does not imply that they will always occur, and certainly not that they will always occur in a particular sequence. It merely suggests that *typically* a negotiation will embrace most or all or these activities.

517

PREPARATORY STAGES AND TASKS

Attempts to identify the stages involved in negotiation have been carried out by a number of writers (Atkinson, 1973; Kennedy, 1978; Kennedy, Benson and McMillan, 1980; Pedler, 1977-78). Morley and Stephenson, in turn, have sought to identify the individual behaviours discernible at each of these stages (Morley and Stephenson, 1977). They employ a different approach to depicting what occurs, and use a different vocabulary to identifying the stages and events.

Two of them offer models in which there is a sequence of activities conducted in stages and punctuated by events which prepare for a subsequent stage. They usually include a preparation stage which is brought to a conclusion with the production of a case or a negotiating handbook. The actual negotiations are then divided into a number of distinct stages based on an activity which is often followed by a transitional event.

Where Kennedy deals with preparation as a single step Atkinson (1973) breaks this down into five distinct tasks, as follows:

1 *Formulating the objective which is to be sought through the negotiation*

This will typically take the form of what settlement of the difference each party hopes to achieve at the end of the negotiating episode. It can be based on hunch or whim, but is now more usually based on research, entailing survey and assessment of the current situation. The purpose of the survey is usually to uncover what passes for the contemporary norm or normal (such as a survey of current levels of settlement of wage claims, or of common practice in handling disciplinary cases). Assessment links the findings of the survey with the present and expected-future position of the unit (for example, whether a particular level of settlement can be afforded by the undertaking, or what precedent value for the undertaking's relationships will be attached to the handling of a rights issue in a particular way).

2 *Evaluating the capacities of both parties to realize their goals*

In the context of negotiation, this will focus mainly upon what is identified as bargaining power. This involves making an informed judgement of the strength of the party and its 'case' in relation to that of the opponent. This entails making estimates of the extent to which the party (and the opponent) can rely upon concurrence amongst the various groups (own side, other side, and outsiders) with the position it takes up, and of the extent to which either can compel compliance with its objectives by taking action in support. In order that judgement may be adequately informed, it is necessary to draw inferences from past and concurrent interactions with the other groups (or representatives of them).

3 Planning and implementing ways of building up the strength of the party prior to actual negotiation

The object here is to increase one's own capacity to win against the other party. These activities are likely to have two main foci. First, they will focus upon action to reduce the risks to the party (for example by building up stocks to lessen the impact of a strike) or to increase the risks to the opponent (for example, by putting it about that the undertaking's financial position is so poor that redundancies might have to be contemplated). Secondly, they will focus upon changing the commitment of the various internal and external interest groups to particular values (for example, by initiating a propaganda campaign designed to bolster the party's position or undermine the opponent's position in the eyes of constituents or outsiders).

4 Planning the strategies and tactics by which each party will seek to reach the main goals and the subgoals which can be separately identied on the route to these

The main object here is to establish what actions in the negotiation itself can be calculated to achieve desired ends. The plans will focus upon the stages which can be identified in the negotiating sequence (see pp 532-33). Separate plans will be developed, therefore, to guide the phases of orientation or argument, propositioning, bargaining (giving and taking) and agreement formulation. At each stage in this sequence, subgoals related to building the strength of own position and weakening that of opponent, will be linked into the strategic conceptions.

5 Formulating the case to be presented by the methods decided in the planning stage, and selection of and allocation of tasks to the negotiating team

This calls not merely for case-drafting skills, but also for judgemental skills in identifying just how the tasks shall be identified and allocated to those with the competence to carry them out. Although strictly not part of this stage, it may also be necessary to secure sufficient commitment, not only of the team, but of the constituents as well, to the proposals embodied in the case (see below, pp 528-31).

These steps in the process may be examined in more detail in turn.

Step one: establishing objectives

Once the occasion for negotiation arises, the first step in preparing for negotiation entails formulating the objectives. The parties may do this either simultaneously or sequentially. Objectives may be distinguished according to whether they represent the underlying purposes of the party or immediate situation-derived objectives. Both of these receive attention in the industrial relations literature, and are often used to distinguish the foundations for open and hidden agenda items.

We have already looked at some of the broad purposes and long-term objectives of the parties in chapters 9 and 10. These may be said to form a constant, underlying agenda for any episode of negotiation but they are not necessarily made explicit on each occasion. The preservation of the party's own position and organization, and the realization of such immediate objectives as are feasible without damage to these long term imperatives, commonly serve as unarticulated objectives.

A negotiating episode will also have some particular and immediate objective for each party. These will develop out of the difference or dispute which develops between the parties. This may involve perception of the inadequacy of the wage rate, a sense of grievance arising out of the treatment of an individual or group by a management representative, a concern that productivity levels have fallen to an unacceptably low level, etc. These are immediate issues which provide the basis for immediate and short-term objectives which are to be achieved in the particular episode.

These cannot stand, nor can they be considered in isolation from, the longer-standing objectives (as outlined above). Securing immediate objectives in the short term must remain consistent with achieving the long-term objectives or at least maintaining the party's preferred position.

The objectives (in the terms of this rational model) will be regarded as constrained by:

1   The interpretation which the parties make of the situational constraints which surround the decision. Objectives are usually regarded as reflecting and responding to the 'needs' developing out of the situation in which the decision (about objectives) is located. The objective of a wage increase is 'derived' from immediately-perceived needs defined as differences between the desired state and the actual state.

2   Norms or expectations held by the principals or members of the constituency, norms of the opposing party, and norms of the society (whether or not expressed in law) In the 'tripolar model' presented by McGrath and Julian (1962) these are expressed as 'forces' on the negotiator and are identified as R-forces, A-forces and C-forces, respectively. The effect of these is often, for example, to make any kind of bargaining an essentially ritualistic process. It is also to keep demands and offers within certain bounds, or to justify expressions of disapproval from some source when they are exceeded.

3   Perceptions of what constitute legitimate means. Harbison and Coleman, for example, imply that agreements between the parties as to the means to be adopted to secure their ends may in themselves diminish the significance of the differences between them about those ends (Harbison and Coleman, 1951, p 18). Similarly, Crouch has argued that trade union strategies may not reflect a choice simply between desired ends, but one between goals 'set in the context of means needed to secure them' (Crouch, 1982, p 139). Whilst this implies that the choice is based on efficiency criteria, it may also import connotations of value and legitimacy as well.

Specifying objectives

Distinct objectives applicable to the particular case will also be established. A trade union may formulate an objective initially of a high or a low settlement figure in a wage negotiation, or it may aim for a high or low settlement only after an industrial action (intended to teach the managment or the members some kind of lesson). Equally, a goal might be established by seeking to trade off an immediate gain (for example, in wages) against a longer term control over the source of higher earnings (for example, of overtime).

Even where management is adopting a posture of reacting to the unions' demands (rather than seeking to be proactive) it faces a similar range of alternatives. It might, in a situation of high unemployment, for example, seek a low settlement of a wage claim and accept whatever consequences might follow in the way of industrial action. In a situation of buoyant product demand, it might aim to concede a relatively high wage increase with the object of securing aceptance of tighter procedures to govern future relations.

However, it is usually considered prudent in determining objectives to establish three positions which may then guide subsequent actions and approaches to negotiation. These 'positions' depict:

1   The *Ideal Settlement* (IS), or the point in the range of possible outcomes which would represent the ideal or most optimistic outcome from the standpoint of the party.

2   The *Realistic Settlement* (RS) point, or that which is most likely to be reached as a result of give and take in the bargaining process, judged to be most likely on the basis of taking into account all the relevant (environmental and internal) factors.

3   The *Fall Back Position* (FBP) or that point in the range of all possible outcomes at which the party would refuse to move further under pressure from the other side, and therefore the point at which the party would withdraw from 'the game' (and, for example, take industrial action rather than continue negotiation).

No one of these is any more real as an objective than any other. They represent the optimistic, realistic and pessimistic forecasts of possible outcomes from the negotiation, but are all necessary to provide structure to the approach and the strategies which the party will make. They reflect the 'reading' which the party makes of the constraints which surround that episode of negotiation.

Objectives are frequently developed in 'package' form, and this factor often assists in the realization of various positions. If the demand is for an increase in, say, four items, the various positions can be expressed in a number of different ways by combining the items in different proportions. This provides a basis for the 'packaging' stage distributive bargaining (see pp 532-33).

Assessing bargaining power

The parties need to deploy some power to secure their objectives and to coerce each opponent to accept a settlement. This bargaining power, as we have seen (see pp 475-83) is an important but nevertheless elusive concept. It is necessary to ensure that each party should secure enough of it to enable it to secure as much of its objective as possible in the actual negotiation.

The bargaining strength of the two parties will usually fluctuate marginally over time. The party which can choose its time to open a negotiation may therefore take advantage of a relatively favourable position and seek to place the other at a disadvantage. This is not always possible, as issues may emerge from a continuing situation in such a manner that a choice of timing is not always possible. The time is never likely to be right, except accidentally, for the party which is forced to respond to a demand from the opponent.

Confronted with a demand to bargain, therefore, either party faces the need both to assess the other's bargaining power and to increase its own within the confines of the bargaining episode itself.

This assessment demands that the abstract concepts of power and bargaining power should be capable of being operationalized. A number of authors have put forward a method of doing this in which the importance of the issue is made paramount. Chamberlain (1965) and Levinson (1966) (in marginally different ways) suggest that two calculations can be made which allow the comparative advantage to be worked out. To describe these as calculations is, perhaps, to impute too great a precision and the mathematical symbolism used in their presentation should be interpreted rather loosely.

These authors suggest that:

$$\text{The bargaining power of A} = \frac{\text{The costs to B of disagreement with A's terms or proposals}}{\text{The costs to B of agreement with A's terms or proposals.}}$$

523

and

$$\text{The bargaining power of B} = \frac{\text{The costs to A of disagreement with B's terms or proposals}}{\text{The costs to A of agreement with B's terms or proposals.}}$$

Using this formula, the assessements necessary for the judgement are the costs of agreement and of disagreement with the other's terms. The cost of agreeing with the other are fairly readily calculable in the case of a wage demand, but the cost of disagreeing is more difficult to estimate, depending as it does on forecasts of what might then happen. Thus, the assessment must take into account not merely the identifiable cost, but also the probability of its occurring. A high cost (for example, arising from a strike or lock-out) might in itself be unacceptable; but if the probability of its happening is very low it might be placed in the category of an acceptable risk (see Armstrong et al, 1977).

In a particular case, it may well be, as Anderson (1979) has suggested, that some measure of these objective factors is necessary. But to measure them as *objective* facts is one thing. To assess them in terms of their influence upon the perceptions and perspectives of the bargainers is more difficult. Nevertheless, in the alternative view of negotiation as something constructed by the individual actors, it is this influence of the external factors and events upon the individual's consciousness which is likely to prove most relevant to outcomes. It is not merely that there is an objective condition of differential bargaining power, but that the negotiators will attempt in various ways to bring it to bear on the resolution of the difference. This view would be consistent with the findings of Anderson (see pp 300-02) but it is so only or mainly to the extent that the measure of the objective fact can be taken as a kind of surrogate measure of its influence on the perspectives and perceptions of the several negotiators.

Increasing own bargaining power

The point of the assessment is to provide a basis for determining strategy, but the outcome of it may be to suggest that the side needs to increase its bargaining power in order to deal with the issue or the problem.

524

This may be done initially by delaying the negotiation as long as possible in the hope or expectation that bargaining power will increase as the relative positions change over time. This response involves the risk that the party may be accused of refusing to bargaining or refusing to do so in good faith. There are therefore limits to the amount of delay which can be brought about.

It is therefore more likely that the party will attempt to use some means of influencing the negotiators or their constituents to accept that the relative position is not as they might think. The sheer giving out of information and interpretations of it may be undertaken to try to undermine the bargaining position of the opponent by seeking to change levels of commitment and orientation.

Management may put it about (whether in formal or informal communications) that they are right in the position they adopt and that the opponent is wrong, or that the assumptions on which the opponent is basing his case are false. They may seek to justify a dismissal for fighting either on the grounds that the rules and conventions support such a course or that this kind of conduct cannot be tolerated because of the danger which it creates for others. They may suggest that the assumption of high productivity or high profitability is totally unsupported by the facts of the situation, and so on. The intention is to change expectations of what might constitute a proper outcome of the negotiation.

The use of a sanction as a means of increasing bargaining power is likely to prove to be a double-edged sword. It can demonstrate that the party is firm and resolute on the issue to the extent that it is willing to suffer high costs in order to inflict cost on the other, but there is always some risk that the necessary solidarity will not be forthcoming and that the name of the game being played will be changed quite drastically even if it is successful from the first point of view. Consequently, this kind of tactical enhancement of bargaining power as seen by the opponent is usually attempted by the device of securing a resolution of the membership to take certain action if..., or alternatively to secure a pronouncement from the board or head office as to the consequences if.... Such tactics have the advantage that they are likely to affect the opponent's perceptions of bargaining strength without either running the risks of industrial action or committing resources to the conflict which might more advantageously be kept in reserve.

The assessment of the relative power of the party and of his chances of improving it, may lead the negotiating team to consider which mode of bargaining is to be emphasized. There are two distinct varieties of negotiation which can be distinguished. One entails negotiation over issues on the assumption that outcomes will form a variable share of a fixed total of something or other, so that what one wins the other will lose. The other treats differences between the parties as problems to be solved, and proceeds on the assumption that if they are solved, the parties may jointly benefit because a higher total quantity to be shared may be generated. Although this is not the usual or the main purpose of making the assessments, they do raise fundamental strategic questions of this kind (see Bacharach and Lawler, 1981).

The kinds of assumption which can be made about the conduct of the opponent in these two situations, vary, and in doing so, highlight the necessity for the members of the teams to be endowed with a capacity for making sound and relevant judgements in circumstances in which it may not be *obvious* what the other party is attempting from what he says or does. This is likely to form the foundation for what are frequently referred to as the 'skills of the negotiator'.

Step two: strategies and tactics

The second step involves the development of strategies which will be adopted to secure the objectives, and the determination of the tactics (or mini-strategies) which may be adopted to support them.

In this context, strategy is defined as 'a plan, method, or series of manoeuvres for obtaining a specific goal or objective' (Brandt, 1973, p 11). Tactics are defined as 'expedient, short-run strategies ... as specific actions or manoeuvres within a strategic plan, that move the action towards the realization of goals' (*ibid*, p 11). Some degree of forward planning is possible in respect of both. This cannot eliminate the need to leave some operating decisions to be taken by the negotiators in response to the situation as it develops. The latter cannot be planned for in advance and have to be left to the skill of the negotiator (which can be developed only or mainly by reinforced experience or specialized training).

526

Decisions about strategy will entail a search for feasible and potentially successful means of influencing the situation to bring about the desired end, and ultimately, a choice of one such 'solution' above the others identified and evaluated. This need not involve a total or rational systems approach, and may in many cases reflect the garbage can model of decision-taking (see pp 52-55). The choice of strategy is also constrained in a similar fashion to the choice of objectives, and perceptions of these factors form significant inputs to the process at this stage.

The presence of the two sets of objectives related to growth and control will, it is thought, tend to constrain the strategies available to achieve them. In Walton and McKersie's view, there are a limited number of basic strategies which may be adopted, according to the nature of the decision to be reached on this joint basis. Thus, a particular objective which implies the existence of a zero-sum situation, will constrain the parties to the extent that they will be committed to an exercise of distributive bargaining (see Walton and McKersie, 1965). Alternatively, an objective which implies that there is a problem to be resolved jointly and that its resolution will enlarge the total advantage which the two parties together may secure, will constrain the parties to attempt a strategy of integrative bargaining (*ibid*).

In addition to this division between integrative and distributive strategies Walton and McKersie also recognize alternative strategies relevant to bargaining within the own side (intra-organizational bargaining) and to maintain and develop the bargaining relationship itself (attitudinal structuring). The first of these is relevant to the situation in which it might prove difficult to secure agreement within the side on what objectives ought to be pursued in the bargaining episode and by what means. The second is essentially a long term strategy which must perforce develop through a number of bargaining episodes.

They are also likely to be constrained by the same sets of values, norms, and rules as apply to the decisions about objectives. This is the equivalent in this (bargaining) context of the recognition of constraint on the choice of means of influence (which we have already noted, see pp 471-73). Not all methods of negotiation with others are accorded the same degree of legitimacy or sanction by the norms of the parties or of society. Differences on this score may therefore lead to different choices of strategy.

The strategies adopted in any one particular episode of

negotiation are likely to be unique to that episode. Nevertheless, once the decisions are taken about the objectives and the kind of bargaining which is to be pursued as appropriate (that is, distributive or integrative, conjunctive or co-operative) certain aspects of strategy are likely to be carried in automatically *and* to be broadly comparable through a number of different episodes of bargaining in that mode.

Threat

A major strategic issue which arises in all negotiations is how industrial action or threat of it is going to be used *within the negotiating process itself*. It is not always necessary for either party to initiate industrial action to enforce demands, but each party must decide whether it is prepared to use it, and if so under what circumstances and at what cost. Because industrial action is known to constitute the 'ultimate sanction' available to compel agreement or compliance, it may more readily be used as a threat in any negotiations on any issue, even though it too risks incurring costs.

'The distinctive character of a threat', Schelling has suggested, is:

> 'that one asserts that he will do, in a contingency, what he would manifestly prefer not to do if the contingency occurred, the contingency being governed by the second party's behaviour' (Schelling, 1960, p 123).

From the standpoint of the second party, such an assertion by the first party is deceiving because it does not *know* the strength of the commitment to act in the event of the contingency arising; it can only guess at this, and could very easily guess wrongly.

Edwards (1969) identifies three main types of threat used in international negotiations, all of which have their place in collective bargaining processes.

1 The deterrent threat, which takes the form that the utterer will do something undesired by the opponent if that opponent does something which is undesired by the party. 'If the management sack this member of the union, the rest of the membership will go on strike.' 'If the union membership call a strike, the management will immediately issue dismissal notices.'

2 The desistent threat, which takes the form that unless the

528

opponent discontinues an action already engaged, the utterer will take action which will be to the detriment of the opponent. 'If the management do not reinstate this dismissed worker, then the union will take strike action.' 'If the union do not immediately call off the strike, the management will issue dismissal notices to all on strike.'

3 The compellent threat, which takes the form of a demand that the opponent shall do something which the utterer wants, on pain of the utterer taking some action which will be to the opponent's disadvantage. 'If the management do not concede a pay increase of x per cent, the union will call a strike.' 'If the union is not prepared to sign a productivity agreement, the management will discontinue negotiations on the pay demand.'

Each of these has different credibility, because of the inherent nature of the threat itself. The desistent threat is less credible than the deterent threat, because the party making it has put up with the opponent's action and has only now thought it necessary to offer a threat in respect of it. The compellent threat is similarly less credible that the other two, because the question of the opponent doing this good act has not been raised before and he can therefore argue that he should go on not doing it, whilst the utterer may find that he has to carry out the threat *until* the other acts (a recipe for a possibly long-lasting action).

The opponent is always in the position where he has to make a response to a threat, and without that response the efficacy of the threat itself is not ascertainable. Edwards suggests that there are four broad categories of response which the opponent might make.

1 Submission, which yields an agreement in the terms dictated by the utterer.

2 Defiance, which leads to disagreement and open conflict if the utterer considers that he must now carry out the threat.

3 Counterthreat may lead to deterrence if it succeeds, but to open conflict if not, and will in any event draw out the same range of responses to the initial threatener as his first threat opened up for the opponent.

4 Integration, by which is meant the development of a community of interest and values between the two parties, as a result of

attempts to persuade the other that in the face of coercive measures threatened by the two parties to each other, there is probably advantage in coming together in a more co-operative relationship.

Clearly, if a threat can coerce the other into accepting a desired course of action, this provides a less costly way of securing agreement. But a threat depends upon industrial action being feasible, and is therefore often associated with bluff, or an intentional deception of the other party as to the true facts of the situation (see pp 561-64). For this reason it is risky and if bluff is called, it may prove costly. Its consideration from a strategic point of view is, therefore, justified on these grounds.

Decisions on tactics

Once the broad strategy has been determined and the relative strength of the two parties assessed, some attention can be given to the tactics to be used in the negotiation. Fundamentally, the establishment of the possible tactics involves the subdivision of the broad lines of attack upon the problem into its component issues or subissues, and the decision as to how these are to be handled in the actual negotiation. It follows from this that once the broad strategy is established certain relevant tactics can be developed which are not necessarily to other strategies.

The major *prior* decisions about tactics usually concern timing and bluff. The employer, for example, may have established a strategy which involves an opening position somewhat distant from that likely to be taken up initially by the union representatives; he may also have established which aspects of the offer may be sacrificed in the give and take leading to the agreement; and he may have determined what are his preferred settlements and his fall-back position. But he must also develop some plan relating to the sequence in which these positions are to be revealed and the time intervals which it is intended shall elapse before moving on in the sequence (see pp 532-38).

Similarly, each party has to establish what kind of impression he will seek to make on the other in an attempt to get him to reveal his position before he would plan to do so. This is the aspect of the process which is often referred to by 'bluff' or

530

'bluffing' (see Bowlby and Schriver, 1978). It is a part of the exercise that each party will try to convince the other that he is stronger (more powerful) than perhaps he is, that he holds higher cards than in fact he does (ie, each will attempt to bluff the other). If one party can get the other to believe something which is strictly incorrect, it may wring a concession or movement from the other. Since both are attempting this, the foundation is laid for the dilemma of trust (see pp 549-54).

In the context of decision about tactics, what becomes important is working through when and under what circumstances of interaction in the negotiating room, bluffs of various types may be attempted. From this it follows that prior decisions might then have to be taken as to the response to be made to the second party when the bluff succeeds; it would be necessary to recognize 'success' here and to respond to it appropriately.

Decisions about tactics which are taken before the actual negotiation, therefore, take the form of answering the question; 'what should we do if in the negotiating chamber a certain type of situation is produced by interchange?' The condition (if) might never materialize, although as part of the strategic plan some attempt might be made to produce such conditions. But tactical planning is essentially different from strategic planning in that where the latter lays down positions to be worked for, the former lays down positions which might be taken if certain eventualities arise.

The inputs at this stage are essentially ones of knowledge, attitude and skill. They are often coloured by previous experience of negotiation in general and negotiation with this party in particular, but derived from the own side's trained capacity to develop appropriate tactics in respect of negotiation.

Preparing the 'case'

The activities associated with preparation will probably be brought to a conclusion with the creation of 'a case'. This may take the form of a set of objectives and strategies which exist in the minds of the negotiators, or it may be put in written form as a written case or as a 'negotiation handbook' (see, Campo in Marceau, 1969, pp 88-89). In the first form, it represents little more than the recollection of what has been talked through in prenegotiation meetings of the team and other representatives of the principals. In the second, it is the product of a relatively skilled activity which gives coherence to the decisions already taken.

The most influential factor in the decision about whether to produce a written statement or not is likely to be the expectation of how complex the negotiation episode is likely to prove. A relatively simple episode may require nothing much more than clearing the minds of the negotiators as to the main requirements upon them. A more complex pattern of negotiation may seem to require a near-complete compendium of relevant data; bargaining objectives in priority ranking; outlines of the broad strategies and indications of the ministrategies which are considered to be worth engaging in to secure some subgoal.

The responsibility for securing the necessary understandings or for producing the written case usually rests with the chief negotiator (although the leg-work involved may be delegated). Once realized, it will serve three main purposes:

1 It provides the basis for the exercise of intra-organizational bargaining in which the own side must engage in order to realize a situation in which the team of negotiators primarily, and the constituency as a whole secondarily, achieve a broad acceptance of, or even consensus about, the way in which the issue is to be dealt with.

2 It provides the outline plan of the activities in which the actual negotiators will engage when actually confronting the other side in the negotiation episode itself. It cannot cover every contingency, particularly because negotiation implies that what one side attempts will occur against the diverse attempts to influence being made by the opponent. There must always be scope or discretion for the negotiators to take operating decisions (on their feet) as they respond to the exigencies of the actual negotiation. The intention of the 'case' is, therefore, that it will provide guidance to those who must necessarily take these kinds of decision.

3 It will eventually serve as the basis for any review of success or otherwise in the actual negotiation.

The 'case' thus terminates a *sequence* of steps in the preparation for negotiation.

532

NEGOTIATING TASKS

Atkinson identifies five stages in the actual negotiation which complement the five which he distinguishes in the preparatory stage. These are offered as guides as to the strategic behaviours the negotiator should be prepared to adopt and recognize in the conduct of the other party. Kennedy adopts a model of the process which includes eight distinct stages or steps (including preparation) which refers to as:

1 Preparation   5 Package
2 Argument   6 Bargain
3 Signal   7 Close
4 Propose   8 Agree

These form a game plan which he uses as a basis for identifying tasks and skills in preparation for training for negotiations.

Putting the two together, however, it is possible to recognize five phases of activity and five transitional actions. Because the two authors use different language to identify a broadly comparable sequence of activities, it is necessary to adopt labels for these which identify the main behavioural activities associated with them. Therefore we may recognize the ideal-typical sequence as including:

1 Preparation, which leads to producing a case (which we have discussed in the immediately preceding pages);
2 Orientation, which leads to communicating a signal.
3 Proposition, which leads to summary packaging.
4 Bargaining, which leads to closure.
5 Agreement, which culminates in endorsement.

The vocabulary used in this may respond to some of the language normally linked with negotiations, but behind the words themselves lies a model of group decision-making which has been widely used in other contexts and with other terms (see Bales, 1951, and pp 509-10). The four latter stages are discussed here.

Orientation and argument

Atkinson's first step involves securing an orientation to the issue between the parties and an evaluation of the strength of the other party relative to one's own. This is not dissimilar to what Kennedy means by 'argument' by which he refers to the opposing statements which establish the basic or opening positions of the two parties to the negotiation. These statements indicate the different perceptions and orientations to the issue which exist and which will provide the basis for the subsequent moves towards a compromise agreement. As Atkinson suggests these activities are carried out before there is much commitment by either party to one position or another, so that much of the information that is exchanged at this time is in a kind of code which the other party has to decode in order to arrive at the necessary meanings.

Pruitt (1981) in common with a number of other writers on the subject, sees this part of the process of bargaining as a necessary preliminary to more serious negotiating activity, but as one in which the parties engage in posturing for the sake of effect. That effect may be to convince the other party that the negotiation will be hard and that the strength of the party is something to be reckoned with. It may be to convince the negotiator's own side that they have their constituents' best interests at heart and the will to pursue them. In either event, the effect might also be to allow the negotiators to convince those not in the negotiating room that any compromise settlement was the 'best that could be obtained' in the seemingly difficult circumstances.

Atkinson's second stage involves persuasion of, and suggestion to the other party, as to how the issue could be handled and dealt with. In this process, the attempt is made to cast doubts on the validity of the other's position but to create more certainty about the validity of the own-side's position. It is a process of creating doubts as to the utility of the position which the other has taken up in the opening stage, and remains a part of the 'competitive' stage which Pruitt (1981) distinguishes. In Kennedy's model, this is also decidedly a part of his first, argumentative, stage, and this the view adopted here. The two processes of argument are subsumed as one.

Kennedy regards this phase as coming to an end only after the two parties offer each other signals as to their willingness to move on to more constructive stages. By 'signal' he identifies the actions (statements) which indicate a willingness by one party to end this 'argumentative' phase in which each has adopted a highly comnpetitive and partisan approach, and to move to the stage of considering proposals for resolution. This is likely to be wrapped up in the onward flight of the arguments, and needs to be disentangled by the negotiators in order that progress can be made.

Proposals for resolution

This will then lead to what Kennedy calls the stage of 'proposition'. By this he means those statements which may be put forward by the two parties as a basis for resolving the differences between them. These are likely to be advanced by the two sides in different terms and forms, as each seeks to preserve the potentiality of his own advantage. The suggestions for resolution may to be more or less numerous, depending upon the readiness of the other to react positively to the suggestions made. This phase corresponds to the search process in decision-models (see Simon, 1965, pp 58-64).

Atkinson identifies as his third stage an activity which is in many ways comparable to this. He suggests that at this stage, the parties will offer compromise settlements of the issue which are cast at points *below* that at which the other party would be prepared to settle. The object here is to test the strength of commitment of the other side to its own position, and to discover a settlement point below that which the proposer regards as his fall-back position, but which the other side shows some willingness to accept.

In this connection, conditional 'logrolling' might occur where the original demands and offers took the form of composite packages. Logrolling involves each party in giving up one (or more) demand(s) which have a relatively low utility or priority in return for a concession which has a higher one for him. A demand for higher rates for night shift working might be retained and conceded by the other party, in return for the acceptance that the other party would not move on an associated demand for a reduction in weekly hours.

In this process, a certain amount of 'bargaining' or 'give and take' must occur. But the main object here is to reduce the differences between the parties to the level where they are 'serious'; it gets rid of the fluff in the original claims and counterclaims. By 'fluff' in this context is meant those elements of a demand (or offer) which were originally introduced either to give the appearance of a stronger case, or to provide something which might be traded later for just such a concession as logrolling implies. It can be argued that the serious bargaining does not occur until after this stage has been passed, or that before this stages the activities remain essentially conflictual whereas after it they become more progressively 'problem-solving' in orientation as the parties *work* towards an agreement (see Pruitt, 1981, pp. 131-35).

Both of these authors recognize as the next step, what Atkinson calls the 'recomposition of the demands and offers' and what Kennedy calls 'packaging'. This is a similar summary-and-transition step to those of case and signal.

Atkinson sees this stage as involving a restatement of the demand/offer position reached, or a reformulation of them in a way which will probably indicate the possible links and trade-offs. As each party attempts this, he will attempt to state the position in the light most favourable to him. In Kennedy's approach, this is what essentially he means by his concept of 'packaging'. He use this term to apply to the process of picking up the different proposals and 'summarizing' them in a way which will protect the party's position and interests. Each negotiator is likely to do this in order to predispose the other party to recognition of a 'package' settlement which might be effected (albeit in the first party's interest). This helps to establish where trade-offs can be attempted in the next stage.

Bargaining and closure

In Kennedy's model, the actual *bargaining* process occurs at this next stage. It is the process of giving and taking, as the parties move towards a resolution of their differences, and, in terms of the packages already articulated, the process of establishing which trade offs might be acceptable. This is thus the part of the process which most directly and bluntly entails bargaining, trading off, or give and take. This need not imply that no give and take occurs at any other stage (because as we have seen, it does occur elsewhere) but in this particular phase, the serious bargaining might be considered to take place.

Atkinson is prepared to see this as leading straight into the stage of settlement, in which, on the basis of such trade offs, the actual agreement is founded, as the final act in the whole episode. He does, however, recognize that it may be necessary

536

at this stage to engage in an exercise designed to convince the other side that it has secured an acceptable and satisfactory outcome.

Kennedy, however, precedes this stage with what he calls 'closure', in which all that has previously been presented conditionally is made firm and explicit. It is not confined to a simple summary of what has gone before, but involves any final detailed concessions which each party may be invited and disposed to make in the interests of securing an acceptable agreement. It is only then that one can talk of the stage of agreeing. Thus, closure is seen to be followed either by agreement in the terms established in the closure stage or by a return to argument.

Agreement and endorsement

Obviously, once the parties have reached the stage of having traded off all which they are willing to trade and have reached the transition of closure, there remains little to be done but formally agree and signify the agreement in some fashion. This is rather like the act of choice which is seen to occur, as a discrete event, at the end of a decision sequence; it is brief and difficult to see and analyse.

This is nevertheless an important stage for two reasons:

1 It is desirable to have the drafting exercise carried out with care and due attention. There are, of course, many examples on record of agreements which have been reached only to fall apart because, as the parties might subsequently argue, they were badly drafted. (The British Rail v ASLEF disputes of 1981-82 seem to fall into this category). This is however not always what it may seem, because poor drafting may in some circumstances be both intentional and functional; it might for example prove to be the only way to get a 'cooling off period' in a heated dispute, and there are probably many unpublicised examples of such bad drafting proving useful from this point of view. The agreeing process may, therefore, require careful attention, even when the intention of both parties might be to produce loose drafts for this kind of reason.

2 It may be desirable and prudent to review the agreement reached from the viewpoints of what it secures for the

several parties. This could, if mishandled, lead to a reopening of issues. But where it is handled sensibly, it can serve to influence either side that it has secured a 'good deal' in the circumstances, as in the suggestion by Atkinson mentioned on the previous page.

The agreement process can be regarded as culminating in the endorsement of the agreement by the parties. Except in more formal national negotiations, this process of signing the agreement on behalf of principals is frequently done after the negotiating session. The agreement will be drafted in the personnel office and despatched to the union representatives with an extra copy for signature and return. This action thus ties off the activity of agreeing in a formal fashion.

There are differences in the practice of who signs agreements at the different levels of negotiation. National agreements may attract the signatures of the officers of the employers' associations and the trade unions, which may be applied in rather formal signing ceremonies. At more local levels of negotiation, however, signatories may be the same as, or different from the negotiators. Negotiations led by a works or personnel manager may lead to agreements signed by board members on the management side, just as those led by shop stewards may be signed by full-time officers of the trade union. Practice varies, and sometimes it does so for purely historical (and perhaps accidental) reasons, sometimes for deliberate reasons (such as keeping agreements 'in house').

Five major categories of activity in the actual process of negotiation, each culminating in some action which allows progress towards the next logical stage, may thus be identified in this manner. These call for different behaviours on the part of the negotiators.

The associated behaviours

The activities which occur within a negotiating episode may take on an extremely wide variety of forms. Detailed discussion of the whole range of them would be virtually impossible and unproductive. However, these behaviours are all essentially strategic, embarked upon deliberately and with the intention to serve a previously chosen purpose. Therefore, some attempt can be made to categorize the main behaviours associated with distributive bargaining. This offers some broad indication of the kinds of activity in which negotiators are usually expected to become skilled.

Morley and Stephenson have attempted to build upon the original (1950) Bales' interaction process model (and some variants which appeared subsequently) to produce a model which proceeds *via* a language more appropriate to distributive bargaining between representatives (Morley and Stephenson, 1977, pp 188-215). They title their model 'conference process analysis' and seek to apply it to negotiations in general, including those which contain some bargaining (or give and take on the way to an exchange). They also provide a language more appropriate to that used in negotiations using terms like concessions, threats, settlement points, procedures, etc (*ibid*) rather than the more neutral concepts used by Bales.

Although they accept that negotiation involves both instrumental and affective behaviours, they take the view that there is a fundamental difference in the way in which instrumental and affective behaviours are related in negotiations from that found in problem-solving:

> 'the principal difference between problem-solving and negotiation groups is that, whereas in problem-solving groups coping with task leads to conflict, in negotiating groups, conflict leads to coping with tasks' (Morley and Stephenson, 1977, p 259).

Although the representatives start with different interests and objectives, they can only secure them by engaging in a kind of co-operative process of negotiation, since neither can succeed without what the other possesses and is willing to put on offer. They must therefore engage in negotiation through which common problems are solved or issues between them are resolved. The beginning stages are therefore more likely to involve high emotion ('hard bargaining from entrenched positions') which gives way to more instrumental behaviour ('problem solving') only with the necessary elapse of time in negotiation.

The activity which occurs in negotiations may be appreciated at two distinct levels, that which seeks the exchange as occurring at the material level, and that which sees it occurring at the informational level. The two are not, perhaps, so different since the first involves the communication of information

539

and argument about the terms of the real (future) exchange rather than a (current) transaction of a physical or material kind. What is therefore exchanged in the verbalization process are the 'resources' of conformity to procedures, relevant information, acknowledgements of the other's right and potentially acceptable settlement points and outcomes (Morley and Stephenson, 1977, p. 193). In that sense, the exchange of 'information' or of 'symbols' is not so very different in nature, although it may be seen as concerned with a different mode of securing agreement.

Table 21

Behaviours in negotiation

Information exchanges	
1 Seeks information	2 Gives information
3 Probes other's position	4 Distorts information
5 Seeks suggestions	6 Offers suggestions
Verbalizations of potential resource exchanges	
7 Demands	8 Offers/counterdemands
9 Threats	10 Counterthreats
11 Concessions	12 Rejections
Affective behaviours	
13 Seeks opinions	14 Offers opinions
15 Acknowledges other's status	16 Provokes other
17 Agrees	18 Disagrees

In a typical negotiating sequence, 'resources' are introduced in what Morley and Stephenson refer to as different 'modes'. They are either demanded or offered, in each case in the form of a statement of what 'might' be demanded or offered. In the nature of this kind of negotiation, however, the demands and the offers will be presented in a way which links them with

540

(explicit or implicit) threats and counterthreats. 'We seek an increase of £3, and if it is not conceded, we will strike'. 'We are prepared to offer £1, and if it is not accepted, we will have to terminate the employment of the people concerned'. This uses the 'language' of distributive bargaining, where agreement can only be compelled either by disabling action or threat of it.

In the face of a request or demand, resources may be either yielded or withheld. In the face of an offer they may be either accepted or rejected. The decisions about which response to make in each case are likely to be influenced by the perceptions of the seriousness of the threats made or implied and of the calculations of the consequences if the threats were to be carried out. This too is the nature of distributive bargaining; threat and counterthreat are instrumental in securing a response from the opponent. Of course, in the absence of 'give and take' and consequent agreement, threats may have to be articulated in order to secure movement; but *actual* exchanges of this kind are what the processes of negotiation are intended to avoid.

These interchanges involve the communication of information. There may be a sense in which what is thus communicated is not 'true' or 'factual'. This is the other 'level' at which the interactions between the parties are to be appreciated. Information is introduced in some mode and form in the negotiating room. This may 'follow' the pattern indicated by Bales (1950) and may be identified in terms of asking for and giving information, opinion, and suggestion (see p 510). But this process of information exchange is also structured by strategic considerations. In the giving of information, both may seek to 'bluff' the other into believing something to be true which is not true. This is a major 'strategic deception' which is designed to secure some advantage for the bluffer over the other party. It is what preserves the element of *difference* between the parties as they tackle the problem of bringing an 'agreement' into existence.

Both of these may then be linked to the affective or emotive aspects of the process. These also focus on tension and its reduction and upon agreement and disagreement within the negotiating processes themselves. But just as the Bales' conceptions acquire a new dimension in the other cases discussed above, so here disagreement is often expressed as 'provocation' (taking the form of derogatory statements about the

541

other) and agreement as (what Morley and Stephenson call 'acknowledgement' (statements which acknowledge or praise an opponent). The stages of 'packaging' and 'interpretation' in the process of negotiation may be associated with Bales' categories of integration (bringing the negotiations *in toto* to a realization that the parties can co-operate with one another in spite of their differences). The final stages of 'agreement' also carry their connotations of emotion, as much as the stages of disagreement and rejection do.

Within something like this framework, it can be argued, as do Morley and Stephenson, that every negotiating behaviour is concerned with the verbalization of some resource or some information. They also suggest that it involves one mode of introduction to the negotiating exercise or another. These behaviours are designed to bring about a final agreement on terms as favourable to the party as its negotiators can make them by the exercise, not only of the skills of communication and argument, but also of those of threatening, bluffing, and provoking.

Stages and behaviours

Morley and Stephenson's original purpose in making their categorization was to enable observations of experimental and actual negotiations to be recorded and analysed, and so to increase our knowledge of what goes on. In the present context, they provide labels for the kind of activity in which negotiators are expected to engage, and in which they are expected to provided a skilled performance.

Morley and Stephenson's Conference Process Analysis has not yet been used as extensively as has Bales' Interaction Process Analysis, and the conclusions which may be drawn from its use are therefore limited. On the basis of their observations in experimental and actual sessions of negotiation, they are able to conclude that their major hypothesis about the difference in direction of movement between instrumental and affective behaviours is confirmed (Morley and Stephenson, pp 292-3). They see the sequence as moving from hard distributive bargaining, to problem-solving, to decision-making and action, and the behaviours involved beoming less partisan and less separately identifiable as the negotiation proceeeds (Morley and Stephenson, 1977, p 292). Pruitt

(1981, pp 131-35) has also concluded on the basis of his work and that of colleagues in the USA, that there is a transition from what he calls 'competitive' behaviours to 'co-ordination' (in which movement towards agreement is facilitated by co-operative problem-solving behaviours).

In the first of these phases, the negotiators are seen to act in a distinctly partisan fashion, as they express their principals' demands. This may be regarded as useful in that it allows the parties to come to a conclusion about the feasibility of their own and the other's demands in the light of how firm the other appears to be in maintaining its position, and of the power which the other might be able to deploy to secure its end. Pruitt suggests that this competitive posturing establishes the negotiator's commitment to his side's position. It clarifies for him what his goals are and ought to be and demonstrates how firm each party is in pursuing ends. It also indicates how far the other side may be pushed and helps to establish what the 'realistic' limits of the differences between the parties are (Pruitt, 1981, p 135).

Transition to the 'co-ordinative' stage is thereby facilitated. This occurs where each party has recognized what is feasible within that negotiating situation. As Pruitt suggests, 'Eventually all of the threats, commitments and debating points that can be made have been made; and the party, while duly impressed, is unwilling to make further concessions' (Pruitt, 1971, p 210) so that avoiding complete breakdown demands a more co-ordinative or problem-solving approach. He also makes the point that this transition will depend upon the negotiators developing a sufficient degree of trust that the opponent will not then move in a way which is not sanctioned by the conventions of bargaining, and that there will, for example, be a degree of equality in the amount of movement or concession which the parties make in order to reach agreement (*ibid*, p. 133-34).

This implies that the most stressful situation in any negotiation is likely to occur at the beginning of the episode, and that both the more effective and the more pleasant activities are likely to follow only after the passage of some necessary time and argument involving the use of those strategic behaviours which are referred to as probing, bluffing, provocation and threat. These become more directly associated with the early posturing phase, and diminish in significance as the negotiators lose their overt partisan associations as the negotiation progresses. As Stevens (1963, p. 11) has argued:

> 'In the early stages the essentially competitive tactics of coercion and deception (tactics by means of which each party attempts to 'move' his opponent's position in his own favour) will be relatively more prominent. In the pre-deadline stages, tactics of co-operation (tactical problems associated with mutual convergence upon an agreed position) will be relatively more prominent'.

By implication, therefore, these less congenial behaviours are associated with the stage at which the parties seek to measure the strength of the opponent and its own case, as a basis for resolving the differences between them in a more problem-solving, co-ordinative fashion.

Summary: distributive bargaining

Distributive bargaining is the kind of bargaining which most have in mind when 'collective bargaining' is thought of. It is that bargaining which occurs where two parties who must co-operate have divergent interests and diverse views about the appropriate terms for that co-operation. It is characterized by the willingness of the parties to exchange of some of their material or symbolic resources in order to secure a basis for future co-operation.

Because distributive bargaining, by definition, involves the parties in a zero-sum game (in which the gains of one are the losses of the other) it is associated with conflict, and, for this reason, depends upon both parties having some *power* to compel or coerce the other to an agreement, preferably on the party's terms. For this reason, too, the actions of the parties are essentially strategic actions, linked to the broad overall strategy developed to ensure that the game is won in the preferred terms.

A number of distinct stages can be identified in the sequence of distributive bargaining activities, beginning with a number of preparatory activities, moving through a number of negotiating and bargaining activities, and culminating in those activities which create and implement an agreement as to terms. This can be no more than a statement of the ideal-typical sequence in which the activities of the parties are structured by the conventions of negotiation. However, the statement does provide a guide to *likely* tasks of the negotiators and an indication of the kinds of skills which the negotiators will be required to bring to the negotiating and bargaining tasks.

A comparison of the kinds of action required for the two modes (integrative and distributive or co-operative and conjunctive) suggests that each makes its own demands on the negotiators. The probability that any episode of negotiation between management and workers will contain elements of both approaches to bargaining, adds to the confusion of negotiators over the appropriate kinds of behaviour to adopt.

Readings

Walton and McKersie: (1965), pp 11-125.
Atkinson: (1975), pp 86-170. Pruitt: (1981), pp 91-135.
Kennedy, Benson and McMillan: (1980), pp 14-114.
Clegg: (1972), pp 20-37. Anthony: (1977), pp 219-67.

20

The dilemmas of negotiation

The mixed motives of negotiation

The models of bargaining and negotiation most commonly employed emphasize the existence of 'mixed motives' within the parties (Nemeth, 1972; Bartos, 1977, p 565). This term is used to indicate that the parties wish to reach a mutually acceptable solution in order that the co-operative relationship may continue, but nevertheless wish to realize as many of their own wants or preferences for the solution as possible (Rubin and Brown, 1975, p 10). This reflects the existence of both co-operative and competitive objectives but it also admits that different views may be taken of the 'essential nature' of the relationship between organized workers and employers, simply by placing more stress on one rather than the other.

We have already noted that there are two very broad alternative approaches to maintaining the relationship between the parties, one stressing the integrative and the other the competitive orientation. This may lead to the conclusion that distributive and integrative bargaining are separate and distinct processes which are mutually exclusive; if one is pursued, the other cannot be countenanced. This is probably to confuse the needs of analysis with a description of reality; in reality, the two may exist happily side by side, and even in an intertwined and interdependent fashion, and it is only for purposes of analysis that one might want to treat them separately.

This interconnection is likely to prove a source of problems and difficulties for both the principals and the negotiators. These are frequently referred to as 'dilemmas' (see, Kelley, 1966) which confront the negotiators because the two motives and the two processes co-exist. These dilemmas are frequently regarded as characteristic of all negotiations which are concerned with different interests and founded on differential control of and access to power bases (see Pedler, 1977, p 21; Walton and McKersie, 1965, pp 121-5; 169-82; 268-80; 340-51). In their nature, however, they focus upon the individual agents or representatives, who conduct the negotiations and assume responsibility for them and their outcomes.

What makes these dilemmas significant, is the possibility that the negotiators, in attempting to resolve them, will make mistakes which adversely affect the negotiating processes and outcomes. The possibility that negotiators might fail in their attempts is widely recognized in bargaining literature. Coping with the dilemmas inherent in negotiation may be one solution to this. At the same time, the inherent problems may not be very amenable to resolution by prior training, as is suggested by the late development of training approaches and programmes in this area (see, CIR Report Nos 33 and 33A; BIM, 1971; Kennedy *et al.*, 1980; Brewster and Connock, 1982).

Error and stress

The scope for making errors in negotiation is considerable. Edwards, for example, suggests that errors might occur at any stage. The party might make an error in perceiving the conditions in which either he himself or his opponent find themselves; he might make wrong calculations about the probabilities of outcomes from various courses of action which might be theoretically open; and he might make errors in carrying out his strategic plans in negotiation with the opponent (Edwards, 1969, p 83).

Errors may stem from the conditions in which the tasks have to be carried out, particularly where stress is present in the situation (see Hopman & Walcott, 1977, p 301). What the negotiators do may reflect the circumstances, but 'events occurring during the negotiations may be affected by the state of the system in which they are embedded and may have an effect on future states of that system' (Hopman & Walcott, 1977, p 301; see also Druckman, 1973, pp 80-1), so that permanent damage is done.

They may also occur because of disabilities or deficiencies on the part of the individual. Provided that these are not fundamental, associated with genetic or physiological deficiencies, they can be made up for by training and experience. But the situation will make it likely that stress will be a constant feature of the negotiating process, and a damaging factor dependent upon the negotiators' tolerance thresholds for stress.

Research into the effects of stress upon individuals and groups engaged in various kinds of tasks, including negotiating tasks, suggests that where this stress moves beyond a certain threshold of intensity, it is likely to have harmful effects upon performance (although below the threshold the effect may be stimulating for some people and some groups).

At the individual level, the outcome of the research suggests that above a certain threshold, the effects of stress are likely to increase 'hostility and rigidity ... in negotiations' by way of limiting perceptions, increasing intolerance of ambiguity, enhancing cognitive rigidity and reducing problem-solving ability (Hopmann and Walcott, 1977, pp 302-3).

At the group level research suggests that stress brought on by external threats may increase group cohesiveness, but where this moves above a threshold, it may adversely affect the group's ability to solve problems and to reach agreements in bargaining situations. Hopmann and Walcott's own simulation study suggests, further, that the findings from different kinds of research tend to be convergent and that therefore they can conclude that:

> 'stresses and tensions generally tend to be dysfunctional for negotiations ... creating ... hostility among negotiators ... harder bargaining strategies, and ... less successful outcomes...' (Hopmann & Walcott, 1977, p 321).

Herein lies the reason for concern about the dilemmas which negotiation creates for the people who are directly involved in it.

In this chapter, we consider three types of dilemma.

1   The related dilemmas of trust and integrity, which most directly concern the nature of the principals, and the relationships between them, even though the dilemmas have to be borne and worked through by their representatives or agents.

2   The dilemmas which are associated with the goals and the means adopted for their realization in the particular situation.

3   The dilemmas of personality and role, which focus most directly upon the negotiators themselves as they seek to meet their role expectations and at the same time live comfortably with their own self-images.

In each case, we look at the main means by which the negotiators may reduce the stress which is occasioned by the presence of a dilemma.

THE DILEMMAS OF INTEGRITY AND TRUST

The dilemma of trust is arguably the most fundamental one to the relationship between the parties because it develops directly from the presence of mixed motives and intentions in the continuous relationship. Inevitably, within that relationship, some interactions will be open, honest and sincere, but others will be intended as strategic deceptions intended to deceive and obfuscate issues. This must be so, because the parties at least partially seek to defend or improve different (interest) positions, and some of the gain to any one party must be at the expense of the other. Even in an exercise in integrative bargaining, the question of the distribution of any pay-off must enter into the process of negotiation at some stage. It is this feature which distinguishes bargaining and negotiation from a simple exercise in philosophical discussion (or 'mere communication') to influence the thoughts of another.

The dilemma that is created here is that which suggests that if one party believes in the sincerity of the other party, he places himself in the position of risking being duped and losing out. If, on the other hand, he regards the other as engaged in strategic deception, he places himself in the position of being too cynical to succeed. In the actual negotiating episode, if the negotiator believes everything that is said by the other party, he places himself at a disadvantage in making counter-proposals or concessions, whilst if he disbelieves everything said by the first party, no agreement on outcome is possible (Kelley, 1966, p 60).

Closely related to the dilemma of trust is that which can be identified as a 'dilemma of integrity'. This refers to the congruence of the party's conduct with his own self image. It manifests itself in the concrete situation as a concern to maintain a position in ethics which may be under threat or challenge from the other party. It is, of course, always possible to define an expendient course of action as being in this category, but the identification of a matter of moral principle is considerably easier where there is a published statement of what the undertaking's or the union's policy is. Whether or not this exists, there are occasions where either party may be unable to move because he regards himself as bound by some higher ethic. In the usual example, this higher ethic is a 'policy' (management or union) which is intended to be binding upon the negotiators for reasons which are not immediately pragmatic or expedient.

The commonest case of this kind is where the party sees a 'principle' to be at stake. What makes the issue a matter of principle is usually connected with the party's underlying objectives. It becomes important to maintain a position. In such circumstances, the party may feel that his opening position is also his final position, and that there can be no give or movement on it in negotiation.

Alternatively, this problem may be expressed in terms of pay-offs. Some issues presented may be such that they provide no potentially positive pay-off for one party. In these circumstances, that party has no incentive to engage in negotiation. The issue is, from its point of view, a non-negotiable one.

The negotiator in these circumstances risks the accusation that he is not prepared to bargain in good faith if he refuses to move on the issue, and jeopardizes his own moral position if he does in the face of a declared policy to the contrary. Such is the basis of his dilemma.

Controls on the dilemma

Controlling the dilemma of trust requires some action either to make it clearer what is the intention of the other in any of his interactions, or to bring about changes in the attitudes which the other holds so that they are more congruent with the party's own. The first of these is attempted by the development of policies by the parties themselves separately and of conventions of bargaining by the parties jointly (see chapter 12). The second is sometimes considered desirable, but frequently regarded as too difficult to accomplish within the negotiating framework except on a long-term basis.

'Trust' may be treated as being based upon attitudes or frames of reference which have developed as a result of socialization and experience. Decisions or choices about whether to trust another respond to predispositions in the individual concerned. These in turn are generally regarded as deep-seated and slow to change. They are thought to be formed gradually during socialization and to change just as gradually. For this reason, they provide the foundation for consistency and pattern in human behaviour, but make behavioural modification a difficult process.

The attitudes on which inter-party trust is based are held in place or modified by pressures from three main sources:

1   The experience which the parties have had of negotiations with one another over a period of time (which may be supported by experience of other negotiations elsewhere or acquired beliefs about negotiation relationships in general). This will have led the negotiators (and their constituents or principals) to expect *as customary* certain approaches by the other party directed towards to certain ends. *Current* negotiating experience will tend either to reinforce these expectations or to challenge them, and in the latter case it will sow the seeds of a change in frames of reference and attitudes.

2   The technological, economic (market), and power environments of the relationship are usually seen to have an important bearing on the formation and modification of attitudes. Where these remain stable, they will contribute to the stability of existing attitudes, but where they change, they may initiate changes (which may still take a long time to mature). This is because, in a dynamic environment, attitudes may get out of phase with the environment and lead to inappropriate or ineffectual behaviours. If the environment could be assumed totally unchanging, existing predispositions would continue to be relevant to action, and there would be little pressure to change them. If the environment changes, however, there may be a need for changes in attitudes or frame of reference. But there is nothing, even in Kelly's scientific perspective of man, which implies that such 'objective' changes will necessarily effect 'subjective' ones without human intervention to reform perceptions (see Katz and Lazarsfeld, 1954, pp 116-33).

3   The ideological (or social belief) systems of those who occupy 'gatekeeper' roles in the process of attitude formation and revision (see, Walton and McKersie, 1965, p 190). This is because direct experience, either of negotiation with the other party or of a changing environment, is unlikely by itself to produce changes in attitude and predisposition. These, consistent with Katz and Lazarsfeld's two-step process of communication and influence, will occur only after some kind of human (or group) mediation.

Therefore, although past experience can be expected to colour or shape the individual's views of the world and his or her perception of desirable and feasible objectives, and although environmental changes may create the presumption of a need to change attitudes, this is not an autonomous and automatic influence, but rather one which depends upon human agency. Moreover, that human agency must be accepted ('trusted') as being in the position of gatekeeper, and not just any old agent (such as a trainer or opposing negotiator) who happens to have an interest in bringing about change to support some objective or strategy of his own.

Effecting changes in conduct through changes in attitudes may be attempted in one of two principal ways. Given that attitudes are the product of responses to the environment over time, modification may be sought by varying that environment. Alternatively, given that attitudes are socially-formed (requiring human agency to provide meanings that the environment does not 'automatically' provide), changes may be sought through human intervention to persuade the 'other'.

Dealing with dilemmas of integrity

The party faces a dilemma of integrity in those circumstances where some demand is made upon him by the other party. The resolution of the dilemma is thus to be considered in the context of an actual negotiation. The party in this position has a number of constrained options open to him.

1   The party might refuse to bargain on the issue, to play that particular game. This involves a risk of industrial action by the other party and would therefore be embarked upon only after a consideration of the likely costs. Bartos argues that negotiation can start only when the opening bids are acceptable to the other party, as allowing some potential (positive) pay-off for him. The 'trick' in negotiation becomes that of finding the opening bid which will be 'just' acceptable to the opponent or acceptable only with the greatest possible reluctance (Bartos, 1977, pp 571-72).

2   The party may seek to condition the other party to accept a particular point of view on the issue, in advance of the negotiation actually commencing. A management might communicate to the union that the economic situation is so

tight that it will be able to give very little in an approaching wage negotiation, and therefore that the union should take care to present an appropriately small demand (for example, one which can be negotiated on the usual conventions).

It might take steps to change the financial position of the company as this will be revealed in the accounts, so that this 'information' will help structure the union's thinking on the issue. It might call a pre-negotiation meeting to say, off the record, but bluntly, to the negotiators that they must recognize that the management's fall-back position will be one which is extremely low. It might also take action to 'communicate' this kind of message to the workforce in general, either by a circular letter or by cutting back on an expected investment or on all overtime.

3   The party might make a number of counter-demands upon the other party in order to produce some room for manoevre as a result of linking them together. If these are presented, as it were 'simultaneously' with the presentation of the first party's demand, then the two may be considered together as a 'package'. Failure to give on the first claim might then be traded off by giving on the counter-demand. A union faced with a demand for changed working practices, for example, may well come back with a demand for an increase in wages or for staff status, which can then be linked and traded off.

This is similar in effect to the approach which can be made to bargaining in the circumstances where a number of different elements of demand are incorporated in the original demand. The responding party may under those circumstances give on one element but stick on another. For this same kind of reason, it is usual for both parties to 'bank' demands immediately prior to a negotiation (see Batstone, Boraston and Frenkel, 1978). But such 'banking' may allow management, which is faced with a no-movement position on some issue for example, to concede *within the main negotiation* what it would probably have conceded anyway and at any time had the issue been allowed to surface.

The general intention of such strategies is, therefore, to establish that there is something on which the individual party is willing to negotiate, even if it is unwilling to bargaining on the first demand. It becomes a particular exercise to try to find an equal and opposite position which can be taken up in the opening statements to allow the conventional give and take to occur.

It may be done by seeking to influence the opposing negotiators or their constituents to regard the party's position as realistic or sensible, or 'in everybody's long term interests'. It might be done by making resolution of this issue dependent upon solving some other problem which the other party has presented for negotiation and which is of comparable value to it. It might also be done by linking this issue with others not yet on the bargaining table but which might be argued to be important to both parties and requiring resolution at this time.

There are therefore strategic and tactical options open to a party which finds itself in a position from which it can make no movement to accommodate the other in accordance with the conventions of bargaining. Each calls for consideration in the light of the likely responses of the opponent and of their impact upon the bargaining process itself.

The dilemmas of goals and means

The 'dilemma of goals' (Kelley, 1966) depends upon the voluntary nature of the negotiating process. The parties meet with one another in negotiation by choice, and must recognize that they have the options of either withdrawing from the relationship (if in their view they might gain more of what they seek by doing so) or continuing within it (if they believe that some solution or outcome out of a possible range will satisfy them more) (Rubin and Brown, 1975, pp 7-8).

They do *have* objectives which they seek to achieve in interaction with the other and these, in the nature of the relationship, must be at least potentially or partially different from one another. The objective may be no more than protecting some position from being undermined by the actions of the other party, but it could involve securing from the other something which it possesses and the negotiating partner wants.

If one party pushes too hard for a particular outcome or solution, it may then risk the withdrawal of the other party from the negotiating process, but if either party does not push hard enough it may have to settle for less than might otherwise have been achieved. This may be illustrated by reference to the problem of determining the opening moves in any negotiation. Where an issue is accepted by the parties as negotiable, the determination in advance of the opening moves to be made is of significance because they set the scene for what follows, and could affect the outcomes.

Establishing limits to settlements

The opening 'demand' by the one party, and the opening 'offer' or counter-claim by the other, set a limit to the interactions and negotiations which will follow. It follows that if the situation is mistaken by either party, or that if one party somehow gets the opening 'wrong', the whole course of the subsequent negotiation is likely to be affected. Misapprehensions and mistakes will be difficult to retrieve in any event and are likely to involve cost. In integrative bargaining, for example, the initiation of the exercise with a 'blank sheet of paper' (p 503 above) can easily be misunderstood by the workers' representatives.

In distributive bargaining, the conventions that the opening moves should leave room for give and take in order to reach a settlement (Stevens, 1966) produces its own dilemmas: the party which makes the first demand will establish by that demand, what kind of a game is to be played (distributive bargaining) and what the parameters to the give and take will be (from zero to the fulfillment of that demand). If the demand made is 'low', then the amount of room for subsequent manoeuvre will be restricted. Given the convention that the parties will have a fall-back position as well as an opening demand, an even narrower set of limits can be detected; if the party wants something, but it is something not far from an opening zero, then its fall-back position (which indicates the range of possible settlement) is likely to be very close, by definition, to its opening demand.

This also has implications for the responding opening move of the other side. The opponent is never in the position where he can dictate the kind of game which is to be played, except by refusing to play the game indicated by the opening openent and risking confrontation. But he does have some scope to influence the limits of the subsequent bargaining process by determining where his opening offer or bid is to be placed, albeit in reaction to the first party. A low initial demand not only allows little room for manoeuvre overall, but it restricts the scope for the opponent's opening move. Given the convention of equal sacrifice in order to reach a settlement, the opponent's opening move can only be a correspondingly low one close to the initial demand.

Similar considerations apply in connection with the high opening demand. If it is so high that the opponent must seek his opening bid at a level which will give up roughly the same amount to settle at what *he* estimates to be the likely settlement point, he may have to open with an offer of a minus quantity (which would be regarded as derisory) or more realistically adopt a position of zero movement after the opening offer. The effect might then well be that the high opening bidder would find himself having to make a considerable concession in return for very little movement on the part of the opponent. In either case, the situation has all the making of confrontation and possible industrial action to compel 'greater realism' on the part of one or the other.

A high opening demand, or one which is expressed in vague terms ('a substantial increase in wages') might risk a response from the other side which involves or implies that he is not willing to play that game. He may refuse to bargain until such time as the other makes a more realistic demand, and in that event the opener may have to consider sanctions as a way of compelling the opponent's return to the game. If that were to be thought likely to occur and to succeed, the effect might be to force the opponent to respond with a relatively high opening bid, one above his original intention. In that event the area for give and take would be lifted up the scale, and the opener could regard this as a victory. But it does entail risks, and many have argued that the normal approach to bargaining does not countenance such risks being taken.

The dilemma of means

The dilemma of means takes two different (but related forms). In the first form it concerns the choices which exist in respect of planning (or the means of arriving at the decisions about what will be looked for as a result of the negotiation). The dilemma arises from the possibility that the choice of any one approach will inevitably block off opportunities for achievement which one of the other methods might have produced. This is not a dilemma which is confined to negotiations: as we saw on pp 51, managers face this kind of choice in any planning or decision-making context.

As it relates to negotiations, however, it presents the two sides with a choice which (in the most general terms) lies between what Lindblom refers to as the root and branch approaches to decision-taking. In the root approach, the 'whole' system (for example, that of the totality of agreements) is considered afresh each time occasion for negotiation presents itself. It is in the nature of collective contracts negotiated in the USA, that this 'root' approach is more likely (but not necessarily) to be adopted to form negotiating issues in a particular round. In effect, everything is looked at in relation to everything else.

The alternative is to approach the whole question of what is to be negotiated and what for in a much more piecemeal fashion, taking the definition of negotiable issues from the recurring situation and pursuing those upon which the negotiators think they might stand some chance of improving at that time and in those circumstances. What effects these might then have upon the rest of the 'system' is something to be determined in later experience, not estimated in advance and in a way which will allow objectives to be shaped by the forecasts. In effect, only limited goals are established and pursued.

The negotiators thus face a wide choice and confront the dilemma of missing opportunities if the wrong one is made. The 'branch' approach might well expose the principals to requirements and rules which will disconcert them; the root approach will prevent the negotiators from securing marginal improvements except at considerable cost occasioned by the reactions of the other side to the wider demands made.

The second part of this dilemma is focused much more directly upon the actual modes of negotiation to be adopted. Decisions have to be taken as to the manner in which the principal will deal with the negotiating partner in any particular episode of bargaining or negotiation. This choice may be oversimplified to regard it as one between distributive and integrative (or co-operative) bargaining. This is sometimes refered to as the 'dilemma of honesty and openness' which develops from any juxtaposition within a particular episode of bargaining of the strategic demands of the two main modes.

In integrative bargaining, it is essential that the approach shall be based on open, frank and honest discussion of the 'facts' and the inferences which can be drawn from them. Where this occurs, however, it raises the question of how frank the negotiator can be in the context of any parallel or subsequent exercise in distributive bargaining over the pay-offs. If he is too frank, he cannot withdraw from the position later; but if he is too covert in his expressions, the other party may deny that he is engaged in good faith bargaining, and may withdraw.

Similarly, where the parties have been accustomed to using strategically deceptive behaviours to win their points in distributive bargaining, problems might arise where the attempt is made to move over to an integrative bargaining mode. In such circumstances, either party may doubt the sincerity of the negotiators and the honesty of any communications made in the context of integrative bargaining. Whilst this is obviously a dilemma which stems, like that of trust, directly from the presence of mixed motives and mixed means to their pursuit, it is also one which in practice is often resolved by compartmentalizing communications and negotiations (for example, between joint consultation and collective bargaining, or between productivity bargaining and the annual round of (distributive) bargaining).

The dilemmas of role and personal behaviour

The dilemmas of role develop out of the multiplicity of expectations which impinge on the roles of negotiators. These may be seen to crystallize in the role of the chief negotiator, the 'person with primary responsibility for negotiations' (Walton and McKersie, 1965, p 282). This is essentially a boundary role (which is shared by the team as a whole) and, therefore, the incumbent of it is liable to experience role conflict (which might explain some of reluctance of some people to take it on). It is this idea of role conflict which identifies the nature of the dilemma which confronts those who do take it on.

The notion of role conflict arises from multiple expectations of conduct to which some roles are subject and this, in turn, follows from the way in which the concept of role is defined. A role is usually defined as the product of the expectations of others as to the way in which the incumbent of that role should act. Where the expectations are compatible with one another (because they are either all the same or because they are complementary even though different) the individual can develop a single conforming perspective of what he is (expected) to do. When he acts in accordance with these expectations he secures approval and avoids the disapproval which usually accompanies failure to conform to them.

Where, therefore, a role is subjected to two or more distinct and incompatible sets of expectations, it may be identified as a boundary role: it rests on the boundary between two sets or systems of expectations. The individual, in conforming to one set and securing the approval of those who hold it, can only secure disapproval from the others with whose incompatible expectations he cannot simultaneously conform. He must, of course, decide for himself in accordance with his own preferences which set he must attempt to conform to, under such circumstances, and having done so, he must tolerate the disapproval of the opposing group.

The negotiator is subject to a number of such pressures or conflicting expectations, as shown in the following diagram. This recognizes that there are a principal and some subsidiary sources of pressure from the negotiator's own side *and* from the opposing side, as well as a pressure from the external social environment. His dilemma stems from the choice he must make. If he conforms to one set, he may jeopardize his chances of securing a return of approval or acceptance from another set. It is unlikely that he can secure a return of approval from all three.

Figure 5

Pressures on the negotiators

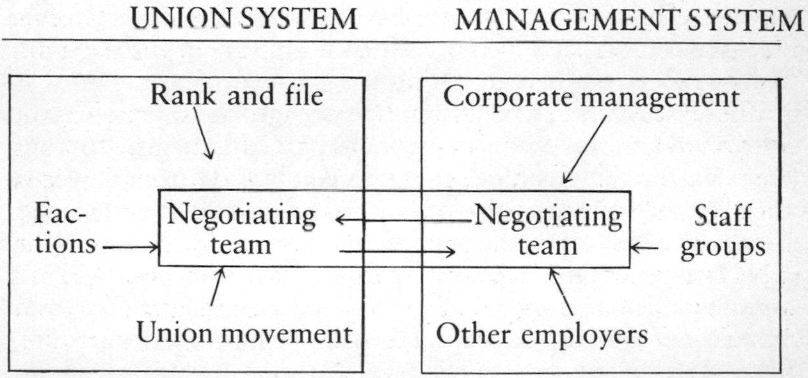

| UNION SYSTEM | MANAGEMENT SYSTEM |

Source: Walton and McKersie (1968)

He will receive from his own side prescriptions of the role (and therefore the behaviour) that he should follow. A works manager (see Winkler, 1973) or a full-time officer (see Batstone, Boraston and Frenkel, 1977, p 112) will be instructed in a more or less formal fashion as to what he is to achieve and how he is to set about it. Even if he has considerable autonomy in framing objectives and strategies, he will still confront expectations of how he will exercise that autonomy in making his choices. If he conforms to those of his own side, he may risk his potentially-fruitful relationship with the opponent.

He will also be subjected to expectations and prescriptions from the opposing side. These are likely to be unwritten, but nevertheless identifiable as the conventions of bargaining (see ch. 12) aimed at preserving the long-term relationship between the opposing negotiators and the opposing sides. Those who do not have to negotiate with the opponent can often afford the luxury of ignoring such questions in their expression of view as to what ought to be aimed for or attempted. Those who do can scarcely avoid these, and must therefore seek to secure some approval from the opponent, at least in the sense of bargaining according to convention and good faith in order to maintain a sufficient level of trust to permit success. Conformity to these expectations may, however, lose the support of one's own principals or constituents.

The negotiator will also be subject to pressures from the general public. How strong these will be is likely to depend on the importance attached to the issue and the threat posed by any failure to agree. How much notice is taken of these kinds of pressure is not likely to vary with the strength of the pressure, but with ideology and commitment on the part of the negotiators and the relative strength of the more immediate pressures. However, they are likely to have some influence and in some circumstances may prove crucial to the settlement.

This aspect of the situation has frequently been observed and commented on (see Katz, 1959, pp 28-40; Barbash, 1961; Rosen and Rosen, 1955, pp 539-45). It is often expressed in terms of the negotiators being out of touch or out of sympathy with the objectives and preferred approaches of the principals or the membership (see Parnes, 1956, p 61). Role conflict may therefore be a natural and normal outcome of a number of factors inherent in the situation:

1   The negotiators on the two sides engage in interaction with one another to an extent which is not possible for the other members of the two sides. This involvement can be expected to give rise to heightened sentiments (although not necessarily of liking) (see Homans, 1951, pp 99-103).

2   The negotiators come to regard themselves as in a continuing relationship which ought to be preserved for 'technical' reasons, that is, to facilitate the carrying out of these responsibilities. They usually have a continuing responsibility for their decisions, being actively involved in implementing the agreements reached and in modifying them in further negotiations where this proves to be necessary.

3   Part of the negotiators' self-image develops from his participation in the negotiations. These then take on a value in themselves so that the negotiators will tend to regard the preservation of the ritual exercise as a necessary and desirable feature of their experience (see Etzioni, 1975, p 5).

For these reasons, therefore, the negotiator may use the main negotiation to further his attempts to bring constituents' expectations of goals and behaviours into line with his own.

Resolution of role conflict

The term, 'intra-organizational bargaining' is used by Walton and McKersie to refer to the process of bringing expectations of constituents into line with those of the negotiators, and vice versa. It refers to the process of bargaining with members of one's own side in the circumstances where one is also engaged in bargaining with the opposing party. This kind of bargaining is, therefore, only to be distinguished from the ordinary or normal processes of influencing others within assumedly-consensual structures (see Abell, 1975; Simon, 1953) by virtue of the circumstances surrounding it. It is the fact of bargaining with colleagues *in the context of* bargaining with an opponent, which distinguishes it.

Because of this, negotiators will not always attempt to maximize the advantage of the side in negotiations with the opponent. In some cases, they will conduct the negotiation in a way which heightens the prospect of the opponent securing something from it which would not otherwise be possible, in order to pressurize members of the own-side into accepting outcomes to which they are opposed. Ross has indicated the way in which union officials seek to manipulate the situation to reduce conflict:

> 'Knowing what seems attainable, sensing the temper of the membership, and bearing in mind the strategic possibilities of the situation (from the standpoint of the union's institutional objectives) the officials must decide whether to 'play it up' or 'play it down'. They can emphasise the employer's exorbitant profits, or his high cost of productionm and difficult marketing problems ... They can praise the employer's co-operative attitude or condemn his lack of good faith' (Ross, 1948, p 41).

The effect is to convince the principal that the negotiation is more or less as difficult as they had originally thought. This has predictable consequences for their expectations of what would constitute a good or fair outcome.

The suggestion is that role conflict can be reduced by changing the expectations of the principal as to the desirability or feasibility of certain outcomes over others. It is one strategy which takes the objectives and methods of the opponent as given and seeks to change those of his own constituents. There are others in this catgegory, just as there are strategies for dealing with the opponent's expectations of his role.

In dealing with the discrepancies between constituents' expectations and his own perceptions of role behaviours and role achievements, the negotiator has, in Walton and McKersie's view, the options of conforming to, ignoring or modifying the former. The first does not eliminate role conflict, but it does take the negotiator into strategies which focus on the opponent's expectations. The second depends upon the power and dependency positions of the constituents and the negotiators. The third is more likely to be adopted, and involves two broad strategic options.

(a) he can seek to bring expectations into alignment with actual or potential achievement, that is either after or before the agreement is reached; or
(b) he can seek to change the constituents' perceptions of the achievement in such a way that these are aligned with their expectations.

Each implies that there will be a successful attempt at influence.

The strategies available to the chief negotiator focus upon the timing and the behavioural focus of his attempts. He can for example seek to effect a change in the expectations of his constituents before, during or after the actual negotiation. He may decide to conform to the constituents' expectations, to modify them, or to ignore them. These are likely to carry their own time location, except in the case of the second one, where modification might be attempted at the different times mentioned. He can also adopt these strategies in relation to either the objectives of his constituents (in relation to what they want) or to the behavioural expectations (how he should proceed in the negotiation).

The achievement of internal consensus might be attempted in advance of negotiations with the opponent in respect of some of the differences (for example, the priorities to be attached to different goals). This is more likely to be feasible where the differences are ones of view or priority. Inter-group differences are, on the other hand, more likely to persist through the sequence of negotiating with the opponent, as they stem from quite different roots. Reduction of internal differences is likely to occur simultaneously whilst negotiating with opponent.

Walton and Mckersie also suggest that the strategy adopted will make use of one or more of six tactical assignments, which are appropriate to different stages of the negotiation with the opponent. These they list as:

(a) avoiding incompatible expectations from the start of the process, by preventing their crystalization until the negotiator is sure of how the opponent is going to react to a claim or counter-claim

(b) persuading the constituents to change their expectations after they have been developed, in the light of superior knowledge or judgment which he might profess

(c) utilizing events in the actual negotiation with the opponent to induce change in expectation on the part of the constituents on his own side

(d) rationalizing any difference between expectation and actual or potential achievement in terms of the latter being 'realistic' in the circumstances

563

(e) covering up the actual discrepancy by emphasizing the benefits achieved on other scores, whether these are real or imagined

(f) using tacit bargaining with the opponent, in which the opponent is convinced that although the negotiator is going through the motions, his arguments are not to be taken seriously.

The power or authority base the chief negotiator has for making the attempt to achieve consensus is, however, likely to vary considerably according to the manner in which the side selects the negotiating team and its leader. That activity is usually seen to depend upon achieving two objectives, one concerned with covering all the technical problems associated with negotiation, and the other with the donation of requisite authority to facilitate the achievement of the desired ends.

THE DILEMMAS OF SELF-CONCEPTION

The dilemmas of personality are no more and no less than the dilemmas which any person may experience in trying to conform to the expectations associated with any role which he might occupy. Performance of the role may demand that the person shall conduct himself in ways which are not congenial to his self-image or to his personality, and he may experience tension as a result. He experiences the dilemma that arises from acting in accordance with his self-conception. He risks failure to achieve or acts in accordance with the task requirements and thus experiences debilitating stresses in himself. In the context of negotiation, this kind of tension can be expected to increase the liability of the performer to make errors, and for this reason needs to be considered in connection with selection of members of the negotiating team.

The *conduct* of the parties in a negotiation is (as we have already seen (see pp 329) guided by conventions, some of which provide for and control these kinds of deception. They have the effect of controlling the strategic behaviours of the parties. They are also to be seen as supplemented by ordinary social conventions relating to social behaviour, in particular where the convention does not explicitly allow for a departure from these. Consequently, behaviour in negotiations might be described as mannered even though it conforms to some of its own conventions which allow strategic deceptions to be made in the special circumstances.

The general belief in the value of sincerity and honesty in dealings with fellow men is most directly associated with the kind of conduct required of negotiators in the integrative bargaining mode. Here, they can be as open, sincere and honest as they might be in other more general relationships. In the distributive bargaining mode, however, the role demands that the individual attempts to create an impression (as distinct from a true awareness on the part of the opponent) by ingratiation and bluff. Deception is used strategically to attempt to secure a more favourable outcome for one's own side, although it is not necessarily attempted at every stage which has been identified (see ch. 19).

The use of the threat might be placed in this category as a means of compelling agreement. Although not quite a deliberate deception, it is similar in the sense that (whether it is articulated in the negotiation or not) the threat of using sanctions is something which both parties would want the other to be aware of, but, as Schelling indicates (see ch. 19) which neither would particularly want to have to implement. It is part of the game of deception.

Naturalness and ingratiation

In the case of 'ingratiation' personal conduct is developed strategically in order to deceive the other party, and is to be contrasted with an open, honest, sincere or friendly approach to the other. Ingratiation is a term used to include all deliberate and clandestine strategies which are employed to increase the attractiveness and acceptability of one person to another, in the hope that the person will secure some benefit as a result (Jones, 1964). Its opposite often does not amount to a 'strategy' but acknowledges the essential equality of those who meet in the relationship and the general value of acting honestly and openly or being one's natural self. There is, however, always an element of 'ingratiation' in personal encounters as the person seeks to develop friendly relations with others (see, Goffman, 1959).

Ingratiation strategies and tactics tend to be used in the belief that the effect will be to simulate friendly relations which most people would consider to be productive of help and reward (just as the opposite effect might be expected to attend the generation of unfriendly relations: see, Bramel, 1969). They can be, and are used, to influence others by any individual in any cirumstances, and they do not depend upon the person using them having a power base. Any interaction, even a casual one, can provide the individual with the access which is necessary to the other. However, where it is used as a substitute for power, as in the case of the grovelling subordinate, its use may be both suspect and counter-productive.

Such strategies take the form of drawing the other's attention to the person's good traits and qualities, offering complimentary or flattering statements about the other, and indicating one's compatibility with the other by means of expressions of agreement with the other's opinions and statements. However, in the power context, such devices might have to be used with some subtlety, and probably indirectly or obliquely in order to avoid disapprobation associated with grovelling (Davis and Florquist, 1965).

Honesty and bluff

The other main type of deception practised, known as 'bluff', is more concerned with specific behaviours and involves the manipulation of information made available to the opponent. The object is to lead him to form a wrong impression or perception of the situation. The alternative to this is the open disclosure of information where it can be established, as the EP Act 1975 has it, that it is material to the collective bargaining process or to the relationship generally.

'Bluff' means the attempt to convince the other party that something which is not the case is the case. It may involve attempts to convince the opponent that one is stronger than one is, or that the external world is different from the way in which he perceives it. It may simply involve the presentation of genuine information in a way which will stand a good chance of leading the other to draw the wrong inference from it. In some way, it will ensure that the other is wrong-footed, and wrong-footed in a way which will assist the bluffer to achieve his objective (see Bowlby and Schriver, 1978).

Within the 'game' of negotiation in the distributive mode, this form of deception is a very important one in those parts of the sequence where the party is attempting to change the orientations, expectations or attitudes of the opponent. All of this may be necessary if what passes for bargaining power is to be sustained or increased in order to facilitate the realization of a successful outcome.

This arises because it is unlikely that the different values or utility functions of the negotiators will permit either party to convince the other by *rational* argument to adopt the terms of its preferred settlement. The 'rationality' of the discussion must therefore be tempered by another kind of perspective, and this is essentially what is intended and meant by bluff in this context. Breaking down the opponent's resistance to one's demands or counter-demands is likely to depend upon succeeding by such means.

The value of bluff in this context is that it may be expected to enhance the bluffer's power if it is carried out successfully, but to detract very litle from it if it should prove unsuccessful. In this, it is different from the concept of a 'threat' where the threatener may be forced to carry out the threat if the other responds in one way. In the case of bluff, however, the bluffer may loose a little face if his bluff is seen through, but this does not involve him in any great loss of power or resources which he cannot retrieve fairly easily. In any event, since bluffing is sanctioned by the conventions of the game, it involves no major points being subtracted if it fails.

Bluff may be used in connection with all the parts of the negotiating process. It may be used to present the objectives in a favourable light, or to convey an incorrect impression of commitment and determination. It may be used to evaluate the statements of the other in a way which might lead him to doubt his own case. It might be employed to create a wrong impression about amounts and directions of movement towards an agreement. It might be used to convey a different meaning to the terms of the settlement than that which the opponent thinks is intended.

Even before the negotiating episode formally commences, the representatives may find opportunity to suggest what the end position might be, or what might happen in the negotiation, and do so in a way which conveys a wrong impression, given the 'reality'. In making opening moves, the parties may similarly exaggerate the position in order to convey false impressions, although this does tend to be restricted by adherence to bargaining conventions designed to protect the process as a whole from abuse. In the trading off process which goes on in the negotiation, bluff may be used to vary perceptions on the part of the opponent of the value which the party places on the elements. Even after the negotiation is over and an agreement is reached, bluff may be used to sell the terms of the agreement to the constituents on the two sides.

Nevertheless, it cannot very effectively be used in certain parts, particularly in those which we have identified above as the transitional acts in the negotiating process. They may however *continue* successful bluffs which have been perpetrated in the immediately-preceding stage. Thus, if management have succeeded in bluffing the opponent during the proposition stage, the effect of this may be swept up in the statements made during the act of closure as if it were 'true'. On the other hand, bluffing, introduced for the first time in closure is likely to delay the closure process, as it will tend to lead back into the proposition phase.

Tensions and selection

Strategically-significant behaviours which do not necessarily lend themselves to acceptance in any context other than that of negotiation, are likely to be sources of stress and tension in the individual. The individual's capacity for tolerating the ambiguities which are thus involved is likely to be a factor to be taken into account in selection team members. Rubin and Brown, for example, argue that there is 'little doubt that personality variables, as well as other individual characteristics, are important determinants of bargaining behaviour' (Rubin and Brown, 1975, p 37).

Individual characteristics are obviously relevant to the capacity to perform in this as in more general social contexts, and the fact that individuals differ provides the justification for the preparation of person specifications for any such role. The variables in this category such as age, race, nationality, intelligence, religion, social background (social class, father's occupation, family income, place of residence), sex have all been shown to have some bearing on performance (Rubin and Brown, 1975, pp 157-74). They have all been shown in various pieces of research to correlate with negotiating ability, but they do not provide a very reliable basis for prediction and therefore for selection.

Amongst the personality differences which might bear most

closely upon performance, and which have been measured in some study or other, Rubin and Brown include propensity to take risks, perceived locus of control, cognitive complexity, tolerance of ambiguity, self-concept, motives, attitudes (generalized trust, co-operativeness, authoritarianism, and internationalism (ibid, pp 174-96). A rigourous selection process, were it thought to be worthwhile, might thus seek to filter through only those who showed themselves to have a ability, for example, to tolerate ambiguity in negotiations, or to accept as consistent with their self-conceptions, the strategic deceits necessary to the performance of this role.

On both sides of the negotiating table, however, the constraints upon decisions about selection are such that this rational and rigorous approach to composing the team is unlikely to be feasible or even desirable. The particular variables which have been identified (and which can be measured) are unlikely to be distributed through the personnel available for the role in such a way that rigorous selection is likely to be fruitful. They are therefore likely to operate at a much more generalized level, informing the selectors in a general way about what might be looked for or what might be avoided. Selection is, in other words, likely to be based on much more generalized criteria, and it is probably the general judgement which is most useful (in bargaining, as in many other areas of decision about human capacity).

Summary: dilemmas of bargaining

The negotiation process is replete with dilemmas of a technical, social and personal kind. It is also stressful and liable to negotiator error. The presence of so many dilemmas may contribute to stress and errors, and to the difficulties of establishing what *really* happens in a typical process and of identifying what are the preparatory and training needs of the negotiators.

The first set of dilemmas are those associated with the underlying conditions of integrity and trust. These make it possible that negotiators might believe to much or too little of each other and might have too much or too little trust in the other, to allow optimization of outcomes. The establishment of the nature of the 'game' and the rules of the game, to be applied at the outset, provides a partial control.

The second set of dilemmas are associated with the choices of goals and the means to establishing and achieving them. Whether, as a whole, negotiations are rational processes is not a question which precludes the adoption of rational models by the negotiations as guides to their planning of objectives or strategies; they can (and apparently in different circumstances, do) adopt very different approaches to the resolution of these issues. By doing so they place themselves in the dilemma of having posibly chosen inappropriately in the circumstances.

The third set of dilemmas are more directly associated with the negotiators themselves. The negotiator is confronted (as a person) with the need to adopt a role or style which is appropriate to the situation in which he finds himself (or herself); but as he does so, he may find himself increasingly uncomfortable in it because it is dissonant with his own personality or self-image. This, in itself, is likely to be a source of stress for many in the negotiating situation, and there is also a sense in which all the other problems and dilemmas are ultimately focused at this level.

Finding people who can cope with these problems and dilemmas, and who can tolerate the potential stresses which are associated with them, thus tends to become a major problem in resourcing the negotiating teams of the two sides. In principle, training ought to provide a way of improving the performance of negotiators, and no doubt it can and does do, especially in respect of the judgemental and social skills which are involved. But in the nature of the processes involved, there are difficult choices which have to be made *in situ*, and for this reason, selection by 'personality' and 'experience' is often preferred to selection on the basis of formally-trained competence.

Readings

Walton and McKersie: (1965), pp 121-5; 169-82; 268-80; 340-51.
Atkinson: (1975), pp 86-170. Pruitt: (1981), pp 71-162.
Anthony: (1977), pp 219-67.
Kennedy, *et al*.: (1980). Druckman: (1977).
Brewster and Connock: (1982).

21

The management of industrial relations

The traditional industrial relations systems

Since the industrial revolution, decisions about basic terms and conditions of employment and of co-operation in the work undertaking have, in Britain, been devolved to employers and workers. This devolved arrangement provides the basis for the 'partnership' between the State, on the one hand, and the employer-employee parties to the basic relationship, on the other.

The State has created and maintained a number of mechanisms through which co-operation may be developed (the contract of employment being a main one), and tried to ensure *order* and *stability* in both product *and* labour markets (to enable confident prediction to be made about behaviour). The State also designates and assigns authority to those 'persons' (real or fictional) who will be expected to take the necessary decisions. The role of the parties is, consequently, a bounded one, and the State retains the 'ultimate' power to determine the terms of the devolution.

Over the past two centuries, the extent of the delegation and the designation of the recipients' authority, have both changed, allowing us to identify at least two fundamental 'systems' of industrial relations.

The first approach was one which delegated authority to decide to individuals (whether masters or workers). The rules governing the establishment of the individual contract of employment set the limits to the means available to the parties to realize their diverse objectives. In effect (because of the inequalities in bargaining power in the labour market and the policies and attitudes of the judiciary) this gave most power to the employer to determine terms and conditions of employment. It produced one *system* of decision-making based on individual bargaining which

571

only slowly gave way to the collective alternative.

The second approach developed gradually alongside this, without necessarily being accorded the status of an accepted social policy. It 'allowed' workers lawfully to combine into associations which could then try to secure the voluntary consent of the employer(s) to negotiate with them with a view to reaching agreements on the terms and conditions applicable to a group or category of workers. This must necessarily reduce the 'unilateral' power of the employer, as the first 'system' gives way to one in which a *joint* negotiating body takes the decisions and monitors their application. The collective agreement has not, however, acquired the same legal status as the contract of employment, nor has the collective system entirely replaced the individual one. Collective bargaining is, nevertheless, a second and distinct system.

The delegation of authority (and power) to decide industrial relations issues remains, therefore, cast in two co-existing modes and the industrial relations structure remains a dual one. Society allows two broad methods of dealing with the commitment problem, one based on the individual contract of employment and the other on the collective agreement. Within the category of collective bargaining, there are also a number of options, and these, too, have to be selected for their relevance to the market and social pressures within which the undertaking seeks to survive.

The basic duality provides both parties with two options (individual and collective bargaining) for ordering their dealings. Any attempt to define *the manager's role* in industrial relations must allow for the possibility that it can involve either unilateral imposition of the rules governing work behaviour, or their joint determination in association with a rival, dual, or external 'organization', usually, that is, with representatives of the workers' unions (see Stagner, 1953). The dual nature of the system also supports the continuation of the choice of residual and trustee theories to explain the managerial position and role (see above ch. 11). Workers, similarly, may also exercise a choice between bargaining for their own terms and delegating this task to representatives.

The manager's position

The manager occupies a central position in both of these systems.

572

His prime function is one of running the production process in a way which results in profitability and efficiency but he becomes necessarily involved in industrial relations issues and problems as he pursues these objectives.

Managers are expected to secure production and productivity at levels which satisfy the aspirations of the various groups of income takers in society, and to do so by means which are both lawful in the eyes of the State and legitimate in the eyes of the various interest groups which surround the production process. In the private sector, the prime end may be subordinated to that of making money or a profit to satisfy the shareholder interest; in the public sector the prime end of service may be comparably subordinated to securing economy in the use of resources, even if the notion of profit as such is absent.

The manager becomes concerned with industrial relations to the extent that industrial relations contributes to or detracts from the achievement of these primary goals. His derived task here is that of securing the necessary amount of commitment from the various interest groups in order to realize the broader economic end. He may either use direct coercion or labour control, or more sophisticated techniques of incentive and persuasion in order to do this, but he will find that these are governed by established laws, conventions and rules which attempt to limit his absolute discretion in these matters.

The role placed upon the manager is supported by law and convention and is reflected in the way in which the institutions of both industry and industrial relations are ordered. They establish his autonomy and the limits to his discretion to act in carrying out the tasks assigned to him. The law establishes the manager's right to make and apply the rules of work in the interests of the members of the enterprise. Convention upholds the managerial privilege or prerogative and is reflected in the frames of reference of those who are subjected to the manager's authority. Both of these have assumed the nature of 'custom' by dint of long usage. The way industry is organized both reflects these underlying values and norms, and helps to ensure that they survive; in other words, that they do assume the nature of custom. The changes wrought by employment legislation in recent years have not removed these basic rights, but the changes in attitude towards authority, evidenced amongst workers, may be more challenging to the hitherto accepted conventions. The shape of industry may therefore be expected to change in response to them.

Any such change in the nature of the institutions is, however, most unlikely to occur in a manner which affects all organizations in the same way and to the same extent. A reading of history should suggest that some things change but other things continue unchanged. This may be accounted for by recognizing that undertakings and even industries which face different situations must respond to their variable situations as well as to the more general rules and demands of the society.

First of all, a management response to changes such as those of legislative change or general economic fluctuations, is likely to be curbed by the market position of the particular undertaking. Firms may face a rising or a falling market demand for their product, and they may hold a different position in relation to the market as a whole. Each is likely to constrain the opportunities for action which management confronts in the immediate situation. Response to a given level of activity for the economy as a whole or to a given law intended to have universal application, may therefore vary (at least within a range) according to the specific circumstances in which the undertaking finds itself.

Similarly, social values and attitudes in a particular organization, may not match those which may be found generally. It is possible to chart the changes in social values and attitudes over the industrial period and show how these have altered the distribution of power, between the managers and the other interested parties. These may have sustained the progression from individual to collective bargaining, but not all groups of workers support this development by their orientations and ideologies. In particular circumstances, worker attitudes, for example, may support a number of different approaches to the industrial relations questions. It is therefore useful to identify some of the middle range categorizations which allow such broad constraints upon the manager's opportunity to act to be recognized.

The challenge of the market

The manager must perform his role within both the economic and social contexts of his enterprise. Both the economic and social frameworks tend to generate some universal demands and constraints, and some specific ones. For example, all undertakings confront a world recession together, and frequently they are subjected to the same laws, but they face distinct markets and encounter particular sets of attitudes and orientations amongst their employees. The manager must necessary respond to both sets in both areas.

In the period since World War II, Britain's diminishing role in world trade has presented general problems to management and workers alike, and the failure to adjust has often been charged to both parties to industrial relations. Similarly, the failure of 'the system' of industrial relations to change to meet the new situation has often been held up as the villain in the economy's performance. Nevertheless, to confine any examination of the problems and possibilities to such broad and general terms may miss the opportunities which exist in the situation to make adjustments of a more situational or contingent kind.

The market of a particular undertaking or establishment is not, of course, a constant. It varies in terms of whether as a whole it is growing or declining, and whether the share which any one enterprise has or can acquire is large or small. These are the main variables used by the Boston Consulting Group (1970) to develop a two-by-two matrix for classifying undertakings. This is used as a basis for predicting appropriate market strategies, and may also be employed to evaluate industrial relations strategies. It defines four broad-brush situations:

The traditional industrial relations systems

The Wildcat undertaking: low share of a rising market
The Star undertaking: high share of a rising market
The Cash Cow undertaking: high share of a falling market
The Dog undertaking: low share of a falling market.

Each of these will have a different cash position and need to develop different product and marketing strategies to survive. In the wildcat, cash will be short and needed for market development; in the star and cash cow undertakings cash will be more plentiful, but in the latter will be needed to improve technology or increase R&D; in the dog cash will be available largely to the extent that productivity can be improved without investment, which will be directed towards new products. This analysis is based upon the concept of a product life-cycle, and there is a presumption that undertakings (or their divisions) will 'move' through the cycle, from wildcat to star to cash cow to dog.

575

However, this is not infallible: wild cats may transform into cash cows without moving through the star position, and cash-cows may move to wildcats without experiencing the dog-house.

This classification is used to suggest that business strategies (as measures of the dependent variable) are likely to be constrained (although not necessarily determined) by the undertaking's current market position. It also admits that the congruent industrial relations strategy will be different, partly because of the availability of cash for it, and partly because securing commitment and performance from the workforce may make different demands. The options open to the 'star' are not as readily available to the 'dog'; there is a presumption that the latter's attempt to emulate the star would be to get it wrong, and the former's attempt to emulate the dog would be to forego the most profitable (or otherwise advantageous) options available to it.

Thus, given the state of the economy, management of particular undertakings within it may still face very different constraint patterns. The general recession may cut everyone's market, but some undertakings may still confront favourable options whilst others go under. Management may find itself adopting quite different strategies in what might otherwise be regarded as a common situation. This might be as true of industrial relations as of business strategies.

The challenge of ideologies and attitudes

The manager also confronts another set of constraints which arise from the attitudes which employees bring to bear and which may be 'organized' by trade unions and other worker organizations. Managers must secure the legitimation of their status and roles in order to secure commitment and performance, and this too must be done in the face of both general and particular demands. Generally, this may have become more difficult because of the failure to satisfy material aspirations, and possibly because of a failure to develop structures and policies which recognize the workers' aspirations to more independent status. In local circumstances, however, these aspirations and attitudes may vary from the general position.

Changed worker attitudes are in evidence in worker behaviour as well as in union advocacy. The statistics of withdrawal behaviours, ranging from sickness and absenteeism, through strike and other forms of industrial action, to sabotage (see Chadwick Jones et al, 1973; Taylor, 1970; Hyman, 1972, pp 34 and 53-56; Taylor and Walton, 1971) suggest a withdrawal, also, of legitimation by workers of the system within which they work. The unions for their part reject the view of the worker as an instrument of production and the demand for independent status, as least on a par with other 'factors of production'. The growth in the power of the trade unions as independent associations of independent workers, of joint regulation as a means of asserting their influence on both industrial decisions and employment law-making, both reflect and succour these underlying changes in attitude.

The trade unions both articulate the worker's traditional demand for a fair share of the product of industry, and the more recent demand for greater participation and control. These are advanced as demands for positive *rights* which, whilst in the usual way they would be associated with workers as individuals, become associated with their representative organizations. Whilst trade unions have always been concerned with the process of 'democratizing' industry, this recent advocacy has become associated with secular shifts in general social attitudes.

It can be represented that the demand for worker rights has produced the present patterns of industrial relations. The growth of collective bargaining over individual bargaining and of agreements on such matters as participation, status, harmoniza-tion and joint control of health and safety and job evaluation projects may be linked to changes in attitude. They may also in turn produce further changes in attitude, leading to the development of 'fashions' in approaches and practice.

But not all workers construe their situation in ways which demand acceptance of collectivization as a prerequisite for improving status. The evidence of union density and work behaviours and orientations suggests, for example, that the same strategic solutions may not have the same relevance in all circumstances because of the differences in attitude demons-trated in them. The evidence on workers attitudes to the employer and the employment relationship suggests that some basically accept the unitary nature of the 'system' whilst others see it as necessarily based on dichotomous fate and conflict. Some therefore offer their commitment in one manner, whilst others give it in a quite different way.

A rough attempt to match the Boston Consulting Group's matrix in this area might be based on the studies of workers' orientations and images of society (following Dubin, Goldthorpe, Popitz *et al*). The four cells of a similar two-by-two matrix might contain the following types or 'climates' of organization, consistent with different worker demands and perspectives of the way the system is seen to operate:

Hiring hall:	narrow demands (for example, for income only) from what is seen as a unitary system of organization
Life-time employer:	broad demands (for general status) from what is seen as a unitary system
Conjunctive bargaining organization:	narrow demands from what is seen as a dichotomized system
Constitutional bureaucracy:	broad demands from what is seen as a dichtomized system.

Casual observation suggests that these 'labels' typify some work organizations more than others, and that the differences can be traced back to some broad independent variable of this general type. Large-scale organization is likely to sustain attitudes which place greater emphasis on conflict than the small-scale undertaking. Undertakings in different market situations and at different phases of their development might also be seen to differ on something like this dimension. The deliberate actions of some managements in propagandizing particular views of the managerial role and status can also be seen in some cases to have an effect. Consequently, it is not to be expected that generalizations about worker attitudes and frames of reference will apply with equal force to all such situations identified. Managerial responses could well vary with the state of this variable as well as with that of the market. In the development of industrial relations strategies, therefore, we should expect both some general developments and some variations which respond to more localized circumstances.

These are no more than broad indications of possible congruencies between the approach to the market and the approach to ordering internal relations. They are by no means automatic in their occurrence in the various circumstances outlined. This may be due to the existence of no more than a loose relationship between situation and approach, or to a failure of managements to recognize (and mobilize support for) desirable adjustments and accommodations of changes (whether in attitudes or other factors). There is, however, a growing feeling that monolithic conceptions of industrial relations approaches, structures and 'solutions' are no more likely to accommodate specific worker attitudes than they are other situational pressures upon undertakings (such as market position).

The need for new strategies

The changes in the country's economic position and in the technological means available to create wealth, appear to call for new industrial relations strategies. These are likely to be constrained by both the market and the ideological situations to which they are to be applied. Developing strategies thus calls for a 'contingent' approach. This is one in which decisions and actions are responsive to immediate situational pressures as well as to general pressures and demands. These may pull or push in quite different directions.

The general requirement of the country's changed economic position in world markets may be for cost-cutting and other increases in productive efficiency, to be achieved by increasing productivity. The general challenge of changed attitudes seems to be one of securing a structure and an approach which will assign legitimacy to the objectives and means of both managements and workers and their associations as independent and autonomous entities.

The manner in which these pressures and demands impinge upon a specific undertaking may vary markedly. The cells of the two matrices (above) may combine to give 16 different combinations of market and social demands. If strategies respond to these, this limited set of variables alone will permit a wide variety of responses. There is, as is frequently observed, some tendency for certain strategies and techniques to become 'fashionable' from time to time and for undertakings to adopt them for their prestige value. However, a more careful examination of managerial action could well suggest that successful undertakings were adopting one of a restricted range of strategies and techniques and that the real correlation was with some set of variables of the kind identified in these matrices. This, if it could be demonstrated on a sufficiently wide scale, might offer a better guide to action than universal generalizations and their associated panaceas.

Strategies for increasing control

The development of appropriate strategies in the undertakings which face unstable and insecure markets, is likely to emphasize opposition or antagonism to independent workers associations. It will probably also involve some modification or rejection of the conventions which currently surround and uphold the institution of collective bargaining. Many of these originated in the need to accommodate union pressures to protect members' pay and status, but they developed within the relatively stable and persistent 'system' of industry-wide bargaining prevalent during the first half of the present century. They may fit inadequately the processes of mutual influence which now occurs on an undertaking or establishment basis. There is some suggestion that changes are occurring in this respect, but it is even less possible to establish at this stage just what substance these have.

The traditional strategy of attempting to hold back the power of the workers and their unions may have been, and may continue to be, relevant in certain kinds of market situation, those in which rapid and flexible managerial responses to the insecure market situation appear to be required. In a period of recession and high unemployment *more* undertakings are likely to find themselves in situations which management construe in this way, and which are thought to need less attention to worker attitudes and aspirations. In these circumstances, the search for commitment is likely to be replaced by application of strict control of work behaviour, whether by personalized and autocratic imposition or by a more impersonal bureaucratic regulation of work behaviours.

The major distinction which may be made in this context, is one between the strategy of maintaining autocratic control in the new firm in a rising market which needs to effect rapid responses to strategic market-based decisions, and the strategy of retrieving managerial influence in the long-established undertaking which has moved into a declining market. The one implies non-acceptance of the right of the workers' asssociation to constrain these 'necessary' decisions and the other involves breaking the mould of the existing conventions of collective bargaining to

580

reduce the 'power' of the workers and their union organizations (for example, through the creation of redundancies).

Management will be constrained in its choice of approach by the perception it makes of the risk of disorder resulting from each of them. Existing conventions may produce relative stability, even if they also necessarily restrict opportunity to change. In the new undertaking, this risk is likely to be associated with 'external' pressures to recognize the union (as in the Grunwick dispute). In the long-standing enterprise, the pressures will stem from more internal sources (as in the case of the miners' dispute of 1983-84). In these circumstnaces, many managements are likely to regard a 'root' approach to decision-taking as too fraught with risk and Lindblom's 'branch' (or even 'twig') approach as more in accord with requirements. For other managements, dependent on the state of the order book or the competitiveness of the undertaking, taking the whole thing up by the roots may prove more appropriate. But this could court disaster in some circumstances, much in the fashion that many believe the Industrial Relations Act did between 1971 and 1974. A more incrementalist approach might then have had more relevance to the problems of many undertakings, just as a more radical approach can bring about a fundamental change if the under-lying conditions are right.

A major constraint here developed from the probability that the unions are not unnaturally reluctant to give up their positions and missions once they have established them. Having attained a role and function, they wish to hang on to it. This causes them to emphasize the continuation, albeit in extended form, of collec-tive bargaining arrangements under which the trade union provides a permanent opposition or acts as a constant watch-dog. If they were to give up this position, they might well lose all the power to influence that they have hitherto secured during their history.

Both the manager who seeks to achieve order and perform-ance in the production system on the employer's terms and the worker representative who seeks to change the system in the interests of greater equality, equity or worker emancipation, face the same kinds of risks, and are likely to adjust their decision-taking strategies accordingly. How people construc the risks, is, however, very likely to vary with experience and frames of reference, and it is not to be expected that everyone will produce exactly similar constructions. Consequently, the modification of

581

conventions and the procedural rules which give them expression can be expected in some situations and their preservation in others.

Strategies for increasing commitment

In the oligopolistic firm which enjoys a relatively high share of a stable or growing market, the main need is likely to be that of fostering high commitment and co-operation to maintain stability. In these situations, therefore, basic direct labour control strategies are likely to be avoided. Holding the unions at arm's length is likely to secure a minimal contribution defined in terms of the least that workers can get away with in the circumstances, and portend a rolling forward of the workers' associations' power as employment circumstances improve for any reason. Commitment may be sought either by increased bureaucratic control which avoids the involvement of workers' associations, or where workers' attitudes are supportive of an independent voice in affairs, by attempting to proceduralize and constitutionalize the relationships between management and organized workers through collective bargaining.

In this kind of situation, 'participation' (which reflects the broad changes of attitude referred to above) is likely to secure greater acceptance by management. Unions may also give greater support where they see profitability as capable of making their objectives easier to attain. Involvement and participation can then become means through which the generalized status of the worker might be upheld or improve (particularly in the larger-scale undertaking). The demand is being addressed by management at various levels and in various ways, so that 'participation' becomes one strategy for securing commitment which stands alongside or extends beyond individual and collective bargaining as strategies.

Other strategies entirely may be needed and adopted in those undertakings which face declining market shares, as managers seek to cope with the problem of international competitiveness and the development of new production technologies. These may, however, focus more readily upon confrontation with the workers and their unions, as management seeks to recover authority to act flexibly, or unilaterally in response to their reading of the situation. Instead of seeking procedural and constitutional solutions to the relationships problem, manage-

582

ment in these undertakings is more likely to demand changes in work practices in order to avoid redundancies.

Strategies for increasing individual commitment

In the more stable undertakings, the first strategy for increasing commitment and one which is most within the discretion of the individual parties is that which relies upon communication and involvement at the level of the job itself. It is the strategy more appropriate to the smaller enterprise where scale has not denuded the interpersonal and informal ties. 'Employee involvement' is a broad strategy which may be adopted by management or demanded by workers and their trade unions, but which contains a number of different elements which will serve diverse ends for different people. It comprises the replacement of methods which rely upon simple hierarchical ('chain of command') structures, by the development of those which depend upon a coalition of management and workers through which informing and involving the worker as an individual at different levels (from the work station to the board room) becomes a major objective.

In a small number of undertakings this has been carried to the extent of instituting common ownership or partnerships of one kind or another, and in a smaller number of cases, private unsdertakings have been turned into co-operatives. But in the general run of undertakings, this strategy has usually focused upon more limited changes which:

(a) seek to inform and involve the individual about his immediate task and contribution. This focuses on two-way communications (such as 'morning prayers') between supervisor and employee within the ordinary 'chain of command', but may be functionally-specialized under titles such as briefing groups (Industrial Society, 1974), quality circles (Collard, 1981), analytical trouble-shooting, behaviourally-anchored rating scales (BARS) or management by objectives (MbO) (Odiorne, 1965), according to the kind of work role involved.

(b) seek to inform, if not involve, the individual about the performance and problems of the establishment or undertaking as a whole, either through Noddy guides to the accounts or through fully-integrated teach-ins on problems and prospects (Jones, 1973). This objective might be more often realized in structures of 'joint consultation' where the emphasis is less upon the consultation and more upon discussion of issues and problems, even though management may acquire more 'understanding' of the problems of implementation through it.

In both cases, there are very real differences in the extent to which the individual is 'involved' as some of these do little more than work on the theory that to inform is to effect change in thinking, feeling or behaving. In some of the more sophisticated approaches, however, theories of small group dynamics, processes of effecting attitudinal change, and learning processes are integrated with the strategy in order to secure greater involvement and commitment.

These managerial initiatives may be regarded with some suspicion by the employees, if only because they leave the worker exposed in the structure of power and authority within industrial organization. One way of reducing the immediate problem, often adopted by management in situations where the necessary degree of trust for doing otherwise does not exist, is to make participation voluntary. Another is to ensure that the union (where it exists) is fully involved in discussions about the introduction of participation and encouraged to carry out its watch-dog role in relation to it, in order to give employee members some guarantee than they will not 'be taken advantage of' by management in the process. Where there is no union, however, workers remain exposed to risk and public policy may either have to legislate for union recognition or provide for a substitute watch-dog as it does in the Wages Council trades in another connection, or in a more radical alternative provide for a more positive right for the worker in relation to his employment.

The development of mutual influence structures

The second strategy is that which finds an independent place for the workers' association in a process of mutual influence which recognizes the status of both (company and union) partners. Usually this develops in larger scale undertakings, and involves the development of new coalitions of interest groups under one guise or another. The existing institutions of collective bargaining and the proposed arrangements for worker participation or industrial democracy present, respectively, a voluntary and an imposed solution to the problem of securing commitment in the light of current attitudes. Given our preference for voluntary solutions to social problems, the first is usually more strongly advocated than the second, although European Economic Community harmonization proposals may produce more action.

The major alternative to collective bargaining is linked to conceptions of involvement, participation and industrial democracy. This now focuses on the options summarized in the EEC's redrafted Fifth Directive (of May 1983). This allows accommodation of the worker interest through one of four main devices:

1   A Supervisory Board system with employee representation on the German or Dutch model.

2   A Unitary Board with a minimum of one-third or a maximum of one-half non-executive directors elected by the employees.

3   A Consultative Committee or Works Council representing employees with clearly established rights to information and consultation at certain intervals.

4   Joint arrangements for participation by collective bargaining.

These also require (as does the Vredeling Directive on disclosure of information in larger multi-plant undertakings) the regular disclosure of information about the performance and problems of the undertaking to the representatives either in the course of their involvement on a Board or by separate presentation where the option adopted is based on consultation or negotiation.

This set of proposals is regarded with suspicion by some unions. It is seen to be associated with the development of 'corporatism' a term used to indicate the subordination of the individual (manager or worker) to the impersonal corporation, as itself an instrument of State control. For the large scale undertaking, corporatism tends to take the place of the concept of 'paternalism' as the term of abuse applied in circumstances of denial of worker interests. Both substitute one form of control for another and denude the independence of both the parties to

585

voluntary individual or collective bargaining (see, Fox, 1978; Winkler, 1976; 1977). The maintenance of an independent source of power to oppose the employer, has therefore been seen as a more desirable alternative.

Both employers and workers are resistant to the notion of a supervisory board, and only the Bullock Committee (1977) expressed strong support for the unitary board. The employer's fear is that such a 'joint' structure would both reduce his unilateral authority and his discretion to decide issues. His preferred option is one which allows discretion to the management to develop consultative structures as may seem appropriate to the situation, taking into account the extent to which workers' attitudes are supportive. British management's preferred option is the third or the fourth one, dependent upon the degree of unionization and the efficacy of existing arrangements within any particular establishment (see Heller *et al.*, 1979). The British unions' fear is that anything other than an extension of collective bargaining will risk much that they have achieved by 'struggle'. Their preferred option (although there are variations between unions of different political complexions and histories) is probably the last one although there is some support for the notion of a unitary board.

Now that the options provided for in the Fifth Directive admit extensions of collective bargaining supported by better information disclosure, alongside the various other forms of representational arrangement, the way is open for the development of a more open and integrative approach to the whole question of joint regulation. If there is to be a development from the present position and pattern, however, negotiations will have to be more open (and informed) and concern themselves with a wider range of issues than the 'pay and hours' questions which have hitherto tended to characterize the British system.

Moreover, the style of collective bargaining will need to emphasize more the integrative approach, itself more consistent in terms of its characteristics with an open approach to management. This does not imply that distributive bargaining will be removed from the agenda, as there is every reason to believe that the two forms are inextricably bound up with one another. It does, however, require that management take a more positive or proactive position in the negotiation of effort or contribution than was traditionally associated with the industry-wide system, and support this with a more open process of

586

informing the workers as well as their representatives.

Market position and industrial relations strategy

The consequences of thinking through the development of strategies with the aid of a contingency approach may therefore be summarized in the following fashion, to indicate the broad possibilities. Strategies are, however, likely to develop only spasmodically and intermittently in response to forces and factors other than those of general 'fashion'. Some strategies are likely to be more congruent with the 'market facts' than others; some dependent upon the perceived 'power' balance may attach greater weight to what we have called the social variables. Given the derived nature of industrial relations, however, it is more realistic to recognize that the social variables are likely to have less weight than the market ones, and for this reason the four Boston Consulting Group categories form the basis for the discussion.

1 The Wildcat

The *wildcat* enterprise, assuming it to be new, young and dynamic, would (a) be short of cash and (b) in need of flexibility and versatility to meet all exigences in what is necessarily a volatile situation. The implication of the one is that it is unlikely to have cash available to 'buy' co-operation at rates over the odds or to 'buy off' (industrial relations) trouble. The implication of the other is, however, that it requires a very willing co-operation to accommodate the exigencies and to avoid 'trouble' in order to penetrate the market. In this situation, transference of the problem to external mechanisms of control may be indicated.

The indicated industrial relations strategy is therefore one which will emphasize autocratic and largely unregulated coercive control of labour with its concomitant avoidance of union organization with the implication of dual loyalty.

Different positions on the social matrix would, however, offer greater or lesser support to this. Stakeholders who regarded the enterprise as a casual source of material satisfaction, would be welcomed as their limited demands and low commitment to the organization would tend to support flexibility. If, however, on the social matrix, the enterprise confronted a pressure for a winning team, it would be impossible to comply; if it confronted a pressure for a conjunctive bargaining system, it could accommodate this, but would probably want to externalize the bargaining process in order to control product cost competition; if it confronted a pressure to develop a constitutional bureaucracy, it would be impossible (and uneconomic) to comply.

The major choices are between the kinds of organization associated with the narrow demands. Where stakeholders accept a subordinate position, the management will have the flexibility which it sees as required by the market position; where union organization occurs in response to a dichotomous perspective, chronic conflict may become an inherent feature, and may be contained only by the acceptance of a district or national negotiating structure and agreement (whether this is voluntary or imposed as in the case of wages councils).

2 *The Star*

The *star* enterprise will have a comparative surfeit of cash available and a need for the maintenance of ordered relationships with the internal (human) environment. The implication of the one is that there will be cash available to work for the realization of the other: order may be purchased, either by the development of an elaborate (and costly) domestic control structure (say through a personnel department) or by the provision of high incentives in the form of cash or kind. It will not particularly want to encourage creativity amongst personnel, but will more clearly want to produce clear objectives, strategies and policies which will hold everyone (if possible) to a particular path, ie one which will ensure the maintenance of the undertaking's position in the growing market.

This enterprise may develop strategies of benevolent paternalism or of a highly rule-bound bureaucracy in order to secure that degree of control over performance internally to match the ordered position in the market. There is a choice between keeping out the unions and recognizing that they could play a significant (if also constitutional) role, assisting management in securing order. The goal *is* order, and the means to its achievement include plentiful resources (some of which may be disbursed in the pay-packet). The industrial relations strategy is therefore able to tolerate or avoid unionization (provided the goal is realized).

The most congruent social position is that which is labelled the constitutional bureaucracy. The 'winning team' situation would also serve, although the sheer size of the undertaking in some instances, may make this less viable. The market position of the undertaking would, in principle make either of these viable: there is enough cash to purchase either. The narrow, instrumental demands, in either mode, are unlikely to provide bases for these kinds of strategy: the elements of noncommitment or dual loyalty, respectively, would render these less apposite. Responding to these social requirements would prove unhelpful in that they would drain resources without securing the degree of commitment to the team or bureaucracy which the position in the market would appear to demand.

3 The Cash-Cow

The *cash-cow* is most likely to be a wildcat or a star which has moved into a different market situation. It is likely therefore to emerge into this position with all the trappings and trimmings of the star.

The fallen star is likely still to have relatively high cash resources and to require the maintenance of an ordered relationship, which it can still afford to 'buy'. The major new requirement, however, is to find a way of coping with the stagnating or declining market in a way which will not diminish profitability. To this end, it may well have to do one or other of two things, either pursue improvements in the 'processes' of production, or move (by R&D or acquisition) into the wildcat situation. Either of these will call for more *flexibility*, even if it is still to be controlled by rule, than might have been necessary in the star position. It may nevertheless expect more conflict, as the expectations of the stakeholders are 'interfered with' and it may need to use its cash resources to buy this out. But in this case, the internal problem of control may prove to be of such a nature that management will see the union as a major ally in securing control of the processes of necessary change, and may therefore, be more ready to encourage unionization and control by agreement, than in the star context.

The wildcat which 'never quite made it to the star' position, will have fewer cash resources, but will have less need to use these to buy out the consequences of interference, since it will never have jelled into a bureaucratic control structure. Securing technological change to cope with the declining market will be perceived as not significantly different for the internal environment than securing the flexibility required. Where, therefore, the fallen star may use its bureaucratic control systems to move to a more flexible position, the untamed wildcat will probably continue to externalize its industrial relations processes and seek technological flexibility by more direct coercive control methods.

This category may be seen as more tolerant of internal social positions. Because more flexibility is required, the pressure for a constitutional bureaucracy may prove a hindrance (but may still be accommodated in time) but the pressure for a winning team may be accommodated also, with more difficulty, may the pressures for the conjunctive bargaining system. What is likely to prove least relevant is the casual source, since this will probably not provide the degree of commitment to task which would be required to cope with the changed products or processes.

4 The Dog

The *dog* is in a very different situation from these. It too has probably come on from some previously more beneficient position in the market. But it now faces the prospect of drawing little cash out of the market and what it does secure will come largely by improving labour productivity without incurring any significant investment in capital equipment or plant. Cash will become progressively scarcer as the undertaking moves down the graph, and the possibilities of 'buying' co-operation will diminish accordingly.

The indicated strategy will place more emphasis on achieving control by direct coercive methods (rather than through bureaucratic control by rule or by manipulation of incentives). The possibility of conflict between management and labour is likely to increase alongside the market pressure and increasing cash shortage.

The social variable here is likely to make its main impact in one of two ways. Either, the labour force will move to become 'casual' (that is, labour as well as stockholders will take out what they can at a minimum contribution) or it will resist through conjunctive bargaining which may have the objective of max-imizing cash benefits or that of protecting status in a more general sense. The workers are, however, likely to see the situation as one in which fate is dichotomous and to respond in a way which emphasizes the relevance of dichotomy. The possibilities of moving the undertaking to the state of universal provider or constitutional bureaucracy are not really on for the workers themselves. What is on, is mobilization of opposition internally or mobilization of political control externally.

Dealing with the perceived social problems may, therefore, lead to external or internal control strategies, depending upon where the undertaking has 'come from'. On the one hand, the workers may (through unionization and oppositional bargaining) attempt to protect what has been gained or shift the market strategy (a more difficult undertaking as the Lucas Aerospace Workers' Campaign indicated). Alternatively, they may try to persuade society at large to support them more directly by enactment of favourable legislation or by the assumption of more direct control over the enterprise. In the one case, society could encourage and facilitate the protection of the workers' living standards through legislation (supporting trade unions or supporting levels of pay) or through policies which seek to facilitate collective bargaining. In the other, society could step in to take the dogs out of the unconstrained market nexus, by, for example, subsidizing or nationalizing them with similar objectives in view. Neither of these is, however, possible unless the social variables are set fair at the collective or institutional level.

Institutional change and the creation of trust

It follows from what has been said, that industrial relations responses to situation are likely to vary according to certain contingent factors in the situation. These responses may not develop, however, because social values and norms, responding to other ideologies and perceptions, inhibit them. Moving industrial relations discourse and activity to a new plane is likely to be frustrated in some cases, by the existence of out-moded or simply generally applied rules and conventions.

Management's capacity to bring about significant changes in the industrial relations system may, in consequence, be restricted by the tendency for the underlying institutional structure to reflect universal theories as to its value and efficacy. The emphasis within collective labour law on the general desirability of collective bargaining may inhibit entrepreneurial management in dealing with their immediate situations. The larger, more oligopolistic undertakings on the other hand, may be restricted by the tendency in the common law to uphold individualistic values, thus preventing the growth of sufficiently high levels of trust between the two parties to allow appropriate strategies to be evolved jointly.

Given the objectives of businessmen and managers and of workers and their trade unions, the role of the State is, at least partly, to establish the conditions under which appropriate strategies for realizing them may be developed. At base this requires the establishment of conditions in which trust will be forthcoming in the necessary forms and amounts. The fundamental imbalance in the respective statuses of the two main parties to industrial relations can be expected to reduce the 'trust' which can be generated in the interactive process and which is arguably extremely important to securing change.

If this necessary trust is not present, the manager is likely to continue in the traditional frame of industrial relations: preserve what exists; advance when possible; but risk as little as possible in the process. This mode of operating (which is likely to fit the trade union's approach as much as the manager's) is unlikely to move activity to any new heights and is more likely to hold activities to their present level of limited subject-matter and limited development. The Donovan Commission's generally unfavourable view of management's performance in this area might be justified in just such terms as these. For this reason, changes in the organization of both corporations and unions may be necessary to provide a firmer foundation for mutual trust between the active parties to industrial relations.

Structural changes

The doubts which have arisen over the capacity of the 'industrial relations system' to support economic growth at the levels which people generally regard as desirable and feasible are usually focused upon the need to alter the institutional structure within which industrial relations activities take place. This raises questions about the industrial relations arrangements themselves, but it also questions the more fundamental economic structures of society and the position which is allowed to competitive and conflictual organizations within the economic structure. These changes may require legislation to provide at least the initial impetus to change, even though they will not be executed simply because legislation is changed.

In addition, society at large may question whether necessary changes can be brought about 'voluntarily' or whether it is necessary to stimulate them by changing the law in a way which more accords with emergent values and attitudes. Although some changes have been made in some contexts, there is a thought that this may be neither broad nor fast enough to deal with the problem. Proposals stemming from the EEC (Vredeling and Fifth Directives) suggest that moves to increase the workers' formal independence may be made for this reason in the next few years. On the other hand, managers and workers have been working away at new structures and approaches to industrial relations problems, partly in response to the new economic climate and partly in the context of what is sometimes referred to as a 'new realism' about what is feasible and sensible in the post-industrial society. But new strategies may demand a prior development of more appropriate structures.

Collective bargaining provides some basis for the representation of the worker interest in the running of a corporate enterprise. It might also lead to the development of other kinds of objectives, such as system overthrow, but for the most part it has stayed within generally acceptable limits of tolerance. It has, however, tended to become hidebound in its acceptance of a limited range of 'collective bargaining subjects'. On the historical evidence, the possibility of voluntarily adapting the institution to cope with the kinds of problems confronting workers and managements in a twentieth-century conglomerate is small. There are those who simply want to extend it, using traditional methods, but others see the need to replace the institution itself.

Governments have sought in the past 20 years to introduce changes into that system in order to steer actors' behaviours in desired directions. Much of this activity has been partisan to the extent that it has sought to tackle 'the industrial relations problem' in isolation and from one ideological position.

For example, legislation has given individual employees more rights *within* the employment contract, but has not removed the right of the employer to establish and apply the rules of work unilaterally, nor provided workers with rights *to* employment which might correspond with the employer's right to dispose it at will. The general effect is, therefore, that those workers who are prepared to associate and sustain a demand upon the employer for recognition of their association as a collective bargaining agent, may secure a voluntary sharing of control. But those who are not, or cannot, must rely upon their individual rights and obligations to secure what they can through individual bargaining.

Collective labour legislation has shown a greater tendency to meander in response to ideology. The Labour administrations have generally sought to increase the immunities and rights of trade unions to enable them to challenge management more effectively. The Conservative administrations have, on the other hand, sought to expose workers more directly to the pressures of the market by reducing trade union immunities and rights in the interests of redressing some notional balance of power. In both cases, it might be said, the intention is to steer the target group, managers or workers as the case may be, into activities which are calculated to be more responsible and more effective.

These policies have prevented the development of more congruent institutional structures and the adoption of more relevant strategies.

Enterprise law

No government has yet sought to tackle the more fundamental issue of whether the way in which enterprise is structured in Britain is adequate to support *any* functional system of industrial relations. At least since the time of publication of the Jenkins Report, the agenda for social change has included a recommendation that changes are needed in company law which may need to be altered to change the position and liabilities of the directors. But the problem may be more extensive than Jenkins suggested because of our commitment to 'a precise and limited conception of the company as a means through which capital may be invested in commercial enterprise' (Hadden, 1977), which in turn restricts the opportunities for both managers and workers to develop initatives. Changes in law may be necessary to open up the situation.

The present conception virtually ignores (ss 46 and 74 of the Companies Act, 1980, apart) the 'true association ... of managers and workers' and the contribution of the workers to the enterprise (Gower, 1979, p 66). It is 'company law' and not (as is developing on the continent of Europe) 'enterprise law' composited of both company and labour law (see Fogarty, 1965, p 187). Schmitthoff defines the problem in the following way:

'It is widely agreed that a company as an economic unit,

594

consists of a combination of three interest groups, the management as the directing brain of the enterprise, the shareholders as the providers of capital, and the employees as the providers of labour. The concept of the company as an instrument of economic capitalism has thus developed into one of the enterprise as an instrument of a new social order' (Schmitthoff, 1975, p. 266).

Acceptance of the implications of this perspective has been slow in Britain, although the case has been argued for some considerable time. Savage, for example, has suggested that:

'Company law in the UK has resisted adapting to a view of the company as an institution with desirable social and economic responsibilities to groups other than shareholders. There has been no significant change in the legal definition of the company's responsibilities since the limited company was conceived' (Savage, 1980, p 5; also, Fogarty, 1965).

The failure to respond has continued the 'fundamental imbalance in the respective rights and duties of the three main groups which contribute to commercial and industrial activity' (Hadden, 1977, p 91). A similar point might be made about the continuation, for different reasons, of the perspective of the State as 'sovereign' employer in relation to its employees, which has potentially similar consequences for the development of appropriate managerial and worker roles in that sector. In both cases, the restriction might inhibit the development of manager commitment to his work as it appears to have inhibited the development of any reasonable consensus on the relationships either of management to society at large or of management to the people who work in their enterprises. People, both inside and outside of industry, are therefore forced to construe work relations which do not fit the realities of a modern economy. Management, for example, must always measure proposed actions against criteria derived from a consideration of shareholder interests; workers, on the other hand, must always suspect an 'ulterior' motive behind any proposals for change.

Trade union status

The other major concern of public policy in recent years has been the achievement of responsible unionism, either by exhortation, regulation of the limits to decision (as in the case of incomes policies) or legislation to control internal processes (as in the case of the Industrial Relations Act). The most recent ventures in this area have reduced immunities and now threaten to change internal organization by requiring particular balloting procedures to be followed. These changes may be instituted for one or both of two reasons: either to increase the potential for control of work behaviour by increasing bureaucratic regulation, or to reduce the power of the unions to confront managements in those circumstances where management attempts to develop a confrontational relationship.

Governments of different political persuasions have sought to achieve more ordered relations by different means, but the underlying thread in this process of effecting change has been that of incorporating the trade union and the external regulation of the roles of responsible officers. The aim is to provide a legal (contractual) basis to the relationship between union members and their union regarded as a distinct entity apart from the members. The aim in regulating the conduct of officers is to subject the latter to direct control by the members through a balloting procedure which can be supervised by the courts.

Achievement is likely only if the distinct independence of the union is established in law. There are those who argue that *this* can only be achieved if the union's present immunities are replaced by positive rights and the worker's present dependency under contract is replaced by rights *to* employment as well as *in* employment, as a foundation for greater independence.

The first would include collective rights to recognition and 'consultation' or negotiation, based on the workers' right to create independent organizations to represent them. This would have to be based on a provision to free the workers' associations from employer involvement or interference (similar to what happened to staff associations and house unions in the Industrial Relations Act, for other reasons) and to guarantee worker-members rights to express their views on who should represent them and on the policies and strategies to be employed by the 'union' in their name in order to assure the absence of other 'external' interferences.

The second would call for the legal recognition of a wider range of job property rights which the worker would acquire with his contract than are currently accorded. This would probably require the adoption of a more punitive orientation by the courts in the adjudication of workers' rights and obligations than they have hitherto been willing to adopt (see Collins, 1982) in order to place a more effective curb on managerial behaviours.

Trade union democracy

The consideration of trade union rights has recently been linked with a concern over the effectiveness of the unions' internal democratic procedures, since these have emerged voluntarily and outside the supervision of the courts. Recently, this question has attracted the attention of government which has proposed, in response to criticism, some reform of the election and decision-making processes under the control of legislation and the courts (DE, 1983).

The Green Paper points to the variety of devices adopted voluntarily by the unions to encourage responsiveness of the leadership to the members' wishes but suggests that these generally operate inadequately for a variety of reasons. The suggestion then is that the various voting procedures (related to election of officers, decisions to strike or decision to operate a political fund) should be placed under legislative control to ensure that:

> 'voting invariably takes place in conditions of secrecy;
> 'all members eligible to vote have the opportunity to do so under a system which provides the best opportunity of a reasonable turnout;
> 'all votes are counted fairly; and
> 'those who take decisions at the highest levels are properly representative of, and accountable to, the membership as a whole' (DE, 1983, p 3)

and that similar restrictions are placed on balloting for strikes or political funds.

Although the unions, as institutions, can be criticized on this score, they remain more representative of worker attitudes than any other we possess. They may not be perfect in this respect, nor have they necessarily developed the most appropriate means of allowing democratic decision and control, but they still *represent* the worker interest better than any other body. Management may understand worker aspirations and attitudes, but it cannot represent them adequately, given the constraints under which it must operate.

Criticism of the unions as representative institutions, is often based on a confusion of the processes of mobilizing power against the employer or government with the general operation of the democratic process within unions. The latter may leave something to be desired in many union constitutions, and may call for reform under the supervision of the law in order to prevent the undemocratic 'take-over' of the union (see Rolph, 1962) and in order to reduce the lack of leadership responsiveness (see Wigham, 1961).

The former is, in contrast, a necessary leadership process which if removed by legislative requirement of referenda before decisions can be taken, will neuter the union as an independent force within the bargaining system. What might be attempted through legislation is not the control of every decision which might have to be taken by trade union officers but the control of the election processes. Provided that it can be established that every member can exercise his right to vote in any election without jerrymandering, the officers elected can be left to take the decisions which they consider necessary in the circumstances. The idea of a referendum on any issue which has to be decided is appealing, but will no more make for good government of trade unions than it does for society at large.

This set of proposals, too, is unlikely to secure its intended ends because corresponding changes are not in contemplation on the other side of the industrial relations scene. There is a body of opinion which suggests that the democratic rights of the shareholders are denied by existing practices (see Rubner, 1966; Sullivan, 1975). The existence of limited liability (which effectively applies to shareholder commitment to enterprise), may in itself be an inhibiting factor in any attempt to secure increased commitment and responsibility (if not exactly liability) from workers. The fictional personality of the corporation (or company) allows the management to shelter behind a shield of impersonality and 'un-responsibility' which is not available to the worker for his protection in the employment situation.

Legitimation of joint regulation

The predilection to accept collective bargaining as the instrument of decision-taking and action in this field is well attested. It is however a predilection to accept *voluntary* collective bargaining, and this helps to establish the significance of conventions in upholding the 'system' as we know it. One consequence of this is that industrial relations arrangements will be untidy, revealing different amounts of reliance upon joint regulation in different situations. Another consequence is the reluctance of the parties to regard change initiated by legislation as itself legitimate or desirable. For this reason, compulsion to change is unlikely to be attempted, or successful if attempted (as it was, for example, under the Industrial Relations Act).

It follows that joint regulation as a legitimate approach to the resolution of differences and conflicts surrounding the employment process is unlikely to be established as a legal right for workers or their associations. In so far as it becomes a right at all, it will be a 'voluntarily' established right, as the employer voluntarily concedes authority to a joint body of some sort, and the trade union voluntarily accepts it. What holds it in place then are the conventions which the parties accept, including the conventions governing the use of industrial action. Effecting change will similarly depend upon the parties going through the same ritualized processes of negotiation or bargaining as have established the present mutually recognized statuses of the parties. This is likely to be both a slow and a piecemeal process.

The possibility of legislating joint regulation into existence on any wider basis is small. The country's experience with tripartite regulation in the form of wages' councils suggests that this is likely to be unproductive as a long-term solution, and therefore such measures are likely to remain temporary expedients applied in exceptional circumstances. Tackling the mainstream problem of industrial relations machinery through legislation is also likely to emphasize the provision of 'opportunity' for action, rather than the compulsion of a limited range of actions. At very least this would require legislation to reduce the fundamental authority of the employer to make and enforce the rules of work. This would then be protected because it is upon that same authority that the present system of joint regulation rests: the trade union does not independently enforce the rules which are decided but merely reserves the right to challenge management's enforcement process when it disagrees with it. Consequently, both parties are likely to resist any attempt to introduce a more *dirigiste* approach based on a greater 'equality' of legally-established rights.

It is difficult to see the British arrangements for solving industrial relations problems proceeding by any other route than the empirical and pragmatic. But this might be the way that change is effected, provided that the parties adopt more proactive (and for that reason possibly more aggressive) approaches. Sufficiently wide differences remain on substantive issues to provide a foundation for 'system change'. The trick to be learned by the managers and the union officers is how to convert this process of change into one of constructive development, and to do so in conditions of considerable uncertainty stemming from the conflict of objectives and means which the parties bring to the negotiating table.

Because the system is likely to remain 'voluntary', it will probably continue in its 'bitty' pattern. Some workers will be covered by joint regulation, some by tripartite regulation and some by unilateral regulation. The concept of 'system' itself is unlikely to apply in an overall descriptive sense to British industrial relations; it is just not that neat that anyone could describe it as an enclosed system. The concept is only likely to have relevance as an aid to the process of thinking through the consequences of any industrial relations initiative in the way of strategy or policy, ie as a heuristic which might assist in the determination of a course of purposive action.

For the same reason, the slavish concern with rules as guides to behaviour is unlikely to provide solutions to current problems. There may be a need for new rules which more adequately reflect current situations, but on the way to developing them, it may be necessary to break existing rules and to abandon some of the conventions which they help to uphold. Certainly, it would be in the spirit of British industrial relations to recognize the probability that what develops will not be a set of abstract rules, but a variable set of pragmatic guides to conduct in the workplace.

Consequently, industrial relations in Britain is unlikely to present itself to the observer as a general 'system', of the kind envisaged by Dunlop. But neither will it appear as a mish-mash of unique structures, as envisaged by the situational school. Some middle range generalizations are possible, linking together the external market variables and the internal social variables with the strategies and practices which develop in response to them. Undertakings are not all the same in the way they pursue industrial relations, nor are they all different: they can be represented as falling into a small range of categories. These, in turn, focus management's attention on appropriate decisions and actions which may be taken in this area.

Bibliography and References

Note: references commencing pp refer to pages in the publication quoted. References commencing ... refer to the pages in this text.

Aaron, B (ed). *Disputes Settlement Procedures in Five Western European Countries* (University of California Press, 1969).

Abegglen, JC. *The Japanese Factory* (Free Press, 1958)...63.

Abell, D. 'Industrial Relations and Safety Representation' in *Personnel Review*, 8 (3), 1979, pp 30-33...159.

Abell, P (ed). *Organizations as Bargaining and Influence Systems* (Heinemann, 1975)...53, 561.

Ackroyd, S. 'Economic Rationality and the Relevance of Weberian Sociology to Industrial Relations' in *British Journal of Industrial Relations*, 12 (2), 1974, pp 236-248...61.

Acton Society Trust. *Size and Morale* (Acton Society Trust, 1953 & 1957).

Adams, JS. 'Towards an Understanding of Inequity' in *Journal of Abnormal and Social Psychology*, 67, 1963, pp 422-36...264.

Adams, JS. 'Inequity in Social Exchange' in Berkowitz, L (ed). *Advances in Experimental Social Psychology*, 2, (Academic Press, 1965) pp 267-99...264.

Advisory Conciliation and Arbitration Service. *Industrial Relations Handbook* (HMSO, 1980)...193, 412, 416.

ACAS. Annual Reports, (HMSO/ACAS, 1975 onwards)...170, 193, 380.

ACAS. *Code of Industrial Relations Practice* (HMSO, 1972)...128, 352.

ACAS. Code of Practice No 1. *Disciplinary Practice and Procedures in Employment* (ACAS, 1977)...123, 174, 376.

ACAS. Code of Practice No 2. *Disclosure of Information to Trade Unions for Collective Bargaining Purposes* (ACAS, 1977)...174, 354, 376.

ACAS. Code of Practice No 3. *Time Off for Trade Union Duties and Activities* (ACAS, 1977)...174, 354, 376.

Alderfer, MR. *Existence Relatedness and Growth: Human Needs in Organizational Settings* (Free Press, 1972)...40, 254.

Aldridge, A. *Power, Authority and Restrictive Practices* (Blackwell, 1976)...274.

Allen, D. 'A Review of Process Theories of Decision-Making' in *Management Education and Development*, 8 (2), 1977, pp 79-94...54, 61.

Allen, GC. *Monopoly and Restrictive Practices* (Allen & Unwin, 1968)...65.

Allen, GC. *British Industry and Economic Policy* (Macmillan, 1979)...115.

Allen, VL. *Power in Trade Unions* (Longmans, 1958)...283.

Allen, VL. *The Sociology of Industrial Relations* (Longmans, 1971)...42.

Allen, VL. 'The Sociology of Industrial Relations' in Barrett et al, *Industrial relations and the wider society* (Collier-Macmillan, 1975), pp 35-39...42.

Allport, FH. 'Attitudes' in Murchison, G (ed). *Handbook of Social Psychology* (Clark UP, 1935)...290.

Allport, GW. *Personality* (Constable, 1937).

Amulree, Lord. *Industrial Arbitration in Great Britain* (Oxford UP, 1929)...166.

602

Anastasi, A. *Individual Differences* (Wiley, 1965)...483.

Anderson, JC. 'Bargaining Outcomes: An IR Systems Approach' in *Industrial Relations*, 18 (2), Spring, 1979, pp 127-43...321, 339, 524.

Angel, J. *How to Prepare Yourself for an Industrial Tribunal* (IPM, 1980)...222.

Ansoff, HI. *Corporate Strategy* (Penguin, 1975)...228.

Anthony, PD. 'Industrial Codes of Discipline' in *Personnel*, 1964, pp 32-36...123.

Anthony, PD. *The Conduct of Industrial Relations* (IPM, 1977a)...61, 72, 86, 87, 133, 194, 253, 371, 398, 458, 487, 545, 570.

Anthony, PD. *The Ideology of Work* (Tavistock, 1977a)...67.

Anthony, PD & Crichton, A. *Industrial Relations and the Personnel Specialists* (Batsford, 1969)...299.

Argyle, M. 'The Concepts of Role and Status' in *Sociological Review*, 44 (3), 1952, pp 39-49...38.

Armstrong, EGA. *Industrial Relations. An Introduction* (Harrap, 1969). 'The Role of the State' in Barrett et al.

Armstrong, EGA. *Industrial Relations and the Wider Society* (Collier-Macmillan, 1975). (1975), q.v. pp 109-19...140, 274.

Armstrong, EGA. 'Management and Multi-Unionism' in Kessler S & Weekes B. *Conflict at Work: Reshaping Industrial Relations*(BBC Publications, 1971), q.v., pp 31-52.

Armstrong, K, Bowers, D & Burkitt, B. 'The Measurement of Trade Union Bargaining Power' in *British Journal of Industrial Relations*, 15 (1), March, 1977, pp 91-100...524.

Armstrong, M & Murlis, H. *A Handbook of Salary Administration* (Kogan Page, 1980)...514.

Armstrong, PJ & Goodman, JFB. 'Managerial and Supervisory Custom and Practice' in *Industrial Relations Journal*, 10 (3), Autumn, 1979, pp 12-24...446.

Armstrong, PJ, Goodman, JFB, & Hyman, JD. *Ideology and Shop Floor Industrial Relations*, (Croom-Helm, 1981)...89, 346.

Arnison, J. *The Million Pound Strike*, (Lawrence & Wishart, 1970)...299, 333.

Ashton, TS. *The Industrial Revolution, 1760-1830*, (Oxford UP, 1948; 1968)...11.

Atkinson, GC. *The Effective Negotiator* (Quest, 1975)...458, 514, 518, 533-38, 545, 570.

Atkinson, JW. 'Motivational Determinants of Risk-Taking Behaviour' in *Psychological Review*, 64, 1957, pp 359-72.

Bacharach, SB & Lawler, EJ. *Bargaining, Power, Tactics, and Outcomes* (Jossey-Bass, 1981)...478, 487.

Bachrach, P & Barratz, MS. 'Two Faces of Power' in *American Political Science Review*, 56, 1962, pp 947-52...70.

Bacon, R & Eltis, W. *Britain's Economic Problem: Too Few Producers* (Macmillan, 1976, 2nd edn 1978)...16, 31.

Bain, GS. *The Growth of White Collar Unionism* (Clarendon Press, 1970)...420.

Bain, GS. 'Management and White Collar Unionism' in Kessler S & Weekes B. *Conflict at Work: Re-shaping Industrial Relations (BBC Publications*, 1971), q.v, pp 15-30.

Bain, GS (ed). *Industrial Relations in Britain* (Blackwell, 1983)...133, 164, 193, 253, 283, 400, 415, 426, 430.

Bain, GS & Clegg, HA. 'A Strategy for Industrial Relations Research in Great Britain' in *British Journal of Industrial Relations*, XII (1), 1974, pp 95-110.

Bain, GS & Price, R. 'Union Growth and Employment Trends in the UK' in *British Journal of Industrial Relations*, X, (3), November, 1972, pp 366-381; see also, Price, R and Bain, GS (1976).

Bain, GS & Price, R. *Profiles of Union Growth: A Comparative Statistical Portrait of Eight Countries* (Blackwell, 1980).

Baker, H & France, KR. *Centralization and Decentralization in Industrial Relations* (Princeton UP, 1954)...231, 237.

Bakke, EW. 'To Join or Not to Join' in Barrett et al, 1975, q.v., pp 43-52...51. *Industrial Relations and the Wider Society* (Collier-Macmillan 1975).

Baldamus, W. *Efficiency and Effort* (Tavistock, 1961)...334.

Bales, RF. Interaction Process Analysis (Addison-Wesley Press, 1951)...509, 512, 533, 539, 541.

Bales, RF & Strodtbeck, FL. 'Phases in Group Problem-Solving', in Cartwright, D & Zander, A, q.v. pp 386-400...509. *Group Dynamics: Research and Theory* (Row Peterson, 1953)

Balfour, C. 'Productivity and the Worker' in *British Journal of Sociology*, IV (3), September, 1953, pp 257-65...14.

Balfour, C. *Incomes Policy and the Public Sector* (Routledge & Kegan Paul, 1972a)...419.

Balfour, C. *Industrial Relations in the Common Market* (Routledge & Kegan Paul, 1972b)

Balfour, C. *Participation in Industry* (Croom Helm, 1973a)...353.

Balfour, C. *Unions and the Law* (Saxon House, 1973b).

Bamber, G. 'Trade Unions for Managers?' in *Personnel Review*, 5 (4), Autumn, 1976, pp 36-41.

Banks, JA. *Industrial Participation: Theory and Practice* (Liverpool UP, 1963).

Banks, JA. *Marxist Sociology in Action* (Faber & Faber, 1970).

Barbarsh, J. *Labor's Grass Roots: A Study of the Local Union* (Harper and Row, 1961)...560.

Barnard, CI. *The Functions of the Executive* (Harvard UP, 1938)...461.

Barnard, CI. 'The Functions and Pathologies of Status Systems in Formal Organizations' in Whyte, WF (ed). *Industry and Society* (McGraw Hill, 1946, pp 207-43...35, 38.

Barrett, B, Rhodes, E & Beishon, J. *Industrial Relations and the Wider Society* (Collier-Macmillan, 1975)...32.

Bartos, OJ. 'A Simple Model of Negotiation: A Sociological Point of View' in *Journal of Conflict Resolution*, 21 (4), 1977, pp 565-579...330, 331, 552.

Bartos, OJ. 'How Predictable are Negotiations?' in *Journal of Conflict Resolution*, 11, 1967, pp 481-96...320.

Basnett, D. 'Disclosure of Information – A Union View' in Kessler, S & Weekes, B. Conflict at Work: Re-shaping Industrial Relations (BBC Publications, 1971), q.v., pp 115-23.

Batstone, E, Boraston, I, & Frenkel, S. *Shop Stewards in Action* (Blackwell, 1977)...292, 332, 335, 368, 388, 391, 392.

Batstone, E, Boraston, I, & Frenkel, S. *The Social Organization of Strikes* (Blackwell, 1978)...264, 332, 333, 374, 382, 394, 395, 475, 480, 481, 553.

Bavelas, A. see Lewin, K in Cartwright, D and Zander, A. *Group Dynamics: Research and Theory* (Row Peterson, 1953) q.v., pp 493-506...394.

Bayliss, FJ. *British Wages Councils* (Blackwell, 1962)...181.

Bean, R. 'The Relationship between Strikes and 'Unorganized' Conflict in Manufacturing Industries' in *British Journal of Industrial Relations*, 13 (1), 1975, pp 98-101...394.

Beaumont, P. *Government as Employer – Setting an Example* (Royal Institute of Public Administration, 1981)...420.

Beaumont, P & Gregory, M. 'The Role of Employers in Collective Bargaining in Britain' in *Industrial Relations Journal*, 11, (5), November-December, 1980, pp 46-52...253, 450.

Beenstock, M & Immanuel, H. 'The Market Approach to Pay Comparability' in *National Westminster Bank Review*, November, 1979, pp 26-41...424.

Beesley, M & Hughes, MD. *Corporate Social Responsibility: A Reassessment* (Croom Helm, 1978)...297.

Behrend, H. 'The Field of Industrial Relations' in *British Journal of Industrial Relations*, I, 1963, pp 383-94...42.

Bell, D. *The Coming of Post-Industrial Society: A Venture in Social Forecasting* (Heinemann, 1974).

Bell, JDM. *Industrial Unionism: A Critical Analysis* (McNaughton & Gowenlock, 1949) (quoted in McCarthy, (1972)), q.v., pp 109-40...273.

Bendix, R. *Work and Authority in Industry* (Wiley, 1956; 2nd edn, 1963).

Benemy, WG. *Whitehall – Townhall* (Harrap, 1960).

Bercusson, B. *Annotations on the Employment Protection (Consolidation) Act, 1978*, (Sweet & Maxwell, 1979)...122.

Berle, AA. *The Twentieth Century Capitalist Revolution* (Harcourt Brace, 1955).

Berle, AA. *Power Without Property* (Sidgwick & Jackson, 1960)...468.

Berle, AA & Means, GC. *The Modern Corporation and Private Property* (Macmillan, 1932)...468.

Beynon, H. *Working for Ford* (Penguin, 1973)...292, 309.

Beynon, H & Blackburn, RM. *Perceptions of Work: Variations within a Factory* (Cambridge UP, 1972)...256.

Birch, R. *Guerrilla Struggle and the Working Class* (Communist Party of Great Britain, 1973)...135.

Blackaby, F. *The Future of Pay Bargaining* (Heinemann, 1980)...69.

Blackaby, F. *De-Industrialization* (Heinemann, 1978).

Blackburn, RM. *Union Character and Social Class* (Batsford, 1967)...140, 163, 262-63, 282.

Blackler, F & Brown, C. *Job Redesign and Management Control* (Saxon House, 1978).

Blackstone, Sir W. Commentaries on the Laws of England, 1813 (in four books, edited by Kerr, EM) (Murray, 1957) ...137, 344-45.

Blain, ANJ. *Pilots and Management: Industrial Relations in the UK Airlines* (Allen & Unwin, 1972).

Blain, ANJ & Gennard, J. 'Industrial Relations Theory: A Critical Review' in *British Journal of Industrial Relations*, 8 (3), November, 1970, pp 389-407.

Blake, R, & Mouton, J. 'Loyalty of Representatives to In-Group Positions during Inter-Group Conflict', in *Sociometry*, 24, 1961, pp 177-84...447.

Blake, R, & Mouton, J. 'The Inter-Group Dynamics of Win Lose Conflict and Problem-Solving Collaboration in Union-Management Relations' in Sherif, M, (ed). *Inter-Group Relations and Leadership*, (Wiley, 1962), pp 95-140.

Blau, P. *Exchange and Power in Social Life* (Wiley, 1964).

Blum, FH. *Work and Community* (Routledge & Kegan Paul, 1968).

Board of Trade. *The Conduct of Company Directors* (HMSO, 1977).

Bolton, JE. *Small Firms: Report of the Committee of Inquiry on Small Firms* (HMSO, 1971, Cmnd. 4811)...82, 239.

Boraston, I, Clegg, HA & Rimmer, M. *Workplace and Union: A Study of Local Relationships in Fourteen Unions* (Heinemann, 1975)...276, 278, 287, 316, 334, 347, 355, 450, 475.

Boseman, FG & Jones, RE. 'Market Conditions, Decentralization and Organizational Effectiveness', in *Human Relations*, 27, 1974, pp 665-76.

Boston Consulting Group. *Perspectives of Experience* (Boston Consulting Group, 1970), 522.

Boulding, K. 'General Systems Theory – The Skeleton of a Science' in *Management Science*, 2, 1956, pp 197-208...4.

Bowen, P & Shaw, M. 'Patterns of White Collar Unionization in the Steel Industry' in *Industrial Relations Journal*, 3 (2), Summer, 1972, pp 8-34...272.

Bowlby, R & Schriver, W. 'Bluffing and 'Split-Difference' Theory of Wage Bargaining', in *Industrial and Labour Relations Review*, 31 (2), 1978, pp 161-71...566.

Bowley, AL. *Wages and Incomes since 1860*, (Cambridge UP, 1937)...11.

Bradford, University of. *Developing Industrial Relations Policies* (University of Bradford Management Centre, 1970).

Bradley, K & Gelb, A. *Worker Capitalism: The New Industrial Relations* (Heinemann, 1983).

Bramel, D. 'Inter-personal Attraction, Hostility and Perception' in Mills, J. *Experimental Social Psychology* (Macmillan, 1969) pp 1-120...566.

Brandt, FS. *The Process of Negotiation* (Industrial and Commercial Techniques Ltd, London, November, 1973)...526.

Brannen, P. *Authority and Participation in Industry* (Batsford, 1983).

Brannen, P, Batstone, E, Fatchett, D, & White, P. *The Worker Directors* (Hutchinson, 1976).

Braybrooke, D & Lindblom, CE. *A Strategy of Decision: Policy Evaluation as a Process* (Free Press/Collier-Macmillan, 1963)...53.

Brech, EFL. *The Principles and Practice of Management* (Longmans, 1953, 3rd edn, 1975), 436, 458.

Brewster, C & Connock, SL. *Industrial Relations Training* (Kogan Page, 1980)...547, 570.

Brewster, C, Gill, CG & Richbell, S. 'Developing an Analytical Approach to IR Policy' in *Personnel Review*, 10, (2), 1981, pp 3-10...440.

Bridge, J. *Economics in Personnel Management* (IPM. 1981)...117, 267.

Bridge, J & Dodds, JC. *Managerial Decision-Making* (Croom Helm, 1975)...51.

Brim, OG & Wheeler, S. *Socialisation after Childhood: Two Essays*, (Wiley, 1966)...44, 54, 55.

British Institute of Management. *Industrial Relations Training for Managers* (BIM, September, 1971)...547.

BIM. *The Board of Directors: A Survey of its Structure, Composition, and Role* (BIM Management Survey Report No 10, 1972).

Brown, K. 'Sub-Postmasters: Private Traders and Trade Unionists' in *British Journal of Industrial Relations*, III, March, 1965, pp 31-45.

Brown, RK. 'From Donovan to Where? Interpretations of Industrial Relations in Britain since 1968' in *British Journal of Sociology*, 29 (4), December, 1978, pp 339-61.

Brown, RK, Curran, MM, & Cousins, JM. *Changing Attitudes to Employment* (DE Research Paper, 1983).

Brown, W. *Some Problems of a Factory* (IPM, 1951)...301, 375.

Brown, W. *Exploration in Management* (Penguin, 1960, 2nd edn. 1971)...51.

Brown, W. 'Reforming Wage Systems' in Kessler, S & Weekes, B. *Conflict at Work: Re-Shaping Industrial Relations* (BBC Publications, 1971), q.v., pp 94-104.

Brown, W. 'A Consideration of Custom and Practice' in *British Journal of Industrial Relations*, X (1), 1972, pp 42-61...102, 344, 389.

Brown, W. *Piecework Bargaining* (Heinemann, 1973)...86.

Brown, W, (ed). *The Changing Contours of British Industrial Relations*, (Blackwell, 1981)...84, 232, 345, 431.

Brown, W, Ebsworth, R, & Terry, M. 'Factors Shaping Shop Steward Organization in Britain' in *British Journal of Industrial Relations*, XVI, (2), 1978, pp 139-59.

Brown, W & Terry, MA. 'The Changing Nature of National Wage Agreements' in *Scottish Journal of Political Economy*, XXV (2). 1978, pp 119-33.

Buckley, W. *Sociology and Modern Systems Theory* (Prentice Hall, 1967).

Bullock, Lord. *Report of the Committee of Inquiry on Industrial Democracy* (HMSO, 1977)...28, 586.

Bulmer, M (Ed). *Working Class Images of Society* (Routledge & Kegan Paul, 1975).

Burkitt, B & Bowers, D. *Trade Unions and the Economy* (Macmillan, 1979)...499.

Burns, T. 'The Sociology of Industry' in Welford, AT (ed). *Society* (Routledge & Kegan Paul, 1962) pp 188-218.

Burns, T. *Industrial Man* (Penguin, 1969)...36.

606

Campo, AF. 'Entering into Negotiations' in Marceau, L (ed). *Dealing with a Union* (American Management Association, 1969), q.v., pp 86-99...532.

Caplow, T. *The Sociology of Work* (McGraw Hill, 1964)...136.

Carr, C. 'Inequality of Bargaining Power' in *The Modern Law Review*, 38, July, 1975, pp 463-66...105.

Carr-Saunders, AM & Wilson, PA. The *Professions* (Cass, 1933, 2nd edn, 1964)...136, 137, 139, 141, 163

Cartwright, D. 'Influence, Leadership and Control' in March, JG. *Handbook of Organizations* (Rand-McNally, 1965) pp 1-47...468, 471, 487.

Cartwright, D (ed). *Studies in Social Power* (Institute for Social Research, University of Michigan, 1959).

Cartwright, D & Zander, A. *Group Dynamics: Research and Theory* (Row Peterson, 1953)...393.

Cawson, A. 'Pluralism, Corporatism and the Role of the State', in *Government and Opposition*, 13 (2), 1978, pp 187-98.

Central Arbitration Committee. *Annual Report*, 1976, onwards (HMSO, 1976, annually)...193, *222*.

Chadwick-Jones, JK, Brown, CA & Nicholson, N. 'Absence from Work: Its meaning, measurement and control' in *International Review of Applied Psychology*, 22 (2), 1973, pp 137-55...577.

Chamberlain, NW. *The Union Challenge to Management Control* (Harper, 1948).

Chamberlain, NW. 'Bargaining Power and the Costs of Disagreeing and Agreeing' in Chamberlain, NW & Cullen, D (eds). *The Labour Sector* (McGraw Hill, 1965)...523.

Chamberlain, NW & Kuhn, JW. *Collective Bargaining* (McGraw Hill, 1965)...324, 368, 370, 484.

Chamberlain, NW & Kuhn, JW. 'Conjunctive and Co-operative Bargaining' in Flanders, A (ed). *Collective Bargaining* (Penguin, 1969), pp 317-332, 132, 500.

Chandler, G. 'NEDC at 21: The Scope and Limits of Consensus' in *RSA Journal*, CXXI (5319), February, 1983, pp 134-43... 278.

Charles, R. *The Development of Industrial Relations in Britain*, 1911-1939, (Hutchinson, 1973)...8.

Child, J. 'Organizational Structure, Environment and Performance: The Role of Strategic Choice' in *Sociology* 6 (1), January, 1972, pp 1-22; and in Salaman and Thompson, 1973, q.v., pp 91-107.

Clay, H. *The Problem of Industrial Relations* (Macmillan, 1929)...32.

Clayton, EH. 'A Proprietary Right in Employment' in *Journal of Business Law*, 1967, pp 139-43...132.

Clegg, CW et al. 'Managers' Attitudes towards Industrial Democracy' in *Industrial Relations Journal*, 9 (3), Autumn, 1978, pp 4-17.

Clegg, HA. *Industrial Democracy and Nationalization* (Blackwell, 1951)...292, 294.

Clegg, HA. 'Employers' in Flanders, A & Clegg, HA. *The System of Industrial Relations in Great Britain* (Blackwell, 1954), pp 200-251.

Clegg, HA. *A New Approach to Industrial Democracy* (Blackwell, 1960).

Clegg, HA. 'The Substance of Productivity Agreements' in Flanders (ed) (1969), pp 352-65.

Clegg, HA. *How to Run an Incomes Policy* (Heinemann, 1971)...188.

Clegg, HA. *The System of Industrial Relations in Great Britain* (Blackwell, 1972), 32, 69, 237, 243, 246-47, 248, 283, 377, 419, 423, 428, 430, 448, 473, 479, 480, 545.

Clegg, HA. *Trade Unionism under Collective Bargaining* (Blackwell, 1976).

Clegg, HA. *The Changing System of Industrial Relations in Great Britain* (Blackwell, 1979), 253, 283, 448, 487.

Clegg, HA. 'Pluralism in Industrial Relations' in *British Journal of Industrial Relations*, XIII, (3), November, 1975, pp 309-16...297.

Clegg, HA. 'Reflections on Incomes Policy and the Public Sector in Britain' in *Labour and Society*, VII, 1982, pp 3-12...426.

Clegg, HA et al. *The Employers' Challenge* (Blackwell, 1957).

Clegg, HA, Killick, AJ & Adams, R. *Trade Union Officers* (Blackwell, 1961).

Clegg, S. *Power, Rule and Domination* (Routlege & Kegan Paul, 1975)...70.

Clegg, S & Dunkerley, D. *Organization, Class and Control* (Routledge & Kegan Paul,, 1980).

Cleland, S. *The Influence of Plant Size on Industrial Relations* (IR Section, Princeton University, 1955).

Clevenger, T & Mathews, J. *The Speech Communication Process* (Scott Foresman, 1971)...464.

Cliff, T. *The Employers' Offensive* (Pluto Press, 1970)...294.

Clifton, R & Tatton-Brown, C. *Impact of Employment Legislation in Small Firms* (DE Research Paper No 6, 1979)...133.

Coch, L & French, JRP. Overcoming Resistance to Change in *Human Relations* (1), 1948, pp 512-532; also in Cartwright, D & Zander, A. *Group dynamics: Research and theory* (Rown Peterson, 1953), q.v., pp 257-79; and in Maccoby, Newcomb & Hartley. (1958), q.v., pp 233-50...491.

Coddington, A. *Theories of Bargaining Process* (Allen & Unwin, 1968).

Cohen, MD, March, JG, & Olsen, JP. 'A Garbage Can Model of Organisational Choice' in *Administrative Science Quarterly*, 17 (1), March, 1972, pp 1-25...53.

Coker, E & Stuttard, G. *Trade Union Negotiations* (Arrow, 1976).

Cole, GDH. *Workshop Organization* (Clarendon Press, 1923; Oxford UP, 1973)...7, 286, 473.

Collard, R. 'The Quality Circle in Context' in *Personnel Management*, 13 (9), September, 1981, pp 26-30...583.

Collins, H. 'Capitalist Discipline and Corporatist Control' in *Industrial Law Journal*, 11, 1982, pp 78-93 and 170-77.

Commission on Industrial Relations. First General Report (Report No 9, Cmnd. 4417, HMSO, July, 1970).

CIR. *Facilities Afforded to Shop Stewards* (Report No 17, Cmnd. 4668, HMSO, May, 1972)...351.

CIR. *Second General Report* (Report No 25, Cmnd. 4803. HMSO, November, 1971).

CIR. *Disclosure of Information* (Report No 31, HMSO, 1972)...156.

CIR. *Industrial Relations Training* (Report No 33 and Report No 33A (Statistical Supplement) HMSO, 1972/1973)...547.

CIR. *The Role of Management in Industrial Relations* (Report No 34; HMSO, 1973).

CIR. *Annual Report for 1972* (Report No 37, HMSO, 1973).

CIR. *Communications and Collective Bargaining* (Report No 39, HMSO, 1973).

CIR. *Annual Report for 1973*, (Report No 65, HMSO, 1974).

CIR. *Industrial Relations in Multi-plant Undertakings* (Report No 85, HMSO, 1974)...83, 231, 236, 237.

CIR. *Final Report* (Report No 90, HMSO, 1974).

CIR. *Employers' Organizations and Industrial Relations* (Study No 1, HMSO, 1973)..253.

CIR. *Industrial Relations at Establishment Level* (Study No 2, HMSO, 1973).

CIR. *Recognition of White Collar Unions in Engineering and Chemicals* (Study No 3, HMSO, 1973)...348.

CIR. *Worker Participation and Collective Bargaining in Europe* (Study No 4, HMSO, 1974).

CIR. *Trade Union Recognition – CIR Experience* (Study No 5, HMSO, 1974)...348.

CIR. *Ballots and Union Recognition: A Guide for Employers*. (HMSO, 1974).

Commons, JR. *Legal Foundations of Capitalism* (Macmillan, 1924)...93.

Confederation of British Industry. *Evidence to the Royal Commission on Trade Unions and Employers' Associations* (CBI, 1965).

608

Confederation of British Industry. *The Provision of Information to Employees: Guidelines for Action* (CBI, 1975).

Corbett, P. *Ideologies* (Hutchinson, 1965)...291.

Coser, L. *The Functions of Social Conflict* (Routledge & Kegan Paul, 1956).

Cowan, I.D. 'Developing and Implementing Personnel Policies' in *University of Bradford Management Centre*, 1970, pp 18-21...28, 435.

Craig, A. 'Framework for the Analysis of Industrial Relations Systems' in Barrett, B et al. *Industrial Relations and the Wider Society* (Collier-Macmillan, 1975) q.v., pp 8-20.

Craig, C, Rubery, J, Tarling, R, & Wilkinson, F. *Labour Market Structure, Industrial Organisation and Low Pay* (Cambridge UP, 1982)...185, 193.

Crouch, C. *Class Conflict and the Industrial Relations Crisis* (Heinemann, 1977).

Crouch, C. *The Politics of Industrial Relations* (Fontana/Collins, 1979)...66, 87, 282.

Crouch, C. *Trade Unions: The Logic of Collective Action* (Fontana, 1982), 266-69, 282, 292, 521.

Crozier, M. *The Bureaucratic Phenomenon* (Tavistock, 1964)...479.

Cuthbert, NH & Hawkins, KH. *Company Industrial Relations Policies* (Longman, 1973)...29, 31, 288, 429.

Cyert, RM & March, JC. *A Behavioural Theory of the Firm* (Prentice Hall, 1963)...53, 226.

Dahl, R: 'The Concept of Power' in *Behavioural Sciences*, 2, 1957, pp 201-18...461.

Dahrendorf, R. *Class and Conflict in an Industrial Society* (Routledge & Kegan Paul, 1959).

Dalton, M. *Men who Manage*, (Wiley, 195urnal of Management Studies, 6, 1969, pp 366-75...256.

Daniel, WW. 'Productivity Bargaining and Orientation to Work. A Rejoinder to Goldthorpe' in *Journal of Management Studies*, 8, 1971, pp 329-35...256.

Daniel, WW. *Wage Determination in Industry* (Political Economic Planning, XLII (563), 1976).

Daniel, WW & McIntosh, N. *The Right to Manage?* (PEP/MacDonald, 1972)...113.

Daniel, WW & McIntosh, N. *Incomes Policy and Collective Bargaining* (PEP, May, 1973)...188.

Daniel, WW & Millward, N. *Workplace Industrial Relatio8)...133.

Davey, HW. *Contemporary Collective Bargaining* (Prentice Hall, 1951)...269, 322.

Davis, KE & Florquist, CC. 'Perceived Threat and Dependence as Determinants of Tactical Usage of Opinion Conformtiy' in *Journal of Experimental Psychology*, 1 (3), 1965, pp 219-36...566.

Dean, LR. 'Union Activity and Dual Loyalty' in *Industrial and Labor Relations Review*, 7, 1954, pp 526-36...436.

Deaton, DR & Beaumont, PB. 'The Determinants of Bargaining Structure: Some Large Scale Survey Evidence in Britain' in *British Journal of Industrial Relations*. XVIII (2), 1980, pp 202-16.

Deeks, J, Farmer, J, Roth, H, & Scott, G. *Industrial Relations in New Zealand* (Methuen, Wellington, 1978).

Deutsch, M. *The Resolution of Conflict* (Yale UP, 1962; 1973).

Dicey, AV. *Introduction to the Study of the Law of the Constitution* (Macmillan, 9th edn, 1939)...88.

Dickens, L. 'Staff Associations and the IR Act. The Effects of Union Growth' in *Industrial Relations Journal*, 6 (3), Autumn, 1975, pp 29-41.

Dickens, L. 'UKAPE: A Study of a Professional Union' in *Industrial Relations Journal*, 3 (3), Autumn, 1972, pp 2-16...140.

Doeringer, P & Piore, M. *Internal Labour Markets and Manpower Analysis* (Lexington, 1971)...33-34.

609

Donovan, Lord. *Royal Commission on Trade Unions and Employers' Associations, Report,* (HMSO, 1968)...2, 22, 23, 25, 27, 28, 29, 31, 45, 142, 178, 207, 241, 246, 248, 263, 364, 431, 473.

Dore, RP. *British Factory – Japanese Factory* (Allen & Unwin, 1973)...63.

Doyle, FP. 'Organizing the Enterprise' in Marceau, I. (ed). *Dealing with a Union* (American Management Association, 1969) q.v., pp 21-34, 237-38, 408-09.

Drucker, PF. *The Practice of Management* (Mercury Books, 1961)...226, 297.

Druckman, D (ed). *Negotiations: Social Psychological Perspectives* (Sage, 1977)...547.

Druckman, D & Zechmeister, K. 'Conflict of Interest and Value Dissensus' in *Human Relations,* 26, 1973, pp 449-66...547.

Dubin, R. 'Industrial Workers' Worlds' in *Social Problems,* III, January, 1956, pp 131-42...459.

Dubin, R. 'Power, Function and Organization' in *Pacific Sociological Review,* 6, Spring, 1963, pp 16-20; and in Dubin, R. *Human Relations in Administration* (Prentice Hall, 4th edn., 1974), pp 305-13...479.

Dubois, P. *Sabotage in Industry* (Penguin, 1979).

Dufty, NF. *Industrial Relations in India* (Allied Publishers, Bombay, 1964).

Dunlop, JT. *Wage Determination under Trade Unions* (Kelley, lst edn, 1944; Blackwell, 1950)...317, 321, 339.

Dunlop, JT. *Industrial Relations Systems* (Henry Holt, 1958)...5, 6, 8, 27, 31, 41, 42, 61, 63, 292, 320, 322, 457.

Durcan, JW & McCarthy, WEJ. 'The State Subsidy Theory of Strikes' in *British Journal of Industrial Relations,* XII, 1974, pp 26-47...13.

Eaton, J, Gill, CR & Morris, RS. 'The Staffing of Industrial Relations Management in the Chemical Industry' in *Chemistry and Industry,* 17 September, 1977, pp 751-754...450.

Edelstein, JD & Warner, M. *Comparative Union Democracy* (Allen & Unwin, 1975).

Edwards, C. 'A Study of Local Union Power in the Coal Industry' in *British Journal of Industrial Relations,* XVI (1), March, 1978, pp 1-15.

Edwards, C & Harper, DG. 'Bargaining at the Trade Union and Management Interface' in Abell, P. *Organizations as bargaining and influencing systems* (Heinemann, 1975) q.v. pp 41-71.

Edwards, DV. *International Political Analysis* (Holt, Rinehart & Winston, 1969)...528-29, 547.

Edwards, PK. 'Strikes and Unorganized Conflict. Some further Considerations' in *British Journal of Industrial Relations,* 17, 1979, pp 95-99.

Edwards, PK. 'A Critique of the Kerr-Siegel Hypothesis of Strikes and Isolated Mass: A Study of the Falsification of Sociological Knowledge' in *Sociological Review,* 1977, pp 551-574.

Edwards, PK. 'Plant Size and Strike-Proneness' in *Oxford Bulletin of Economics and Statistics,* 42, May, 1980, pp 145-56.

Edwards, PK. 'Strike-Proneness of British Manufacturing Establishments' in *British Journal of Industrial Relations,* XIX (2), July, 1981, pp 135-48.

Edwards, R & Paul, S. *Job Evaluation* (Association of Professional, Executive, Clerical and Computer Staff, 1977)...358, 367.

Eldridge, JET. *Industrial Disputes* (Routledge & Kegan Paul, 1968)...23, 398.

Eldridge, JET & Cameron, GC. 'Unofficial Strikes: Some Objections Considered' in Eldridge, JET. *Industrial Disputes* (Routledge & Kegan Paul, 1968), pp 68-90...23.

Eldridge, JET. *Sociology and Industrial Life* (Nelson, 1971).

Elliott, D. *The Lucas Aerospace Workers' Campaign* (Fabian Society, 1977)...367.

Elliott, J. *Conflict or Cooperation* (Kogan Page, 1978)...31, 189, 193.

610

Emerson, RM. 'Power-Dependence Relationships' in *American Sociological Review*, 27, 1962, pp 31-41.

Emery, FE. *Systems Thinking* (Penguin, 1969).

Employment, Dept of. *Reform of Collective Bargaining at Company and Plant Level* (Manpower Paper No 5, HMSO, 1971), 231.

Employment, Dept of. *Industrial Relations Procedures* (Manpower paper No 14, HMSO, 1975)...170

Employment, Dept of. *Code of Industrial Relations Practice* (DE, 1972; reissued by ACAS)...128, 352, 361.

Employment, Dept of. *Code of Practice on Picketing* (HMSO, 1980)...174.

Employment, Dept of. *Code of Practice on Closed Shop Agreements and Arrangements* (HMSO, 1983).

Employment, Dept of. *Training for the Management of Human Resources* (The Hayes Report) (HMSO, 1972).

Employment, Dept of. *Trade Union Immunities* (HMSO, 1980).

Employment, Dept of. *Democracy in Trade unions* (HMSO, 1983)...597.

Engineering Employers' Federation. *Business Performance and Industrial Relations* (EEF, 1972, reprinted, 1976)...21.

England, GW. *The Manager and His Values* (Ballinger, 1975)...65.

England GW, Agarwal, NC, & Trevise, RE. 'Union Leaders and Managers: A Comparison of Value Systems' in *Industrial Relations*, 10, (2), 1971, pp 211-26...65.

England, J. 'How UCATT Revised its Rules: An Anatomy of Organizational Change' in *British Journal of Industrial Relations*, XVII (1), 1979, pp 1-18...273.

Etzioni, A. *A Comparative Analysis of Complex Organizations* (Free Press, 1961; 1975)...305, 338, 470, 561.

Etzioni, A. *Modern Organizations* (Prentice Hall, 1964).

Etzioni, A. *A Sociological Reader on Complex Organizations* (Holt, Rinehart & Winston, 2nd edn, 1969).

Etzioni, A. *The Active Society: A Theory of Social and Political Processes* (Collier-Macmillan, 1968)...54.

Evans, EO. 'Works Rule Books in the Engineering Industry' in *Industrial Relations Journal*, 2 (1), 1971, pp 54-65.

Eysenck, HJ. *The Structure of Human Personality* (Methuen, 2nd edn, 1960)...55.

Falk, R and Clark, I. 'Planning for Growth' in *Management Today*, June, 1966, pp 85-88 and 151...51.

Farnham, D & Pimlott, J. *Understanding Industrial Relations* (Cassell, 1979; 2nd edn, 1983)...253.

Fatchett, D & Whittingham, HA. 'Trends and Developments in Industrial Relations Theory', in *Industrial Relations Journal*, 7 (1), Spring, 1976, pp. 50-60.

Ferris, P. *The New Militants: Crisis in the Trade Unions* (Penguin, 1972).

Festinger, L. *A Theory of Cognitive Dissonance* (Row Peterson, 1957).

Fisher, MR. *The Economic Analysis of Labour* (Weidenfeld & Nicholson, 1971)...317.

Fisher, M. *Measurement of Labour Disputes and their Economic Effects* (OECD, 1973).

Flanagan, RJ & Weber, AR. *Bargaining Without Boundaries* (University of Chicago Press, 1974).

Flanders, A. *Trade Unions* (Hutchinson, 1952; 1968).

Flanders, A. *Industrial Relations: What's Wrong with the System?* (IPM, 1965); and in Flanders, A. *Management and Unions*, 1975, pp 86-99.

Flanders, A. *Collective Bargaining: Prescription for Change* (Faber and Faber, 1967); and in Flanders, A. *Management and Unions*, 1975, pp 155-211...344, 358.

Flanders, A. *Collective Bargaining* (Penguin, 1969); Ch. l; also in Flanders, A. *Management and Unions* (1970), pp 213-40...315-16, 323-24, 439.

Flanders, A. 'Can Managers be Taught Industrial Relations?' (BIM Conference papers, 1968).

Flanders, A. *The Fawley Productivity Agreements* (Faber & Faber, 1968)

Flanders, A. *Management and Unions* (Faber, 1970)...31, 61.

Flanders, A. 'The Tradition of Voluntarism' in *British Journal of Industrial Relations*, November, 1974, pp 352-70.

Flanders, A & Clegg, HA (eds). *The System of Industrial Relations in Great Britain* (Blackwell, 1954)...4, 31, 181, 287, 288, 334, 355.

Flanders, A, Pomeranz, R & Woodward, J. *Experiment in Industrial Democracy. A Study of the John Lewis Partnership* (Faber & Faber, 1964).

Fleishman, EA. *Studies in Personnel and Industrial Psychology*, (Dorsey, 1961; rev. edn, 1967).

Florence, PS. *The Logic of British and American Industry* (Routledge & Kegan Paul, 1953, 2nd edn, 1961)...82, 239.

Fogarty, MP. *The Rules of Work* (Chapman, 1961).

Fogarty, MP. *Company and Corporation – One Law?* (Chapman, 1965)...28, 594, 595.

Follett, MP. see Metcalf, HC and Urwick, L. *Dynamic Administration* (Pitman 1981)...500.

Foster, J. ' The Redistributive Effects of Inflation' in *Scottish Journal of Political Economy*, 23 (1), February, 1976, pp 73-98.

Foulkes, D. *Law for Managers* (Butterworths, 1971)...120.

Fowler, A. *Personnel Management in Local Government* (IPM, 1980)...406, 407, 412, 430.

Fox, A. *The Milton Plan* (IPM, 1965)...386.

Fox, A. *Industrial Sociology and Industrial Relations* (RCTUEA, Research Paper, No. 3; HMSO, 1966); and in Flanders, A. *Collective Bargaining* (Penguin, 1969) q.v., pp, 390-409...55, 297, 300, 458.

Fox, A. 'Management's Frame of Reference' in Flanders, A. *Collective Bargaining* (Penguin, 1969), q.v., pp 390-409...55.

Fox, A. *A Sociology of Work in Industry* (Collier-Macmillan, 1971)...37, 61, 344.

Fox, A. *Beyond Contract: Power Work and Trust Relations* (Allen & Unwin, 1974a)...32, 89, 112, 439, 440.

Fox, A. *Man-Mismanagement* (Hutchinson, 1974b).

Fox, A. 'Collective Bargaining, Flanders and the Webbs' in *British Journal of Industrial Relations*, 13 (2), July, 1975, pp 151-74.

Fox, A. 'Industrial Relations. A Social Critique of the Pluralist Ideology' in Child, J (ed). *Man and Organization* (Allen & Unwin, 1973) pp 182-233; and in Barrett, et al. *Industrial Relations and the Wider Society* (Collier-Macmillan, 1975), q.v., pp 261-9...297.

Fox, A. 'Ideologies of Management and Collectivities' in Barrett, B, et al. *Industrial Relations and the Wider Society* (Collier-Macmillan, 1975), q.v., pp 261-9.

Fox, A. 'Corporatism and Industrial Democracy' in SSRC. *Industrial Democracy. International Views* (SSRC, 1978)...586.

Fox, A & Flanders, A. 'The Reform of Collective Bargaining: From Donovan to Durkheim' in *British Journal of Industrial Relations*, 7 (2), 1969, pp 151-80.

Fox, A. 'A Note on Industrial Relations Pluralism' in *Sociology*, 13 (1), January, 1979, p 105...297.

Fraser, WH. *Trade Unions and Society: The Struggle for Acceptance, 1850-80*, (Allen & Unwin, 1974)...134.

French, JRP. 'A Formal Theory of Social Power' in *Psychological Review*, 63, 1956, pp 181-94.

French, JRP & Raven, B. 'The Bases of Social Power' in Cartwright, D. *Studies in Social Power* (Institute for Social Research, University of Michigan, 1959) q.v. pp 150-67...461.

Frey, R, & Adams, J. 'The Negotiator's Dilemma. Simultaneous In-group and Out-Group Conflict' in *Journal of Experimental Social Psychology*, 8, 1972, pp 331-46...446.

Friedman, H & Meredeen, S. The *Dynamics of Industrial Conflict* (Croom Helm, 1980)...294, 309, 321, 332, 333, 336, 369, 390, 391, 392, 396.

Friedman, M. 'The Social Responsibility of the Business Enterprise is to Increase its Profits' in *Issues in Business and Society*, 1977, p 168...297.

Friedman, M. *Capitalism and Freedom*, (Phoenix Books, 1963)...297.

Fulton, Lord. *The Civil Service, Vol 1, Report of the Committee* (HMSO, 1968, Cmnd. 3638)...404.

Galbraith, JK. *Economics and Public Purpose* (Deutsch, 1974).

Galbraith, JK. *The New Industrial State* (Hamish Hamilton, 2nd edn, 1974)...404.

Galenson, W. *Comparative Labour Movements* (Prentice Hall, 1952a)...3, 4.

Galenson, W. *The Danish System of Labor Relations* (Harvard UP, 1952b)...4.

Gamson, WA. *Power and Discontent* (Dorsey, 1968)...257.

Gayler, JL & Purvis, RL. *Industrial Law* (Harrap, 2nd edn, 1972)...104.

Gennard, J. *Financing Strikers* (Macmillan, 1977)...13.

Gennard, J, Dunn, S & Wright, M. 'The Extent of the Closed Shop Arrangements in British Industry' in *Employment Gazette*, January, 1980, pp 16-22...155.

George, M & Elliott, D. 'The Lucas Aerospace Workers' Campaign' in *Employee Relations*, 1 (1), 1979, pp 24-29...367.

Gerhart, PF. 'Determinants of Bargaining Outcomes in Local Government Labour Negotiations' in *Industrial and Labour Relations Review*, XXIX, (3),April, 1976, pp331-51...320.

Gill, CG. 'Industrial Relations in a Multi-plant Organization' in *Industrial Relations Journal*, 5 (4), Winter, 1974-5, pp 22-35.

Gill, CG & Concannon, H. 'Developing an Explanatory Framework for IR Policy within a Firm' in *Industrial Relations Journal*, 7 (3), Winter, 1976-77, pp 13-20.

Gill, CG, Morris, RS & Eaton, J. 'APST. The Rise of a Professional Union' in *Industrial Relations Journal*, 9 (1) Spring, 1978, pp 37-47...140, 240.

Gill, RWT & Taylor, DS. 'Training Managers to Handle Discipline and Grievance Interviews' in *Journal of Education and Training*, May, 1976, pp 217-227.

Giner, S. *Sociology* (Martin Robertson, 1972).

GKN-Shotton. *A Charter for the Workpeople* (GKN-Shotton, 1973)...493, 495.

Glaser, R (ed). *The Nature of Reinforcement* (Academic Press, 1971)...44.

Glueck, WF & Jauch, LR. *Business Policy and Strategic Management* (McGraw Hill, 1984).

Glyn, A & Sutcliffe, *British Capitalism, Workers and the Profits Squeeze*, (Penguin, 1972)...16.

Goffman, E. *The Presentation of Self in Everyday Life* (Doubleday, 1959)...565.

Goffman, E. *Encounters* (Bobbs-Merrill, 1961)...38, 39.

Goldthorpe, JH, Lockwood, D, Bechofer, F & Platt, J. *The Affluent Worker: Industrial Attitudes and Behaviour* (Cambridge UP, 1968)...256, 282, 294, 300, 312.

Goldthorpe, JH. 'Industrial Relations in Great Britain: A Critique of Reformism' in *Politics and Society*, 1974, pp 419-52.

Goldthorpe, JH. 'Social Inequality and Social Integration in Modern Britain' in Wedderburn, D (ed). *Poverty, Inequality and Class Structure* (Cambridge UP, 1974), pp 217-38.

Goodman, JFB & Whittingham, TG. *Shop Stewards in British Industry* (McGraw Hill, 1969)...287.

Goodman, JFB. 'The Role of the Shop Steward' in Kessler & Weekes. *Conflict at work: Re-Shaping Industrial Relations* (BBC Publications, 1971), q.v., pp 53-74...377, 398.

Goodman, JFB, Armstrong, EGA, Davis, JE & Wagner, A. *Rule-Making and Industrial Peace* (Croom Helm, 1977), 240, 449-50.

Goodman, JFB, Armstrong, EGA, Wagner, A, Davis, DJ & Wood, SJ. 'Rules in Industrial Relations Theory: A Discussion' in *Industrial Relations Journal*, 6 (1), Spring, 1975a, pp 14-30...6.

Goodman, JFB, Armstrong, EGA, Wagner, A, Davis, DJ, & Wood, SJ. 'The Industrial Relations System Concept' in *British Journal of Industrial Relations*, XIII (3), November, 1975b, pp 291-308...6.

Goodrich, C. *The Frontier of Control* (Bell, 1920: Pluto Press, 1975)...79, 292.

Gospel, HF & Littler, CR. *Managerial Strategies and Industrial Relations* (Heinemann, 1983).

Gottschalk, AW, 'A Behavioural Analysis of Bargaining' in Warner, M (ed). *The Sociology of the Workplace* (Allen & Unwin, 1973, pp 36-81...80, 326.

Gould, J, & Kolb, WL (eds). *A Dictionary of the Social Sciences* (Tavistock, 1964).

Gouldner, AW. *Wildcat Strike*, (Routledge & Kegan Paul, 1955a)...336.

Gouldner, AW. *Patterns of Industrial Bureaucracy*, (Routledge & Kegan Paul, 1955b)... 296, 389.

Government Social Survey. *Workplace Industrial Relations* (SS 402, HMSO, March, 1968).

Gower, LCB. *Principles of Modern Company Law* (Stevens, 4th edn, 1979)...197, 594.

Grant, W & Marsh, D. *The CBI*, (Hodder & Stoughton, 1977)...241, 250.

Gregson, D and Ruffle, K. 'Rationalizing Rewards at Rogerstone' in *Personnel Management*, 12 (10), October, 1980, pp 62-64... 274, 346, 358.

Griffith, JAG. *The Politics of the Judiciary* (Fontana, 1977; 2nd edn, 1981)...135.

Guest, D & Fatchett, D. *Worker Participation: Individual Control and Performance* (IPM, 1974).

Guest, D & Knight, K. *Putting Participation into Practice* (Gower, 1979).

Hadden, T. *Company Law and Capitalism* (Weidenfeld & Nicholson, 1972, 2nd edn, 1977)...116, 595.

Hahlo, HR & Trebilcock, MJ. *Casebook on Company Law* (Sweet & Maxwell, 2nd edn, 1977)...136.

Halsbury, The Earl of. *Report of the Committee of Inquiry into the Pay and Related Conditions of Service of Nurses and Midwives*, (HMSO, 1974)...414.

Hambrick, DC, MacMillan, IC & Day, DL. 'Strategic Attributes and Performance in the Four Cells of the BCG Matrix. A PIMS-based Analysis of Industrial-Product Businesses' in *Academy of Management Journal*, 25 (3), 1982, pp 510-531.

Hambrick, DC, MacMillan, IC & Day, DL. 'The Product Portfolio and Profitability - A PIMS-based Analysis of Industrial-Product Businesses' in *Academy of Management Journal*, 25 (4), 1982, pp 733-755.

Hammerhesh, D. 'Who Wins in Wage Bargaining?' in *Industrial and Labour Relations Review*, 26 (4), 1973, pp 1146-49.

Handy, C. 'The Changing Shape of Work and Life' in *Policy Studies Institute Journal*, 1982, pp 189-98.

Hanika, F de P. *New Thinking in Management* (Hutchinson, 1965)...4.

Hanson, CG. *Trade Unions. A Century of Privilege* (Institute of Economic Affairs, Occasional Paper No 38, 1973)...146.

Hanson, C, Jackson, S, & Miller, D. *The Closed Shop. A Comparative Study in Public Policy and Trade Union Security in Britain, the USA and West Germany* (Gower, 1982)...155.

Harbison, FH & Coleman, JR. *Goals and Strategy in Collective Bargaining* (Harper & Bros, 1951)...225, 270, 521.

Harbison, F, & Myers, CA. *Management in the Industrial World. An International Analysis* (McGraw-Hill, 1959)...297.

Harsanyi, JC. 'Measurement of Social Power, Opportunity Costs, and the Theory of Two-Person Bargaining Games' in *Behavioral Science*, 7 (1), 1962, pp 67-80...461.

Hartmann, H. 'Managerial Employees –New Participants in Industrial Relations' in *British Journal of Industrial Relations*, XII (2), July, 1974, pp 268-81...98.

Harvey, J. *Elementary Economics* (Macmillan, 3rd edn, 1971)...499.

Hawes, WR & Brookes, CCP. 'Change and Renewal. Joint Consultation in Industry' in *Employment Gazette*, April, 1980, pp 353-61...490, 513.

Hawkins, K. 'Company Bargaining. Problems and Prospects' in *British Journal of Industrial Relations*, 9 (2), July, 1971, pp 198-213; and in Cuthbert, N & Hawkins, K (eds). *Company Industrial Relations Policies*, (Longmans, 1973) pp 34-49, 429.

Hawkins, K. *The Management of Industrial Relations* (Pelican, 1978)...365.

Hawkins, K. *Industrial Relations Practice* (Kogan Page, 1979)...438, 458.

Health and Safety Commission. *Code of Practice: Time off for Training of Safety Representatives* (H&SC, No 9, 1978a)...161.

Health and Safety Commission. *Safety Representatives and Safety Committees* (H&SC, 1978b)...159.

Healy, JJ (ed). *Creative Collective Bargaining* (Prentice Hall, 1965).

Heller, F, Wilders, M, Abell, P, & Warner, M. *What do the British Want from Participation and Industrial Democracy?* (Anglo-German Foundation, 1979)...586.

Henderson, BD. *Henderson on Corporate Strategy* (Abt Books, 1979).

Heneman, HG. 'Towards a General Conceptual System of Industrial Relations. How do we Get there?' in Somers, GG, *Essays in Industrial Relations Theory* (Iowa State University, 1969), q.v., pp 3-24.

Heneman, HG & Schwab, DP. 'An Evaluation of Research on Expectancy Theory Predictions of Employee Performance' in *Psychological Bulletin*, 78, 1972, pp 1-9...40.

Hepple, BA & O'Higgins, P. *Employment Law* (Sweet & Maxwell, 3rd edn, 1979 4th edition, 1981)...104, 112, 120, 133, 163, 205, 209, 210-11, 222, 407.

Herzberg, F. *Work and the Nature of Man* (Staples, 1968)...40, 47, 54.

Hicks, JR. *The Theory of Wages* (Macmillan, 1st edn, 1932; 2nd edn, 1963).

Hickson, DJ, Hinings CR, Lee, CA, Schneck, RE & Pennings, JM. 'A Strategic Contingencies Theory of Intra- Organizational Power' in *Administrative Science Quarterly*, 16, 1971, pp 216-29; and in Salaman, G & Thompson, K. *People and Organisations*, (Longmans, 1973), pp 174-89...479.

Hill, L, & Hook, C. *Management at the Bargaining Table* (McGraw Hill, 1945)...297.

Hill, S. 'Norms, Groups and Power: The Sociology of Workplace Industrial Relations' in *British Journal of Industrial Relations*, XII (2), July, 1974, pp 213-35...481.

Hill, S. 'The New Industrial Relations?' in *British Journal of Industrial Relations*, XIV (2), July, 1976, pp 214-19.

Hill, S. *Competition and Control at Work* (Heinemann, 1981)...478.

Hiller, AT. *The Strike* (Arno, 1969)...395.

Hinton, J. *The First Shop Stewards Movement* (Allen & Unwin, 1973)...266.

Hobsbawm, EJ. *Labouring Men* (Weidenfeld & Nicholson, 1964).

Hofer, CS. 'Towards a Contingency Theory of Business Strategy' in *Academy of Management Journal*, 18 (4), December, 1975, pp 784-810.

Homans, GC. *The Human Group* (Routledge & Kegan Paul, 1951)...36, 39, 271, 561.

Homans, GC. *Social Behaviour* (Routledge & Kegan Paul, 1961).

Honzik, JF. 'The Management Bargaining Team' in Marceau (ed): *Dealing with a Union* (American Management Association, 1969), pp 78-85...451, 454, 457, 458.

Hopmann, PT & Walcott, C. 'The Impact of External Stresses and Tensions of Negotiations' in Druckman, D (ed). *Negotiations: Social and Psychological Perspectives* (Sage, 1977)...547, 548.

Howells, R & Barrett, B. *The Manager's Guide to the Health and Safety at Work Act* (IPM, 1976; 2nd edn, 1982)...164, 222.

Hughes, J. *Trade Union Structure and Government* (RCTUEA Research Paper No 5, HMSO, 1966)...140.

Hughes, J. *Membership Participation and Trade Union Government* (RCTUEA Research Paper No 5, HMSO, 1968).

Hughes, J & Moore, R. *A Special Case? Social Justice and the Miners* (Penguin, 1972)...424.

Hughes, J & Pollins, H. *Trade Unions in Great Britain* (David & Charles, 1973)...264.

Hutt, WH. *The Theory of Collective Bargaining, 1930-75* (Institute of Economic Affairs, 1975)...77, 499.

Hyman, HH. 'The Value Systems of Different Classes: A Social-Psychological Contribution to the Analysis of Stratification' in Bendix, R & Lipset, SM (eds). *Class, Status and Power* (Free Press, 1953), pp 426-42...65.

Hyman, R. *Disputes Procedure in Action* (Heinemann, 1972).

Hyman, R. *Strikes* (Fontana, 1972)...398, 577.

Hyman, R. *Industrial Relations: A Marxist Introduction,* (Macmillan, 1975)...61, 67, 87.

Hyman, R, & Fryer, B. 'Trade Unions' in McKinlay, JB (ed). *Processing People* (Holt, Rinehard and Winston, 1975), pp 150-213...6, 268, 270, 292.

Hyman, R & Brough, I. *Social Values and Industrial Relations* (Blackwell, 1975)...65.

Hyman, R: 'Pluralism, Procedural Consensus and Collective Bargaining' in *British Journal of Industrial Relations*, XVI (1), 1978, pp 16-40...297.

Indik, BP. 'Some Effects of Organizational Size on Member Attitudes and Behaviour' in *Human Relations*, 16, 1963, pp 369-84.

Indik, BP. 'Organization Size and Member Participation: Some Empirical Tests of Alternative Explanations' in *Human Relations*, 18, 1965, pp 339-49.

Industrial Facts and Forecasting, Ltd. *Workplace Industrial Relations in Manufacturing Industry, 1978: Key Results* (IFF, 1978)...84.

Industrial Society. *Practical Policies for Participation* (Industrial Society, 1974)...583.

Ingham, GK. 'Organizational Size, Orientation to Work and Industrial Behaviour' in *Sociology*, 1 (3) September, 1967, pp 239-58...229.

Ingham, GK. 'Plant Size and Political Attitudes and Behaviour' in *Sociological Review*, 17 (2), July, 1969, pp 235-49...229.

Ingham, GK. *Strikes and Industrial Conflict* (Macmillan, 1974).

Jackson, D, Turner, HA & Wilkinson, F. *Do Trade Unions Cause Inflation?* (Cambridge UP, 1972).

Jackson, M. *Industrial Relations on the Docks* (Saxon House, 1973).

Jackson, MP. *Industrial Relations: A Textbook* (Croom Helm, 1977)...61, 87, 371.

Jackson, MP. *Trade Unions* (Hutchinson, 1982)...272, 273.

Jackson, P & Sisson, K. 'Employers Confederations in Sweden and the UK: The Significance of the Industrial Infrastructure' in *British Journal of Industrial Relations*, XIV (3), 1976, pp 306-323.

Jackson, P. *Local Government,* (Butterworth, 1976)...403.

Jaques, E. *The Changing Culture of a Factory* (Tavistock, 1951)...491, 493-94.

Jeffery, K & Hennessy, P. *States of Emergency* (Routledge & Kegan Paul, 1983).

Jefferys, JB. *The Story of the Engineers* (Lawrence & Wishart, 1945)...316.

Jenks, E. *The State and the Nation* (Dent, 1919)...66, 405-06.

Jenkins, C & Sherman, B. *Collective Bargaining* (Routledge & Kegan Paul, 1977).

Jenkins, Lord. *Report of the Company Law Committee* (Cmnd 1749, HMSO, June, 1962)...594.

Jenner, R. 'Analysing Cultural Stereotypes in Multi-national Business: United States and Australia', in *Journal of Management Studies*, 19 (3), 1982, pp 309-25...63.

Jensen, L. 'Soviet-American Bargaining Behaviour in Post-war Disarmament Negotiations' in *Journal of Conflict Resolution*, 7, 1963, pp 522-41...326.

Johnson, DM. *The Psychology of Thinking* (Harper & Row, 1972)...53, 54, 65.

Johnston, E. *Industrial Action* (Arrow, 1975)...385.

Jones, DMC. *Disclosure of Financial Information to Employees* (IPM, 1978)...584.

Jones, EE. *Ingratiation* (Appleton-Century-Crofts, 1964)...565.

Jones, GP. *Workers Abroad* (Nelson, 1939)...4.

Jones, K. *The Human Face of Change – Social Responsibility and Rationalization at British Steel* (IPM, 1974).

Jones, P. 'Incomes Policy and the Public Sector' in *Personnel Management*, 10 (2), February, 1978, pp 38-43...419.

Jones, PR. 'The British Medical Association and the Closed Shop' in *Industrial Relations Journal*, 5 (4), Winter, 1974-75, pp 36-45...139.

Jones, RM. *Absenteeism* (DE Manpower Paper No 4, HMSO, 1971). Joyce, P & Woods, A. 'Management Attitudes on Industrial Relations' in *Employee Relations* 2 (5), 1980, pp 30-32.

Kahn-Freund, O. *Labour and the Law* (Stevens, 1972, rev edn, 1977)...71, 72, 87, 94, 108, 109, 112, 306.

Kahn-Freund, O. 'Industrial Democracy' in *Industrial Law Journal*, 6, 1977, pp 65-84.

Karsh, B. *Diary of a Strike* (University of Illinois Press, 1958)...327.

Kast, FE & Rosenzweig, JE. 'General Systems Theory: Applications for Organization and Management' in *Academy of Management Journal*, December, 1972, pp 447-65...4.

Katz, D. 'Consistent Reactive Participation of Group Members and Reduction of Intergroup Conflict' in *Journal of Conflict Resolution*, 5, March, 1959, pp 28-40...560.

Katz, E & Lazarsfeld, PF. *Personal Influence* (Free Press, 1955)...56, 392, 551.

Keenoy, T. *Invitation to Industrial Relations* (Blackwell, 1984).

Keenoy, T. 'The Employment Relationship as a Form of Socio-Economic Exchange' in Dlugos, G & Weiermair, K (eds). *Management Under Different Value Systems* (Walter de Gruyter, 1981), pp 405-46...316.

Kelley, HH. 'A Classroom Study of the Dilemmas in Interpersonal Negotiations' in Archibald, K (ed). *Strategic Interaction and Conflict* (Institute of International Studies, University of California, 1966), pp 49-73...549.

Kelly, GA. *A Theory of Personality: The Psychology of Personal Constructs* (Norton, 1963)...39, 40, 47, 54.

Kelly, J. *Is Scientific Management Possible?* (Faber & Faber, 1968)...301.

Kelly, J & Nicholson, N. 'Strikes and Other Forms of Industrial Action' in *Industrial Relations Journal*, 11 (5), Nov/Dec, 1980, pp 20-31...398.

Kennedy, G. 'Negotiating Skills Training: The 8-step Approach' in *ATM Journal*, 9 (3), December, 1978, pp 189-96...327, 514, 518, 533-34.

Kennedy, G, Benson, J & McMillan, J. *Managing Negotiations* (Business Books, 1980)...514, 518, 545, 547, 570.

Kerr, C. 'Labour's Income Share and the Labour Movement' in Taylor, GW & Pierson, FC (eds). *New Concepts in Wage Determination* (McGraw Hill, 1957), pp 269-79...12.

617

Kerr, C & Siegel, A. 'The Inter-Industry Propensity to Strike – An International Comparison' in Kornhauser, A, Dubin, R & Ross, AM (eds). *Industrial Conflict* (McGraw Hill, 1954) pp 186-212...336.

Kerr, C, Dunlop, JT, Harbison, FH, & Myers, CA. *Industrialism and Industrial Man* (Heinemann, 1962; Penguin, 1960).

Kessler, S & Weekes, B. *Conflict at Work: Re-Shaping Industrial Relations* (BBC Publications, 1971)...283.

King, B, Streufert, S & Fiddler, FE (eds). *Managerial Control and Organizational Democracy* (Winston, 1978).

Kipping, Sir N. *Summing Up* (Hutchinson, 1972)...113.

Kleingartner, A. 'The Organization of White Collar Workers' in *British Journal of Industrial Relations*, VI (1), March, 1968, pp 79-93...262.

Kluckhohn, C. *Culture and Behaviour: Collected Essays* (Free Press, 1962)...64.

Kluckhohn, FR. 'Dominant and Variant Cultural Value Orientations' in Cabot, H & Kahl, JA. (eds). *Human Relations, Vol. 1, Concepts* (Harvard UP, 1953), pp 88-98...64.

Kluckhohn, FR & Strodtbeck, FL. *Variations in Value Orientations* (Row Peterson, 1961).

Knight, IB. *Company Organization and Worker Participation* (HMSO, 1979)...230.

Kniveton, B & Towers, B. *Training for Negotiation* (Business Books, 1978).

Knowles, KGJC. *Strikes: A Study in Industrial Conflict* (Blackwell, 1954)...335.

Kochan, TA & Wheeler, HN. 'Municipal Collective Bargaining. A Model and Analysis of Bargaining Outcomes' in *Industrial and Labour Relations Review*, XXIX, (1), October, 1975, pp 44-6...339.

Kornhauser, A et al. *Industrial Conflict* (McGraw Hill, 1954).

Kotter, JP. 'Power, Dependence and Effective Management' in *Harvard Business Review*, Nov-Dec. 1956, pp 25-29.

Kroeber, AL, & Kluckhohn, C: *Culture: A Critical Review of Concepts and Definitions* (Vintage Books, 1952).

Kruisinga, HJ. (ed). *The Balance Between Centralization and Decentralization in Managerial Control* (Stenfert Kroese NV, Leiden, 1954).

Kuhn, JW. *Bargaining in Grievance Settlement* (Columbia UP, 1961).

Labour, Ministry of. *Dismissal Procedures* (HMSO, 1967).

Labour, Ministry of. *A National Minimum Wage*, (HMSO, 1967)...180.

Labour, Ministry of. *Industrial Relations Handbook* (HMSO, 1944; 1961)...166.

Lammers, CJ & Hickson, DJ. *Organizations, Alike and Unlike* (Routledge & Kegan Paul, 1979).

Landsorganisationen (LO). *Trade Unions and Full Employment* (Swedish Confederation of Trade Unions, 1953)...22.

Lane, T & Roberts, K. *Strike at Pilkingtons* (Fontana, 1971)...333, 381, 390, 391.

Lansbury, R. 'Professionalism and Unionization Among Management Service Specialists' in *British Journal of Industrial Relations*, XII (2), 1974, pp 292-302...262.

Larson, MS. *The Rise of Professionalism* (University of California Press, 1977)...135.

Leary, M. 'Industrial Relations: The Training Contribution' in *Journal of European Training*, 4 (4), 1975, pp 195-227 (MCB Monograph, Bradford).

Leighton, P. *Contractual Arrangements in Selected Trades* (DE Research Paper, 1983)...93.

Leighton, PE & Dumville, SL. 'From Status to Contract – Some Effects of the Contract of Employment Act, 1972' in *Industrial Law Journal*, 6, 1977, pp 133-148.

Leiserson, MW. 'Wage Determination and Wage Structure in the US' in Hugh-Jones, EM (ed). *Wage Structure in Theory and Practice* (North Holland, 1966),pp 1-70.

Lemon, N. *Attitudes and their Measurement* (Batsford, 1963; 1968)...291.

Lerner, SW. *Breakaway Unions and the Small Trade Union* (Allen & Unwin, 1961)...280.

Lester, RA. *As Unions Mature* (Princeton UP, 1958).

Levinson, HM. *Determining Forces in Collective Wage Bargaining* (Wiley, 1966)...339, 523.

Levinson, HM. *Collective Bargaining by British Local Authority Employees* (Institute of Labour and Industrial Relations, University of Michigan, 1971)...412.

Levy, A. *Private Corporations and their Control* (Routledge & Kegan Paul, 1950).

Lewin, K. 'Studies in Group Decision' in Cartwright, D & Zander, A. *Group Dynamics: Research and Theory* (Row Peterson, 1953) q.v., pp 287-301. and in Maccoby EE, Newcomb, TM & Hartley, EL. *Readings in Social Psychology* (Henry Holt, 1958) q.v., pp 197-211...394.

Lewin, K. *Resolving Social Conflicts* (Harper and Row, 1967).

Lewis, R, & Stewart, R. *The Boss*, (Phoenix House, 1958).

Lindblom, CE. 'The Science of Muddling Through' in *Public Administration Review*, 19, 1959, pp 79-88...54.

Lindblom, CE. *The Policy Making Process* (Prentice Hall, 1968)...581.

Lindrop, E. 'Workplace Bargaining: The End of an Era?' in *Industrial Relations Journal*, 10 (1), Spring, 1979, pp 12-21.

Lipset, SM et al. *Union Democracy* (Free Press, 1956).

Little, EM. *History of the BMA, 1832-1932* (BMA, 1933).

Littler, C. *The Development of the Labour Process in Capitalist Societies* (Heinemann, 1982).

Lockwood, D. *The Blackcoated Worker: A Study in Class Consciousness* (Allen & Unwin, 1958).

Lockwood, D. 'Sources of Variation in Working Class Images of Society' in *Sociological Review*, 14 (3), 1966, pp 249-58; and in Bulmer, M. *Working class images of society* (Routledge & Kegan Paul, 1975), q.v. pp 16-31.

Lockyer, JR. *Industrial Arbitration in Great Britain* (IPM, 1979)...193.

Lover, J. 'Shop Stewards. Conflicting Objectives and Needs' in *Industrial Relations Journal*, 7 (1), 1976, pp 27-39.

Loveridge, R. *Collective Bargaining by National Employees in the UK* (Institute of Labour and Industrial Relations, University of Michigan, 1971)...417.

Lowndes, R. *Industrial Relations: A Contemporary Survey* (Holt, Rinehart & Winston, 1972).

Lowry, P. 'A Matter of Attitudes. Penetrating the Platitudes' in *Personnel Management*, 13 (10), October, 1981, pp 46-47.

Lukes, S. *Power: A Radical View* (Macmillan, 1974)...70.

Lumley, R. *White Collar Unionism in Britain* (Methuen, 1973).

Lumley, R. 'A Modified Rules Approach to Workplace Industrial Relations' in *Industrial Relations Journal*, 10 (4), Winter, 1979-80, pp 49-56.

Lupton, T. *On the Shop Floor* (Pergamon, 1963)...271, 473.

Lyman, EL. 'Occupational Differences in the Values Attached to Work' in *American Journal of Sociology*, 61, 1955, pp 138-44.

Maccoby, EE, Newcomb, TM, & Hartley, EL. *Readings in Social Psychology* (Henry Holt, 1947; 1958), 393.

MacDonald, DE. *The State and the Trade Unions* (Macmillan, 1960; 2nd edn, 1976).

Maitland, I. 'Disorder in the British Workplace. The Limits of Consensus' in *British Journal of Industrial Relations*, XVIII, November, 1980, pp 353-364...26.

Makeham, P & Creigh, S. 'Variations in Strike Activity within UK Manufacturing Industry' in *Industrial Relations Journal*, 11 (5), Nov/Dec, 1980, pp 32-37.

Mansfield, R & Poole, M. *International Perspectives on Management and Organisation* (Gower, 1981)...63.

Mansfield, R, Poole, M, Blyton, P, & Frost, P. *The British Manager in Profile* (British Institute of Management, 1981).

Mansfield Cooper, W and Wood, JC. *Outlines of Industrial Law* (Butterworths, 1966; 1974)...90, 96.

Mant, A. *The Rise and Fall of the British Manager* (Macmillan, 1977)...21, 26.

Marceau, L. *Dealing with a Union* (American Management Association, 1969)...409, 451, 454, 531.

March, JG (ed). *Handbook of Organisations* (Rand McNally, 1965).

March, JG, Olsen, JP, et al. *Ambiguity and Choice in Organisations* (Bergen, Universitetsforlaget, 1976).

Marchington, M. *Managing Industrial Relations* (McGraw Hill, 1982)...253, 339, 371, 513.

Margerison, CJ. 'What do we Mean by Industrial Relations?' in *British Journal of Industrial Relations*, VIII (2), July, 1969, pp 273-86.

Margerison, C & Leary, M. *Managing Industrial Conflicts: The Mediator's Role* (MCB Books, 1975).

Marquand, H. *Industrial Relations in the USA* (University of Wales Press, 1934)...4.

Marquand, H (ed). *Organised Labour on Four Continents* (Longmans, 1939)...4.

Marsden, D. *Industrial Democracy and Industrial Control in West Germany, France and Britain* (DE Research Paper No 4, September, 1978).

Marsh, AI. *Industrial Relations in Engineering* (Pergamon, 1965), 304, 365, 366, 371.

Marsh, AI. 'Why not Teach More Industrial Relations?' in *Personnel Management*, XLVII (373), 1965, pp 144-50...26.

Marsh, AI, Evans, EO & Garcia, P. *Workplace Industrial Relations in Engineering* (Kogan Page, 1971)...450.

Marsh, AI. 'The Staffing of Industrial Relations Management in the Engineering Industry', in *Industrial Relations Journal*, 2 (2), Summer, 1971, pp 14-23...452.

Marsh, AI. 'Company Policy' in Parkinson, CN (ed). *Industrial Disruption* (Leviathan, 1973).

Marsh, AI. 'Employers' Associations' in Towers, B, Whittingham, TG, & Gottschalk, AW (eds). *Bargaining for Change* (Allen & Unwin, 1973).

Marsh, AI. *Managers and Shop Stewards* (IPM, 1963)...294, 458.

Marsh, AI, Hackmann, M & Miller D. *Workplace Relations in the Engineering Industry in the UK and the Federal Republic of Germany* (Anglo-German Foundation, 1981)...63.

Marsh, AI. *Employee Relations Policy and Decision-Making* (CBI/Gower, 1982)...84, 87, 98, 248, 253, 289, 345, 428, 431.

Martin, R. 'The Concept of Power. A Critical Defence' in *British Journal of Sociology*, 22, September, 1971, pp 240-56...70.

Martin, R. *The Sociology of Power* (Routledge & Kegan Paul, 1977)...70.

Maslow, AH. 'A Theory of Human Motivation' in *Psychological Review*, 50, 1943, pp 370-96...40, 47, 54, 254.

Maurice, M, Sorge, A & Warner, M. 'Societal Differences in Organising Manufacturing Units' in *Organisation Studies*,1, 1980, pp 63-91...63.

McCarthy, WEJ. *The Closed Shop in Britain* (Blackwell, 1964)...155.

McCarthy, WEJ. *The Role of Shop Stewards in British Industrial Relations* (RCTU&EA Research Paper No 1, HMSO, 1966)...377.

McCarthy, WEJ. 'Changing Bargaining Structures' in Kessler, S & Weekes, B.*Conflict at Work: Re-shaping Industrial Relations* (BBC Publications, 1971) q.v., pp 83-93.

McCarthy, WEJ, Parker, PA, Howes, WR, & Lumb, AL. *The Reform of Collective Bargaining at Plant and Company Level* (DE Manpower Paper No 5, HMSO, 1971)...26.

McCarthy, WEJ (ed). *Trade Unions* (Penguin, 1972).

McCarthy, WEJ. *Making Whitley Work* (Dept of Health and Social Security, 1977)...412, 417, 418, 430.
McCarthy, WEJ. 'Trade Unions and the Limits of Law' in *New Society*, 21 April, 1983, pp 97-98...132, 153, 201.
McCarthy, WEJ & Collier, AS. *Coming to Terms With Trade Unions* (IPM, 1973).
McCarthy, WEJ & Ellis, ND. *Management by Agreement* (Hutchinson, 1973).
McCarthy, WEJ & Parker, SR. Shop Stewards and Workshop Relations (RCTUEA Research Paper No 10, HMSO, 1968).
McConnell, CR (ed). *Perspectives on Wage Determination: A Book of Readings* (McGraw Hill, 1970).
McCormick, B. 'Managerial Unionism in the Coal Industry' in *British Journal of Sociology*, ll (4), December, 1960, pp 356-68.
McCormick, B. *Wages* (Penguin, 1969).
McGaw, Sir John. *Inquiry into Civil Service Pay* (Cmnd 8590, HMSO, 1983)...419, 421, 423, 425, 428, 430.
McGrath, JE. 'A Social Psychological Approach to the Study of Negotiation' in Bowers, R, (ed). *Studies on Behaviour in Organisations: A Research Symposium*, (University of Georgia Press), 1966, pp 10l-34.
McGrath, JE & Julian, JW. *Negotiation and Conflict: An Experimental Study* (University of Illinois, 1962)...521.
McGrath, JE & Julian, JW. 'Interaction Process and Task Outcomes in Experimentally-created Negotiation Groups' in *Journal of Psychological Studies*, 14, 1963, pp 117-38.
McGregor, D. *The Human Side of Enterprise* (McGraw Hill, 1960)...459.
McIver, RM. 'Professional Groups and Cultural Norms' in Vollmer, HM & Mills, DL (eds). *Professionalization* (Prentice Hall, 1966) pp 50-54.
McIver, RM & Page, CH. *Society – An Introductory Analysis* (Macmillan, 1953)...76.
McKersie, RB & Hunter, LC. *Pay, Productivity and Collective Bargaining* (Macmillan, 1973).
McKersie, R, Perry, C, & Walton, R. 'Intra-Organisational Bargaining in Labour Negotiations' in *Journal of Conflict Resolution*, 9, 1965, pp 463-81.
Meakin, D. Man and Work. *Literature and Culture in Industrial Society* (Methuen, 1976)...35.
Mechanic, D. 'Sources of Power of Lower Participants in Complex Organizations' in *Administrative Science Quarterly*, 7, December, 1962, pp 349-62; and in Dubin (1974), q.v., pp 323-27.
Megginson, LC & Gullett, CR. 'A Predictive Model of Union-Management Conflict' in *Personnel Journal*, June, 1970, pp 495-503; Armstrong (1970) pp 49-52.
Mellish, M. *The Docks after Devlin* (Heinemann, 1972).
Mellish, M & Collis-Squires, N. 'Legal and Social Norms in Discipline and Dismissal' in *Industrial Relations Journal*, 5 (3), September, 1976, pp 164-77...123.
Metcalf, D. 'Unions, Incomes Policy and Relative Wages in Britain' in *British Journal of Industrial Relations*, 15 (2), 1977, pp 157-75...186.
Metcalf, HC & Urwick, L. *Dynamic Administration* (Pitman, 1941).
Michels, RWE. *Political Parties* (Free Press, Glencoe, 1959; original German edition, 1911).
Miller, S. 'Relationships of Personality to Occupation Setting and Function', in *Journal of Counselling Psychology*, 9 (2), 1962, pp 115-21...35.
Millerson, G. *The Qualifying Associations* (Routledge & Kegan Paul, 1964)...138, 163, 244, 262.
Milliband, R. *The State in Capitalist Society* (Weidenfeld 89 & Nicholson, 1969)...66,

Millward, N. 'Workplace Industrial Relations: Results of a New Survey of IR Practices' in *Employment Gazette*, 97 (7), July, 1983, pp 280-89.
Milne-Bailey, E. *Trade Union Documents* (Macmillan, 1929).
Milne-Bailey, W. *Trade Unions and the State* (Allen & Unwin, 1934).

Mintzberg, H. *The Nature of Managerial Work* (Harper & Row, 1973).

Mintzberg, HB. 'The Manager's Job: Folklore and Fact' in *Harvard Business Review*, July/August, 1975, pp 49-61.

Mintzberg, HB. *Power In and Around Organizations* (Prentice Hall, 1983).

Mitchell, E. *The Employer's Guide to the Law on Health, Safety and Welfare at Work* (Business Books, 1974).

Mitchell, F, Sams, I, Tweedie, D, & White, P. 'Disclosure of Information: Some Evidence from Case Studies' in *Industrial Relations Journal*, 11 (5), Nov/Dec., 1980, pp 53-62.

Moore, R. 'The Cross-Cultural Study of Organisational Behaviour' in *Human Organisation*, 33, 1974, pp 37-46.

Morley, I, & Stephenson, G. *The Social Psychology of Bargaining* (Allen & Unwin, 1977)...326, 477, 514, 518, 539-43.

Mortimer, J. 'Collective Bargaining; the Key to CAS' in *Personnel Management*, 7 (1), January, 1975, pp 27-30 & 38...171.

Moulding, T & Moynagh, M. 'Pay Bargaining in Britain: Too Many Players in the Game of Leap-frog' in *Personnel Management*, 14 (4), April, 1982, pp 38-41...345.

Muir, J. *Industrial Relations Procedures and Agreements* (Gower, 1981)...269, 371.

Mulvey, C. *The Economic Analysis of Trade Unions* (Martin Robertson, 1978).

Munns, VG & McCarthy, WEJ. *Employers' Associations* (RCTU&EA Research Paper No 7) (HMSO, 1967)...240, 248, 253, 258, 312.

Myers, CA. 'The American System of Industrial Relations: Is it Exportable?' *(Proceedings of the 15th Annual Meeting of the IR Research Association*, 1962)...4.

Myers, MS. *Managing Without Unions* (Addison-Wesley Press, (1976)...436, 438, 441.

Nash, J. 'The Bargaining Problem' in *Econometrica*, 18 (2), 1950, pp 155-62.

National Board for Prices and Incomes. *The Pay and Conditions of Manual Workers in Local Authorities, the National Health Service, Gas and Water Supply* (NBPI Report No 29, Cmnd. 3230, March, 1967).

NBPI. *Productivity Agreements* (Report No 36, HMSO, 1967), 501, 508.

NBPI. *Payment By Results* (Report No 65, HMSO, 1968).

NBPI. *Job Evaluation* (Report Nos 83 and 83S, HMSO, 1968)...501.

NBPI. *Salary Structures* (Report No 132, HMSO, 1969).

NBPI. *Top Salaries in the Private Sector and Nationalized Industries* (Report No 107, HMSO, 1969).

NBPI. *The Pay and Conditions of Service of Ancillary Workers in the National Health Service* (NBPI Report No 166, Cmnd, 4644, April, 1971).

NBPI. *General Problems of Low Pay* (NBPI Report No 169, Cmnd. 4648, April, 1971)...420.

National Economic Development Office. *Management Training in Industrial Relations* (NEDO, 1975).

Nemeth, C. 'Bargaining and Reciprocity' in *Psychological Bulletin*, 74, 1970, pp 297-308.

Nemeth, C. 'A Critical Analysis of Research utilising the Prisoner's Dilemma Paradigm for the Study of Bargaining' in Berkowitz, L (ed). *Advances in Experimental Social Psychology*, 6, (Academic Press, 1972), pp 2032-34...546.

Hewby, H & Bell, C. 'The Sources of Variation in Agricultural Workers' Images of Society' in Bulmer, M (ed). *Working Class Images of Society* (Routledge & Kegan Paul, 1977), pp 83-97...312.

Newcomb, TM. *Social Psychology* (Tavistock, 1952)...64.

Newcomb, TM. 'Attitude Development as a Function of Reference Groups. The Bennington Study' in Maccoby, EE Newcomb, TM & Hartley, EL. *Readings in Social Psychology* (Henry Holt, 1958) q.v., pp 265-75.

Newstrom, JW, Reif, WE, & Monczka, RM. *A Contingency Approach to Management: Readings* (McGraw Hill, 1975).

Nichols, D. *Three Varieties of Pluralism* (Macmillan, 1974)...297.

Nichols, TH. *Ownership, Control and Ideology* (Allen & Unwin, 1969).

Nichols, TH & Beynon, H. *Living with Capitalism* (Routledge & Kegan Paul, 1977).

Nicholson, M. *Conflict Analysis* (English Universities Press, 1954)...326.

Nicholson, N. 'The Role of the Shop Steward' in *Industrial Relations Journal*, 7 (1), Spring, 1976, pp 20-25.

Norgren, PH. *The Swedish Collective Bargaining System* (Harvard UP, 1941)...4.

Norstedt, JP & Aguren, S. *The Saab-Scania Report* (Swedish Employers' Confederation, 1972).

North, DTB & Buckingham, GL. *Productivity Agreements and Wage Systems* (Gower, 1969)...371, 513.

Northrup, HR. *Boularism* (University of Michigan, 1964)...299.

Odiorne, GS. *Management by Objectives* (Pitman, 1965)...583.

Office of Population Censuses and Surveys, Social Survey Division. *Workplace Industrial Relations*, 1972 (by S Parker) (HMSO, 1974).

Ogden, SG. 'Bargaining Structure and the Control of Industrial Relations' in *British Journal of Industrial Relations*, XX (2), July, 1982, pp 170-85.

O'Higgins, P. *Workers' Rights* (Hutchinson, Arrow Books, 1976)...101.

Oldfield, FE. *New Look Industrial Relations* (Mason Reed, 1966)...508.

Orzack, LH. 'Work as a Central Life Interest of Professionals' in *Social Problems*, 7, 1959, pp 125-32.

Padfield, CF. *British Constitution Made Simple* (Allen & Unwin, 1972)...88, 96, 196.

Page Arnot, R. *The Miners* (Allen and Unwin, 1949; 1953)...294.

Pahl, RE & Winkler, JT. 'Corporatism in Britain: Why Protecting Industry Need Not Mean More Bureaucracy' in *The Times*, 26 March, 1976...65.

Pahl, RE & Winkler, JT. 'The Coming Corporatism' in *New Society*, 30 (627), 10 October, 1974, pp 72-76...65.

Paine, FT, Deutsch, DR & Smith, RA. 'Relationship between Family Backgrounds and Work Values' in *Journal of Applied Psychology*, 51, (4), 1967, pp 320-23...56.

Panitch, L. *Social Democracy and Industrial Militancy* (Cambridge UP, 1976).

Panitch, L. 'The Development of Corporatism in Liberal Democracies' in *Comparative Political Studies*, 10 (1), 1977, pp 61-90.

Panitch, L. 'Recent Theorisations on Corporatism. Reflections on a Growth Industry' in *British Journal of Sociology*, 31, 1980, pp 159-87.

Parker, SR. *Workplace Industrial Relations*, 1972 (HMSO, 1974).

Parker, SR. *Workplace Industrial Relations Survey*, (HMSO, 1977).

Parker, SR. *Workplace Industrial Relations*, 1973 (HMSO, 1975).

Parker, SR & Scott, MH. 'Developing Models of Workplace Industrial Relations' in *British Journal of Industrial Relations*, 9 (4), 1971, pp 214-224.

Partridge, BE. 'The Process of Leadership on the Shop Floor' in King, B, Streufert, S & Fiddler, FE. *Managerial control and organizational democracy* (Winston 1978) q.v., pp 187-200...372-73, 389, 392, 398.

Paterson, TT & Willett, FJ. 'Unofficial Strike' in *Sociological Review*, XLIII, 1951, pp 57-94.

Peach, DA & Livernash, ER. *Grievance Challenge & Resolution* (Harvard Business School, 1974).

Pedler,M. 'Negotiation Skills Training', in four parts in *Journal of European Industrial Training*, Part I, 1 (4), 1977, pp 18-21 & 26; Part II, 1 (5), 1977, pp 12-16; Part III, 1 (6), 1977, pp 25-27 & 34; Part IV, 2 (1), 1978, pp 20-25...325, 327, 513, 515, 517, 547.

Pedler, M. 'The Training Implications of the Shop Steward's Leadership Role' in *Industrial Relations Journal*, 5 (1), 1974, pp 57-70.

Pelling, H. *A History of British Trade Unions* (Penguin, 1963)...31.

Pen, J. 'A General Theory of Bargaining' in *American Economic Review*, 42, 1952, pp 24-42.

Pen, J. *The Wage Rate under Collective Bargaining* (Harvard UP, 1959)...77, 339.

Peterson, R & Tracey, L. 'A Behavioural Model of Problem Solving in Labour Negotiations' in *British Journal of Industrial Relations*, 14 (2), 1976, pp 159-73.

Peterson, F. 'Management Efficiency and Collective Bargaining' in *Industrial and Labour Relations Review*, 1, October, 1947, pp29-49.

Pettigrew, A. *The Politics of Organizational Decision-Making* (Tavistock, 1973)...53.

Pettman, BO. *Strikes* (Management Centre Bradford, 1976).

Phelps-Brown, EH. *The Growth of British Industrial Relations* (Macmillan, 1959)...31, 269.

Phelps-Brown, EH. *The Economics of Labour* (Yale UP, 1962).

Phelps-Brown, EH. *Pay and Profits* (Manchester UP, 1968).

Phelps-Brown, EH. *The Inequality of Pay* (Oxford UP, 1977).

Phelps-Brown, EH. *Collective Bargaining Reconsidered* (Athlone Press, 1971).

Phelps-Brown, EH with Browne, M. *A Century of Pay* (Macmillan, 1964)...12, 22.

Phelps-Brown, EH & Hart, PE. 'The Share of Wages in the National Income' in *Economic Journal*, 62 (246), 1952, pp 276-83...11, 17, 22.

Phelps-Brown, EH. *The Origins of Trade Union Power* (Oxford UP, 1983).

Pigou, A. *Principles and Methods of Industrial Peace* (Macmillan, 1905).

Pilkington, Sir A. 'Science and Technology' in *RSA Journal*, CXXIV (5241), August, 1976, pp 523-36...27, 72.

Pollard, HR. *Developments in Management Thought* (Edward Arnold, 1965).

Pollard, S. *The Genesis of Modern Management* (Edward Arnold, 1965).

Poole, M. *Workers' Participation in Industry* (Routledge & Kegan Paul, 1975).

Poole, M. 'A Power Analysis of Workplace Labour Relations' in *Industrial Relations Journal*, 7 (3), 1976, pp 32-43.

Poole, MJR. 'Managerial Strategies and Industrial Relations' in Poole, MJR & Mansfield, R (eds). *Managerial Roles in Industrial Relations* (Gower, 1980), pp38-49...339.

Poole, M, Mansfield, R, Blyton, P, & Frost, P. 'Managerial Attitudes and Behaviour in Industrial Relations; Evidence from a National Survey' in *British Journal of Industrial Relations*, 20,(3), 1982, pp 285-307.

Poole, M, Mansfield, R, Blyton, P, & Frost, P. *Managers in Focus* (Gower, 1981).

Poole, MJF & Mansfield, R (eds). *Managerial Roles and Industrial Relations* (Gower, 1980).

Poole, M. 'A Power Analysis of Workplace Labour Relations' in *Industrial Relations Journal*, 7(3), 1976, pp 31-43.

Popitz, H, Bahrdt, HP, Jueres, EA & Kesting, A. 'The Worker's Image of Society' in Burns, T. *Industrial Man* (Penguin 1969) q.v., pp 281-324...55, 256-57, 282, 290, 294, 312.

Porter, AR. *Job Property Rights* (King Crown Press, 1954)...113.

Posses, F. *The Art of International Negotiation* (Business Books, 1978).

Prandy, K. *Professional Employees* (Faber and Faber, 1965)...140, 163.

Pratten, CF. *A Comparison of the Performance of Swedish and UK Companies*, (Cambridge UP, 1976)...63.

Prentice, DD. 'A Company and Its Employees. The Companies Act, 1980' in *Industrial Law Journal*, 10 (1), March, 1981, pp 1-9...118.

Prest, AR. 'National Income of the UK, 1870-1946, in *Economic Journal*, 58 (229), March, 1948, pp 31-62...11.

Prest, AR & Coppock, DJ. *The UK Economy: A Manual of Applied Economics* (Weidenfeld & Nicholson, 1966, 6th edn, 1976).

Pribicevic, K. *The Shop Stewards' Movement and Workers' Control, 1910-22* (Blackwell, 1959)...294.

Price, R & Bain, GS. Union Growth Revisited: 1948-74 in Perspective' in *British Journal of Industrial Relations*, XIV (3), 1976 pp 339-55.

(Priestley) *Royal Commission on the Civil Service, 1953-5*, (Cmnd 9613, HMSO, 1955)...424.

Pritchard, RD. 'Equity Theory· A Review and Critique' in *Organisational Behaviour and Human Performance*, 4, 1969, pp 176-211.

Pruitt, DG. *Negotiation Behaviour* (Academic Press, 1981)...379, 484, 506, 514, 534, 536, 543, 545.

Purcell, J. *Good Industrial Relations: Theory and Practice* (Macmillan, 1981).

Purcell, J. 'A Strategy for Management Control in Industrial Relations' in Purcell, J & Smith, N. *The Control of Work* (Macmillan, 1979) q.v., pp 27-58.

Purcell, J & Earl, MJ. 'Control Systems and Industrial Relations' in *Industrial Relations Journal*, 8 (2), Summer, 1977, pp 41-54.

Purcell, J & Smith, N (eds). *The Control of Work* (Macmillan, 1979)...439.

Raimon, RL. 'The Indeterminateness of Wages of Semi-Skilled Workers' in *Industrial and Labour Relations Review*, 6, January, 1953, pp 180-94.

Ramsey, JC. 'Negotiating in a Multi-Plant Company, in *Industrial Relations Journal*, 2 (2), Summer, 1971, pp 42-48.

Ramsey, JC & Hill, JM. *Collective Agreements – A Guide to their Content and Drafting* (IPM, 1974)...351.

Randle, CW & Wortman, MS. *Collective Bargaining Principles and Practice* (Houghton Mifflin, 1966).

Raza, MA. *The Industrial Relations System of Pakistan* (Bureau of Labour Publications, Karachi, 1963)...4.

Redgraves Factories Acts (eds. Thompson, J & Rogers, HR) (Butterworths, 1966)...114.

Renold, GC. *Joint Consultation over Thirty Years* (Allen & Unwin, 1950).

Revans, RW. *Scale Factors in the Management of Coal Mines* (National Coal Board, 1954).

Revans, RW. 'Industrial Morale and Size of Unit' in Galenson W & Lipset, SM (eds). *Labour and Trade Unionism* (Wiley, 1960), pp 295-300, 229.

Rheinstein, M (ed). *Max Weber on Law in Economy and Society* (Simon & Schuster, 1954).

Rhenman, E. *Industrial Democracy and Industrial Management* (Tavistock, 1968).

Rhys, DG. 'Employment, Efficiency and Labour Relations in the British Motor Industry' in *Industrial Relations Journal*, 5 (2), Summer, 1974, pp 4-26...21.

Richardson, JH. *Industrial Relations in Great Britain* (ILO, 1933)...4.

Richardson, JH. *Introduction to the Study of Industrial Relations* (Allen & Unwin, 1954)...4.

Richbell, S. 'Participation and Perceptions of Control' in *Personnel Review*, 5 (2), Spring, 1976, pp 13-19.

Richter, I. *Political Purpose in Trade Unions* (Allen & Unwin, 1973)...278.

Rideout, RW. 'Trade unions: Some Social and Legal Problems', Part 1 in *Human Relations*, 17 (1), February, 1964, pp 73-95; Part II in *Human Relations*, 17 (2) May, 1964, pp 169-198.

Rideout, RW. 'The Contract of Employment' in *Current Legal Problems*, 19, 1966, pp 111-27...94.

Rideout, RW. *Reforming the Redundancy Payments Act* (IPM, 1969).

Rideout, RW. *Principles of Labour Law* (Sweet & Maxwell, 3rd edn, 1979)...112, 133, 407.

Rideout, RW. *Industrial Tribunal Law* (McGraw Hill, 1980)...222.

Robens, Lord . Safety and Health at Work: Report of the Committee (HMSO, 1979).

Roberts, BC. *Trade Union Government and Administration* (Bell, 1956)...279, 282.

Roberts, BC (ed). *Industrial Relations: Contemporary Problems and Prospects* (Methuen, 1962).

Roberts, BC & Gennard, J. 'Trends in Plant and Company Bargaining' in *Scottish Journal of Political Economy*, XVII (2), June, 1970, pp 147-66.

Roberts, BC, Loveridge, R, & Gennard, J. *Reluctant Militants* (Heinemann, 1972)...262.

Roethlisberger, FJ & Dickson, WJ. *Management and The Worker* (Harvard UP, 1939)...36, 392.

Rogaly, J. *Grunwick* (Penguin, 1977)...155.

Rokeach, M. 'Political and Religious Dogmatism: An Alternative to the Authoritarian Personality' in *Psychological Monographs*, 70 (18), 1956, pp 1-43.

Rolph, CH. *All Those in Favour? The ETU Trial* (Deutsch, 1962).

Ronken, HO & Lawrence, PR. *Administering Changes* (Harvard UP, 1952).

Rose, AM. *Human Behaviour and Social Processes* (Routledge & Kegan Paul, 1962).

Rosen, H & Rosen, RAH. *The Union Member Speaks* (Prentice Hall, 1955)...560.

Ross, AM. *Trade Union Wage Policy* (University of California Press, 1968)...339, 562.

Ross, AM & Hartman, PT. *Changing Patterns of Industrial Conflict* (Wiley, 1960)...37, 335.

Ross, MG & Hendry, CE. *New Understandings of Leadership* (Association Press, 1957).

Ross, NS. 'Organized Labour and Management in the United Kingdom' in Hugh-Jones, EM (ed.) *Human Relations and Modern Management* (North Holland 1958) q.v., pp 101-32.

Rubin, JZ & Brown, BR. *The Social Psychology of Bargaining and Negotiation* (Academic Press, 1975)...477-78, 546, 568.

Rubner, A. *The Ensnared Shareholder* (Penguin, 1966)...598.

Ruddick, R. *Roles and Relationships* (Routledge & Kegan Paul, 1969).

Runciman, WG. *Relative Deprivation and Social Justice* (Routledge & Kegan Paul, 1966)...267.

Russell, B. *Power: A New Social Analysis* (Allen & Unwin, 1938)...468.

Salaman, G & Thompson, K. *People and Organizations* (Longman, 1973).

Samuels, H. *Industrial Law* (Pitman, 1967).

Saunders, C. *Engineering in Britain, France and West Germany* (European Research Centre, Brighton, 1979)...63.

Savage, N. *The Companies Act, 1980: A New Business Code* (McGraw Hill, 1980)...118, 595.

Sayles, L. *The Behaviour of Industrial Work Groups* (Wiley, 1958)...33, 36, 257, 271, 391, 392, 480.

Sayles, L. *Managerial Behaviour* (McGraw Hill, 1964)...446.

Sayles, L & Strauss, G. *The Local Union: Its Place in the Industrial Plant* (Harper & Bros, 1953).

Scarman, Lord. *Report of a Court of Inquiry into a Dispute between Grunwick Processing Laboratories, Ltd, and Members of APEX* (HMSO, 1977)...87, 299.

Schelling, TC. *The Sociology of Conflict* (Harvard UP, 1960)...528, 565.

Schmitthoff, C. 'Employee Participation and the Theory of Enterprise' in *Journal of Business Law*, 1975, pp 265-272...28, 594-95.

Schumacher, C. 'Personnel's Part in Productivity Growth' in *Personnel Management*, 13 (7), July, 1981, pp 26-30.

Sealy, LS. 'Undue Influence and Inequality of Bargaining Power' in *Cambridge Law Journal*, 1975, pp 21-5...105.

Seidman, J. *The Worker Views his Union* (University of Chicago Press, 1958).

Selekman, BM. *A Moral Philosophy for Management* (McGraw Hill, 1959).

Selekman, BM; Selekman, SK; & Fuller, SH. *Problems in Labor Relations* (McGraw Hill, 1958).

Selwyn's Law of Employment (Butterworths, 1976).

Selznick, P. 'An Approach to a Theory of Bureaucracy' in *American Sociological Review*, VIII, (1), 1943, pp 47-54; and in Coser, L & Rosenberg, M (eds). *Sociological Theory – A Reader* (Collier-Macmillan, 1969) pp 459-72...91, 93.

Sethi, AJ & Dimmock, SJ. *Industrial Relations and Health Services* (Croom Helm, 1982)...430.

Seyfarth, Shaw, Fairweather, & Geraldson, . 'Labour Relations and the Law in the United Kingdom and the United States' in *Michigan International Labour Studies*, 1, 1968.

Shackle, GLS. 'The Nature of the Bargaining Process' in Dunlop, JT (ed). *The Theory of Wage Determination* (Macmillan, 1957), pp 292-314.

Shackle, GLS. *Expectation, Enterprise and Profit: The Theory of the Firm* (Allen & Unwin, 1970)...430.

Shackleton, V & Davies, J. 'The Unionized Manager' in *Management Today*, June, 1976, pp 19-28...99.

Shafto, TAC. *Introducing Economics* (Nelson, 1971)...499.

Shalev, M. 'Industrial Relations Theory and the Comparative Study of Industrial Relations and Industrial Conflict' in *British Journal of Industrial Relations*, 18 (1), 1980, pp 26-43.

Shanks, M. *The Stagnant Society* (Penguin, 1961).

Shannon CE & Weaver, W. *The Mathematical Theory of Communication* (University of Illinois Press, 1949).

Sharp. IG. *Industrial Conciliation and Arbitration in Great Britain* (Allen & Unwin, 1951).

Shimmin, S & Singh, R. 'Industrial Relations and Organizational Behaviour' in *Industrial Relations Journal*, 4 (3), Autumn, 1973, pp 37-42...45, 61.

Shorey, J. 'The Size of Work Unit and Strike Incidence' in *Journal of Industrial Economics*, 23, March, 1975, pp 175-88...229.

Silberberg, H. 'Gratuitous Payments for the Benefit of the Company' in the *Journal of Business Law*, 1968, pp 213-228...118.

Silver, M. 'Recent British Strike Trends – A Factual Analysis' in *British Journal of Industrial Relations*, II, 1973, pp 66-104.

Silverman, D. *The Theory of Organizations* (Heinemann, 1970)...49, 58, 61.

Simitis, S. 'Workers' Participation in the Enterprise – Transcending Company Law' in *Modern Law Review*, 38, 1975, pp 1-22.

Simmel, G. *Conflict* (trans. Wolff, KH), (Free Press, 1955)...467.

Simon, HA. *Administrative Behaviour* (Macmillan, 1953)...49, 461, 469-70, 561.

Simon, HA. *Models of Man: Social and Rational* (Wiley, 1957).

Simon, HA. 'Theories of Decision-Making in Economics and Behavioural Science' in *American Economic Review*, XLIX, June, 1959, pp 253-83.

Simon, HA. *The Shape of Automation* (Harper & Row, 1965)...447, 535.

Simpson, DH. *Commercialisation of the Regional Press* (Gower, 1981).

Simpson, DH. 'Managers in Workers' Trade Unions: The Case of the NUJ' in Thurley, K & Wood, SJ (eds). *Industrial Relations and Management Strategy* (Cambridge UP, 1983), pp 19-26.

Singleton, N. *Industrial Relations Procedures* (DE Manpower Paper No 14; HMSO, 1975)...371.

Sisson, K. *Negotiating in Practice* (IPM, 1977)...371.

Sisson, K & Brown, W. 'Industrial Relations in the Private Sector' in Bain GS, *Industrial Relations in Britain* (Blackwell, 1983) q.v., pp 137-54...31.

Slater, PE. 'Social Bases of Personality' in Smelser, NJ (ed). *Sociology* (Wiley, 1967), pp 548-600.

Slichter, SH. 'The American System of Industrial Relations' in *Arbitration Today* (Proceedings of the Eighth Annual meeting, National Academy of Arbitrators, January, 1955) (BNA Inc. Washington, 1955)...4.

Smelser, N. *Sociology. An Introduction* (Wiley, 1967)...55, 258.

Smith, A. *The Wealth of Nations* (1776) (Methuen, 1904)...76, 239, 243-44, 285.

Smith, CG & Tannenbaum, AS. 'Organizational Control Structure' in *Human Relations*, November, 1963, p 299-316.

Smith, CTB, Clifton, R, Makeham, P, Creigh, SW, & Burn, RV. *Strikes in Britain* (DE Manpower Paper No 15, 1978).

Smith, H. *The Wage Fixers* (Hobart Paper No 18, Institute of Economic Affairs, 1962)...193.

Smith, IG. *Wage and Salary Administration* (IPM, 1983).

Somers, GG. 'Bargaining Power and Industrial Relations Theory' in Somers, GG (ed). *Essays in Industrial Relations Theory* (Iowa State university, 1969), pp 39-53.

Sorge, A & Warner, M. 'The Societal Context of Industrial Relations in Britain and West Germany' in *Industrial Relations Journal*, ll, 1980a, pp 41-50.

Southgate, GW. *English Economic History* (Dent, 1934; rev. edn, 1970)...32, 146.

Stagner, R. 'Dual Loyalty in Modern Society' in *Monthly Labour Review*, 76, 1953, pp 1273-1274...572

Steers, RN & Porter, HW. *Motivation and Work Behaviour* (McGraw Hill, 1977)...37, 40, 54, 56, 256.

Stephenson, GM. 'Inter-Group Relations and Negotiating Behaviour' in Warr, 1971, pp 347-73.

Stephenson, GM, Kniveton, B, & Morley, I. 'Interaction Analysis of an Industrial Wage Negotiation' in *Journal of Occupational Psychology*, 50, 1977, pp 231-41.

Stevens, CM. *Strategy and Collective Bargaining Negotiation* (McGraw Hill, 1963).

Stevens, CM. 'On the Theory of Negotiations' in *Quarterly Journal of Economics*, February, 1958, pp 77-97.

Stevens, CM. 'Regarding the Determinants of Union Wage Policy' in *Review of Economics and Statistics*, 35, 1953, pp 221-8.

Stinchcombe, AL. 'Formal organizations' in Smelser, NJ. *Sociology* (Wiley, 1967), pp 151-202...258.

Storey, J. 'Workplace Collective Bargaining and Managerial Prerogatives' in *Industrial Relations Journal*, 7, Winter, 1976-7, pp 40-55.

Strauss, A. *Negotiations* (Jossey Bass, 1978).

Strinati, D. *Capitalism, the State and Industrial Relations* (Croom Helm, 1982).

Sullivan, GR. 'The Relationship between the Board of Directors and the General Meeting in Limited Companies' in *Law Quarterly Review*, 93, October, 1977, pp 569-80...598.

Sullivan, J, Peterson, RB, Kameda, N, & Shimada, J. 'The Relationship between Conflict Resolution Approaches and Trust. A Cross-Cultural Study' in *Academy of Management Journal*, 24 (4), 1981, pp 803-15.

Sykes, AJM. 'A Study in Changing the Attitudes and Stereotypes of Industrial Workers' in *Human Relations*, 17 (2), May, 1964, pp 143-54.

Sykes, AJM. 'Work Attitudes of Navvies' in *Sociology*, 3, 1969, pp 21-34; and in Weir, D (ed) *Men and Work in Modern Britain* (Fontana 1973), q.v.,.pp 203-20.

Sykes, AJM. 'The Ideological Basis of Industrial Relations in GB' in *Management International*, 6, 1965-6, pp 65-72.

Szakats, A. 'Compulsory Unionism: A Strength or Weakness? – The New Zealand System Compared with Union Security Agreements in GB & USA' in *Alberta Law Review*, X (2), 1972, pp 313-43...155.

Taft, R. 'The Ability to Judge People' in Whisler, TL & Harper, SF (eds). *Performance Appraisal* (Holt, Rinehart & Winston, 1962), pp 28-52.

Tannenbaum, AS. *Control in Organizations* (McGraw Hill, 1968).

Tannenbaum, R. 'The Manager Concept: A Rational Synthesis' in *Journal of Business*, 22 (4), October, 1949, pp 225-41; and in Tannenbaum, R, Weschler, IR, & Massarik, F. *Leadership and Organization* (McGraw Hill, 1961) pp 243-64...113.

Taylor, FW. *Shop Management* (Harper & Bros, 1910).

Taylor, I. & Walton, P. 'Industrial Sabotage' in Cohen, S. *Images of Deviance* (Penguin, 1971) pp 577.

Taylor P. 'Absenteeism – the English Sickness' in *Industrial Society*, July, 1970...577.

Taylor, PJ. *Absenteeism – Causes and Control* (Industrial Society Notes for Managers No 15, 1973).

Tedeschi, JT, Schlenker, BR, & Bonoma, TV. *Conflict, Power and Games* (Aldine Press, 1973).

Terry, M. 'The Inevitable Growth of Informality' in *British Journal of Industrial Relations*, XV (1), 1977, pp 76-88.

Terry, M. 'Organizing a Fragmented Work Force: Shop Stewards in Local Government' in *British Journal of Industrial Relations*, March, 1982, pp 1-19...421.

Thelen, HA & Withall, J. 'Three Frames of Reference. The Description of Climate' in *Human Relations*, II (2), 1979, pp 159-76...55, 61.

Thomas, JL & Robertson, M. *Trade Unions and Industrial Relations* (Business Books, 1976).

Thomas, RE. *Business Policy* (Phillip Allen, 1977).

Thomason, GF. *The Management of Industrial Relations* (UCCP, 1971).

Thomason, GF. *Experiments in Participation* (IPM, 1971)...501, 508, 513.

Thomason, GF. *The Individual, the Trade Union and the State: Some Contemporary Issues* (Irish Association for Industrial Relations, 1978).

Thomason, GF. *Job Evaluation. Objectives and Methods* (IPM, 1980a)...358, 367, 426.

Thomason, GF. 'Corporate Control of the Professional Association' in Poole, MJF & Mansfield, R (eds). *Managerial Roles and Industrial Relations* (Gower, 1980b), pp 26-37.

Thomason, GF. *A Textbook of Personnel Management* (IPM, 1975; 4th edn, 1981)...37, 56, 61, 87, 133, 179, 256, 458.

Thomason, GF, Doughty, G, and Spear, H. *Relations in the London Fire Brigade* (ACAS, 1977)...296.

Thomson, AWJ & Beaumont, PB. *Public Sector Bargaining. A Study of Relative Gain* (Saxon House, 1978)...399, 403.

Thomson, AWJ & Hunter, L. 'The Level of Bargaining in a Multi-plant Company' in *Industrial Relations Journal*, 6 (2), 1975, pp 23-40, 232.

Thompson, EP. *The Making of the English Working Class* (Penguin, 1967).

Thompson, J & Rogers, HR (eds). *Redgrave's Factories, Truck and Shops Acts* (Butterworth, 19th edn, 1956).

Thurley, K & Wood, SJ (eds). *Industrial Relations and Management Strategy* (Cambridge UP, 1983).

(Tomlin) *Royal Commission on the Civil Service, 1929-31* (Cmnd 3909, HMSO, 1931)...424.

Torrington, D. *Comparative Industrial Relations in Europe* (Associated Business Programmes, 1978)...186, 193.

Towers, B, Whittingham, TG & Gottschalk, AW (eds). *Bargaining for Change* (Allen & Unwin, 1972).

Trades Union Congress. *Trade Unionism* (TUC, 1966).

TUC. *Evidence to the Donovan Royal Commission*, (TUC, 1965).

TUC. *Costs and Profits: Financial Information for Trade Unionists* (TUC, 1970)...156.

TUC. *Good Industrial Relations. A Guide for Negotiators* (TUC, 1971).

TUC. *Collective Bargaining and the Social Contract* (TUC, 1974)...189.

TUC. *Industrial Democracy* (TUC, 1974).

TUC. *Guide to the Bullock Report on Industrial Democracy* (TUC, February, 1977).

TUC. *Paid Release for Union Training* (TUC, 1977)...161.

TUC. *TUC Handbook on Safety and Health at Work* (TUC, 1978)...161.

Treitel, GH. *The Law of Contract* (Stevens, 1975 edn)...90, 105, 112.

Turner, HA. *Trade Union Growth, Structure and Policy* (Allen & Unwin, 1962); quoted in McCarthy, WEJ. *Trade Unions*, (Penguin, 1972) q.v., pp 80-108...140, 163, 272.

Turner, HA. *Is Britain Really Strike Prone?* (Cambridge UP, 1969)...12, 23, 335.

Turner, HA, Clack, G, & Roberts, G. *Labour Relations in the Motor Industry* (Allen & Unwin, 1967)...335.

Turner-Samuels, M. *Industrial Negotiation and Arbitration* (Solicitors' Law Society, 1951)...166.

Ulman, L. 'Collective Bargaining and Competitive Bargaining' in *Scottish Journal of Political Economy*, 21 (2), June, 1974, pp 97-109...500.

Unwin, G. *The Gilds and Companies of London* (Methuen, 1908)...136.

Vickers, Sir G. *The Art of Judgement* (Chapman & Hall, 1965).

Vollmer, HM & Mills, DL (eds). *Professionalization* (Prentice Hall, 1966).

Walker, J. *British Economic and Social History*, 1700-1977 (McDonald & Evans, 1979).

Walker, KF. 'The Comparative Study of Industrial Relations' in *International Institute for Labour Studies Bulletin*, 3, November, 1967, pp 105-32.

Walker, KF. 'Strategic Factors in Industrial Relations Systems – A programme of International Comparative Industry Studies' in *International Institute for Labour Studies Bulletin*, 6, June, 1969, pp 187-209.

Walker, KF. *Personnel and Social Planning on the Plant Level* (International Institute for Labour Studies, 1970).

Walker, KF. 'Towards Useful Theorising About Industrial Relations' in *British Journal of Industrial Relations* XV (3), 1977, pp 307-16.

Walker, P. *The Courts of Law* (David & Charles, 1970)...195.

Wall, TD & Lischeron, JA. *Worker Participation* (McGraw Hill, 1977).

Walsh, K. 'Centralization and Decentralization in Local Government Bargaining' in *Industrial Relations Journal*, 12 (5), September/October, 1981, pp 43-54...417.

Walton, CB. *Corporate Social Responsibilities* (Wadsworth, 1967)...297, 300.

Walton, RE & McKersie, R. *A Behavioural Theory of Labour Negotiations*, (McGraw Hill, 1965)...290, 291, 293, 298-99, 301, 302, 304, 305, 307, 308, 310, 339, 434, 446, 452, 484-85, 487, 496, 500, 506, 507, 513, 514, 527, 545, 547, 551, 558, 559, 561-62, 570.

Warr, P. *Psychology and Collective Bargaining* (Hutchinson, 1973).

Webb, B. *The Co-operative Movement* (Swan Sonnenschein, 1899)...286, 315.

Webb, S & B. *History of Trade Unionism* (Longman, 1894; 2nd edn 1920)...94, 140, 146, 259, 263, 292, 315.

Webb, S & B. *Industrial Democracy* (A S E, 1898; Longman, 1920)...286.

Weber, M. *Economy and Society* (Bedminster Press, 1968)...44, 58-59.

Weber, M. *The Theory of Economic and Social Organisation* (Free Press, 1947; 1964)...44, 55, 58-59, 328, 345, 460-61.

Wedderburn, K. *The Worker and the Law* (Penguin, 1971)...65, 94, 107-08, 148, 164.

Wedderburn,K & Davies, PL. *Employment Grievances and Disputes Procedures in Britain* (University of California Press, 1969).

630

Weekes, B, Mellish, M, Dickens, L & Lloyd, J. *Industrial Relations and the Limits of Law* (Blackwell, 1975)...140-41, 144, 151, 164, 280.

Weir, D. 'Radical Managerialism: Middle Managers' Perceptions of Collective Bargaining' in *British Journal of Industrial Relations*, XIV (3), November, 1976, pp 324-38.

Wensley, R. 'PIMS and BCG. New Horizons or False Dawn?' in Strategic Management Journal, 3, 1982, pp 147-58.

Westergaard, J. 'The Power of Property' in *New Society*, 11 September, 1975, pp 574-7.

Westergaard, J. 'Class, Inequality and Corporatism' in Hunt, A (ed). *Class and Class Structure* (Lawrence & Wishart, 1977).

Westergaard, J & Resler, H. *Class in a Capitalist Society: A Study of Contemporary Britain* (Penguin, 1976).

Wheeler, HN. 'Punishment Theory and Industrial Discipline' in *Industrial Relations*, 15 (2), May, 1976, pp 235-43.

Whisler, TL & Harper, SF. *Performance Appraisal* (Holt, Rinehart & Winston, 1962).

White, JL. *The Limits of Trade Union Militancy* (Greenwood, 1978).

Whitley, JH (Chairman). *Report of the Committee on the Relations between Employers and Employed* (HMSO, 1916).

Whitley, RD. 'Concepts of Organization and Power in the Study of Organizations' in *Personnel Review*, 6 (1), Winter, 1977, pp 54-9.

Whittingham TG & Gottschalk, AW. *Bargaining for Change* (Allen & Unwin, 1972).

Whyte, WF. *Street Corner Society* (Chicago UP, 1943)...36.

Wigham, E. *What's Wrong with the Unions?* (Penguin, 1961)...21, 23.

Wigham, E. *The Power to Manage. A History of the Engineering Employers' Federation* (Macmillan, 1973)...113, 241, 244, 245, 247.

Wilders, MG & Parker, SR. 'Changes in Workplace Industrial Relations, 1966-72' in *British Journal of Industrial Relations*, 1975, 13 (1), pp 14-22.

Williams, F. *Magnificent Journey* (Odhams, 1954).

Wilson, K. 'Social Responsibility and Management Perspectives' in Poole MJF & Mansfield R(eds), *Managerial Roles and Industrial Relations* (Gower, 1980), q.v., pp 50-62.

Winchester, D. *Workers, Management and Government* (Open University, 1976).

Winchester, D. 'Industrial Relations in the Public Sector' in Bain GS, *Industrial relations in Britain* (Blackwell, 1983) q.v., pp 155-178.

Winkler, JT. 'The Ghost at the Bargaining Table: Directors and Industrial Relations', in *British Journal of Industrial Relations*, XII (2), 1974, pp 191-212...456.

Winkler, JT. 'Law, State and Economy. The Industry Act in Context' in *British Journal of Law and Society*, 2 (2), Winter, 1975, pp 103-28.

Winkler, JT. 'Corporatism' in *Archives Europeens de Sociologie*, 17 (1), 1976, pp 100-136...586.

Winkler, JT. 'The Corporate Economy: Theory and Administration' in Scase, R (ed). *Class Cleavage and Control*, (Allen & Unwin, 1977) pp 43-58...586.

Wood, SJ et al. 'The Industrial Relations System Concept as a Basis for Industrial Relations' in *British Journal of Industrial Relations*, XIII, (3), November, 1975, pp 291-308...6.

Wood, SJ. 'The Radicalization of Industrial Relations Theory' in *Personnel Review*, 5 (3), Summer, 1976, pp 52-7.

Wood, SJ & Elliott, R. 'A Critical Evaluation of Fox's 'Radicalization' of Industrial Relations Theory' in *Sociology*, 11, January, 1977, pp 105-25.

Woodward, J. *Management and Technology* (HMSO, 1958)...33, 37.

Woodward, J. *Industrial Organization: Theory and Practice* (Oxford UP, 1965)...37.

Woodward, J. *Industrial Organization: Behaviour and Control* (Oxford UP, 1970).

Woodworth, RT & Peterson, RB. *Collective Negotiation for Public and Professional Employees* (Scott Foresman, 1969).

Wooton, B. *The Social Foundations of Wage Policy* (Allen & Unwin, 1962)...344.

Wortman, MS & Randle, CW. *Collective Bargaining: Principles and Practices* (Houghton Mifflin, 1966).

Yoder, D. 'Personnel Adminsistration' in Somers, CG (ed.) *The Next Twenty Five Years of Industrial Relations.* (IRRA, Madrson, 1973), q.v., pp 141-56.

Young, AF. *Social Services in British Industry* (Routledge & Kegan Paul, 1968).

Young,, DE & Findlater, JE. 'Training and Industrial Relations' in *Industrial Relations Journal*, 2 (1), 1972, pp 3-22.

Young, S. 'The Question of Managerial Prerogatives' in *Industrial and Labour Relations Review*, 16 (2), 1963, pp 240-53...93.

Subject Index

arbitration, 8, 81, 166-79, 377-80, 422-23
armed forces, 406
Armed Forces Pay Review Body, 415
attitude(s), 42-47, 299, 576
   to authority, 299, 462-63, 571-72
   to collective bargaining, 290-91, 482
   to collective bargaining partner, 293-94, 296-312, 433, 446, 474
   and bargaining relationship, 292-96, 457, 460-62, 477-80, 551-52
attitudinal structuring, 291

bargaining power, 10-11, 69, 71, 77-81, 105, 317-22, 364, 379, 388, 474-82, 499, 518-19, 523-26
bargaining relationships, 284-312
board of directors, 115-18, 240, 301
Boulwarism, 299, 330
British Institute of Management, 249

capitalism, 3, 35, 37, 260
car industry, 294, 335, 390
cases cited:
   Amalgamated Society of Railway Servants v Osborne, 143
   Bonsor v Musicians' Union, 144
   Boychuk v H J Symons Holdings Ltd, 123, 125
   British Home Stores Ltd v Burchell, 130
   Dalton v Burton's Gold Medal Biscuits Ltd, 124
   De Francesco v Barnum, 200
   Elliott Bros (London) Ltd v Colverd, 124
   Ford Motor Company Ltd v A E F, 100
   Greenslade v Hoveringham Gravels Ltd, 123

Grunwick Processing Laboratories Ltd and others v ACAS and others, 87, 171, 299, 309
Hill v C A Parsons and Co Ltd, 106
Hunt v Broome, 199
Hutton v West Cork Railway Co, 118
R v Jones (John) and others, 199
Langston v AUEW, 106
Larkin v Belfast Harbour Commissioners, 198
Laws v London Chronicle (Indicator Newspapers) Ltd, 124
Mears v Safecar Security Ltd, 105
Meridan v Gomershall, 124
Meyer Dunmore International Ltd v Rogers, 125
Monterosso Shipping Co Ltd v I F W F, 100
National Coal Board v Galley, 101
Piddington v Bates, 199
Rookes v Barnard, 101
Singh v Lyons Maid Ltd, 123
Taff Vale Railway Company v Amalgamated Society of Railway Servants, 142-43, 201
Talbot v Hugh M Fulton Ltd, 123
Taylor v Parsons Peebles NEI Bruce Peebles Ltd, 124
Thompson and others v Eaton Ltd, 198
Turner v Manson, 124
Tynan v Bulmer, 199
UKAPE v ACAS, 171
Central Arbitration Committee, 156, 178-79, 202-07
centralization, 68, 73, 228-38, 408
Chambers of Commerce, 249-50
Codes of practice, 73, 122-31, 174, 352, 354, 361, 376, 454-56, 532, 558-64

objectives of, 74, 76, 78-79,
  223, 243-50
structures of, 240, 250-51
Employment Appeal Tribunal,
  202, 209-10
enforcement, 194-222
Engineering Employers'
  Federation, 241, 244, 247,
  249, 348
equity, 129-31

Fair Wages Resolution, 177, 179,
  204, 419
foremen, supervisors, 393, 497
frames of reference, 55-57,
  256-59, 461, 550
freedom of contract, 303, 315

general labour unions, 272
GKN-Shotton, 301, 354, 495
Glacier Metal Company, 300-01,
  354, 493-95
grievances, 126-131, 201, 335,
  372-81, 388-92
Gross Domestic Product, 14-19

health and safety, 28, 158-61

ideology, 5, 14-15, 43, 45, 57,
  257, 264, 290-92, 310, 432,
  551, 594
images of society, 257-58
incentives, 367
incomes policy, 186-91, 419-20
individual bargaining, 75-81,
  98-99, 160, 295-96, 299
individualism, 47-49, 55-60,
  64-65, 75, 134, 298-99
Industrial action, 383-87, 393,
  528-30
Industrial Court, 168-69, 171,
  178, 202-03, 411
industrial democracy, 264
Industrial Disputes Order, 1951,
  176-77
Industrial Disputes Tribunal, 176
industrial tribunal(s), 129-31,
  202-22
industrial tribunal jurisdictions,
  206-10, 215

industrial unions, 140, 280
informal groups, 271
inquiries, 172
Institute of Directors, 249
Institute of Personnel
  Management, 249
integrative bargaining, 484-85,
  496-513, 542, 557-58, 565,
  586
integrity, 552-54
inter-union conflict, 418, 446-48

job satisfaction, 236
joint consultation, 80, 275,
  351-54, 367, 375, 462,
  490-98, 584-86, 598-600
joint negotiation, 275
jurisdictional disputes, 209, 475

labour cost, unit, 19-20
law, 27-28, 59, 64, 68, 86-112,
  145-54, 192-222, 323-24,
  594-95
local authorities, 399-407
LACSAB, 421, 425
local bargaining, 26, 431-58

magistrates, 146
managing director, 113-17
manipulation, 467-70
mediation, 81, 166-79
models,
  decision-making, 51-53,
    514-17, 534-44
  emergent IR, 47-60, 501-03,
    593-95
  influence, 33-41
  systems, 4-13, 320-21, 587-91,
    600
  traditional IR 2-3, 23-26, 32,
    41-47, 575, 592
motivation, 37-40, 44, 49, 54-55,
  59, 254-56, 446, 505-07
multinational enterprise, 230-31

National Board for Prices and
  Incomes, 188, 414, 500-01
National Economic Development
  Council, 251